AF504900

Redaktion und Bildarchiv: Gabriele Ruff, Wien
Translation into English by Katja Steiner, Ehingen

Library of Congress Cataloging-in-Publication Data
A CIP catalogue record for this book is available from the
Library of Congress, Washington D.C., USA.

Die Deutsche Bibliothek – CIP– Einheitsaufnahme
Podrecca, Boris:
Boris Podrecca: Arbeiten, works 1980 –1995 / Walter Zschokke.
Einl.: Friedrich Achleitner. [Transl. into Engl. by Katja Steiner].
Basel; Boston; Berlin: Birkhäuser, 1996
ISBN 3–7643–5441–0 (Basel; Boston; Berlin) Gb.
ISBN 0–8176–5441–0 (Boston) Gb.
NE: Zschokke, Walter [Mitarb.]

Layout and Cover design: Loys Egg, Wien

Cover Photographs: © Gerald Zugmann, Wien

Printed on acid-free paper produced of chlorine-free pulp. TCF ∞
Printed in Austria by Holzhausens Nfg., 1070 Wien

ISBN 3-7643-5441-0
ISBN 0-8176-5441-0

9 8 7 6 5 4 3 2 1

Fotonachweis / *Photo credits:*
Bernhard Angerer: 208/209 / Archiv MA 19: 206/207 / Atelier Podrecca: 84, 112, 129 / Javier Azurmendi: 64/65 / Gert v. Bassewitz: 158–163 / Alex Bauer: 207 / Bigelli Marmi: 210 / Elio Ciol: 125–127 / Oskar Dariz: 68–72, 192–195 / Patrick Delauney: 184–185 / Foto Abuja: 72 / Damjan Galé: 58 – 63, 76, 78, 80/81, 169–171, 176–177 / Landesbildstelle: 112 / Marko Lavrenčič: 131–133 / Eleonore Littasy: 15–17 / Gerhard Luckner: 31, 33, 39, 42, 47, 54, 56/57, 76, 80, 201–204 / Wolfram Otlinghaus: 53, 55/56 / Boris Podrecca: 54, 71, 89, 111, 143, 147/148, 150/151, 153–157, 166/167, 173–174, 176 / Marko Prestor: 102/103 / Claus Radler: 196 / Uwe Rau: 197–199 / Georg Riha: 187–191 / P. Rosselli: 182/183 / Franz Schachinger: 30–33 / Herbert Schwingenschlögl: 42, 47–51, 97–99, 104, 106/107, 110/111, 115, 140–146, 149–151, 153,155/156, 209 / Vaclav Sedy: 63 / Manfred Seidl: 207 / Rupert Steiner: 122/123 / Teatro delle Muse: 209 / Hans-Joachim Wuthenow 116–119 / Gerald Zugmann: 28/29, 35–37, 39–41, 43–45, 74–79, 81/82, 84–95, 100/101, 105, 107–109, 111, 137–139,180/181, 209, 211

Walter Zschokke

BORIS PODRECCA

ARBEITEN / WORKS   1980 - 1995

Mit einem Essay von Friedrich Achleitner

Birkhäuser Verlag
Basel · Boston · Berlin

Friedrich Achleitner

Statt einer Einführung

Es hat sich wohl herumgesprochen, daß mit der Sprache allein Architektur nicht erreichbar ist. Und man muß, zumindest nach der x-ten Einführung zugeben, daß man auch einen Menschen mit Wörtern einem anderen nicht vermitteln kann. Trotzdem werden Einführungen zu Monographien bestellt und, was noch schlimmer ist, sie werden auch geschrieben, obwohl außerdem eine fast hundertprozentige Garantie besteht, daß sie nicht einmal von einem Prozent der Buchdurchblätterer (Buchdurchblätterinnen) gelesen werden. Was tun?

Geradezu fatal wird die Lage, wenn von einem Architekten, wie etwa von Boris Podrecca, intelligente, wenn auch in Teilen anzweifelbare Aussagen bestehen, so daß der *Einführer* eher in die Rolle eines *Zusammenfassers* gedrängt wird. Dem möchte ich entgehen. Denn jeder Text über einen Architekten ist ja mehr oder weniger der *Entwurf* eines Architekten, so daß der Einführer, sprich Zusammenfasser, eine Verantwortung übernehmen müßte, die er gar nicht übernehmen kann. Das Folgende ist also höchstens ein *Vorentwurf*, vielleicht ein Zugang zum Werk unter vielen, das sich ohnehin außerhalb der Monographie befindet und nur vom Objekt der Monographie selbst beeinflußbar ist, das selbstverständlich (nicht im Wiener oder im Nestroy'schen Sinne) ein *Subjekt* ist.

Die Wirklichkeit ist Experiment genug

Boris Podrecca nimmt in der österreichischen, speziell in der Wiener Architektur eine Außenseiterstellung ein, obwohl man nach den Klischeevorstellungen von Wien ihn als typischen Repräsentanten dieser Stadt ansehen könnte. Einerseits ist man verführt zu behaupten, daß sein universalistischer Ansatz im «klassischen» Rollenverständnis von Architektur, sein Changieren zwischen Geschichte und Gegenwart - ja, seine Gleichsetzung der Wahrnehmung von Gegenwart und Geschichte - sein kultureller Pluralismus und seine formale Beredsamkeit eben etwas typisch Wienerisches seien, andererseits muß man heute zur Kenntnis nehmen, daß gerade im sprachsensiblen Milieu von Wien, nichts unduldsamer und penibler bewacht wird, als die Trennungslinien zwischen architektonischen Positionen.

Ebenso kann man nicht umhin, daran zu erinnern, daß die kulturelle Sozialisation Boris Podreccas in einem mehrsprachigen Milieu stattfand und zwar jeweils zumindest in einer slawischen, in einer romanischen und und in einer germanischen Sprache. Die Übersetzung oder das simultane, parallele oder überlagernde Denken und Reden war ihm in die Wiege gelegt. So ist er auch, könnte man weiter behaupten, zwar in jeder

Instead of an introduction

Word must have spread that with language alone, architecture is not accessible. And one has to admit, at least after the umpteenth introduction, that words alone cannot bring one person closer to another. Nevertheless, introductions and monographs are requested, and what's even worse is that they are being written even though, on top of everything else, there is almost a 100% guarantee that they will not be read by even 1% of those who will flip through the book's pages. So, what to do? The situation becomes nearly fatal if there are statements by an architect, such as Boris Podrecca, that are intelligent (even if somewhat equivocal), putting the introducer *into the role of a summarizer. I would like to avoid that because each text on an architect is more or less the* design *of an architect, meaning that the introducer – say summarizer – would have to take on a responsibility which he really cannot assume. The following is, at most, a pre-design; perhaps one approach among many. And it will remain outside the realm of a monograph and can be influenced only by the object of the latter, which of course is (not in the Viennese or Nestroy sense) a* subject.

Reality is enough of an experiment

Boris Podrecca takes on an outsider's role in Austrian and especially Viennese architecture although, according to the stereotypical ideas on Vienna, one could consider him a typical representative of this city. On one hand, it is tempting to claim that his universal approach in the "classic" understanding of architecture's role – his alternating between past and present giving the perception of present time and historic times an equal value, his cultural pluralism, and his formal eloquence – would be something typically Viennese. On the other hand, one has to recognize today that in the Viennese milieu sensitive to language, nothing is observed more indulgently and precisely as the dividing lines between architectural standpoints.

One can not help but remember that the cultural socialization of Boris Podrecca took place in a multi-lingual milieu in at least one Slavic, one Roman, and one Germanic language. The translation or the simultaneous parallel or overlapping thinking and speaking was placed in his cradle. One could say that he is at home in each language; however, in none of them is he completely "present". His speaking is not non-reflective; it does not have the unsuspecting characteristic of someone at home in a different language. He always speaks out of a different way of thinking or evokes this impression with his very own and private linguistic artistry. I came to understand Boris Podrecca only on the day that I drove with him to a meeting in

Sprache zu Hause, aber in keiner Sprache ganz «anwesend». Sein Sprechen ist nicht unreflektiert, es hat nicht die Ahnungslosigkeit eines in einer Sprache Beheimateten, er spricht immer aus einer anderen Denkweise oder erweckt mit seiner ganz privaten Sprachartistik diesen Eindruck. Ich habe Boris Podrecca erst verstehen gelernt, als ich mit ihm zu einer Tagung nach Piran fuhr. Nach Udine war er ein veränderter Mensch, in Triest ein anderer.

Podreccas Architekturbegriff ist ein mediterraner, dem Leben (was immer das sei) zugewandter, ein sinnlicher, der sich aus unterschiedlichen kulturellen Ebenen und Traditionen strukturiert. Seine Begriffskonstruktion *Archikultur* ist keine Attitüde, obwohl dies manchem monokulturellen Wächter so erscheinen mag. Podrecca fehlt jeder Sinn für grundsätzliche, prinzipielle, totale, moralistische, puristische oder gar orthodoxe Positionen, sie sind ihm unverständlich, ich vermute sogar widerlich. Daß sie gerade heute wieder in seinem Geburtsland besonders blutig urgiert werden, zeigt, wie zerbrechlich das multi- oder interkulturelle Konstrukt geblieben ist. Ja selbst in Wien wurde seine Haltung lange nicht ernst genommen; Wien neigt trotz seiner langen Assimilationsgeschichte zu sektiererischen Gruppierungen, die alle den Anspruch auf Ausschließlichkeit erheben. Und ausschließlich war Boris Podreccas Denken nie.

Die ersten Positionen seines Werksverzeichnisses, das vor rund dreißig Jahren beginnt, zeigen den Entwurf einer Platzgestaltung in Salzburg, ein Projekt für Bulgarien (Stadtzentrum für Varna) und die Gestaltung der Ausstellung *Josef Plečnik* für die *Österreichische Gesellschaft für Architektur* in Wien. Seine Begegnung mit dem universalistischen Architekturbegriff der *Arbeitsgruppe 4* (vor allem mit Friedrich Kurrent, dessen Assistent er später in München wurde) haben vermutlich seine eigene Architekturanschauung mehr gefestigt als das Studium und die Diplomarbeit bei Roland Rainer. Diese ersten Arbeiten umreißen auch schon die thematischen Schwerpunkte, stecken aber auch das Spannungsfeld seiner späteren Tätigkeiten ab, das zwischen städtebaulichem Projekt (vor allem als Eingriff in bestehende Strukturen) und der Gestaltung von Ausstellungen liegt, die bis heute für ihn *Werkstatt*, also Experimentierfeld geblieben sind. Und wie von selbst ergibt sich daraus das breite «Zwischenfeld» für den sich bewußt nicht spezialisierenden Architekten: Umbauten in allen Facetten, von der Wohnung bis zum städtischen Ensemble, Neubauten vom Bürohaus bis zum Einkaufszentrum, von der Schule bis zum Flußkraftwerk, vom Hotel bis zum Wohn- oder Siedlungsbau, von der Galerie bis zum Einfamilienhaus, vom Möbel bis zum Schmuckstück. Diese Mischung, die durchaus dem «klassischen Rollenverständnis» des Architekten entspricht, wäre an sich nicht erwähnenswert,

Piran. When we got past Udine, he was a different person; in Trieste he was yet another.

Podrecca's architectural idea is Mediterranean. Oriented towards life (whatever this may be), it is sensual and structured from the most varying cultural levels and traditions. His construction of the term archiculture is not an attitude, although some mono-cultural guardians may perceive it as such.

Podrecca has no sense for basic, principle, total, moralistic, purist, or even orthodox positions. He can not understand them and I suspect that he truly despises them. The fact that they have been urged back in a particularly bloody way in the country of his birth shows the fragility of the multi- or intercultural construct. Even in Vienna his attitude was for a long time not taken seriously. Despite its long history of assimilation, Vienna tends towards sectarian formations, all of which claim to be exclusive. Boris Podrecca's thinking has never been exclusive.

The first items on his list of works which begins about thirty years ago show the design of a square in Salzburg, a project for Bulgaria (city center and Varna), and the design of the Josef Plečnik exhibition for the Austrian Society for Architecture in Vienna. His encounter with the universalist architectural ideas of Arbeitsgruppe 4 (work group 4; above all with Friedrich Kurrent, whom he later on assisted in Munich) probably have strengthened his own architectural approach more than the studies and the diploma work with Roland Rainer. These first works already outline the contextual focal points but also measure out the potential field of his later activities lying in between the urban projects (above all as an operation on existing structures) and the design of exhibitions which, up to this day, has remained a kind of workshop, i.e., an experimental field. And almost by itself, the wide "intermediate field" results for the consciously non-specialized architect: conversions in all facets – from apartment to urban ensemble; new buildings – from office building to shopping mall, from school to river power plant, from hotel to housing development, from gallery to one-family-home; and accessories – from furniture to jewelry. This mixture, which conforms to the "classical understanding of roles" of the architect, would by itself not be worth mentioning if these works did not come out of a superior net of relationships which seems to be the basis for all designs. Podrecca is a bit suspicious of, and yes, may even have an aversion towards, the isolated object. He would most likely integrate a brooch into a larger ensemble, if he didn't have a city on which to operate. And so, we have already entered the design-stage of the portrait of Boris Podrecca, the architect.

wenn diese Arbeiten nicht in einem übergeordneten Beziehungs-
netz entstünden, das für alle Entwürfe grundlegend erscheint.
Podrecca hegt eine Art von Argwohn, ja Widerwillen gegen das
isolierte Objekt. Er würde vermutlich noch eine Brosche in ein
größeres Ensemble einbinden, wenn dafür schon keine Stadt zur
Verfügung steht. Hier befinden wir uns bereits in der Entwurfs-
phase des Bildes vom Architekten Boris Podrecca.

Das dialogische Prinzip
und die Geschichte mit den Geschichten

Boris Podrecca muß reden. Auch in der Architektur. Er sucht
das Gespräch. Seine Recherchen sind Gespräche und Fragen.
Und wenn keine Antworten kommen, werden sie notfalls selbst
gegeben. Seine Ideen - und mögen sie zunächst noch so formal
erscheinen - sind aus realen Situationen entwickelt, sie artiku-
lieren einen Bedarf, der oft erst später als solcher erkannt wird.
Wenn heute etwa ein rundes Dutzend Platzgestaltungen vorliegen (Aufträge, die vorwiegend aus Wettbewerbserfolgen stammen), so hat das seine handfesten Gründe. Diese Erfolge liegen
in der Fähigkeit, nicht nur die materialisierte Geschichte einer
Stadt (typologische Substanz, morphologische Besonderheiten,
Bewegungsrelationen, Sichtbeziehungen, gesellschaftliche Ge-
wichtungen, Bedeutungen, Symbole, Lichtverhältnisse, Mängel,
Leerräume, potentielle Angebote an Nutzungen etc.) zu «lesen»,
sondern sie in einem neuen «Lebenszusammenhang» darzustel-
len. Der Dialog wird auf mehreren Ebenen geführt, sicher einmal ganz unsentimental auf der praktischen, zweckorientierten,
aber auch auf der inhaltlichen und symbolischen. Podrecca hat
eine spannende, vergnügliche und «entwaffnende» Art, Stadt-
strukturen zu lesen, wobei Geschichte ebenso aus Geschichten
wie aus realen Befunden entsteht.
Städte haben nicht nur das Bedürfnis, ihre Plätze neuen Nutzungen und Bedeutungen zuzuführen, sondern dies auch zu zeigen.
Es geht nicht nur um zeitlich wechselnde oder simultan
ablaufende Ereignisse, sondern es geht um die Lesbarkeit der
Totalität aller möglichen Ereignisse. Podreccas Plätze wirken
unbenutzt nicht leer, ihre latente Leistung bleibt sichtbar, sie
bleiben als Erzähler präsent und als ästhetischer Bestandteil
der Stadt erlebbar, ja ihre Erscheinungsform liefert zunächst
einen Blick auf die Stadt, als gäbe es keinen andern.
Boris Podrecca hat keine Hemmungen, realen Forderungen,
Konventionen und Wünschen nachzugehen und nachzugeben.
Für ihn sind Anschaubarkeit, Verdeutlichung, Inszenierung,
ja naive «Zurschaustellung» keine Tabus. Seine Architektur
schafft die Erzählung und die Illustration in einem.
Beispiel: Der Tartini-Platz von Piran machte als Projekt, ja noch
während der Bauzeit den Eindruck eines ästhetisch vollkommen

The dialogue principle
and history through narratives

*Boris Podrecca has to speak. And that applies to architecture,
as well. He is looking for the dialogue. His investigations are
conversations and questions. And if there are no answers, he
supplies them himself if necessary. His ideas – as formal as
they may appear at first glance – have been developed out of
real situations. They articulate a need which very often is recognized as such only later. If, for example, around a dozen new
designs for city squares exist today (orders resulting mainly
from a success in a competition), there are very good reasons
for this. These successes stem from the ability not only to
"read" the materialized history of a city (typological substance, morphological characteristics, relationships of movement and perception, societal weights, meanings, symbols,
light conditions, deficiencies, empty spaces, potential possibilities for utilities, etc.), but also to show them in a new "context
of life". The dialogue takes place on several different levels.
One time, it may be very unsentimental on the practical, use-
oriented level; the next time, on the contextual and symbolic
one. Podrecca has a suspenseful, entertaining and "disarming"
way of reading city structures, where history develops from narrative stories as well as from real facts.
Cities do not only have the need to bring their squares towards
new uses and meanings, but also to show this. It is not only
about events changing in time or taking place simultaneously,
but also about the legibility of the totality of all possible events.
Podrecca's squares, even if unused, do not have the feeling of
being empty. Their latent performance remains visible and they
remain present as story-tellers and can be experienced as an
esthetic component of the city. Their form of appearance, at
first, gives you one look onto the city, as though there were no
other.
Boris Podrecca does not shy away from going after and giving
in to real demands, conventions and wishes. To him, distinct-
ness, clarity and staging, even a naive "showing-off" are not
taboo. His architecture creates the tale and the illustration
in one.
One example is the Tartini-square in Piran. As a project and
even during the building phase, it gave the impression of esthe-
tically being a completely exaggerated and excessive design.
The large white marble oval slightly curved in two planes,
lying there like an egg sunny-side-up in a pan, and the extended edges of the discharging streets, drawn as if with a razor
blade, seemed to overwhelm the modest (but still Venetian) conditions of the small city. Today, this square (with or without
tourists) is a show, play and "action space", with constantly*

überzogenen Entwurfs. Das große, leicht bombierte Oval aus weißem Marmor (das wie ein Spiegelei in der Pfanne daliegt) und die wie mit einem Rasiermesser gezogenen verlängerten Kanten der einmündenden Straßenfluchten schienen die bescheidenen (aber immerhin auch venezianischen) Verhältnisse der kleinen Stadt zu überfordern. Heute ist dieser Platz (ob mit oder ohne Touristen) eine Schau-, Spiel- und «Aktionsfläche», die ständig ihre Aktivisten wechselt, wobei die Kinder und Halbwüchsigen die Oberhand behalten. Die *Geschichte* des Architekten, der mit dieser polierten Fläche an das einstige (schon lange zugeschüttete) Hafenbecken erinnern wollte, ist wohl lange vergessen. Das Geheimnis des Platzes liegt aber nicht so sehr im rigorosen formalen Eingriff, in der plakativen Darstellung und Überhöhung der Geschichtlichkeit des Ortes, oder in den präzise designten Vorbereichen vor den öffentlichen Bauten (Kirche, Tartini-Haus etc.) und den Einmündungen der Gassen, sondern im «normal» gepflasterten breiten Rand zwischen Oval und Hausfronten, in dem sogar Autos parken dürfen. Die scheinbar plakative Idee ist also in einer stärkeren *Normalität* aufgefangen und abgesichert, die vielleicht gerade durch die Transformation einer historischen Situation (Hafen mit Kai) entstanden ist und in ein neues, analoges Nutzungsmuster übergeführt wurde. Die Fläche, die einst dem Leben auf dem Wasser gehörte, gehört jetzt in einer spielerischen Weise dem Leben der Stadt.

Diese Art des Denkens, die vielleicht einem Camillo Sitte viel näher liegt als dem immer wieder bemühten Josef Plečnik, die vermutlich weniger kontextuell als (dia)logisch, weniger rational als real ist, und das in seinen kaum entwirrbaren Bahnen und Anspielungen vielleicht auch *taube Formen* produziert, dieser Arbeits- und Denkstil ist mit Sicherheit eine ernste und ernst zu nehmende Alternative im Spektrum heutiger *Stadtdiskussionen*. Selbstverständlich ist Boris Podreccas *Stadtbild* ein mediterran-mitteleuropäisches, seine Interventionen haben noch die planbare Stadt im Auge, es geht eher um «Stadtreparatur» oder um das Weiterführen bestehender, bewohnbarer Stätten. Seine Städte oder städtebaulichen Arbeiten setzen die Überschauberkeit voraus, ja urgieren diese; überhaupt das Schauen als Wert und Gradmesser von urbaner Lebensqualität.

Seine Projekte haben alle, oft mit mehr oder weniger guten Argumenten, diese ganzheitliche, zusammenschauende, ja auch ausufernde Rhetorik. Es gibt genaugenommen keinen Entwurf, der nicht «städtebaulich» oder «städtisch» argumentiert.
Ein anderes *Beispiel:*
Das Gebäude der Basler Versicherung am Wiener Donaukanal hat eine «Wasserseite», eine Quartierseite und eine Zone des Übergangs. Die eine Seite ist gekennzeichnet durch Bewegun-

changing activities. In this environment, the presence of children and teenagers is ubiquitous. The story of the architect who wanted to commemorate the former harbor basin (which has long since been filled), has probably been long forgotten. However, the secret of the square is not to be found so much in the rigorous formal operation, in the graphic demonstration and over-accentuation of the location's history, or in the precisely designed areas in front of the public buildings (church, Tartini-house etc.) and the intersections of the alleys. It lies rather in the "normal" cobble-stone broad edge between the oval and the building fronts, where cars may even park. The seemingly graphic idea is therefore caught and assured in a stronger normality which, perhaps just because of the transformation of a historic situation (harbor with a quay), has come into being and has been brought towards a new analogue pattern of utilization. The surface which once belonged to life on the water, now belongs in a playful way to life in the city.
This kind of thinking – which may be closer to a Camillo Sitte than to the always endeavoring Josef Plečnik – is probably less contextual than (dia)logical, less rational than real, and which, in its barely able to be unraveled ways and insinuations, may produce deaf forms. This way of working and thinking is definitely a serious alternative which must be taken seriously within the spectrum of today's city discussions.
Of course, Boris Podrecca's city image is a Mediterranean based, middle-European one. His interventions keep the future plan of the city in sight. The cause is more the "city's repair", or the continuation of existing, livable places. His work on towns or urban development presume a certain manageability; they even urge it. Anyway, looking has the urban living standards as a value and measure.

Podrecca's projects all have, and often with good argument, this holistic, synoptic rhetoric which at times may even get out of hand. To be precise, there is no design which would not argue in an "urban" way.
Another example:
The building of the Basel Insurance Company on the Vienna Danube canal has a "water side", a quarter side, and a zone of transition. One side is marked by the movements of water and traffic. It is the side of the river and of a flowing with an urban spatial distance; the show-side. The opposite side (towards the district) speaks with the residential quarter which was built in the 1870s' time of wild speculation. An autistic, self-indulgent, contemporary star architecture would hardly have thought of not forcing its own "standards" onto this situation (especially given the self-serving need for insurance). Podrecca cares for the play of this dialogue; whether as a kowtowing in front of

gen des Wassers und des Verkehrs. Sie ist die Seite des Flusses und Fließens mit stadträumlicher Distanz, *die* Schauseite. Die entgegengesetzte Seite (zum Bezirk hin) *redet* mit dem gründerzeitlichen Wohnquartier. Autistischer Selbstbezogenheit heutiger Stararchitektur wäre es wohl kaum in den Sinn gekommen (noch dazu beim Selbstdarstellungsbedürfnis einer Versicherung), dieser Sitatuation nicht die eigenen «Maßstäbe» aufzuzwingen. Podrecca liegt am Spiel dieses Dialogs, ob als Verneigung vor dem Ort oder «Leutseligkeit» bleibt gleich, es ist ihm ein Bedürfnis, auf diese Situation mit einer *nautischen* Fassade - was immer das sei - und einer den Verhältnissen des Wohnquartiers entsprechende zu antworten. Die Rhetorik der Fassaden ist also eine abgeleitete, eine auf den Ort bezogene, eine auf eine städtische Situation eingehende und antwortende. Gerade in dieser Haltung liegt natürlich auch etwas Herausforderndes, das die Frage provoziert: Wo kommt die heutige Architektur hin, wenn sie nicht mehr redet (mitteilt, Statements abgibt oder gar Botschaften verbreitet) sondern nur mehr antwortet?

Nun, gerade das *Reden* muß man bei Podrecca wirklich nicht einfordern. Diese Haltung ist ja keine unterwürfige, sich verleugnende, sondern sie ist methodisch, sie führt zum eigentlichen Entwurf.

Der bisherige Ansatz ist ein Erkärungsmodell, aber nicht eine Erklärung. Spricht Podrecca in seinen Arbeiten tatsächlich mehrere Sprachen oder nur eine, die mit Vokabeln aus mehreren Sprachen angereichert ist? Auch das ist eine Scheinfrage, die man an den Entwürfen schwer belegen kann.

In Podreccas Vokabular gibt es, wenn man von Schnürlsamthosen, Jeans und Dreitagebart absieht, nur einen eindeutig negativ besetzten Begriff: *Avantgarde.* Wie man weiß, konnte die militärische Avantgarde nur dann weit vorstoßen, wenn sie eine starke Truppe hinter sich hatte, also mit leichtem Gepäck. Die architektonische lebt vom Ausschluß möglichst vieler Aspekte des Bauens. Je weniger Ballast, desto größer der Sprung. Über die Bedeutung von Avantgarden zu diskutieren, wäre wohl am Ende des 2o. Jahrhunderts müßig. Aber die Einforderung des Gegenteils, die *peinliche Beobachtung der Wirklichkeit* (um es Otto-Wagnerisch zu sagen), ist zumindest eine theoretische Herausforderung. Und für Boris Podrecca scheint sie mehr zu sein. Wenn kulturelle Wirklichkeit (also Gegenwart) nach Josef Frank die *ganze uns bekannte historische Zeit ist*, dann ist der Umgang mit dieser Wirklichkeit das Abenteuer der Zeitmaschine. Podreccas Abenteuer und Entdeckungen liegen im Bewußtsein dieser Zeitmaschine, und daß diese auch zum Experiment verführt (ohne sich an der Speerspitze der Avantgarde zu befinden) hat uns ja auch schon Josef Plečnik vorgeführt.

Im Zusammenhang mit den zahllosen Umbauten von Boris Podrecca findet man den Hinweis, daß es ihm weniger auf die

the location or merely an affability, it does not matter. He has the desire to answer to this situation with a nautical *facade – whatever that may be – and in a way that is appropriate to the conditions of the residential quarter. The rhetoric of the facades is thus derived in relation to the location, constantly considering and answering to an urban situation. It is this attitude which naturally poses a challenge and provoking the question: where does today's architecture end up if it no longer speaks (informs, makes statements or even spreads messages), but merely answers?*

Well, speaking *is not something we have to ask of Podrecca. This attitude is not subordinate or self-denying, but it is methodical and leads to the design.*

The approach, so far, has been a model of explanation but not the explanation itself. Does Podrecca really speak several languages in his work or is it only one, enriched with vocabulary from several languages? This is a pseudo-question as well, and it can hardly be proven through the designs.

There is only one negatively imprinted term in Podrecca's vocabulary – leaving aside tied velvet pants, jeans and a three-day-beard: Avant-garde. *As we know, the military avant-garde could advance well only if it had strong troops behind itself, which means with light baggage. The architectural avant-garde gets its life from the exclusion of as many aspects of construction as possible. The lesser the load, the greater the leap. It would be vain to discuss the importance of the avant-garde at the end of the 20th century; however, the demand for the contrary, the embarrassing observation of reality (to use Otto Wagner's words), is at least a theoretical challenge. And for Boris Podrecca, it seems to be more. If cultural reality (read: the present and contemporary) is the entire historic time known to us according to Josef Frank, then dealing with this reality is the adventure of the time machine. Podrecca's adventures and discoveries lie in the consciousness of this time machine and Josef Plečnik has already shown us that this can also cause a seduction into experimentation (without having to be at the spear head of the avant-garde).*

In connection with the numerous conversions of Boris Podrecca, one can gather that he does not care as much about the single solution; he rather cares for the development of a grammar or, at the very least, an obliging method. On one hand, this can lie in the systematics of the development of questions (e. g., wrapped into stories), on the other, in a kind of grid search for sensual particles leading to a surprising construct or, in a compressed form, a just as surprising solution.

(This claim has to be treated carefully, because the functionally incorrect image could arise that solutions are the automatic result of a method. The method as an instrument does

Einzellösung ankäme, eher auf die Entwicklung einer *Grammatik* oder zumindest einer verbindlichen Methodik. Diese kann einerseits in der Systematik der Entwicklung von Fragen (etwa in Geschichten verpackt), andererseits in einer Art Rasterfahndung nach Sinnpartikeln liegen, die zu einem überraschenden Konstrukt oder, komprimiert, zu einer ebenso überraschenden *Lösung* führen.

(Diese Behauptung ist mit Vorsicht zu behandeln, denn es könnte das funktionalistische Trugbild entstehen, daß sich Lösungen automatisch aus einer Methodik ergeben. Die Methodik als Instrument entbindet den Architekten nicht vom Entwurf, das weiß Podrecca sehr genau, auch wenn er manchmal den Eindruck zu erwecken versucht, seine Entwürfe wären Ergebnisse seiner Pirschgänge und Recherchen.)

Drittes Beispiel: Die Schule von Liesing, wenn man einmal vom Korsett des Raumprogramms absieht, thematisiert das Andocken an eine bestehende Schule ebenso wie den städtebaulichen Übergang von einem Zentrum in eine Parklandschaft. Allein schon die thematische Aufbereitung führt in eine Auseinandersetzung mit den Begriffen Natur, Landschaft, künstliche Natur, künstlerische Perzeption von Natur, so daß das Thema Schule in einem größeren Themenkreis abgehandelt wird, was schließlich die Terrassierung der Klassentrakte, die räumliche Entwicklung des durchlässigen Hallenbereiches (über die Turnhalle hinweg in den Park) bis hin zur Farbgebung der ganzen Schule und zum zentralen Kunstwerk (von Franta Lesák) bestimmt.

Doch ein dialogisches Prinzip?

Diese Frage führt uns wieder zum Ausgang zurück. Die Sehnsucht nach einer ganzheitlichen Vermischung aller Kulturen und Stile ist ein Kind der Romantik. Im Historismus (einhergehend mit den Forschungen der Kunstgeschichte), mit dem wissenschaftlichen Blick auf die Kunst und der enzyklopädischen Ordnung ihrer Formen entstand eine distanzierte «Verfügbarkeit» (oder die Illusion davon) über und die Abkoppelung der Formen von Inhalten. Die postmoderne Bewegung (soweit sie etwas bewegte) hat diese Problematik wieder aufgegriffen, sich aber, bis auf wenige Ausnahmen, nicht wirklich auf sie eingelassen.

Boris Podrecca versucht gegenüber *Moderne* und *Postmoderne* einen dritten Weg. Er beruft sich hier vor allem auf Adolf Loos und die Dissidenten der Otto-Wagner-Schule, die entweder, wie Loos, das Risiko des konfliktreichen Dialogs mit einer Stadtkultur eingingen, oder, wie Leopold Bauer, sich auf die kollektiven Ergebnisse einer umfassenden *Baukultur* stützten.

not free the architect from the design, and Podrecca knows this very well, even if at times he tries to evoke the impression that his designs were the results of his hunting sprees and research.)

Third example: *The school in Liesing – leaving aside the corset of the spatial program – takes up the theme of a docking onto an existing school as well as the transition from a municipal center into a park landscape. The thematic preparation alone leads to a confrontation with the terms nature, landscape, artificial nature, artistic perception of nature, so that the theme of the school is dealt with in a larger context of themes. Finally, this determines the terracing of the classroom blocks, the spatial development of the pervious lobby area (above the gymnasium into the park), the coloring of the entire school and the central work of art (by Franta Lesák).*

A dialogue principle after all?

This question takes us back to the beginning. The desire for a holistic mixture of all cultures and styles is a child of romanticism. In historiography (going hand in hand with the research of art history), with the scientific look on art and the encyclopedic order of its forms, a distanced "availability" (or an illusion of such) of forms and their detachment from contexts has come into being. The post-modern movement (if it has moved anything) has taken up this problem; however, with very few exceptions, it has not really dealt with it.

Boris Podrecca, facing modernism *and* post-modernism, *tries out a third way. Above all, he refers to Adolf Loos and the dissidents of the Otto-Wagner-school who, like Loos, either took on the risk of a dialogue with an urban culture, or based themselves on the collective results of an extensive* building culture, *like Leopold Bauer.*

Modernism can no longer be the subject of his design interest in so far as he is more interested in the dynamics of the existing relationships of time – of the present – than of some progress, no matter how it is declared. Post-modernism has disavowed itself because it has not really taken its own program seriously enough and has confused the precise quote with a discretionary exploitation.

Podrecca's architecture is an architecture of effects, messages, and reactions in an already existing, multifaceted world which, after all, can still be sensually experienced and affirmed. He is searching for a realistic look at its problems and conditions. This world, due to its rich cultural experience, also has the methods at hand by which it can be improved and

Die *Moderne* kann insoferne nicht mehr Gegenstand seines Entwurfsinteresses sein, weil ihn an der Zeit, an der Gegenwart eher die Dynamik der bestehenden Beziehungen interessiert als ein wie immer deklarierter Fortschritt. Die *Postmoderne* hat sich desavouiert, weil sie genaugenommen ihr Programm selbst nicht ernstgenommen und das präzise Zitat mit beliebiger Ausbeutung verwechselt hat.

Podreccas Architektur ist eine Architektur der Wirkungen, Mitteilungen und Reaktionen in einer bereits eingerichteten, vielfältigen und noch immer auch sinnlich erfahrbaren und zu bejahenden Welt. Er sucht den realistischen Blick für ihre Probleme und Verhältnisse. Diese Welt hält durch ihre reiche kulturelle Erfahrung auch die Methoden bereit, sie zu verbessern und zu verschönern. Die *Ausstellungen* sind ein Mittel, diesen Schatz zu heben und die Methoden zu überprüfen. Die städtebauliche Intervention ist deren Überprüfung an der Realität des Lebens. Die Projekte sind Pirschgänge auf jeweils neu gesehenen Territorien. Die Wirklichkeit ist die Herausforderung, der Umgang mit ihr: Experiment.

Man soll keinen Architekten entwerfen. Die ersten Striche scheitern schon an der Entwurfsmethode. An der Entwurfsmethode des Architekten? Nein, der eigenen, natürlich.

Friedrich Achleitner

Wien, am 3. August 1996

made more beautiful. The exhibitions are one means to excavate this treasure and to reconsider the methods. The urban intervention is its verification with the reality of life. The projects are hunting sprees on territories seen anew each time. Reality is the challenge; dealing with it – an experiment.

One should not design an architect. The first lines would fail because of the design method. The design method of the architect? – No, our own, of course.

Friedrich Achleitner

Vienna, August 3, 1996

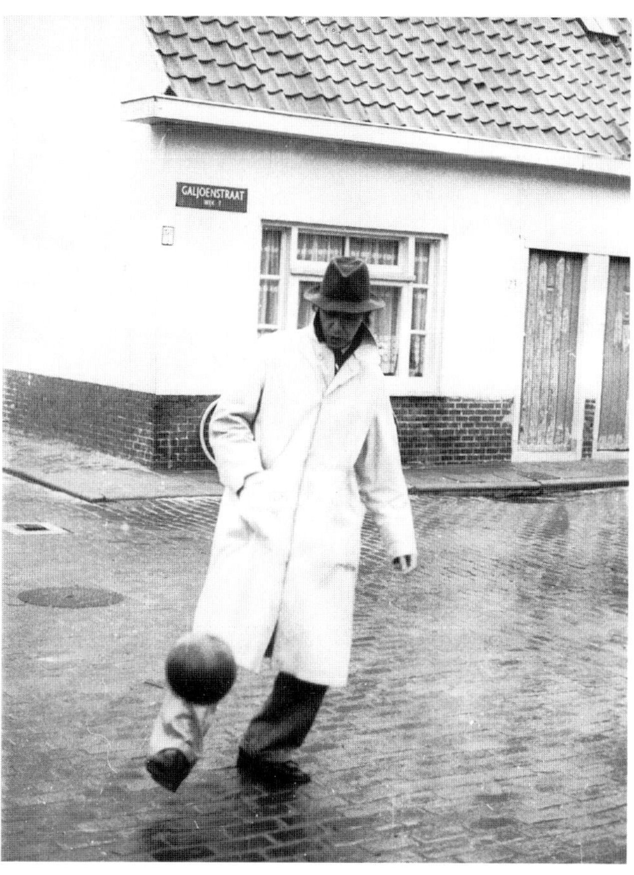

Walter Zschokke

In der Republik Österreich, dem Kernland der vor mehr als einem Menschenalter geschrumpften und zerfallenen Donaumonarchie, sind jene Persönlichkeiten rar geworden, die sich gleichermaßen im deutschsprachigen wie im slawisch sprechenden Raum auskennen. Boris Podrecca, in dessen Namen sich bereits die kulturellen Sphären mischen, ist in Belgrad geboren und in Triest aufgewachsen. Er hat in Wien Architektur studiert und lehrte an Hochschulen beidseits des Atlantiks, bevor er in Stuttgart die Professur an der Technischen Universität übernahm. Vielsprachig wie er ist, bewegt er sich südlich und nördlich der Alpen wie zu Hause, kann in Los Angeles spontan mit einem Taxichauffeur über Boxen diskutieren, um fast übergangslos mit den verblüfften Begleitern ein Spezialproblem der Architektur zu erörtern, denn er ist ein Vermittler zwischen den sozialen Schichten, den Kulturen und Zeiten.

In seiner Arbeit steht neben einer bildhaften Sprache, mit der er seine Überlegungen erläutert, die Zeichnung im Vordergrund. Podrecca ist ein zeichnender Entwerfer, der, ständig skizzierend, seine Entwurfsgedanken in der suchend insistierenden Zeichnung überprüft und vorantreibt. Von großen Projekten, wie beispielsweise der Basler Versicherung am Donaukanal, gibt es daher zahlreiche Skizzen aus verschiedensten Phasen der Entwicklung, die das prozeßhafte Arbeiten spiegeln.

Vom Werden eines Architekten

Anhand der frühen Arbeiten Podreccas, den Umbauten und Anbauten, kleinen Einfamilienhäusern oder etwa dem pavillonartigen Holzbau für die Werbeagentur GGK im Garten der Villa Vojcsik läßt sich nachvollziehen, daß für ihn jeder Bau dieser Phase auch eine bewußt gewählte Auseinandersetzung mit bestimmten Prinzipien und Formen ist, mit denen er sich gerade beschäftigte. Meist stammen diese Prinzipien und Formen von Bauwerken, die von wichtigen Persönlichkeiten des österreichischen Architekturschaffens am Anfang dieses Jahrhunderts entworfen wurden. Aber die trockene Analyse der Raumkompositionen von Adolf Loos, der texturierten Oberflächen von Josef Hoffmann, der Materialsensibilität Jože Plečniks und der kritischen Modernität von Josef Frank reichte ihm nicht aus. Wie das Kleinkind, das die ergriffenen Gegenstände in den Mund steckt, um sie zu schmecken und auch mit der Zunge tastend zu erfassen, was es da zu lernen geben könnte, suchte Podrecca im praktischen entwerferischen Nachvollzug der Prinzipien und Formen nach den dahinterliegenden Gedanken, aber auch nach den spezifischen Problemen der entsprechenden Detaillösungen. Diese gezielte Selbstschulung mag den einen als Nachahmung erscheinen, ist aber etwas anderes und daher wesentlich mehr. Das Ausprobieren und Durchspielen von gestalterischen Mustern oder grundrißlichen Typologien führt zu einem direkten, vorsprachlichen Erkennen von Materialgefühl, von Formgedanken und vom Verhältnis zwischen Material, Form und Herstellung. Im gleich-

In the Republic of Austria – the core country of the Danube monarchy which diminished in size and was dismantled more than a generation ago – those personalities have become rare who are familiar at the same time with the German as well as the Slavic speaking areas. Boris Podrecca, in whose name the cultural spheres are already mixed, was born in Belgrade and grew up in Trieste. He studied architecture in Vienna and taught at universities on both sides of the Atlantic ocean before taking over the professorship at the Technical University in Stuttgart.

Speaking as many languages as he does, he feels at home both North and South of the Alps and is capable of spontaneously discussing boxing with a cab driver in Los Angeles while almost simultaneously talking about a specific architectural problem with his astounded companions. He is a mediator between social classes, cultures, and times.

In his work, side by side with a pictorial language with which he explains his thoughts, drawing plays an important role and is always in the foreground. Podrecca is a draftsman who, always sketching, verifies his design concepts through searching, persistent drawing, thus pushing them forward. Consequently, many sketches of his large projects exist – the Basel Insurance Company building on the Danube Canal is but one example – which clearly illustrate the various stages of development, reflecting the process oriented nature of his work.

On becoming an architect

Podrecca's earlier works – conversions and expansions, small single family homes, and more specifically, the pavilion-like wooden construction for GGK advertising agency in the garden of Villa Vojcsik – make it possible to understand that each building of this phase represents a consciously chosen confrontation with certain principles and forms that he was dealing with during this period. Most of the time these principles and forms stemmed from buildings which were designed by important personalities in Austrian architecture in the beginning of this century. However, a dry analysis of the spatial compositions by Adolf Loos, the textured surfaces by Josef Hoffman, Jože Plečniks sensibility for materials, and the critical modernity of Josef Frank were not enough for Podrecca. Similar to the toddler sticking all seized objects into his mouth in order to taste them and understand all things to be learned by touching them with his tongue, Podrecca searched not only for the underlying thoughts but also for the specific problems of the appropriate detailed solutions with his methodically designed reconstruction of the principles and forms. This purposeful self-education may appear to some as an imitation; however, it is something else and therefore, much more. The trying-out and playing-through of fashioning patterns or ground plan typologies leads to a direct, pre-language recognition of a feeling for the material, of thoughts on form, and of the ratio between material,

wertigen Nebeneinander der Arbeiten der Vorväter, wie es sich durch dieses Durcharbeiten präsentiert, liegt auch der Schlüssel für das Verständnis unterschiedlicher Herangehensweisen und eigenständiger formaler Auffassungen, was im strikten Nachfolgen und Befolgen der Spur eines einzigen Meisters mangels Vergleichsmöglichkeiten eher zu kurz kommt. Natürlich besteht auch die Gefahr der Verwirrung ob der vielen Bilder, Muster und Theorien, aber das entwerferische Durcharbeiten und die Umsetzung bis hin zum gebauten Objekt schützt vor Oberflächlichkeiten und läßt eine praktische Erfahrung anwachsen, die parallel zum architekturtheoretischen Gewinn immer stärker an Reichtum zunimmt.

Das Bekleiden klimatisierter Lufträume

Die systematische Selbstschulung kennzeichnet Boris Podreccas Arbeiten der ersten Jahre als freischaffender Architekt. Das Risiko unzeitgemäß zu wirken, hat ihn unter anderem nicht gehindert, sich intensiv mit der Bekleidungstheorie Gottfried Sempers zu befassen, während andere der Postmoderne huldigten. Auch hier ging es ihm nicht nur darum, zu wissen, sondern durch praktisches Ausprobieren an Bauten sich den Inhalten dieser Theorie anzunähern, ihren Möglichkeiten mit heutigen Mitteln nachzuspüren und ihre Wirkung im zeitgenössischen Kontext zu verifizieren und nutzbar zu machen. Dies läßt sich beispielsweise an der steinverkleideten Rückfassade der Villa Moralić in Cavtat erkennen, deren Platten vor der verputzten Wand montiert sind. Tür- und Fensteröffnungen wurden jeweils exakt in der Fugenachse, eigentlich entgegen dem System der Steinteilung eingeschnitten, um deutlich zu machen, daß keine tektonische Ordnung vorliegt. Mit der Verlagerung der Türen und Fenster in die äußerste Ebene der Steinplatten wird der schicht- oder hautartige Charakter des vorgeblendeten Wandelements verdeutlicht. Andererseits ist die steinverkleidete Fläche kleiner als die gesamte Hausmauer. Sie wird damit zum Wandschirm, zu einem Bestandteil einer größeren Fassade, wobei die geringe Materialstärke dieser Steinhaut nicht ausgeblendet, sondern an der seitlichen Kante explizit gezeigt wird.

Umgekehrt und dennoch ähnlich verhält es sich beim Wohnhaus Schlamminger in München: Der Rahmen einer massiven Mauer umfaßt die Doppelreihe hochformatiger Fenster; Zwischenpfeiler und Brüstungen sind mit einer Vertikalschalung versehen, deren Fugen mit halbrunden Leisten gedeckt sind. Obwohl diese Verkleidung aus festem Material gefertigt ist, entsteht der Eindruck eines Vorhangs, das heißt eines textilen Elements. Die am oberen Abschluß ornamentartig aufgesetzten kleinen Ringe verstärken noch diesen Eindruck. Unter verschiedenen Voraussetzungen hat sich Podrecca in beiden Fällen mit dem Prinzip der Bekleidung auseinandergesetzt, mit formalen Analogien und strukturellen Verwandtschaften, aber auch mit der eher abstrakten Problematik von Fugenbildern und mit deren klassischen beziehungsweise gegenklassischen Aussagen gespielt.

form and production. In the side by side comparison of the progenitors' work as it is presented through this working-through lies also the key to understanding different approaches and independent formal opinions which, lacking a possibility for comparison, is rather neglected when one strictly follows in the footsteps of a single master. Of course, the danger of confusion is close at hand considering the many pictures, patterns and theories that exist, but the working-through of the concept and the translation of the design into the actual completed project fights off superficialities and lets a practical experience grow, whose wealth increases parallel to the theoretical architectural gain.

The attire of climate control spaces

The systematic self-education marks Boris Podrecca's works of his first years as an independent architect. Among other things, the risk of having a non-contemporary effect did not prevent him from dealing intensively with the clothing theory of Gottfried Semper while others were paying homage to postmodernism. Here as well, his point was not to know outright, but rather to approach the contents of this theory by practical experiments, to follow the subsequent revealed possibilities with the currently available means, and also to verify and utilize their effect in a contemporary context. This can be seen, for example, in the stone-clad rear facade of Villa Moralić in Cavtat, whose panels are mounted in front of the plastered wall. The door and window openings were cut out right in the seam axis which stands contrary to the normal system of stone division. This was done in order to clarify that there is no tectonic order. By moving the doors and windows to the outer level of the stone panels, the layered or skin-like character of the curtain wall element becomes even more clear. On the other hand, the stone-clad surface is smaller than the surface of the entire wall of the house. It thus becomes a protective screen and an integrated component of a larger facade. In the process, the slight thickness of the material of this stone shell, rather than being minimized, is instead shown explicitly on the lateral edge.

Conversely and yet similar is the case of the apartment building, Schlamminger, in Munich: the frame of a massive wall encloses the double row of high format windows; interstitial columns and parapets have a vertical form work whose joints are covered with semi-circular strips. Although this paneling is made of a firm material, it calls forth the image of a curtain, i.e., a textile element. The small rings placed like ornaments on the upper termination increase this impression. In both cases, Podrecca has come to terms with the principle of clothing under differing conditions not only with formal analogies and structural relationships, but also with the rather abstract problem of seam line appearance and has played with their classical or counter-classical statements.

Suche nach Form

Die Arbeiten Podreccas zeigen entgegen einer gerade aktuellen Modeströmung einen großen Formenreichtum. Diese Vielfalt entsteht jedoch nicht durch die quasi mechanische Erzeugung von Varianten, sondern als Folge der Suche nach Greifbarem, nach Anknüpfungspunkten in der Vielfalt des Vorhandenen. Zugleich gilt die Suche aber auch dem Ende des vorangegangenen Abschnitts der architektonisch-kulturellen Erzählung. Wenn Podrecca so ein dreidimensional konkretisiertes Ende einer gebauten Geschichte wie ein Fundstück in Händen hält, drängt ihn die Lust nach Form in assoziativen und dissoziativen Denkfiguren zu immer neuen Interpretationen, Weiterungen und Ergänzungen. Oft steht dabei auch der Schalk nicht weit entfernt, jedenfalls erfolgt das Fabulieren in Formen locker und frei von engstirniger Dogmatik.

Das Bauwerk als Erzählwerk

Das Erzählen von skurrilen Erlebnissen und hintergründigen Zusammenhängen liegt in der Natur Boris Podreccas. Dabei erinnert er manchmal an einen orientalischen Märchenerzähler, der Menschenschicksale, Spannung, Mythen und Wunder geschickt mit Lebensweisheit verbindet. Ein häufiges Muster ist die Schachtelerzählung, in der eine Geschichte aus der anderen hervorgeht, wie wir es von russischen Märchen kennen. In den Entwürfen für seine Bauten spielt das Erzählmotiv ebenfalls eine wichtige Rolle, doch ist seine Erzählung in diesem Fall nicht eine in Worten oder folgt anderweitig einem sprachlichen Aufbau; vielmehr sind es Materialien, Oberflächentexturen, Formen, Konstruktionsweisen usw. die Bedeutungen tragen. Als Bezugsebene dient dabei die Architektur- und die Kulturgeschichte. Natürlich versteht man die in der Sprache der Dinge vorgebrachten Inhalte umso besser, je genauer man das Wesen der Architektur und die Möglichkeiten des Bauens kennt. Aber nicht alle Betrachter sind Architekten. Nun gibt es bei Podrecca eine weitere Bezugsebene, jene der Lebensvorgänge, die dem Verstehen auf die Sprünge hilft.

Es ist im Mittelmeerraum durchaus üblich und verbreitet, auch technische Sachverhalte in sprachliche Bilder zu kleiden, die unmittelbar aus dem Leben gegriffen sind. Was im Deutschen etymologisch bereits stark verschliffen ist, etwa bei dem Begriffspaar Nut und Kamm, das die Verbindungsprofile zum Aneinanderfügen von Brettern benennt, wird beispielsweise im Italienischen in einer kulturell vernetzteren Form ausgedrückt. Zwar ist «Nut» grammatikalisch weiblich und «Kamm» männlich. Es bedarf aber einer weiterzigen Freudschen Auslegung dieser Worte, um sie mit dem männlichen bzw. weiblichen Geschlecht in Beziehung zu setzen. In der italienischen Handwerkersprache heißt die Nut «femmina» und der Kamm wird als «maschio» bezeichnet.

Bei einer Verschalung wird nun die jeweils männliche und die

In search of form

Podrecca's work shows a tremendous wealth of form running contrary to current fashionable movements. This diversity, however, does not develop through the quasi-mechanical creation of versions. Instead, it is the result of a search for something tangible; reference points in the multitude of the existing. At the same time, the search is directed towards the end of the preceding chapter, the architectural-cultural tale. When Podrecca is holding such a three-dimensional concrete end of a constructed history in his hands like a found object, his lust for form in associate and dissociate thought figures urges him towards ever new interpretations, expansions and additions. Oftentimes, roguery is not far away. At any rate, the invention of stories takes place loosely and without narrow-minded dogmas.

The building as a narrative tale

Telling about strange experiences and background contexts is Boris Podrecca's nature. In doing so, he sometimes reminds one of an oriental fairy tale teller who smartly connects human destinies, suspension, myths and miracles with the wisdom of living. A frequent pattern is the staggered tale in which one story comes out of the other, as we know from Russian fairy tales. The motif of story-telling plays an important role in the designs for his buildings. However, in this case his tale is not worded nor does it follow a linguistic structure; moreover, it is the materials, surface textures, forms, construction methods, etc., which carry the meaning. Architectural and cultural history serve as a level of reference. Of course, the contents told in the language of things can be understood better if one knows the essence of architecture and the possibilities of construction. But not all observers are architects. With Podrecca, there is yet another level of reference, the level of life processes, which helps the understanding to come into being.

It is a rather common and wide-spread practice in the Mediterranean countries to garb even technical facts in linguistic images taken directly from every-day life. For example, the vernacular pair "tongue" and "groove", which describe the connecting profiles for putting together boards, is rather exhausted etymologically in the German language. In Italian, however, this is expressed in a culturally more complex and interwoven form. "Groove" (Nut) in German is feminine and "tongue" (Kamm) masculine. However, it takes a rather open-hearted Freudian interpretation of these terms to relate them to the masculine or feminine gender. In the Italian trade language the groove is called "femmina" and the tongue "maschio".

In case of a planking, the male and the female sides of the boards are pushed together and fixed to the sub-construction by nails which are hammered in at an angle above the tongue. The term for these narrow sides which are shaped differently with

weibliche Seite der Bretter ineinander gestoßen und mit Nägeln, die schräg über dem Kamm eingeschlagen werden, auf der Unterkonstruktion befestigt. Die Bezeichnung der zum Fügen verschieden ausgebildeten Schmalseiten ist nun nicht etwa schlüpfrig, sondern trocken volkstümlich. Überdies ist so eine Verschalung zugleich ein einfaches Modell einer homogenen dörflichen Gemeinschaft und Gesellschaft des Zusammenhaltens und der Nachbarschaftshilfe. Alltägliches Leben findet auf diese Weise eine Entsprechung in der sprachlichen Interpretation verbreiteter handwerklicher Prinzipien. Derartige Bilder sind allgemein verständlich und benötigen keine Erläuterungen.

Die Metaphern und Bilder in Podreccas Schaffen sind vornehmlich von dieser letzteren, das Leben interpretierenden Art; etwa wenn er bei der Schule Dirmhirngasse den großen Steg über die Straße zum alten Schulgebäude als männlich, die abgehängte Passerelle, die im ersten Obergeschoß durch die Pausenhalle führt, als weiblich bezeichnet. In diesem Fall sind die Benennungen weniger mit Mann und Frau oder mit dem Geschlecht in Beziehung zu sehen, als mit Eigenschaften, die wir sowohl bei Männern als auch bei Frauen vorfinden können, aber als weiblich oder männlich identifizieren. Das ingenieurmäßige Fachwerk des Stegs unterscheidet sich von dem nicht minder genau berechneten Hängewerk der Passerelle. Die formale Ausbildung des Fachwerks mit Schweiß- und Schraubverbindungen in der Tradition des Stahlbaus steht im Gegensatz zu jener der Passerelle, die wie aus Seilen geknüpft und gespannt wirkt, obwohl die Hängestäbe durchaus ebenfalls aus Stahl bestehen. Dennoch kommen einem die Hängebrücken aus Ziegenhaarseilen in den Sinn, wie sie im Himalaya gebräuchlich waren oder jene aus geflochtenen Graszöpfen, wie sie von den Inkas in den Anden errichtet wurden. Männlich und weiblich stehen auch für das analytische, geometrisch-rechnerische Prinzip des Fachwerks einerseits und für das handarbeitsmäßig-textile Zusammenwirken ganzheitlicher Ansätze andererseits. Beide Prinzipien finden in Podreccas Schaffen Eingang, sie sind für ihn keine einander ausschließenden Gegensätze, sondern Ausdrucksmittel bestimmter räumlich-konstruktiver Konstellationen wie auch der Formgebung im Detail.

Arbeiten an der Stadt

Bei städtebaulich relevanten Projekten ist die Suche nach möglichen Anknüpfungspunkten eine wichtige Voraussetzung für den späteren Entwurf. Podrecca will die Geschichten erfahren und ergründen, die sich städtebaulich und architektonisch im Umfeld des zu bearbeitenden Grundstücks abgespielt haben. Ob nun in den Ablagerungen und Schichten eine Ordnung zu erkennen ist oder ob nur mehr Fragmente vorliegen, nach einer inhaltlich und formal bestimmten Gewichtung nimmt er darauf Bezug, um mit seiner neuen Erzählung einen Beitrag zur Fortsetzung der Kulturgeschichte zu liefern.

Beim Entwurf für den Slomškov Trg in Maribor nimmt er bei-

the purpose of putting them together, however, is not lascivious but simply a dry popular expression. Furthermore, such a planking is a simple model for a homogeneous rural community and society which sticks together with neighbor helping neighbor. In this way, the every day life finds an equivalence in the linguistic interpretation of widely-spread principles of the trades. Such images can be commonly understood and need no further explanations. The metaphors and pictures in Podrecca's work relate mainly with this latter way – as a means for interpreting life. For example, he describes the small bridge across the street leading from the new school in Dirmhirngasse to the old school building as masculine, and the suspended walkway leading to the school recess hall on the first floor, as feminine. In this case, the choice of terms is not referring to the sexes, but rather to characteristics which we find in men as well as women yet identify to be either masculine or feminine. The engineered Tudor construction of the bridge is different from the not less calculated truss frame of the walkway. The formal execution of the Tudor with welding and screw joints in the tradition of steel work opposes that of the walkway which has the appearance of knotted ropes and of being stretched, although the hanging rods are made of steel as well. Still, one remembers the suspended bridges made of goat hair ropes as they used to be made in the Himalayas, or those made of grass plaits built by the Inca in the Andes. Masculine and feminine also represent the analytical geometric calculation principle of the Tudor on the one hand, and the needlework textile co-effect of holistic approaches on the other. Both principles enter into Podrecca's work. They are to him not opposites that exclude one another. They are instead a means of expression of certain spatial-constructive constellations as well as the forms in detail.

Works on the city

When it comes to projects that are relevant in an urban sense, the search for possible points of reference is an important precondition for the subsequent design. Podrecca wants to learn and understand the stories which took place on an urban and architectural level in the surroundings of the property to be worked on. Whether there is a recognizable order in the layers and deposits or whether there are only fragments, he refers to them to a formally and content-defined extent in order to contribute to the continuation of cultural history with his tale.

In his design for the Slomškov Trg in Maribor, for example, he takes up the suggestion of Jože Plečnik who decades ago proposed to embrace the cathedral in the center of the square with a huge ellipse. Although it never left the planning stage, Podrecca took this idea as seriously as though it had been realized once before and had actually existed for a while. However, he reinterprets it. With the surface of stones, he chooses an old method of pavement and thus points to the fact that this idea is older than the remaining square design.

spielsweise den Vorschlag Jože Plečniks wieder auf, der vor Jahrzehnten vorschlug, die mitten im Platz befindliche Kathedrale mit einer riesigen Ellipse zu fassen. Obwohl Projekt geblieben, nimmt Podrecca diese Idee so ernst, wie wenn sie schon einmal ausgeführt worden wäre und einige Zeit bestanden hätte. Allerdings deutet er sie um. Mit dem Belag aus großen halbierten Kieselsteinen wählt er eine alte Methode der Pflästerung und deutet damit an, daß diese Idee älter ist, als die übrige Platzgestaltung. Das Gebäude der Basler Versicherung, das im oberen Bereich des Donaukanals in eine nahezu homogene, gründerzeitliche Bebauung mit Zinshäusern zu stehen kam, hat eine strukturelle Veränderung des Quartiers zur Folge. Podrecca, der das Defizit des Bezirks an öffentlichen Räumen erkannte, schlug einen zur Allee aufgewerteten Straßenzug vom Bezirkszentrum bis zur Uferpromenade vor, die an an der Gelenkstelle durch den Neubau der Basler Versicherung mit einer Markierung versehen wurde. Die wegen der Baumpflanzung verlorenen Parkplätze kompensierte die Basler mit einem weiteren Parkgeschoß.

Die Ansprüche der großen Versicherung, ihren Wiener Hauptsitz mit einer signifikanten Fassade zu versehen, die im Rahmen des Uferprospekts auffällt und auf die mittlere Distanz über den als «Donaukanal» ungenügend gewürdigten alten Donauarm hinweg wirken soll, verstand Podrecca zu verbinden mit den allgemeinen Interessen der vorgegebenen städtebaulichen Gesamtsituation. Das sich von seinen Nachbarn angemessen unterscheidende Bauwerk ist nicht bloß ein Zeichen höherer Ordnung im Flußraum der kleinen Donau, vielmehr wirkt es zugleich als Kopf der neuen Binnenpromenade durch das dahinterliegende Quartier. Podrecca denkt damit nicht nur an die gebaute Stadt, sondern auch an die gelebte Stadt, in der erst durch die kollektive Beanspruchung der öffentlichen Räume Bedeutungen verdichtet werden und in der Folge Strukturelemente einer kollektiven Erinnerung entstehen können. Die Öffnung des Hofes als Durchgang zur Uferpromenade ist eine Komponente; die deutliche Zurücknahme des Anspruchs bei jenen Fassaden, die zu den Quartiersstraßen des angrenzenden 20. Bezirks orientiert sind, ist die andere Komponente. Podrecca schafft damit einen Ort, der benennbar ist, der eine qualitative Veränderung durchgemacht hat, aber nicht arrogant wirkt, denn der Neubau ist auf verschiedenen Ebenen mit seiner Umgebung verwoben. Podreccas Vorgehen kommt einem Anknüpfen und einem Weitererzählen gleich, auch wenn die Fortsetzung nicht in demselben Rhythmus weitergeht.

Architektur als Bindeglied

Jedem Betrachter wird sofort klar, daß die Bauten Podreccas keine abstrakten Kuben sind, deren Fassaden einem strengen Raster gehorchen, oder wie eine Tapete allseitig von Kante zu Kante herumlaufen. Seine Bauten haben – im übertragenen Sinn – Füße, Kopf und Bauch; zwar gehorcht ihr Aufbau einer Ordnung, sie enthält aber immer auch Störungen eben dieser

The Basel Insurance Company's building, which was erected in the upper section of the Danube Canal in an almost homogenous development of the 19th century's so-called "time of wild speculation", initiates a structural change of the quarter. Podrecca, who recognized the district's lack of open public spaces, suggested a street running from the district's center to the quay, revalorized towards the avenue. At the juncture, it was met by the new building of the Basel Insurance Company. The parking spaces lost to the tree plantings were compensated for with a new level for parking purposes.

The demands of the large insurance company to give a significant facade to their main seat in Vienna, which would stand out in the surrounding quay setting and, on a medium distance, to have an effect beyond the old branch of the Danube, which the description "Danube Canal" does not honor sufficiently, were understood by Podrecca and fulfilled by connecting them with the general interest of the given urban situation. The building which appropriately distinguishes itself from its neighbors is not only a sign of a higher order in the river's space of the small Danube. It also has the effect of being a head-building for the new promenade, given by the quarter lying to its rear. Podrecca thus not only thinks of the built city but also of the lived city, in which meanings are condensed by the collective use of the public spaces and, as a consequence, structural elements of a collective memory can come into being. The opening of the yard as a passageway leading to the promenade is one component. The clear reduction of the demand for those facades oriented towards the quarter streets of the adjoining 20th district, is the other component. Thus, Podrecca creates a location which can be named and which has undergone a qualitative transformation but does not have an arrogant feel to it because the new building is interwoven with its surroundings on different levels. Podrecca's procedure resembles a connecting link and a continuation of the tale, although the continuation has a different rhythm.

Architecture as a connecting link

Each observer realizes instantly that the buildings of Boris Podrecca aren't simply abstract cubes whose facades conform to a strict grid or which, similar to tapestry, run around on all sides from edge to edge. His buildings, in a figurative sense, have feet, head, and torso; their arrangement follows an order, but it always contains disturbances of this order or enhancements of specific points. This, however, does not serve an egotistical purpose, but is usually the result of contextual reasons. At the same time, the disturbance points to the order and, vice versa, the order exposes the inconsistency.

Contrary to concepts which declare one aspect of the building to be absolute and which radically place it into the foreground while at the same time increasing its gravity one-sidedly, with Podrecca it is always a bundle of architectural measures of

Ordnung oder Auszeichnungen bestimmter Stellen. Dies ist nicht Selbstzweck, sondern erfolgt meist aus inhaltlichen Gründen; aber zugleich macht die Störung auf die Ordnung aufmerksam und umgekehrt exponiert die Ordnung die Unstetigkeit.

Im Gegensatz zu Konzepten, die einen Aspekt des Bauwerks absolut setzen und radikal in den Vordergrund rücken, gleichsam eindimensional zuspitzen, ist es bei Podrecca immer ein Bündel architektonischer Maßnahmen, die, im einzelnen etwas leiser auftretend, gemeinsam als komplexes Ganzes wirken. In ihrer Mehrdimensionalität liegt auch die Chance zur Kommunikation mit dem Umfeld. Das Beispiel der Hauptschule Dirmhirngasse in Wien-Liesing illustriert diese Haltung sehr gut. Der Baukörper ist in vier Teile gegliedert: da sind die beiden Klassentrakte, dann die Eingangshalle, die als Gelenk wirkt und die Klassentrakte verbindet, und als vierter Teil der Ateliertrakt. Mit dem Steg über die Dirmhirngasse wird auch der Altbau respektvoll angebunden, der quergestellte Ateliertrakt als Nordabschluß faßt den Raum und schließt ihn ab, so daß die offene Mitte mit den großen alten Bäumen zu einem wesentlichen Element der Gesamtkonzeption wird.

Die Fassaden unterscheiden nicht zwischen den einzelnen Klassenzimmern, wirken also eher integral, dafür wird die Massenwirkung durch die Terrassierung relativiert. Der Steg schießt von dem am weitesten zurückliegenden Teil des Verbindungstrakts nach vorn und erreicht mit einer einzigen Öffnung den Pfeiler auf dem gegenüberliegenden Gehsteig. In einem von diesem ersten verschiedenen, zweiten Schritt nähert sich dann der verglaste, innerhalb des Tragwerks verlaufende Gang dem Altbau, in den er respektvoll neben dem Mittelrisalit eindringt. Man kann nun nicht sagen, daß Podrecca vor starken Gesten zurückschrecken würde, doch er spürt und weiß zugleich, wo innehalten, um die begonnene Bewegung mit einer abgestuft feineren Maßnahme zuende zu führen. Damit erhält das Bauwerk einen verbindlichen Ausdruck, der unangenehme Arroganz vermeidet.

Etwas anders verhält es sich bei der Stadtbücherei in Biberach, wo die starken Elemente in Form des großen autonomen Baukörpers und des darin enthaltenen Zimmermannswerks bereits vorhanden waren. Das architektonische Vorgehen ist daher einerseits von Respekt gegenüber dieser Ganzheit geprägt, andererseits galt es doch, deren Absolutheit zu relativieren, um aus dem reinen Zweckbau ein öffentlich nutzbares Kulturbauwerk zu machen. Während der gläserne Windfang als Zeichen für den Eingang vor das Gebäude verlegt wird, so daß die Grenze zum großen Innenraum weiterhin von der kräftigen Mauerschale gebildet wird, hat Podrecca im Mittelbereich einen Teil des raumfüllenden Zimmermannswerks geopfert, um eine räumliche Vertikalverbindung und zugleich Belichtungsquelle für den Innenraum zu schaffen. In diese Lücke kommen zwei weitere neue Elemente, der verglaste Lift und das betonierte Fluchtstiegenhaus zu stehen. Alle weiteren Maßnahmen bewegen sich bereits in einem untergeordneten Verhältnis zum Bestand und

which each by itself is more like a whisper – but all of them together have the effect of a complex whole. In their multidimensionality lies the chance for communication with the surroundings. The example of the school at Dirmhirngasse in Vienna-Liesing illustrates this attitude very well. The building volume is structured in four parts: there are the two classroom blocks, the entrance lobby acting as an articulation connecting the classroom blocks, and the studio block acting as a fourth element. The old building is respectfully integrated through the bridge across Dirmhirngasse. The perpendicular studio block serving as a northern termination point, seizes the space and closes it up making the open center with the large old trees an essential element of the entire concept.

The facades do not make a distinction between the classrooms and therefore have a more integral effect. However, the mass effect is made relative by the terracing. The bridge shoots forward from the most remote part of the connecting block and, with a single opening, reaches the column on the opposite walkway. In a second step different from this first one, the glassed-in walkway inside the supporting structure approaches the old building, respectfully penetrating it next to the central projection. Now, it can not be said that Podrecca shies away from strong gestures; however, he feels and at the same time knows where to pause in order to bring the initiated movement to an end with a more subtle, gradual measure. Thus, the building acquires an obliging expression, avoiding an uncomfortable arrogance.

The municipal library in Biberach is yet a different case. The strong elements of the large free-standing building and the timber work inside were already there. The architectural procedure is therefore marked by a certain respect for this entity on one hand; on the other, this entity's absoluteness was to be made relative in order to turn the utility building into a cultural building for public use. While the glassed-in vestibule is moved to the front of the building signaling the entrance, and the border to the spacious interior is still defined by the thick masonry layer, Podrecca sacrificed some of the space-filling timber work in the middle area in order to create a spatial vertical connection and, at the same time, a lighting source for the interior. This gap is filled by two new elements: the glassed-in elevator and the concrete emergency staircase. All other measures move within a subordinate relationship to the existing structure and remain at a relative distance. The new staircase touches the ground only through an elliptically formed "pillow" of steel. This detail illustrates two facts: first, the refusal of a constructive functionalism, and secondly, the departure from the dogma of a so-called material justice. Podrecca opens the doors to a new architectural understanding, nurturing the joy of a formally differentiated expression beyond the monomaniac pathos and dogmatic narrowness.

halten relative Distanz. So berührt der neue Treppenlauf den Erdboden nur über ein elliptisch verformtes «Kissen» aus Stahl. Dieses Detail illustriert zwei Sachverhalte: erstens die Verweigerung eines konstruktiven Funktionalismus und zweitens den Abschied vom Dogma einer sogenannten Materialgerechtigkeit. Damit öffnet Podrecca die Türen zu einem Architekturverständnis, das jenseits von monomanischem Pathos und dogmatischer Enge die Freude an einem formal differenzierten Ausdruck pflegt.

Muskeln, Sehnen und gefrorene Bewegung

Konstruktion ist für Podrecca eine Möglichkeit, um Kraft, Bewegung, Hülle und Oberfläche sichtbar zu machen. Dies zeigt sich bei Mazda-Lietz in Waidhofen/Ybbs an dem dynamisch aufgestützten Vordach und an der gefächerten Glaswand entlang der aufgeständerten Fahrbahnkurve, aber auch bei der Basler Versicherung in Wien-Brigittenau an den geschuppten Brüstungsbändern der Hauptfassade. Wenn Podrecca das heute allgemein beliebte Structural Glazing anwendet, dient dies der Erzielung einer architektonischen Aussage, nicht dem Beweis, die neueste Mode auch schon zu kennen. Mit Gelassenheit wählt er daher für die Fensterwände der Pausenhalle seiner Schule in Wien-Liesing die klassische Metallrahmenkonstruktion, weil er das konstruktive Gespinst hinter der Glasebene vermeiden will. Beim Geländer im nahen Stiegenhaus kommt ihm wiederum das Prinzip der punktgestützten Glastafeln entgegen, aber nicht etwa deshalb, weil er nur die reine Durchsichtigkeit des Glases gesucht hätte, sondern weil ihm die formale Lebendigkeit der Stützkonstruktion für diesen schwallartig genützten, in der übrigen Zeit eher ruhigen Raum richtig schien. In den konstruktiven Elementen und Verbindungen steckt aus Podreccas Sicht architektonisches Leben, das genutzt sein will. Seine Fassaden sind nicht nur als Oberflächen aus mehr oder weniger edlen oder profanen Materialien konzipiert, sondern sprechen aus der Tiefe ihrer konstruktiven Schichten heraus. Dies gilt für die zwischen die weißen Betonpfeiler gespannte Metall-Glaskonstruktion der Liesinger Schule, wie für die flußseitige Fassade der Basler Versicherung mit ihren verschieden getönten, geschuppten Glastafeln. Der komplexe Aufbau dieser Fassadenkonstruktionen wird dabei weniger demonstriert als vielmehr symbolisiert.

Stein – Holz – Metall

Es ist wahrscheinlich der Stein, zu dem Podrecca die tiefste Beziehung entwickelt hat, nachvollziehbar etwa bei den vielfältigen Bodenbelägen der Plätze oder bei skulpturalen Elementen und ab und zu einem Brunnen. In verfeinerter Form kommt diese Liebe zum Stein dort zum Ausdruck, wo er den Stein als Tapete einsetzt, wie beim Café Platana in Ljubljana oder gar als Bild, wie bei der Sitzplatzwand am Wohnhaus Glaser in Liesing. Metall wird über den konstruktiven Bereich hinaus als plastisch verformbares Material betrachtet und behandelt. Beispiele sind die

Muscles, tendons and frozen movement

For Podrecca, construction makes possible the visualization of force, movement, shell, and surface. This is apparent in the Mazda-Lietz building in Waidhofen/Ybbs in the dynamically supported canopy and the fanned glass wall along the stilted roadway curve. But it also can be seen at the Basel Insurance Company building in Vienna-Brigittenau, with the scale-like parapet strips on the main facade. If Podrecca applies the generally well-liked structural glazing, it serves only to achieve an architectural statement, not a declaration of his knowledge concerning the latest fashion. With definite calmness he therefore chooses the classical metal frame construction for the Vienna-Liesing school hall because he wants to avoid the constructive web behind the glass level. The principle of the point-supported glass panels serves him well for the stairway banisters not because he strove merely for the transparency of the glass, but because he felt that this formal vitality of the supporting construction was appropriate for this space which tends to be rather crowded during specific times of the day, and is rather quiet for the remaining time. In Podrecca's view, there is an architectural life in these constructive elements and connections waiting to be used. His facades are not only conceived as mere surfaces made of more or less noble or profound materials, but also because they speak from the depths of their constructive layers. This is the case with the metal-glass-construction stretched in between the white concrete columns of the school in Liesing and with the facade of the Basel Insurance Company building facing the river with its differently hued and scale-like glass plates. Here, the complex arrangement of these facade constructions is not being demonstrated so much as it is being symbolized.

Stone – wood – metal

It is probably to stone that Podrecca has developed the closest relationship, as can be seen in the multifaceted surfacing of squares, in sculptural elements and occasionally, in a fountain. In a more subtle way, this love for stone is expressed where he uses stone as a tapestry – the Platana café in Ljubljana – or even as a picture – the wall of the sitting area in the Glaserhouse in Liesing.
Metal is considered and used beyond the constructive realm as a sculptural and malleable material. Some examples are: the bent hanging rods in the Liesing school's walkway and the details in the Biberach municipal library's staircase. The search for a material expression that goes beyond the material's appropriate use – and also beyond a rather pathetic pretension of the "material just as material" – becomes clear with these examples.
Wood often appears in Podrecca's work as seen through the eyes of the stone-lover and as such, it is worked; however, this slightly antagonistic use provides it with a specific expression. Often, it is dematerialized by the use of color and finds its

umgebogenen Hängestäbe bei der Passerelle in der Liesinger Schule oder die Details der Treppe in der Stadtbücherei Biberach. Die Suche nach einem materialen Ausdruck jenseits werkbündischer Materialgerechtigkeit, aber auch fern einer pathetischen Pose des «Material nur als Material», wird daran deutlich.

Holz erscheint bei Podrecca oft durch die Brille des Steinliebhabers gesehen und verarbeitet, doch gibt ihm gerade das im Sinne einer leichten Verfremdung einen spezifischen Ausdruck. Oft ist es durch Farbe dematerialisiert und kommt eher in der leichtgewichtigen Form zu Ausdruck. Ob dies nun Stein, Holz, Metall oder Beton, Glas und Kunststoff ist, die Materialien werden nicht absolut, sondern immer als Mittel zur Erzielung einer architektonischen Wirkung gesehen.

Zivile Grundhaltung

Im Beruf des Architekten ist vieles eine Haltungsfrage, nicht zuletzt deshalb, weil die fertige Arbeit noch unbekannte Auswirkungen in die Zukunft verbergen kann. Wenn städtebauliche und architektonische Entscheidungen vermehrt von außerdisziplinären Faktoren beeinflußt werden, unter anderem auch durch den Tanz um eine von gesellschaftlichen und baupraktischen Überlegungen unbekümmerte, an Starkult orientierte verselbständigte Architekturpublizistik, gewinnt die zivile Grundhaltung eines Architekten immer mehr an Bedeutung.

Boris Podrecca selber meint dazu: «Ich bin in Triest aufgewachsen. Triest hat eine wunderschöne Architektur, die nicht arrogant ist und den Autor vermitteln muß – eben eine architettura civile, zurückhaltend nach außen, reich, bunt und individuell im Bauch. Heute, in einer Zeit des Bewußtseins für ökologische Probleme, müssen wir mit wenig arbeiten; in einer Zeit, die nicht mehr prospektiv, aber auch nicht retrospektiv, sondern faktisch heute ist, brauchen wir eine Architektur, die nicht mit den Ohren wackelt. Ich glaube, es ist eine interessenlose Architektur notwendig geworden. (...) Die Absage soll nicht zur intellektuellen, kunstnahen Ästhetik werden; das ist ein Malheur. Die Architektur muß den Menschen befreien und in einer gewissen Form eine joie de vivre vermitteln.»

Es kann durchaus sein, daß sich der formale Ausdruck der Bauwerke Podreccas in einigen Jahren wieder ändert, und sei es als Kommentar zu ideologiebefrachteten Architekturen. Die lebensfrohe, erzählerische Grundhaltung jedoch ist ein Konstante seiner Enwürfe, nach der zu suchen sich weiterhin lohnt.

expression rather in the light-weight form. Whether stone or wood, metal or concrete, glass or plastics, the materials are not considered in absolute terms, but always as a means for achieving an architectural effect.

Civil attitude

In the architectural profession, many things are a question of attitude, not in the least because the finished work can conceal unknown effects for the future. If urban and architectural decisions were to be influenced more and more by non-disciplinary factors, e.g., among others, such as through a dance free from society related and practical constructive thoughts or architectural publicity oriented towards cult stardom; the civil attitude of an architect becomes ever more important. Boris Podrecca comments as follows: "I grew up in Trieste. Trieste has a beautiful architecture which is not arrogant and does not have to mediate for the author – an architettura civile, restrained towards the outside and yet rich, colorful and individual in the belly. Today, in a time of a heightened awareness for ecological problems, we have to work with less. In a time which is no longer prospective and not retrospective either, but factually is today, we need an architecture which does not wiggle its ears. I believe that an architecture free of interest has become necessary. (...) The refusal should not become an intellectual and artistic esthetic; this would be unfortunate. Architecture has to free the individual and, in a specific way, communicate a joy of living."

It is possible that the formal expression of Boris Podrecca's buildings will change again a couple of years from now, be it even as a commentary on ideologically laden architectures. Still, the joyful and narrative attitude is a constant in his designs, the search for which continues to be worth the effort.

Die gestalterische Bearbeitung und der Umbau architektonisch wertvoller Bauten steht – gerade in Städten wie Wien mit einer dichten Ansammlung interessanter bis ausgezeichneter Bauten aus mehreren Jahrhunderten – oft am Beginn der selbständigen Tätigkeit eines Architekten. Die Auseinandersetzung mit bestehenden Ordnungen, vorhandenen Elementen, Bauteilen und Oberflächen, deren maßhaltende Integration in das zu schaffende neue Ganze, haben mit unbeirrbarer Beiläufigkeit zur Folge, daß der entwerfende und bauende Architekt einen Erkenntnisprozeß durchläuft. Es beginnt mit dem Einblick in den Bestand, wenn beim Teilabbruch die Schichten freigelegt werden und die tragenden, füllenden, trennenden und dämmenden Elemente zum Vorschein kommen. Aus der Anschauung und einer entsprechenden Erkenntnisarbeit ergeben sich nicht selten weitere Implikationen für den Entwurf.

Ein Blick auf die Werkliste Boris Podreccas zeigt, daß es sich bei ihm nicht viel anders verhält. Sehr gut zeigt dies der Einbau des neurophysischen Instituts in das barocke Palais Starhemberg: In einem denkmalgeschützten Saal, wo das raumfüllende System der Behandlungskojen mit säulenartigen Stehern unübersehbar präsent ist, die breiten Basen aber von den Skrupeln künden, auf dieses herrliche Parkett überhaupt eine derartige Struktur aufzustellen. Aber das Konzept hält: die Beziehung des Patienten zu Stuckdecke und Parkettboden, die je ein intergrales Ganzes bleiben, geht von der durch Vorhänge definierten Kabine immer auf den ganzen Raum, der auf diese Weise bewahrt wurde.

Anders liegt es bei der Renovation der Villa Vojcsik, die Otto Schönthal unter dem Szepter Otto Wagners erbaut hatte. Hier stießen die Forschungen zum Entwurfsprozeß vor, zum Verhältnis Meister und Schüler; und nicht zuletzt kam es zu einem sukzessiven Emanzipationsprozeß von der rein denkmalpflegerischen Arbeit, der in den völlig neu gestalteten Räumen im Souterrain kulminierte.

Es gibt aber auch die sparsame Variante, etwa die Boutique Lilli Pilli, wo mit geringen Mitteln ein größtmöglicher Effekt erzielt wird. Podrecca scheut sich nicht, beim Thema des Verkaufs von Kleidern, ja selbst von Dessous, den unweigerlich vorhandenen Aspekt der Erotik auch anzusprechen und mit Ernst und Augenzwinkern in den Entwurf einzuarbeiten. Dabei vermeidet er die platte Demonstration. Dazu gehören jedoch der Flirt, das ambivalente Spiel von Herzeigen und Verdecken, der entwaffnende Blick über die Schulter und weitere urmenschliche Verhaltensweisen, die Podrecca beobachtet und an die er gedacht hat, und die er bei der Gestaltung des Ambientes berücksichtigt hat. Dieser Bezug zum alltäglich-menschlichen Leben steht bei diesen Projekten vor dem schulmäßig denkmalpflegerischen Umgang, der bei normaler Altbausubstanz jedenfalls sekundär ist.

Die beiden Umbauten «Platana» und «Dessa» in Ljubljana markieren das Ende der 80er Jahre. Wieder werden Detailsorgfalt

The creative process and the conversion of architecturally precious buildings often marks the beginning of the independent work of an architect - especially in cities such as Vienna, with dense accumulations of buildings from several different centuries, ranging from the merely interesting to the exceptional. The occupation with existing orders, elements, components, and surfaces, and their dimensionally stable integration into the new whole with an imperturbable casualness, has the consequence that the designing and constructing architect is going through a cognitive process. It starts with an insight into the existing substance when, during a partial demolition, the layers are brought to light and the supporting, filling, dividing, and insulating elements become visible. From observation and with an appropriate cognitive effort, further implications for the design are often the result. A glance at the list of works by Boris Podrecca reveals that this is much the same with him. This is shown well illustrated in the example of the integration of the institute for neurophysiology into the baroque Palais Starhem- berg. It is a historically listed hall, where the room-filling system of treatment cabins, with its column-like support stanchions, is unmistakably present. The wide bases of the stanchions instill some doubt in the decision to place such structures at all on top of the glorious parquet. But the concept works: the relation of the patient to the stucco ceiling and parquet floor, each forming an integral whole, always refers from the cabin defined by curtains to the entire room which was preserved in this way.

Things take a slightly different turn with the renovation of the Villa Vojcsik, built by Otto Schönthal under the guidance of Otto Wagner. Here, the research proceeded to the design process. The relationship between teacher and student not in the least, led to a successive emancipation process from the exclusively conservation oriented work and culminated in the complete redesign of the rooms in the sub-level. However, there are also the cost-efficient versions, e.g., the Boutique Lilli Pilli, where the greatest possible effect was reached with scant means. Podrecca does not shy away from addressing the unavoidable aspect of eroticism when it comes to the theme of selling clothes or even underwear and working it into the design with seriousness and a wink of the eye. He avoids the dully demonstrative but considers the subtle yet exciting flirt, the ambivalent play between showing off and covering up, the disarming glance over the shoulder and other human behaviors - which is observed and kept in mind and which is integrated into the design of the ambiance. This reference these projects make to daily human life is placed above the scholarly historical preservation aspect for which, in the case of an "ordinary" old building, substance is secondary. The two conversions, "Platana" and "Dessa", in Ljubljana, mark the end of the '80s. Again, a care for the details and the glorious development of the materials are worked out in a symbiotic harmony, considering that an architectural deficit needed to be compensated for.

und materiale Prachtentfaltung zu einer harmonischen Symbiose verarbeitet, galt es doch, ein architekturkulturelles Defizit zu kompensieren.

Die Arbeiten der 90er Jahre weisen eine kontrastierende Spannung auf zwischen Bestand und Intervention, was natürlich auch mit vorgefundenen Qualitäten zusammenhängt. Bei der Galerie A+A in Madrid erlaubten die egozentrisch wirkenden Säulen ein polares Verhalten, doch bedingte auch dies eine sensible Lektüre des Vorhandenen. Podrecca ist der Auseinandersetzung nicht ausgewichen. Andere hätten vielleicht mit puristischem Eifer die Säule zur Rundstütze abstrahiert und damit die Aura der beiden Räume verabschiedet.

Der ehemalige Kornspeicher in Biberach, der heute die Stadtbücherei enthält, weist eine außerordentlich robuste Substanz auf. Die mächtigen Mauern und das raumfüllend dichte Zimmermannswerk dieses Zweckbaus erlaubten eine Beschränkung auf wenige elementare Eingriffe, wobei Teile der Substanz mit Gewinn für die Neukonzeption entfernt wurden. Dieses äußerst kraftvolle Vorgehen gegenüber dem Vorhandenen verdankt sein Resultat nicht zuletzt einer langjährigen Erfahrung mit Aufgaben, die einen vorsichtigeren Umgang mit architektonisch empfindlicherer Substanz erforderten. Doch auch in Biberach ging es um unsentimentale Angemessenheit im Spannungsverhältnis von alt und neu. Dabei hat Podrecca zielsicher die richtige Tonlage gefunden.

Die beiden Interventionen in Venedig, Ca' Pesaro und der Vorschlag für eine Umnutzung des Arsenale, sind wieder unterschiedlich. Während beim Arsenale der Bestand der historischen Zweckbauten fast den Charakter einer geologischen Landschaft annimmt, die als eigenständiger Hintergrund den Rahmen für das Neue setzt, ging es bei der Ca' Pesaro um die Auseinandersetzung mit einem komplexen architektonischen System. Sie äußert sich nach außen in einer markanten Gebäudeflanke, die wie eine zweite, zeitgenössische Stirnseite wirkt, als Gegenstück zur Prachtfassade am Kanal.

The works of the '90s show a contrasting tension between the existing and the intervention, which of course has to do with the given substantive and stylistic qualities. In the case of the A+A gallery in Madrid, the egocentric columns allowed a polar behavior; however, this caused a sensible lecturing on the existing. Podrecca did not avoid the confrontation. Others, out of a purist endeavor, might have abstracted the column into a round support and thus done away with the aura of the two rooms.

The former grain storage building in Biberach, today housing a library, exhibits an extremely robust substance. The massive walls and the dense, room-filling timber work of this functional structure allowed a limitation to a few elementary operations - removing parts of the substance effecting a gain for the new construction. This considerably powerful procedure with respect to the existing is not in the least due to a long-standing experience with tasks asking for a more careful treatment of architecturally sensitive substances. And yet, in Biberach as well, the cause was an unsentimental appropriation of the suspenseful relationship between the old and the new. In this endeavor, Podrecca has decisively found the right pitch.

The two interventions in Venice, Ca' Pesaro and the proposal for a change of use of the Arsenale, are again different. While the existing functional structures in the Arsenale almost take on the character of a geological landscape, setting the framework for the new as an independent background, the Ca' Pesaro dealt with a complex architectural system. It is expressed on the outside in a very striking and profound side elevation creating the effect of a second but contemporary front side as an opposition to the stately facade along the canal.

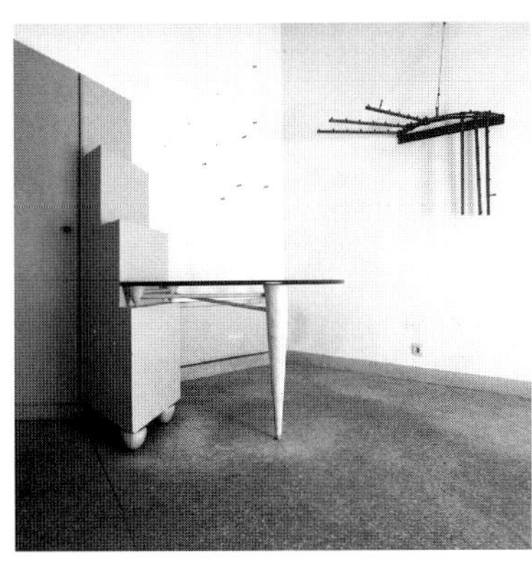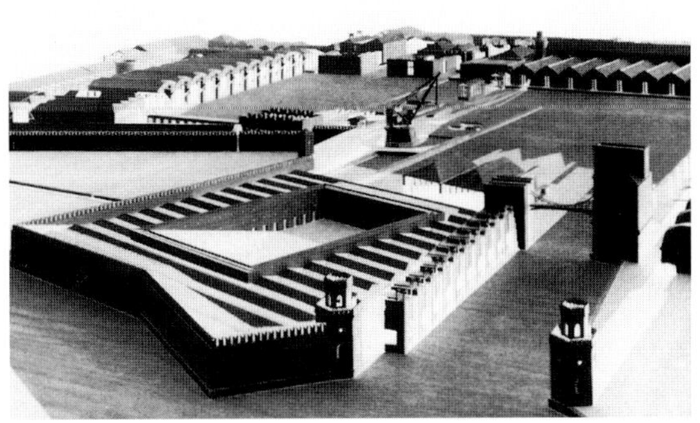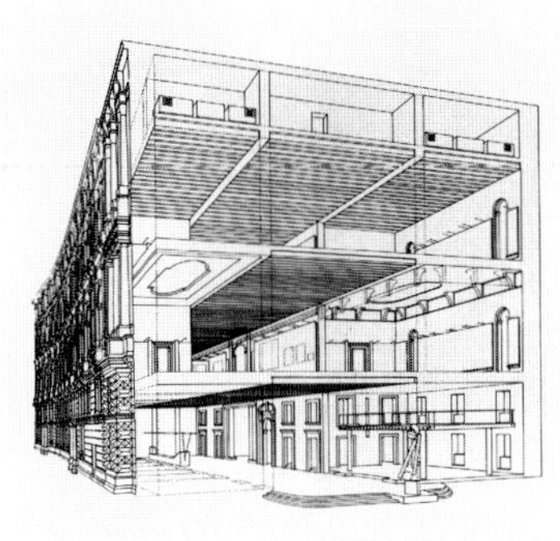

Wien - Innere Stadt / *Vienna - Inner City* 1982

Alte Ansicht mit neuer Positionierung des Säulengerüstes /
An old view showing the new positioning of the column structure

Der barocke Grundriß des Palais Starhemberg (Matthias Steinl, 1733) weist hinter der Schaufassade drei Prunkräume auf, zwei, vier und drei Fensterachsen breit - der große Saal liegt nicht mittig. Dahinter drängt ein Innenhof die Räume der Seitenflügel und des Hoftrakts an die nachbarlichen Feuermauern. Ein neues Strukturelement bildet der Rundgang - ähnlich einem Klosterhof. In den Innenräumen erfolgte der Umbau teils mit intensiver Bezugnahme, wie bei dem denkmalgeschützten Straßentrakt, teils gänzlich neu. Das Intarsienparkett schonend, aber visuell berücksichtigend, sind im Saal 15 Säulen - Steher verschiebbar zu einer Schar formiert. Flache Verbindungsgestänge tragen Vorhänge und trennen acht Behandlungskojen ab, die Stuckdecke bleibt dabei unangetastet. Obwohl die «ausmessende» Raumbeanspruchung beträchtlich ist, auch bei zurückgeschobenen Vorhängen, bleibt sie temporär. Der schmale Saal für physikalische Therapie im Hoftrakt ist mit stark geflammten Platten aus grauem Carrara-Marmor verkleidet. Für die Entspannungstherapie wurden sechs Kabinette mit ruhigerer Raumstimmung geschaffen. Die zwei Ordinationen der Inhaber für Psychoanalyse und Hypnose besetzen die beiden kleineren Säle des Fronttrakts. Weil die Patienten meist liegend therapiert werden, erfolgt die abwechslungsreiche Beleuchtung mit relativ großen blendfreien Flächen.

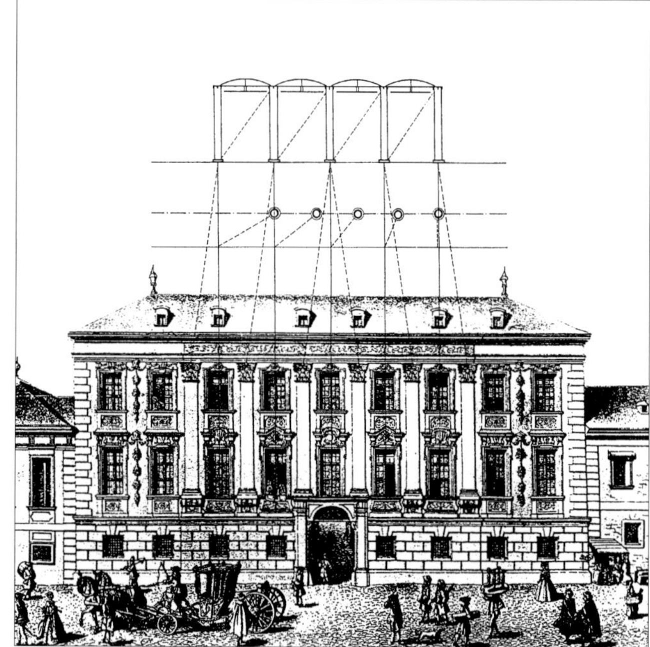

The baroque ground plan of Palais Starhemberg (Matthias Steinl, 1733) contains three stately rooms behind the facade, stretching across two, four, and three window axes with the effect being that the main hall is not situated in the center. In the rear, a courtyard pushes the rooms of the side wings and the courtyard block to the fire walls of the neighboring buildings. In this environment, the intervention for the conversion was effected in part with an intensive self-reference, as in the case of the historically listed block and, in part, with a completely new design. In the main hall, the inlay parquet floor was preserved and, with its visual appearance taken into consideration, 15 free-standing support columns were installed forming a modular grouping. Between the columns, flat connecting rods support the curtains, leaving the stucco ceiling untouched and separating the eight medical therapy treatment cabins. Although the visual and spatial impact of the installation is considerable even when the curtains are open, it is still a temporary structure. The narrow physical therapy hall is located in the courtyard block and stimulatingly encased with strongly flamed Carrara marble panels. In another wing, six cabins with a more quiet atmosphere were created for relaxation therapy. Two departments, psychoanalysis and hypnosis, occupy the two smaller halls of the front block. As the patients are, for the most part, treated lying down, the variable lighting is attained through relatively large, glare-free surfaces.

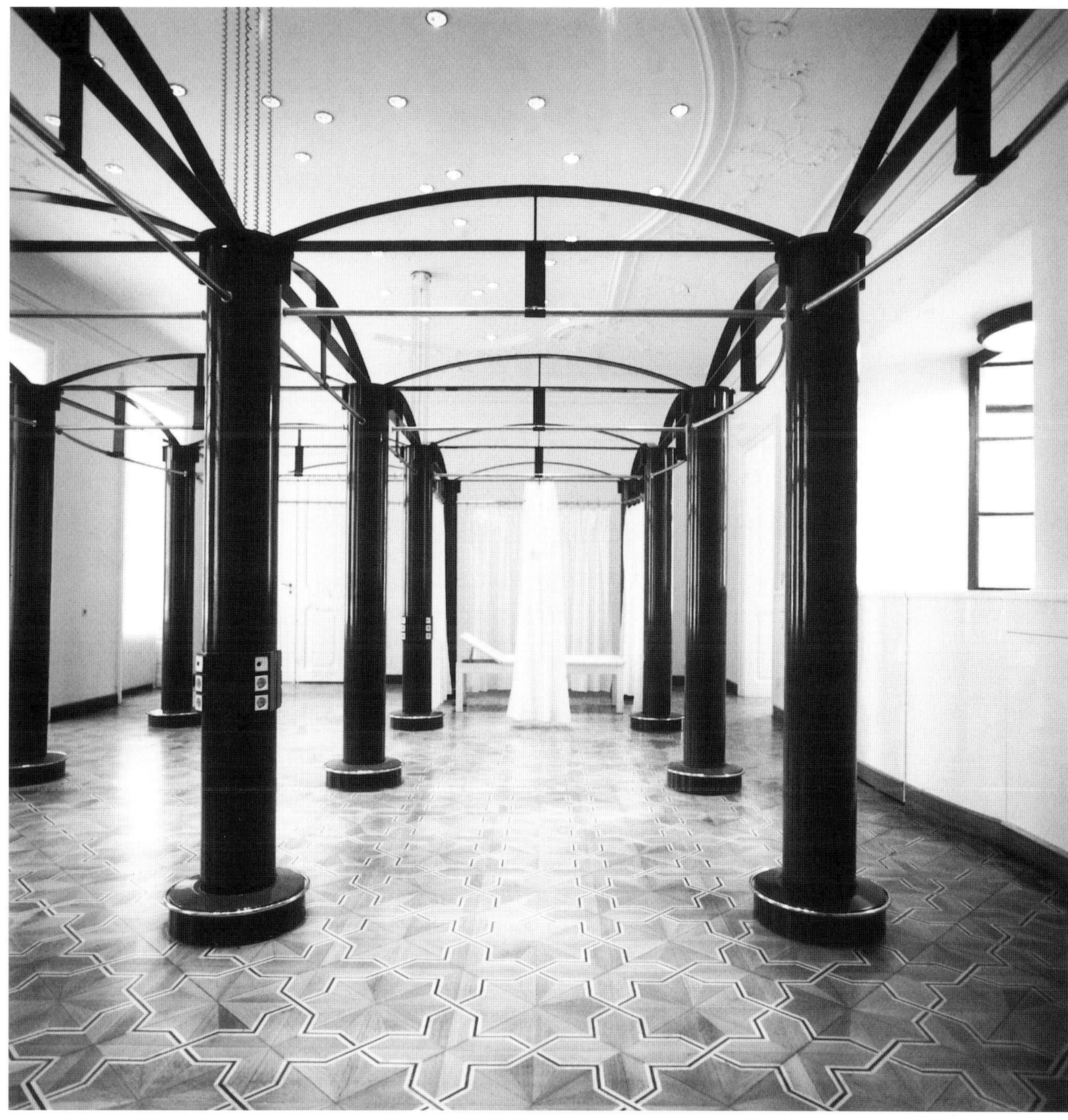

Therapieraum II, Beleuchtungskörper / *Therapy room II, light fixtures*

Therapieraum II, Hypnose / *Therapy room II, hypnosis*

Therapieraum I, Einzelkoje / *Therapy room I, single cabin*

Therapieraum III, Wassertherapie, Detail / *Therapy room III, water therapy, detail*

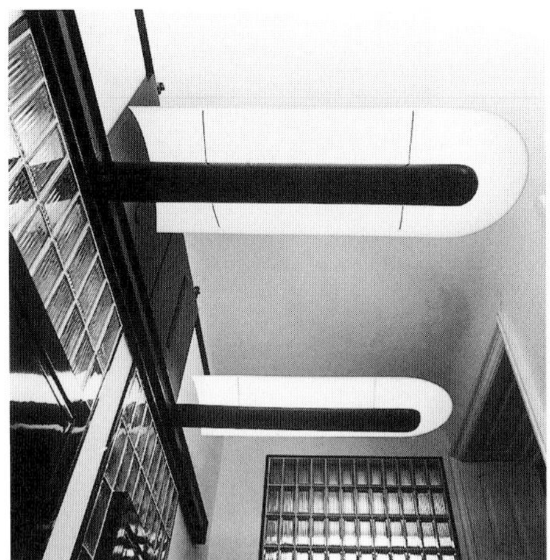

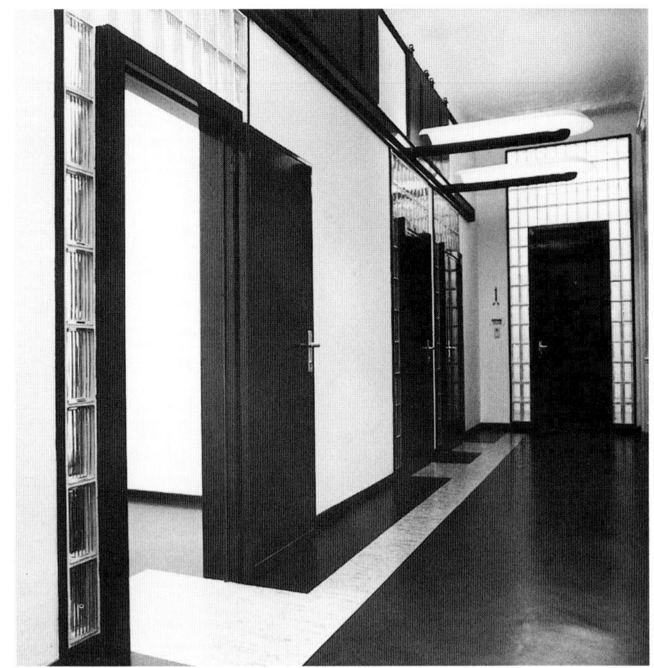

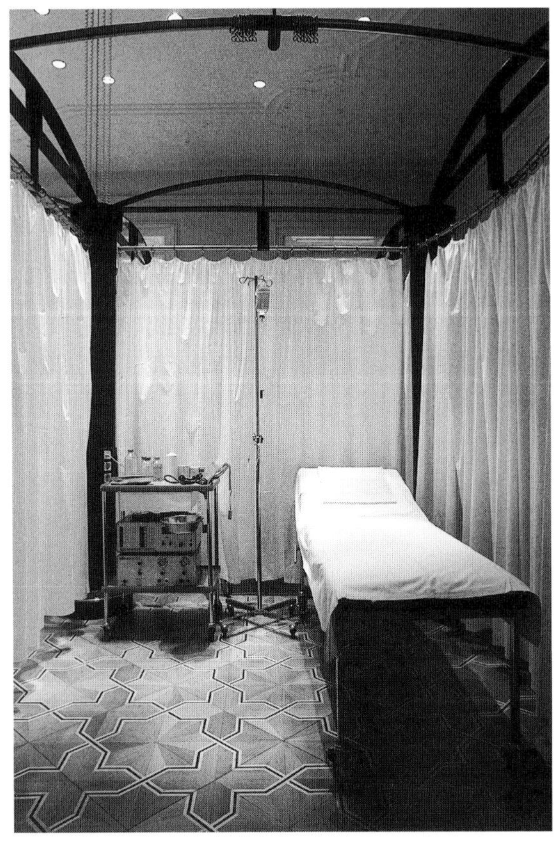

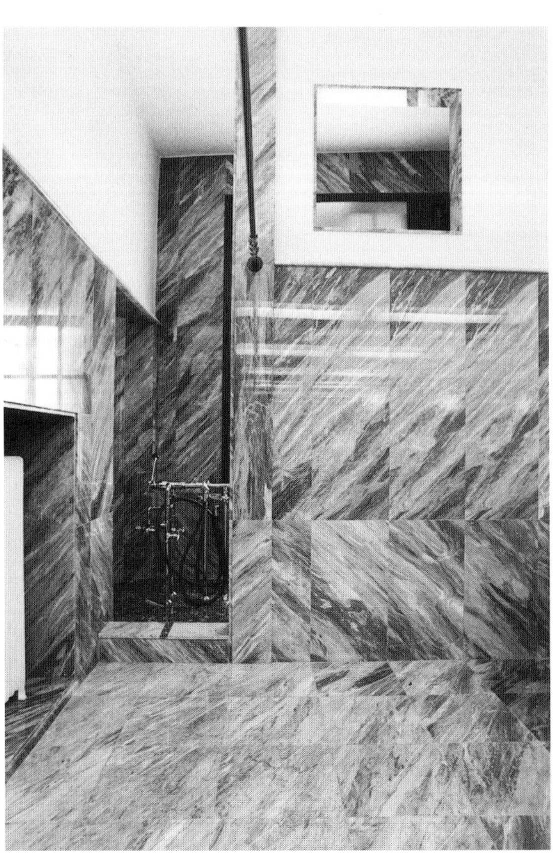

Therapieraum III, Physikalische Therapie /
Therapy room III, physical therapy

Axonometrie der Gesamtanlage /
Axonometric projection of the entire complex

Therapieraum III, Eingangszone / *Therapy room III, entrance zone*

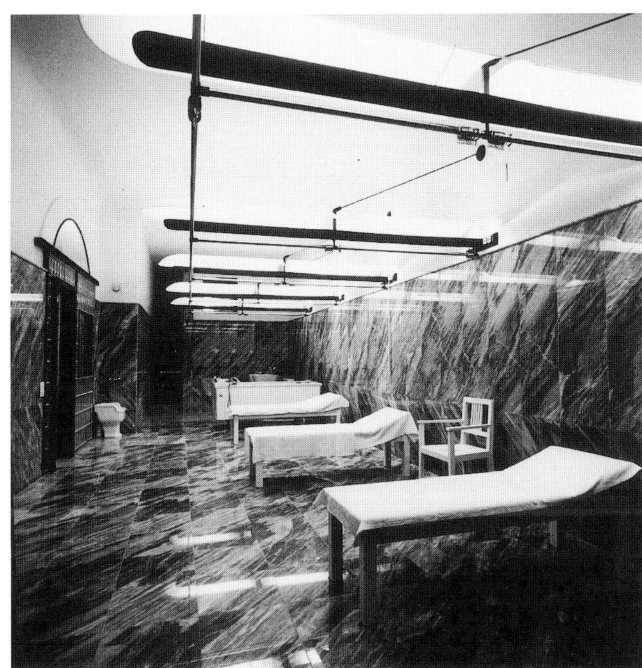

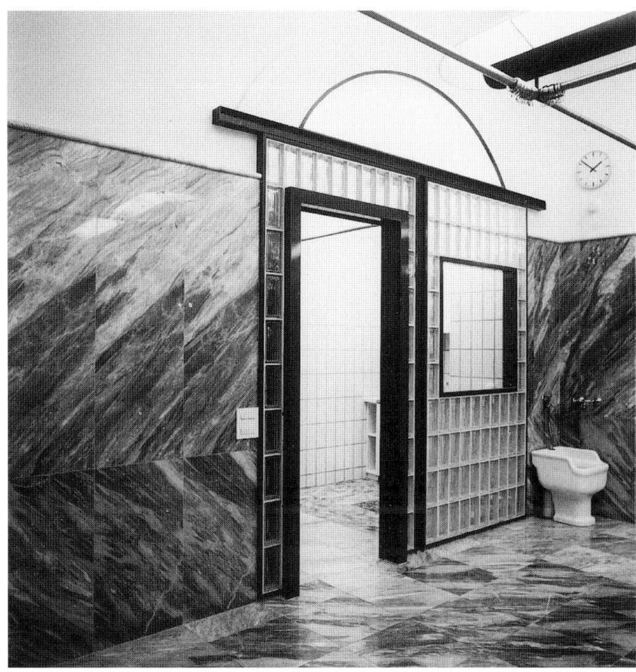

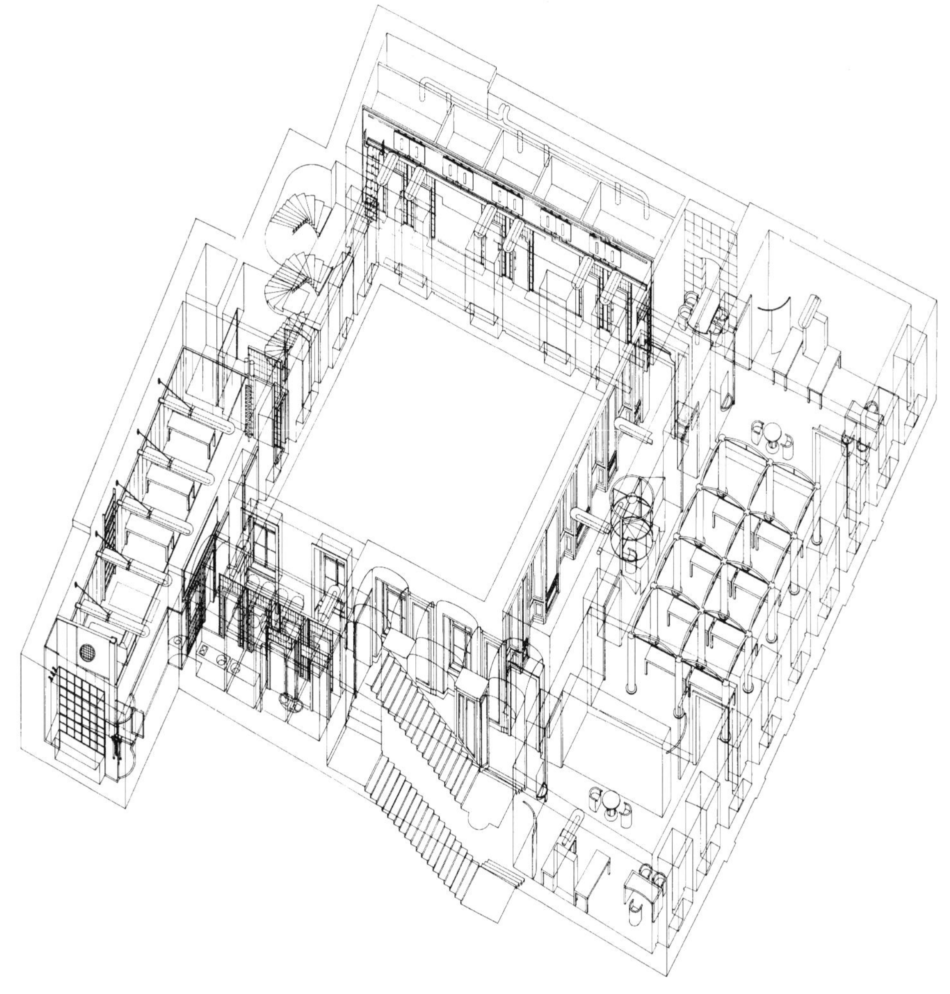

Wien-Penzing / *Vienna-Penzing* 1982, 1986

Straßenansicht / *Street view*

Bürotrakt, Detail / *Office block, detail*

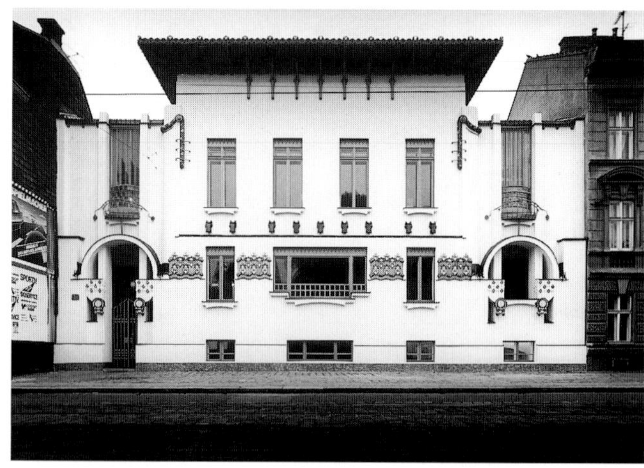

Die von Otto Schönthal 1902 unter dem regen Interesse seines Lehrers Otto Wagner an einer Ausfallstraße im Westen Wiens errichtete Villa Vojcsik war desolat und wurde für eine Werbeagentur etappenweise revitalisiert und mit einer Dependance am unteren Ende des Gartens erweitert. Der Holzbau – baurechtlich ein Provisorium – steht auf einer Schar Kanalrohr-Punktfundamente zwischen den alten Bäumen. An der mittig liegenden Halle, in der die gerade Stiege hinaufführt und die von oben durch ein langes Glasdach belichtet wird, liegen zu beiden Seiten Büros. Zwei Reihen gedrechselter Holzsäulen veredeln hier den Raum. Ein flaches Grabendach gibt dem Bau ein pavillonartiges Aussehen, und das äußere Kleid, eine dunkel imprägnierte Vertikalschalung mit weißen Rundholzstäben über den Fugen, gibt ihm den Eindruck textiler Leichtigkeit. In perspektivischer Sicht verdichtet sich das Weiß der vorstehenden Stäbe im hinteren Bereich, so daß jede Erinnerung an Masse aufgehoben wird. Die Autonomie des Pavillons gegenüber dem Haupthaus wird noch betont durch eine parallele Verschiebung aus der vom Gartenweg eingenommenen Mittelachse. Ausgleichend springt daher über dem Eingang ein schmaler Balkon vor. Zwischen den beiden aneinander vorbeizielenden Achsen dehnt sich die verbindende Eingangsplattform, von wo der Blick zurück gleitet und auf die im Wasser eines herzförmigen Teiches stehende, elegante kleine Brücke fällt, die alt und neu verknüpft.

Villa Vojcsik was originally built on a western arterial road in Vienna by Otto Schönthal in 1902 under the tutelage and great interest of his teacher Otto Wagner. Being in a desolate state, it was renovated for an advertising agency in several different phases and extended with an addition at the lower end of the garden. The wooden structure – a temporary solution with regard to building regulations – is set on a grid of concrete piles among the trees. The central hallway, with its straight, ascending staircase illuminated from above by a long glass skylight, is surrounded on both sides by offices. Two rows of lathed columns lend refinement to the space. A flat roof gives the building a pavilion-like appearance and the outer garb, a darkly impregnated vertical encasing with white painted wooden flutes mounted over of the exterior surface plane gives it the impression of having a textile-like lightness. In a perspective view, the white of the fluting condenses as it recedes toward the back so that any recollection of mass is suspended. The autonomy of the pavilion compared to the main building gains additional significance by a parallel dislocation of the middle axis taken by the garden path. Therefore, a small balcony juts out above the entrance. The connecting platform of the entrance stretches between the two unaligned axes. From there, the view is guided back and falls on an elegant footbridge over the water of a heart-shaped pond, connecting old and new.

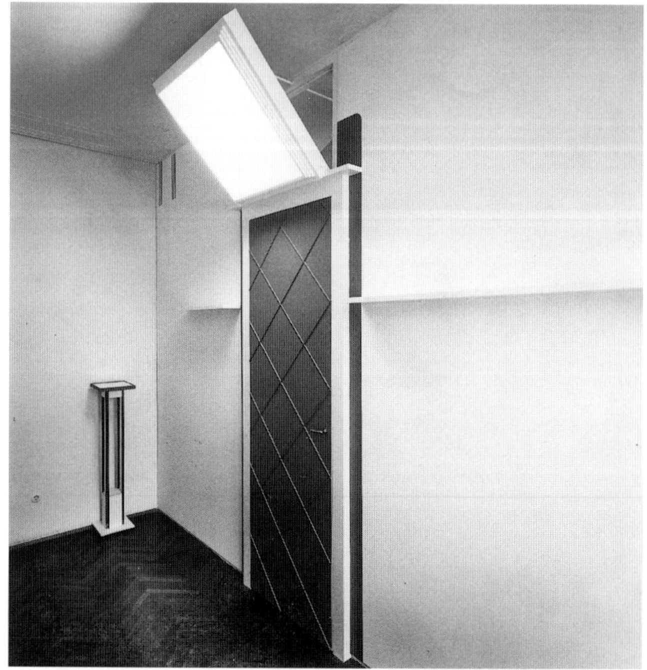

Untergeschoß, Korridor / *Lower floor, hallway*

Untergeschoß, Eingang Dunkelkammer / *Lower floor, dark-room entrance*

Untergeschoß, Details / *Lower floor, details*

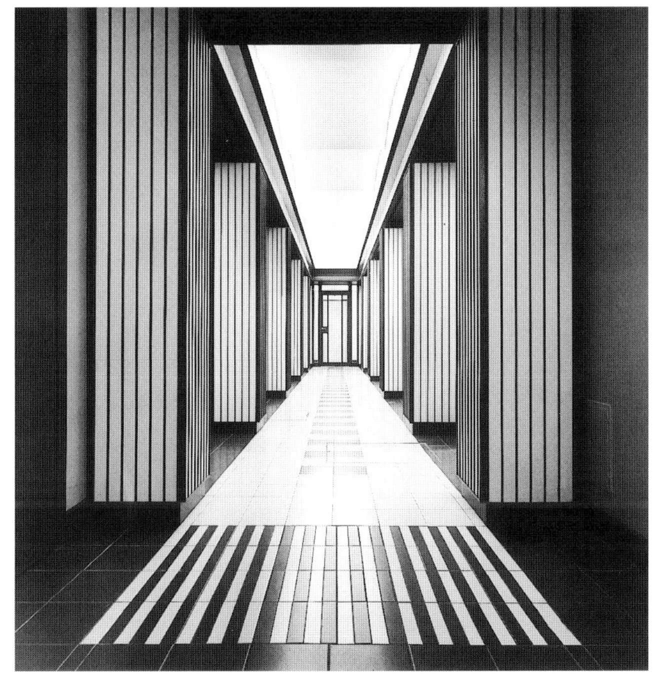

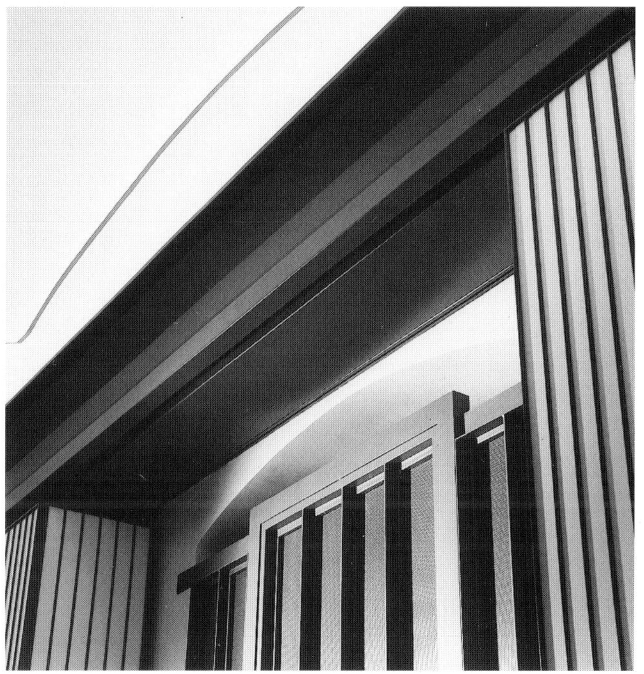

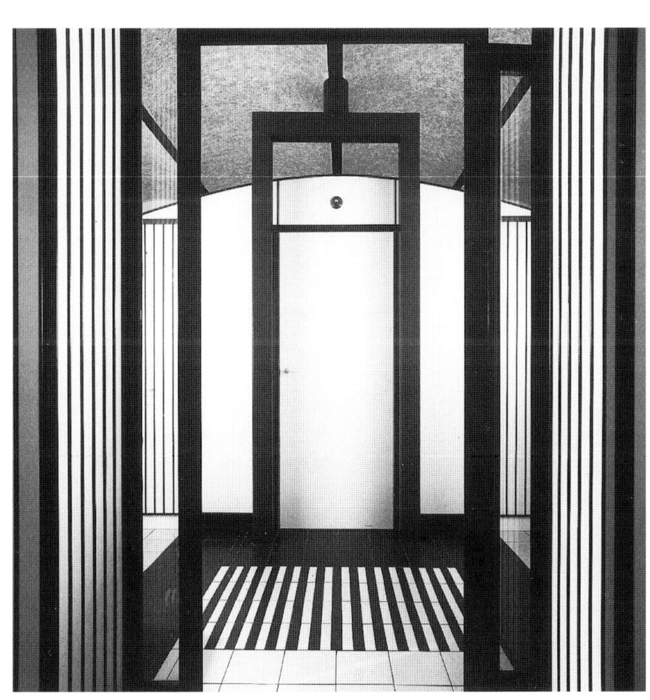

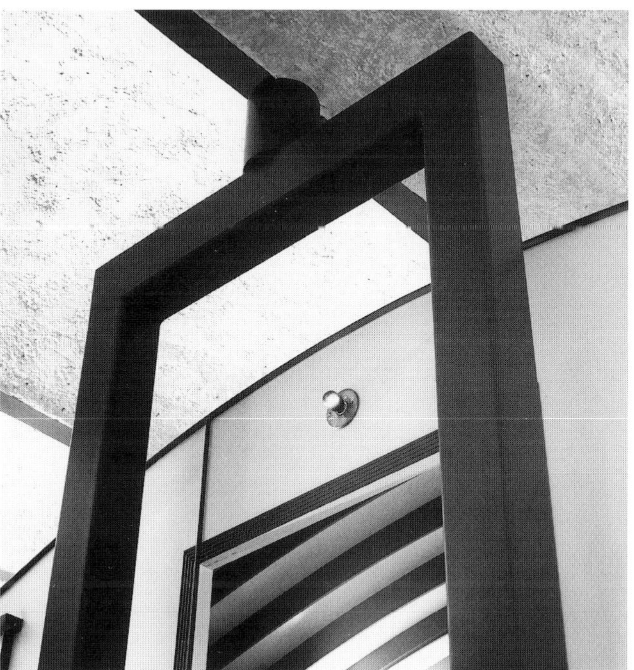

Axonometrie der Brücke / *Axonometric projection of the bridge*

Axonometrie / *Axonometric projection*

Atelierhaus / *Studio building*

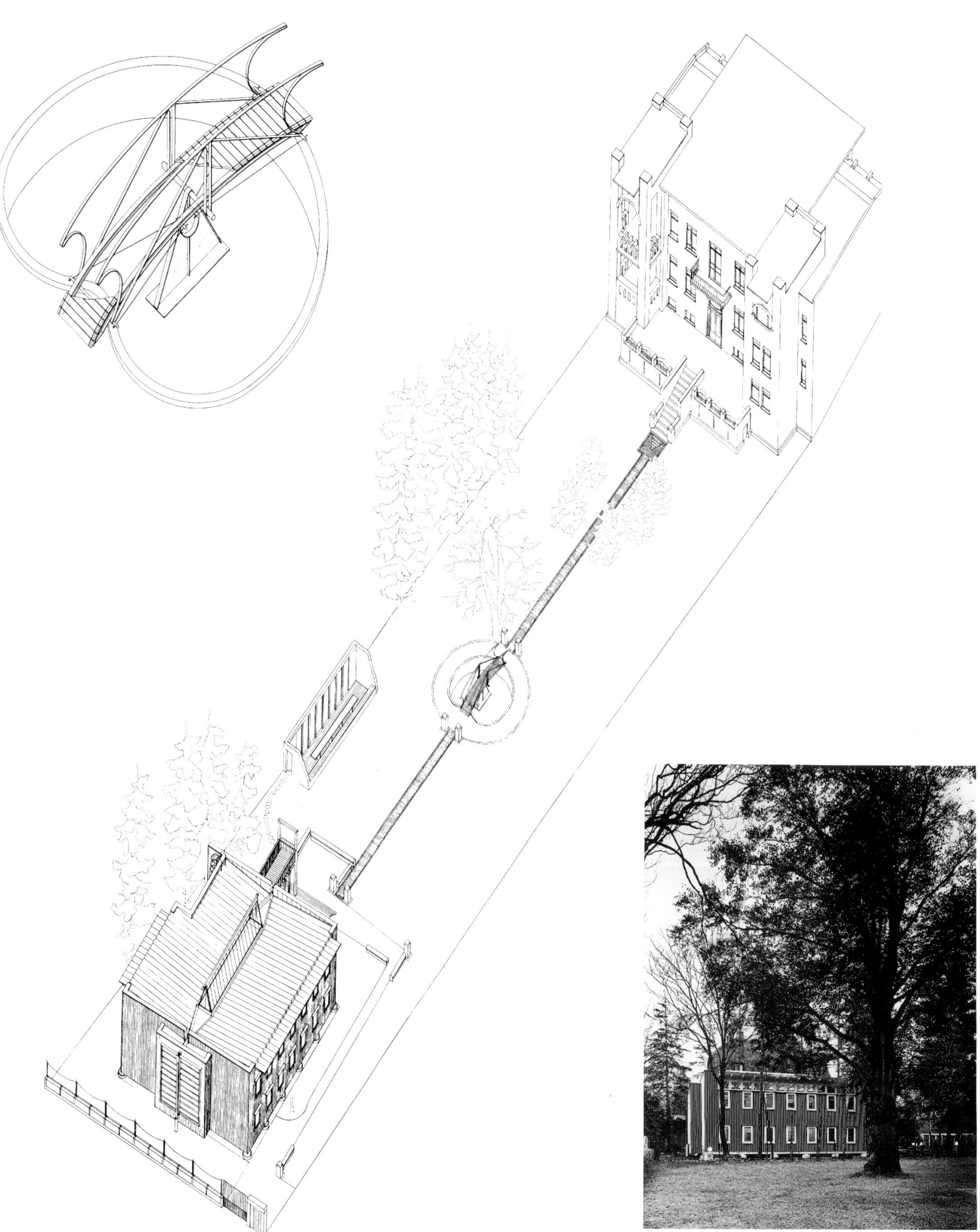

Ansicht Atelierhaus / *View of studio building*

Axonometrie Atelierhaus / *Axonometric projection of studio building*   Fundament, Detail / *Foundation, detail*

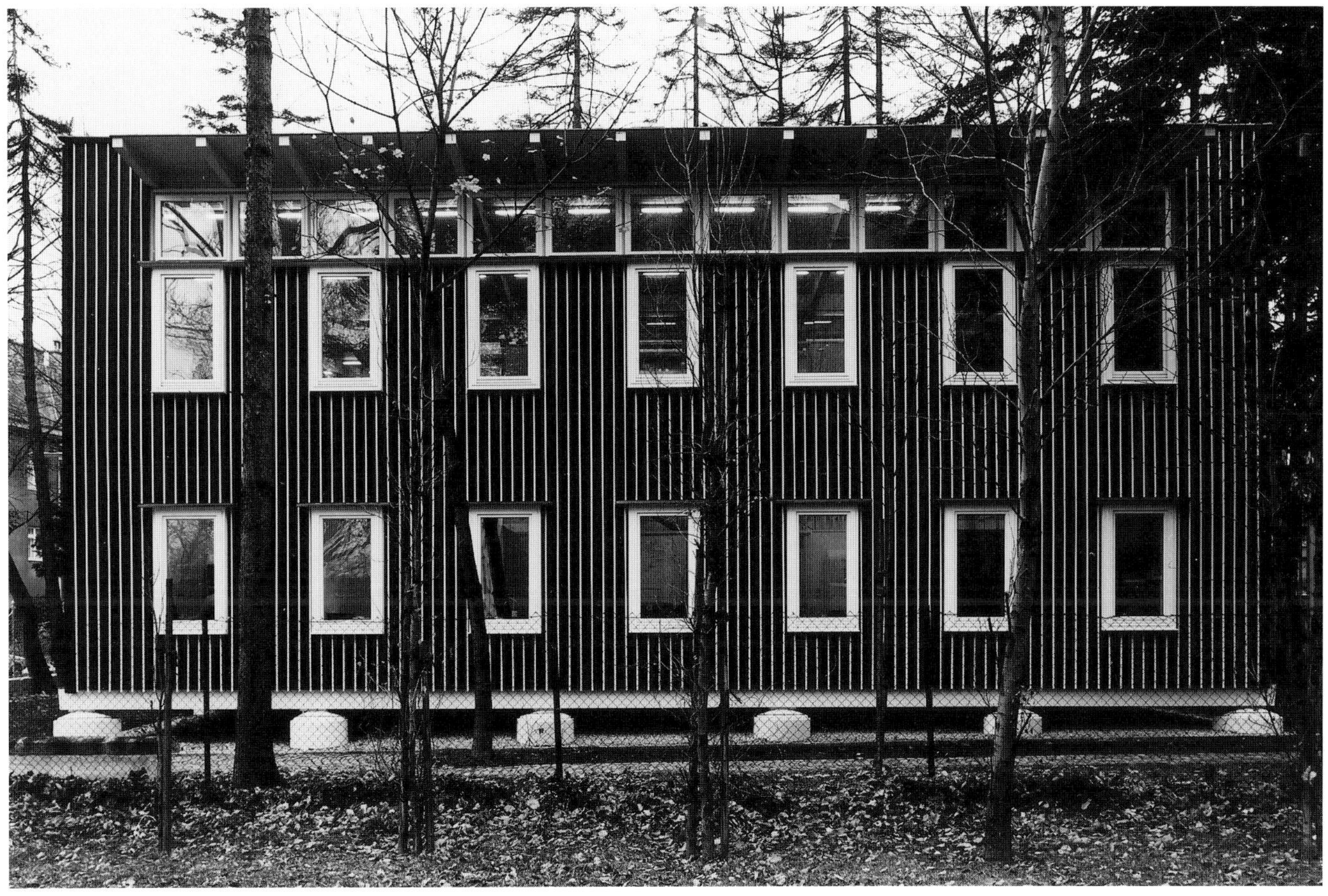

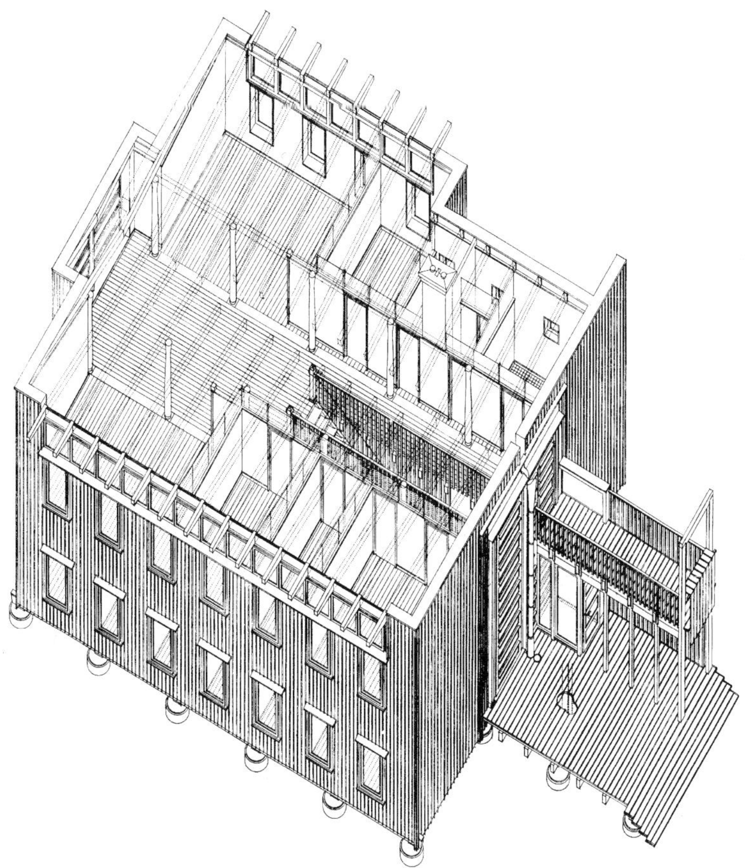

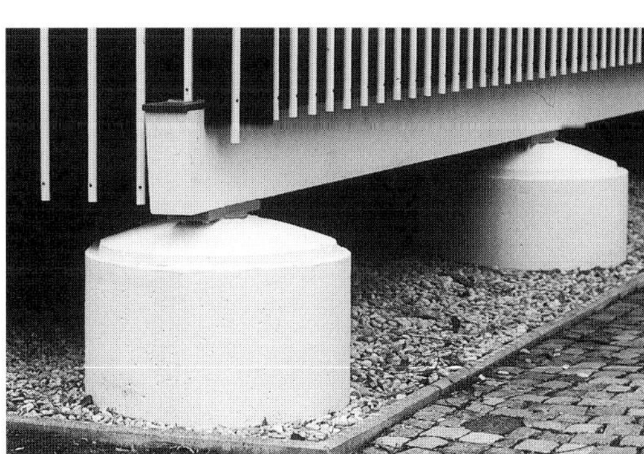

Ansichten Atelierhaus / *Views of the studio building*

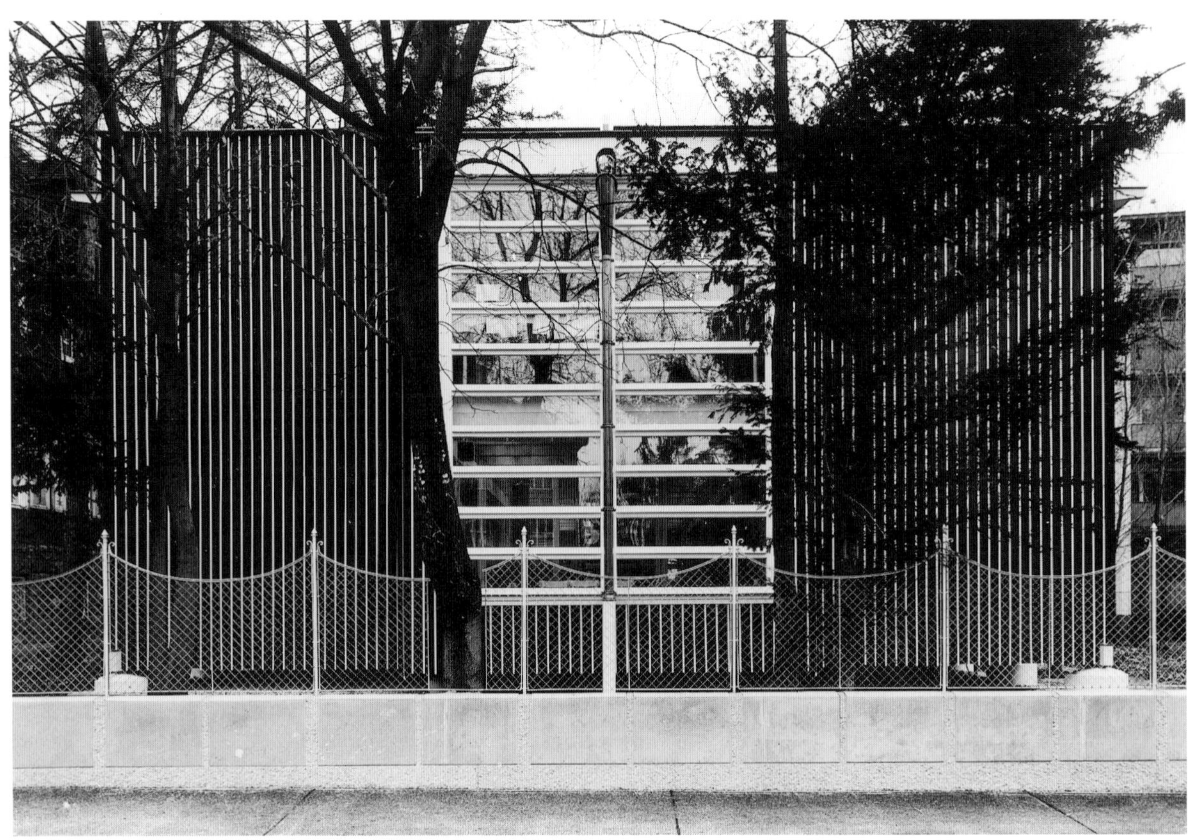

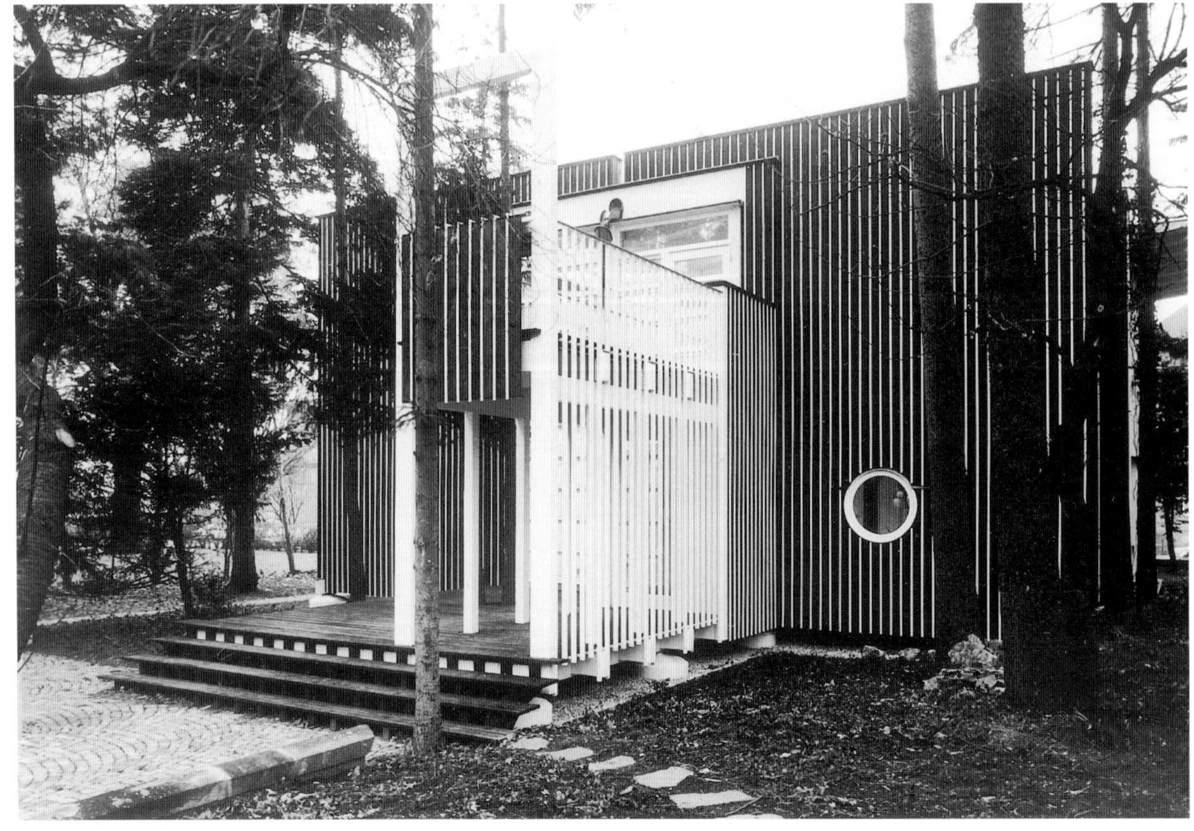

Mittelhalle, Stiege / *Central hallway, stairway*

Säulenköpfe in Erdgeschoß und 1.Obergeschoß /
Column capitals on first and second floors

Mittelhalle, Seitenansicht / *Central hallway, side view*

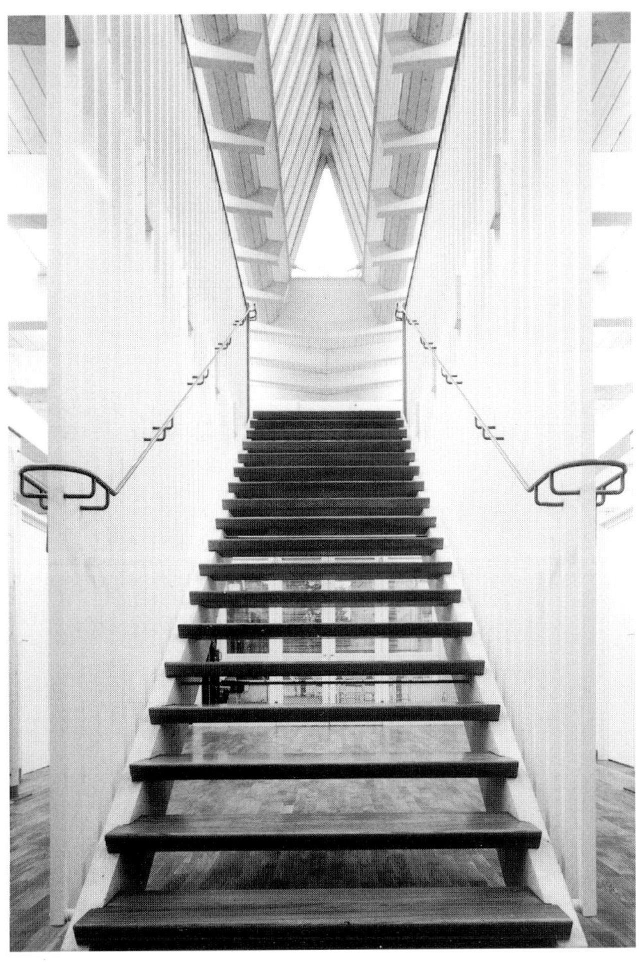

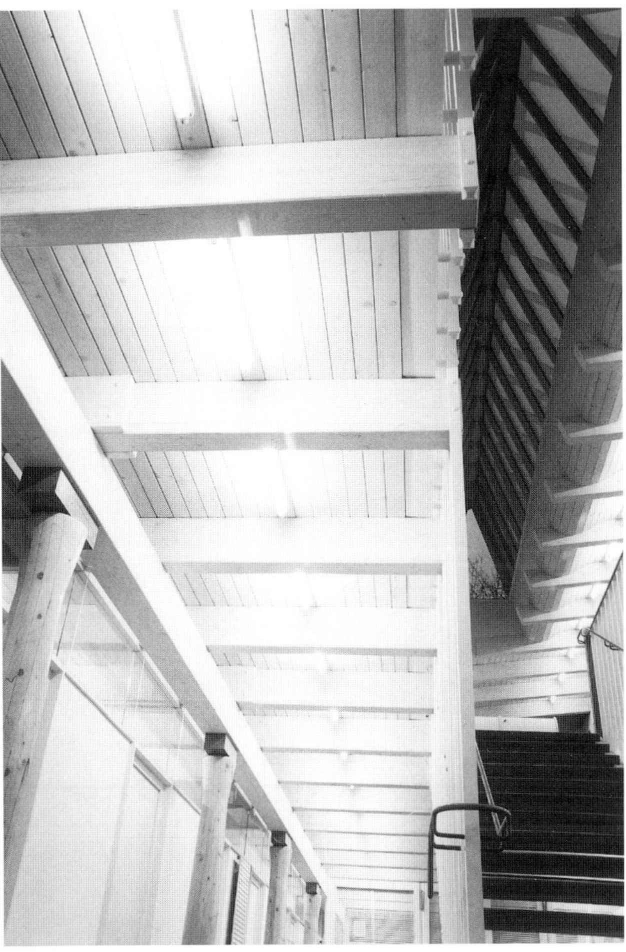

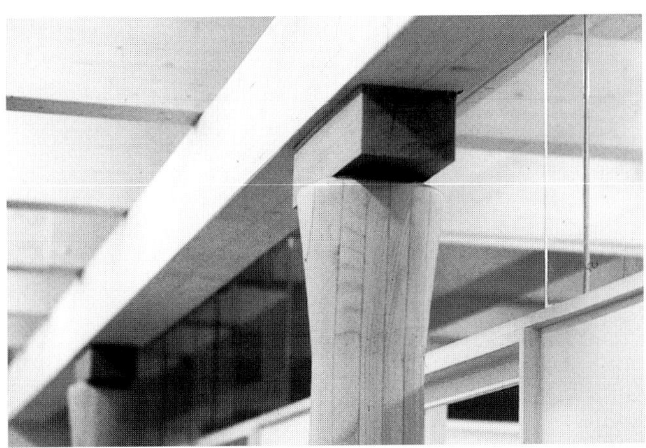

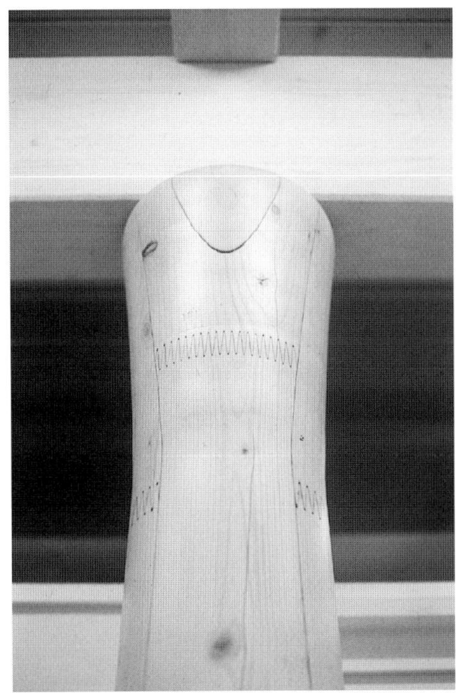

Wien-Mariahilf / *Vienna-Mariahilf* 1985

Entwurfskizzen / *Design sketches*

Die Mündung der Mariahilfer Straße in das ehemalige Glacis ist städtebaulich mehrdeutig, weil die Stirnfront der Ringstraßenverbauung an der Babenbergerstraße über den Außenring hinausgreift und mit der platzartigen Ausweitung und der Geländestufe bei der Rahlgasse eine Zäsur entsteht, die an der rundgeschliffenen Ecke der ehemaligen Hofstallungen kein Gegenüber findet. Mit der Erneuerung des Schuh- und Lederwarengeschäfts in den Räumen des ehemaligen Café «Casapiccola» sollte der kultur- und stadtgeschichtlichen Dichte des Ortes städtebaulich, architektonisch und bedeutungsmäßig Rechnung getragen werden. Der in die Gebäudeecke eingeschnittene Eingangspavillon markiert daher den eigentlichen Beginn der berühmten Geschäftsstraße, wobei der darüber aufragende gründerzeitliche Eckturm sich mit einer koaxialen Kuppel schon auf Distanz bemerkbar macht. Die äußere Erscheinung wurde aber bewußt gegensätzlich gehalten, was die komplexe Situation zu entschlüsseln hilft. Die guterhaltenen Reste des in den 30er Jahren von Carl Witzmann eingerichteten Cafés wurden bewahrt, und eine eigenständige Verkaufsgalerie im mittleren Schiff des von zwei Pfeilerreihen gegliederten Raumes eingebaut. Die schlanken Stahlprofile verleihen dem Einbau Leichtigkeit und systemische Autonomie. Er mischt sich maßstäblich nicht mit den Verkaufsgestellen, so daß die bauliche und die historische Ordnung getrennt erlebbar bleiben.

The intersection of the Mariahilfer Strasse and the former Glacis is ambiguous in an urban sense. The head of the ring road-development at Babenbergerstrasse reaches beyond the outer ring and, together with the square-like expansion and the slope in the landscape, creates a caesura at Rahlgasse which does not find an opposite in the round corner of the former stables. The renovation of the shoe and leather goods store on the premises of the former Café "Casapiccola" was supposed to honor the cultural and historical density of the location in an urban, architectural and symbolic sense. The entrance pavilion cut into the corner of the building therefore marks the true beginning of the famous business street. The corner tower with its bi-axial dome dating back to the early 1870's – the so called "time of wild speculation" – already attracts attention from a distance. The outer appearance, however, was consciously kept antithetical, thus helping to decipher the complex situation. The well-preserved remains of the Café, which was furnished in the '30s by Carl Witzmann, were saved, and an independent sales gallery was built into the middle nave, divided by two rows of columns. The thin steel profiles provide the inset with a certain lightness and structural autonomy. It does not mingle with the sales racks according to scale. Thus, the constructive and the historic order can still be experienced as separate entities.

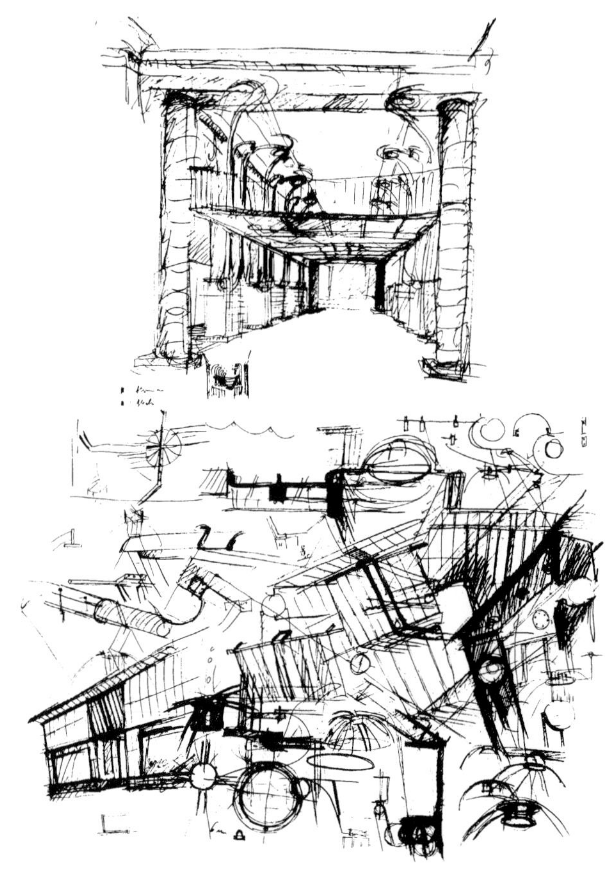

Axonometrie / *Axonometric projection*

Grundriß, Schnitte, Ansichten / *Plan, cross sections, elevation*

Eingangspavillon / *Entrance pavilion*

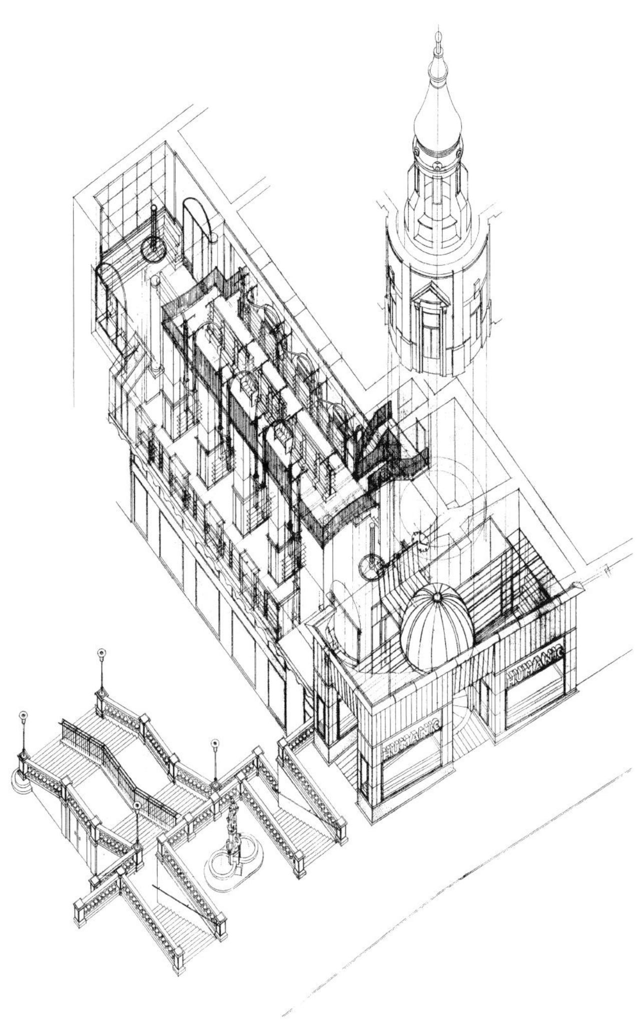

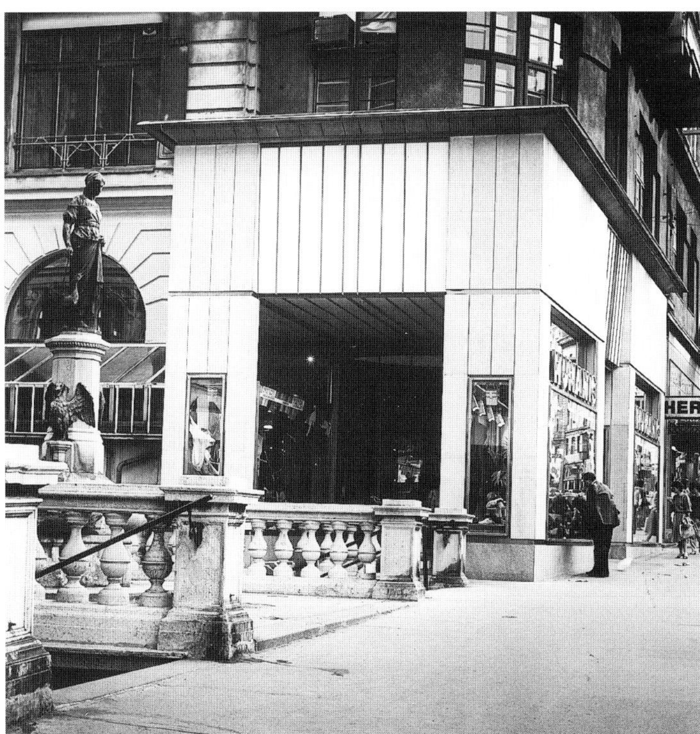

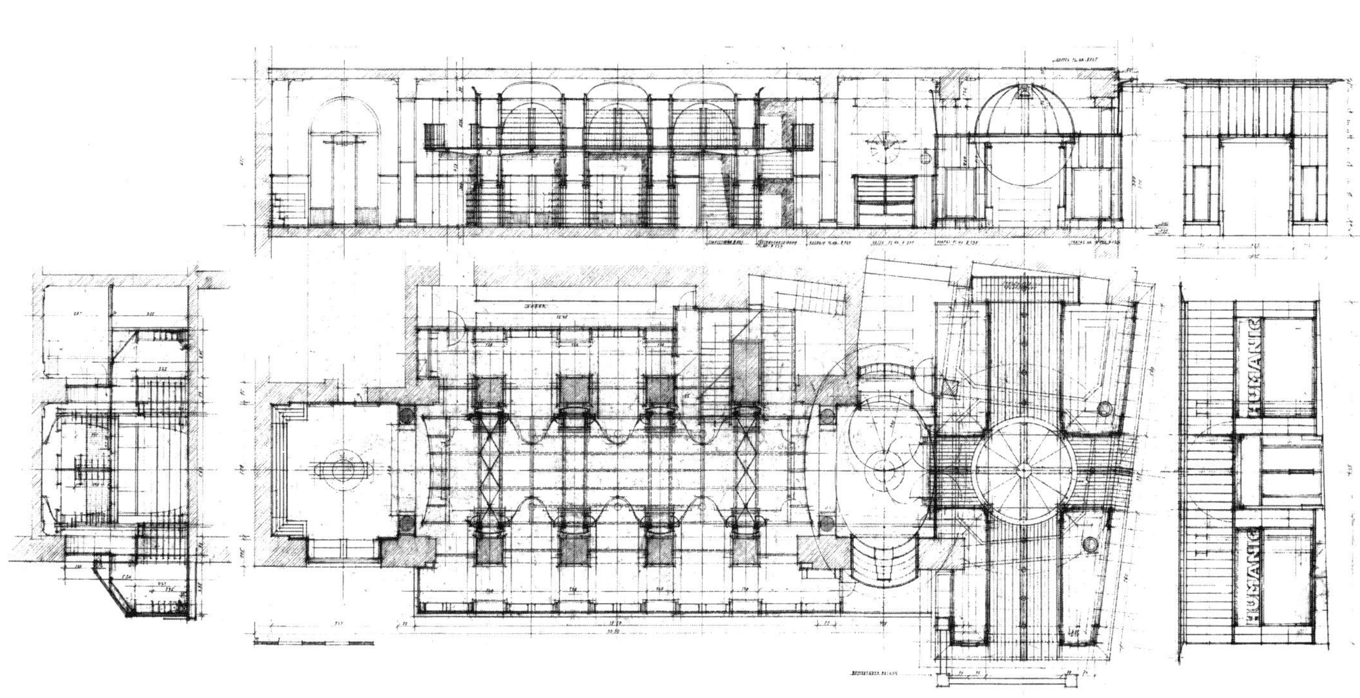

Eingangspassage, Kuppel / *Entrance passage, cupola*

Galerie, Untersicht / *Gallery, visible underside*

Fassadenschnitt, Detail / *Facade cross section, detail*

Galerie, Detail / *Gallery, detail*

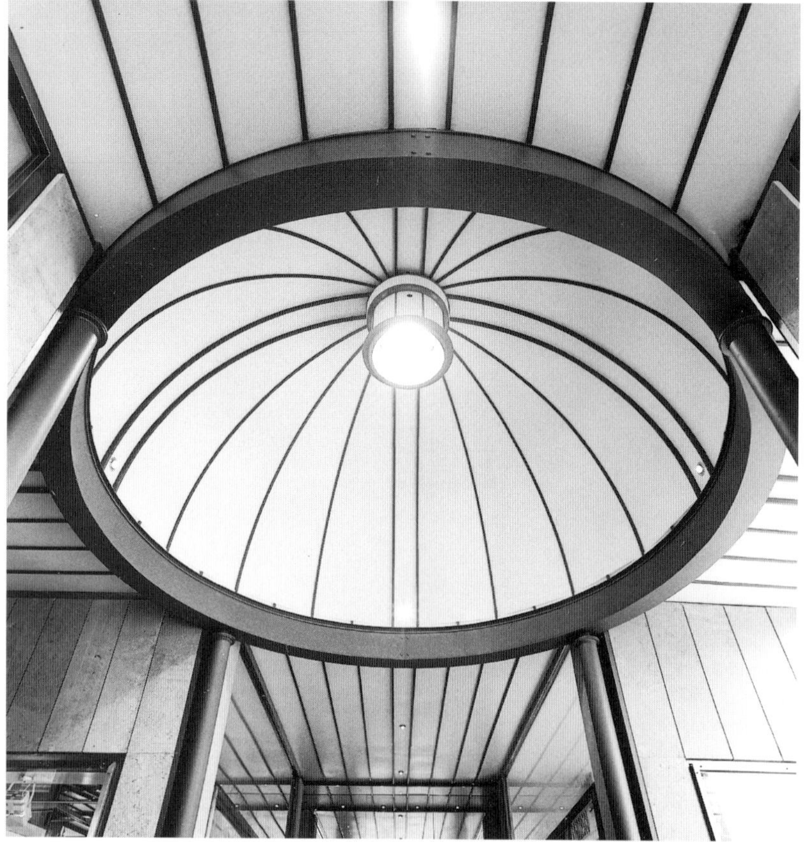

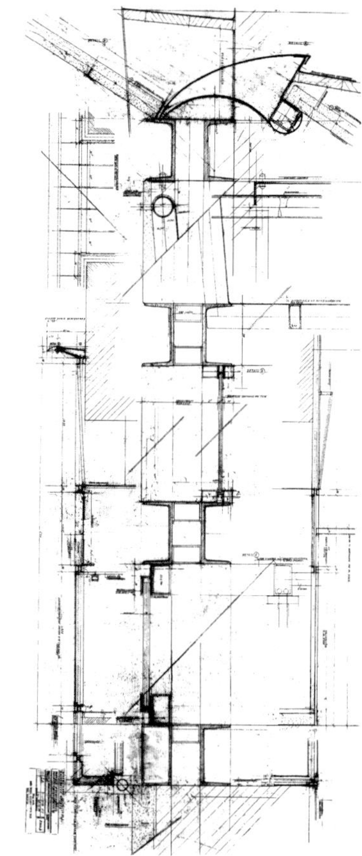

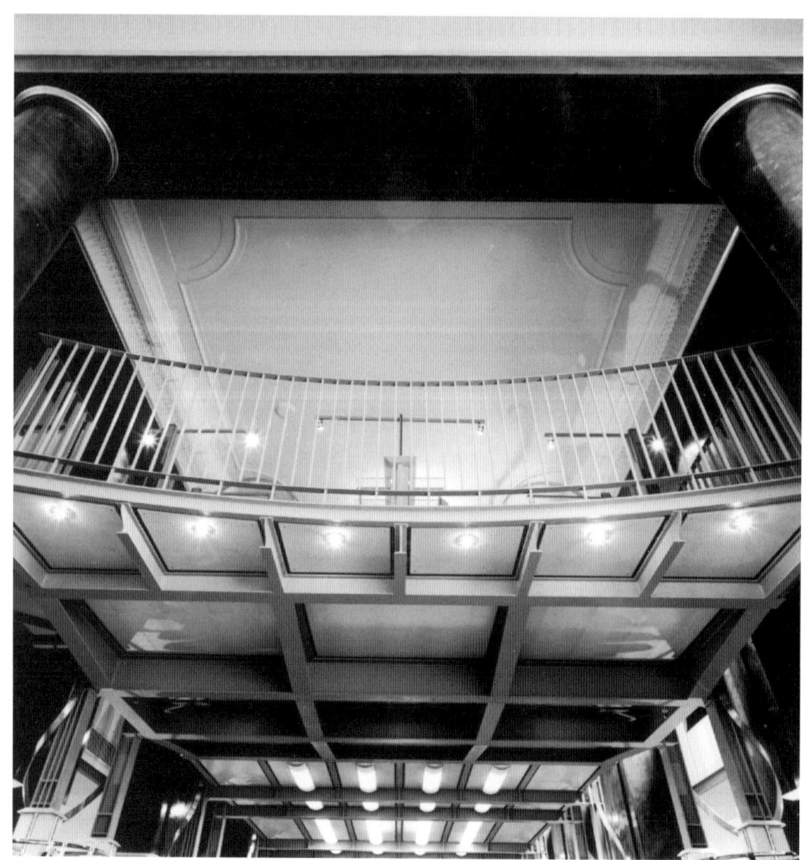

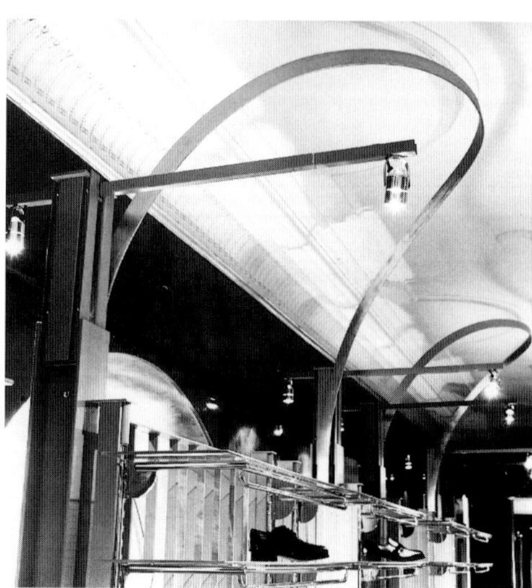

Verkaufsraum / *Sales room*

Aufgang, Galerie / *Stairway, gallery*

Galerie, Ausschnitt / *Gallery, partial view*

Präsentationssäule / *Display column*

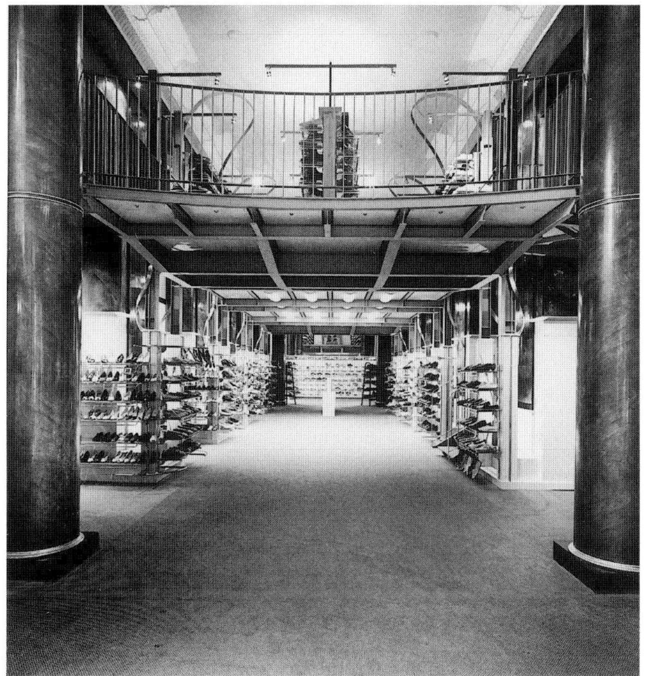

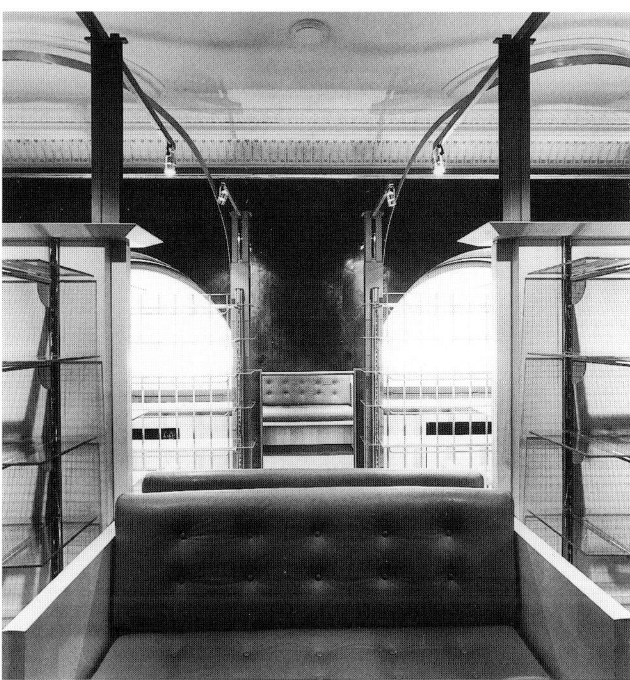

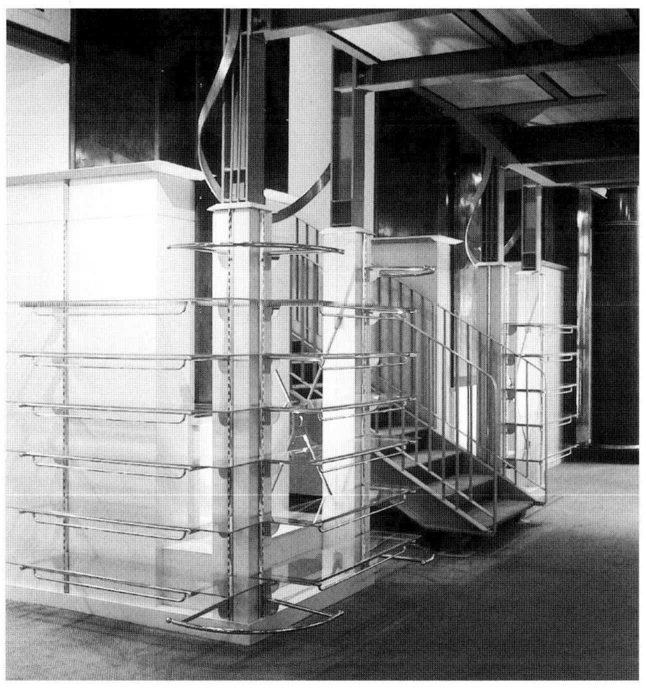

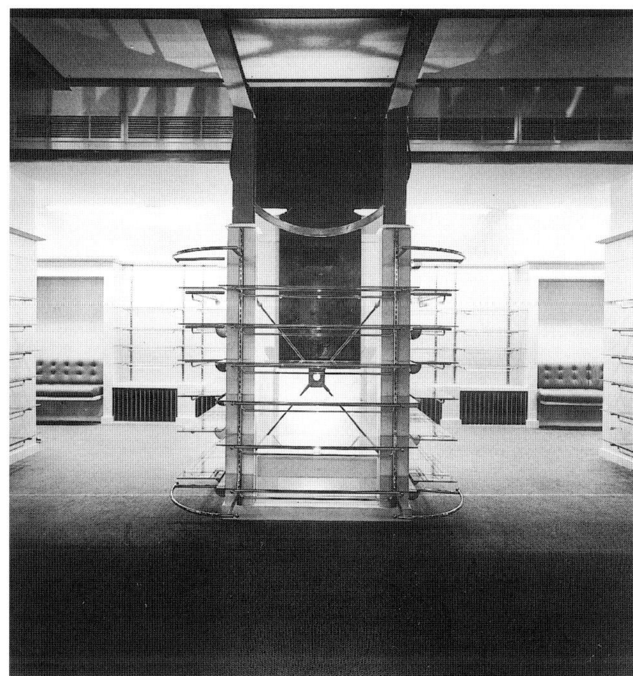

Wien-Josefstadt / *Vienna-Josefstadt* 1989

Eingangsportal, Ansicht, Grundriß / *Entrance portal, elevation, plan*

Axonometrie / *Axonometric projection*

Die Pflege des Corporate Design hat bei Palmers Tradition: Denn das Verkaufen feiner Damenstrümpfe und zarter Dessous ist eine delikate Angelegenheit und fordert einen ansprechenden Rahmen. Die Kombination Schweinfurter grün mit gold und der klassische Palmers-Schriftzug, seit Jahrzehnten im Bereich der Erdgeschosse fester Bestandteil des Stadtbildes, wurden mittlerweile zu einem Permanent. Mit diesen starken Prämissen hatte sich der Entwurf zu befassen. Grün hinterfärbtes Glas rahmt daher das Portal. Den Eingang markieren zwei starke Halbzylinder aus Labradorgranit; ihre polierten, progressiv sich verengenden Rundungen verlocken zum eleganten Einbiegen. Nach dem Eintreten folgt eine Orientierungszone, die zugleich Präsentierbühne ist und von Verkaufspulten flankiert wird. Zwei eng gestellte Pfeiler fangen die axiale Eintrittsbewegung ab und verdecken die interne Treppe zur Galerie. Der Raster schlanker Mauerscheiben vor den Lagergestellen im hinteren Raumdrittel bietet Einblicke in ein ausgedehntes Sortiment, eine Versicherung, daß für jede Kundin etwas da ist. Starker Kontrast und geometrische Strenge prägen das Muster der Natursteinbodenplatten; Pulte, Regale und Präsentationsflächen wahren einen warmen Holzton; Mauerpfeiler und Wände sind in glattem Weiß dematerialisiert. Dies ergibt einen neutralen Hintergrund für die duftigen Waren auf den Ladentischen, dem Ort des Schauens, Auswählens und Kaufens.

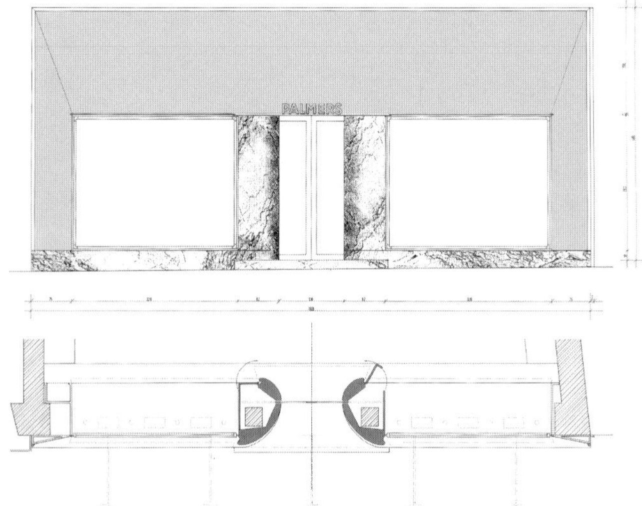

The care and fostering of the corporate design has been a longstanding tradition at Palmers: the sale of fine silk stockings and exquisite undergarments is a delicate matter and asks for an appealing environment. The combination of Schweinfurt green with gold and the classic Palmers logo on the ground floor, which has long been an institution in the cityscape, has meanwhile become a permanent fixture. The design had to contend with these strong preconditions. Therefore, green-tinted glass frames the portal. The entrance is marked by two strong semi-cylindrical forms made of Labrador granite; their polished curves, progressively narrowing, invite an elegant turn. After entering the store, an orientation zone follows which at the same time is a presentation stage and flanked by sales tables. Two tightly arranged columns stop the axial movement of the entrance and cover the interior staircase leading to the gallery. The slender, screen-like wall surface slicing in front of the storage shelves in the back third of the room offers an insight into a wide range of selection – an assurance that each customer will find something matching her taste. Strong contrasts and geometrical strictness dominate the pattern of the natural stone floor tiles while the tables, shelves and display areas are kept in a warm wooden shade. The masonry columns and walls have been dematerialized in a flat white creating a neutral background for the ephemeral goods on the store's display tables – the place for looking, choosing and buying.

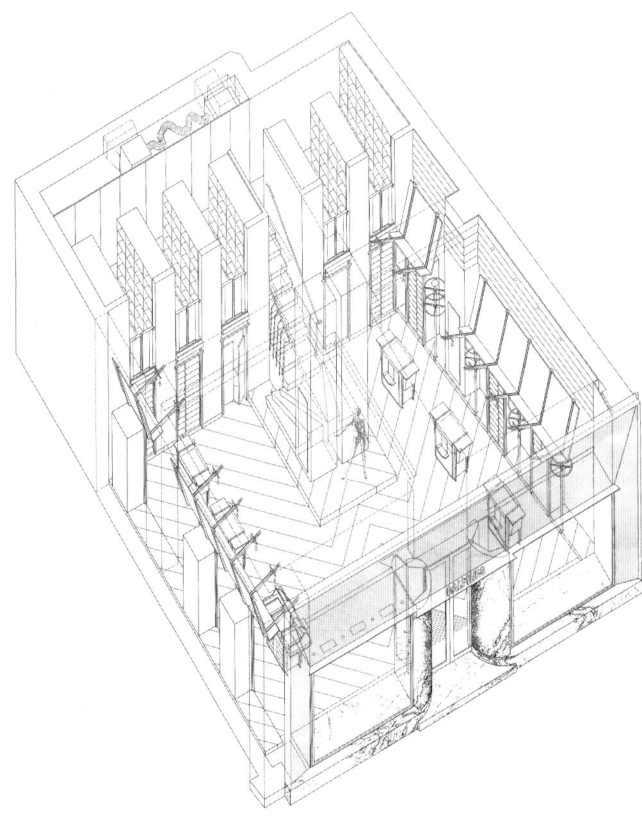

Eingang, Detail / *Entrance, detail*   Stiegenachse, Detail / *Staircase axis, detail*   Aufgang, Galerie / *Stairway, gallery*

Verkaufsraum / *Sales room*

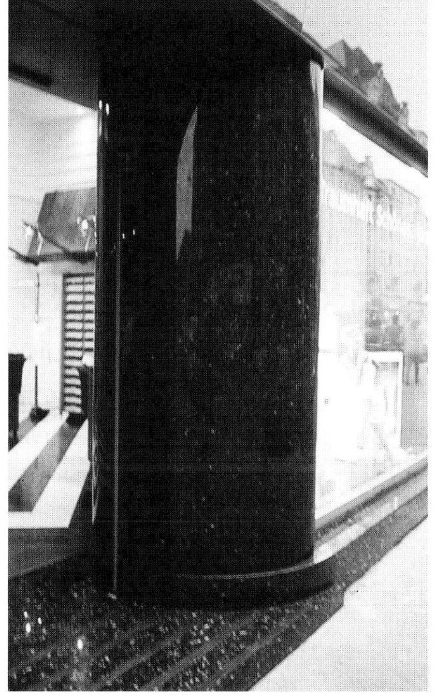
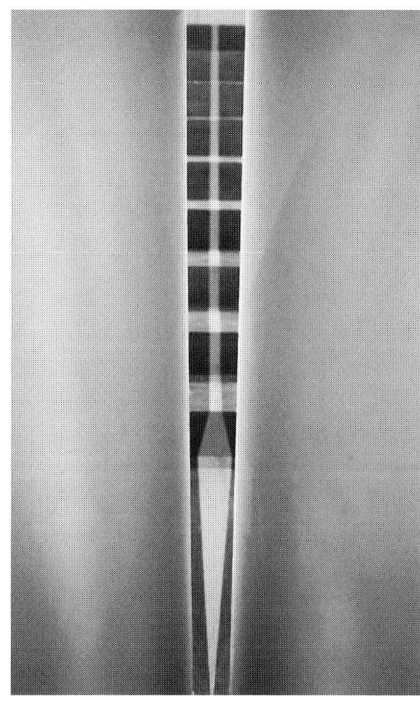
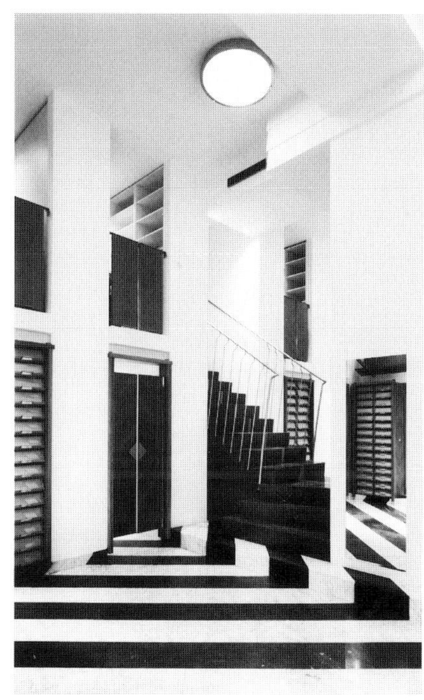

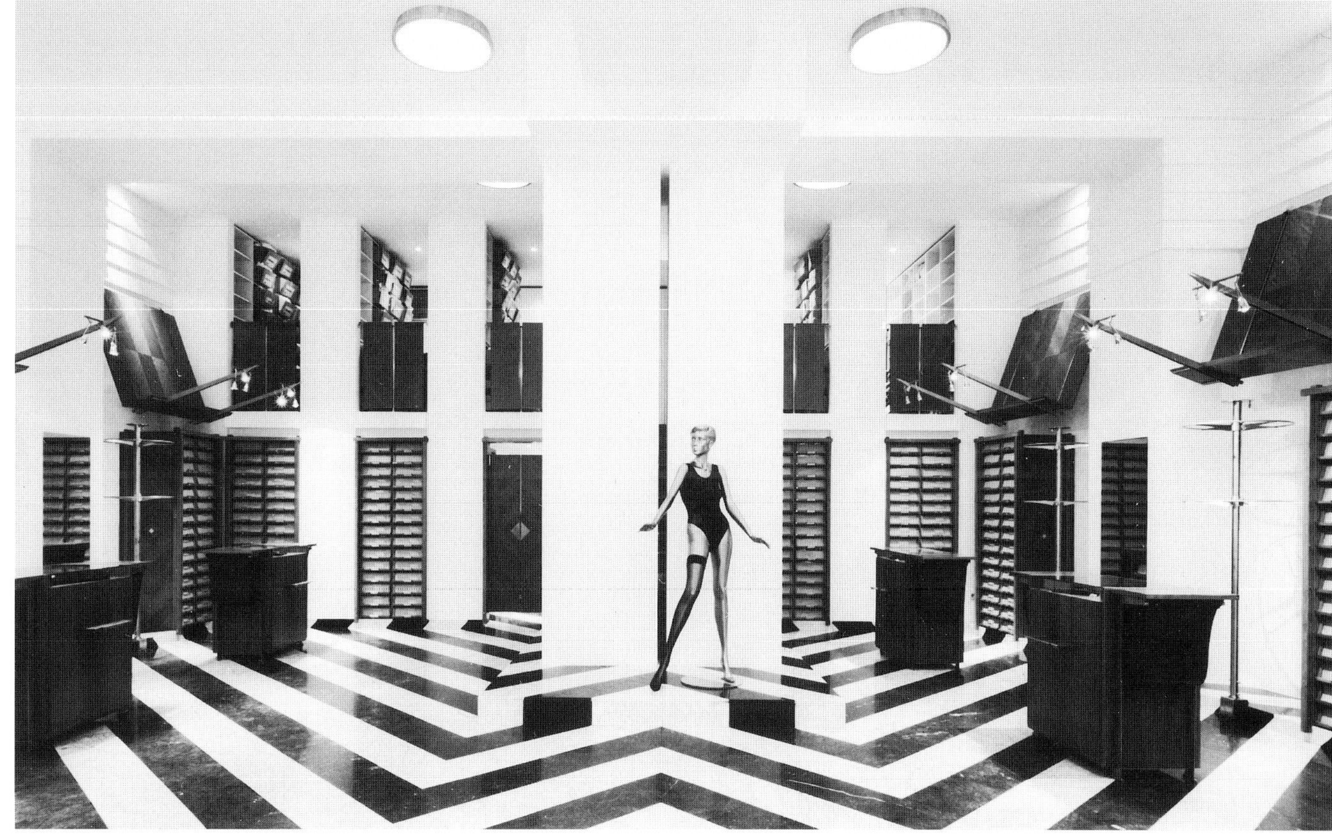

Abgang von der Galerie / *Stairway from the gallery*

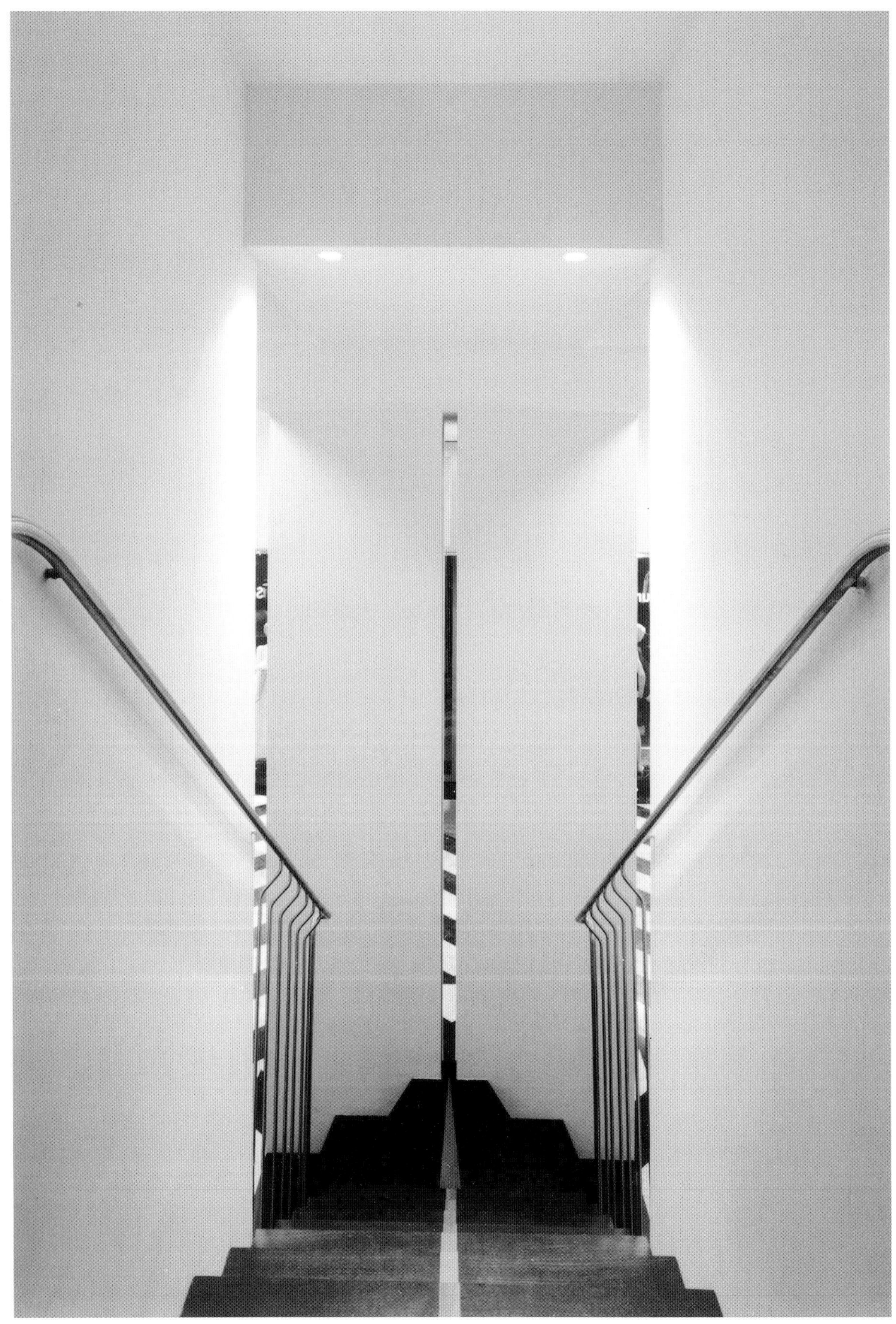

Wien - Josefstadt / *Vienna - Josefstadt* 1993

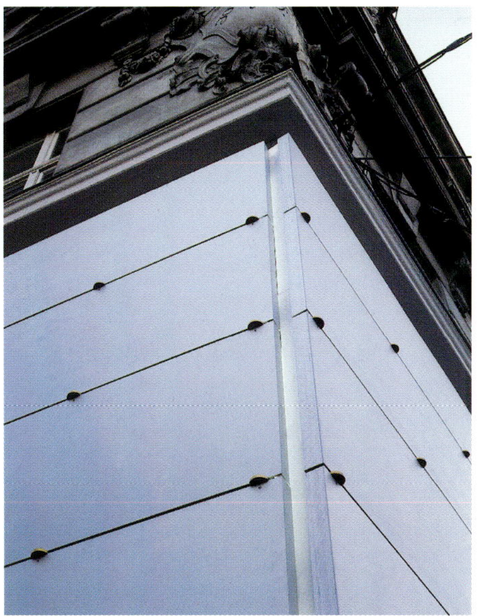

Fassadenbekleidung, Detail / *Facade, detail*

Außenansicht / *Exterior view*

Ein kleines Vorstadtkino in einem gründerzeitlichen Eckgebäude, dessen längerer Flügel auf die vom Verkehr beanspruchte platzartige Ausweitung an der Radialstraße blickt, wird zur Vorstadtbankfiliale umgebaut. Dabei wurde der rustizierte Gebäudesockel mit Alupaneelen wieder evoziert, was dem Eingangsbereich Gewicht verleiht und den dahinterliegenden Räumen Schutz und Schirm bietet. Zur Albertgasse ist die Mauer glatt verputzt und weist hohe Fensteröffnungen auf. Der hohe Innenraum wird für die Schalterhalle genutzt, hinter der in Pfeiler aufgelösten Mittelmauer ist eine Galerie eingezogen, deren Geometrie und Ausrichtung sich auf die Eingangsfront beziehen, die zur Seitenfassade in einem stumpfen Winkel steht. Aus dieser leichten Verdrehung erwächst räumliche Spannung und gestalterische Modernität. Verstärkt wird dieser Effekt durch eine nahezu raumhohe, verkippte Holztafel, welche die Stiege zur Galerie hinauf begleitet. Mit Birke im Fladernmuster furniert, kontrastiert sie zu den starken Farben kobaltblau und pompeianisch rot anderer Einbauelemente oder zu dem schwarzen Keramikboden. Ein würfelförmiges Büro für den Filialleiter, das an den Ort der Projektionskabine erinnert, befindet sich im vorderen Teil der Galerie. Ausblicke auf die Schalterhalle, die Straße und in den Eingangsbereich mit dem Geldautomaten verschaffen dem Chef den nötigen Überblick.

A small suburban movie theater in a corner building, dating back to the so-called "time of wild speculation", whose long wing is oriented towards the square-like extension of the traffic-laden radial street has been converted into a suburban bank branch. The rustic base of the building was evoked through the use of aluminum panels, thus giving weight to the entrance area and protection and shelter to the rooms beyond it. Towards Albertgasse, the wall is plastered with a smooth finish and has high window openings. The high inner room is used as a hall for customer service counters. Behind the middle wall and diluted into columns, a gallery is situated. Its geometry and orientation refer to the entrance front, forming an obtuse angle. The spatial suspense and the modern design grow out of this slight contortion. This effect is strengthened by an almost room-high slanted wooden panel which accompanies the staircase up to the gallery. With its speckle patterned birch veneer, it stands in stark contrast to the strong colors of other builtin elements, e. g. cobalt blue and pompeian red, or the black ceramic tiles. An office for the branch manager, reminding one of the location of the projection cabin, is located in the front area of the gallery. The view across the service counter hall, the street and into the entrance area with the cash machine provide the manager with the requisite view.

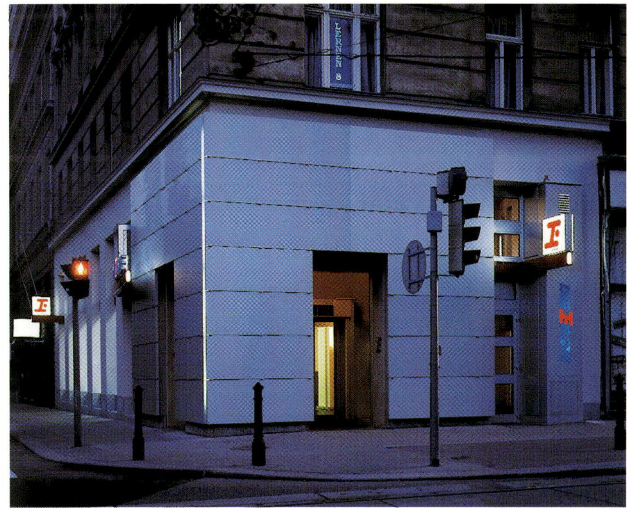

Axonometrie / *Axonometric projection*

Innenraummodell / *Interior model*   Struktur und Textur / *Structure and texture*

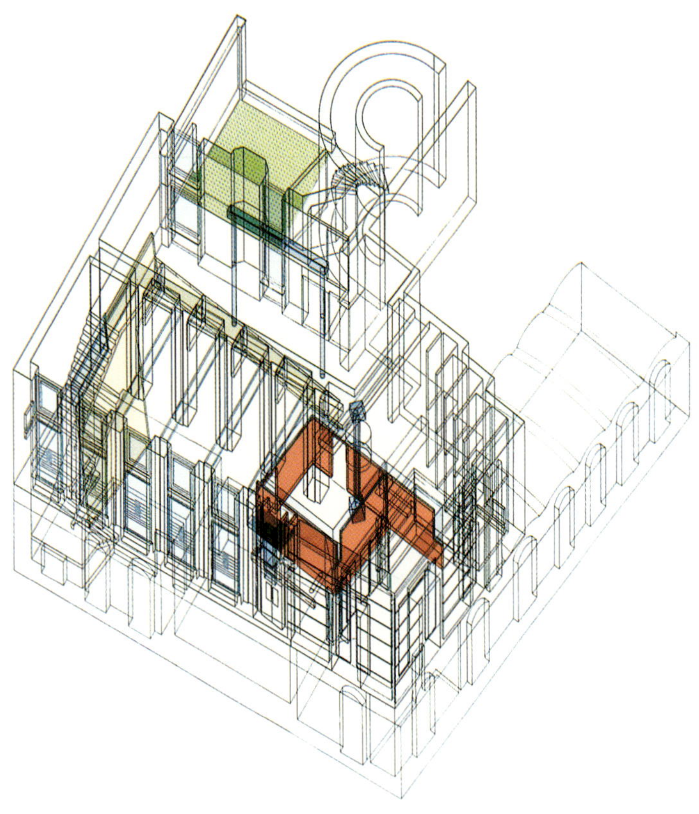

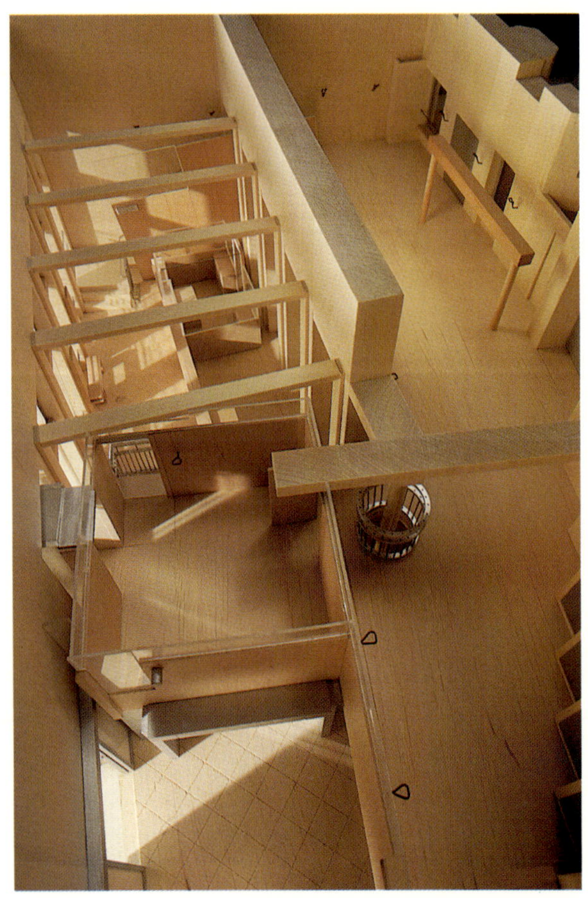

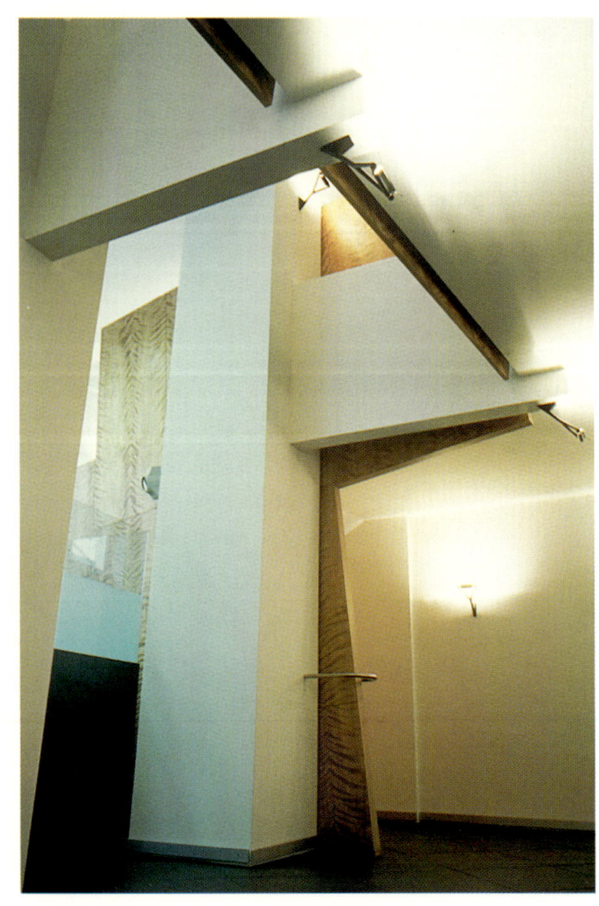

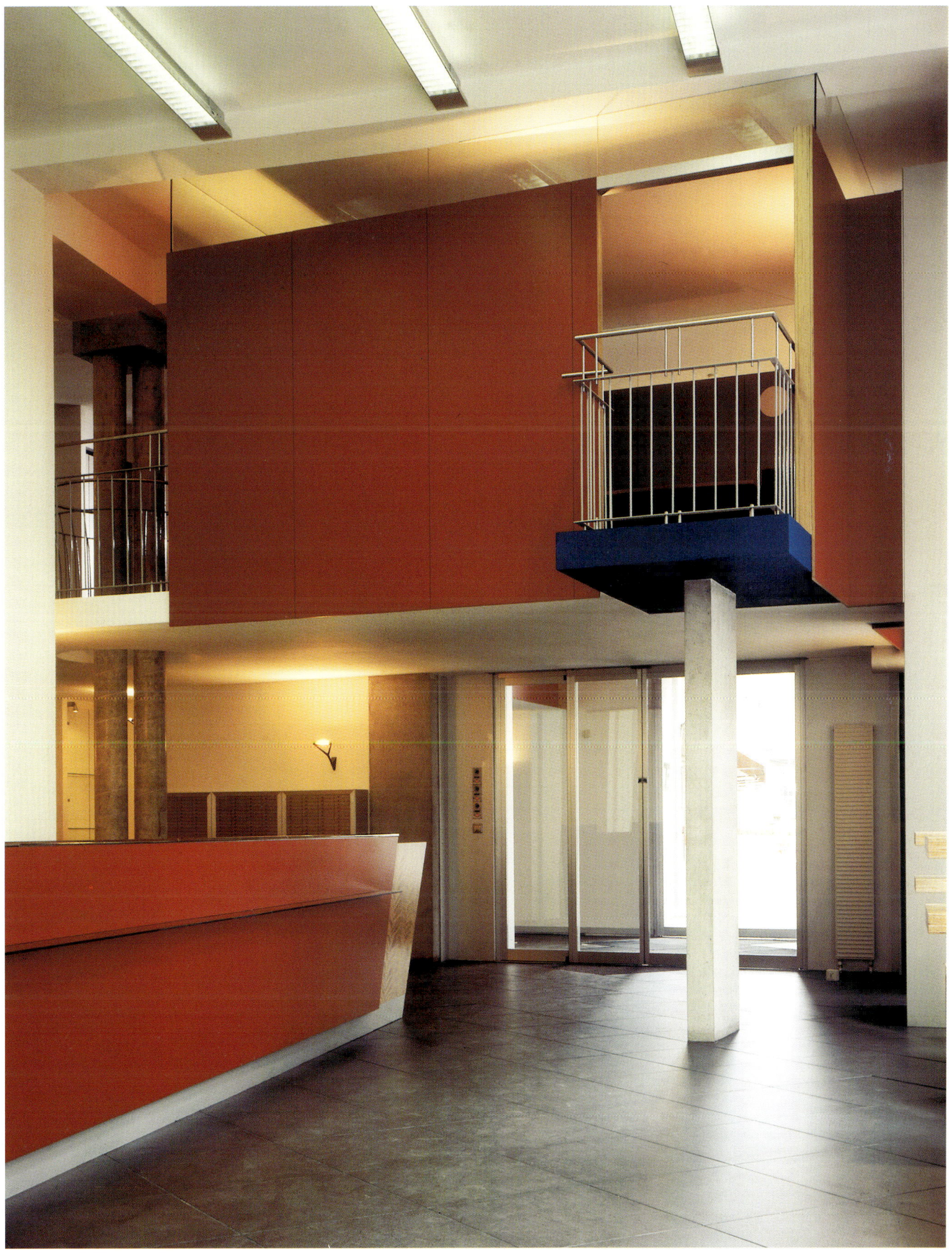

Zwillingssäule, Erdgeschoß und Galerie / *Double column, first floor and gallery*

Blick in die Kassenhalle /
View into the customer service lobby

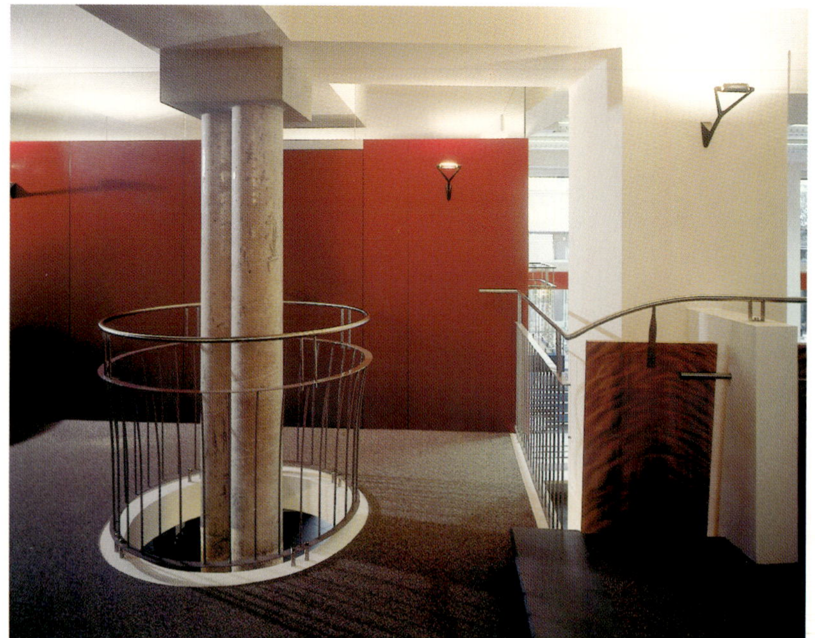

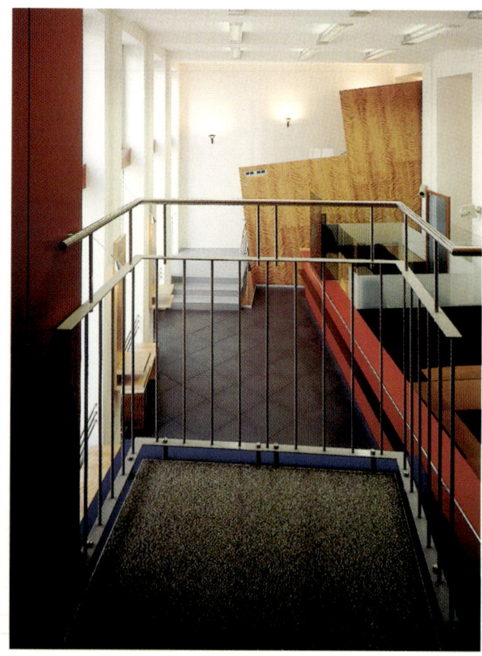

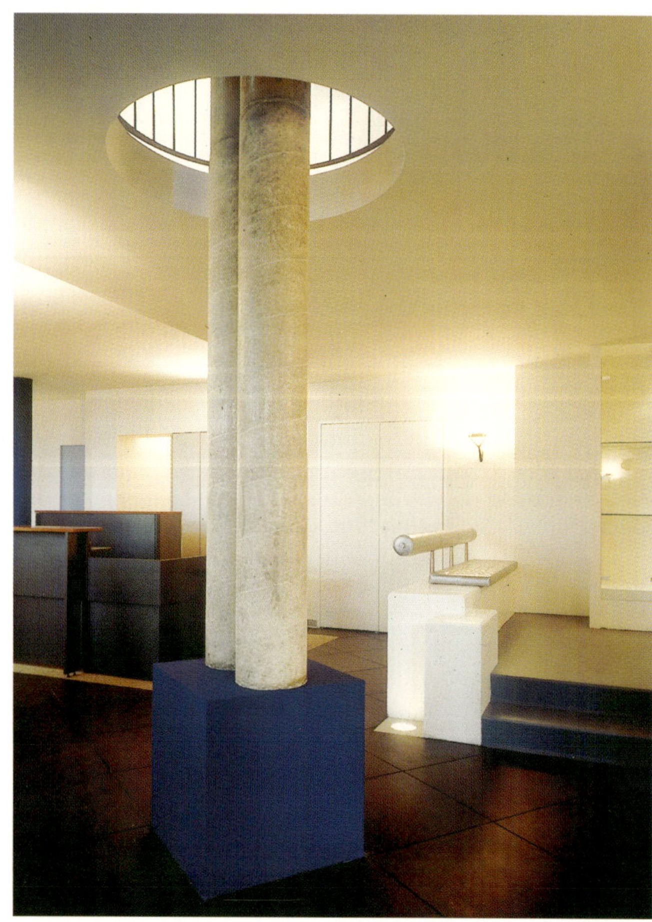

Trennwand, Detail / *Partitioning wall, detail*   Aufgang, Galerie / *Stairway, gallery*

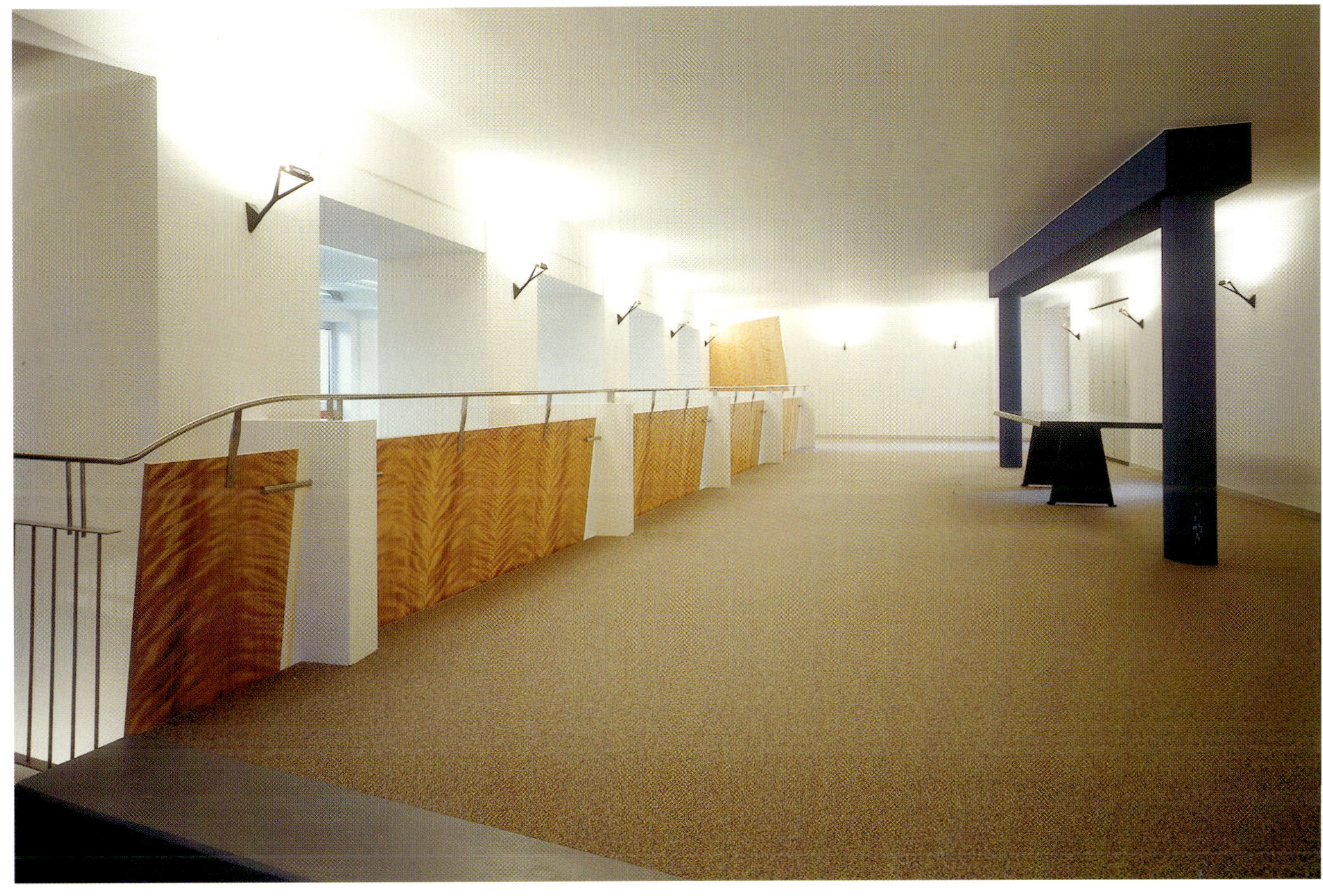

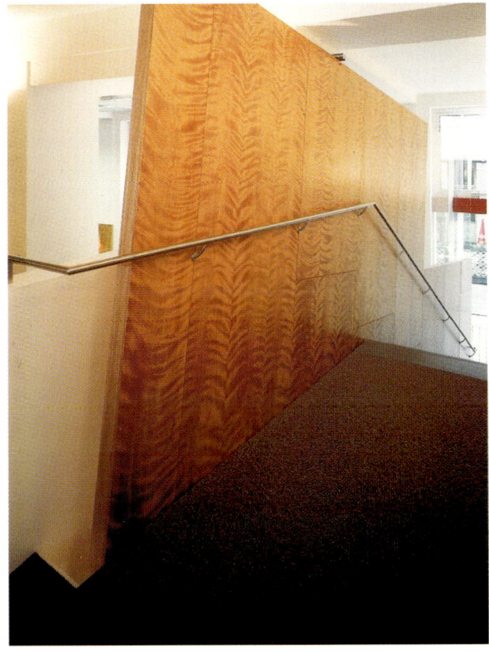

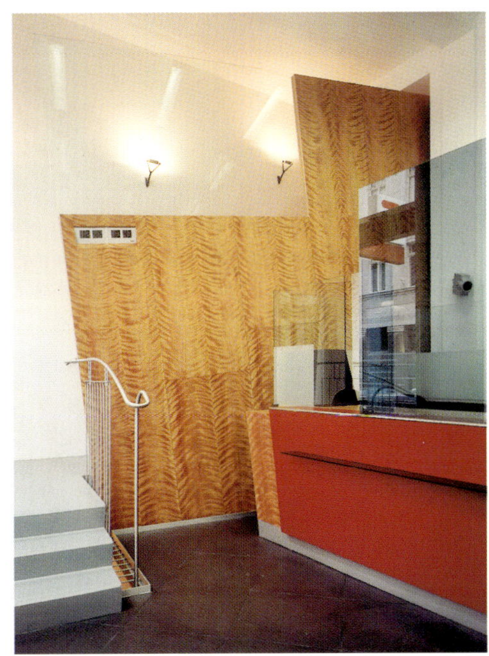

Wien-Josefstadt / *Vienna-Josefstadt* 1995

Grundriß Erdgeschoß / *Plan of first floor*

Perspektive / *Perspective*

Auf Sichtweite des von Boris Podrecca zur Bankfiliale umgebauten Albertkinos galt es, ein slowenisches Studentenheim zu erneuern und zusätzlich Räume für kulturelle Aktivitäten einzurichten. Das Erdgeschoß ist straßenseitig zwei Etagen hoch geöffnet und dient zu Ausstellungszwecken. Die geschuppt eingesetzten Glastafeln wirken weniger hermetisch als eine glatte Metall-Glaskonstruktion, so daß der Straßenraum in das Haus hineinzugreifen vermag. Eine darin eingezogene Galerie beherbergt die Bibliothek und erlaubt den Zugang zu einem Mehrzweckraum, der auch als Kapelle verwendbar ist. Das Erdgeschoß des Hofflügels wird von einem teilbaren Saal ausgefüllt. Einige Zimmer des Heims werden hotelmäßig betrieben; die Mehrzahl ist jedoch mit einfachen, dauerhaften Möbeln eingerichtet und dient Studierenden. Die Fenster sind kastenartig einen knappen halben Meter vor die Fassade gesetzt. Seitliche Verglasungen erlauben den Ausblick die Straße hinauf und hinunter. Dieser erkerartige Raumteil wertet die nicht sehr großen Zimmer entscheidend auf, man kann sich sogar «ins Fenster legen» und sich gleichsam vor die Fassade begeben. Ähnlichen Zwecken dienten in der Biedermeierzeit gewölbte Fensterflügel. In städtischen Verhältnissen ist so ein Erker wertvoller als die meist schlecht nutzbaren Balkone. Die stark plastische Wirkung nach außen verleiht dem Gebäude Signifikanz und kompensiert die knapp bemessenen Umbaumittel mit architektonischem Ausdruck und Identität.

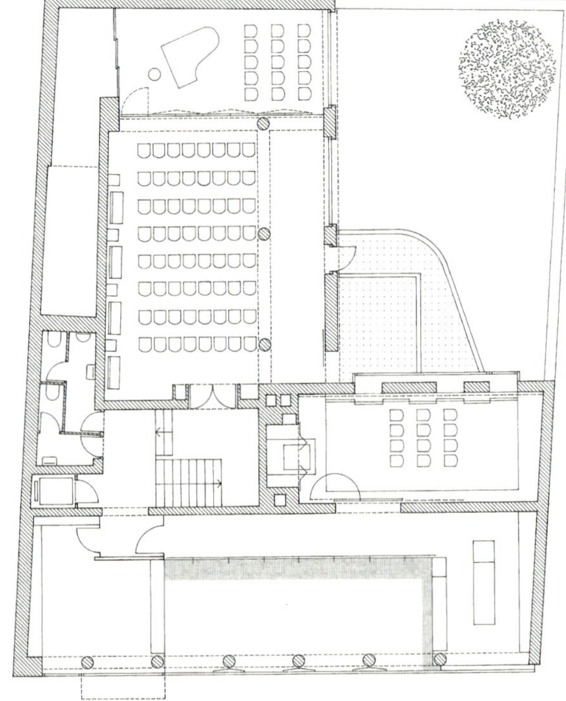

In the vicinity and within view of the Albert movie theater which was converted into a bank branch by Boris Podrecca, a Slovenian student housing unit was converted and at the same time spaces for cultural activities were created. The ground floor is opened up over two stories towards the street and serves for exhibition purposes. The scale-like glass panels have a less hermetic effect than a flat metal-glass construction, thus allowing the street space to enter into the house. An inserted gallery houses the library and allows access to a multi-purpose room which, among other things, can be used as a chapel. The ground floor of the courtyard wing is dominated by a dividable hall. Some dorm rooms are used as hotel rooms, but most of them are furnished with simple, durable furniture and used by students. The windows are placed box-like and extend out from the front of the facade by approximately half a meter. The glass casements on their sides allow a view up and down the street. These outward extensions not only decisively increase the functional value of the rather small rooms, but one can even "lie within the window" and move beyond the facade. The curved window sashes of the Biedermeier period served a similar purpose. In an urban setting, these oriels are more valuable than small, hardly usable balconies. The strong sculptural effect on the outside provides the building with a significant appearance and compensates for the tightly calculated budget of the conversion with an architecturally expressive identity.

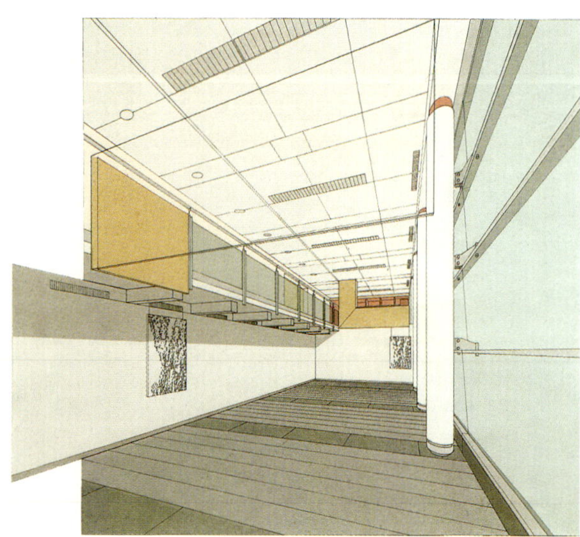

Ansicht Albertgasse / *View Albertgasse*

Ausstellungshalle / *Exhibition hall*

Bezugsachse Bank - Studentenwohnheim /
Reference axis, bank - student housing

Ansicht Albertgasse / *View Albertgasse*

Geschuppte Glastafeln / *Scale - like glass panels*

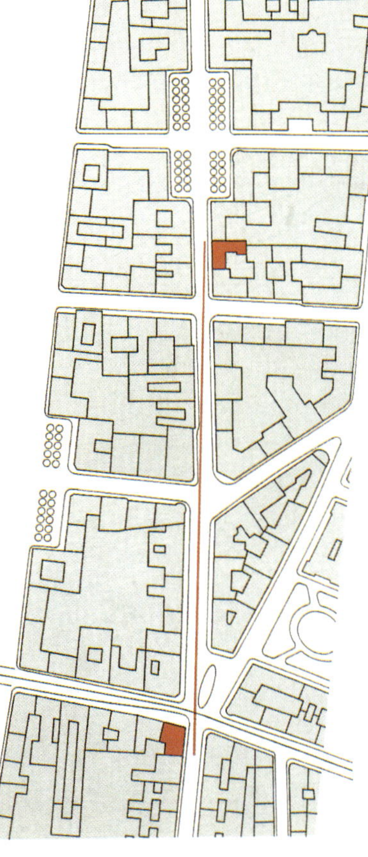

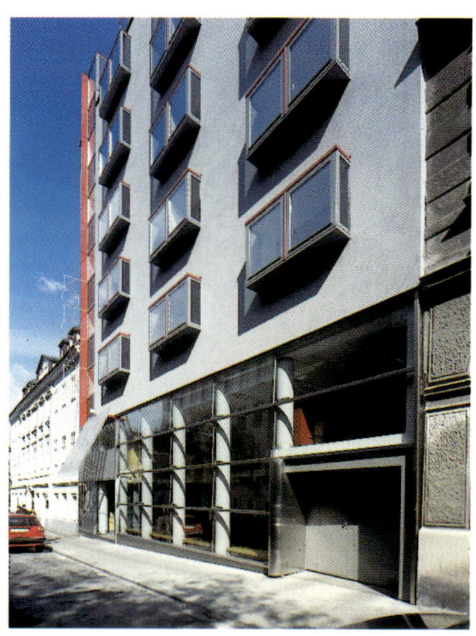

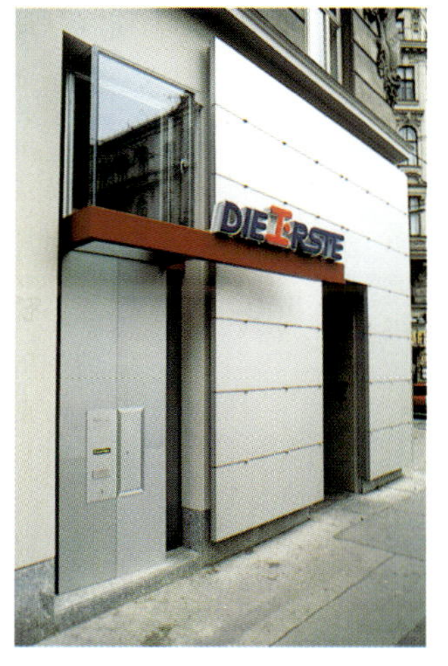

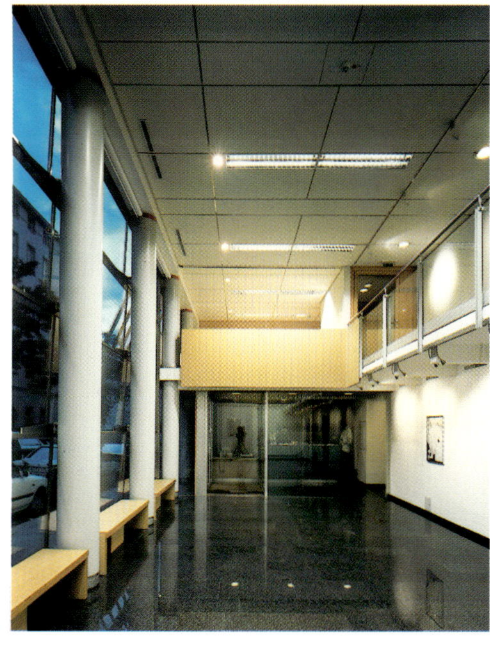

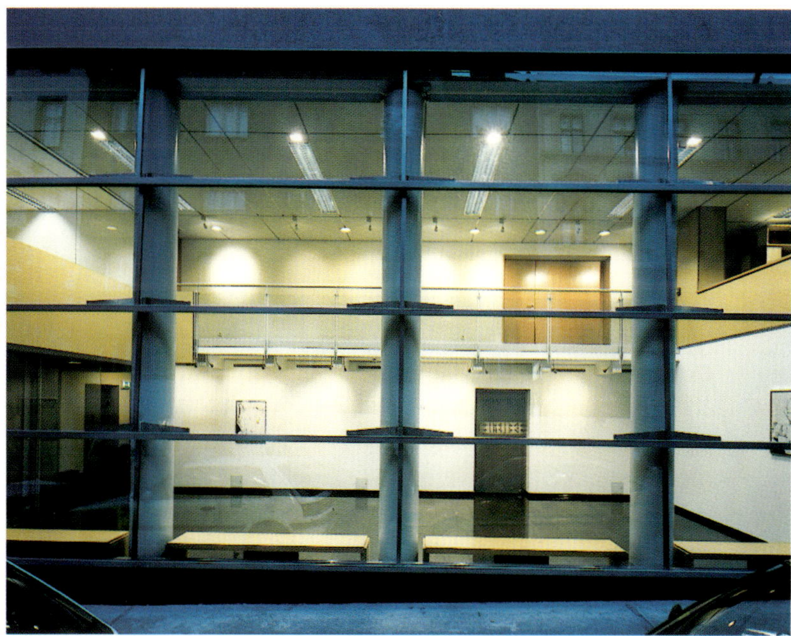

Ansicht Albertgasse / *View Albertgasse*

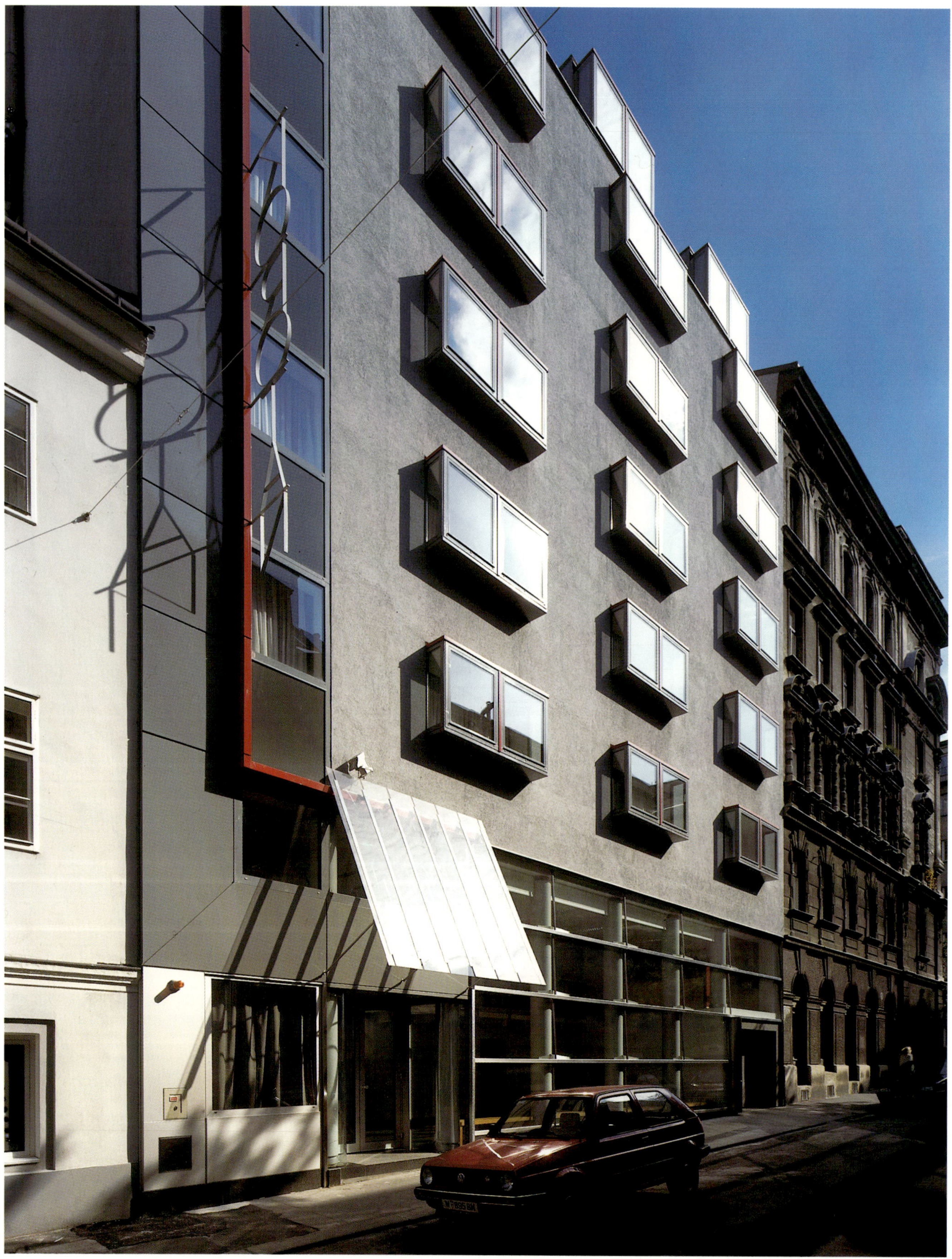

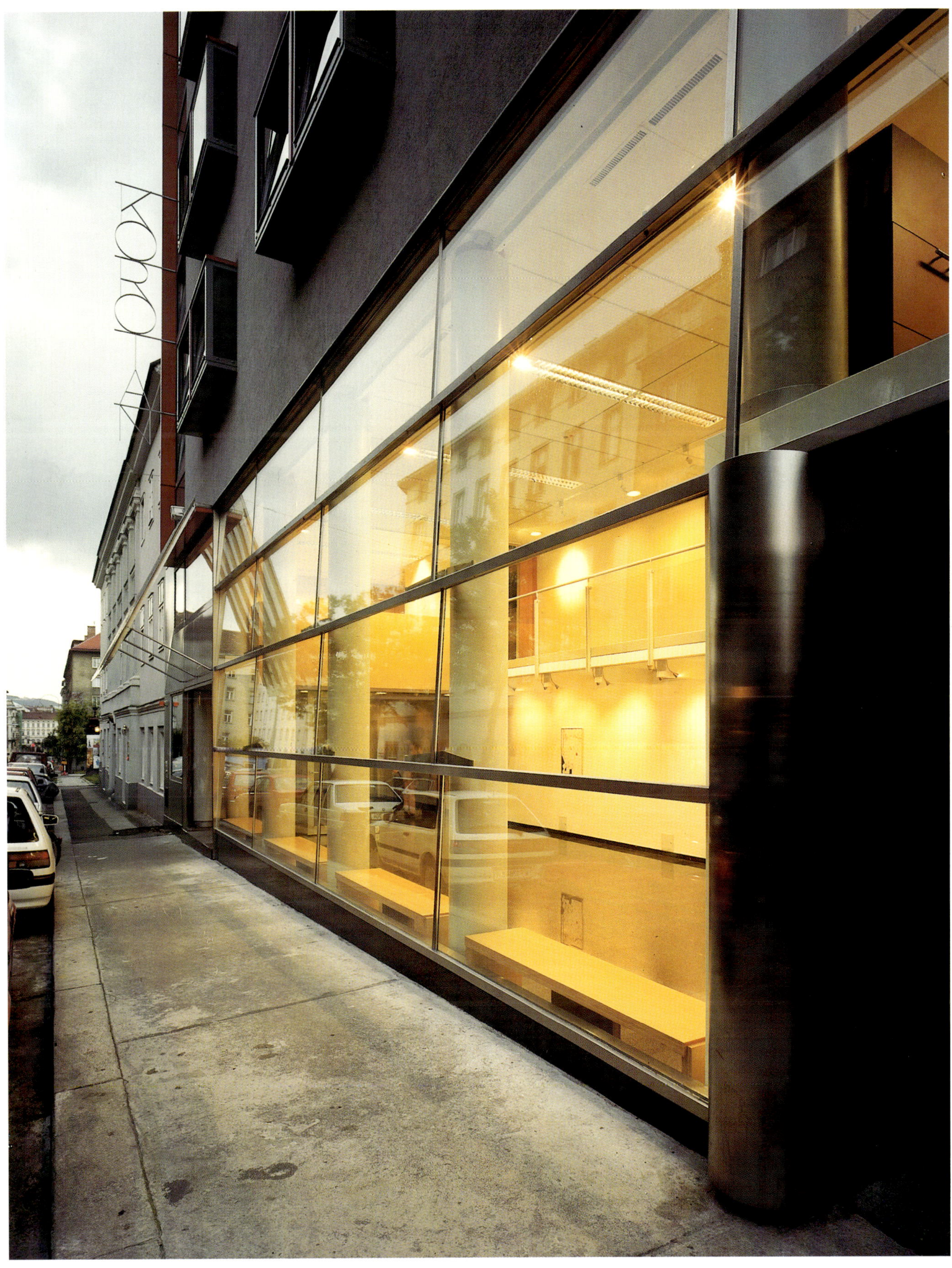

Galerie, Bibliothek / *Gallery, library*   Galerie, Bibliothek / *Gallery, library*

Galerie, Direktion / *Gallery, Direction*

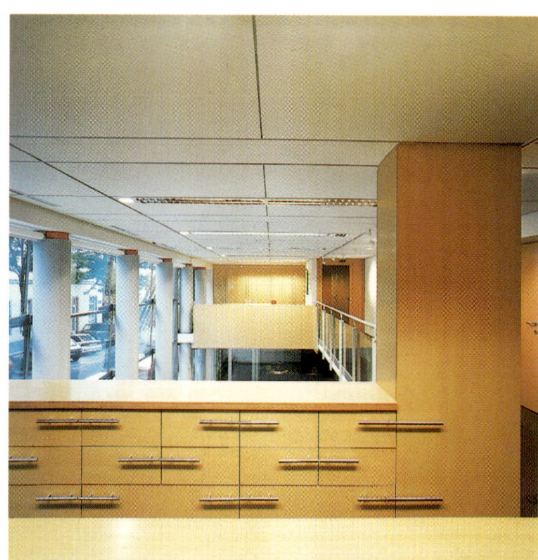
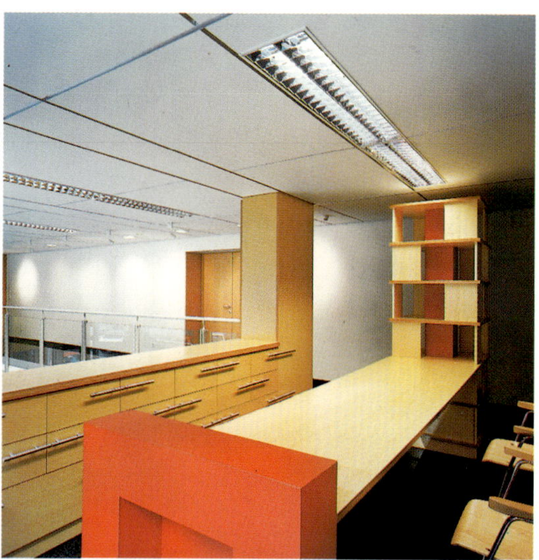

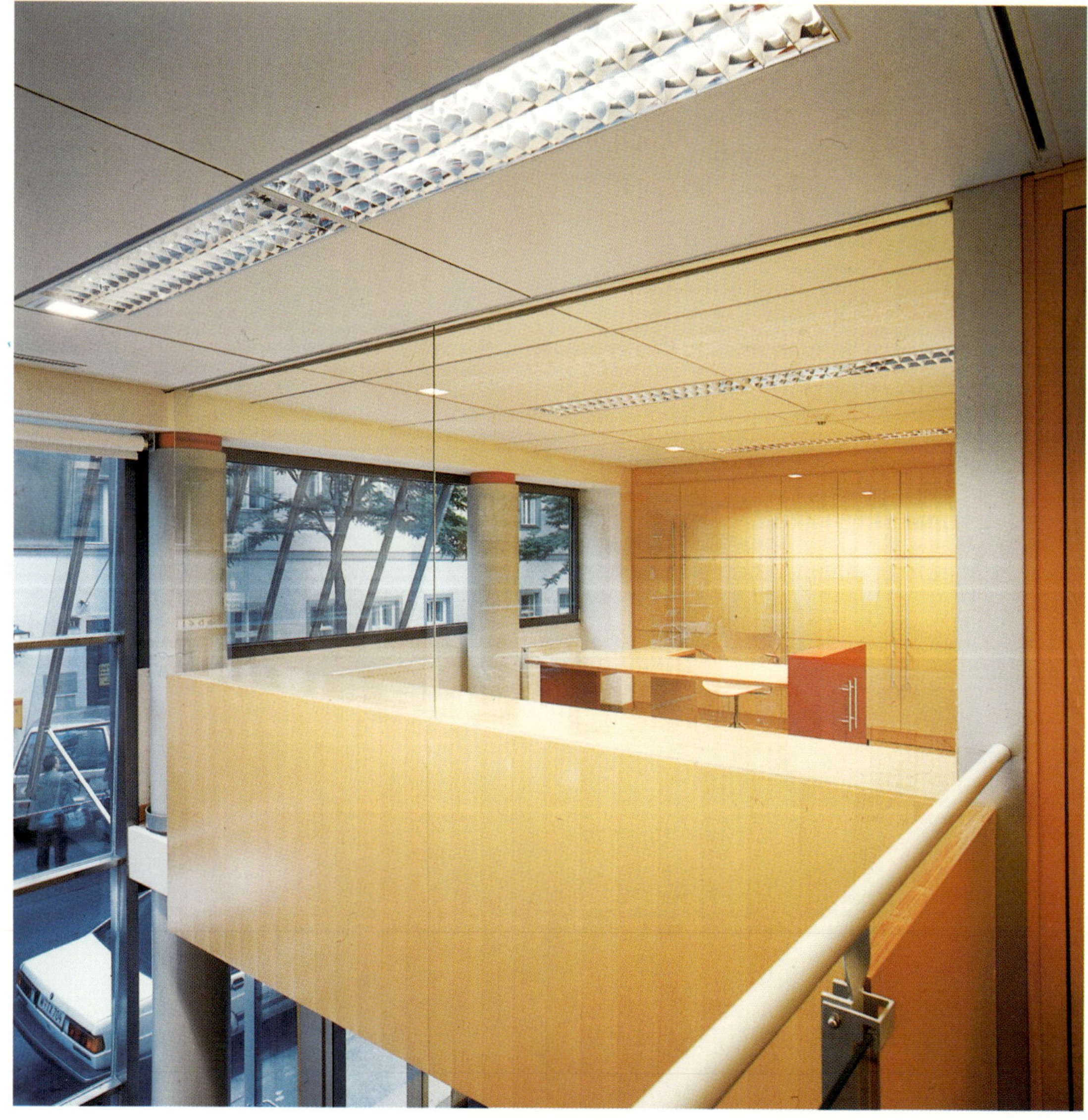

Auffaltbarer Altarschrank /
Altar cabinet, can be flipped open

Versammlungsraum, Kapelle / *Meeting hall, chapel*

Schiebewand, Detail / *Sliding wall, detail*

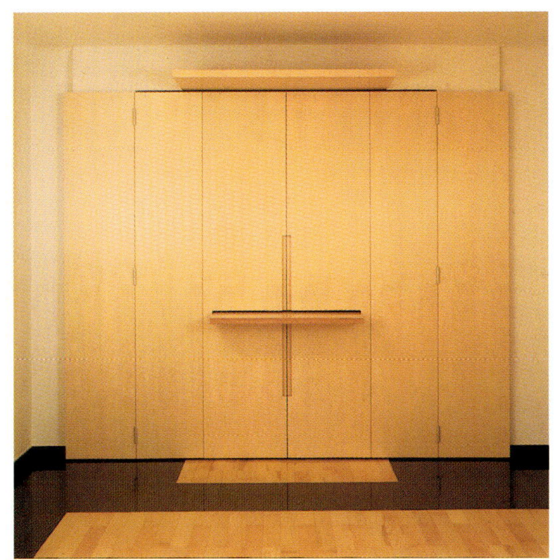

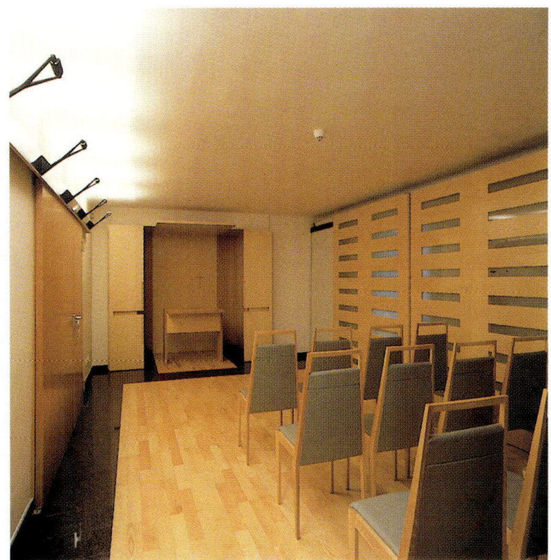

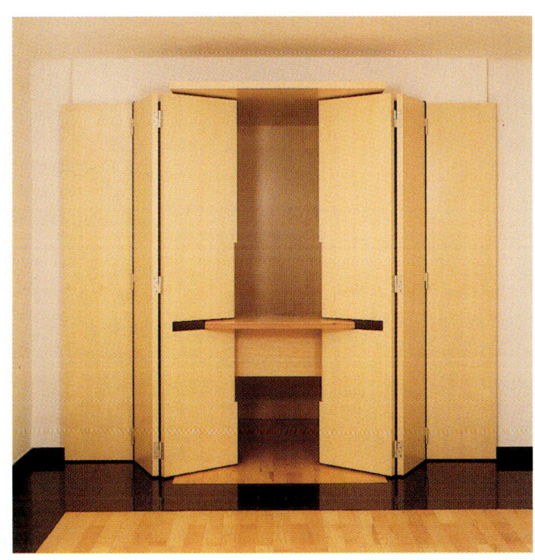

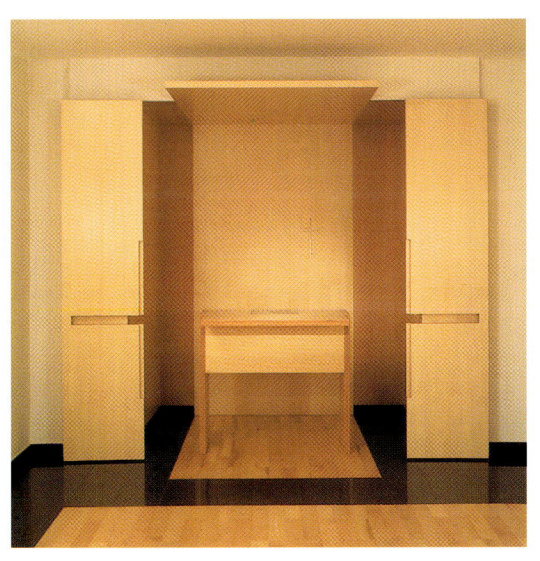

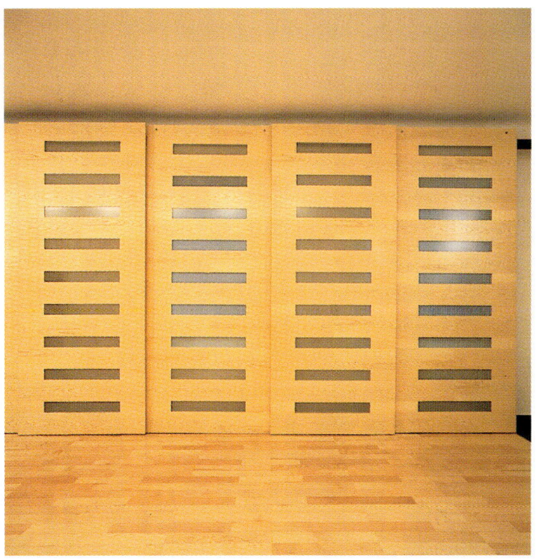

Biberach, Deutschland / *Germany* 1995

Längsschnitt / *Longitudinal section*

Grundriß Obergeschoß / *Plan of upper floor*

Grundriß Erdgeschoß / *Plan of first floor*

Das «Neuer Bau» genannte Gebäude diente früher als Kornspeicher. Über zwei breitgelagerten Vollgeschossen und mächtigen Mauern steigt ein steiles Satteldach auf, das insgesamt noch vier begehbare Ebenen enthält. Das kräftige, überaus eindrückliche Zimmermannswerk für Schüttböden und Dach galt es weitestgehend zu bewahren. Da die kleinen Lüftungsöffnungen nur wenig Licht hereinlassen, wurde am First ein großes Oberlicht eingesetzt, das den Zentralbereich des dreischiffigen Grundrisses aufhellt. Der alle Geschosse durchstoßende Licht- und Luftraum nimmt das Fluchtstiegenhaus aus Stahlbeton sowie den verglasten Liftschacht auf. Bis zur zweiten Ebene zieht sich auch die Diagonale einer Kaskadentreppe hinauf. In den drei nichtöffentlichen Obergeschossen dient die Fluchtstiege als Erschließung. Die empfindliche Substanz des großen Solitärbauwerks bleibt in ihrer imposanten Wirkung unangetastet. So wird der Windfang deutlich vor die hohe Giebelwand gesetzt, wo er als separates Element zum Gesamtbau in Beziehung tritt. Ein weiteres Problem boten die erforderlichen Belichtungsöffnungen in der Dachfläche, die zuvor geschlossen war. Mit einer geometrisch geformten Ausstülpung aus Kunststoff, die bewußt nicht an Gaupen erinnern, gelingt es, dem Dach einen zeitgenössischen Ausdruck zu geben und den Wandel vom Zweckbau zum öffentlichen Bauwerk, ohne Anbiederung, in differenzierter Weise zu vermitteln.

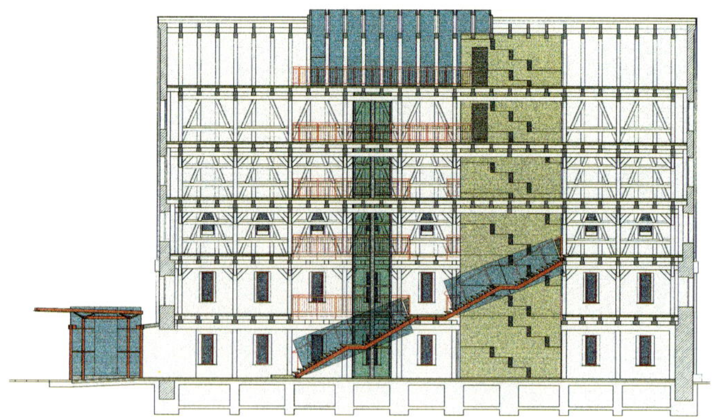

The building, known as "New Building", was originally used as a grain storage building. A steeply pitched saddle-back roof rises above the two wide, full floors and the massive walls, and contains four more accessible levels. The heavy and very impressive timber work for the floors and the roof was for the most part supposed to be preserved. Since the small ventilation openings allowed only a very little light to enter, a large skylight was set into the ridge, illuminating the central area of the ground plan with its three naves. The light and air space going through all three stories contains the reinforced concrete emergency escape stairs as well as the glassed-in elevator shaft. The diagonal line of a cascading staircase reaches the second level. In the three upper, non-public floors, the emergency stairway serves as the access. The delicate substance of the large solitary building remains untouched in its impressive appearance. Thus, the entrance porch is placed noticeably in front of the high gable wall, thus entering into a relationship as a separate element with the entire building. Another problem was posed by the necessary openings in the roof plane for natural lighting. It was mastered by adding plastic geometric forms projecting out from the roof surface, which were intentionally designed not to resemble dormers. The roof thus received a contemporary expression and the transformation from a functional structure to a public building was achieved in a discriminating way without intruding on the original exemplary form.

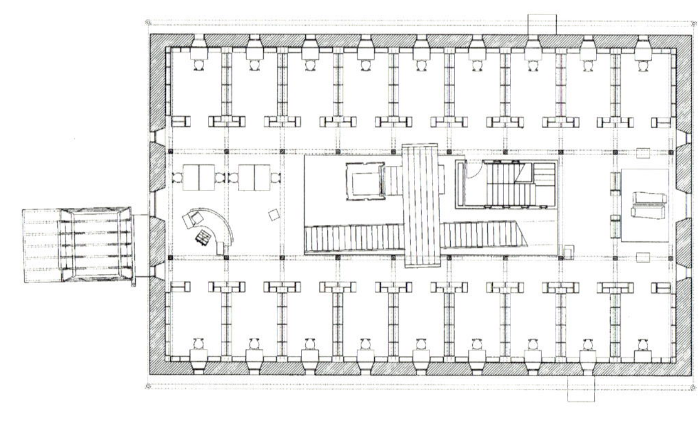

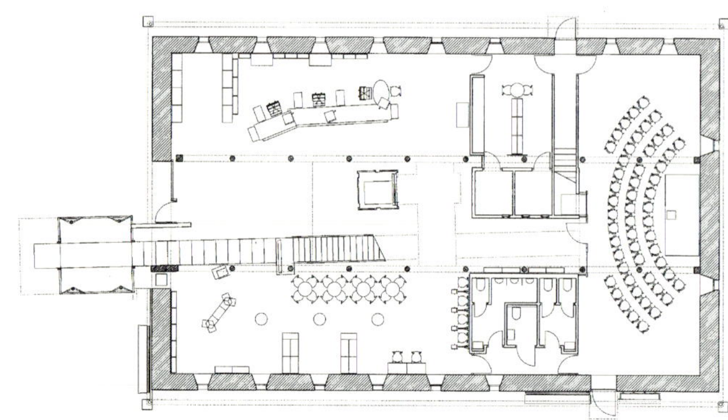

Nachtansicht / *View at night*

Gesamtansicht mit Eingangsvorbau / *View showing entrance porch*

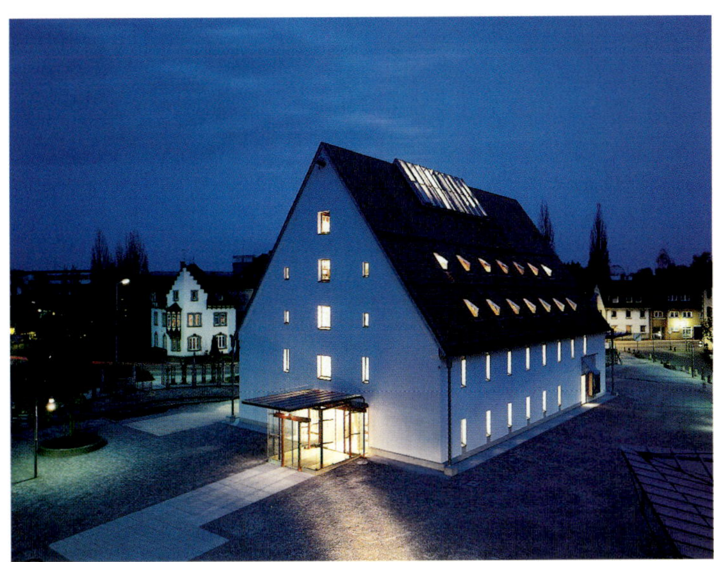

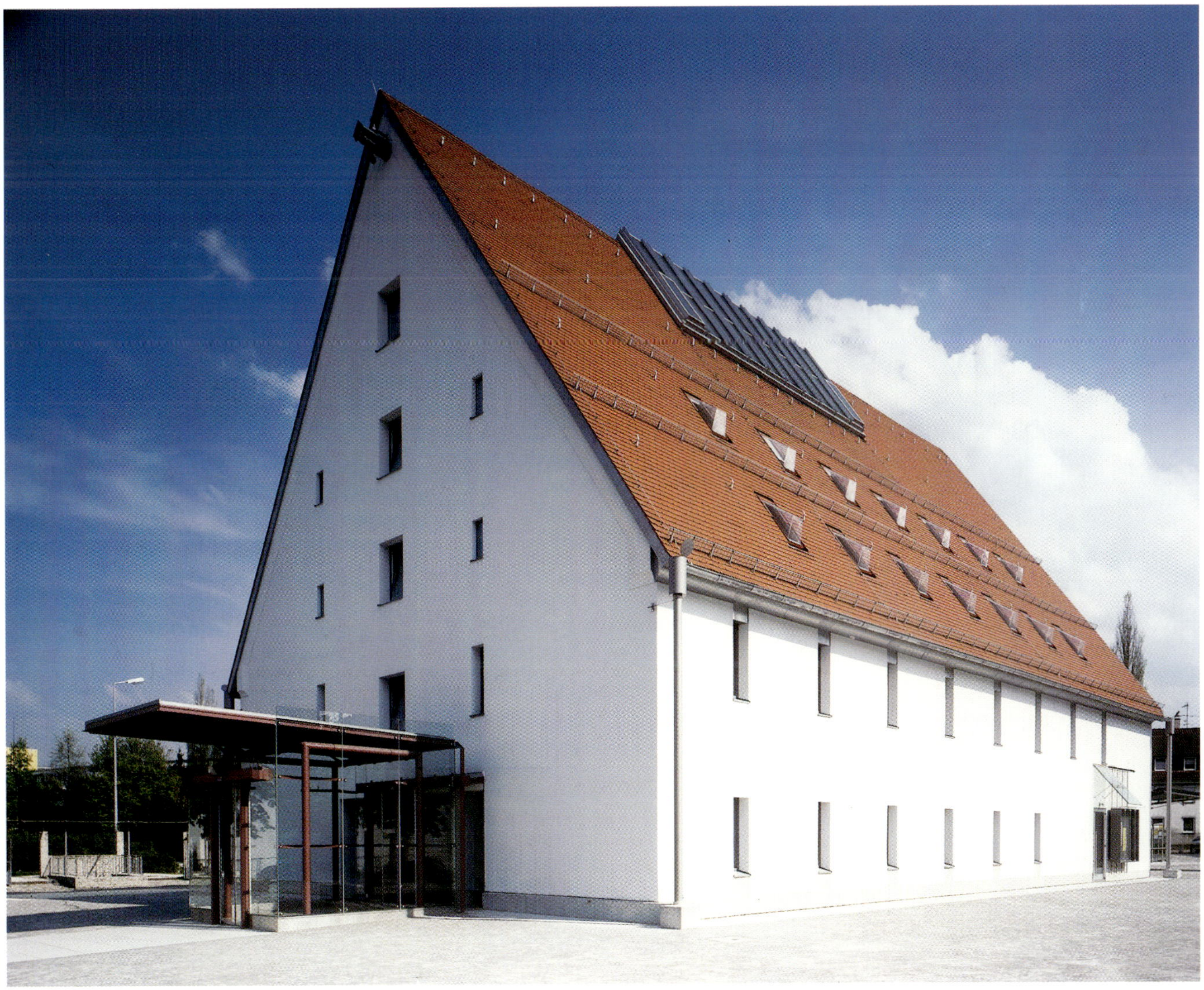

Westansicht, Ausschnitt / *West view, partial*

Eingangsvorbau, Details / *Entrance porch, details*

Eingang Veranstaltungsraum / *Entrance to entertainment room*

Regenrohr, Detail / *Drain pipe, detail*

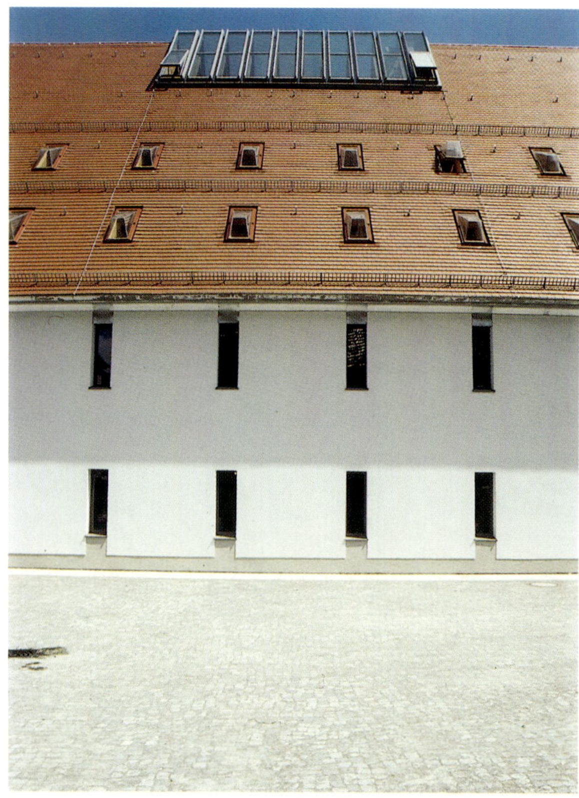

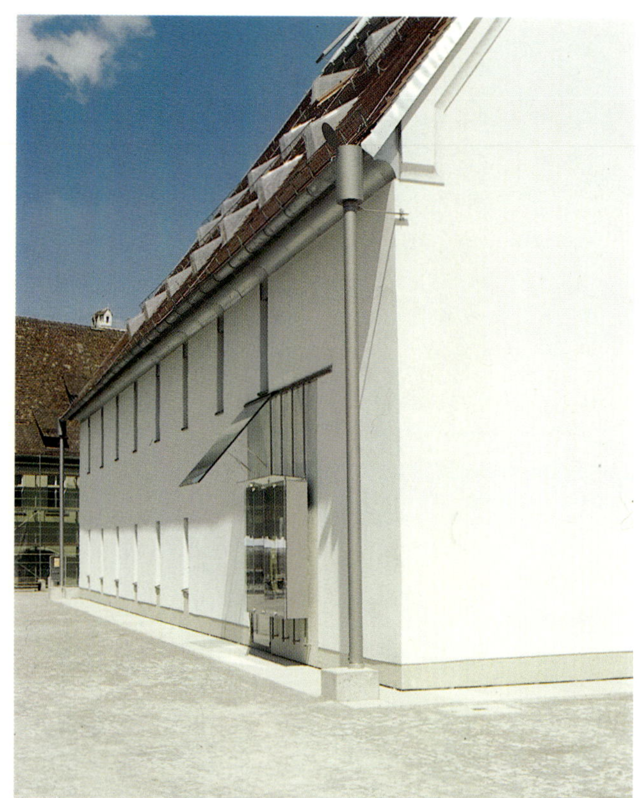

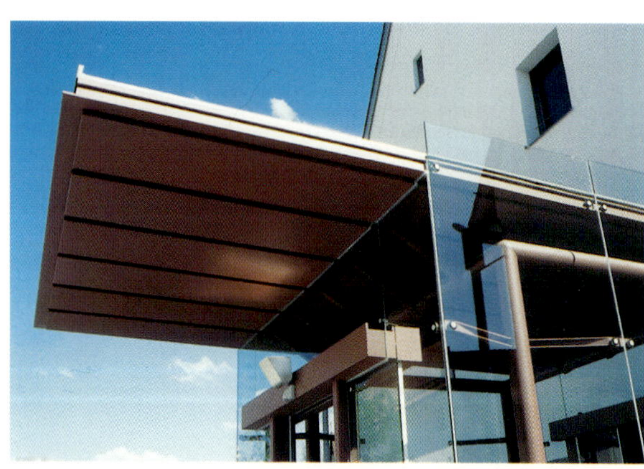

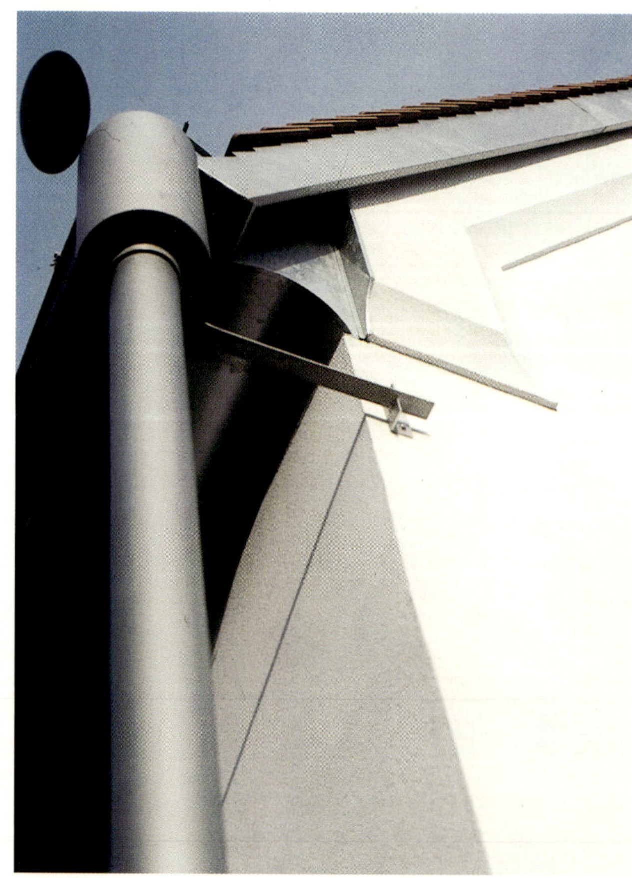

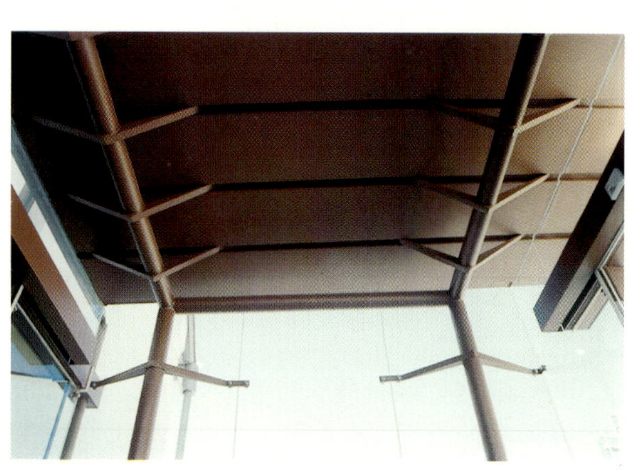

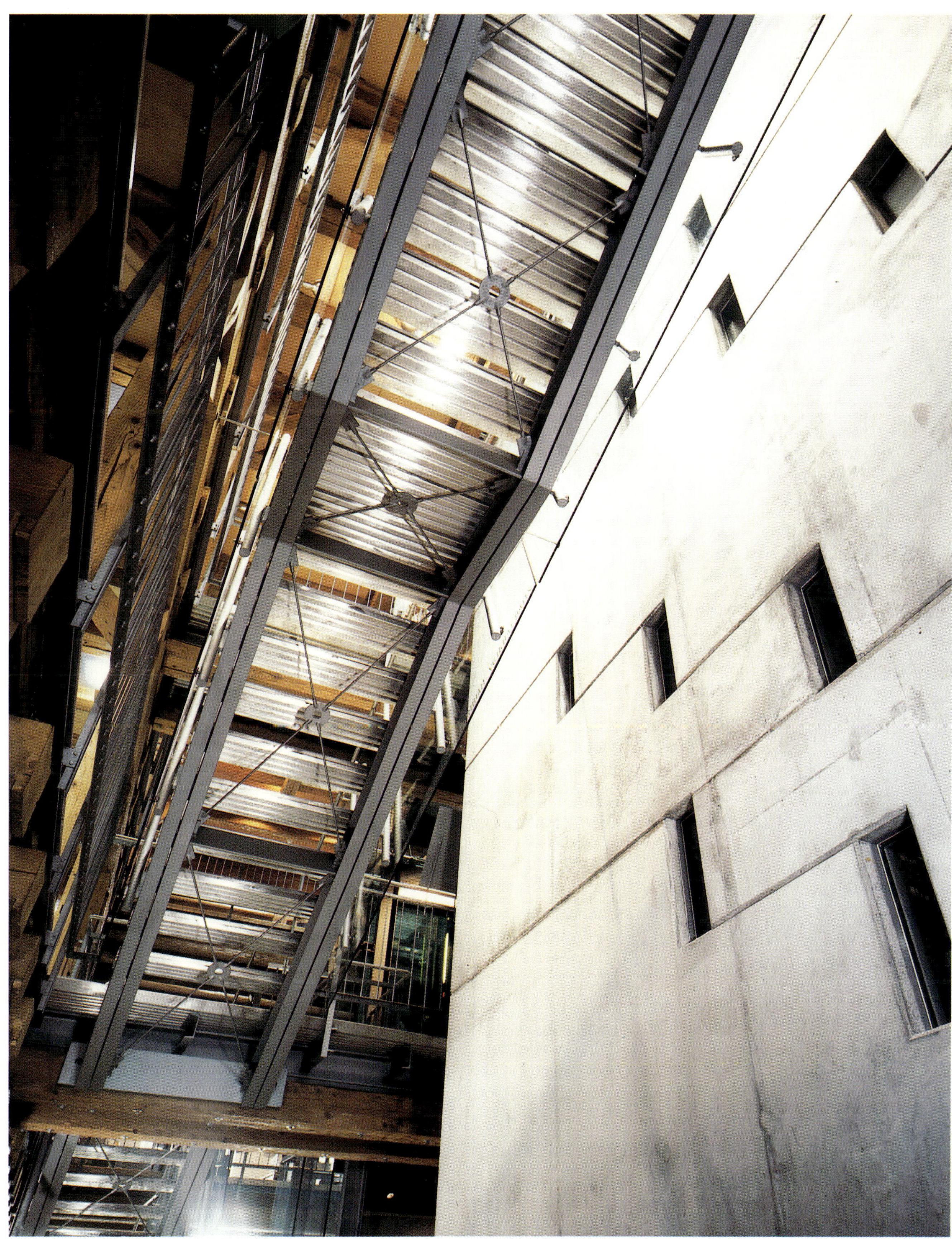

Mittelhalle, Aufzugsprisma / *Central hall, elevator prism*   «Himmelsleiter» / *"Celestial ladder" stairway*

Mittelhalle, Stiegenaufgang und Aufzug
Middle hall, stairway and elevator

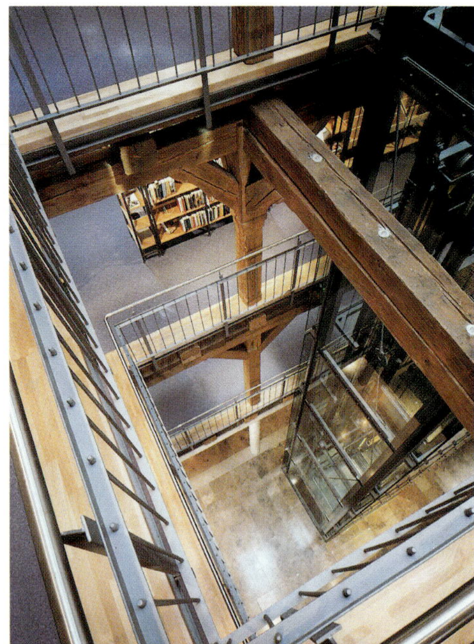
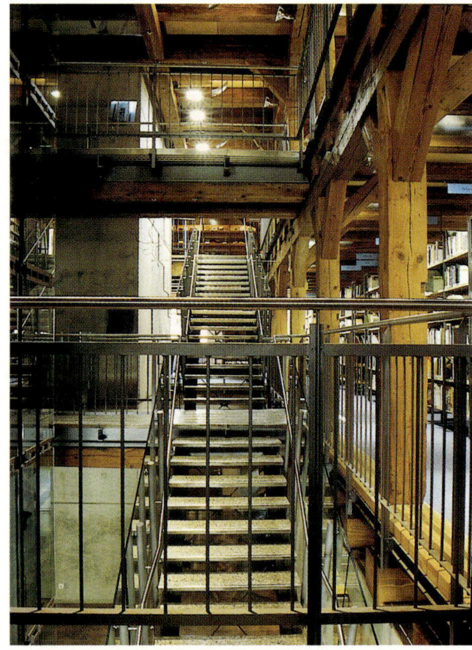

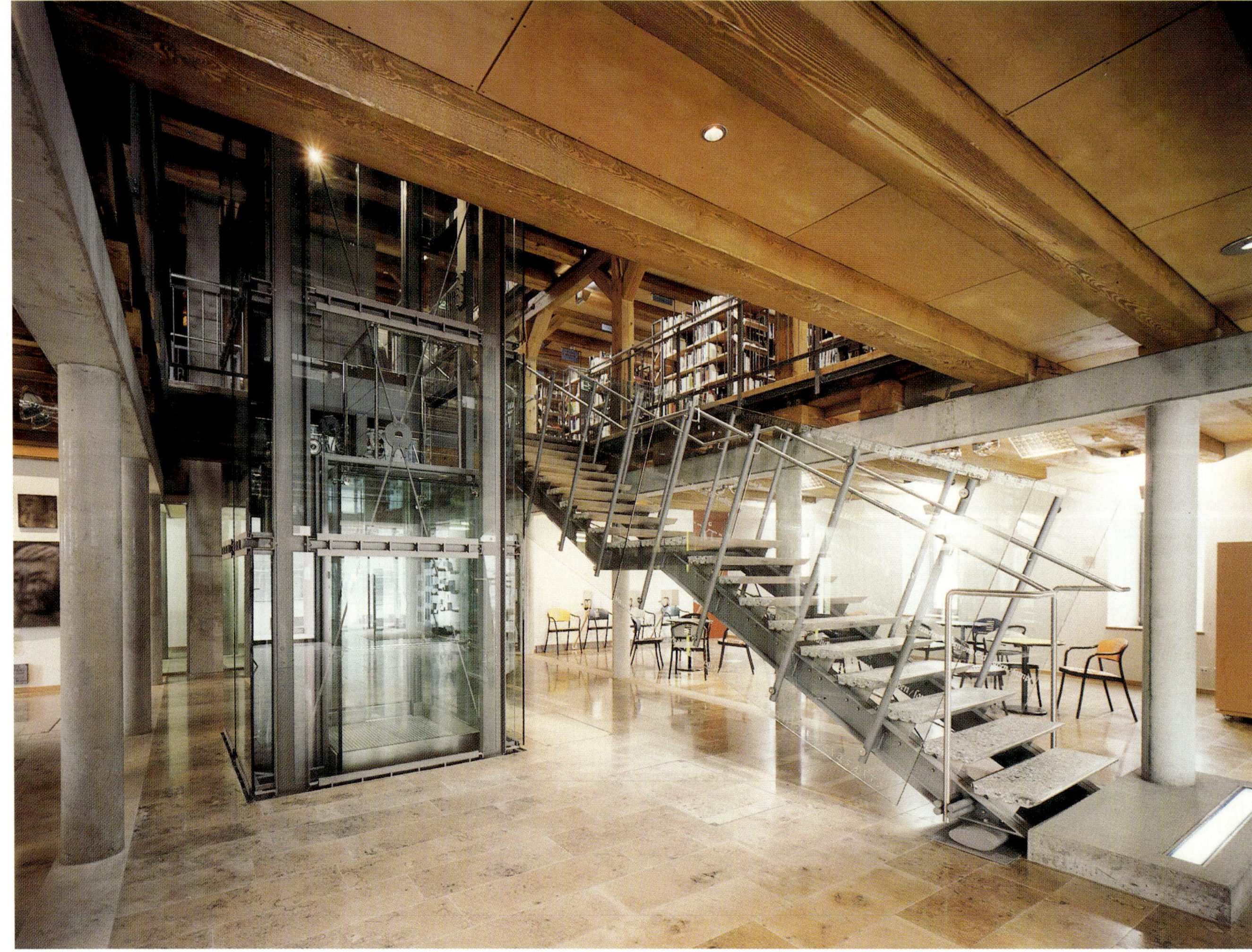

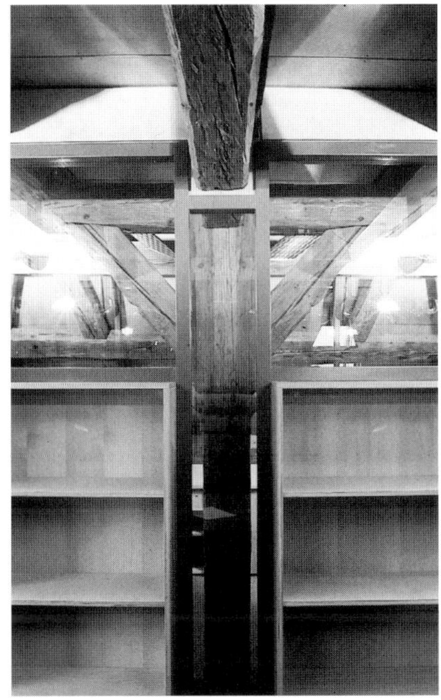 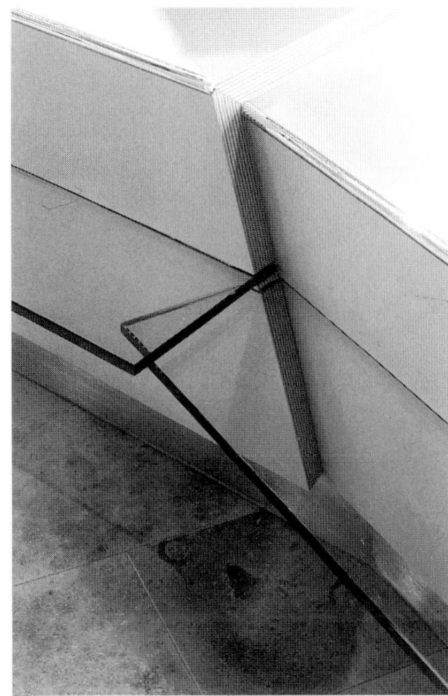 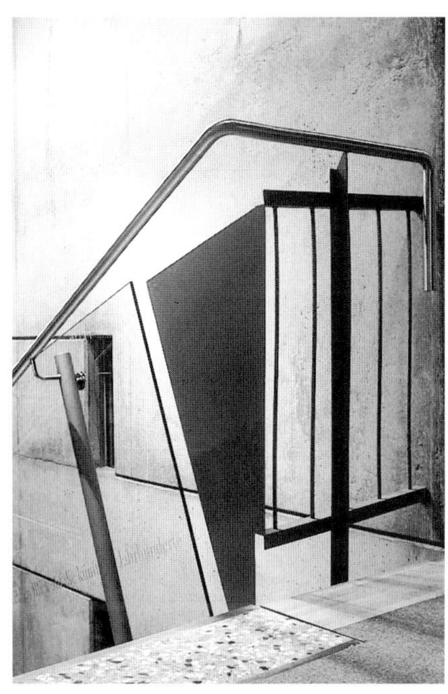

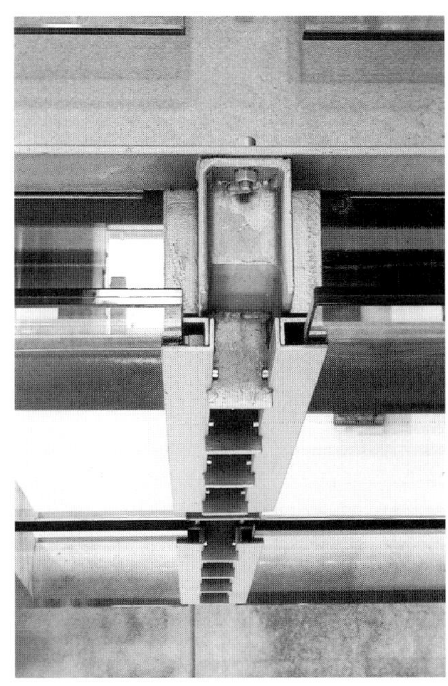 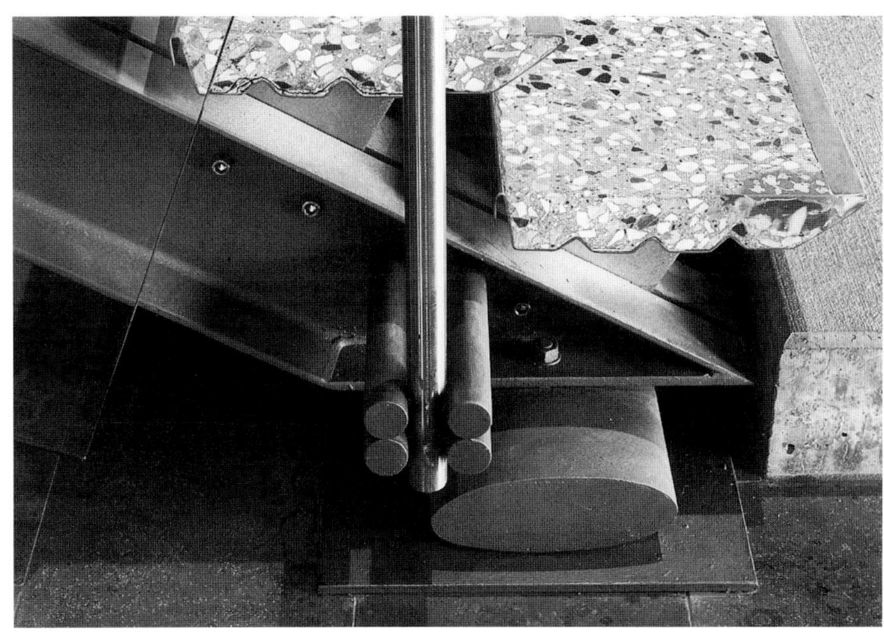

Ljubljana, Slowenien / *Slovenia* 1989

Eingang / *Entrance*

Axonometrie Bar und Bistro /
Axonometric projection of bar and bistro

Das «Platana» war schon vor dem Umbau ein beliebter Treffpunkt der Künstler und Intellektuellen in Ljubljana. Am Kongresni Trg gelegen, einem baumbestandenen Platzraum in der Innenstadt, fokussiert es die Ende der 80er Jahre aufbrechenden Sehnsüchte nach kultureller Vielfalt, nach Entfesselung des formalen Kanons und nach materialer Pracht. Der spiegelnde Glanz der polierten Oberflächen von Stein, Glas und Metall, die edlen Hölzer und das währschafte Leder der Polster bekräftigen die Ansprüche einer Zugehörigkeit zur mitteleuropäischen wie zur mediterranen Tradition und Hochkultur. Hinter dem historistischen Geschäftsportal liegt eine fast verwirrende Welt von Räumen, die vom Bestand vorgegeben ist. Das entwerferische Konzept verlieh jedem Raum seine spezifische Identität. Da ist die Stehbar mit langer Theke und verspiegelter Wandvertäfelung, die den begrenzten Raum überkopf virtuell ausweitet; dahinter liegt ein Speisezimmer für kleinere Imbisse, überwölbt von einer Sternenhimmelbeleuchtung. Das Café bietet zahlreiche Sitzplätze, während für die winzigen Moccatassen und Aperitifgläser ein paar runde Tische mit stabilem Fuß ausreichen. Der Marmorraum mit seinen matt durchscheinenden Tischflächen, der organisch-sinnlichen Maserung des Steins an Wänden und Decke und der geordnet darin eingelassenen Punkteschar leuchtender Rechtecke nähert sich einem parasakralen Raumeindruck, wie ihn auch die Wiener Loos-Bar aufweist.

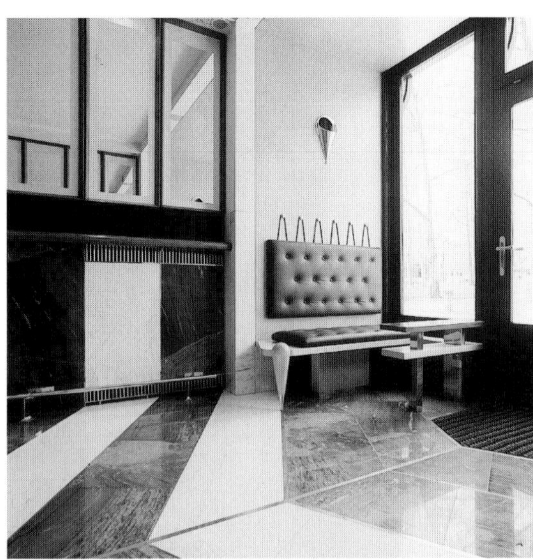

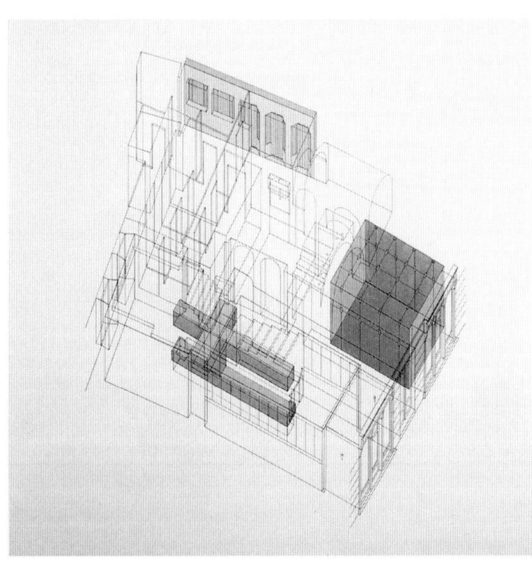

Even before its conversion, the "Platana" had already been a favorite meeting-place for artists and intellectuals in Ljubljana. Situated at Kongresni Trg, a wooded square in the center of the city, it focuses the desires for a cultural multitude – a breaking-free from the formal canon and for material splendor – all of which had begun by the end of the eighties. The mirroring glamour of the polished stone, glass, and metal surfaces, the noble woods, and the upholstery leather all support the demands for a participation in the middle European as well as Mediterranean tradition and high culture. Beyond the historic business portal lies an almost confusing world of rooms created by the existing building. The design concept provided each room with its own specific identity. There is the bar with its long counter and mirrored wall cladding, virtually enlarging the physical limitations of the room; beyond, there is a dining room for snacks, with ceiling lighting reminiscent of a starry sky. The café offers numerous seats, while a few round tables with sturdy bases suffice for the small mocha cups. The marble room with its translucent mat table surfaces, the sensual organic pattern of the stone on the walls and ceiling and the arranged inset masses of glossy rectangles approach a para-sacral room impression, comparable to the Loos-Bar in Vienna.

Details, Sitz- und Stehbar / *Details, sitting booth and bar*

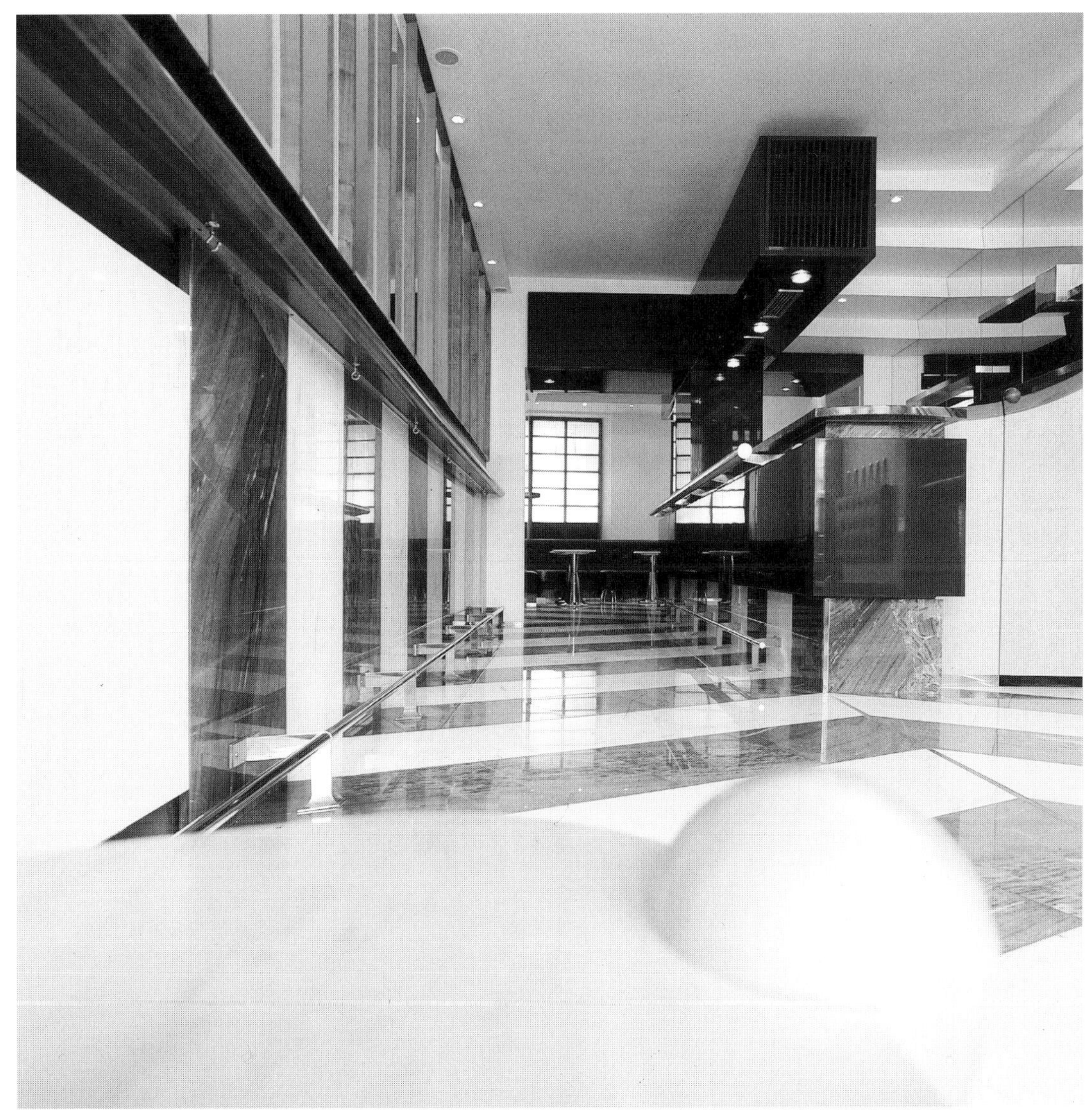

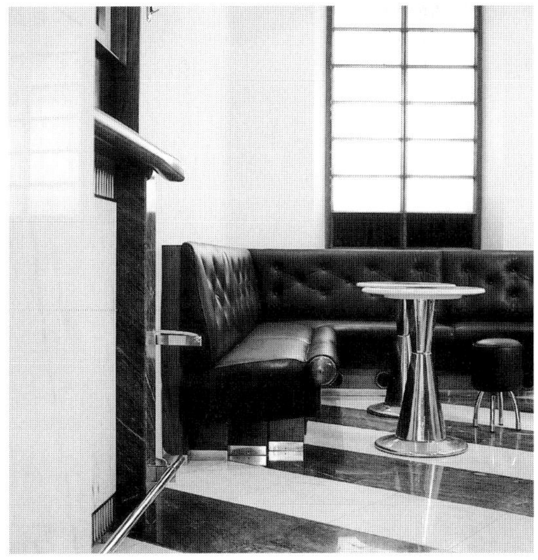

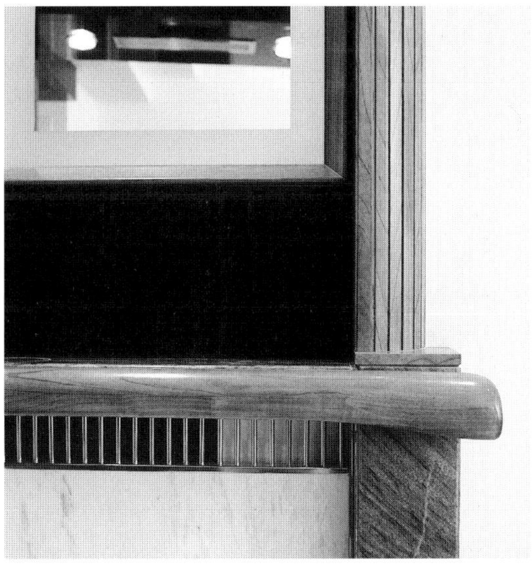

Bistrobereich, Durchblick / *A view through the bistro area*

Bistrobereich, Ausschnitte / *Bistro area, partial views*

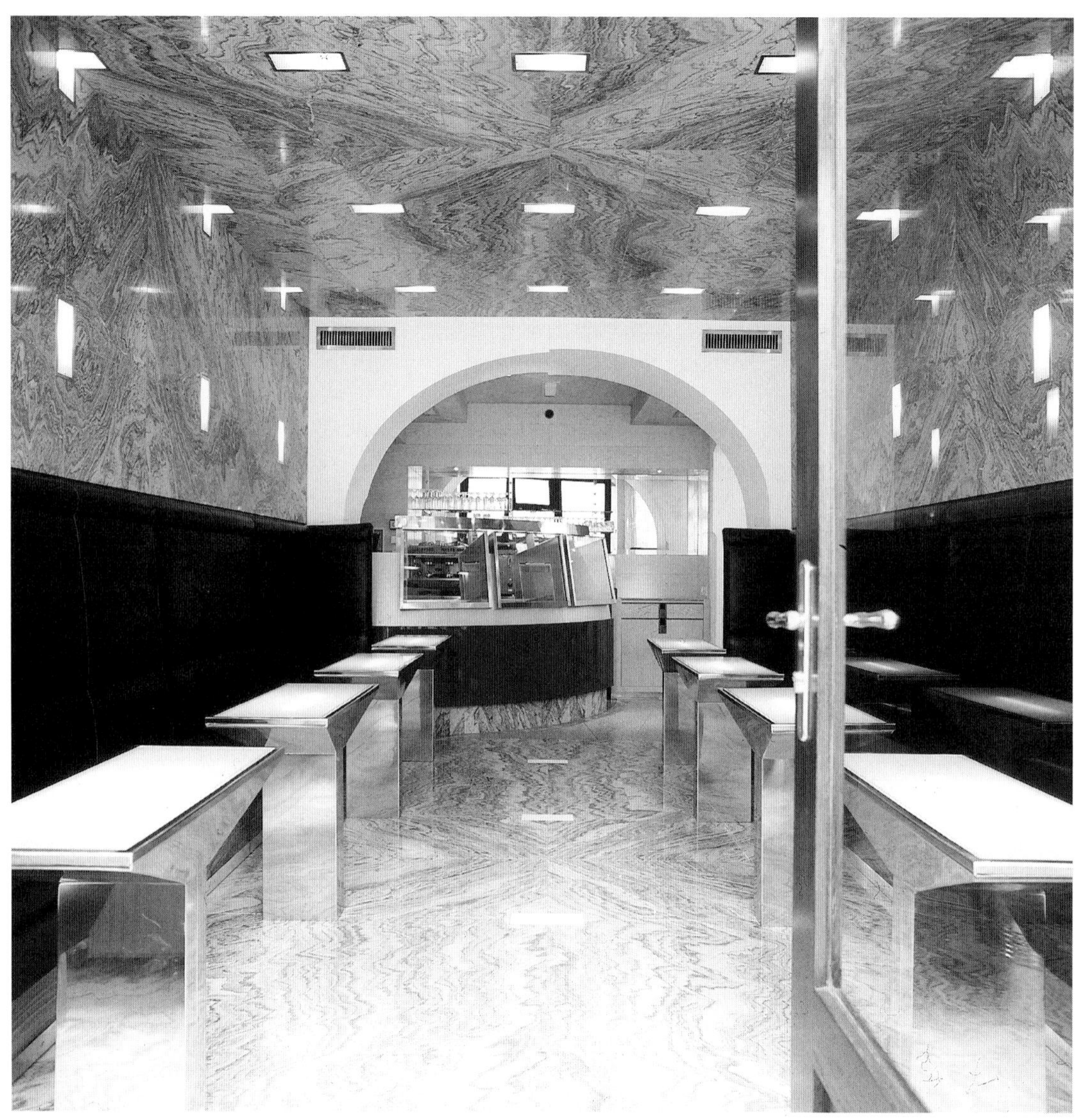

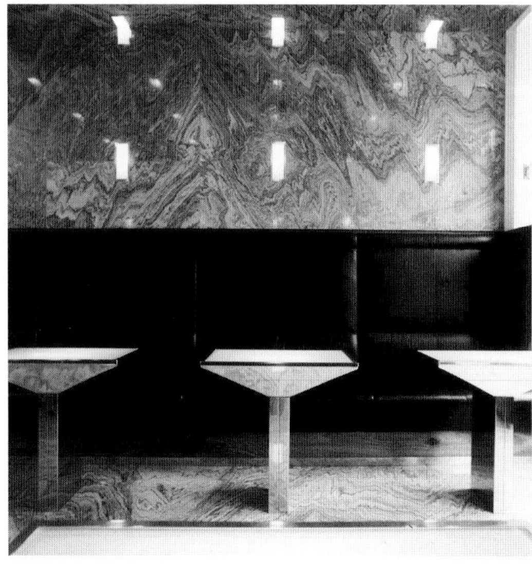

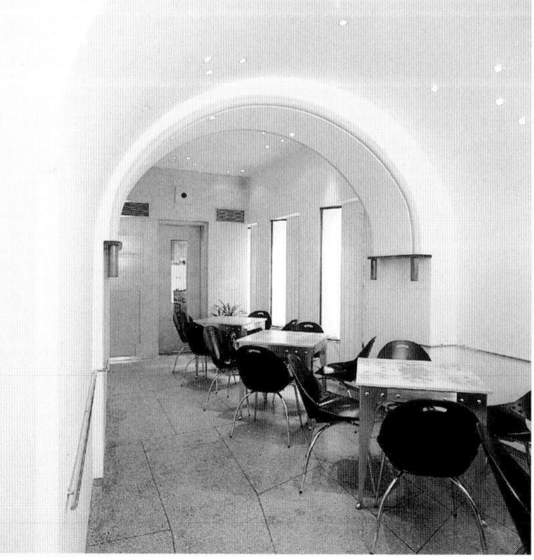

Ljubljana, Slowenien / *Slovenia* 1989

Portalansicht Judengasse / *Entrance portal view Judengasse*

Axonometrie / *Axonometric projection*

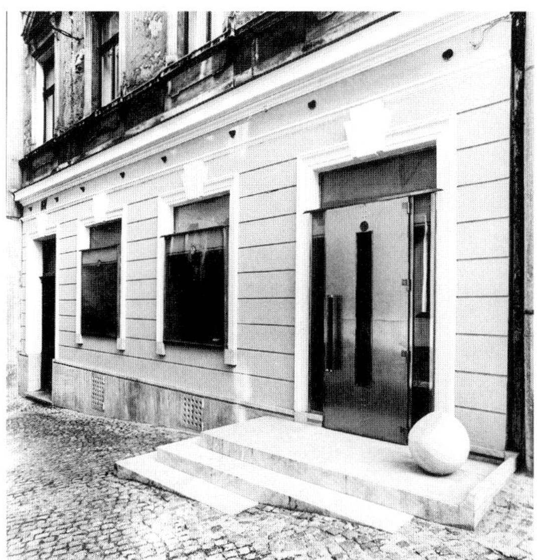

An einer leicht abfallenden Gasse nahe dem Zentrum liegt der Sitz der 1982 gegründeten Vereinigung unabhängiger slowenischer Architekten (Dessa). Drei Stufen aus hellem Naturstein sind vor dem Eingang in die holperig gewordene Pflästerung eingesenkt; einladend breit die oberste, eine die Schwelle relativierende Vorzone andeutend. Hinter der metallbeschlagenen Türe und den zwei breiten Gassenfenstern liegt quer ein Galerieraum für kleine Architekturausstellungen. Eine schranktiefe Schicht läuft an allen vier Seiten des Raumes herum, glättet die Unregelmäßigkeiten des Altbaus und enthält Stauraum und Serviceelemente für Vorträge. Vom öffentlichen Bereich vermittelt ein runder Raum – eine Handbibliothek aktueller Fachbücher und -zeitschriften – zum dahinterliegenden Büro, wo kräftige, pfeilerartig im Raum stehende, ihrerseits geräumige Schränke diesen unterteilen und beanspruchen, so daß ein starker Gegensatz zum Gassenlokal entsteht. Zwischen den Schrankprismen liegen nischenartig abgegrenzte Arbeitsplätze. An diesen Raum schließt seitlich ein Sitzungszimmer an. Im Publikumsbereich entfalten Naturstein, Edelhölzer und Leder ihre Materialwirkung; die Sekretariatsräume sind karger, aber zeugen dennoch von der Qualität slowenischen Handwerks. Der attraktive Einbau auf knapper Fläche, gebaut als Kurzbrevier über Umgang mit Raum und Räumen erscheint als idealer Sitz einer Architektenvereinigung.

The home for the association of independent Slovenian architects (Dessa), founded in 1982, is located near the center of town on a small and slightly sloping alley. Three steps made of light, natural stone are lowered into the uneven cobblestone pavement in front of the entrance. The upper step is invitingly wide, pointing the way to an anteroom, making the stoop highly relative. Behind the metal clad door and the two wide alley windows, a gallery space for small architectural exhibitions is located. A closet-deep layer surrounds all four sides of the room, smoothing out the irregularities of the old building and containing storage space and service elements for lectures. From the public area, a round room – a reference library of current special literature and magazines – mediates for the offices behind it, where strong, column-like, free-standing, and spacious closets divide and claim the room so that a stark contrast to the alley location comes into being. In between the closed prisms, alcove-like separated work spaces are located; to the side is an adjoining conference room. Natural stones, fine wood, and leather develop their material effect in the public area. The secretarial rooms are more simply furnished, but still document the quality of Slovenian craftsmanship. The attractive interior in limited confines, designed and built as a short treatise on the handling of space and rooms seems an ideal home for an architectural association.

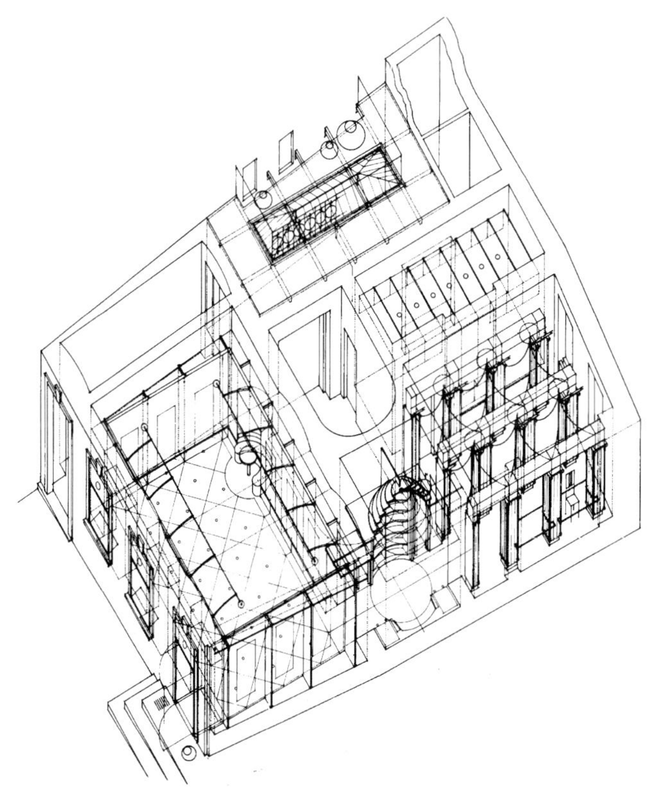

Perspektivischer Schnitt: Architekturgalerie, Bibliothek, Büros / *Perspective section: architectural gallery, library, offices*

Architekturgalerie / *Architectural gallery*

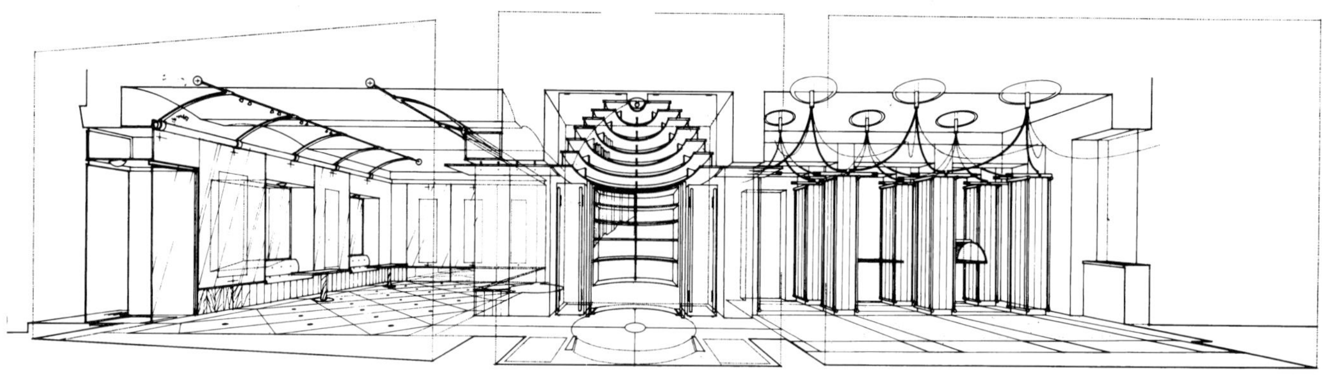

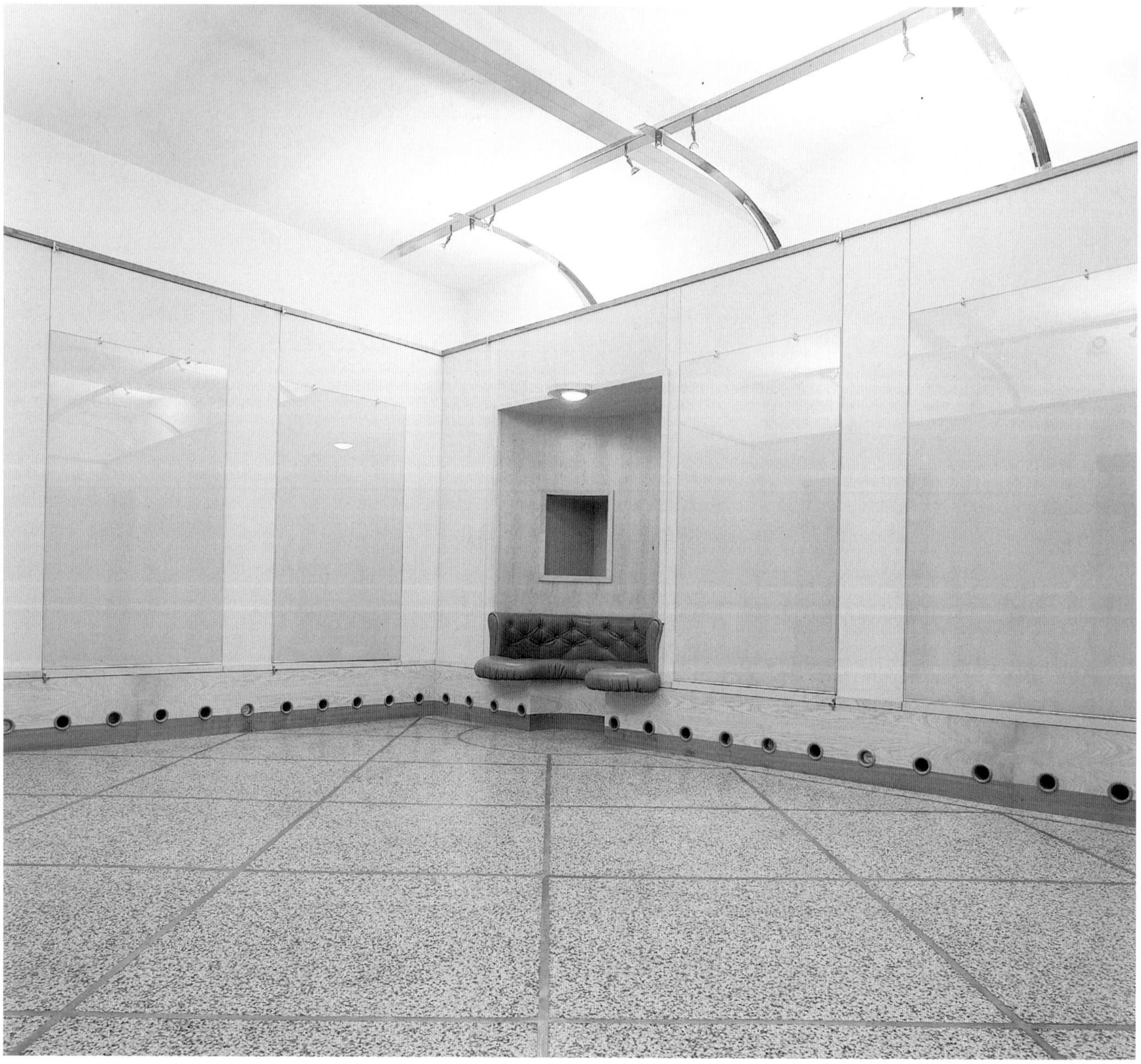

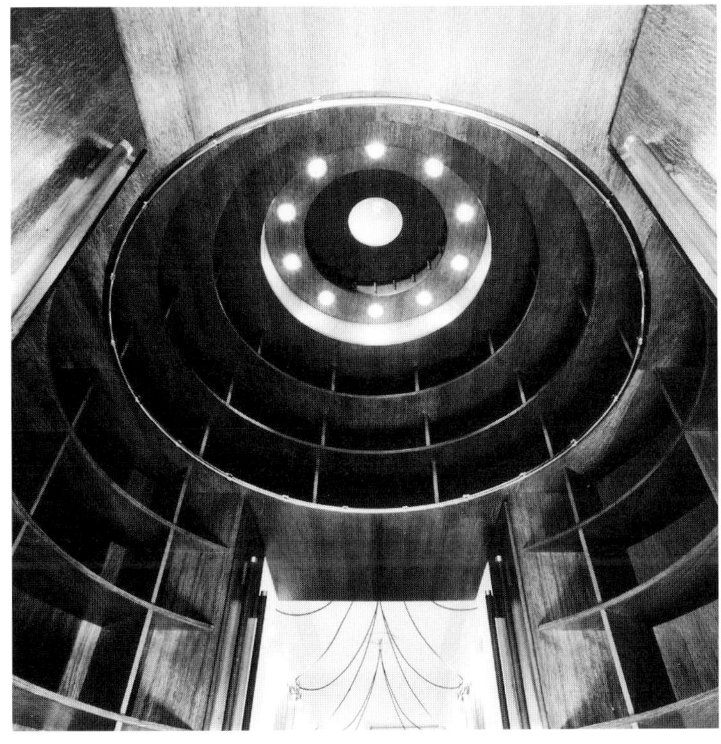

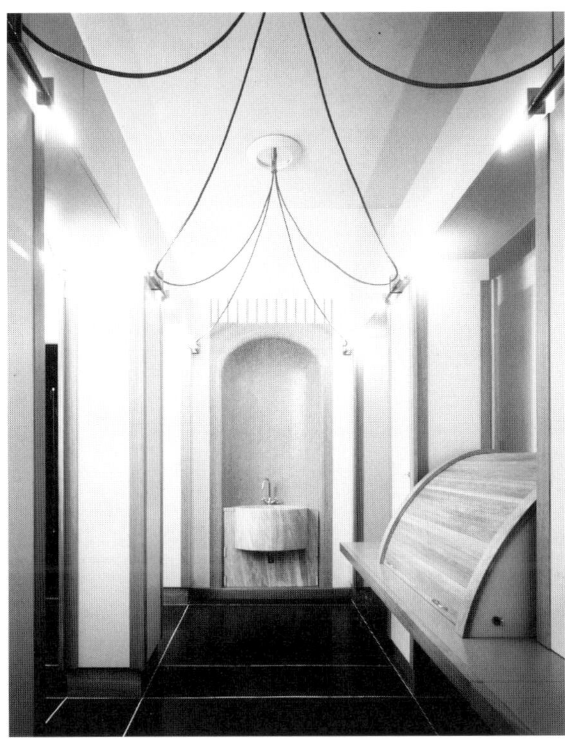

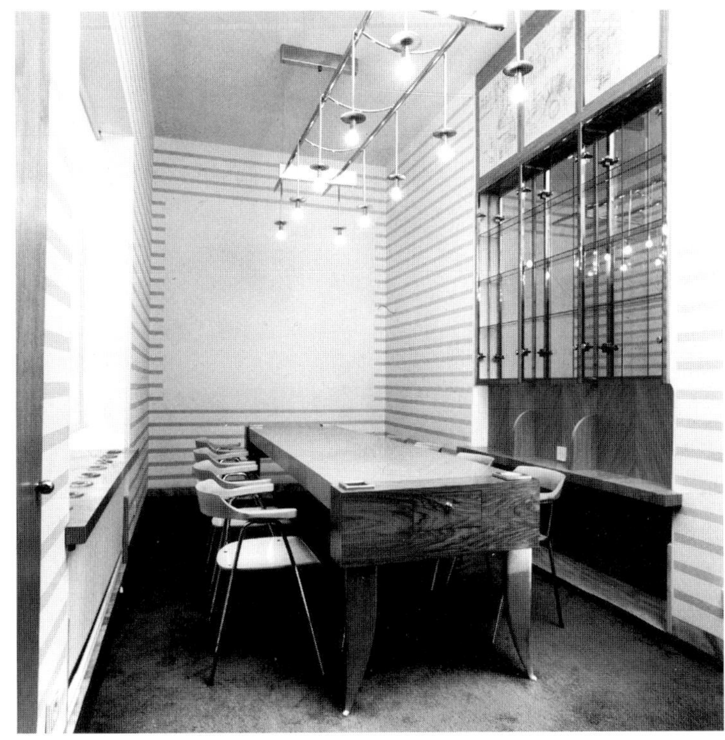

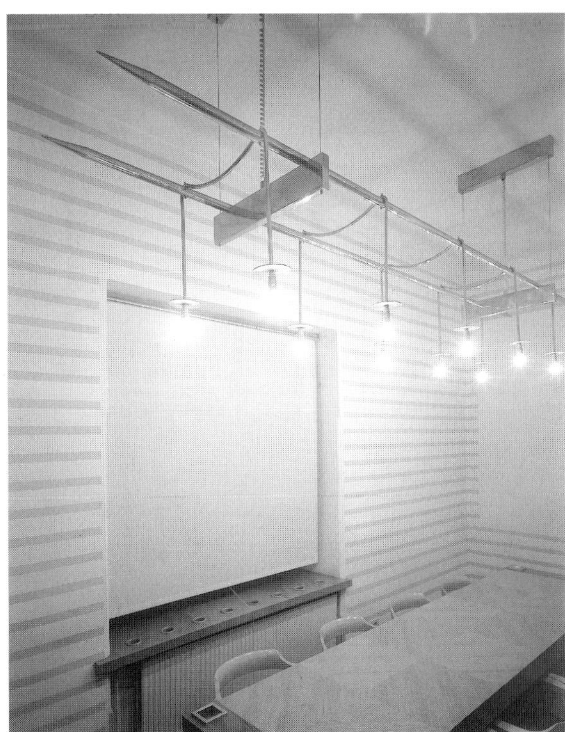

Madrid 1992

Portalansicht San Pedro / *Entrance portal San Pedro*

Axonometrie / *Axonometric projection*

Die kleine Galerie für slowenische Kunst in der Madrider Innenstadt umfaßt zwei kabinettartige, direkt vom Gehsteig her zugängliche Räume, die durch den dazwischenliegenden Hauseingang getrennt werden. Eine zum Bestand gehörende gußeiserne Säule mit plastischem Schmuck dominiert jeweils das Lokal. Obwohl leicht außermittig stehend, degradieren sie den Raum zu Umraum. Im linken Raum befindet sich in der hinteren Ecke ein schrankartiger, mit hellem Holz furnierter Einbau, der die Toilette enthält. Außerdem läßt sich aus dem Volumen seitlich ein Arbeitstisch herunterklappen und nach vorn eine Schranktür öffnen. Die seitlich vor der Rückwand hervortretende Stufenkonstruktion führt zu dem auf dem Schrankdeckel befindlichen winzigen Sitzplatz für zwei Personen. Die zu Bücherregalen umgedeuteten Stufen und die kragenden Zwischentritte entfernen sich vom gewohnten Bild einer Treppe und wirken wie ein neoplastizistisches Relief, das beiläufig auch als Aufgang dient. Im rechten Raum weist die Rückwand ein auf einem Holzrad herausdrehbares Schrankelement auf; in demselben Muster furniert, wie das Möbel im anderen Raum, deutet es Zusammengehörigkeit an. Über den Säulenkapitellen nach vorn und nach hinten auskragende Konstruktionen tragen jeweils die Beleuchtungskörper. Wie Masten messen sie den Raum aus und relativieren mit ihrer schirmenden Wirkung die zentrierenden Kräfte der Säulen.

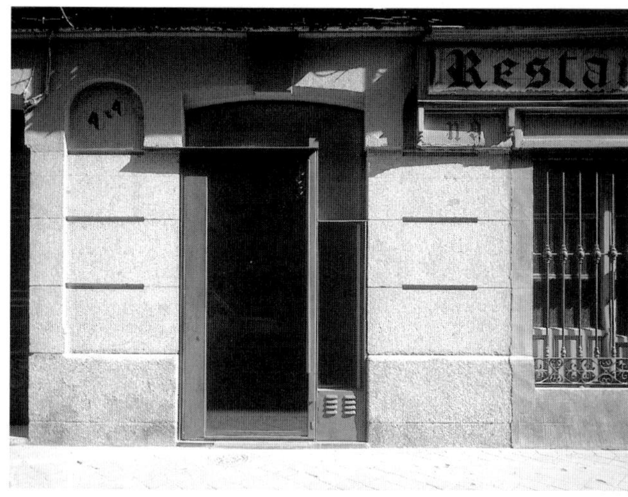

The small gallery for Slovenian art in the center of Madrid consists of two closet-like rooms, directly accessible from the walkway, which are separated by the building entrance in between them. In each room, a cast-iron column with sculptural ornaments is part of the inventory and dominates the location. Although they are not placed in the center, they reduce the room to an environment. In the left room, a built-in cabinet-like enclosure, veneered with light wood, contains the powder room. It is located in the rear corner. On the side of this volume is a working table which can be flipped down; at its front, a closet door opens. The stair construction standing out from the side of the back wall leads to the tiny seating area for two people on the top surface of the enclosure. The steps, which are given a new interpretation and used as book shelves, and the cantilever interstitial steps, are removed from the usual image of a staircase and have the effect of a neo-plastic relief casually serving as a stairway. In the right room, a cabinet element can be turned out on a wooden wheel. Veneered in the same pattern as the furniture in the other room, it points to the correlation between the two. Construction overhangs to the front and back above the column capitals in each room carry the lighting fixtures. Like masts, they measure out the room and with their shielding effect make the centric forces of the columns relative.

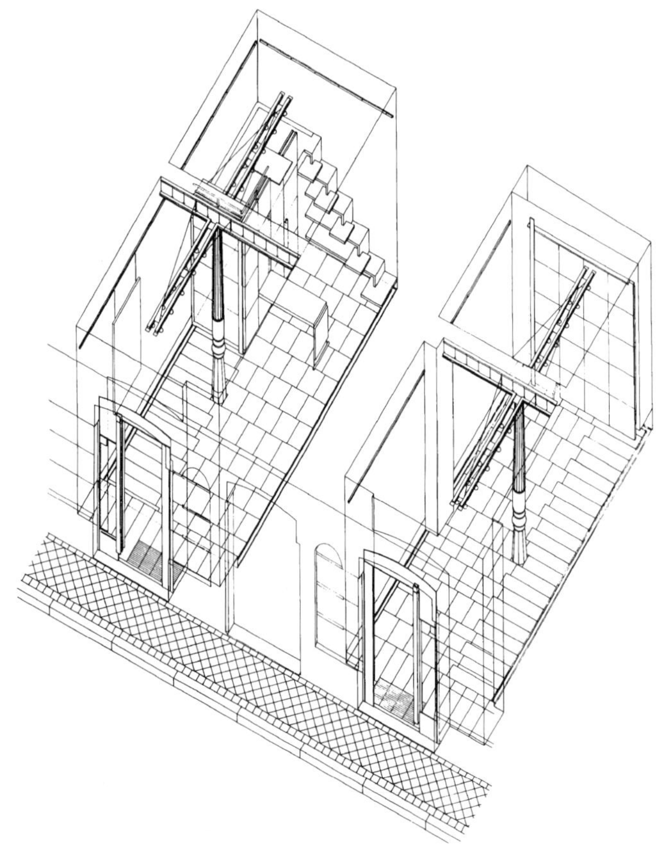

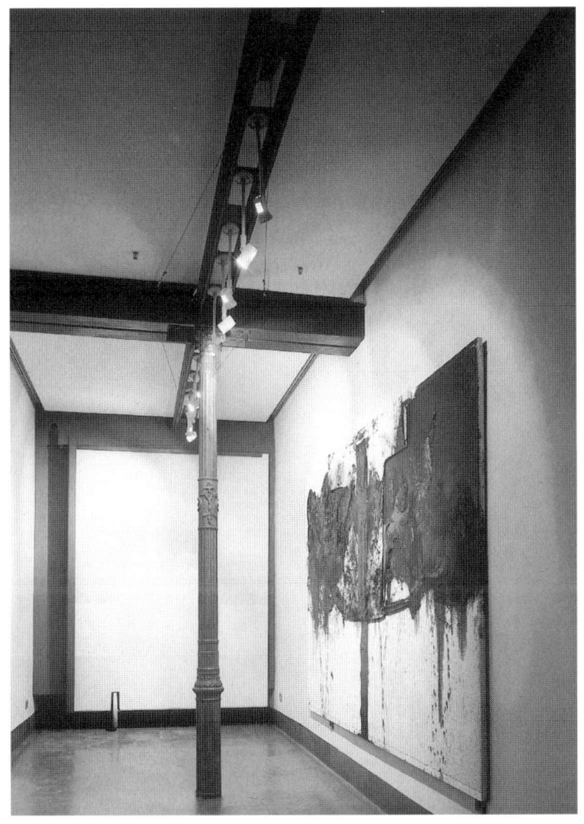
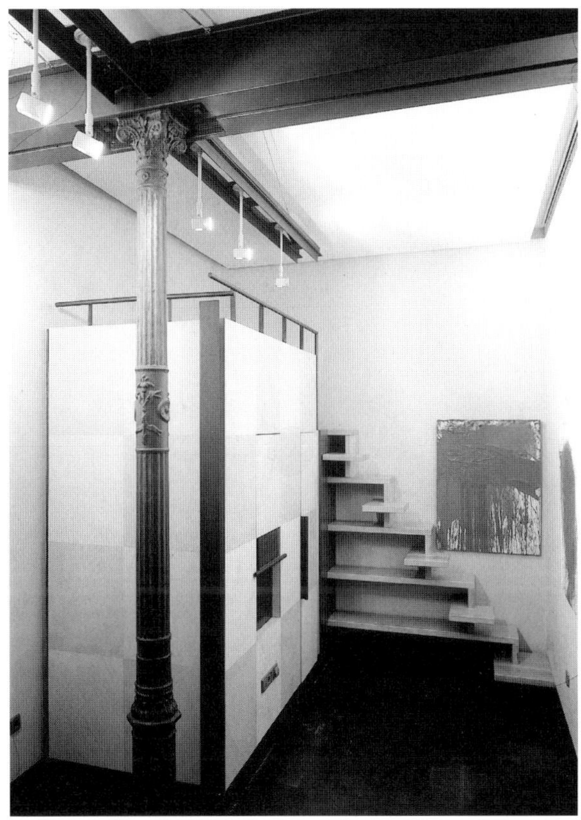
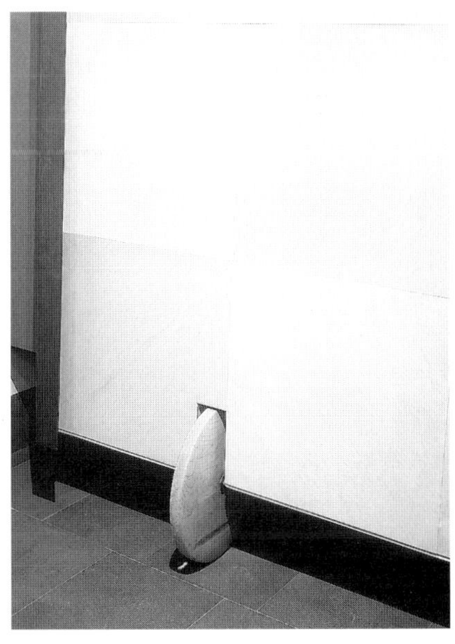
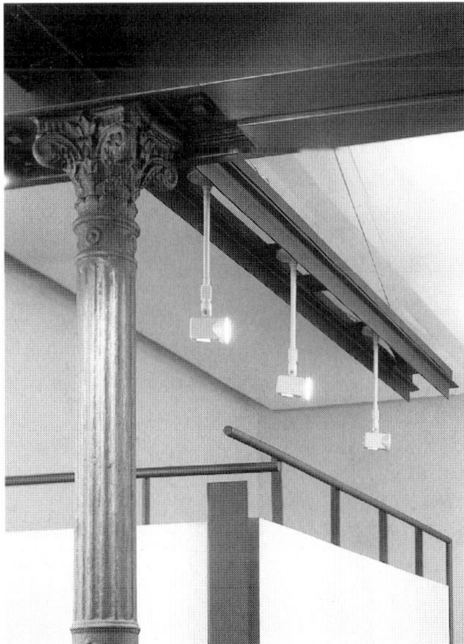
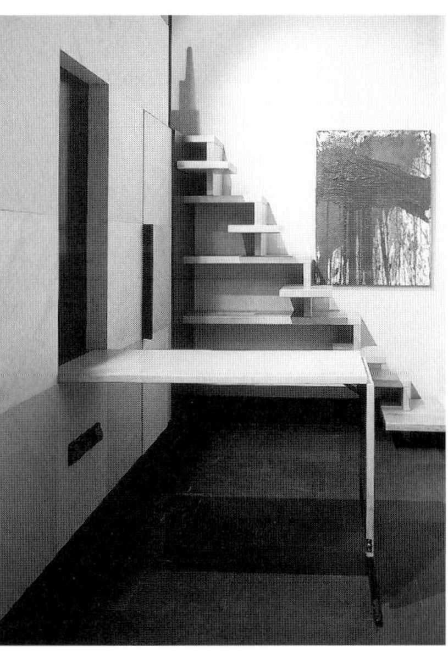

Boris Podrecca gehört zu jener Generation Architekten, der das Ethos der Stadt wichtig ist. Da er selber mehrere Sprachen versteht, registriert er bei der Lektüre einer städtebaulichen Situation Signale, Strukturen und Zeichenkonglomerate aus verschiedensten Bereichen und sieht auch ihre systemübergreifenden Vernetzungen. Dies läßt sich aus der Art und Weise seines Reagierens, seiner Interventionen und seiner Konzepte herauslesen. Dabei sind ihm Details so wichtig wie strukturelle Aspekte. Neben dem Realitätssinn steht immer auch der optimistische Möglichkeitssinn; zwischen eindeutigen Setzungen spannen sich Bereiche für mehrdeutige Entwicklungen.

Selbst wenn ein Bauwerk wie die Autowerkstätte Mazda-Lietz in Waidhofen a.d. Ybbs in den noch weitgehend landwirtschaftlich bestimmten Kontext eines wachsenden Gewerbegebiets zu stehen kommt, ist es auf den Großraum des Tales und auf die vorhandenen Strukturelemente wie Straße, Bahn und Fluß bezogen. Verstärkt kommt dies zum Ausdruck in einer dichteren, vorstädtischen Situation, etwa der Schule in Liesing, wo nicht bloß mit dem Altbau aus dem 19. Jahrhundert ein Dialog aufgenommen wird, sondern ebenso mit den auf den ersten Blick fragwürdigen Betongebirgen aus den 70er Jahren. Weil sie stadträumlich vorhanden sind und zwar auf längere Zeit, werden die Augen davor nicht verschlossen, wird das – aus heutiger Sicht – visuelle Ärgernis oder zumindest problematische Bauwerk nicht ausgegrenzt, sondern nach einem korrekten städtebaulichen Verhältnis gesucht, das scheinbare Ärgernis aufhebend. Dasselbe gilt beim Projekt für die Berliner Wasserbetriebe: der Bestand wird akzeptiert, die Blockrandbebauung sinnvoll weiter-, das heißt, zuende geführt; mit einer sowohl selbständigen als auch auf den Hauptbau bezogenen, ausgedehnten Setzung im Kernbereich wird Bestand und Neubau zu einer neuen attraktiven Gesamtanlage integriert.

Anders stellte sich die Problematik in dem eher vernachlässigten und abgewohnten Baublock im historischen Zentrum von Ljubljana, dessen Innenbereiche für ein Luxushotel vorgesehen waren. Hier mußte sowohl stadträumlich als auch soziokulturell eine qualitativ um einiges höhere Wertigkeit angestrebt werden. Dies erfolgte einerseits durch städtebauliche Bezüge zu primären Elementen des Stadtbildes und durch funktionale Anschlüsse an das urbane Netzwerk, andererseits wird ein erstrangiger Attraktor in Form eines prächtigen Binnenraumes vorgeschlagen, in dem sich die Bezüge zum Netzwerk der Stadt fokussieren. Ähnlich verhält es sich bei der Basler Versicherung, die als neuartiges Element die Urbanisierung des bisher mehrheitlich homogenen Gefüges im 20. Wiener Gemeindebezirk vorantreibt. Auch mit der Kirche in Fontanafredda wird ein vergleichbarer Impuls gesetzt, diesmal in einem präurbanen Neubaugebiet. Entsprechend ist das städtebauliche Vorgehen: die breite Vorhalle ruft und empfängt die Menschen, die sich dahinter im Zentralraum versammeln.

Boris Podrecca belongs to that generation of architects who consider the ethos of the city as being important. As he understands several languages, he is capable of perceiving signals, structures and symbolic aggregates from a wide multitude of realms when 'reading' an urban situation. At the same time, he sees their overlapping and interwoven system of connections. This can be seen by way of his reactions, his interventions and his concepts. To Podrecca, those things which are important stem from different categories and levels of scale. Besides a sober realistic sense, there is always the optimistic sense for what is possible; between clearly perceived settings stretch areas for ambiguous development.

Even if a building like the car repair shop Mazda-Lietz in Waidhofen on the Ybbs comes to be placed in the predominately agriculturally determined context of a growing industrial area, it relates in various ways to the greater space of the valley and the existing structural elements, such as, the road, the railroad tracks, and the river. This expression becomes stronger in an already denser suburban situation, e.g., the school in Liesing, where he takes up a dialogue not only with the old 19th century building, but also with the concrete "mountains" from the '70s which, at first glance, appear to be questionable. But because they exist in the urban space and will continue to do so for a long period of time, he does not close his eyes towards them. He does not exclude the (in today's view) visually annoying or, at the very least, problematic building. Instead, without intrusion, the correct urban relationship is searched for which will repeal the apparent annoyance. The same applies to the project for the Berlin Water Works. The extant situation is being accepted, the block perimeter development is continued purposefully, i.e., brought to a conclusion. With an independent as well as expanded setting into the core area, referring to the main building, the existing structure and the new construction are integrated into an attractive new complex system. The situation in the rather neglected and run-down block in the historic center of Ljubljana, whose interior was to be turned into a

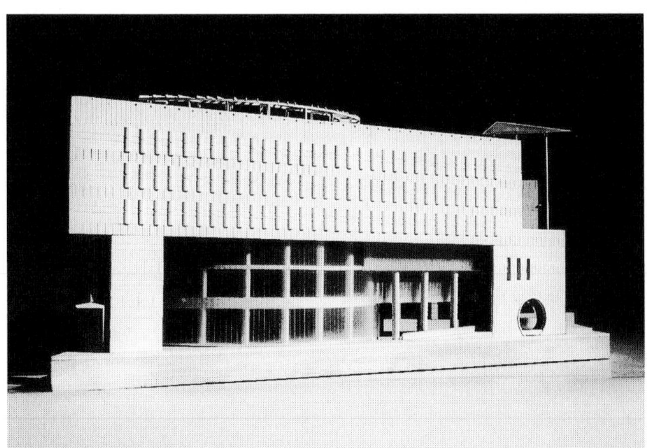

Büroturm für EKZ-Südpark, Klagenfurt, Projekt /
*Office tower for the EKZ-Südpark, Klagenfurt,
project* 1992

Bürohaus Universale, Wien, Projekt / *Office
building Universale, Vienna, project* 1991

Österreichisches Kulturinstitut New York,
Wettbewerb / *Cultural Institute of Austria,
New York, competition* 1992

Zentrum Handelskai, Geschäfts- und Wohn-
hausanlage mit Bürohochhaus, Wien /
*Business and housing complex with office
high rise building, Vienna* 1995

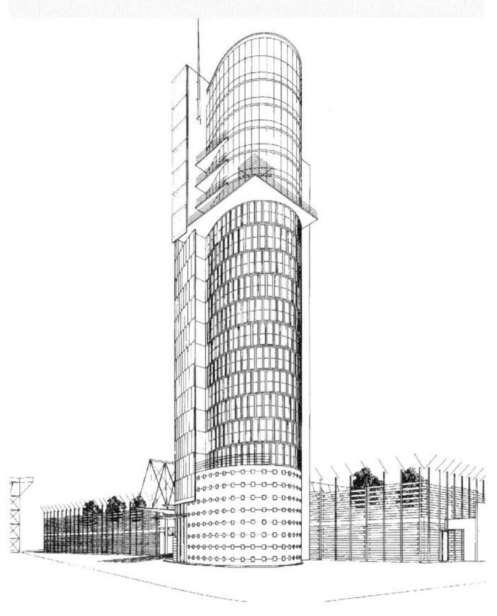

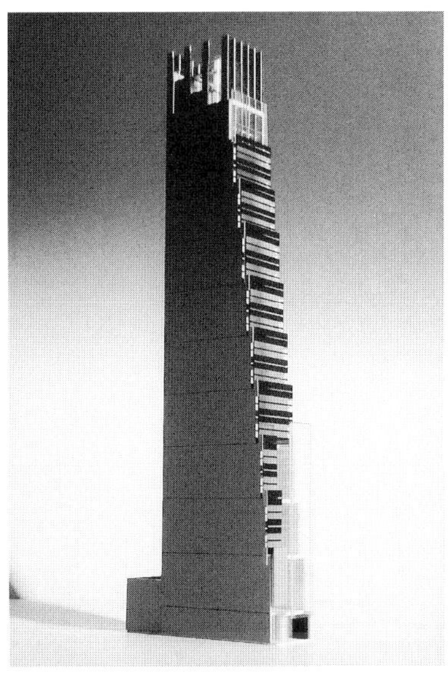

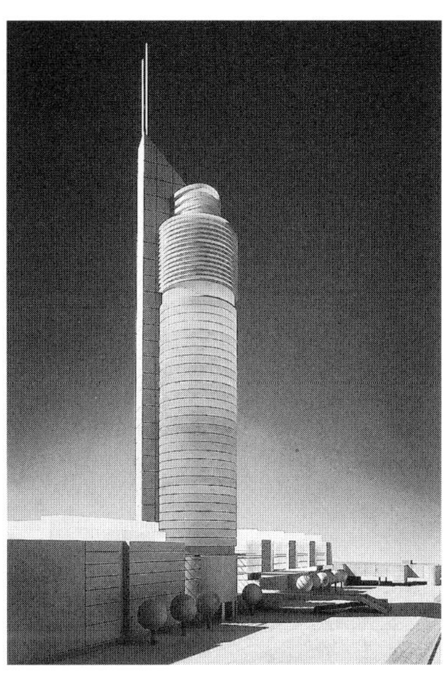

Bei größerflächigen Interventionen zeigt sich, daß Boris Podrecca
der Versuchung zur Überinterpretation nicht erliegt. Sein Vorschlag für Breite Straße/Berlin-Mitte bewegt sich im Bereich der
städtischen Substanz; es werden keine aufgesetzten Superzeichen
vorgeschlagen, vielmehr wird ergänzend verdichtet, wobei in den
Randbereichen, etwa zur Spree, durchaus spezifisch agiert wird.
Ausgeprägter ist dies bei dem größeren Nordbahnhofgelände der
Fall, das von den Rändern her mit den angrenzenden Quartieren
vernetzt wird. Vor allem werden Baublöcke für ein städtisches
Gefüge vorgeschlagen, das nur von wenigen übergeordneten
Strukturelementen durchzogen ist.
All diese Stadtinterventionen zeugen von einer differenzierten
und lebendigen Vorstellung der Stadt. Sie erfolgen mit der nöti-
gen Zurückhaltung und Angemessenheit. Auf vordergründige
Radikalismen wird ebenso verzichtet wie auf Pseudoharmonie,
sie sind vielmehr ein Bekenntnis zur dichten und vielfältigen
mitteleuropäischen Erscheinungsform der Stadt.

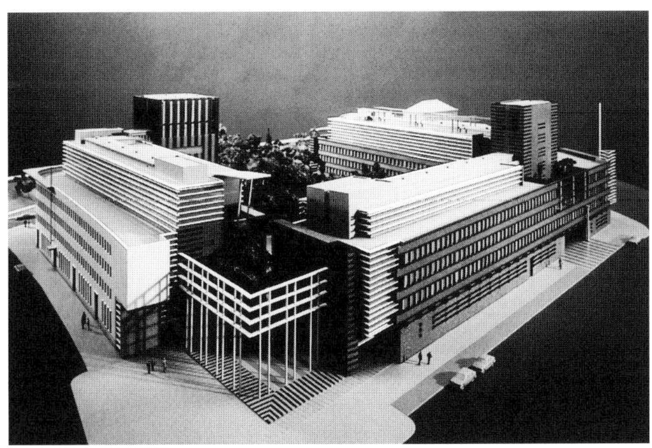

*luxury hotel, represented a different problem. Here, in an urban-
spatial as well as a socio-cultural sense, a qualitatively much
higher value had to be endeavored. This was realized on one hand
by urban relationships with primary elements of the city picture
and functional connections to the urban network. On the other
hand, a first-rank attractor in form of a stately inner space is being
suggested where the relations with the city's network could focus.
We have a similar situation with the building for the Basel insurance company which, as a new element, advances the urba-
nization of the mostly homogenous structure of Vienna's 20th
district. With the church in Fontanafredda, a comparable impulse
is given, but in a new building area with pre-urban conditions. The
urban procedure corresponds – the wide foyer calls and welcomes
people who gather behind it in the central room.
When it comes to larger interventions, we find that Boris Podrecca
does not give in to the temptation for hyper-interpretation. His
proposal for Breite Strasse/Berlin-Center stays within the realm
of the urban substance. There are no fake super-symbols being
suggested, but a complimentary condensation is made with specific
actions in the peripheral areas, such as towards the Spree river.
This has developed into a stronger and more clear expression in the
case of the North Station grounds which are connected with the
adjoining quarters starting from the periphery. Above all, buildings
are proposed for an urban structure which is interspersed by only a
very few higher structural elements.
All these city interventions give proof of a differentiated and living
imagination of the city. They are executed with the necessary
discretion and appropriateness. Superficial radicalism and pseudo-
harmony are left aside. They are much more an acknowledg
ment of the dense and versatile middle-European appearance of
the city.*

Klagenfurt, *Austria* 1989

Grundriß Dachgeschoß / *Plan of top floor*

Ansicht rückwärtige Front / *View of rear*

Dem an der Nordeinfahrt Klagenfurts gelegenen Kaufhaus, einem Dutzendzweckbau aus den 70er Jahren, sollte mit einem großen Annexbau ein Gesicht gegeben werden. Vom Altbestand strebt straßenparallel ein langgezogener Baukörper weg mit halbzylinderförmiger Stirnseite, die den in die Stadt hinein fahrenden Automobilisten zeichenhaft empfängt. Nach hinten wird das Gebäude abgestuft tiefer. Jede Staffelung deckt ein gläserner Turm der Fluchttreppen. Auf der Eingangsseite drängt sich im Winkel zwischen Altbau und Längstrakt ein rund verglaster Turm mit außen spiralig abgebildetem Treppenlauf. Seine Zinne krönt ein luftiger Aussichtstempel unter gefiedertem Dach. Der Aufbau des Längstrakts scheint klassisch: Sockel, Wand, Dachgeschoß mit Attikaaufbau. Aber der Sockel ist nicht rustiziert, sondern besteht aus Betonelementen, die Pfahlbündeln gleichen; darüber steigen horizontale Bänder des Wandaufbaus sich überschuppend in die Höhe, der Wand in Licht und Schatten Leben einhauchend. Der große Abstand der hochformatig-schmalen Fenster und ihr Einschneiden in den oberen Wandabschluß machen den Bekleidungscharakter der Fassade deutlich. Unter dem auf Stichbalken vorkragenden Dach verläuft kontinuierlich ein Glasband. Einem Treibriemen gleich, scheint es die Fassade um die Rundung zu ziehen und vorn bei der Walze des Spiralturms in ein dynamisches Spiel geometrischer Volumen zu verwickeln.

The department store situated at the northern entrance to Klagenfurt was a '70s utility building and was given a new look with the addition of a large annex construction. Parallel to the street, a long volume with a semi-cylindrical front side stretches away from the old section, symbolically receiving the motorists driving towards the city. To the back, the building gradually becomes lower. Each step is covered by a glassed-in tower in which the emergency staircases are situated. On the entrance side, in the angle between the old section and the long extension, we find a round, glassed-in tower with a spiral staircase within which is patterned on the outside. Its pinnacle is crowned by a lookout platform beneath a pinnal roof. The arrangement seems to be classical – base, wall, and roof surface with a roof parapet. However, the base is not rustic, but rather consists of concrete elements resembling bundles of posts. Overlying horizontal strips of the wall fabrication rise above into the heights, breathing light and life into the wall. The large distance between the high-formatted, narrow windows and their cutting into the upper wall termination line clarify the banded character of the facade. Below the roof, overhanging on visible beams, a glass strip runs continuously around the structure. Akin to a drive belt, it seems to pull the facade around the curve and involves it in a dynamic play of geometric volumes in the front, where it meets the spiraling cylinder of the stairway tower.

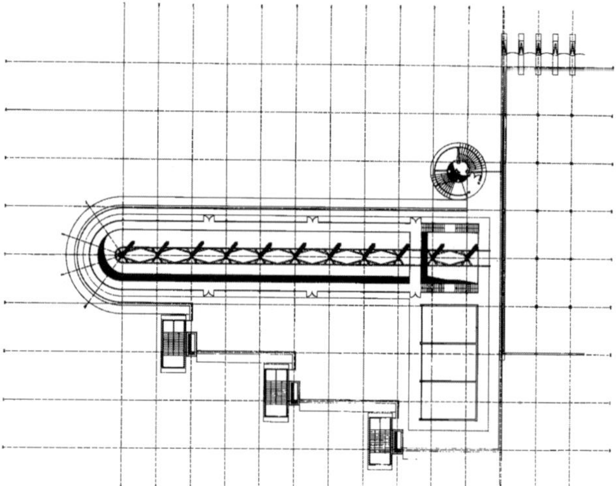

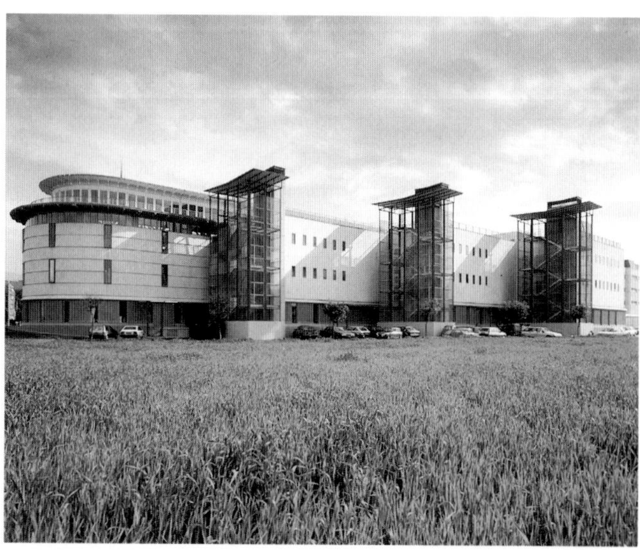

Schrägansicht von der Straße / *Three-quarter view from the street*

Perspektive / *Perspective*

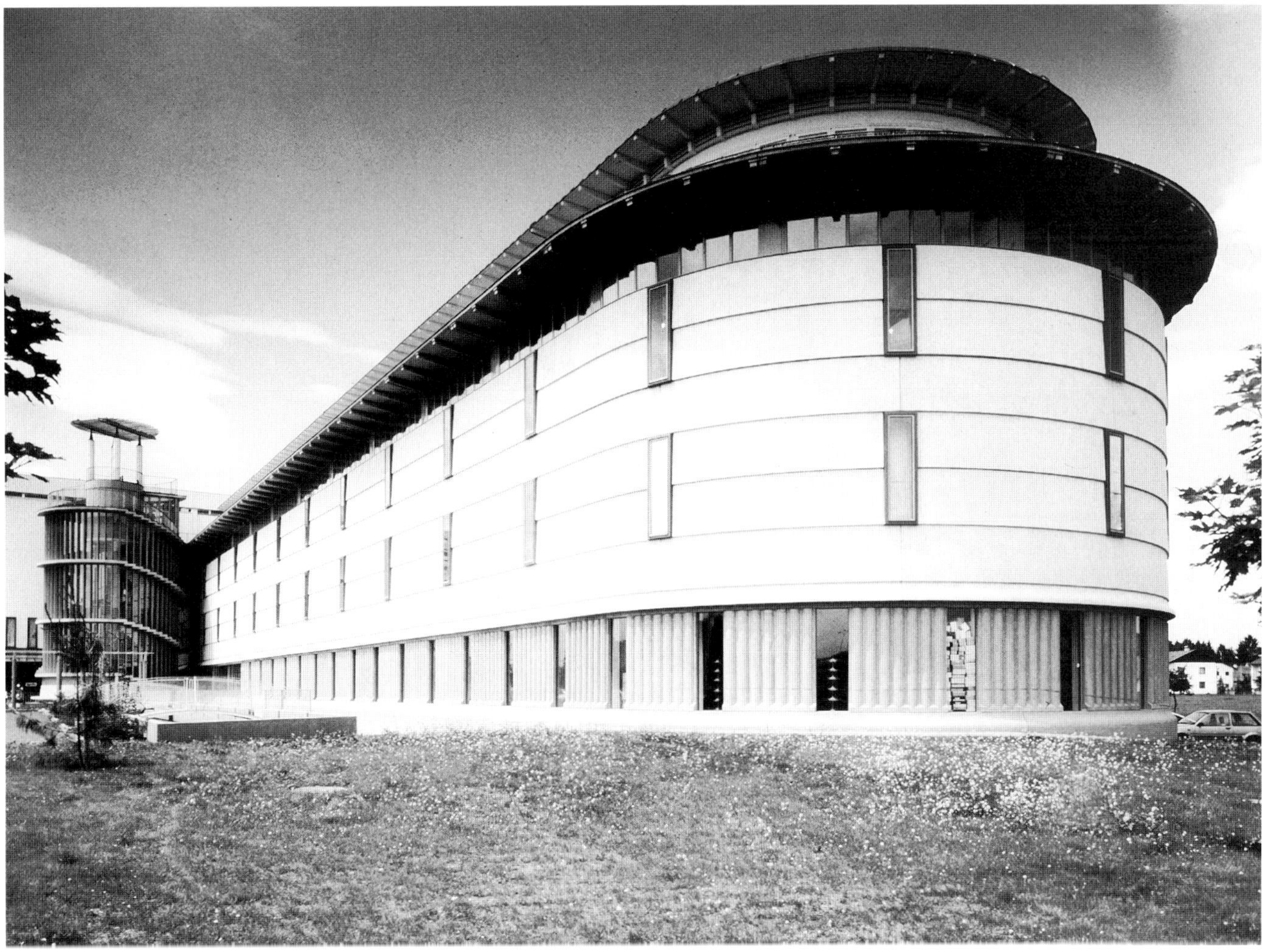

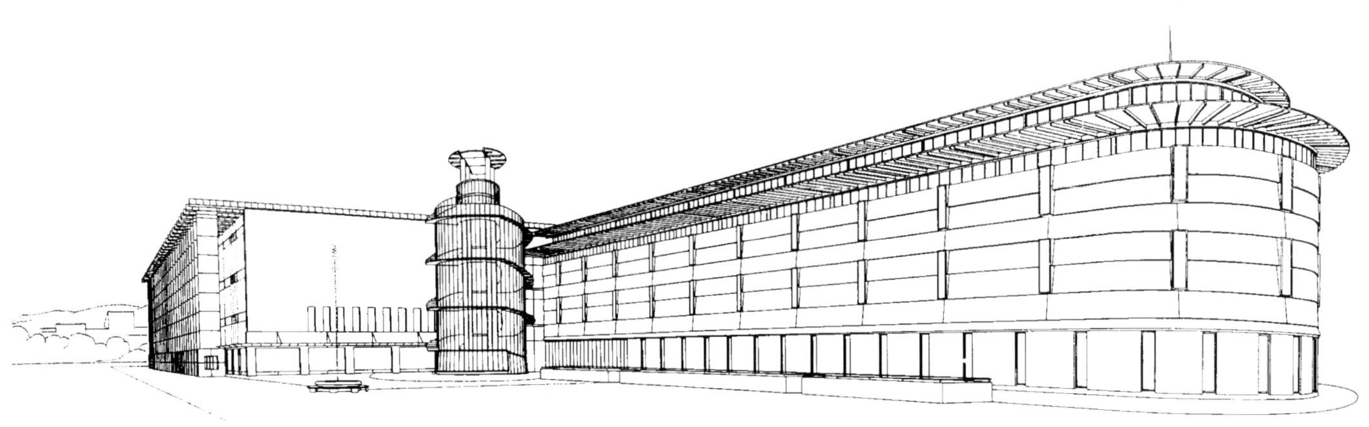

Eingangspiazetta / *Entrance plaza*

Pergola, Detail / *detail*   Vordach, Detail / *Canopy, detail*

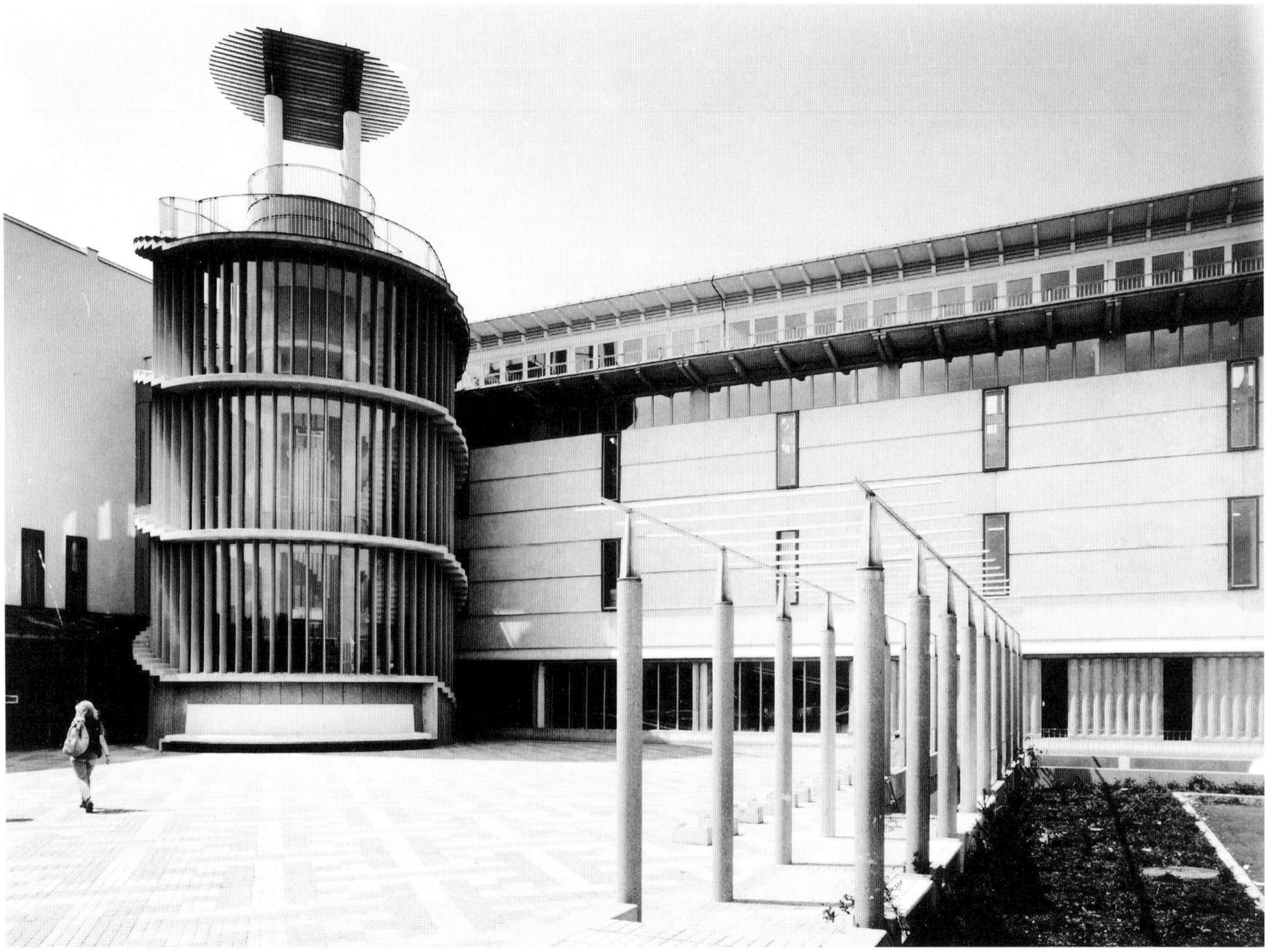

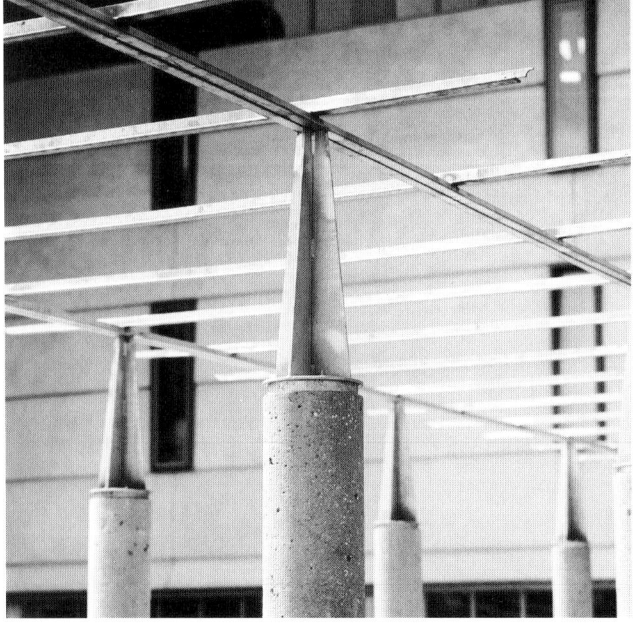

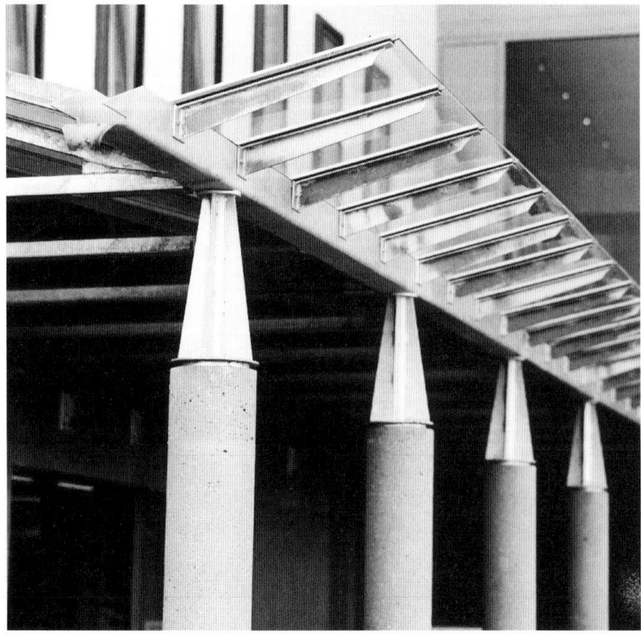

Eingangsfront / *Entrance front*

Sockeldetail / *Base detail*

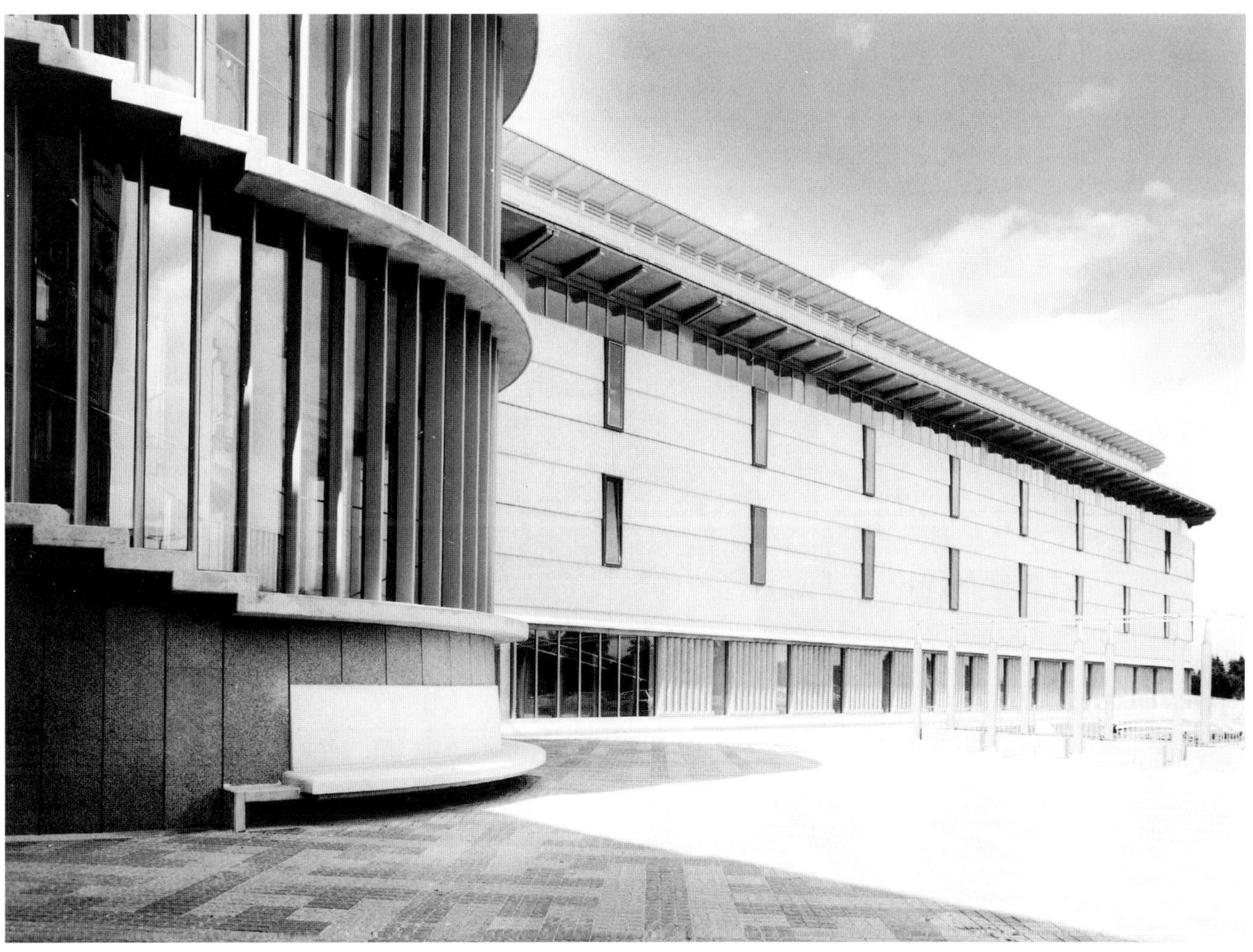

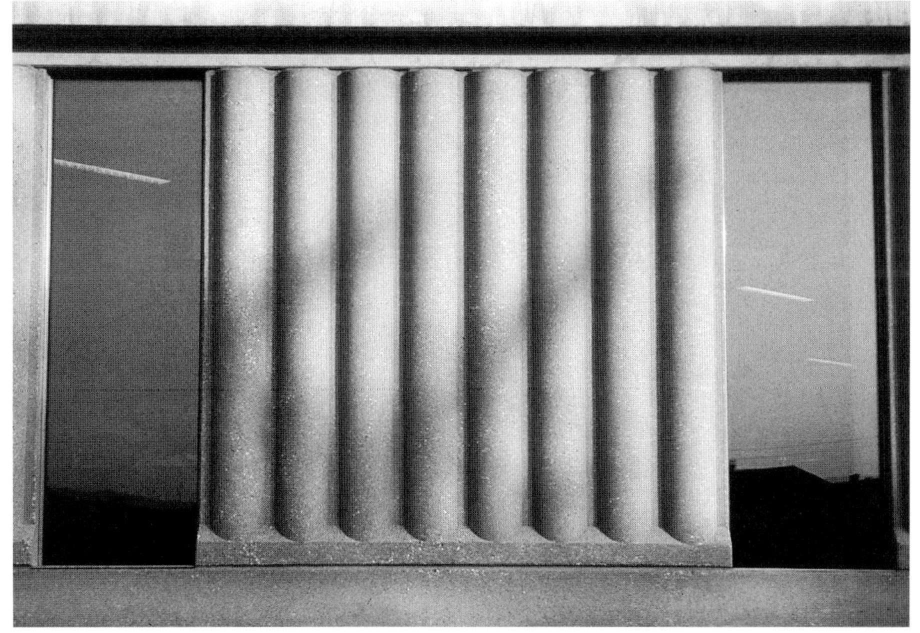

Dachpavillon / *Roof pavilion*

Dachgeschoß, Details / *Top floor, details*

Stiegenhaus, Details / *Staircase, details*

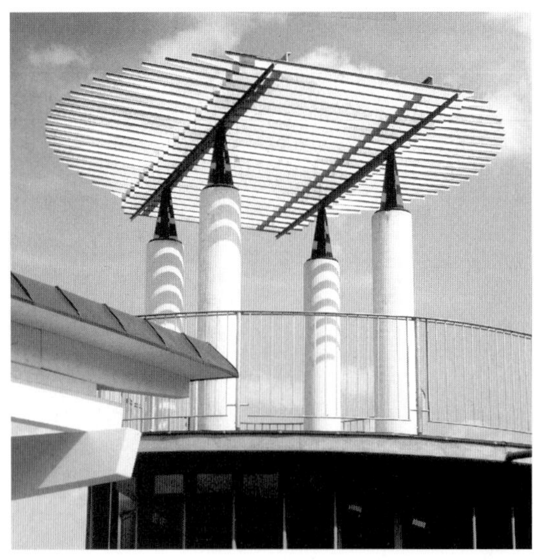

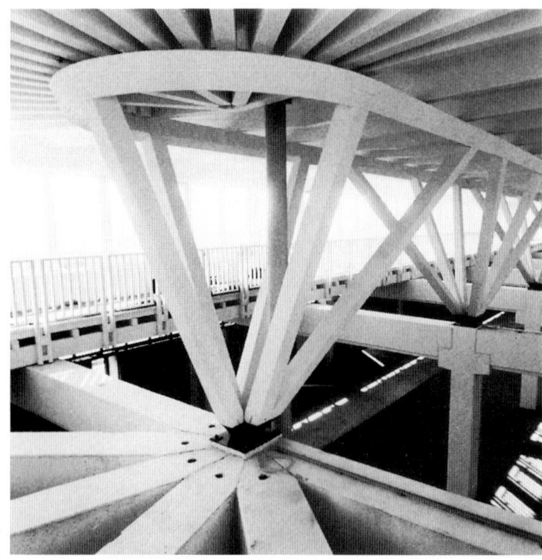

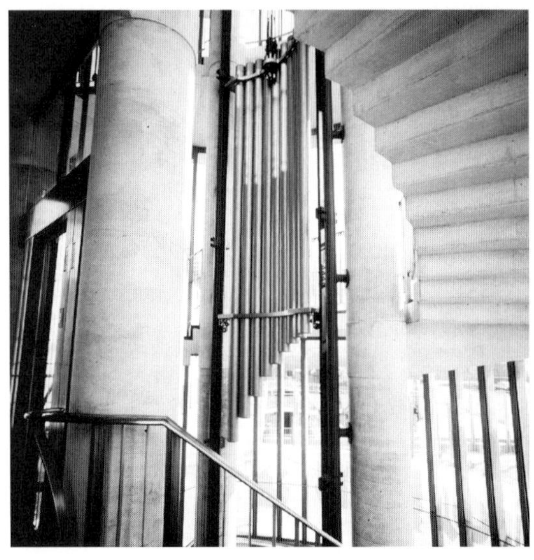

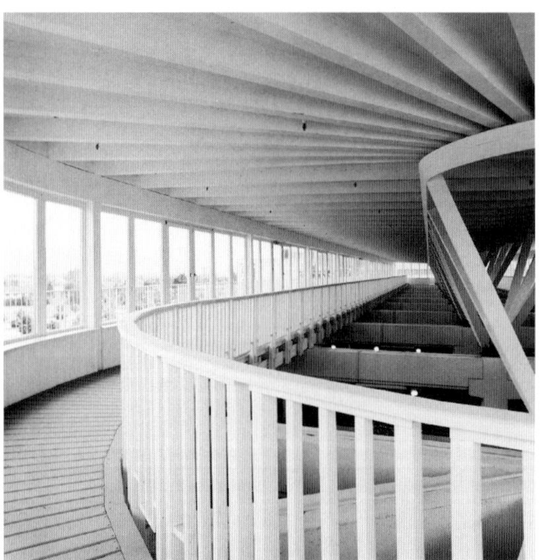

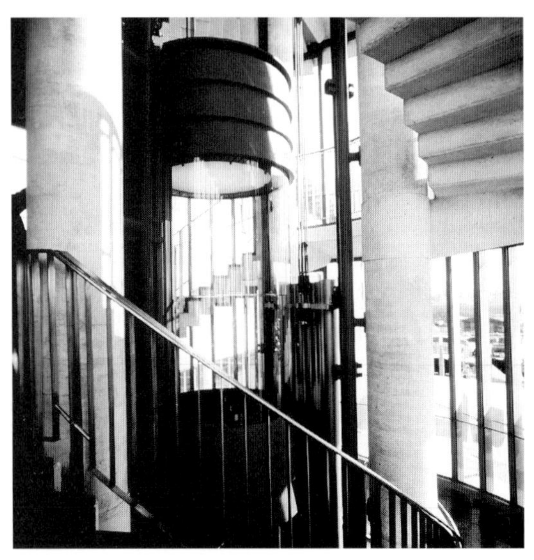

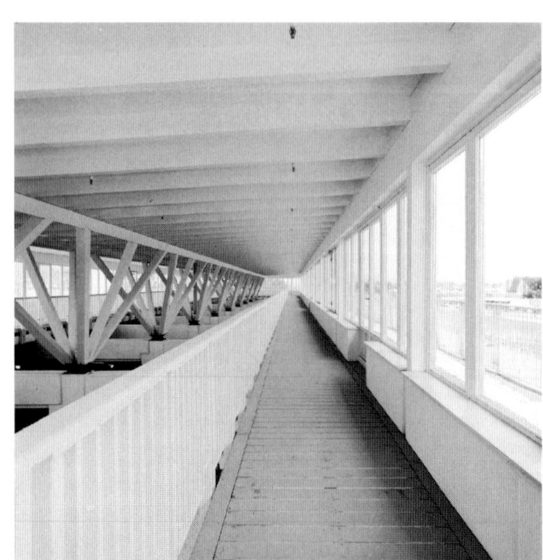

Waidhofen/Ybbs, *Austria* 1992

Entwurfskizze / *Design sketch*

Im grünen Talgrund, parallel durchschnitten von Bundesstraße und Bahngeleise, reihen sich südlich von Waidhofen einige Industrie- und Gewerbebetriebe. Den Abschluß bildet das Autohaus Mazda-Lietz, dessen Gebäudeteile statisch und dynamisch ineinandergreifen. Die klassisch-kubische Hülle für Werkstatt und Magazin übernimmt den statischen, der Wartung und Pflege dienenden Part, während dynamisch bewegte, zeichenhafte Hüllenfragmente Verkauf und Modellausstellung schirmen; dazwischen ziehen sich gläserne Wände. Die Teile formen sich zu einem Viertelkreis, akzentuiert und gefaßt von einem aufgeständerten Fahrbahnabschnitt. Das vielfältige Spektrum zeitgenössischer Automodelle findet hier seinen Raum. In Talrichtung steigt von hinten ein Rampenkeil massig aus der Ebene an und dringt in den gläsernen Viertelzylinder vor, wo die Fahrspur auf das aufgeständerte Brückenfragment, aber zugleich auf einen ruhigeren Aufenthaltsbereich stößt. Die sanft begonnene Dynamik der Rampe setzt sich nun verstärkt in horizontaler wie vertikaler Ebene fort und kulminiert einerseits in dem in Talrichtung blickenden, breit aufgestelzten Flugdach, das die gläserne Schauwand schirmt. An ihrer vorderen Ecke stößt andererseits das Brückenfragment durch das Glas, ragt kühn über den Zugang und trägt zuvorderst das jeweils neueste Automodell als Blickfang.

On the green floor of the valley, bisected and paralleled by the state road and railroad tracks, a couple of industrial and business buildings are arranged in a line to the south of Waidhofen. The Mazda-Lietz car dealership, whose various building segments reach into each other statically and dynamically, forms the end of the row. The classical-cubic shell for the repair shop and the storage room appropriates the static part of the structure in which maintenance and care are attended to. In contrast, dynamically moving, symbolic shell-like fragments shelter the sales and model exhibition area. In between and separating these two very distinct sections are glass walls. The elements of the latter form a quarter circle, accentuated and framed by a studded pavement zone. The diverse spectrum of contemporary car models finds its proper place here. From the back, towards the valley, a ramp wedge massively rises from the plain and forges ahead into the quarter cylinder at the point where the lane meets the bridge fragment and, at the same time, a more quiet lounge area. The soft dynamics which started with the ramp now continues strongly in the horizontal and vertical direction and culminates in the stilted, wing-like roof structure facing in the direction of the valley and shielding the glassed-in showroom wall. At its front corner, the bridge fragment pushes through the glass and boldly rises above the access, where, as an eye-catcher, the latest car model is always displayed.

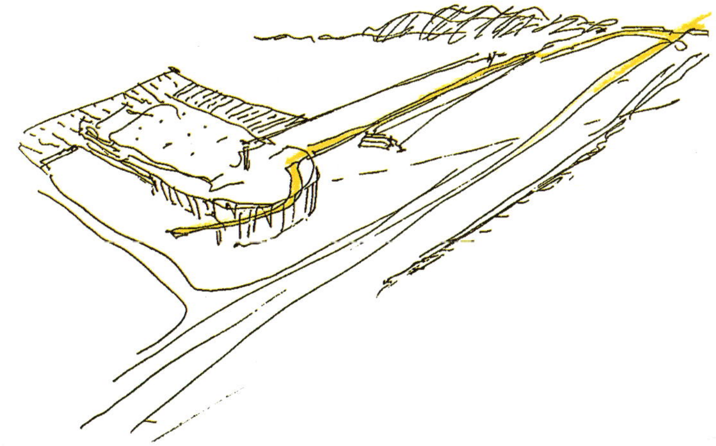

Lageplan / *Site plan*

Werkstättentrakt / *Workshop block*

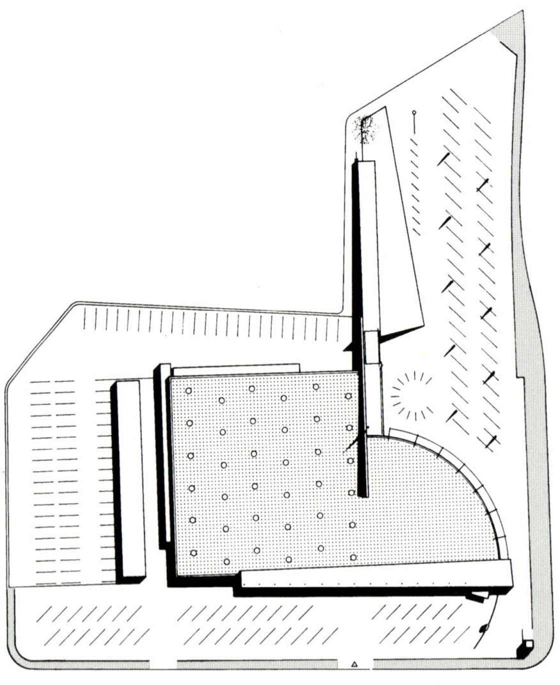

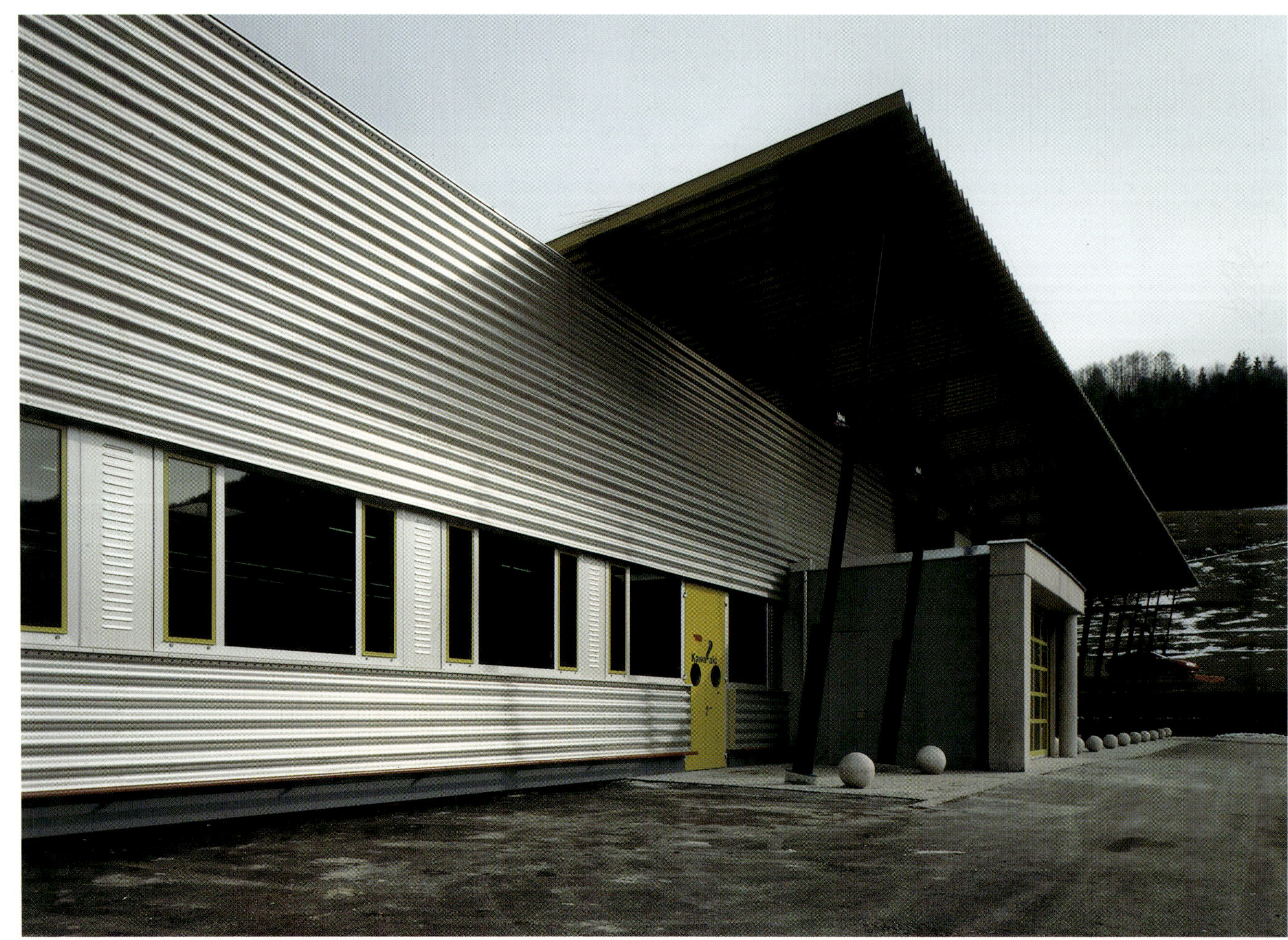

Entwurfskizzen / *Design sketches*

Ansicht Verkaufs- und Ausstellungshalle / *View of sales and show room*

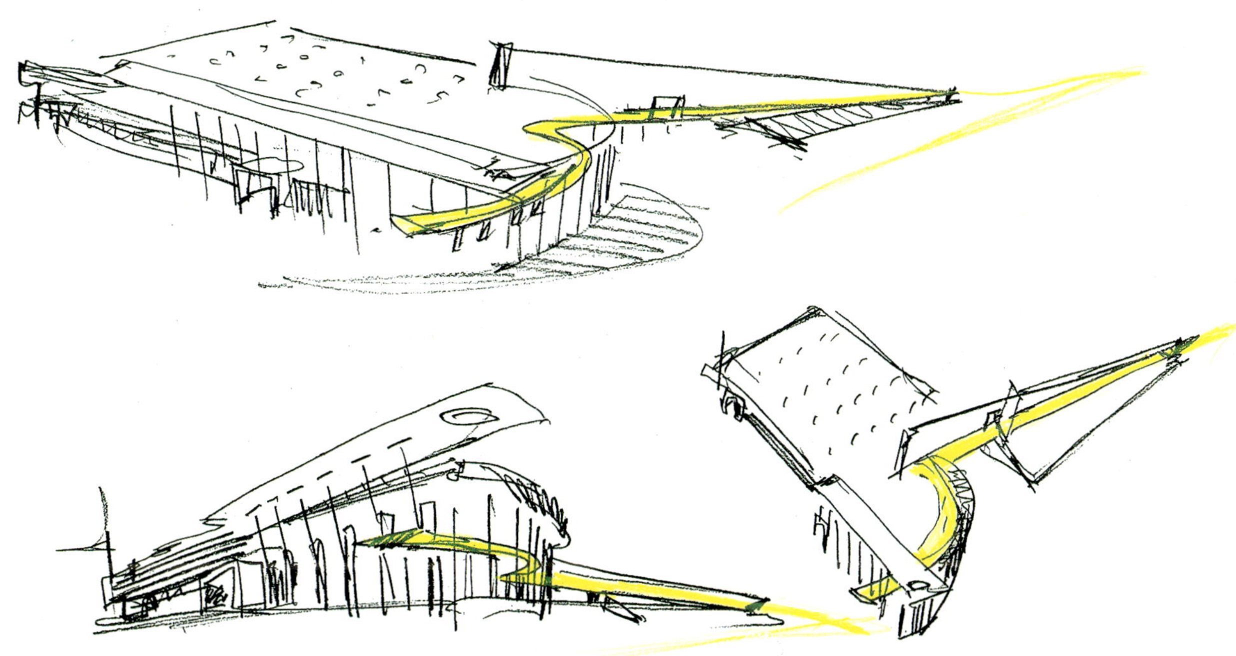

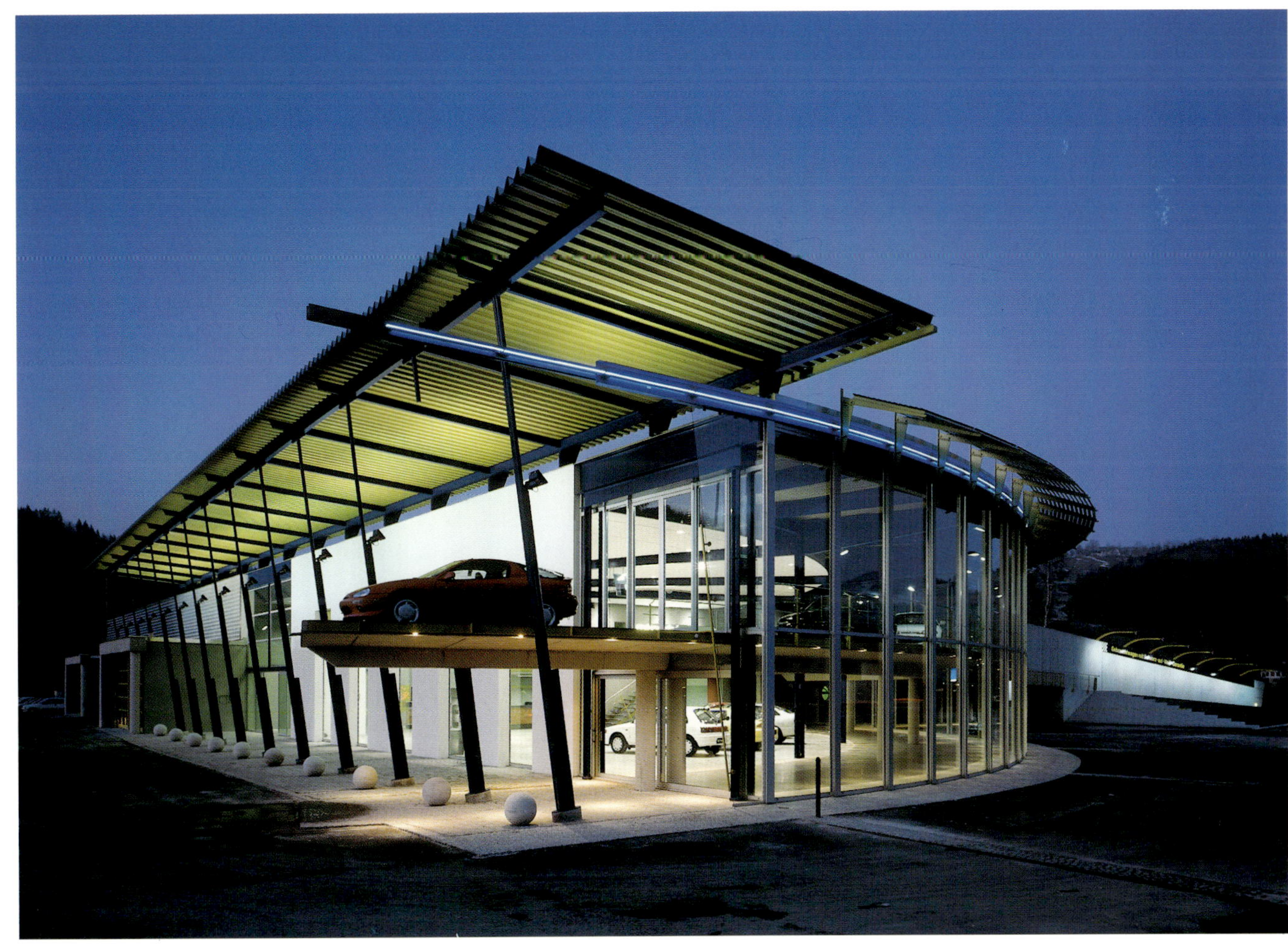

Details / *Details*

Ausstellungsraum, Oberlicht / *Show room, skylight*

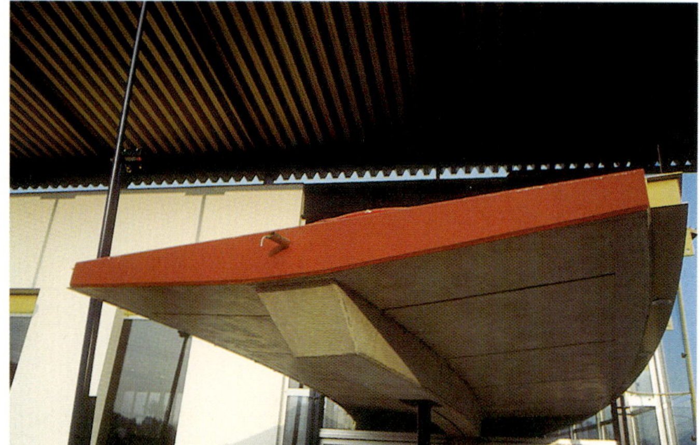

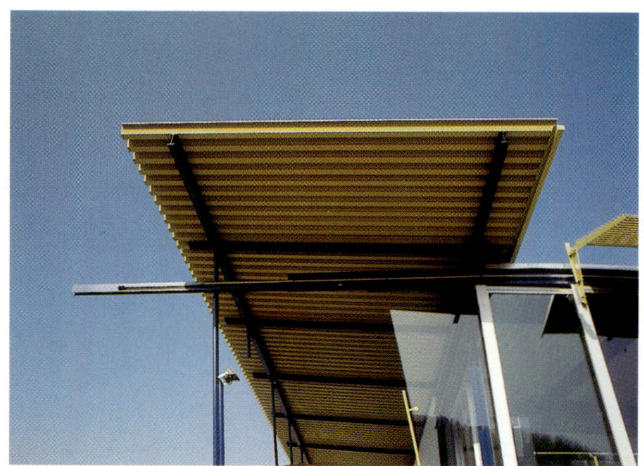

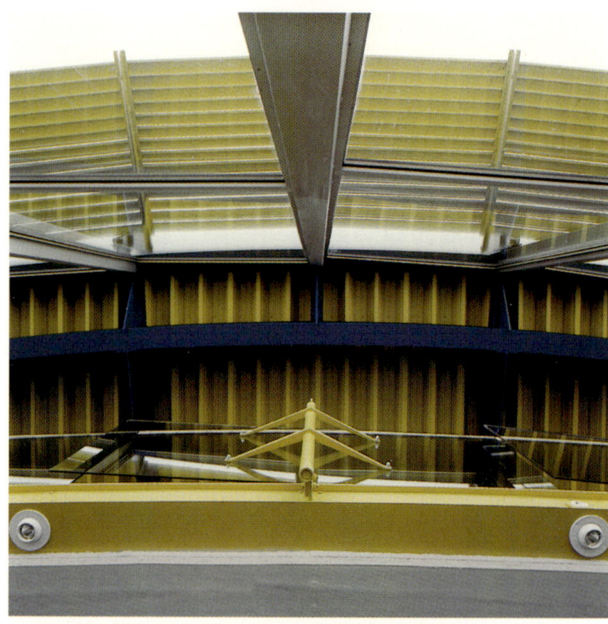

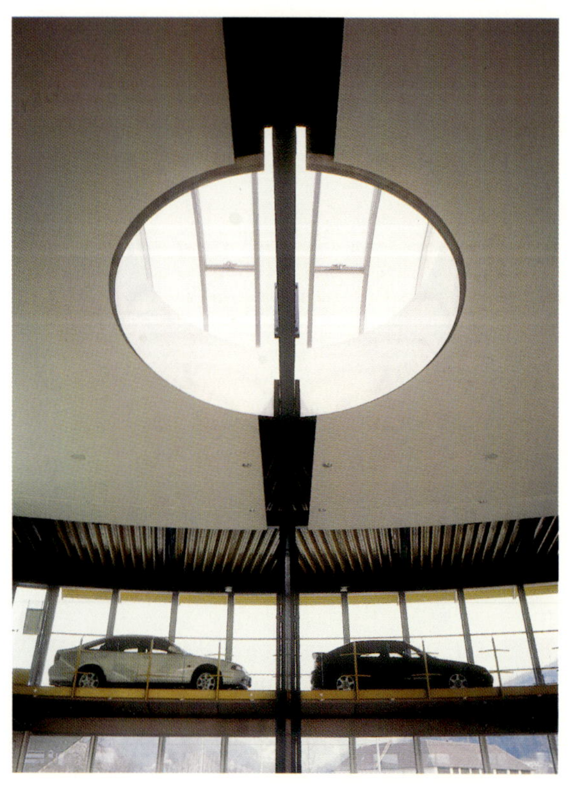

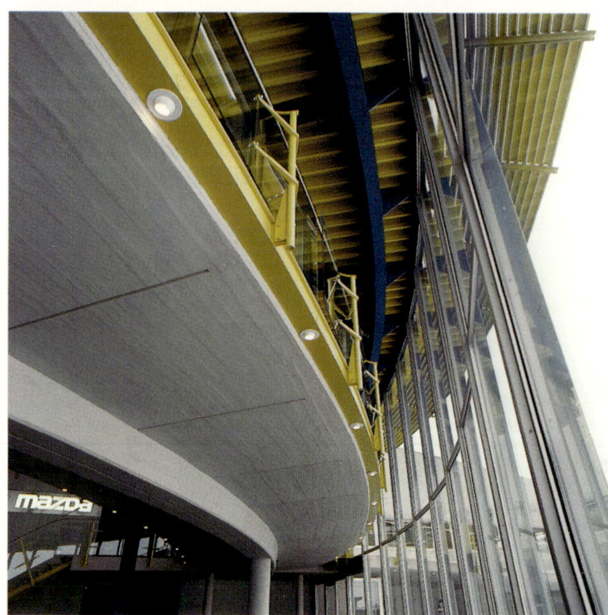

Details / *Details*

Details / *Details*

Ausstellungsraum, Oberlicht / *Show room, skylight*

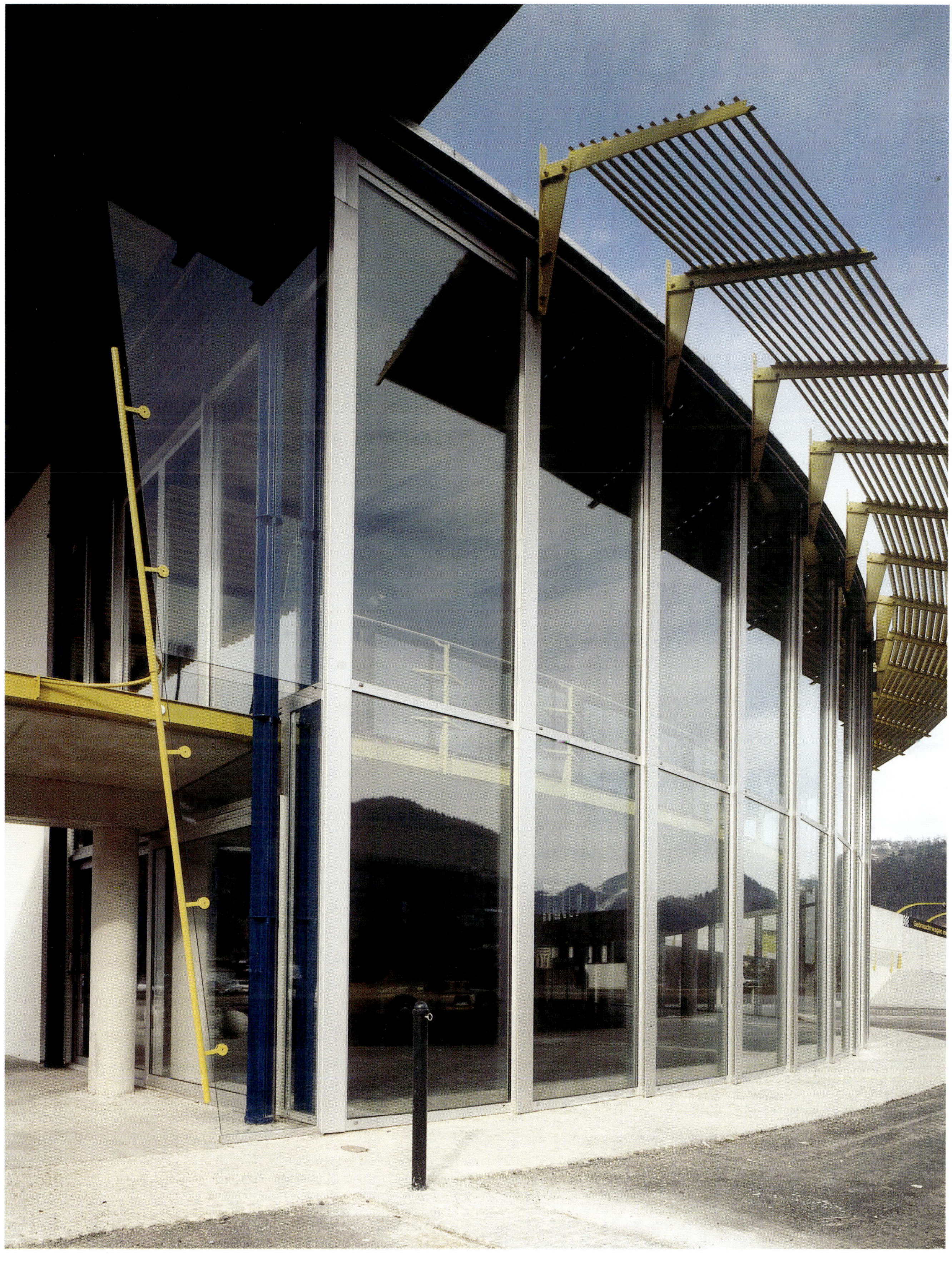

Ausstellungsgalerie / *Exhibition gallery*

Untersicht, Ausstellungsbrücke / *Visible underside of exhibition bridge*

Windfang / *Entrance wind barrier*

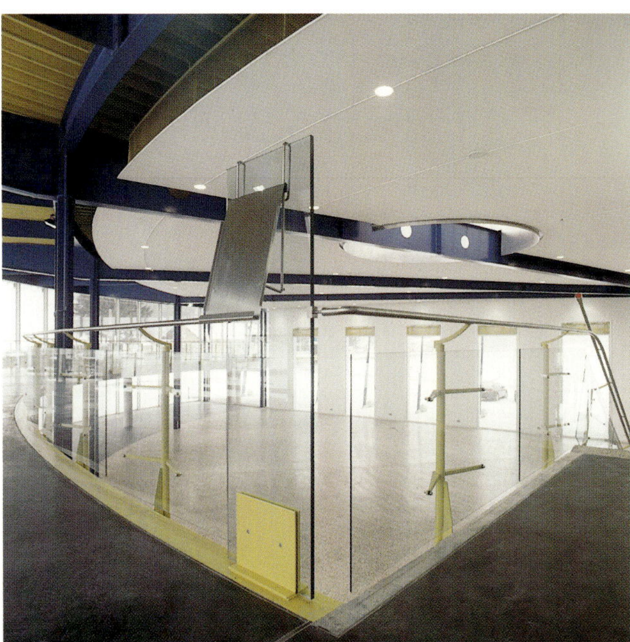

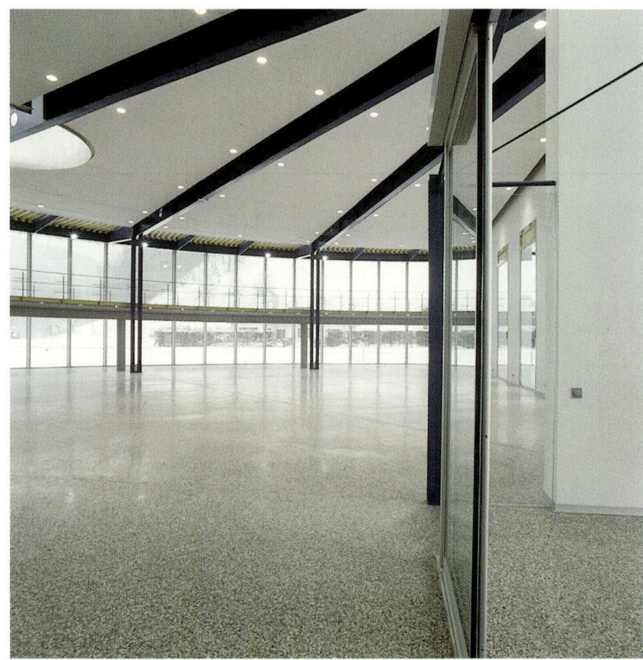

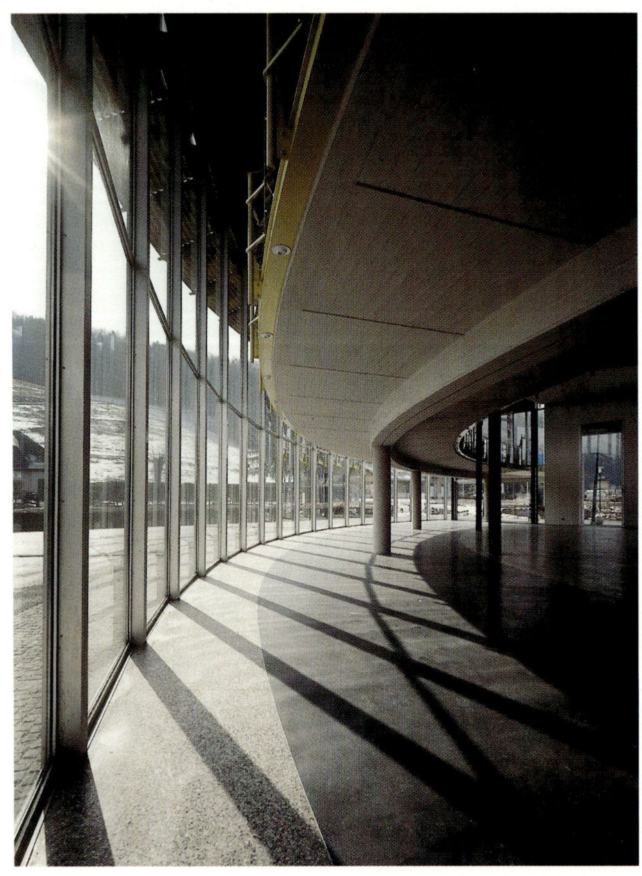

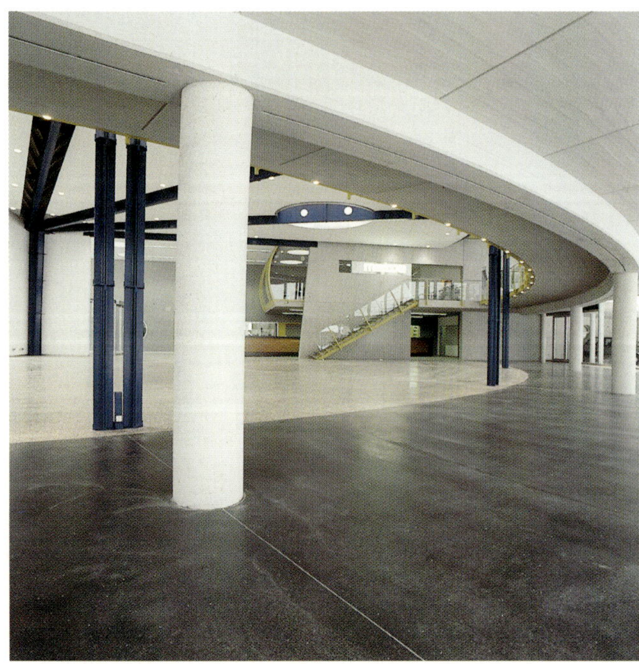

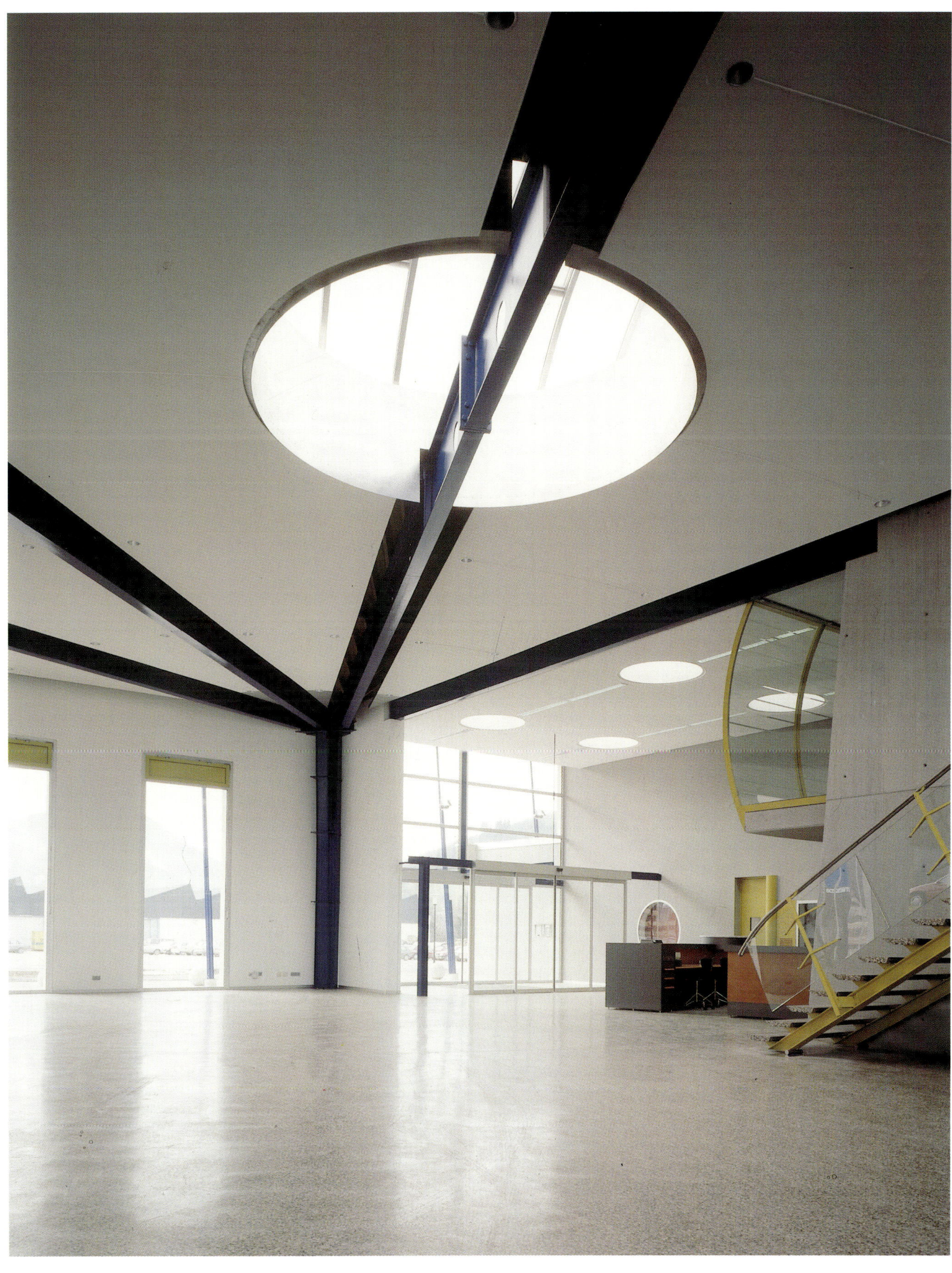

Bürotrakt / *Office block*

Schalttafel / *Control panel*

Empfangsbereich / *Reception area*

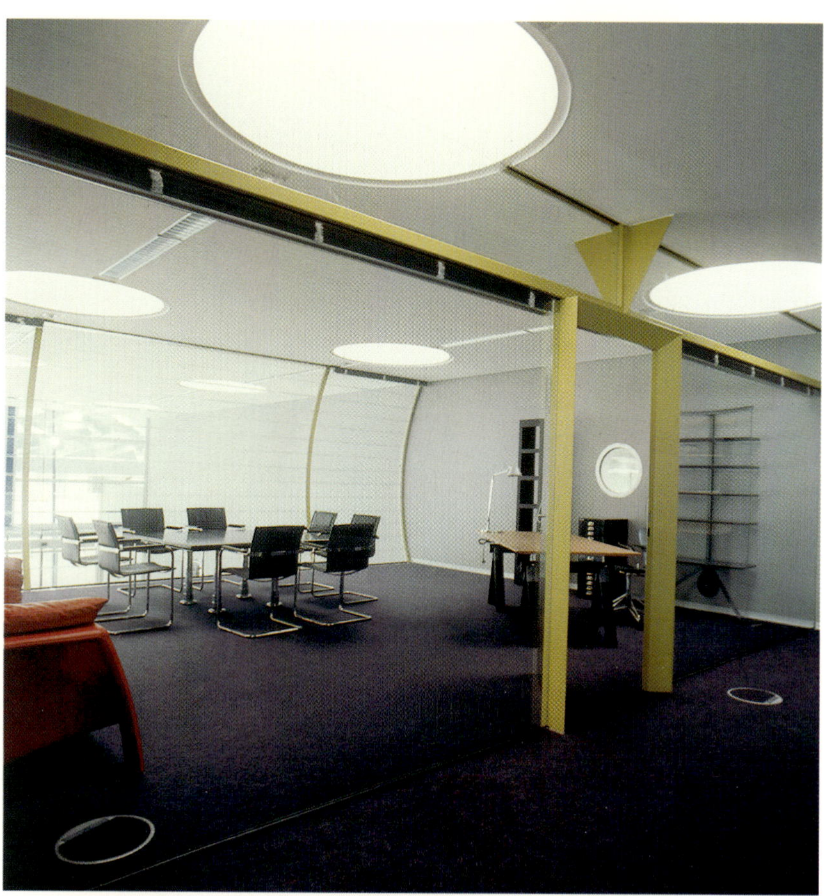

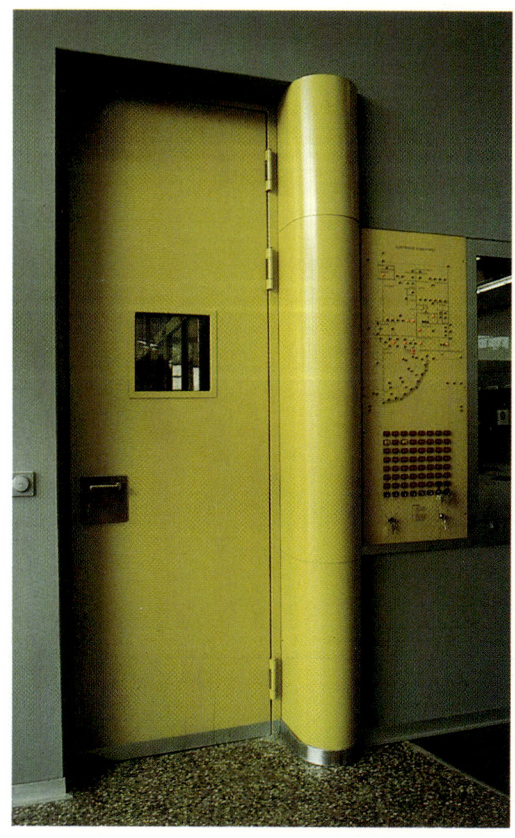

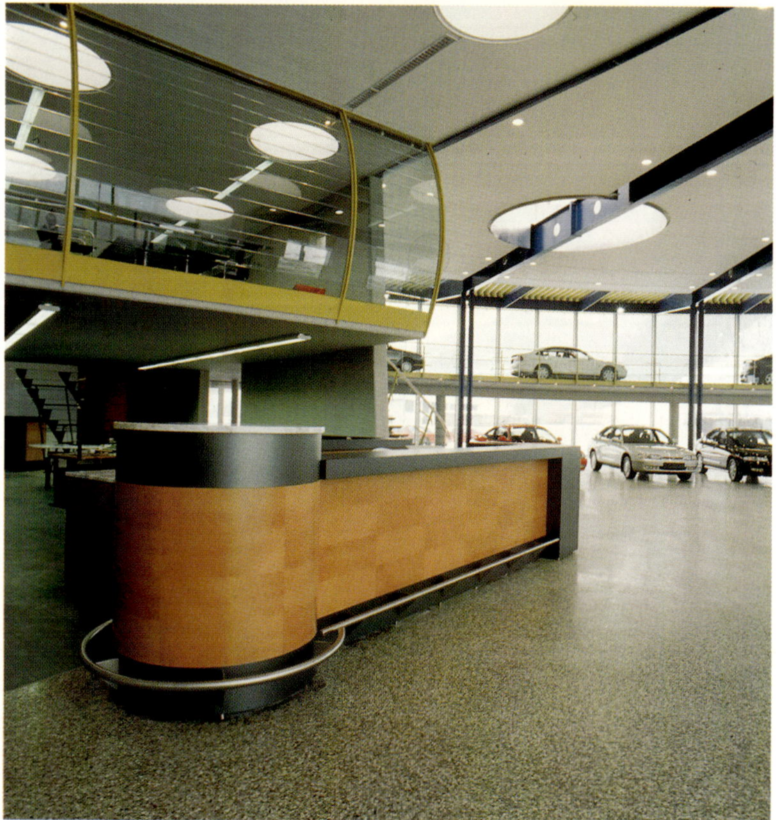

Ausstellungshalle / Exhibition hall

Aufgang Galerie, Details / Stairway gallery, details

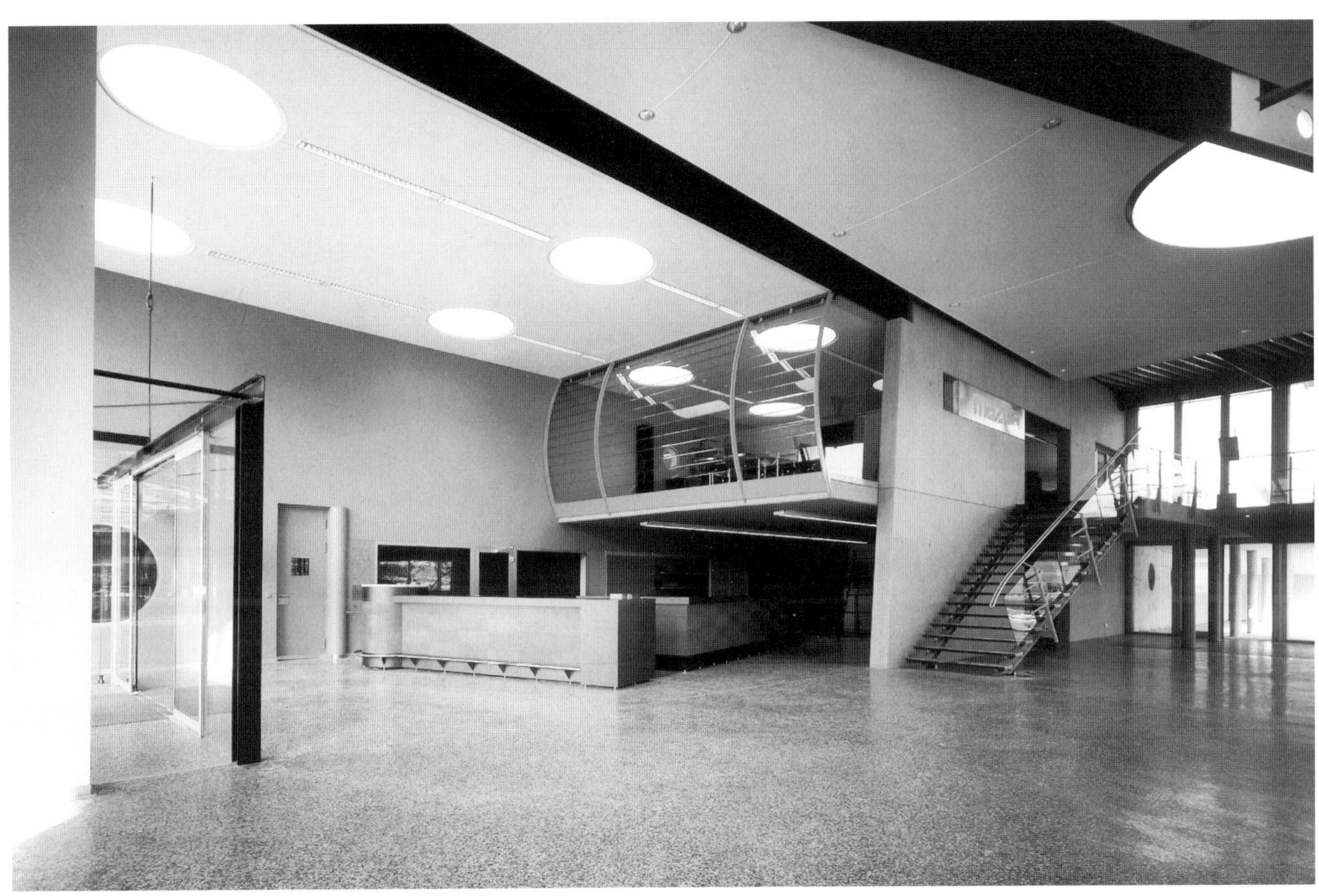

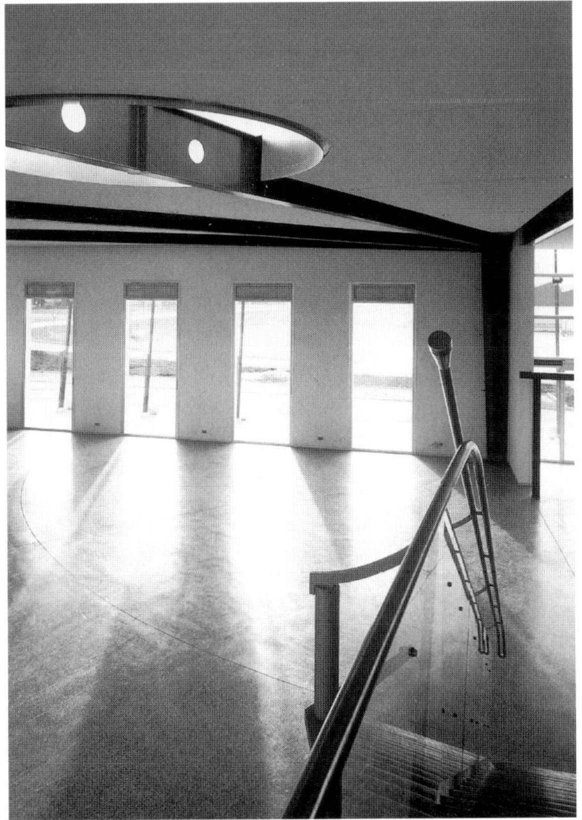

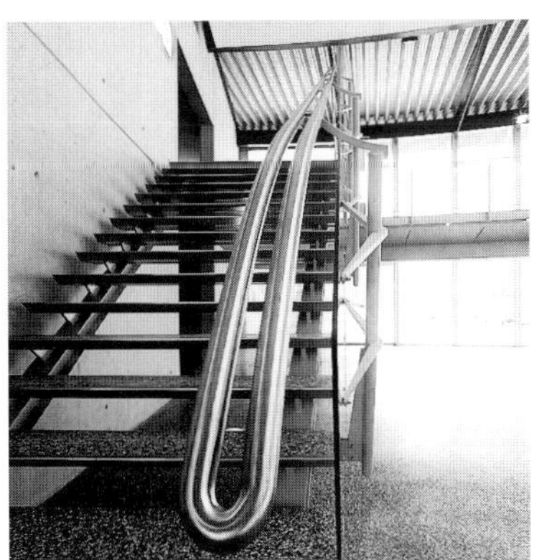

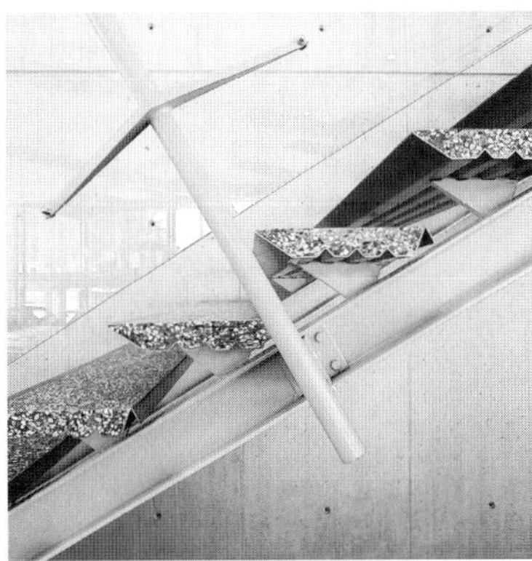

Trennende Mauerscheibe, Ausstellungshalle und Werkstätte / *Dividing wall of exhibition hall and workshop*

Längsschnitt, Südansicht / *Longitudinal section, south elevation*

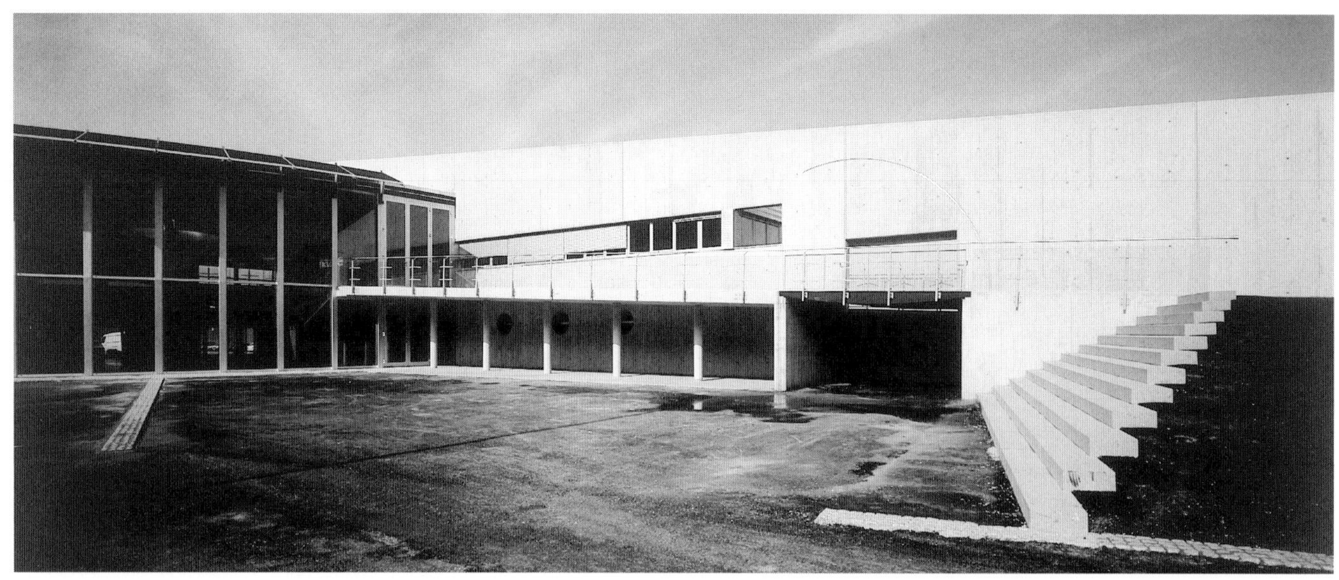

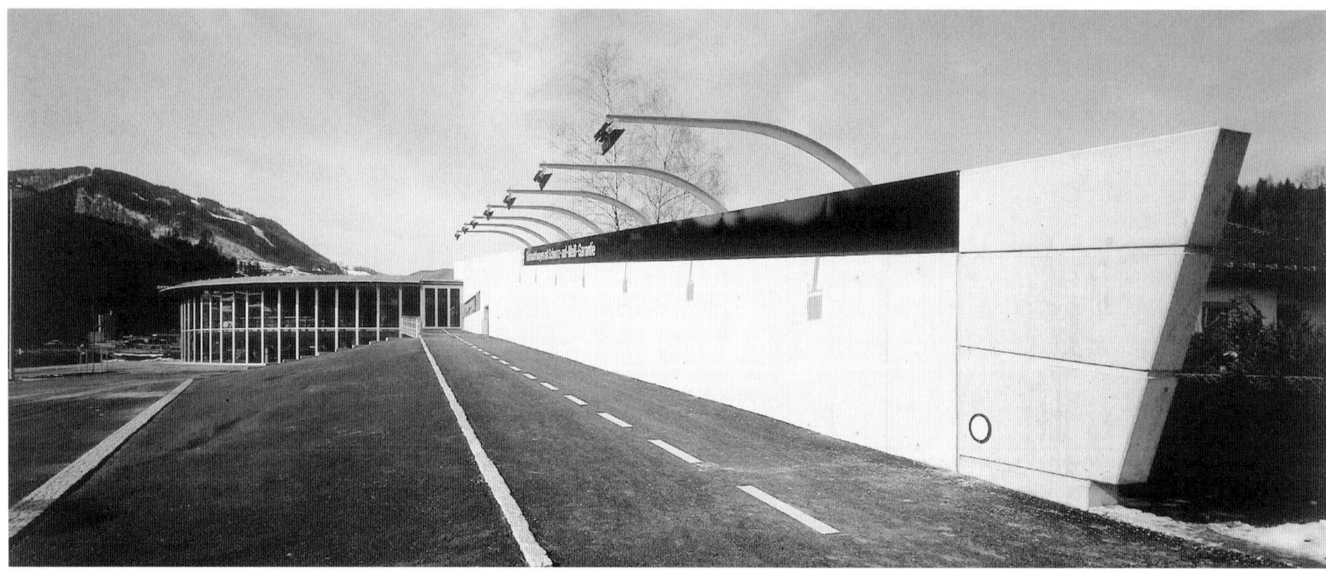

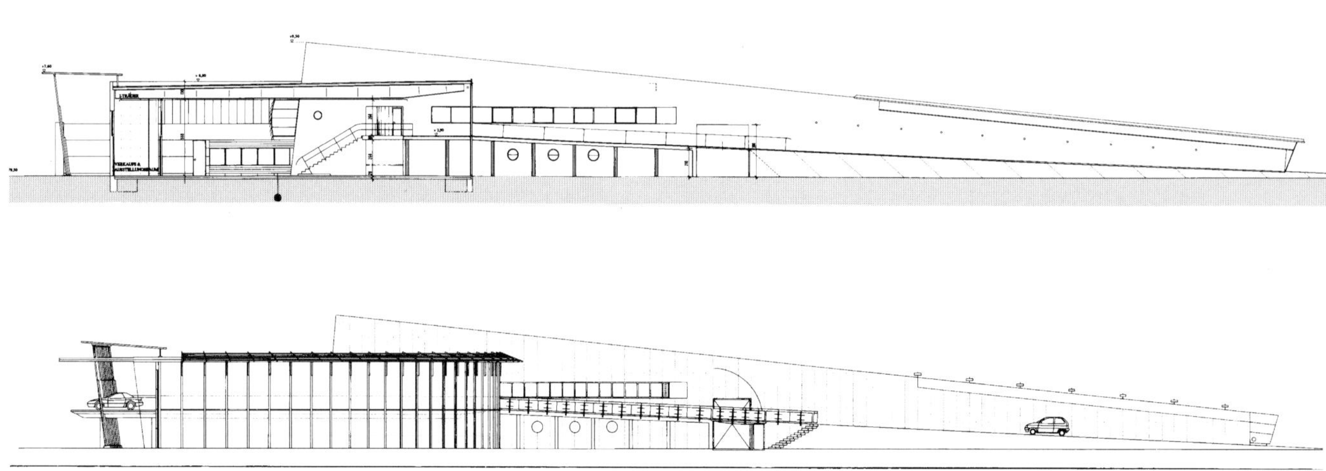

Wien-Brigittenau / *Vienna-Brigittenau* 1993

Lage im Bezirk / *Location in the quarter*

Mit dem Neubau eines den bisherigen Bebauungsmaßstab überschreitenden Geschäftshauses für die Basler Versicherung im oberen Bereich des Wiener Donaukanals wurde an diesem primären städtebaulichen Sturkturelement ein stadtbildendes Gebäude errichtet und ein Zeichen gesetzt für die Aufwertung des 20. Bezirks. Das Verhältnis zum Stadtgefüge wird zum einen bestimmt durch eine auf mittlere Distanz konzipierte Fassade zur Brigittenauer Lände und zum Fluß. Sie interpretiert dessen Fließen und wirkt ihm zugleich entgegen, indem die Glasbänder von Brüstungen und Fenstern mit rundem Schwung aus dem Gebäudevolumen herausschießen und in langen Bahnen nach vorn streben, wo eine große kopfartige Tafel, verkleidet mit schwarzem Naturstein, das Ende und zugleich die Ecke des Gebäudes markiert. Sie lenkt den Drive leicht aus der Fassadenflucht heraus und erzeugt damit eine gerade merkbare Unstetigkeit in der Abfolge der Gebäude. Obwohl keine solitäre städtebauliche Position auf dem Vorquai besetzt wird, wie mit der Urania (Max Fabiani, 1910) oder dem Schützenhaus (Otto Wagner, 1908), bildet das Haus einen städtebaulichen Akzent im Raum des oberen Donaukanals. Zur anderen Seite, zum dicht mit Zinskasernen verbauten 20. Bezirk, weist das Gebäude eine ruhige Putzfassade auf, in der querrechteckige, fast klassische Bürofenster in einfach rhythmischer Folge eingesetzt sind. Spezifische Stellen am Gebäude, etwa beim Eingang oder an der Ecke, werden durch Fenster mit kräftigen roten Rahmen hervorgehoben. Damit gelingt es, den großen Gebäudemaßstab zu relativieren und zu den gegenüberliegenden Mietshäusern eine Beziehung aufzubauen. Die Öffnung des Hofes für die Fußgänger und die urbane Aufwertung der in der Tiefe des Bezirks verankerten und auf die Rückfront zielenden Othmarstraße bewirken, daß das Geschäftszentrum städtebaulich den Charakter eines Kopfgebäudes erlangt, obwohl es im Gefüge verbleibt. Es setzt die urbane Fußgängerachse fort, interpretiert sie durch den Hof leitend neu und verknüpft sie mit der beliebten Uferpromenade. Die Bürogrundrisse sind betriebswirtschaftlich optimiert. Der architektonische Ausdruck konzentriert sich auf die Gliederung der Volumen und auf den konstruktiven Aufbau der sichtbaren äußeren Hülle. Dabei beschränkt sich die Durcharbeitung nicht auf die Oberfläche, sondern reicht in die Tiefe des Wandaufbaus. Die Tafeln und Platten überschuppen sich, greifen ineinander, scheinen von virtuellen Kräften verformt und im Augenblick erstarrt, wie geologische Formationen des Erdaltertums.

With the new construction of an office building exceeding the given building scale for the Basel Insurance Company in the upper section of the Vienna Danube channel, an important building was erected and a mark set for the revaluation of the 20th district at this primary urban structural element. On one hand, the relation with the city structure is defined by a facade designed at a medium distance towards the Brigittenau pier and the river. It interprets the river's flow and at the same time works towards it with the glass strips of parapets and windows. They shoot out of the building volume with a curved swing and strive toward the front in long bands, to where a big head-like panel, covered with black natural stone, marks the end and the corner of the building at the same time. It directs the drive slightly out of the facade flight and thus creates a subtle inconsistency in the sequence of the buildings. Although no solitary urban position is taken up in the area before the pier, as is the case with the Urania (Max Fabiani, 1910) or the Schützenhaus (Otto Wagner, 1908), the house forms an urban aspect in the area of the upper channel of the Danube. On the other side, towards the 20th district densely built up with rental barracks, the building shows a calm, plastered facade into which cross rectangular, almost classical office windows are placed in a simple rhythmic sequence. Specific areas of the building, such as the entrance or the corner, are emphasized by windows with a bright red frame. The attempt to make the large scale of the building relative and to establish a relationship with the opposing rental buildings thus succeeds. The opening of the yard for pedestrians and the urban revaluation of Othmar street, anchored in the depth of the district and aiming towards the back wall, have the effect that the business center attains the character of a head building in an urban sense, although it remains within the structure. It continues the urban pedestrian axis, reinterprets it by leading through the yard and connects it with the well-liked boardwalk. The office ground plans are optimized in an industrial economic sense. The architectural expression concentrates on the arrangement of the volumes and the constructive build-up of the visible outer shell. The execution of these aspects is not limited to the surface but reaches into the depth of the wall erection. The boards and plates overlap, pass into each other, seem to be deformed by virtual forces and frozen in the moment, similar to geological formations of antiquity.

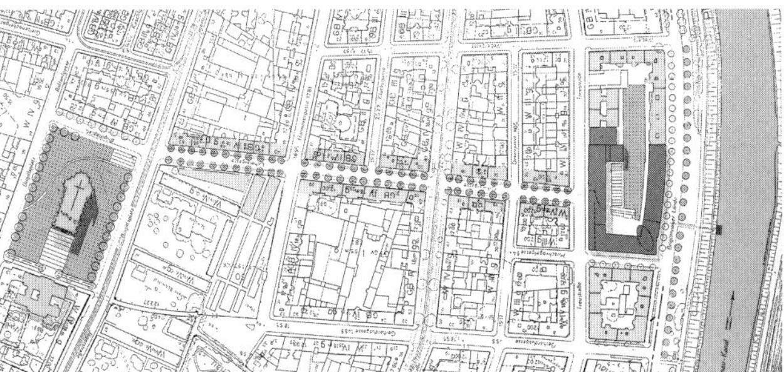

Arbeitsmodell / *Working model*

Entwurfskizzen / *Design sketches*

Lage am Donaukanal / *Location at the Danube canal*

Modell / *Model*

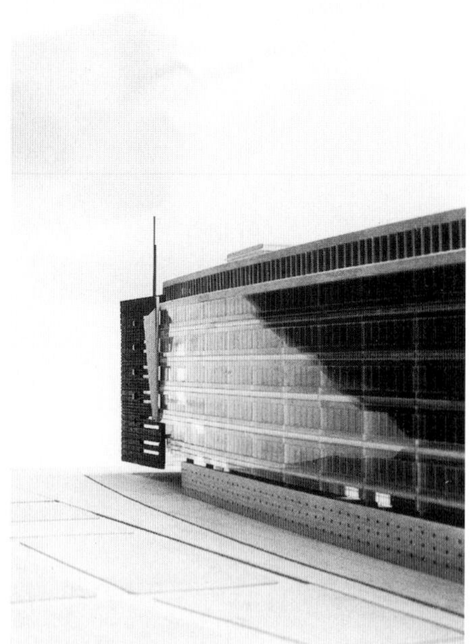

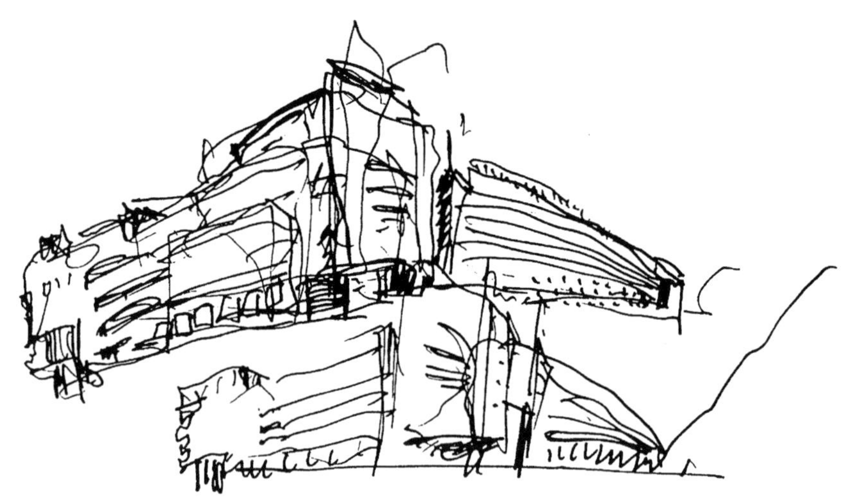

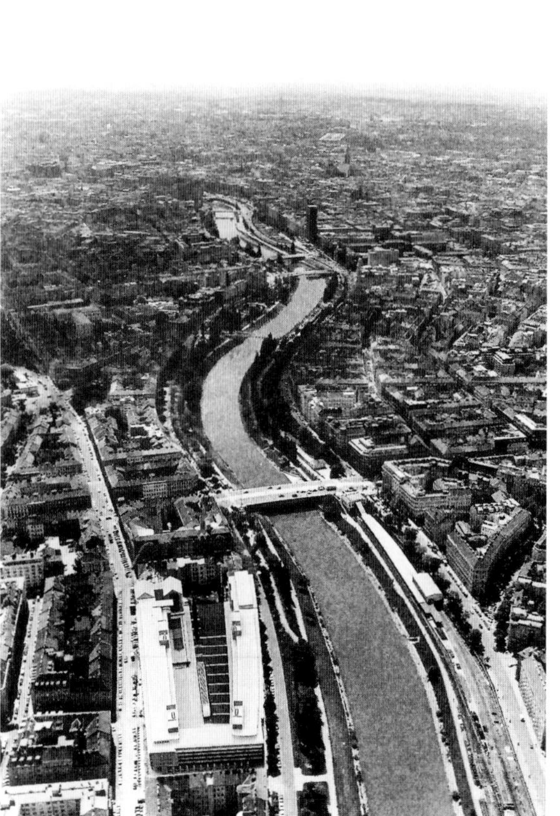

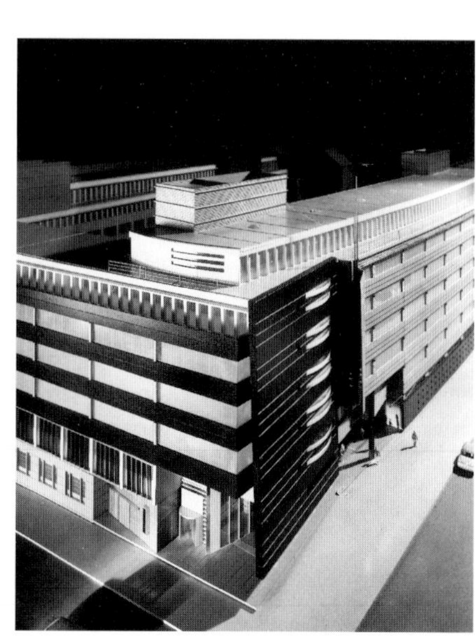

Modell / *Model*

Entwurfskizzen / *Design sketches*

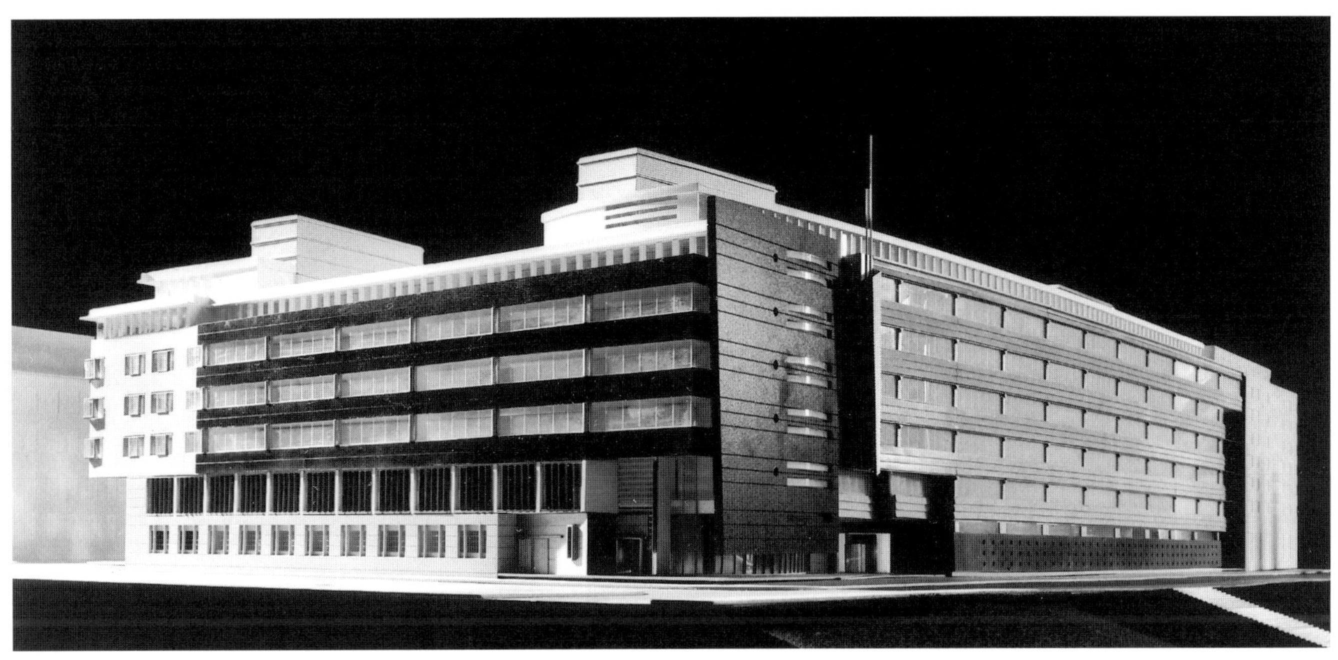

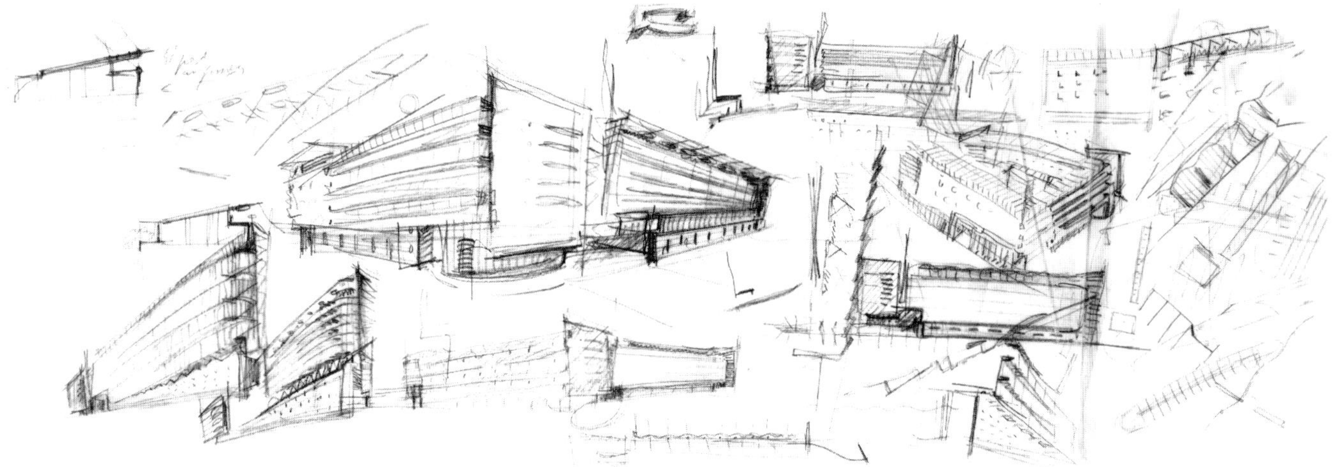

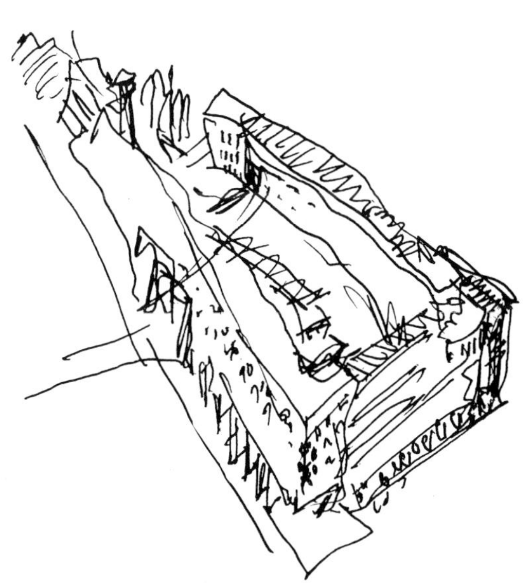

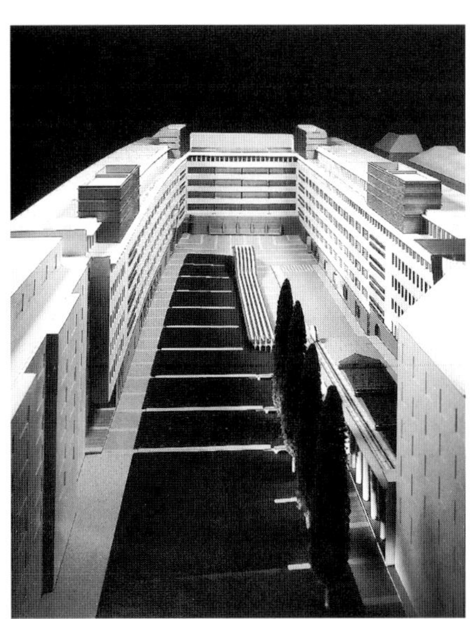

Ansicht von der Donaukanal-Promenade / *View from the Danube canal pier*

Fassade von der Brigittenauer Lände / *Facade from Brigittenauer Lände*

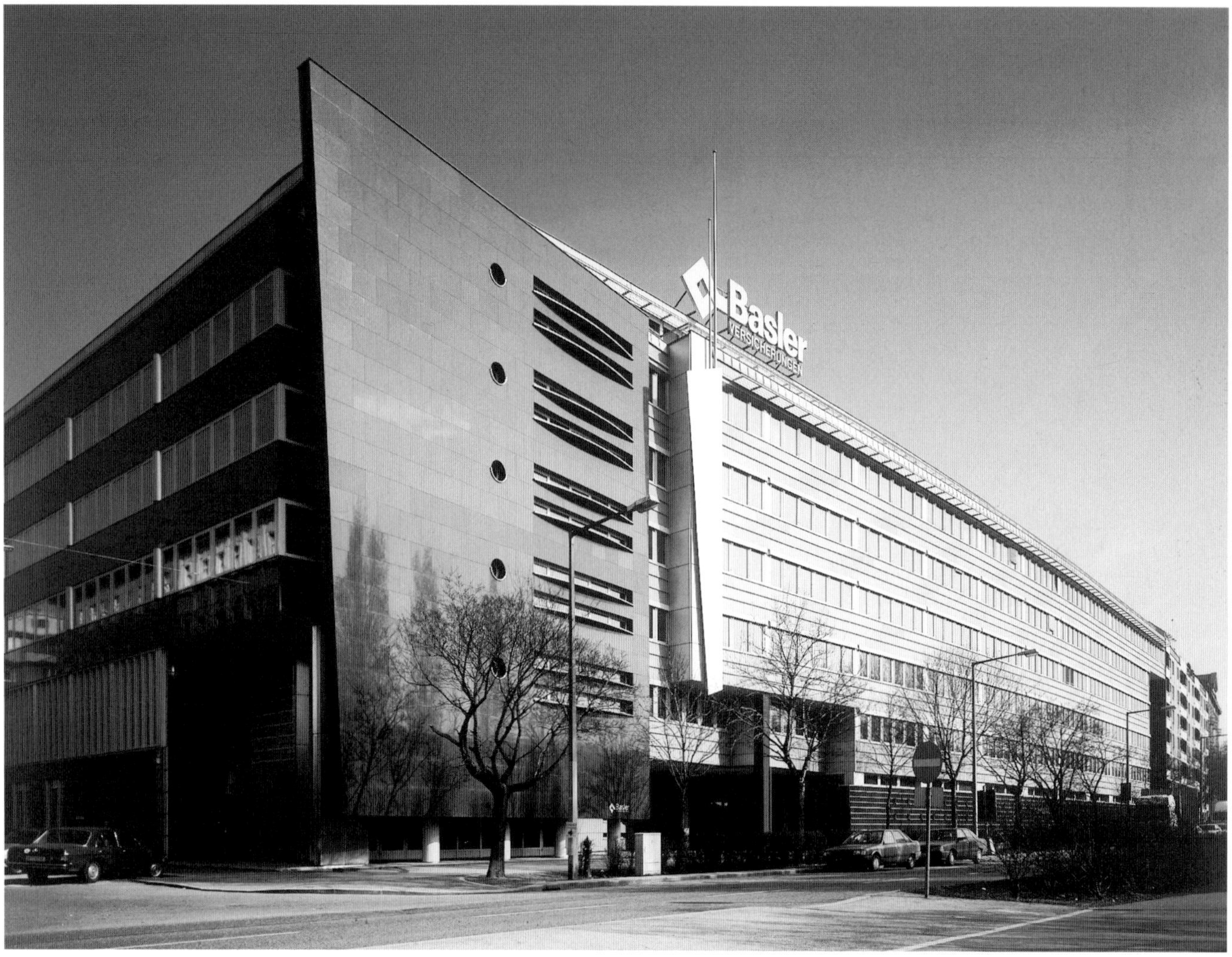

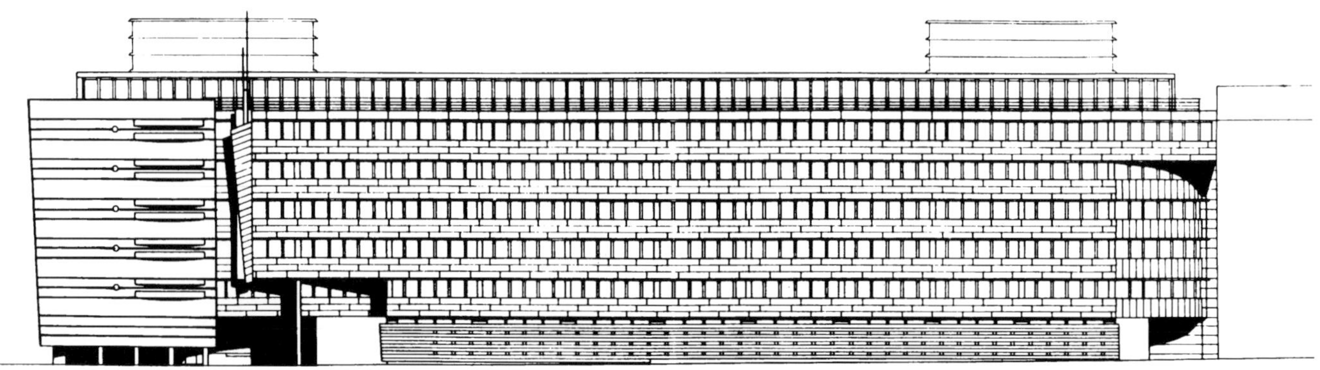

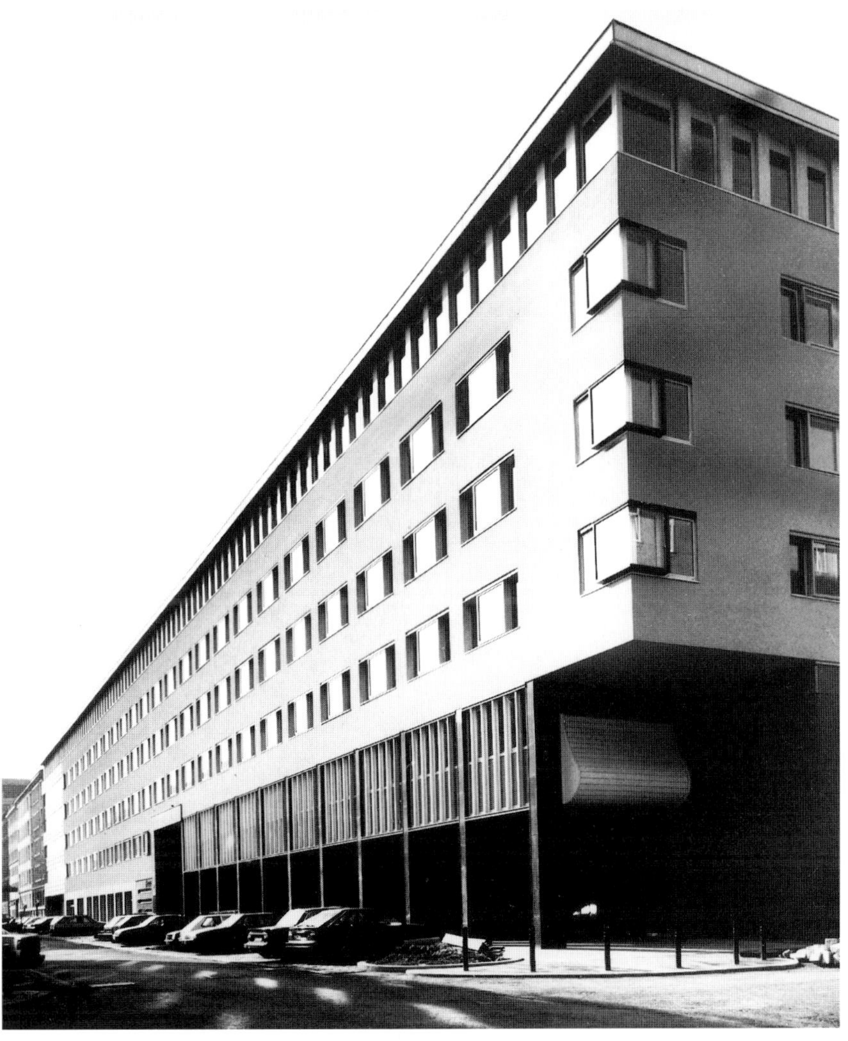

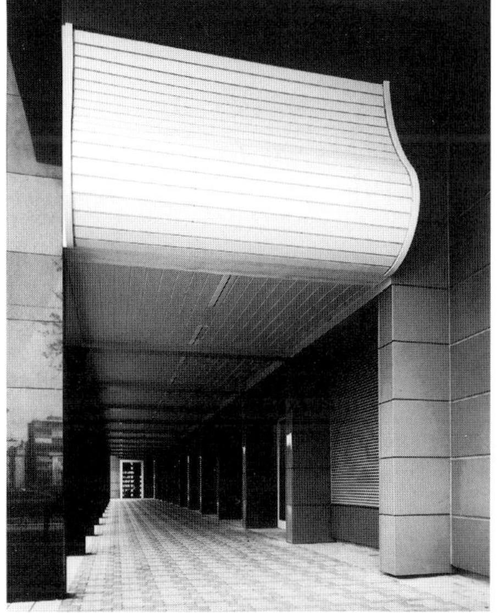

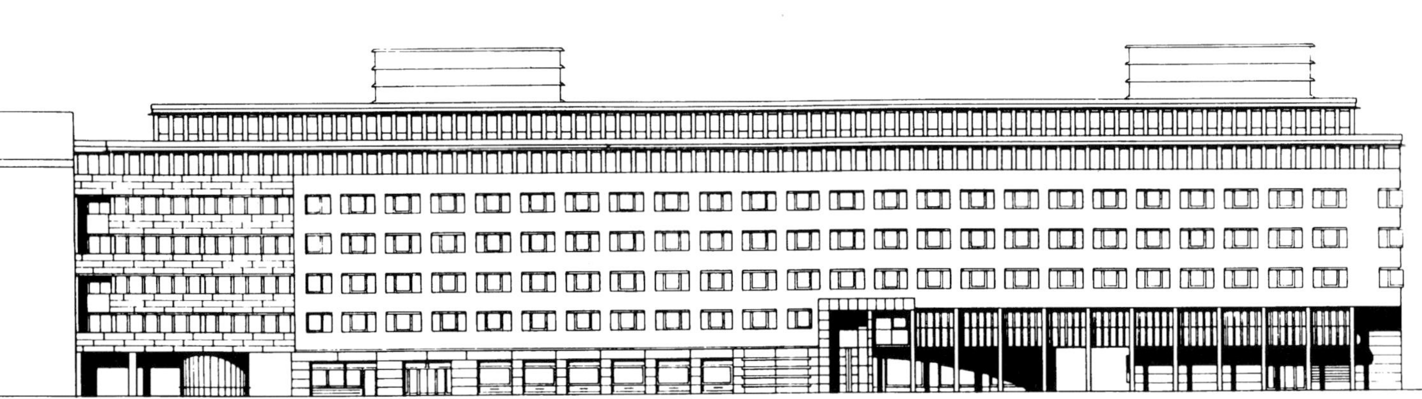

Steinschild, Detail / *Stone panels, detail*

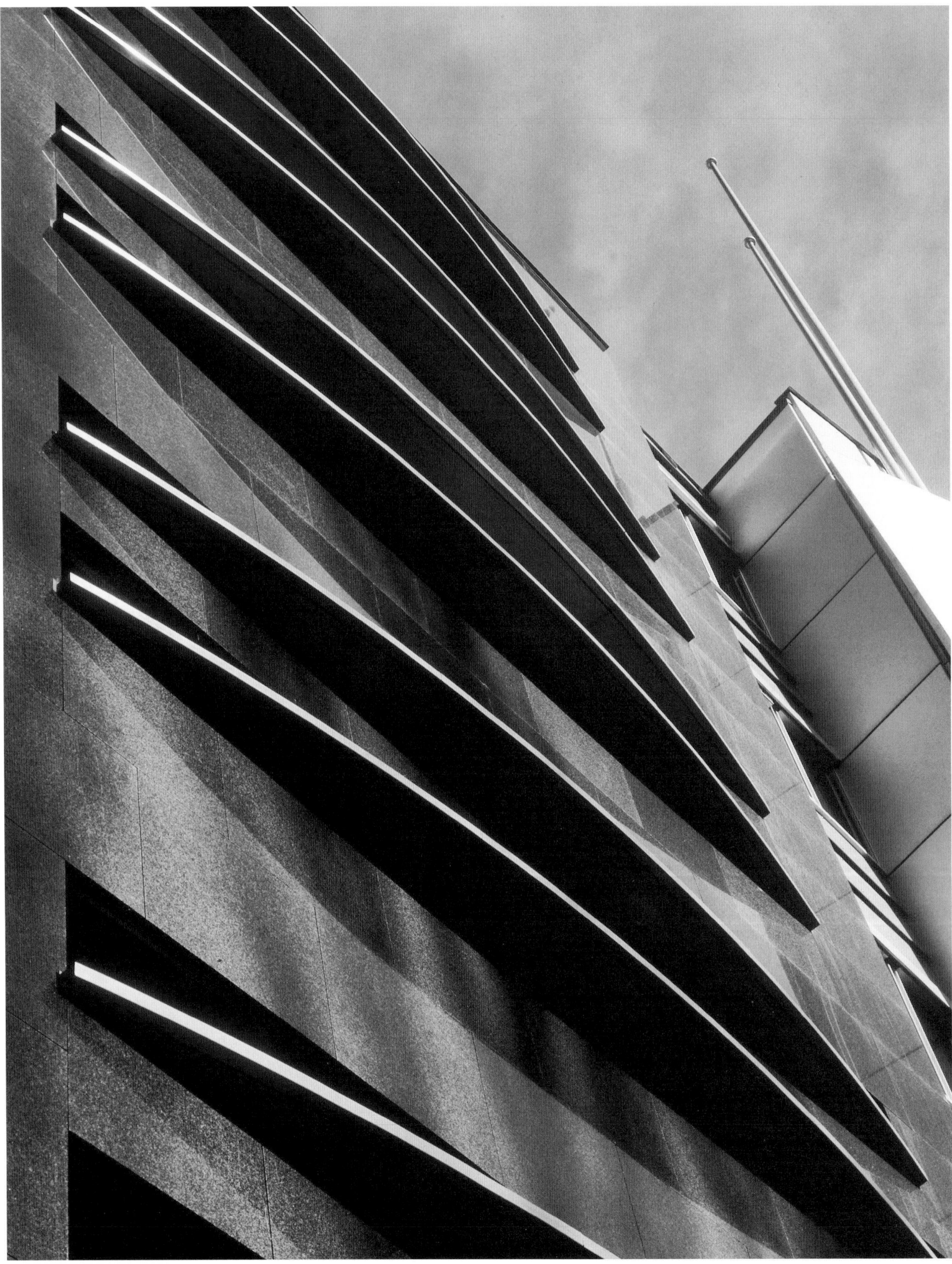

Steinschild, Gesamtansicht / *Stone panels, entire view*

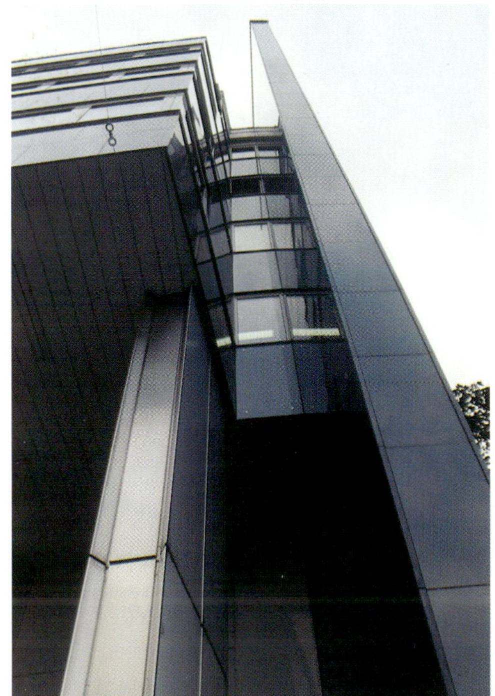

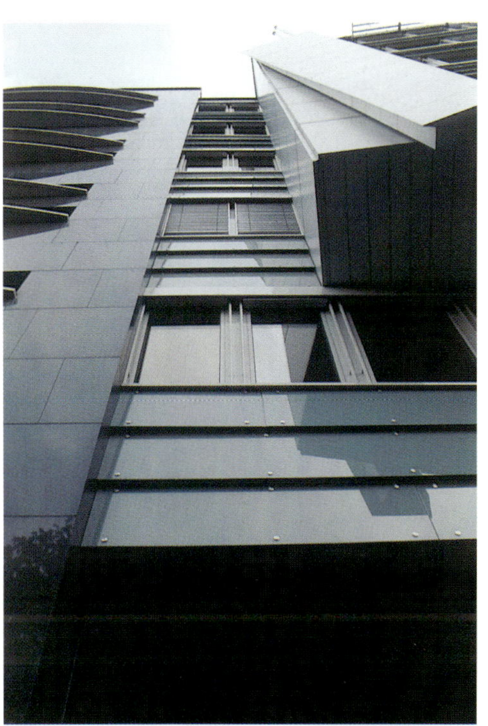

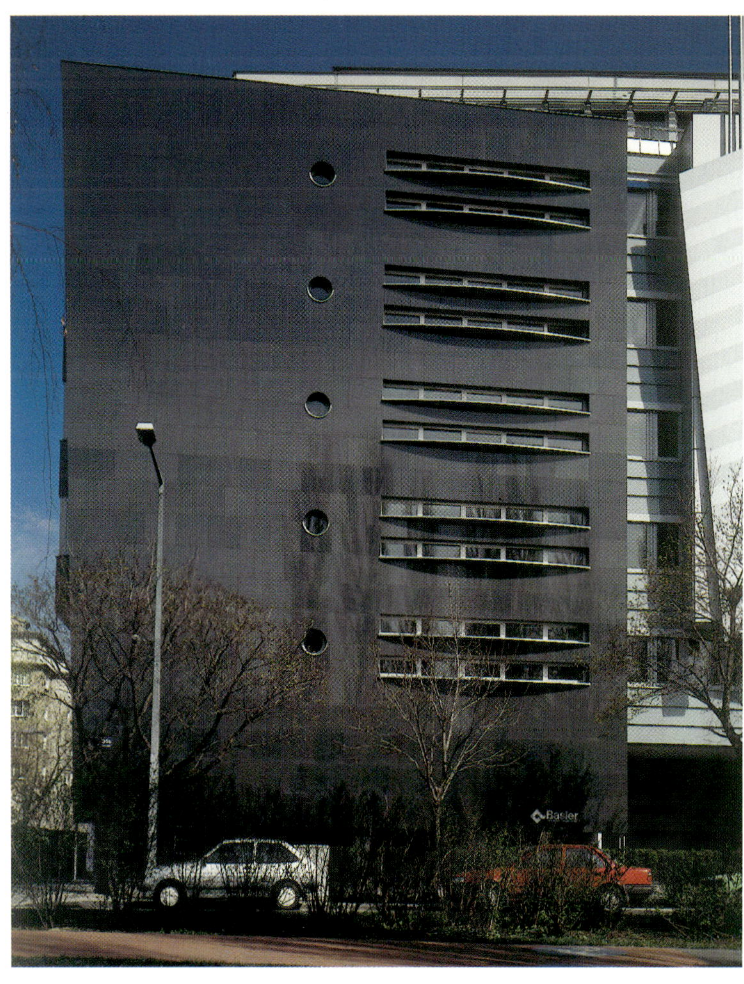

Passage zum Hof / *Passageway to the courtyard*

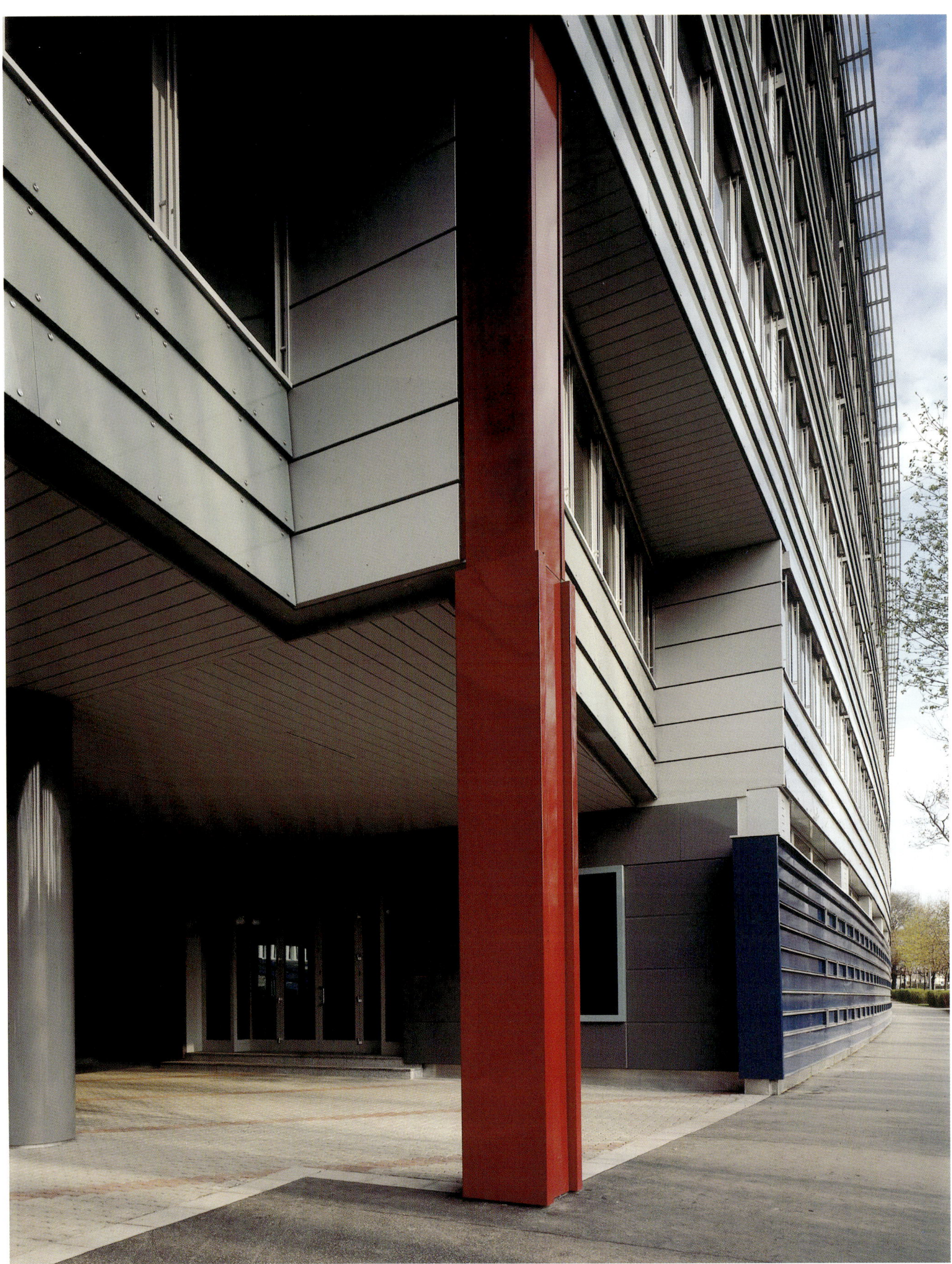

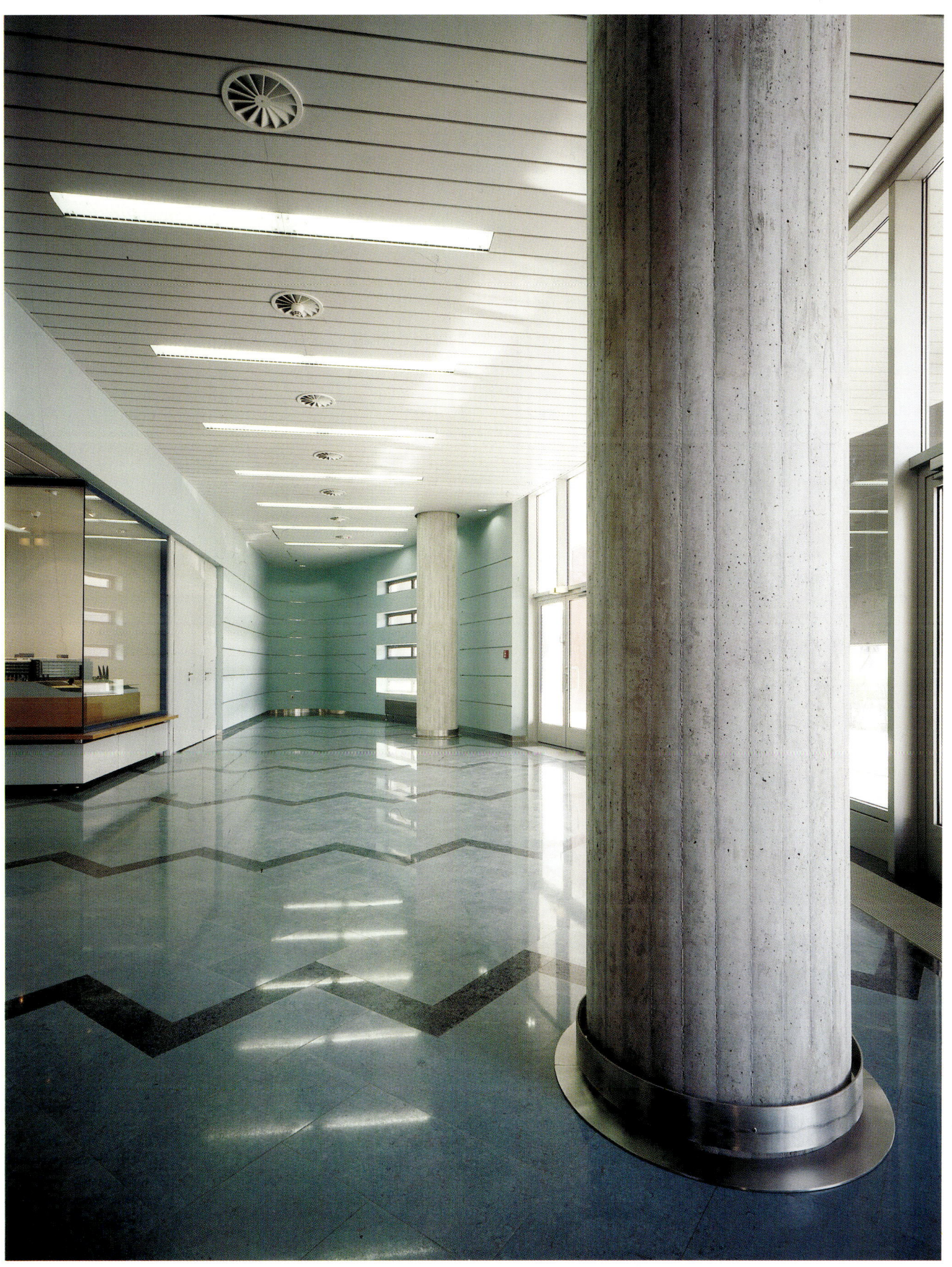

Axonometrie Hof / *Axonometric projection of courtyard*

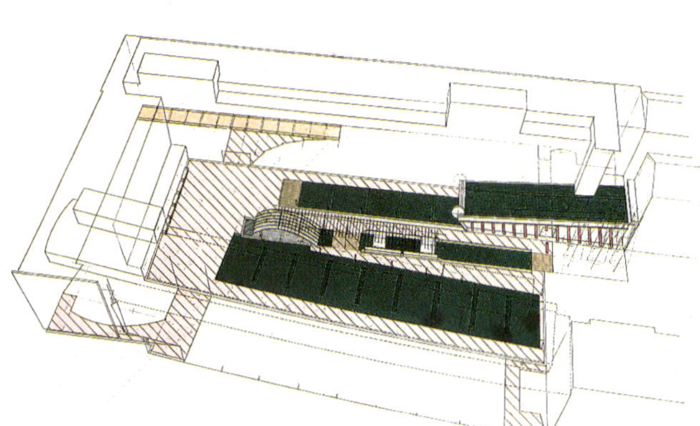

Grundriß Regelgeschoß / *Typical floor plan*

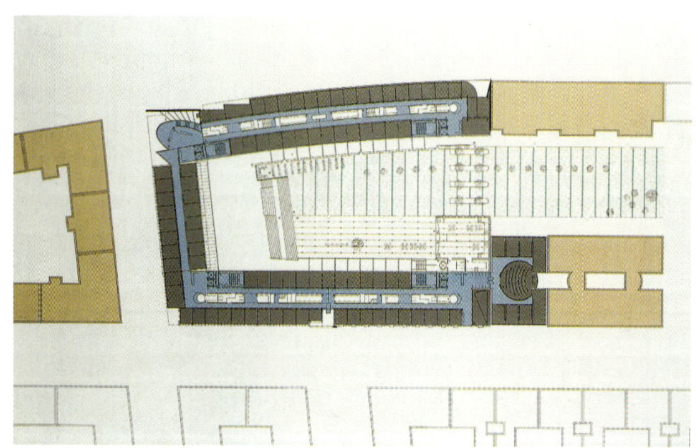

Hofraum mit Brunnenanlage / *Courtyard space with fountain*

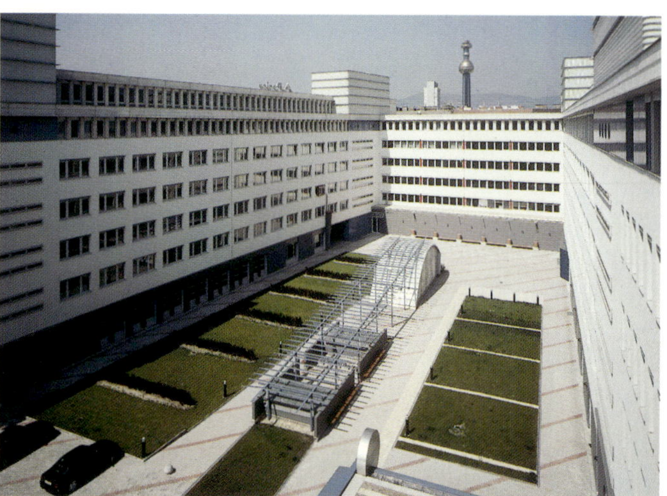

Hofeinbauten, Detail / *Courtyard installations, detail*

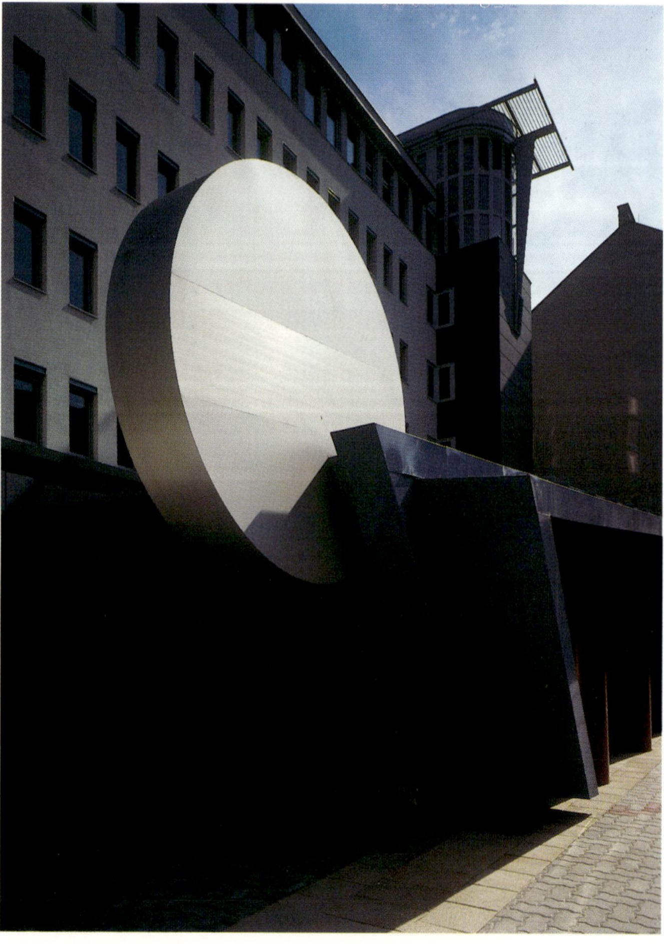

Brunnen an Hofpassage / *Fountain at the courtyard passageway*

Hofeinbauten und Fassade / *Courtyard installations and facade*

Hofeinbauten und Fassade / *Courtyard installations and facade*

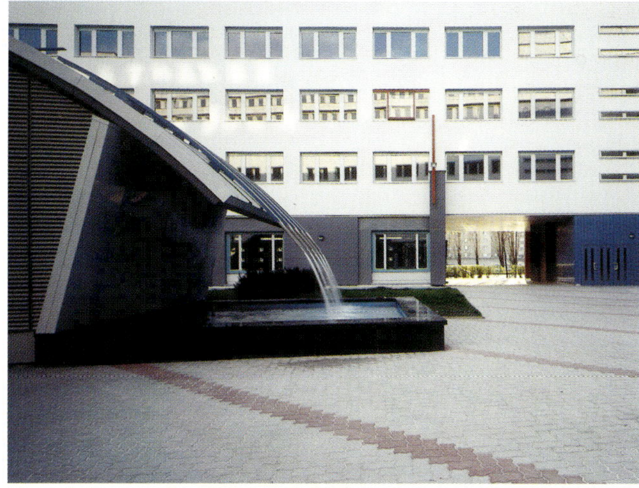

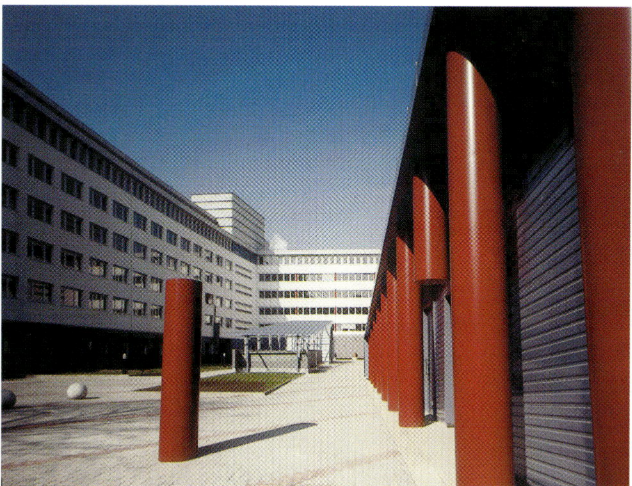

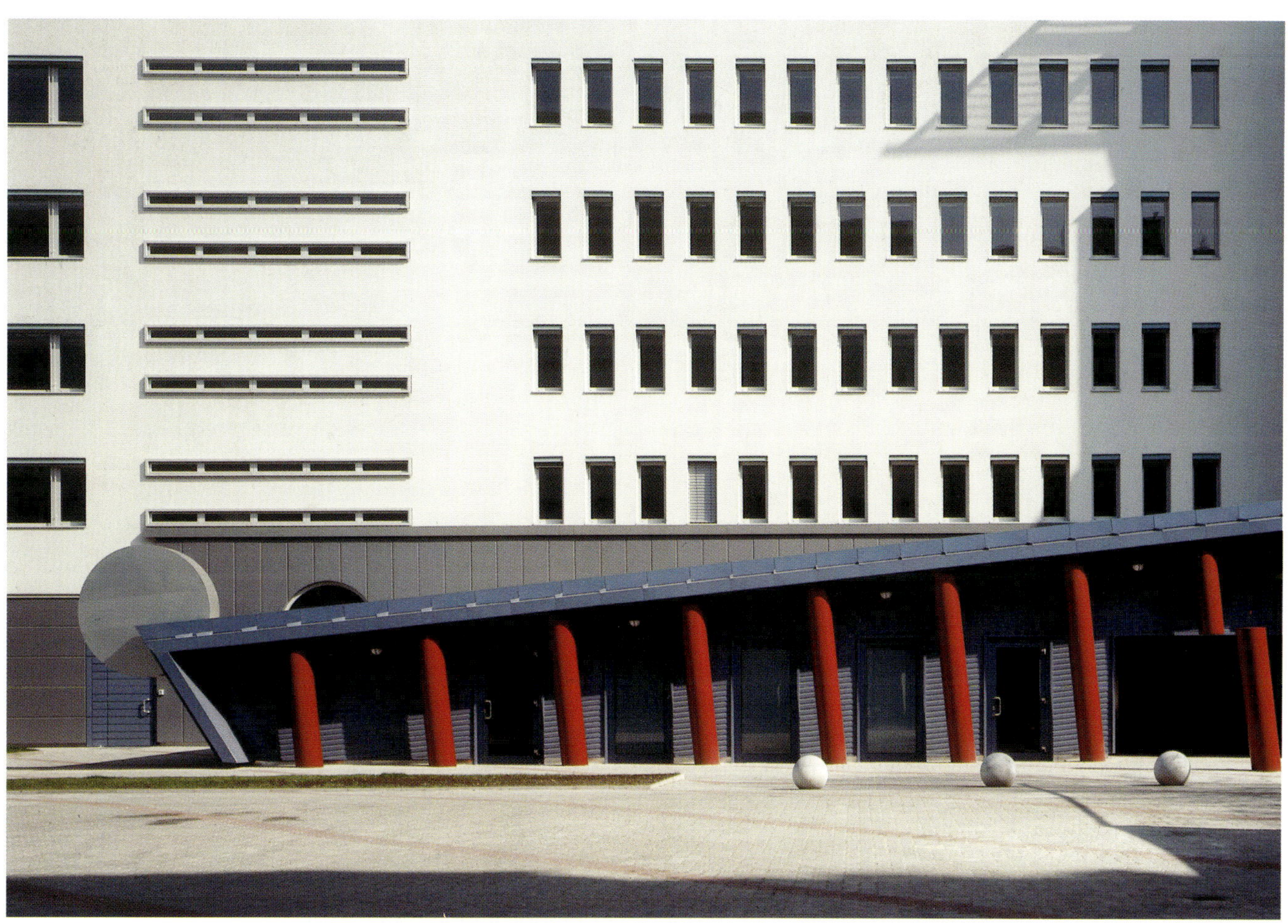

Fassadenabschnitte Hirschvogelgasse und Treustraße /
Facade sections Hirschvogelgasse and Treustrasse

Detail bei der Hofpassage / *Detail at the courtyard passageway*

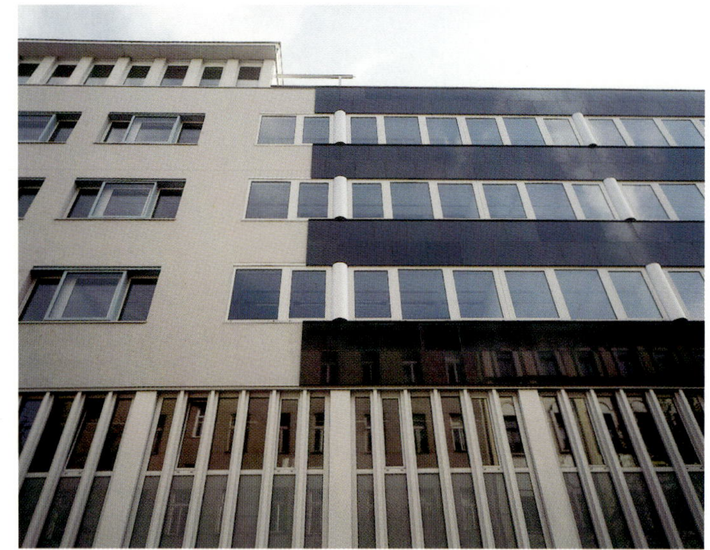

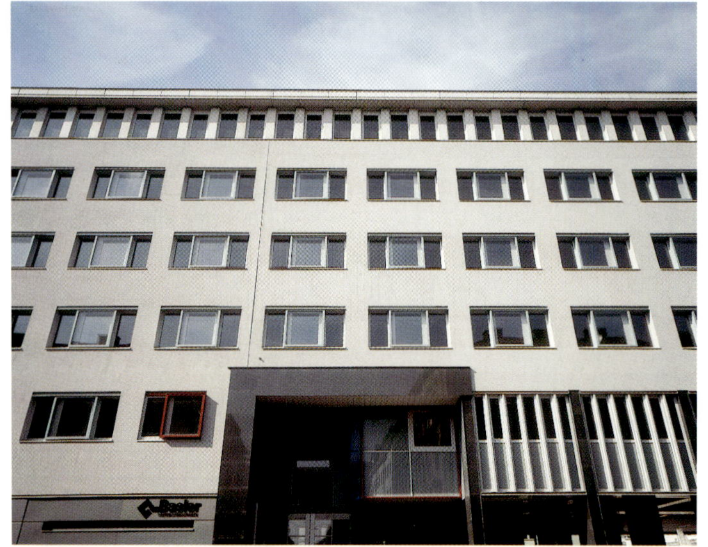

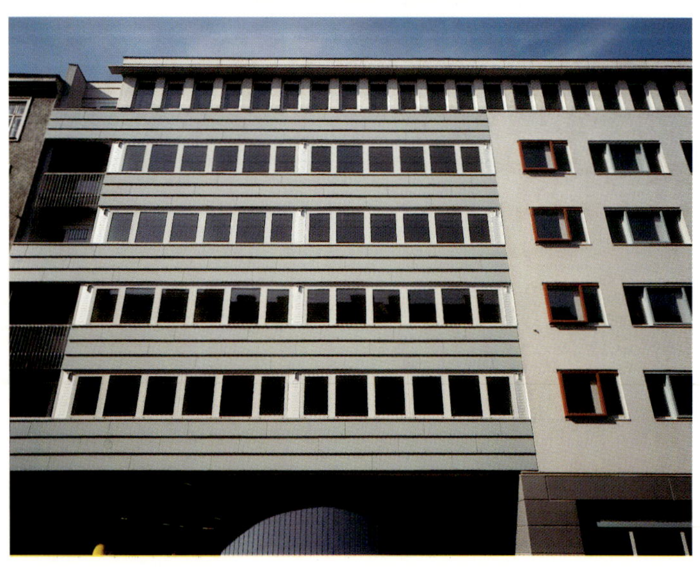

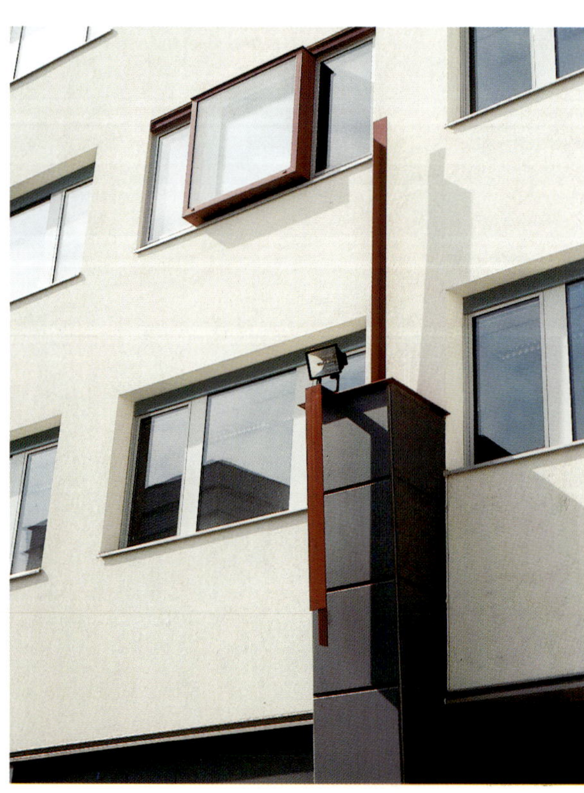

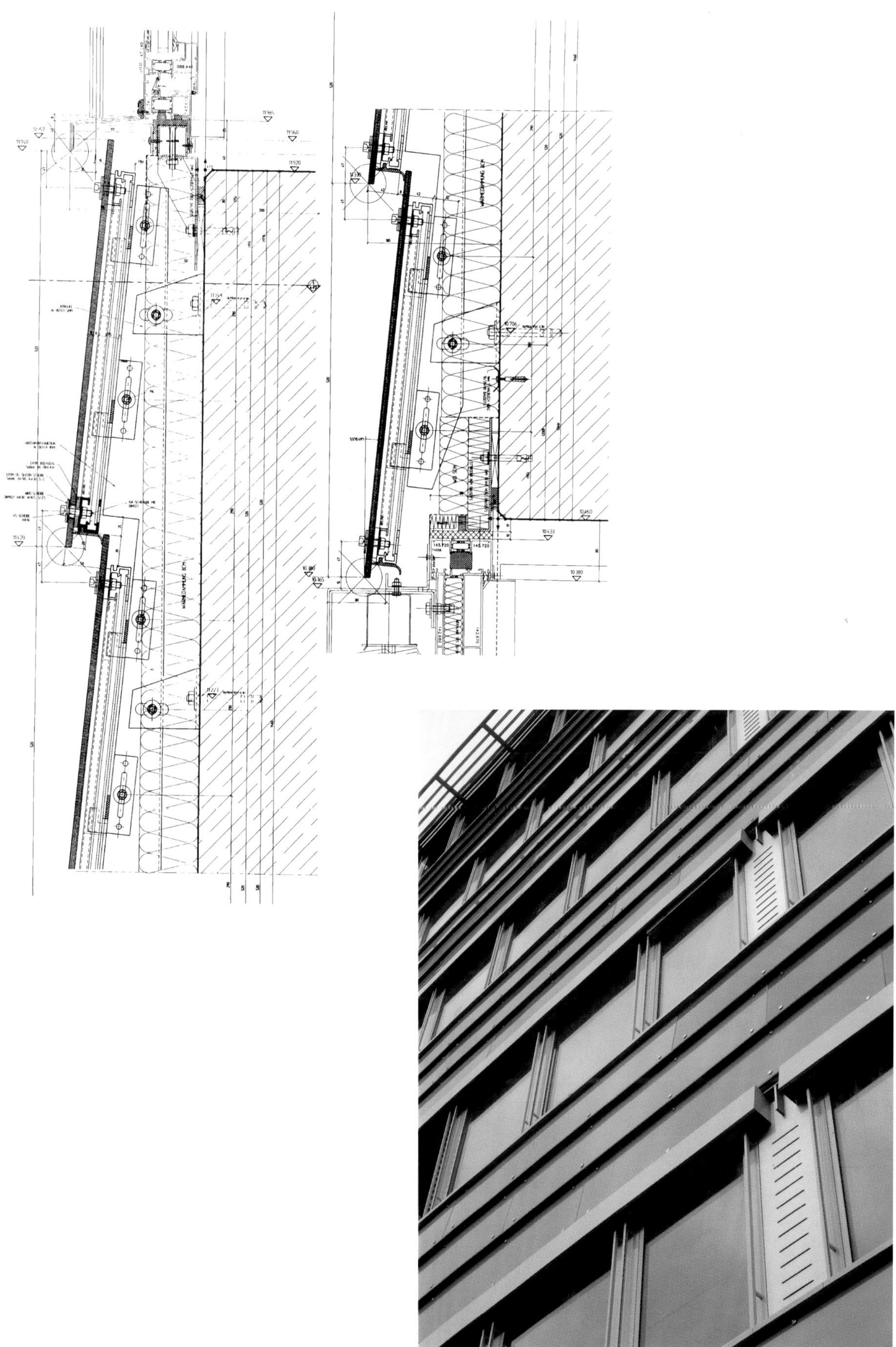

Wien-Liesing / *Vienna-Liesing* 1995

Entwurfskizzen / *Design sketches*

Hinter den Betongebirgen einer Wohnbebauung aus den 70er Jahren, die das ehemalige Dorfzentrum von Liesing markiert, war ein kleines Normalschulhaus aus der Kaiserzeit in ansprechendem Backsteinhistorismus übrig geblieben. Sportanlagen und Villengärten schließen auf der anderen Straßenseite an. Hier stehen nun zwei neue, terrassenförmig zurückgestufte Klassentrakte, verbunden durch das Gelenk einer großen verglasten Halle und gehalten durch ein hohes, scheibenförmig-querstehendes Ateliergebäude für die musische Bildung. Zum Altbau herüber spannt sich ein stählerner Fachwerksteg mit verglastem Gang. Achtungsvoll stützt sich das Haupttragwerk mit einem Pfeiler auf dem Gehsteig ab, so daß nurmehr die schlanke Glashülle bis zum Altbau vordringt. Orthogonal zum Steg verläuft im Neubaukomplex die innere Erschließung, welche die Eingangshalle ebenfalls als Brücke, in Form einer abgehängten Konstruktion durchquert. Podrecca apostrophiert sie als feminin, im Gegensatz zur ersten, die er als maskulin bezeichnet. Im Eingangshof vor der Halle konnten drei eindrucksvolle Bäume erhalten werden, die als Vertikalelemente zu Steg und Ateliergebäude in Beziehung treten. Das Verhältnis zur Natur wird noch auf anderen Ebenen gesucht, sei dies von der Halle zu den Bäumen, von den Klassenzimmern zu den davor liegenden immergrün bepflanzten Terrassen oder mit der subtilen Farbgebung, bei der das Blattgrün im Sommer- und im Winterzustand, einmal moosfarben, einmal gelblich, als Vorlage diente. Beide Farbtöne harmonieren zu allen Tages- und Jahreszeiten mit der belebten Natur vor den Schulzimmerfenstern. Der Entwurf zeichnet sich durch eine affirmative Haltung aus. Er integriert Altbau und Baumbestand und nützt deren Alterswert optimal aus, schafft aber dennoch Raum für den eigenständigen Neubau, der auf seine Weise sogar mit den Bauten der 70er Jahre zu kommunizieren versteht. Damit wird die schwierige städtebauliche Situation in prägnanter Weise klärend geregelt.

A small, normal school building dating back to the emperor's times and constructed in an attractive historic brick style was left over behind the concrete mountains of a housing development from the '70s, marking the former village center of Liesing. Sports complexes and villa gardens adjoin on the other side of the street. Now there are two new classroom blocks, terrace-like and set back. They are connected by an articulation of a large glassed-in hall and supported by a diagonally placed high, disc-like studio building for art education. A steel bridge with a glassed-in hallway stretches towards the old building. Respectfully, the principal bearing structure supports itself with a column on the walkway. Thus, only the slender glass shell reaches to the old building. Perpendicular to the bridge runs the interior development in the new building complex which also crosses the entrance lobby as a bridge in the form of a suspended construction. Podrecca describes it as being "feminine", contrary to the first one, which he thinks masculine. In the entrance yard in front of the hall, three impressive trees are preserved and enter into a relationship with the bridge and the studio building as vertical elements. The relationship with nature is striven for on other levels, too: from the hallway to the trees, from the classrooms to the evergreen-planted terraces in front; or with the subtle color-coding, for which the green of the leaves during summer and winter, i. e., moss green and a yellowish-green, served as a palate. Both shades enter into a harmony with the lively nature in front of the classroom windows during all times of the day and of the year. The design stands out as an affirmative attitude. It integrates the old building and the trees and uses their value of age optimally. However, it still creates a space for the new independent construction which, in its own way, knows how to communicate with the '70s buildings. The difficult urban situation is thus dealt with in a clarifying and striking way.

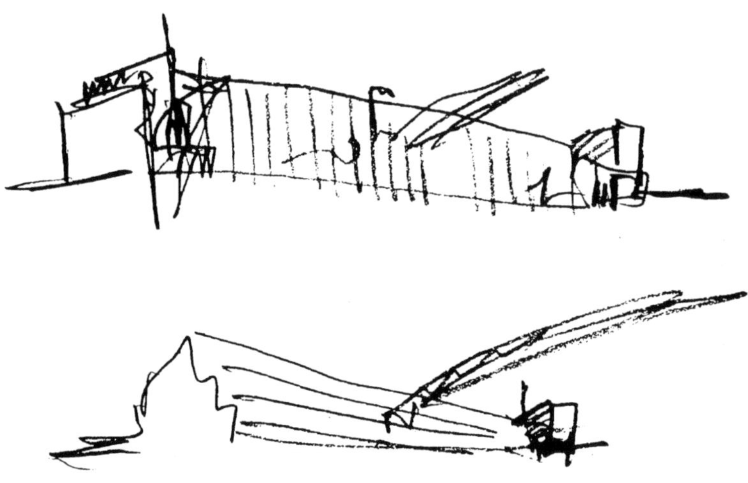

Modellausschnitt / *Model detail*

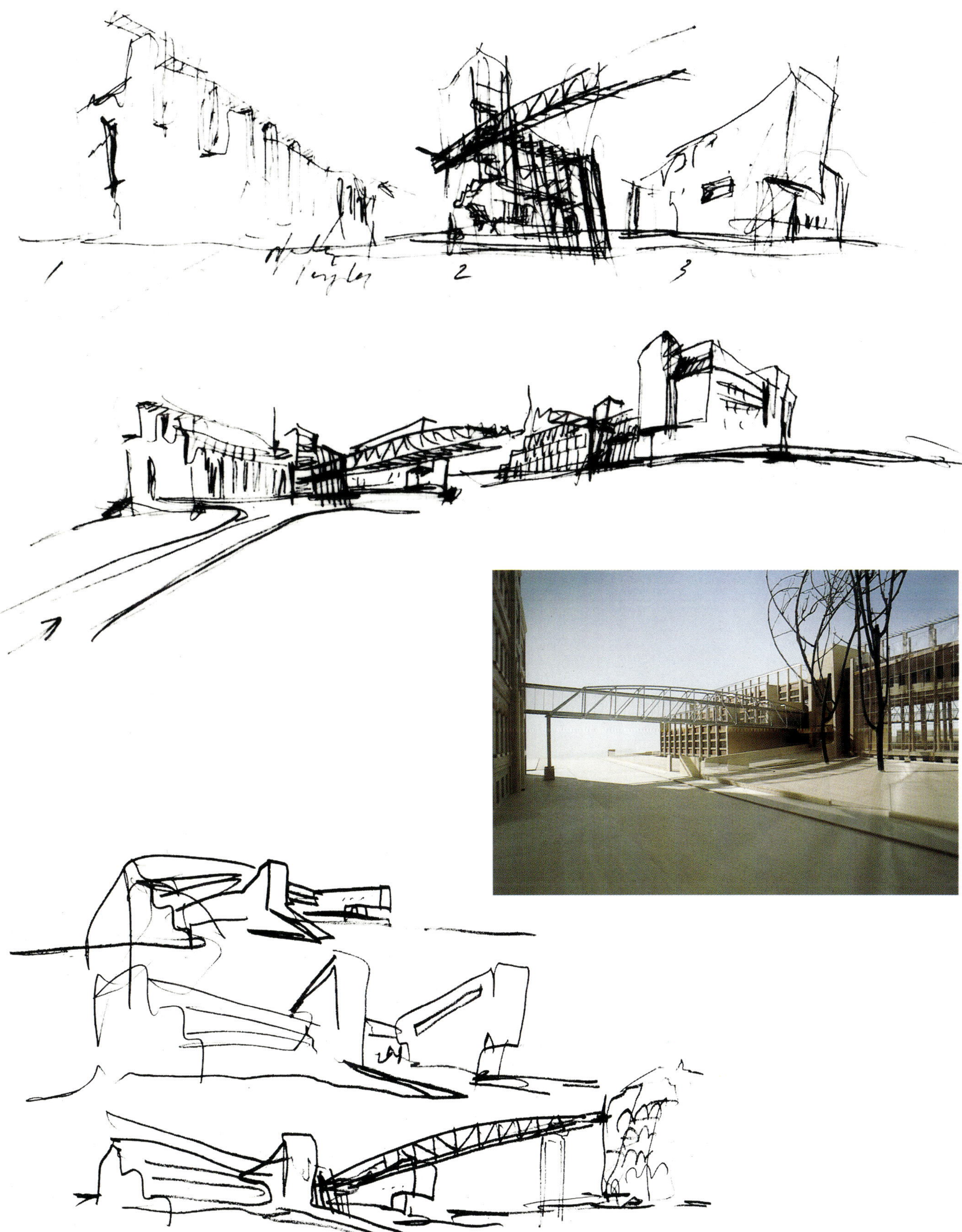

Straßenfassade / *Street facade*

Seitenfassade / *Lateral facade*

Grundriß Erdgeschoß / *Plan of first floor*

Modell / *Model*

Grundriß 2.Obergeschoß / *Plan of third floor*

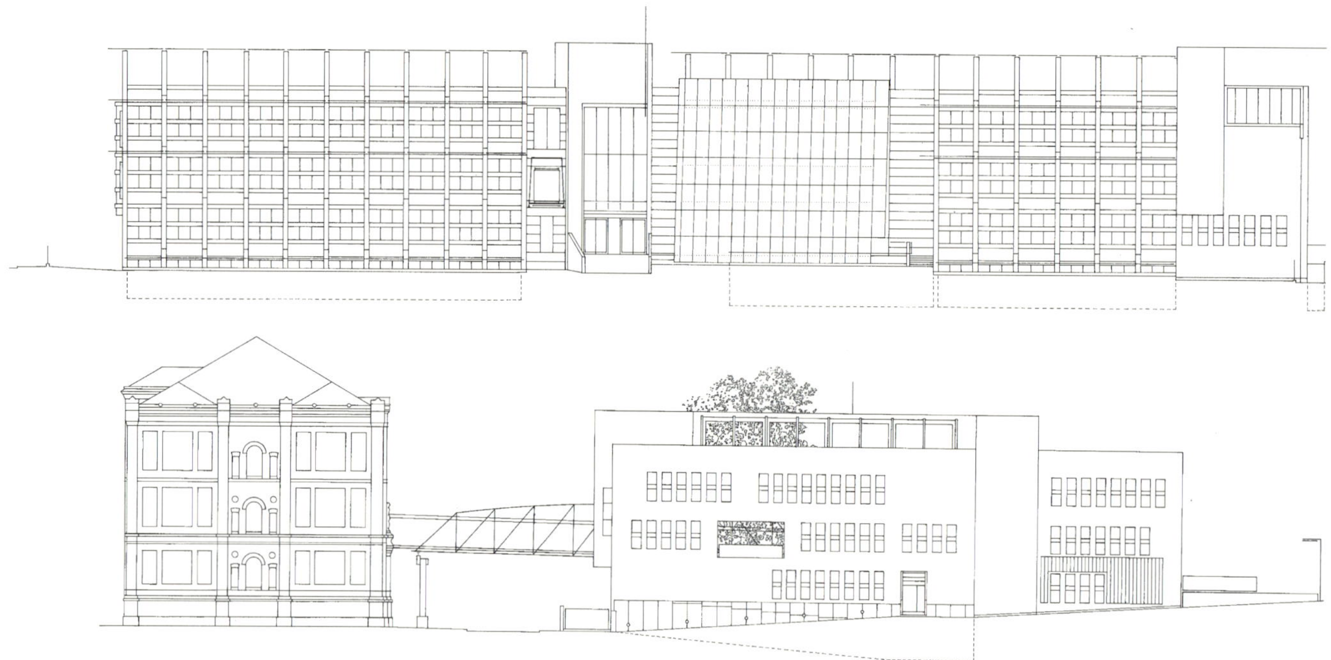

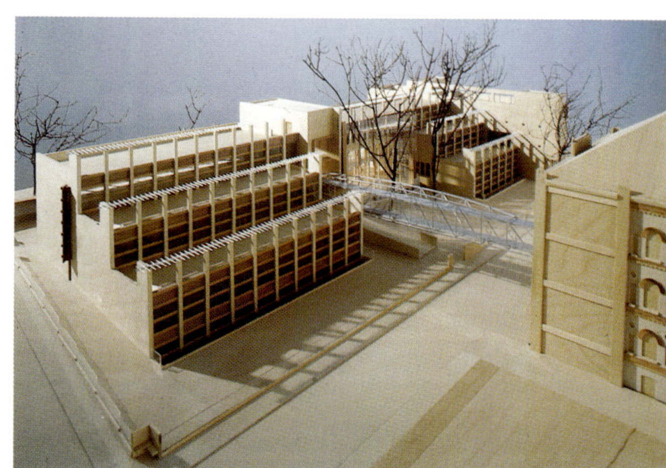

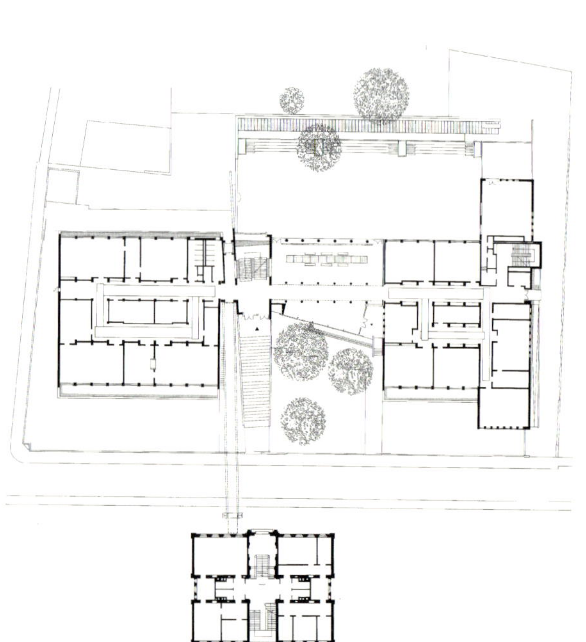

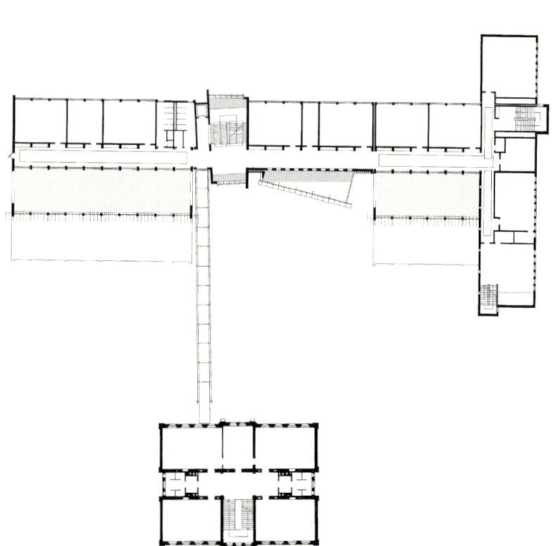

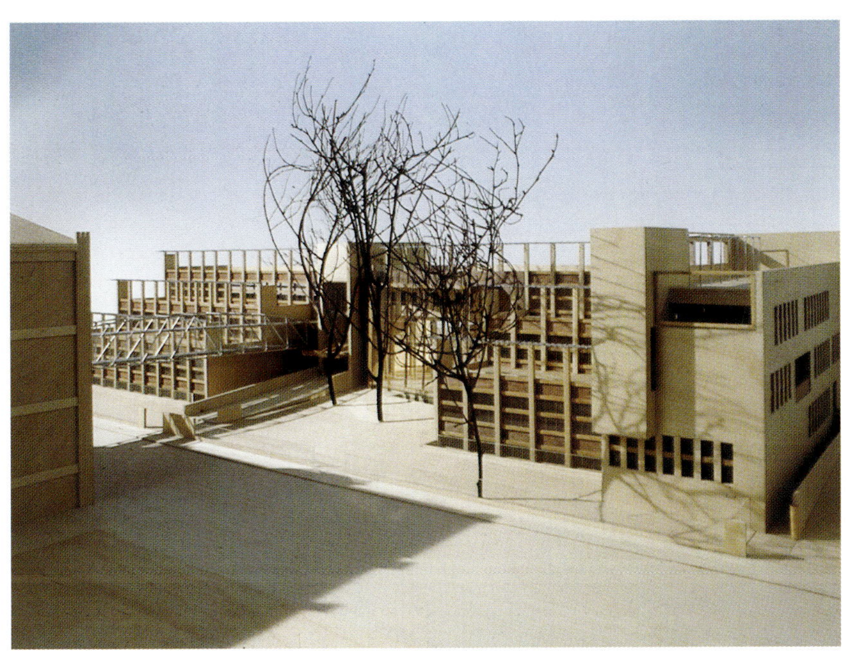

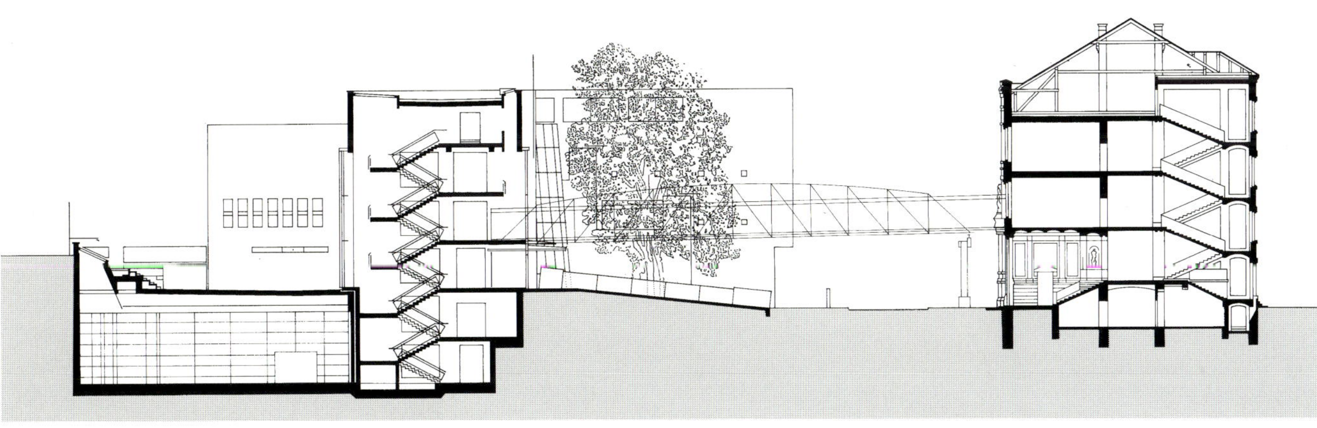

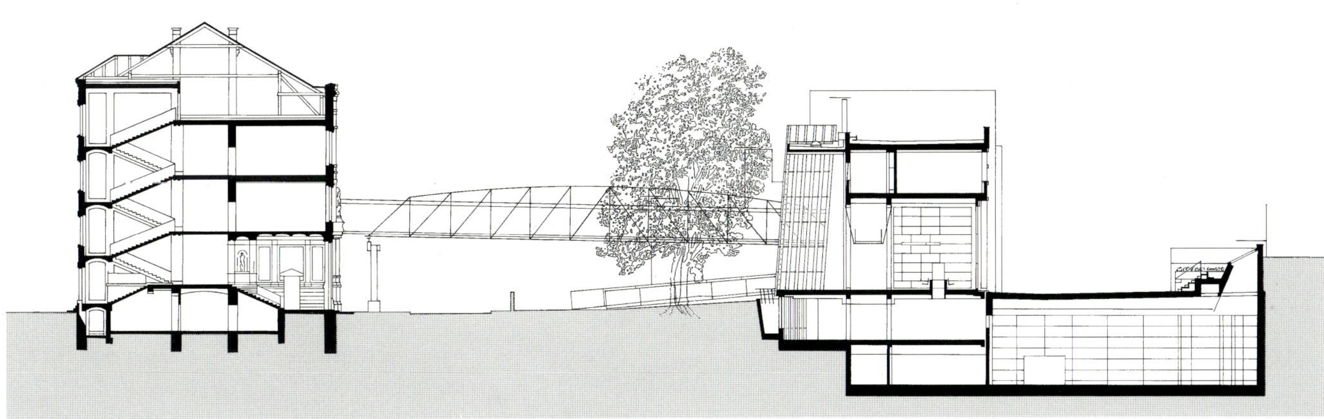

Ansicht Klassentrakt und Brücke / *View of classroom block and bridge*

Lageplan / *Site plan*   Eingang / *Entrance*

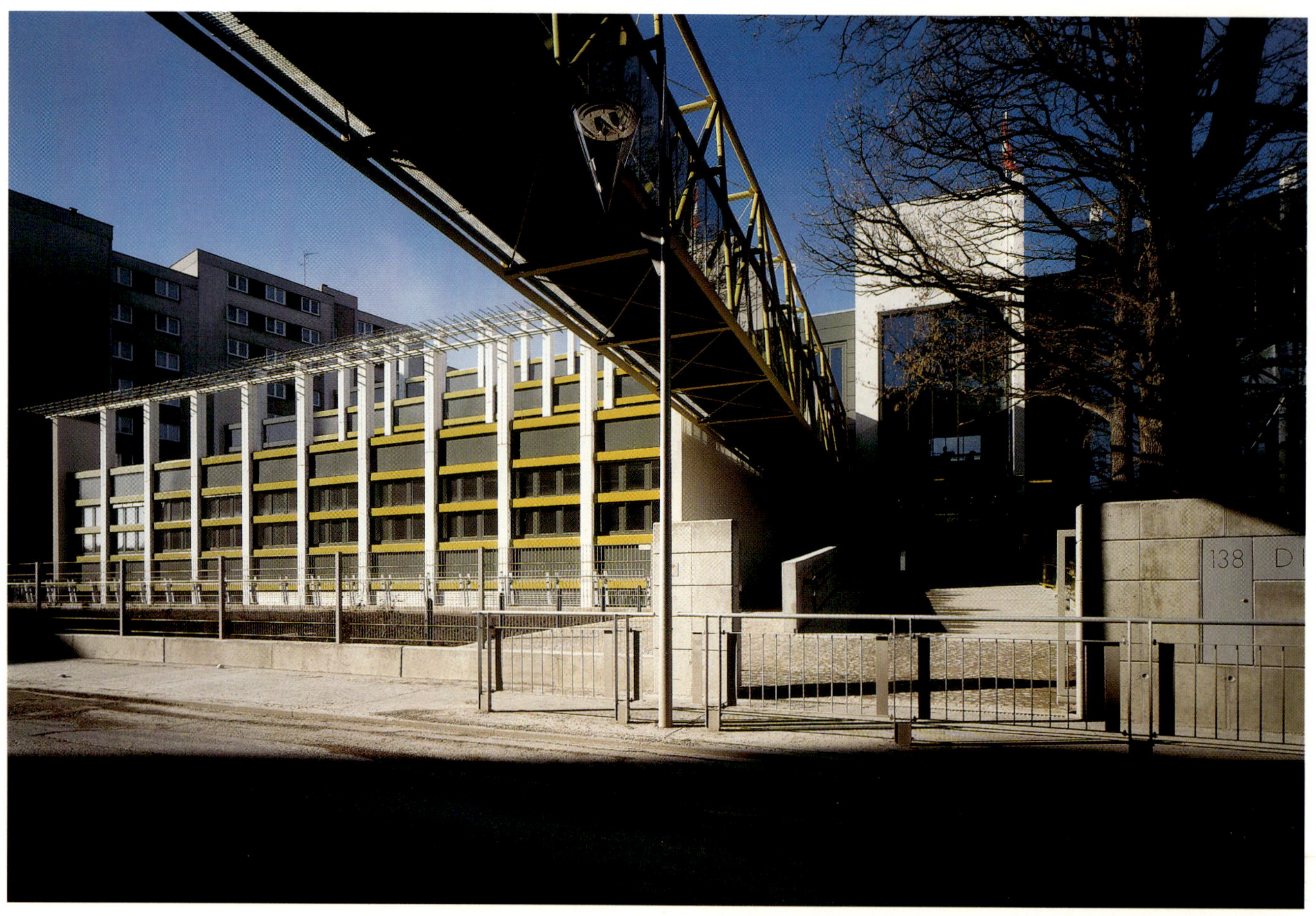

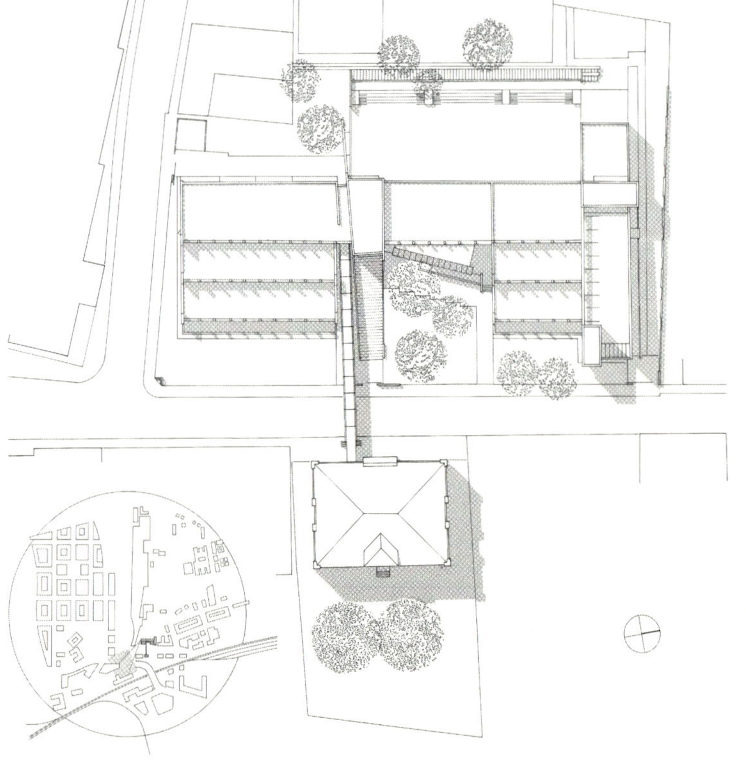

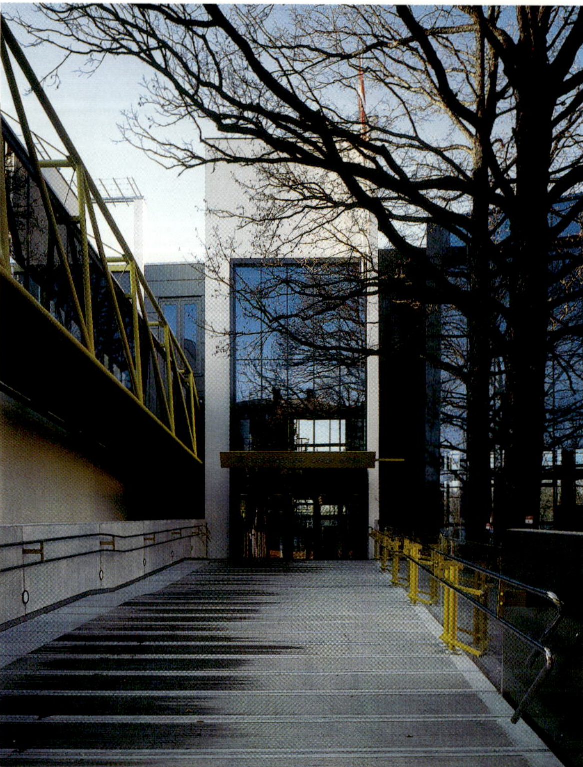

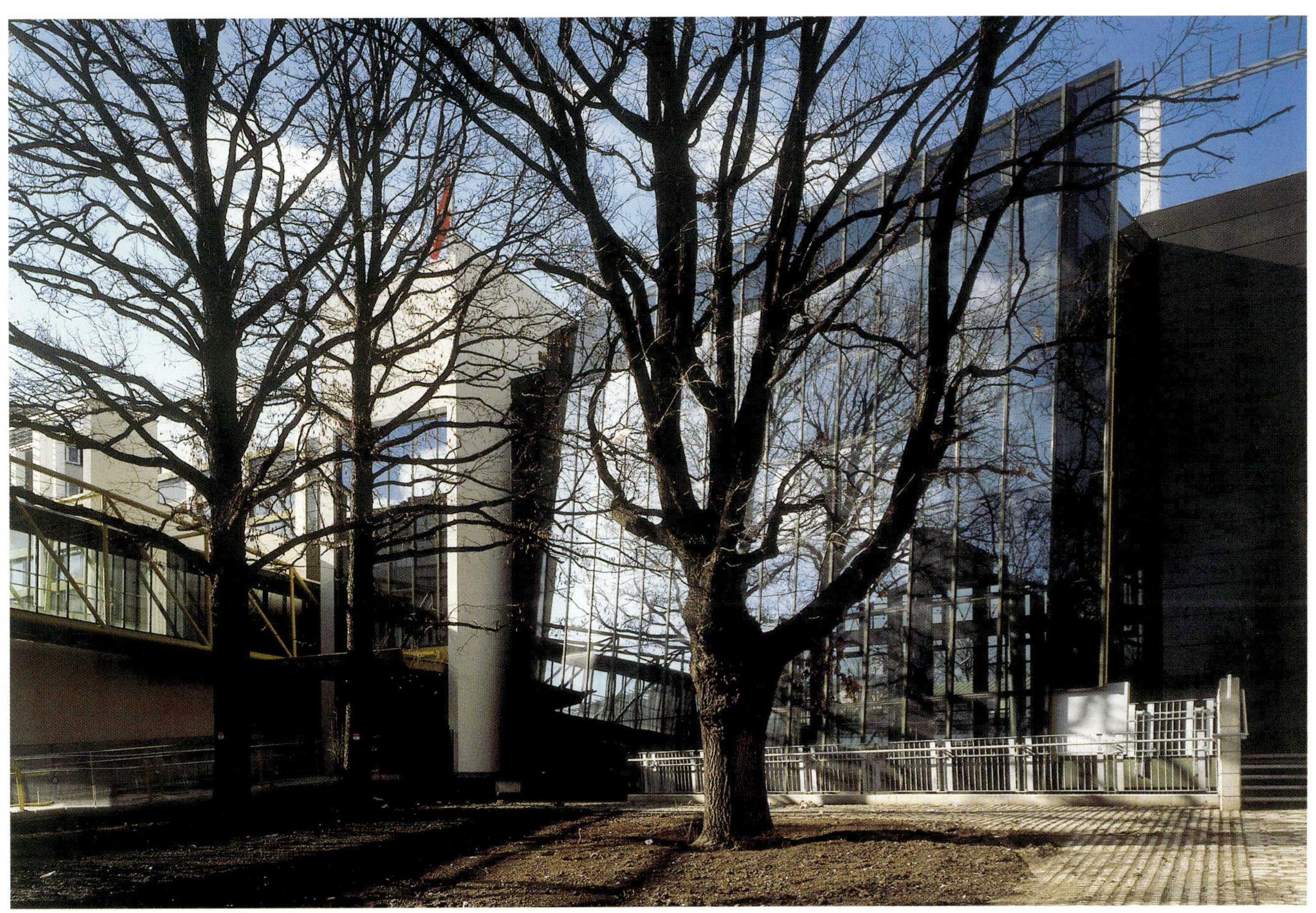

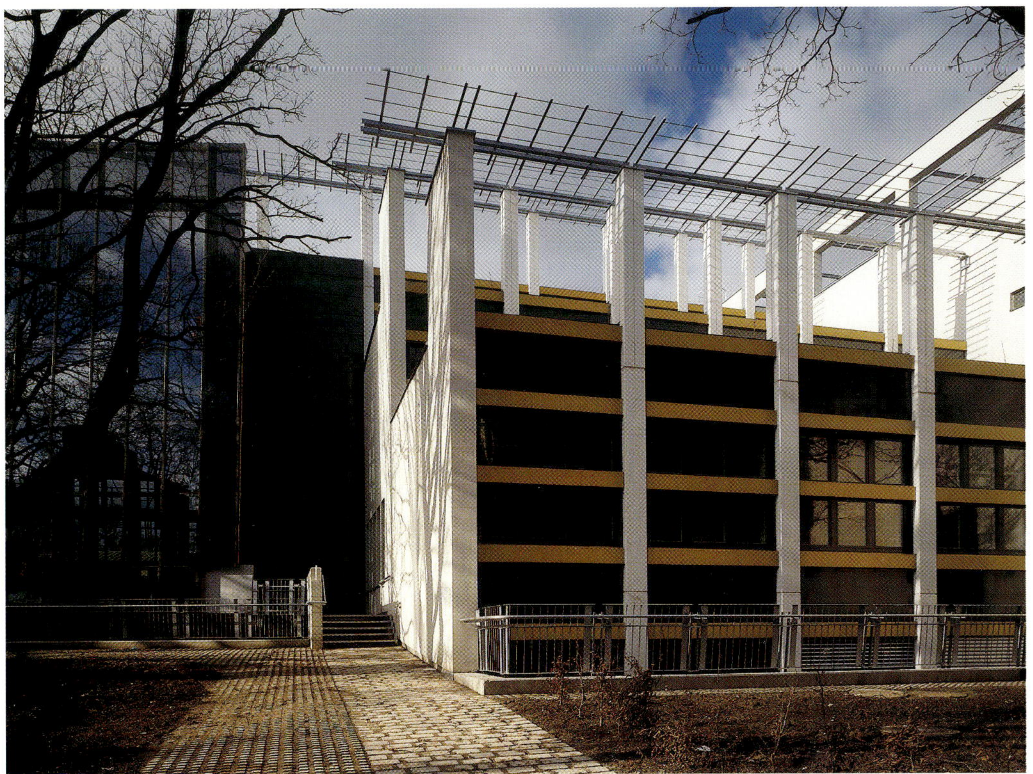

Fassadenausschnitt / *Facade detail*

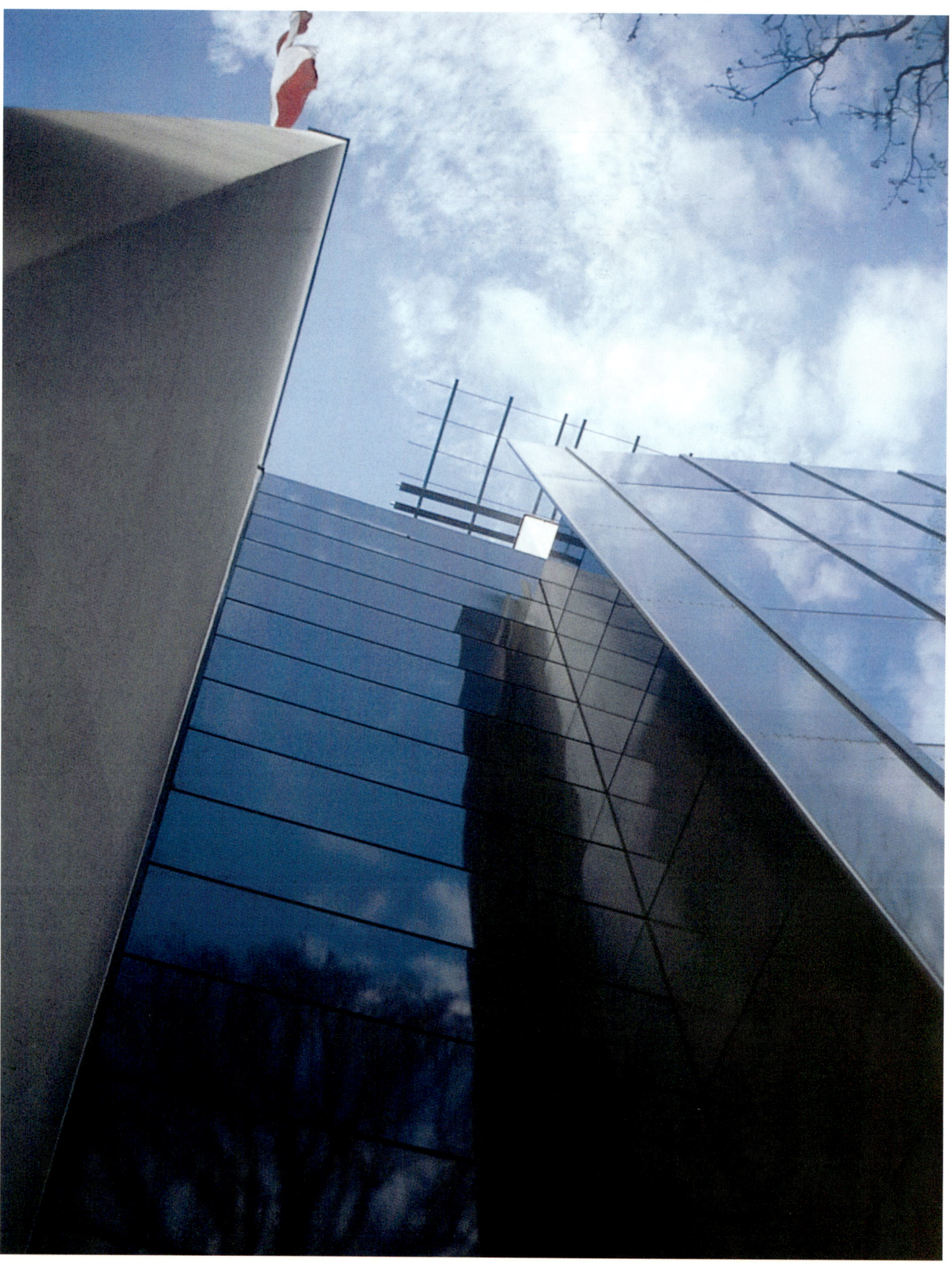

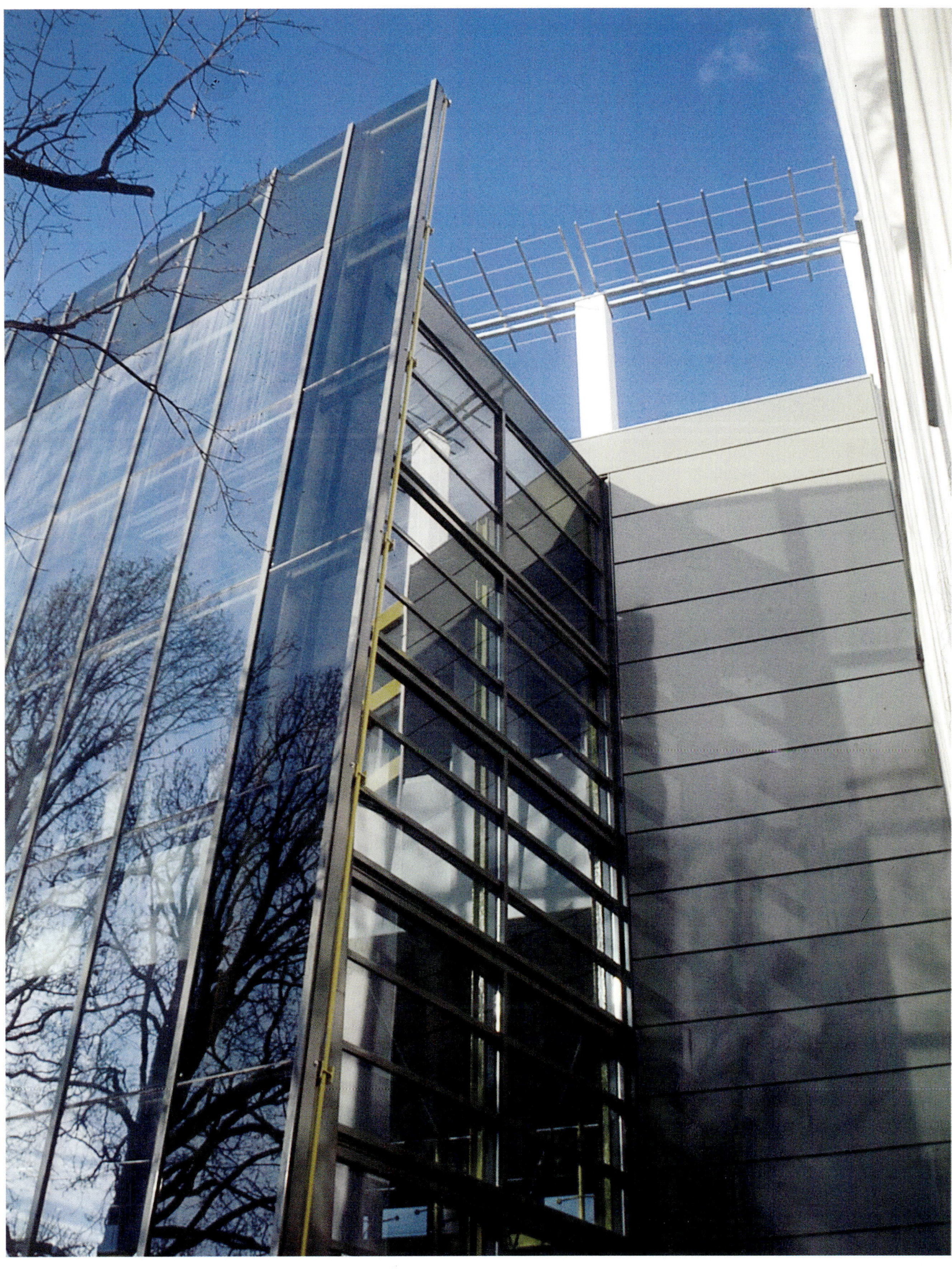

Verbindungsgang / *Connecting passageway*

Brückendetails / *Bridge details*

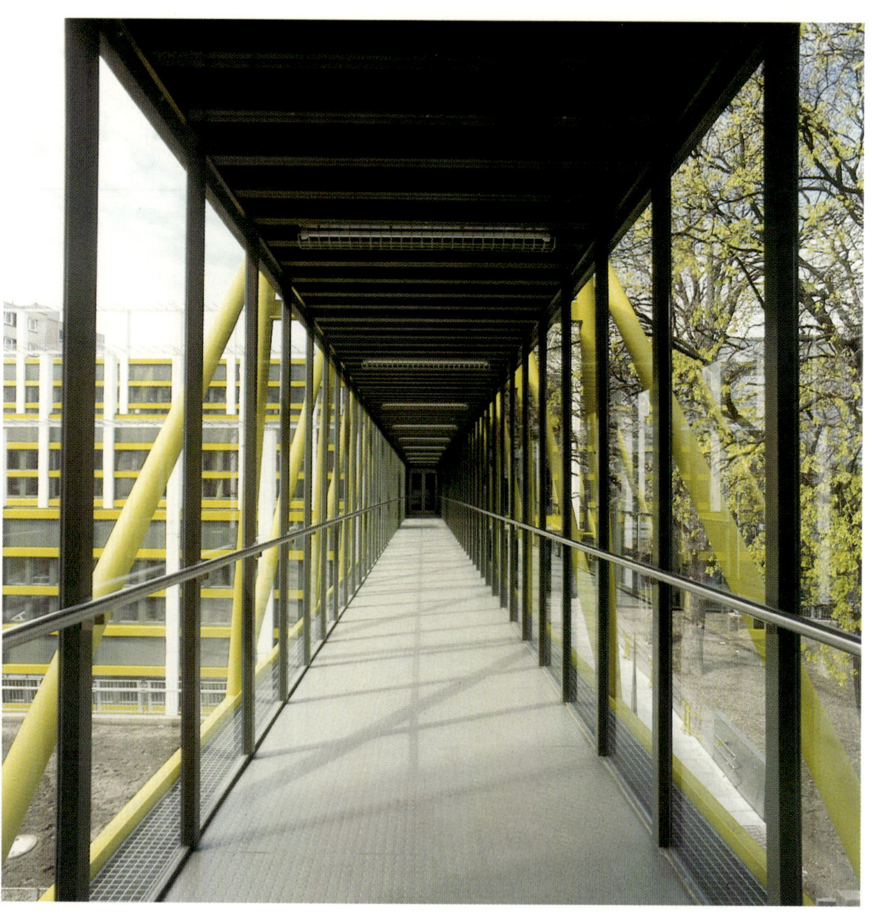

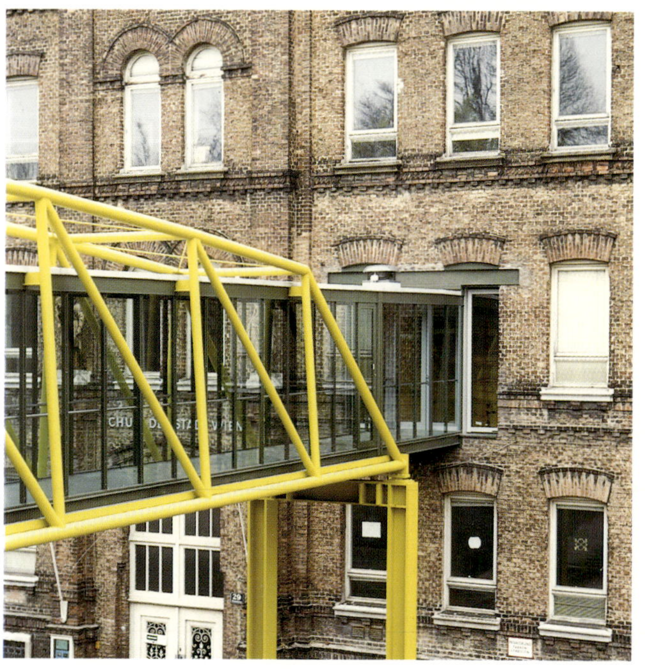

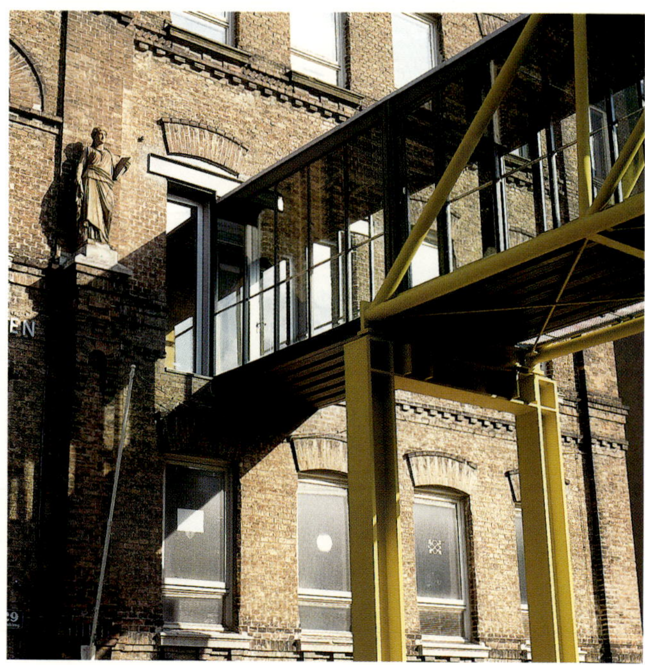

Hängesteg über der Pausenhalle / *Suspending bridge above the commons area*

Speisesaal / *Dining room*

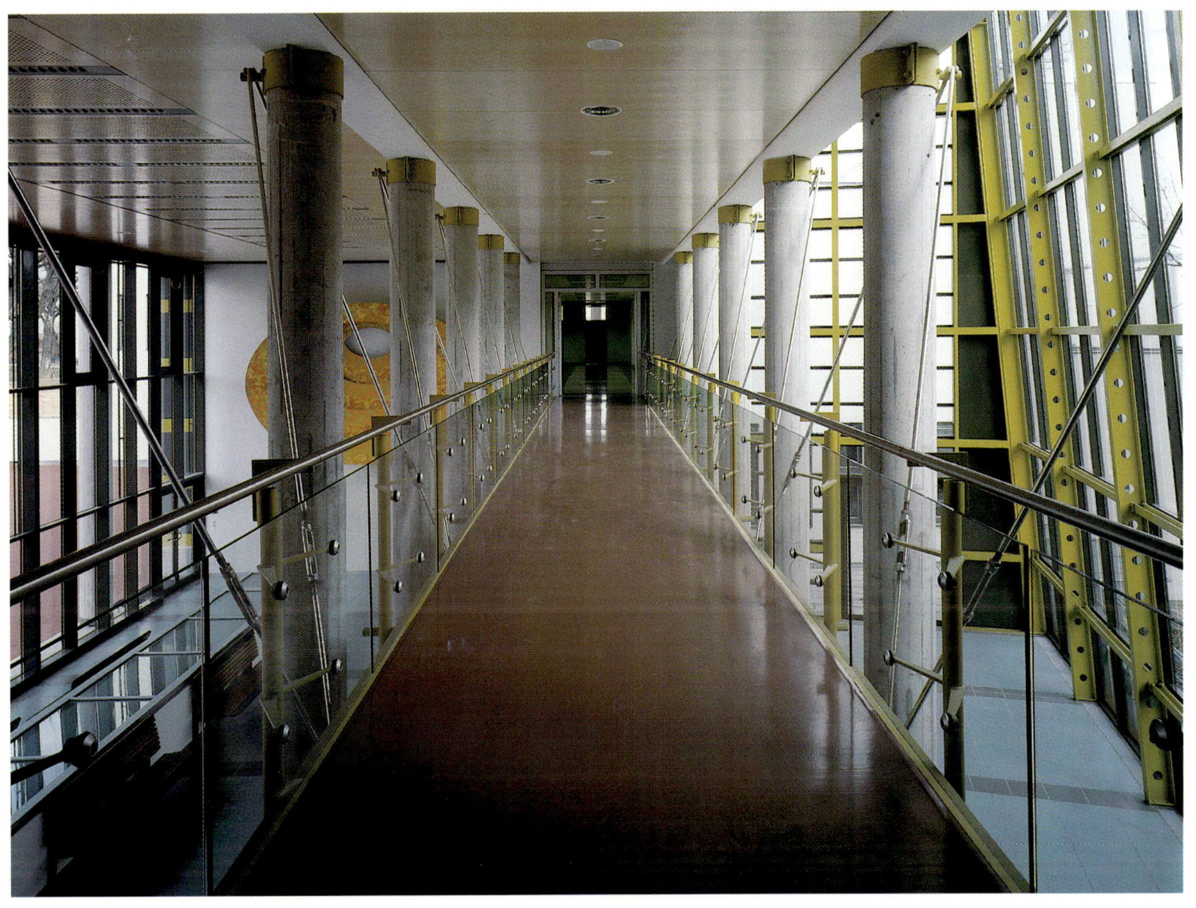

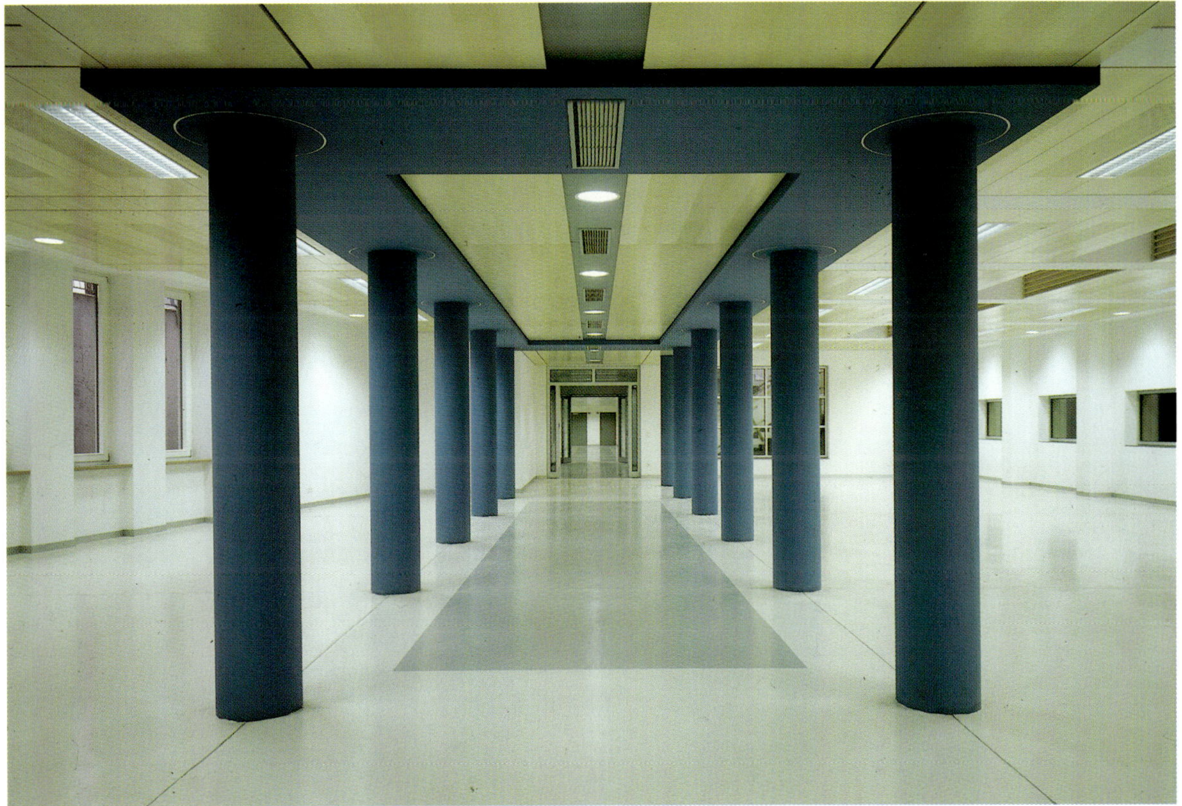

Ansicht Pausenhalle zur Hauptstiege / *View from commons area towards main staircase*

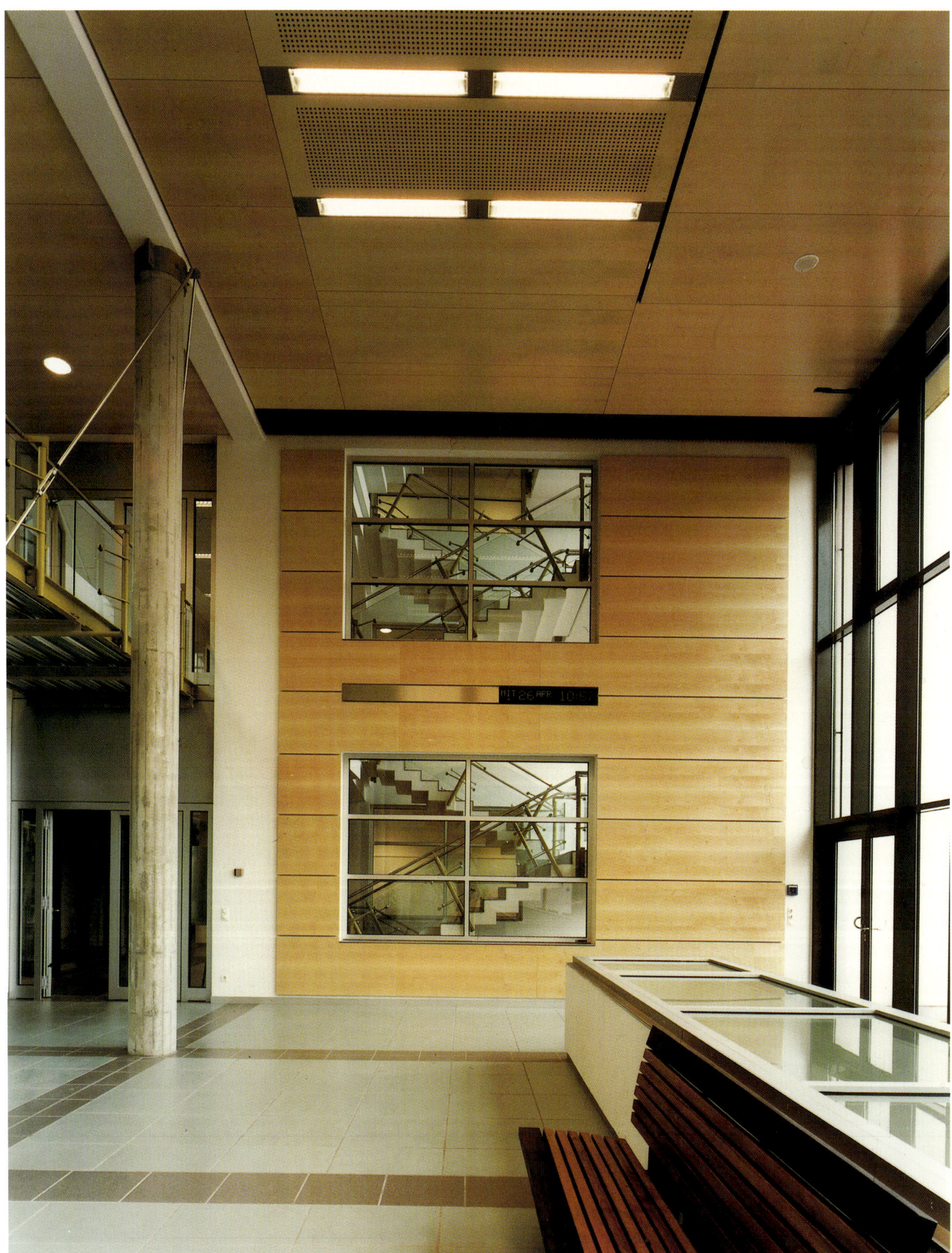

Hauptstiegenhaus / *Main staircase*

Pausenhalle mit Wandrelief von Frantisek Lesák /
Common area with wall relief by Frantisek Lesák

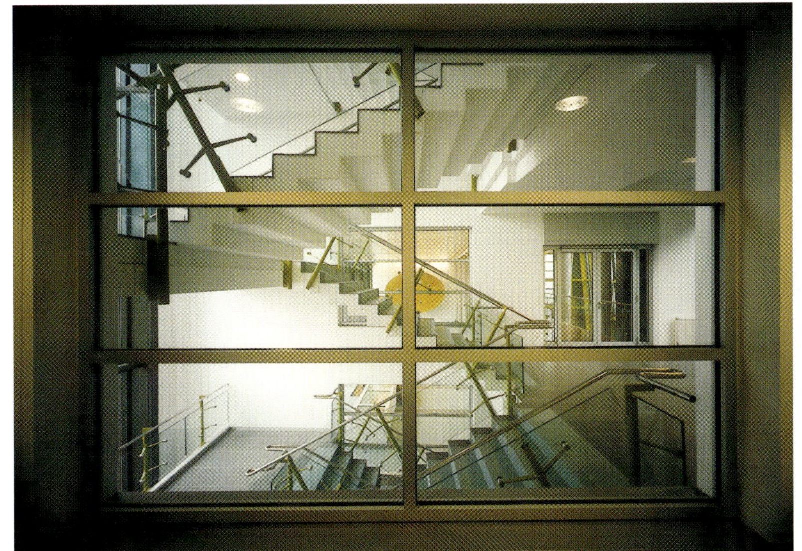

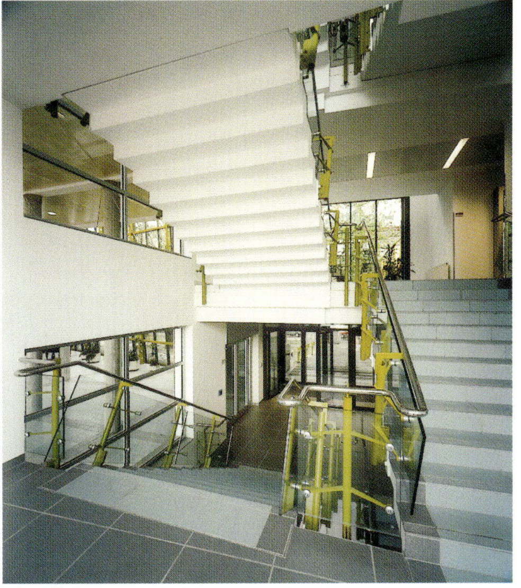

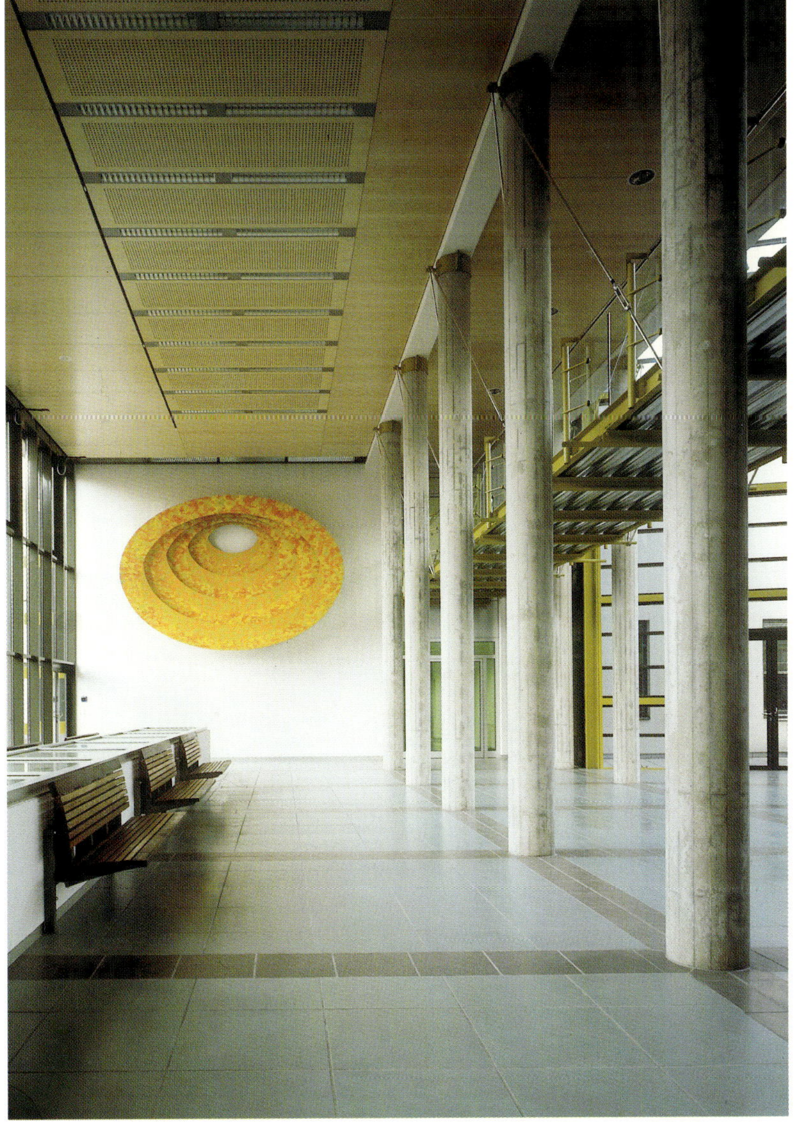

Hängesteg, Detail / *Suspended bridge, detail*

Pausenhalle, Ausschnitte / *Common area, details*

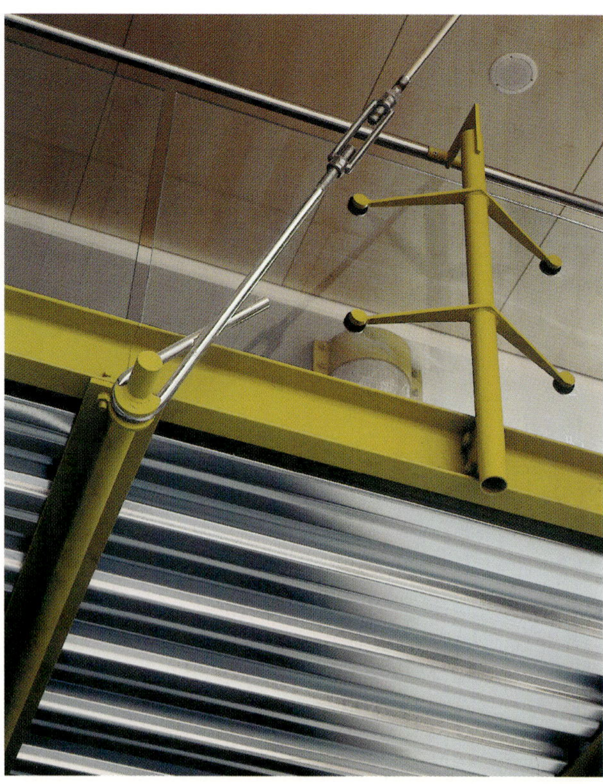

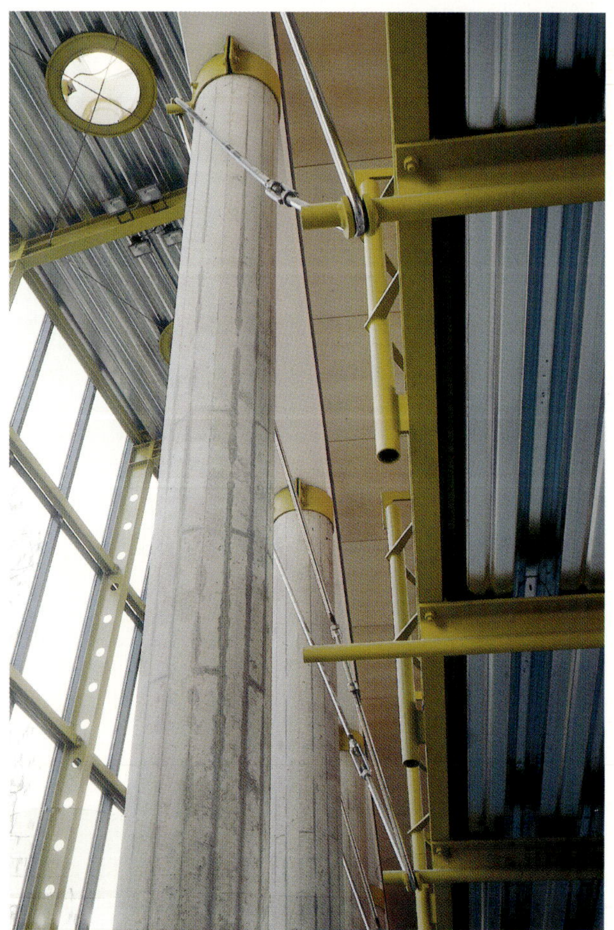

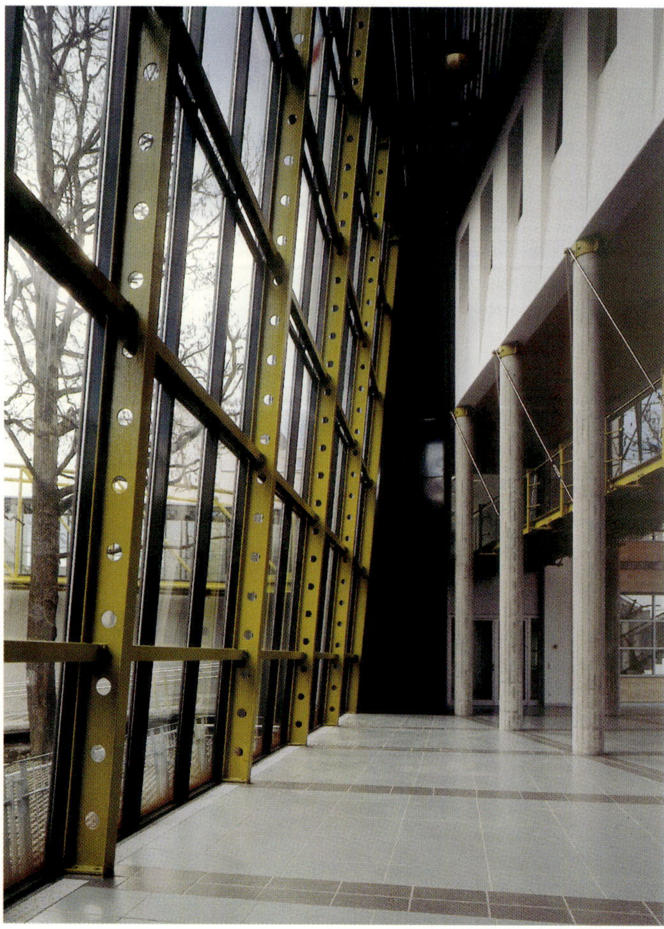

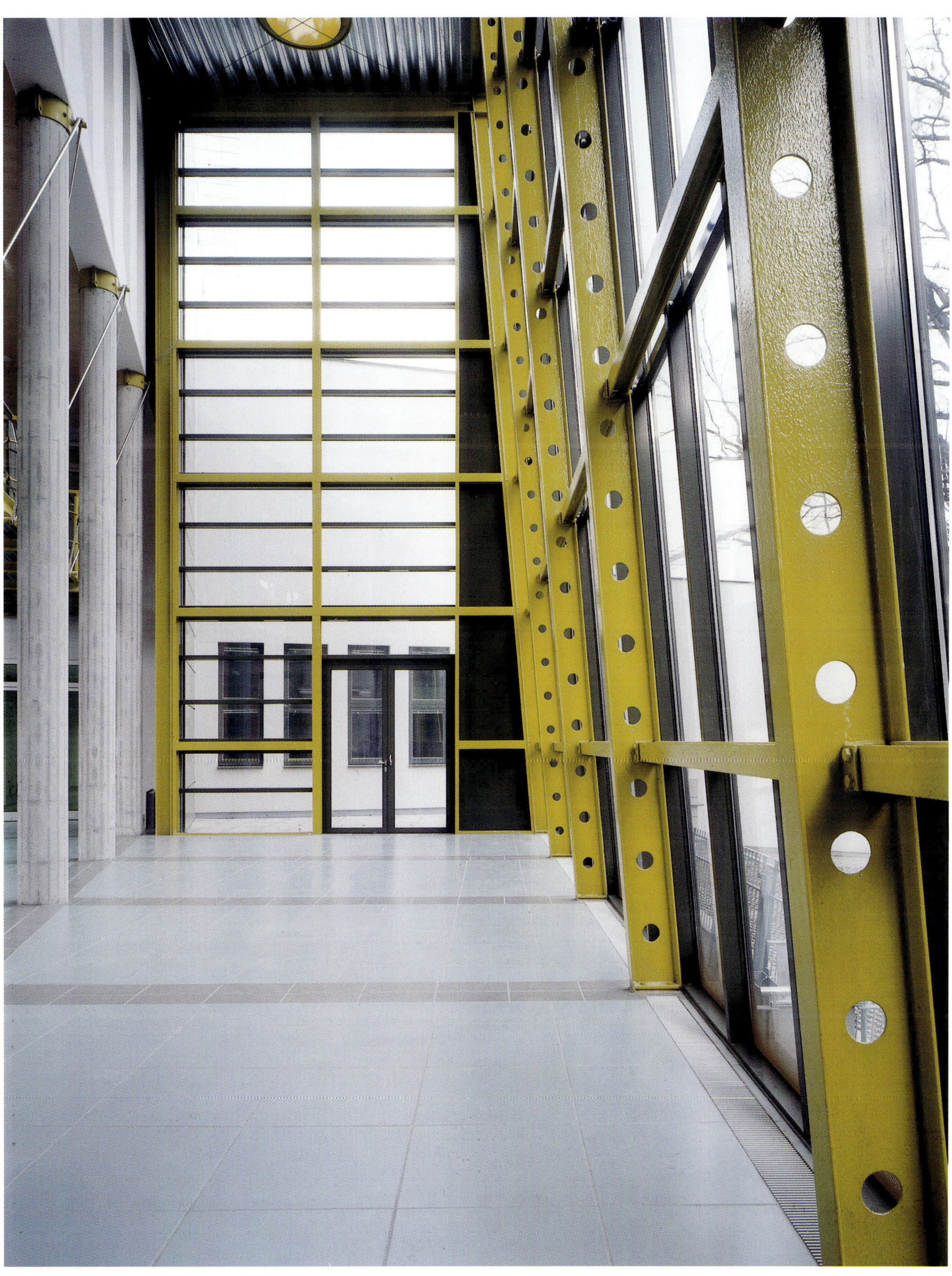

Turnsaal / *Gymnasium*

Bibliothek / *Library*

Atelierklassenzimmer / *Studio classroom*

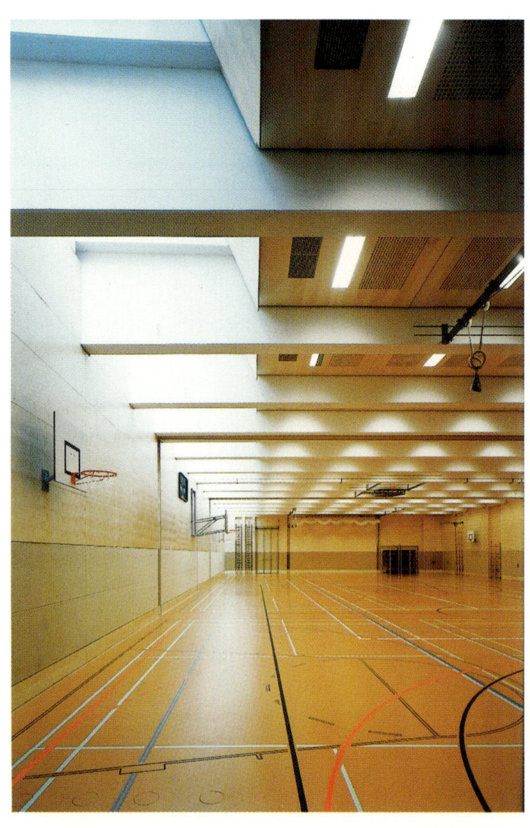

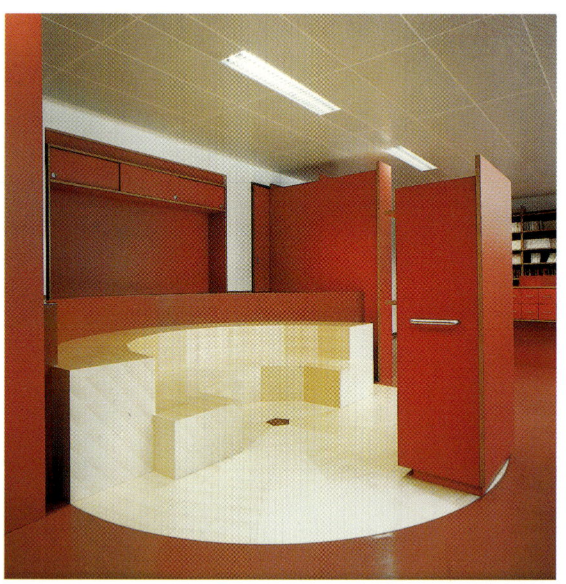

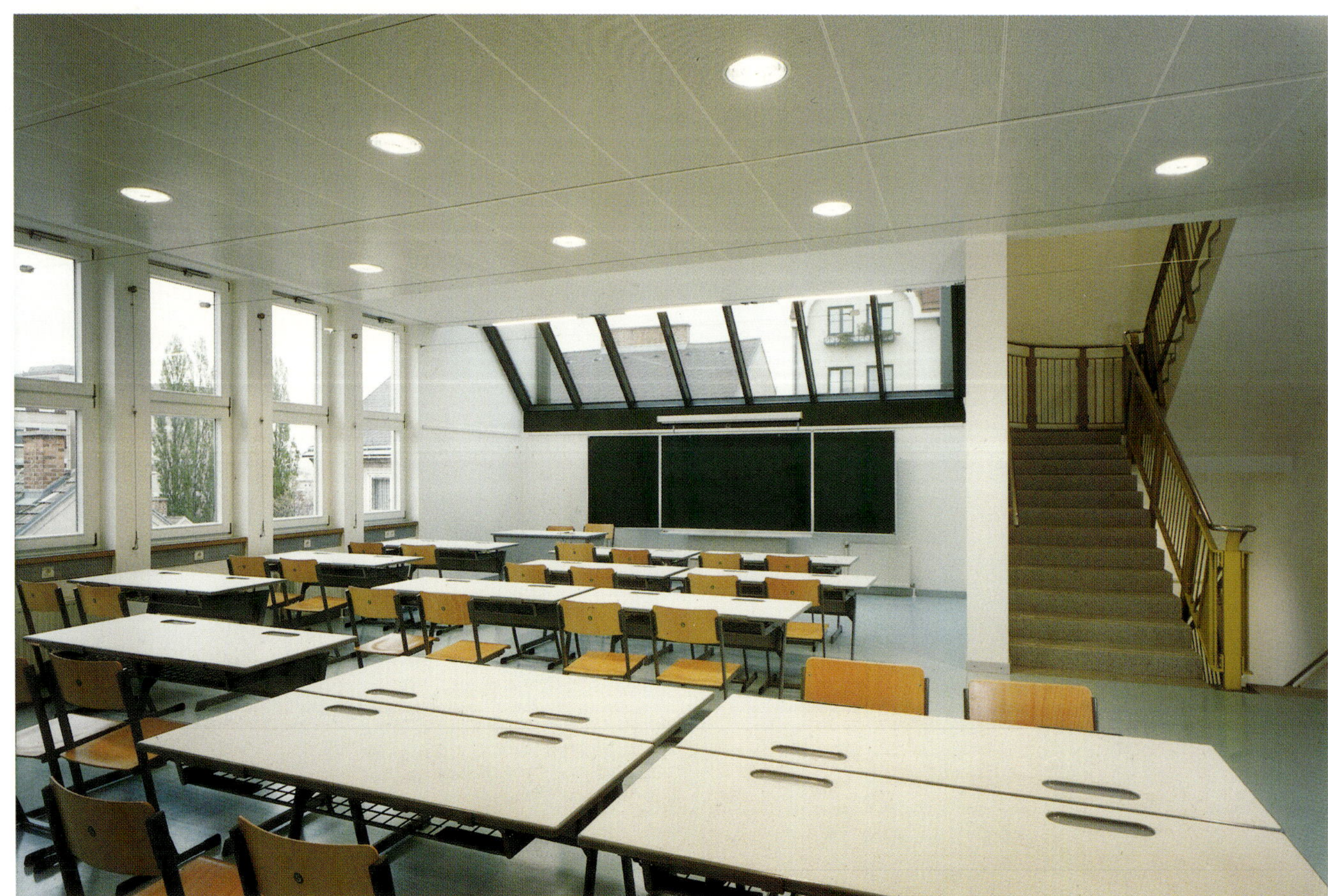

Ateliertrakt / *Studio block*

Ansicht Stiegenhaus / *View of stairway*

Schulhof / *School yard*

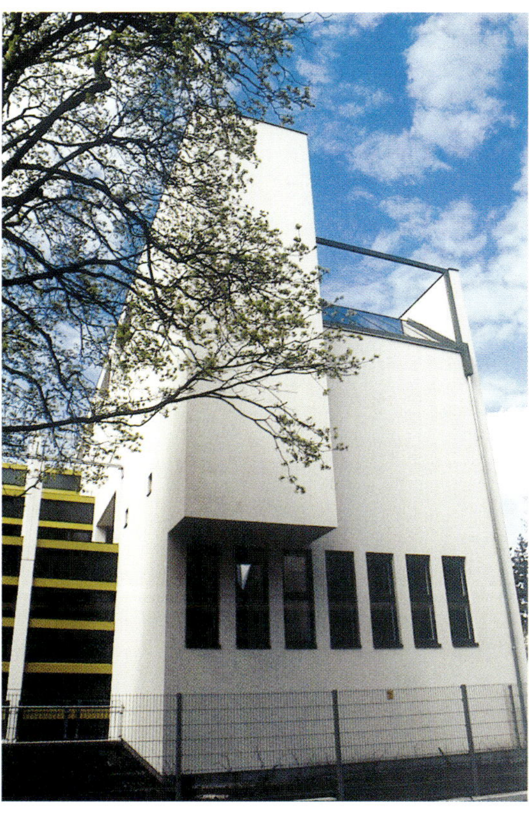

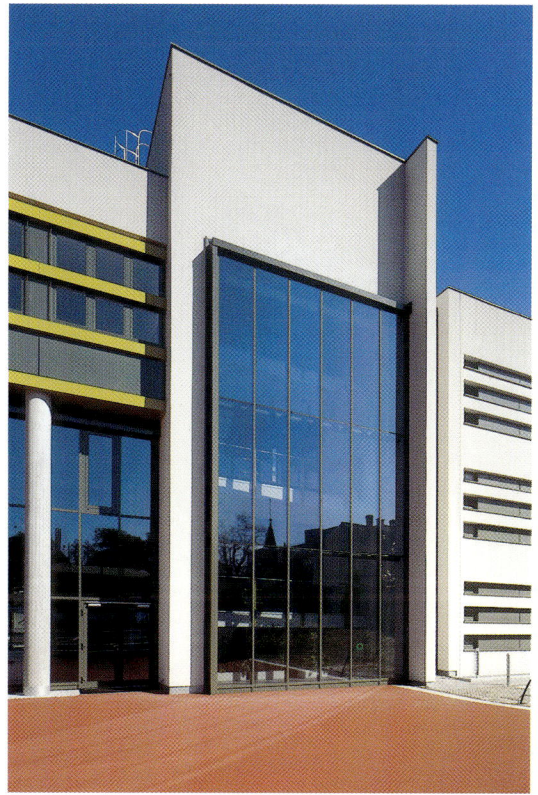

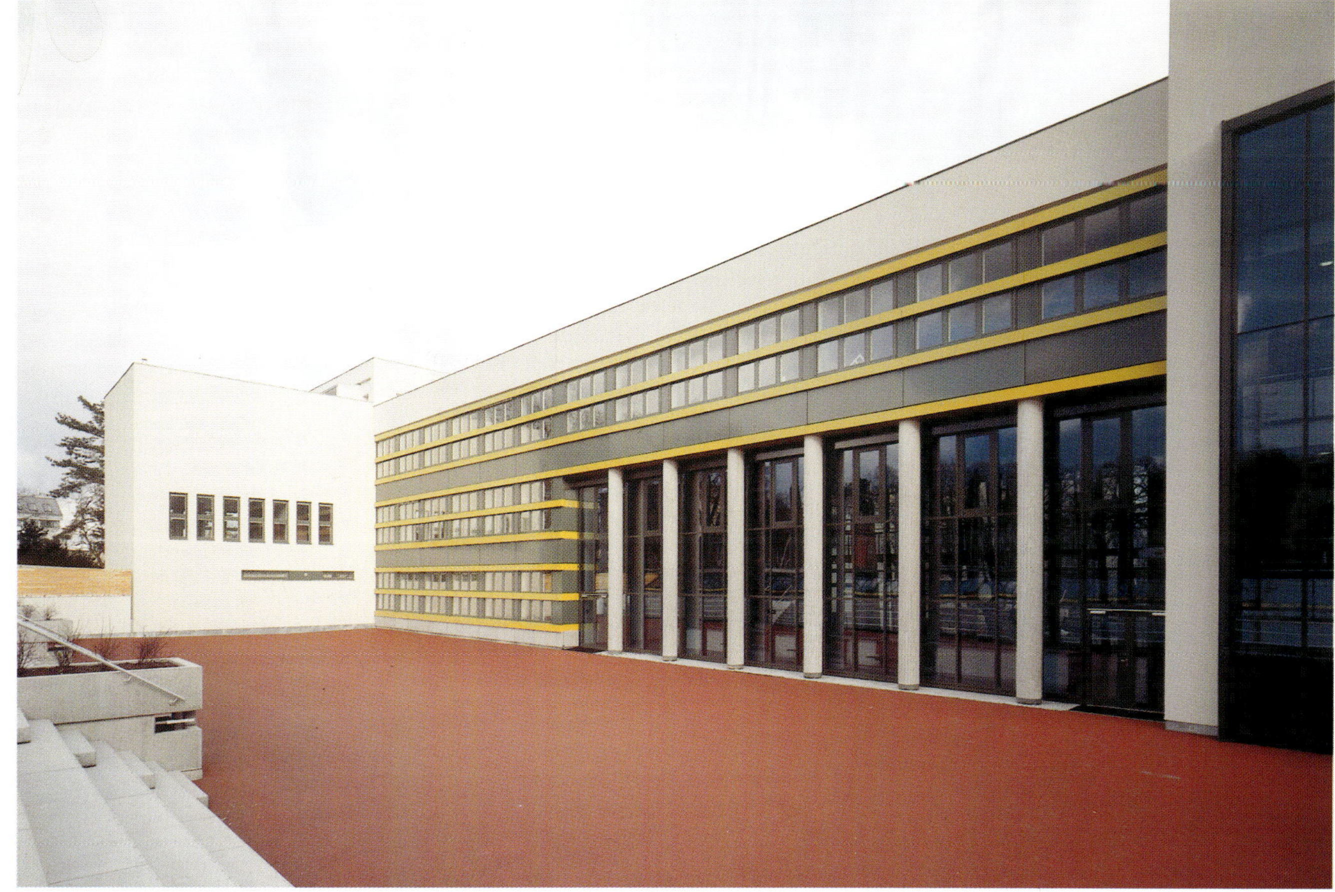

Wien, Wettbewerb / *Vienna, competition* 1992
REMISEBEBAUUNG / *TROLLEY CAR DEPOT* 1995

Luftbild, Nordbahnhofgelände / *Aerial view of north station grounds*

Modell, Studienphase / *Model, study phase*

Lage im weiteren Stadtgebiet /
Location in the larger context of the city

Das ausgedehnte Gelände des Nordbahnhofs und der dahinter liegenden Verschiebegeleise trug als Sperre dazu bei, daß Wien die Beziehung zur Donau bis heute nicht den Möglichkeiten entsprechend entwickeln konnte. Der Nordbahnhof, vor allem für Güterverkehr mit dem Osten gebaut, verlor nach 1945 an Bedeutung. Nach der Öffnung nahm Wien bevölkerungsmäßig wieder zu; das Gelände gilt heute als wichtigstes inneres Stadtentwicklungsgebiet. Das gemeinsam mit Heinz Tesar, dem anderen Preisträger, überarbeitete Projekt bietet Lebensraum für 20.000 Menschen. Auf der ehemaligen Geleisetrasse wird, als Bindeglied zwischen Prater und Augarten, ein langer Grünraum geschaffen, der bis zum Donaukanal und weiter zu Stadtrand und Wienerwald vermittelt. Dahinter wird eine dichte Blockbebauung vorgeschlagen, mit Infrastrukturbauten und Arbeitsplätzen in durchmischter Form. Zwei wesentliche Ordnungselemente, eine diagonal verlaufende, an die Bahntrasse erinnernde Straße und ein großer Platz prägen das Gesamtbild. Mit der Blockbebauung wird ein Bekenntnis zur urban verdichteten Stadt, zum Straßen- und Hofraum ausgesprochen. Die Entwicklung von den Rändern nach innen, in der Art der angrenzenden Quartiere Leopoldstadt und Brigittenau, befürwortet ein Fortschreiben der klassisch-städtischen Lebensweise, wohl wissend, daß das Einwohnen der Neubauquartiere seine Zeit braucht.

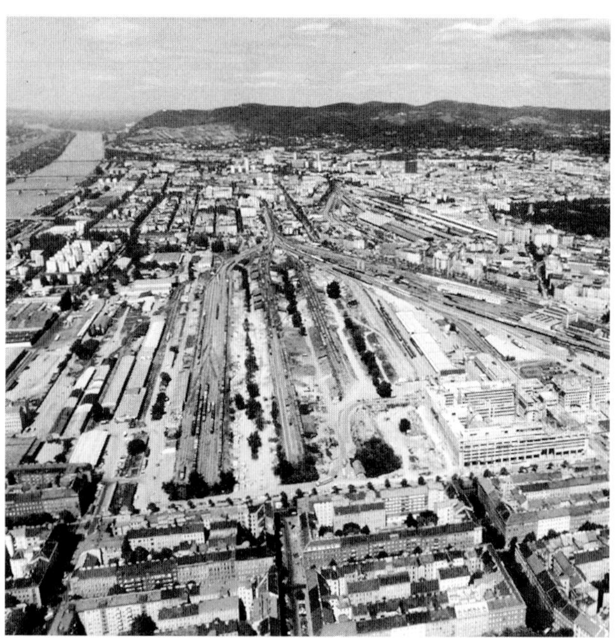

The extensive grounds of the north station and the switching yard beyond them have always been a barrier and have had the effect that, up to this day, Vienna could not develop the relationship with the Danube according to the existing possibilities. The north station lost its importance after 1945 since, above all, it served for the trafficking of goods with the East. After the opening, Vienna's population increased again and today the grounds are considered the most important inner city development area. The project, worked out together with Heinz Tesar, the other award winner, offers living space for 20.000 people. Along the former railroad line a long park will be created serving as a link between the Prater and Augarten, mediating further on to the Danube channel, the city borders, and the Vienna forest. Behind that, a dense block development is being suggested with infrastructure buildings and working places in a mixed format. Two essential elements of order mark the entire picture: a diagonal road reminiscent of the railroad line, and a large square. With the block development, the charcteristics of the dense urban city, the street areas, and the courtyard space are being acknowledged. The development from the edges to the inside in the style of the adjoining quarters, Leopoldstadt and Brigittenau, advocates a continuation of the classic urban lifestyle while knowing full well that the integration and acceptance of the new quarters will require some time.

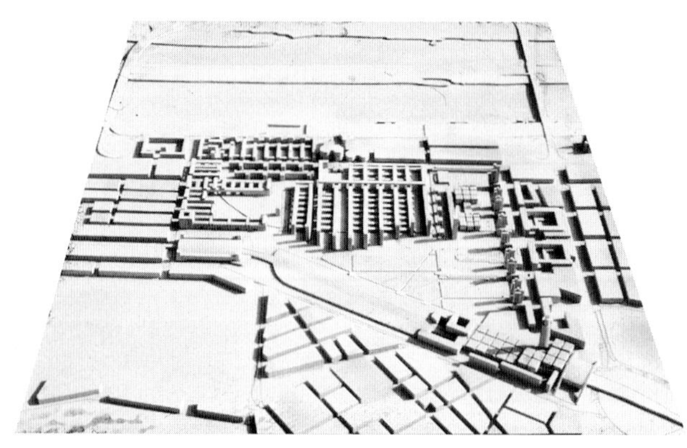

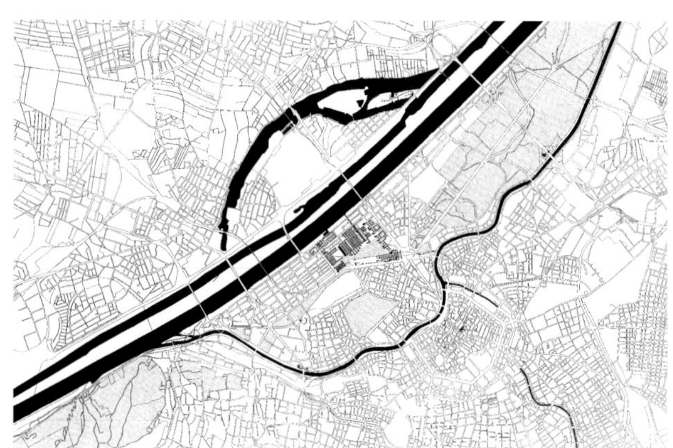

Flugperspektive Wettbewerbsprojekt /
Aerial perspective of competition project

Lage im engeren Stadtgebiet /
Location in denser city area

Axonometrie / *Axonometric projection*

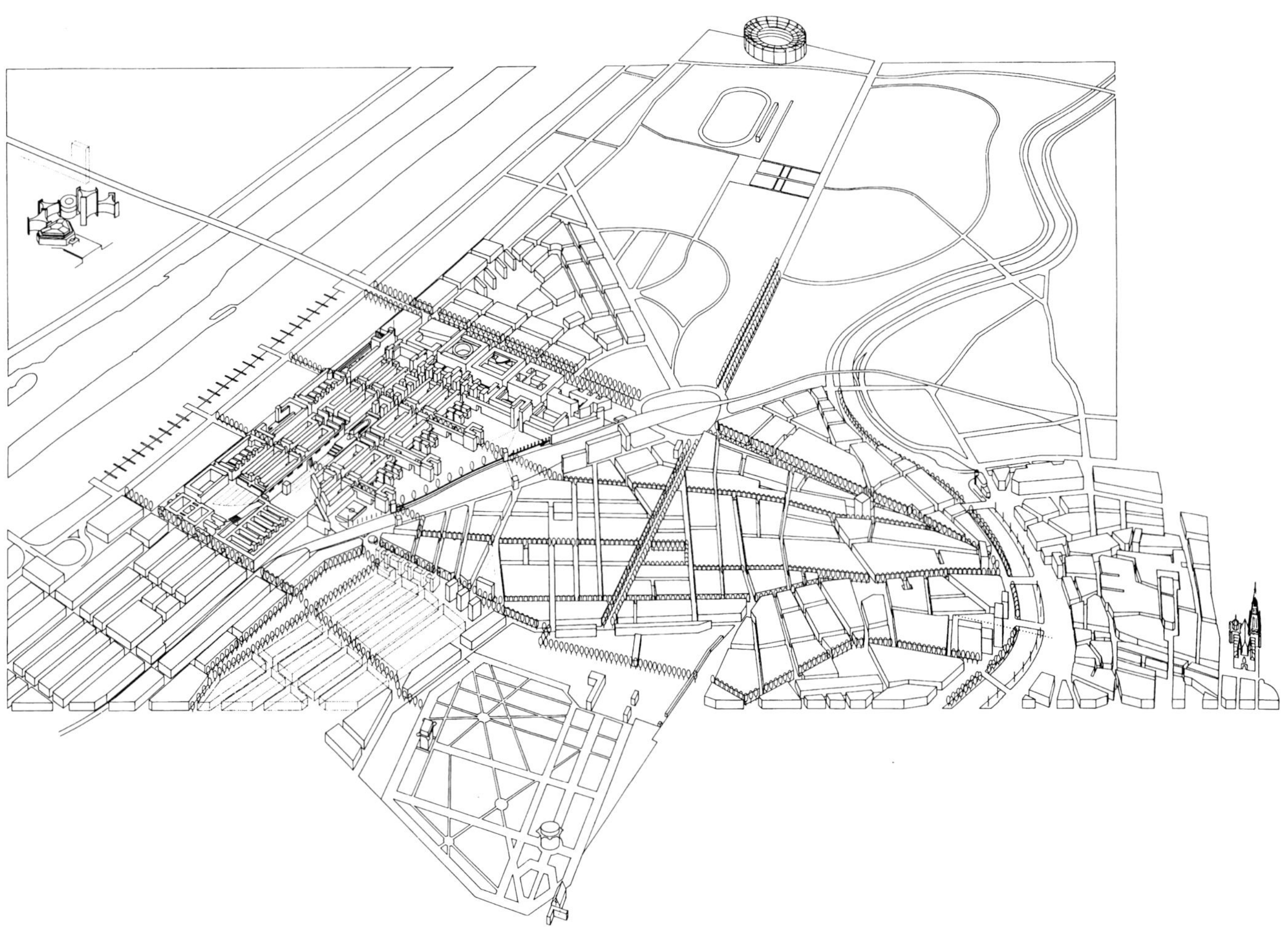

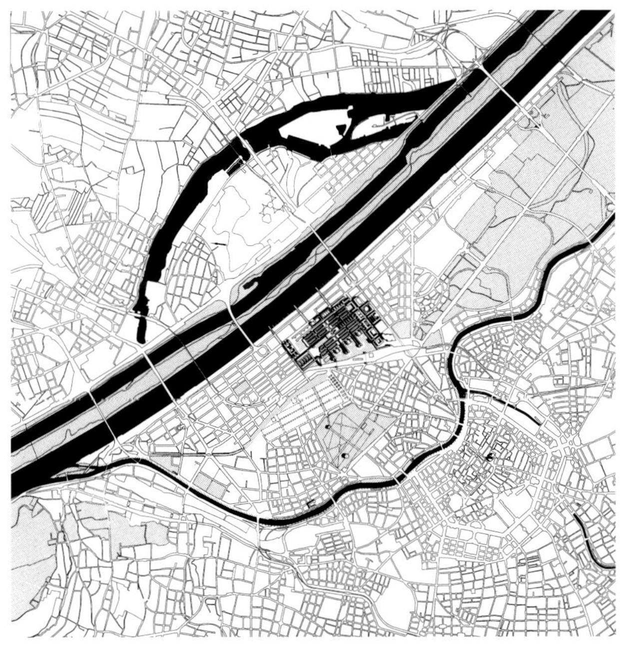

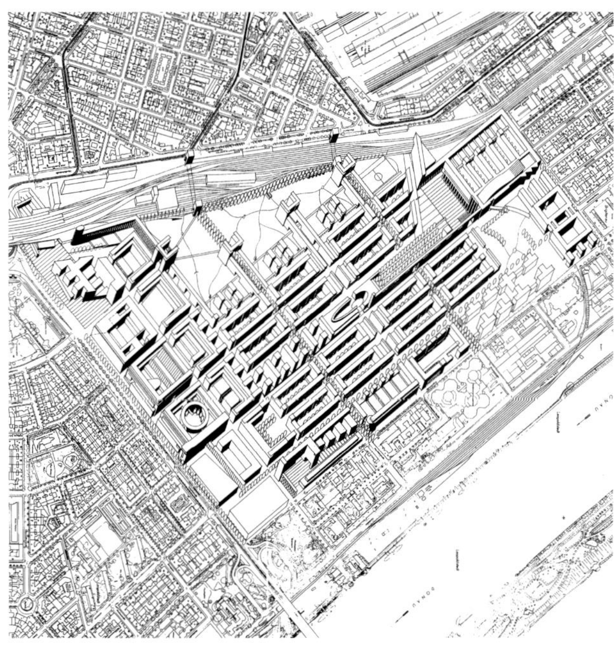

Flugperspektive / *Aerial perspective*

Gültiger Lageplan / *Valid site plan*

Studien der Bauetappen / *Studies of the building phases*

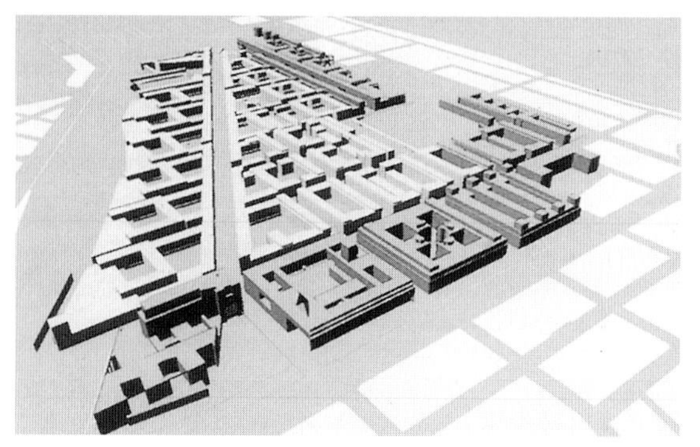

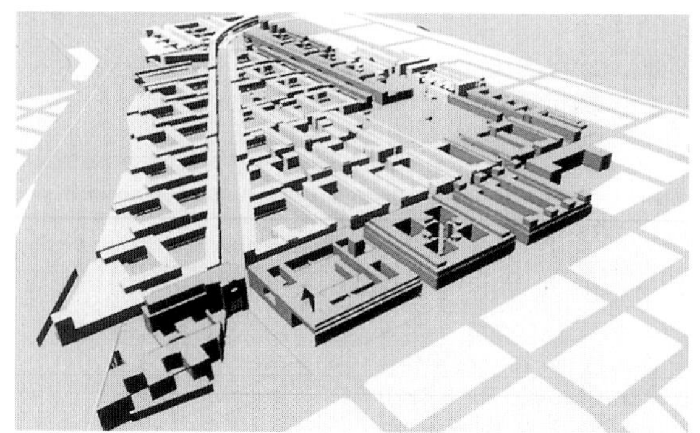

Hauptfassade Remisebebauung, Vorgartenstraße /
Main facade of trolley car depot, Vorgartenstrasse

Modell / *Model*

Lageplan Bauteile / *Site plan of building components*

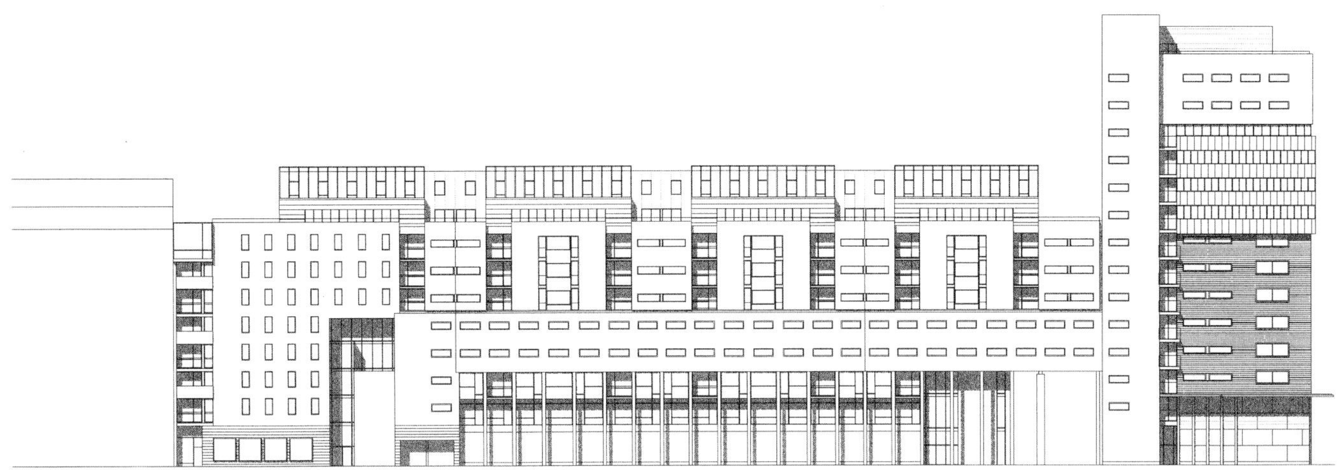

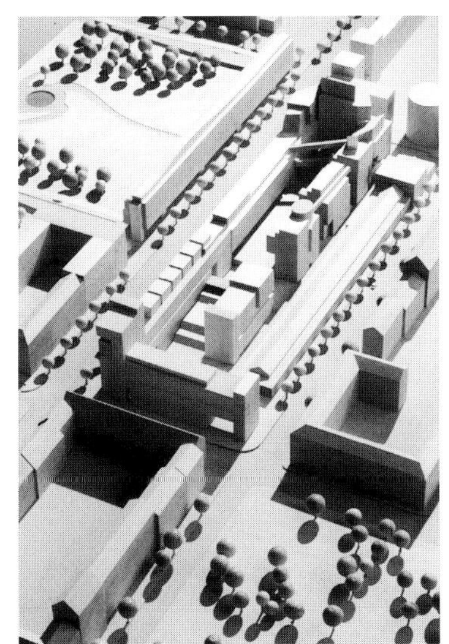

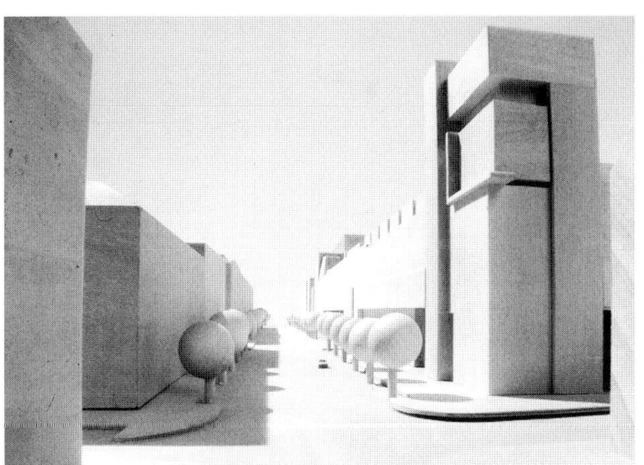

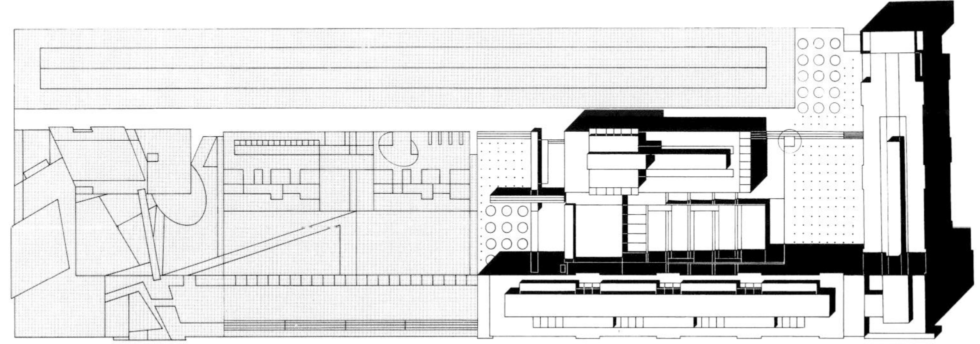

Bauteil
Coop Himmelb(l)au

Bauteil
Neumann & Steiner

Bauteil
Podrecca

Berlin, Wettbewerb / *Competition* 1993

Grundriß Erdgeschoß / *Plan of first floor*

Modell, Ausschnitt / *Model, detail*

Der Baubestand auf dem Geviert stammt aus verschiedenen Jahrzehnten dieses Jahrhunderts und folgt ansatzweise dem Blockrand. Das erstprämierte Projekt führt zum einen das vorhandene Konzept quartierbildend weiter im Sinne einer Vervollständigung der stadträumlichen Struktur. Zum anderen unterteilen zwei zwischen die Seitenflügel gespannte niedere Verbindungstrakte und ein U-förmiger Baukörper in der Mitte den ehemaligen Freiraum in fünf begrünte Höfe. Die symmetrische Vorgabe des Aral-Gebäudes am Hohenzollerndamm wird als Ordnungs- und Orientierungsprinzip zwar aufgenommen, aber auf einer unteren Maßstabsebene relativiert. In der Achse zwischen den beiden Schenkeln des U entsteht ein attraktiver Binnenraum; unter dem hinteren Quertrakt hindurch geht er über in den freier gestalteten Park, der zur Wohnanlage im Norden vermittelt. Die Höfe in den vier Quadranten sind intimer und bieten für die umgebenden Bürotrakte angenehme Ausblicke. Der Haupteingang bleibt vorn in der Mittelachse. Eine neue, lange Eingangshalle reicht in die Tiefe des Grundstücks hinein, wo die Verteilung T-förmig erfolgt. Mit Vertikalbezügen und freistehenden Elementen wird dieser Bereich räumlich aufgewertet. Unspezifische Flächen, die verschiedenen zukünftigen Aktivitäten offen stehen sollen, erlauben eine urbane Verdichtung nach Maßgabe der wachsenden Ansprüche, so daß dieser Bereich mit den Jahren zum lebendigen Herz des gesamten Gebäudekomplexes werden kann.

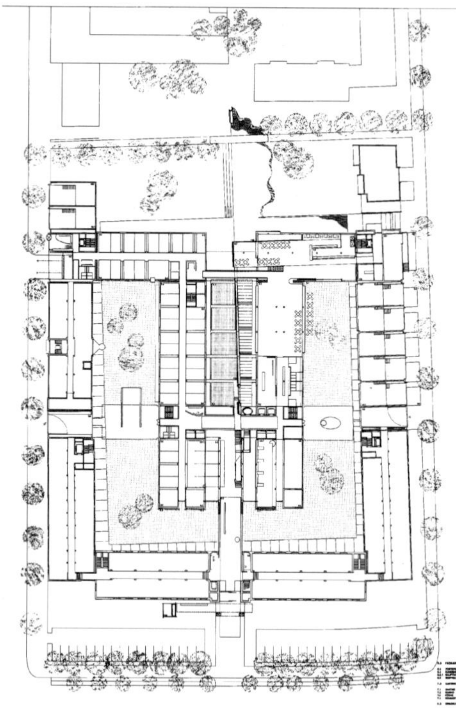

The buildings on the square date back to various decades of our century and tentatively follow the block perimeter. The winning project continues with the existing concept and expands the formation of a quarter in the sense that it completes the urban spatial structure. On the other hand, two low connecting structures squeezed in between the side wings and a U-shaped building volume in the middle separate the former free area into five planted courtyards. The existing symmetrical form of the Aral-building at Hohenzollerndamm is taken up as a standard of order and orientation; however, it is made relative on a lower scale. In the axis between the two arms of the U, an attractive inner space comes into being. Below the rear transverse section it enters into the more freely designed park, mediating towards the apartment complex to the North. The courtyards in the four quadrants are more intimate and provide the adjoining office buildings with pleasant views. The main entrance remains in the front, in the middle axis. A new long entrance hall reaches into the depth of the property, from where the distribution is made in a T-shape. With vertical relations and free-standing elements, this area is spatially reevaluated. Nonspecific areas which are open to various future activities, allow an urban densification according to the growing demands. Thus, this area can become the living heart of the entire building complex after a couple of years.

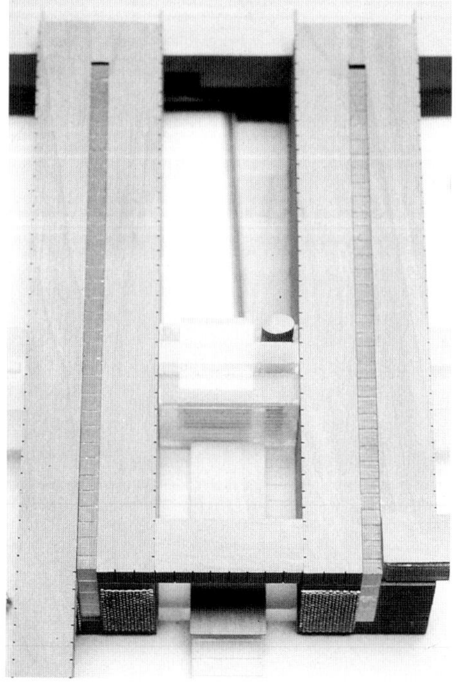

Lageplan / *site plan*

Modell / *Model*

Schnitte und Ansichten / *Sections and elevations*

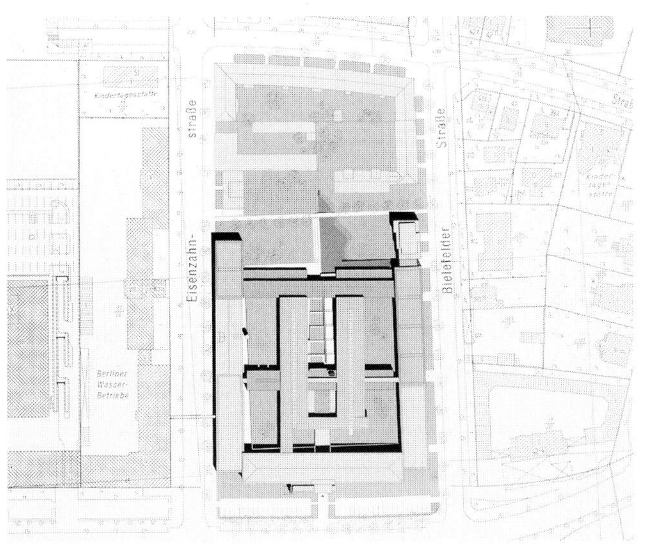

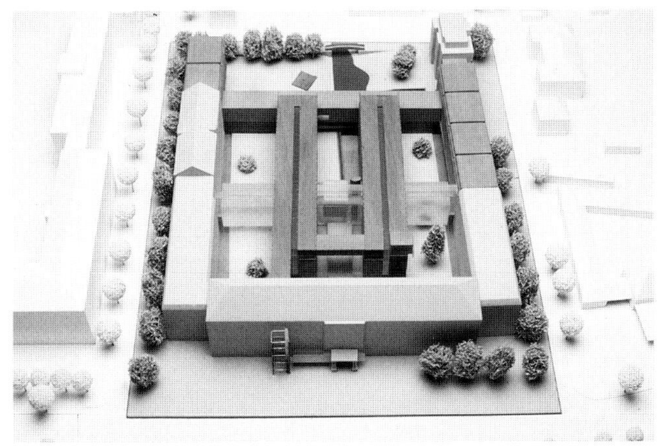

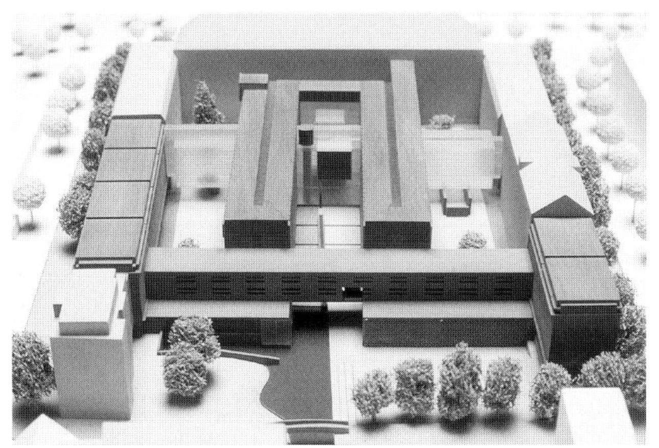

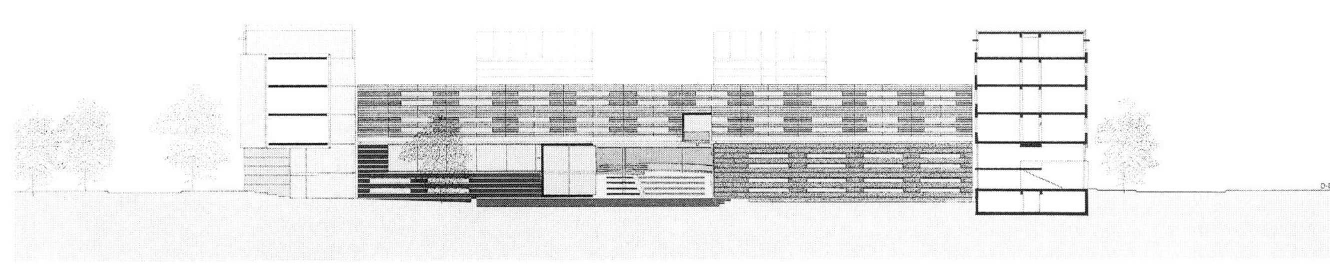

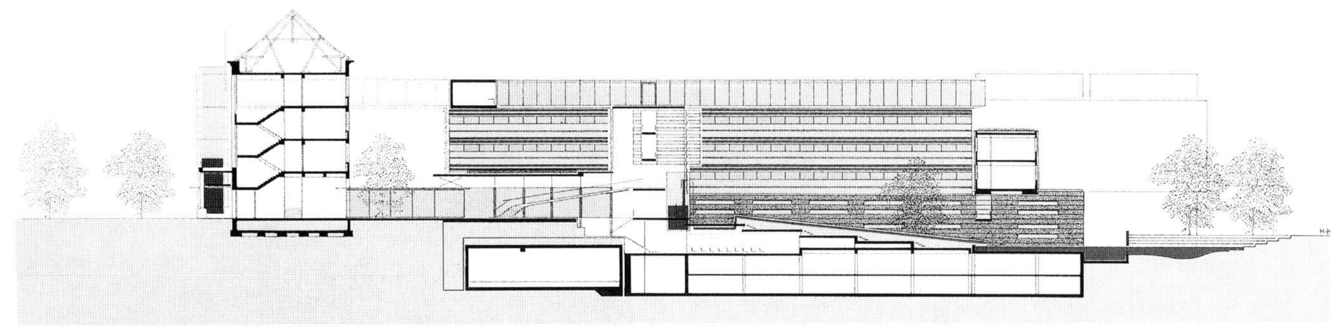

Berlin, Wettbewerb / *Competition* 1993

Modell / *Model*

Lageplan / *Site plan*

Zwischen Spree und Breite Straße, in Fortsetzung des Marstallgebäudes und der Stadtbibliothek, war für das Kopfgrundstück zur Gertraudenstraße eine Bebauung mit Verwaltung, Büros, Geschäften und Wohnungen zu planen. Das Konzept sieht eine klassische Blockrandbebauung vor, wobei der vordere Abschnitt, Sitz des Deutschen Industrie- und Handelstags (DIHT), auf die städtebauliche Richtung der Mühlendammbrücke reagiert und um einige Grade weggedreht ist, so daß im Zwickel eine perspektivische Galerie von der Breite Straße zum Spreeufer Platz findet. Der doppelt so große hintere Abschnitt besteht aus drei Trakten, die U-förmig um einen mit Einbauten versehenen Hof stehen. In den Erdgeschossen sind Läden und Publikumsbereiche des DIHT vorgesehen. Eine breite Passage führt ans Ufer zu Café und Restaurant. Die Obergeschosse enthalten Büros, der zur Spree hin orientierte Block enthält Wohnungen. Volumetrisch umschlingen und durchdringen einander zwei parallele Systeme: Die Bereiche serieller Normalnutzung – ob Büros, Läden oder Wohnungen – sind als dreidimensional mäandrierendes, homogenes Band gestaltet, verkleidet mit Naturstein. Erschließungen, Sonder- und Einzelnutzungen – vom Architekten zusätzlich vorgeschlagen – bilden ein mit ersterem verschränktes, heterogenes Partnersystem, dessen Oberfläche aus emailliertem Glas besteht. Die daraus resultierende kompakte Großform vermeidet unerwünschte Monumentalität.

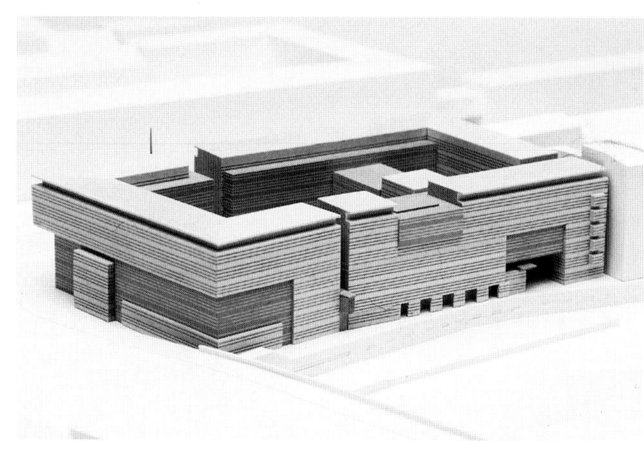

Between the Spree and the Breite Strasse, as a continuation of the Marstall building and the municipal library, a development with the administration, offices, shops and apartments was to be planned for the principal property facing Gertraudenstrasse. The concept projects a classic block perimeter development. The front section, headquarters of the German Association of Industry and Commerce (DIHT), reacts to the urban direction of the Mühlendamm bridge and is turned to the side by a few degrees. In the angle, a perspective gallery from Breite Strasse to the Spree river bank thus finds its proper place. The back section, which is twice the size, consists of three blocks, arranged in a U-shape around a courtyard providing installations. Shops and public areas of the DIHT are planned for the ground floors. A wide passageway leads to the river bank and to a café and restaurant. The upper floors contain office spaces and on the side facing the Spree river there are apartments. Volumetrically, two parallel systems embrace and penetrate one another: the areas of serial normal use – whether offices, shops or apartments – are designed as a three-dimensional, meandering homogenous strip, encased with natural stone. Additional connections for special and single use were suggested by the architect together with the previously mentioned one to form an interlaced, heterogeneous partner system whose surface would be covered with enameled glass. Thus, a compact large scale form comes into being while avoiding an undesired monumentality.

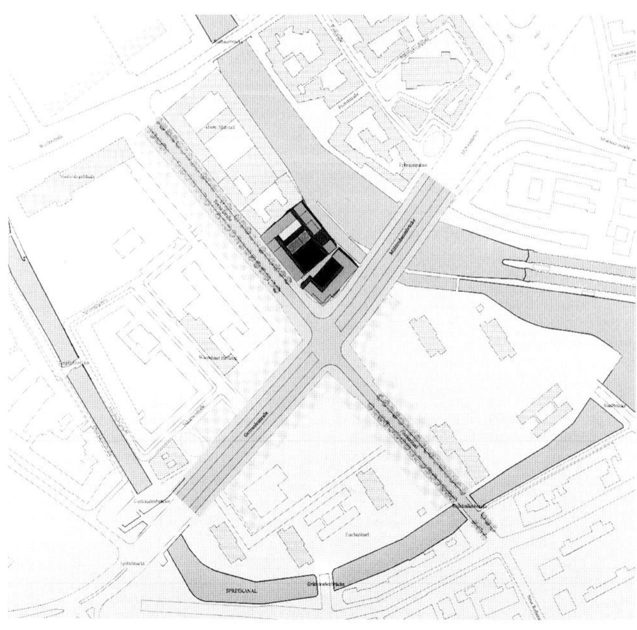

Modell / *Model*

Perspektive, Studie / *Perspective, study*　　　　　　　　　　Fassade, Detail / *Facade, detail*

Räumliche Einlagerung / *Spatial composition*

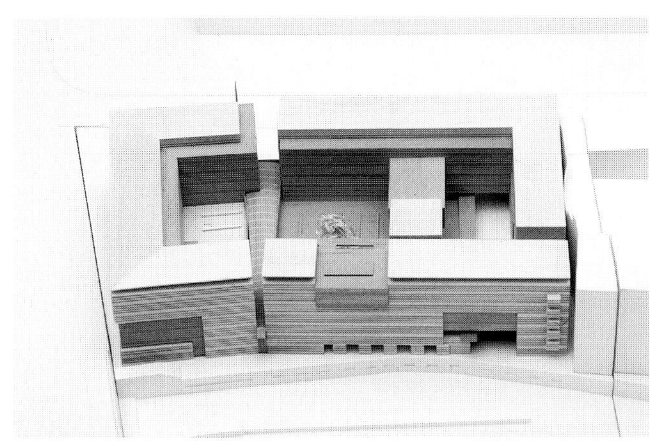 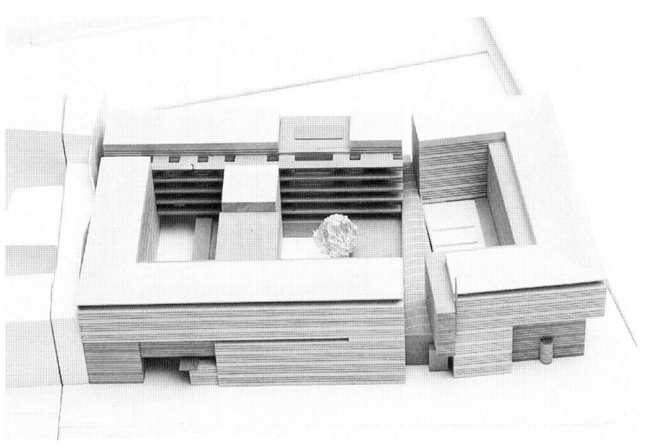

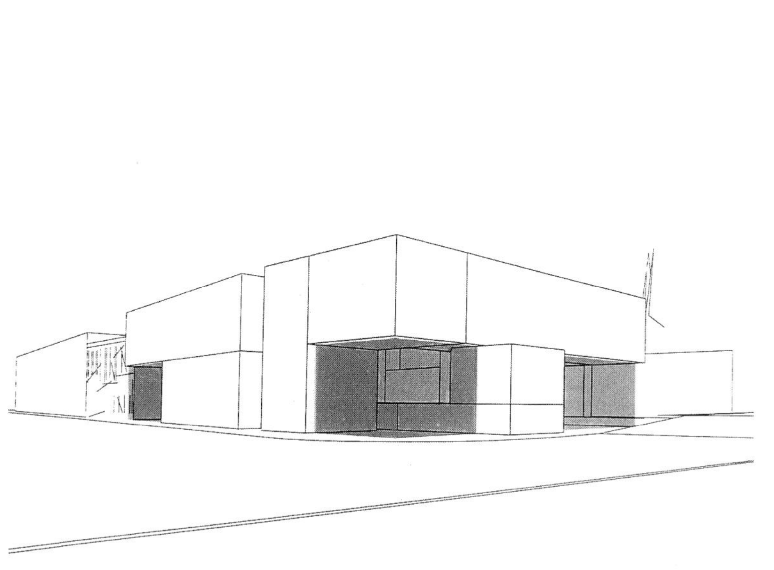 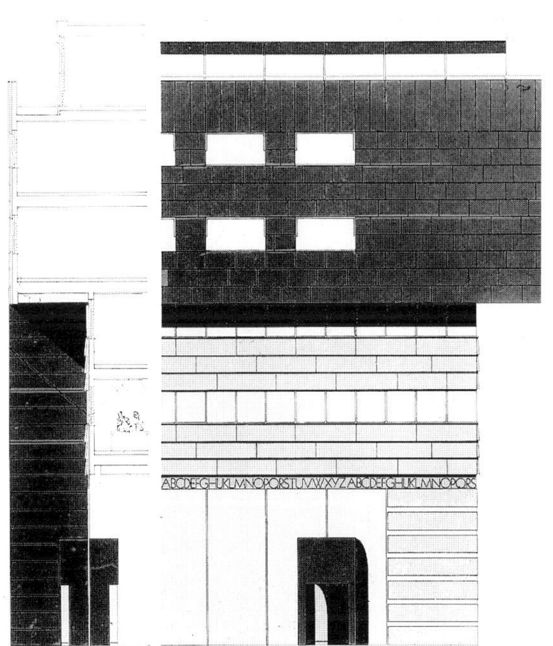

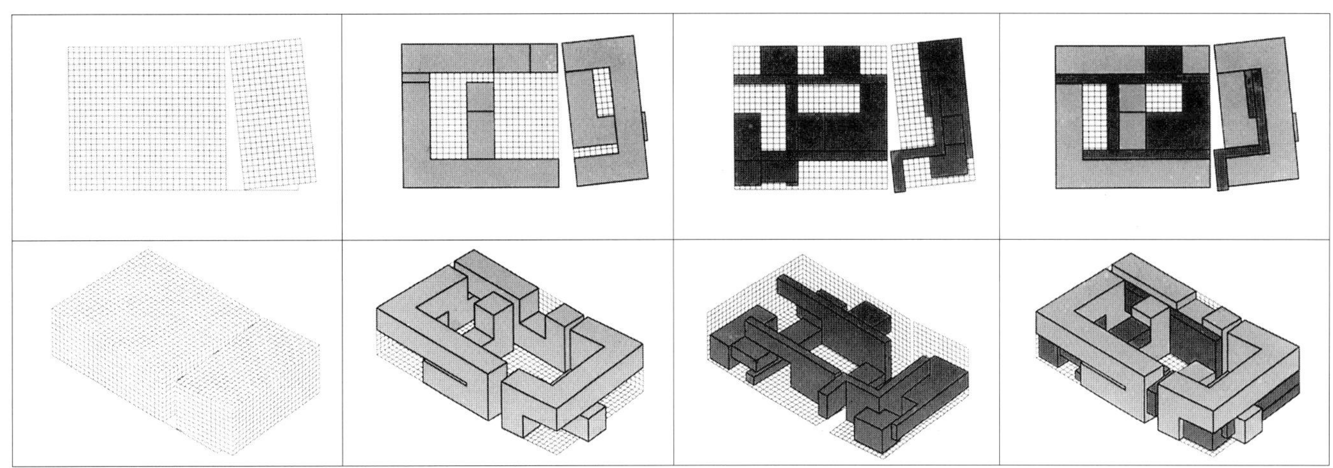

Berlin, Wettbewerb / *Competition* 1994

Flugperspektive / *Aerial perspective*

Der Vorschlag für den Neubau des Regierungssitzes stellt das Bundeskanzleramt in eine Sicht- und Raumbeziehung zu den Bauten für Bundestag und Bundesrat. Der von zwei mächtigen Gebäudetrakten gebildete Winkel öffnet sich in Richtung Bundestag. Die Außenseiten des Gevierts zur Spree sowie die Stirnseiten werden bestimmt von Schildwänden mit konstanter Traufenhöhe. Sie bestehen aus abwechselnd rustizierten und sandgestrahlten horizontalen Steinbändern, die von Glasfeldern unterbrochen werden. Rückseitig ist die tragende Stahlkonstruktion zu sehen. Mit etwas Abstand folgt als zweite Schicht eine Vollglasfassade, der die offenen Felder im Steinmantel Durchblick gewähren. An der Innenseite des Gebäudewinkels sind die Fassaden heterogener. Der Aufbauraster von 1.50 m und eine variable Anordnung der Bürotrakte ermöglichen dauernde Flexibilität. Für die Gesamtorganisation ist das komplexe Energiekonzept bestimmender. Während der westliche Gebäudeflügel weiträumige offene Hallen mit stegartigen Verbindungen und filigranen Treppenläufen aufweist, wird der etwas längere, nördliche Gebäudeflügel durch ein System von Lichthöfen strukturiert. Die virtuelle Form des Gevierts, zugleich des klassisch-stadtbildenden Baublocks, wird durch eine Stadtpergola aus gespannten Kabeln angedeutet, die den Zeremonienplatz definiert. Das Eckelement sollte als technisch-skulpturales Element zusammen mit einem Künstler gestaltet werden.

The proposal for the new construction of the government's headquarters puts the Bundeskanzleramt into a visual and spatial relationship with the buildings of the Bundestag (Federal Assembly) and Bundesrat (Federal Council). The angle created by two massive building tracts opens up towards the Bundestag. The outsides of the square towards the Spree river, as well as the fronts, are defined by face masonry walls with a constant eaves height. They consist of alternating rustic and sand-blasted horizontal stone strips, interrupted by glass fields. On the back, the supporting steel construction is visible. At some distance away, a full glass facade follows as a second layer. Openings in the stone shell provide for a vista. The facades are more heterogeneous on the inside of the building's angle. The construction grid of 1.50 m and a variable arrangement of the office blocks provide the means for an enduring flexibility. The complex energy concept has a more decisive role for the over-all organization. While the west wing of the building has large open halls with bridge-like connections and filigree stairways, the somewhat longer northern wing is structured by a system of inner courts. The virtual form of the square, which at the same time represents the classic, urban-forming building blocks, is hinted at by a municipal pergola of stretched cables, defining the ceremonial square. The corner element should be designed together with an artist as a technical-sculptural element.

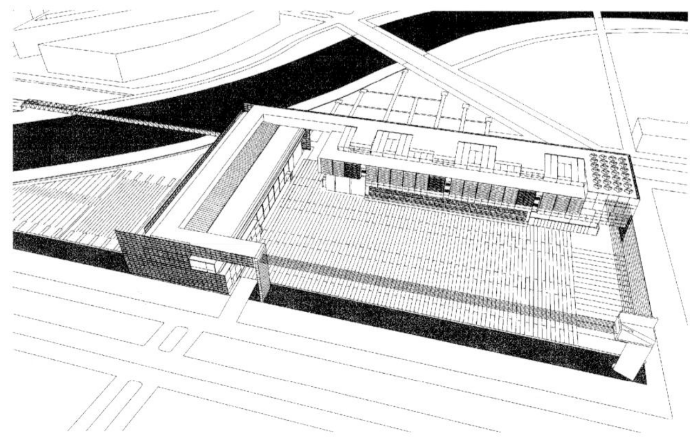

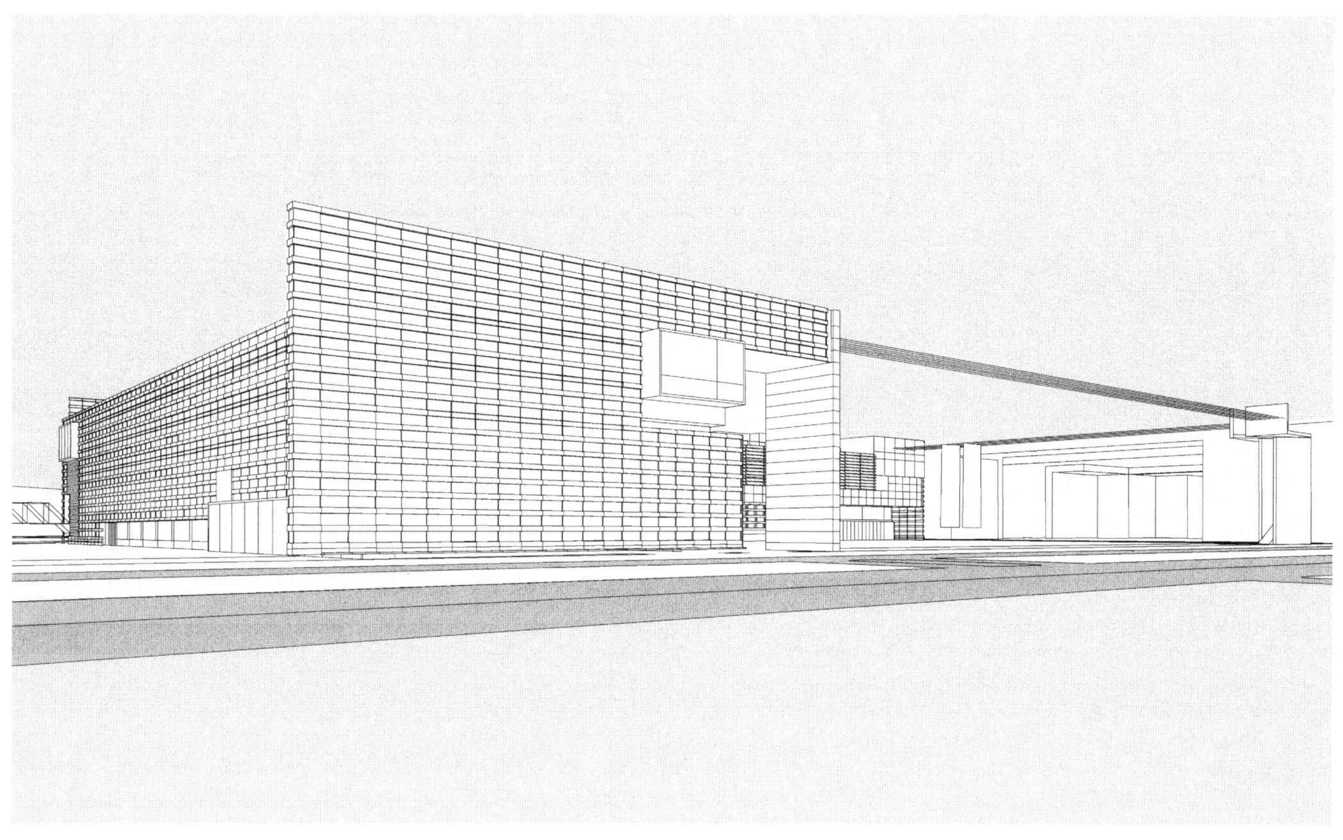

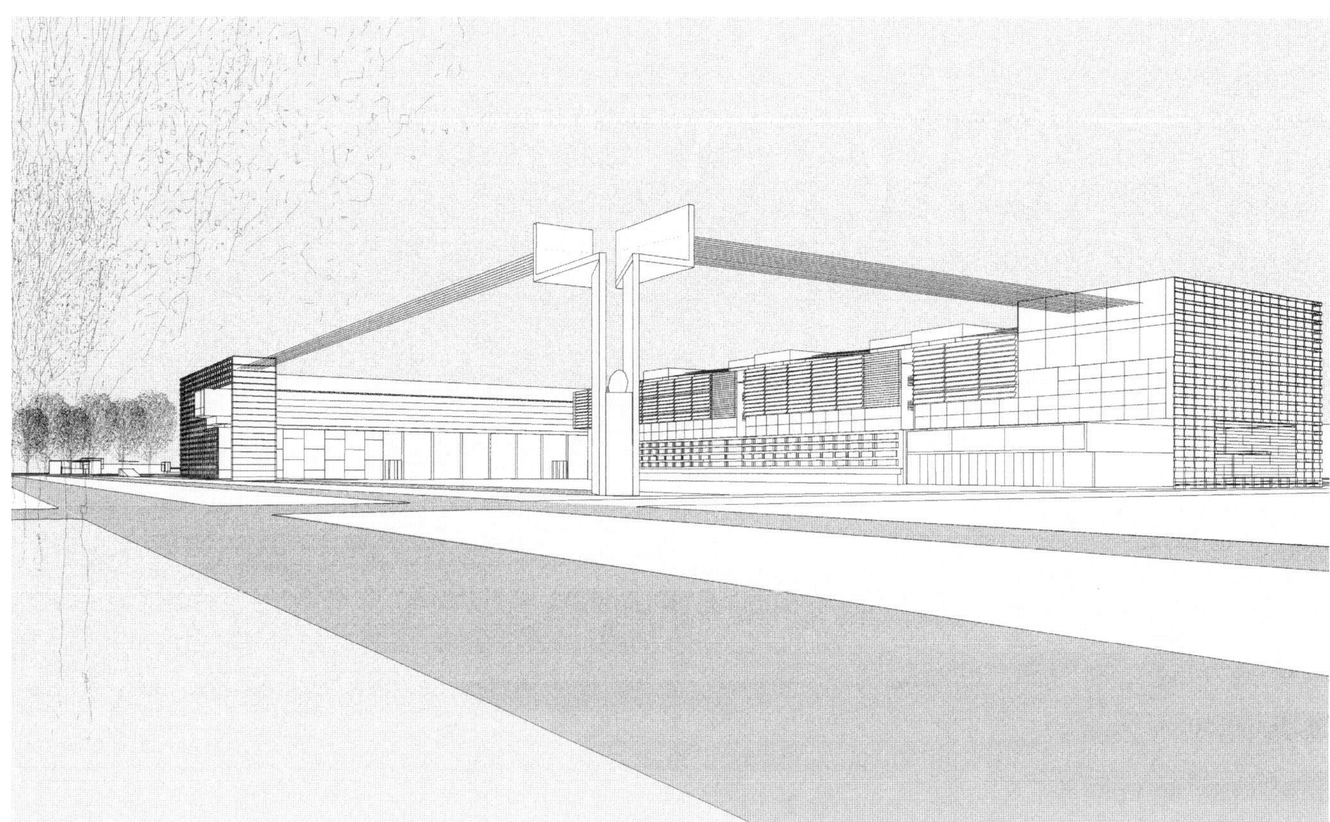

Modell / *Model*

Flugperspektive / *Aerial perspective*

Hauptfassade zur Spree / *Main facade facing the Spree river*

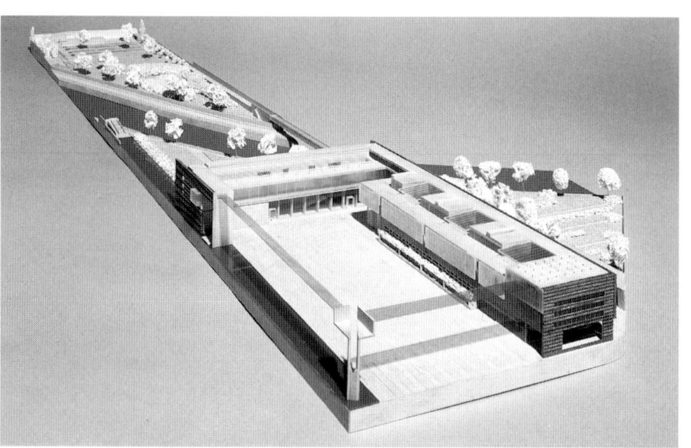

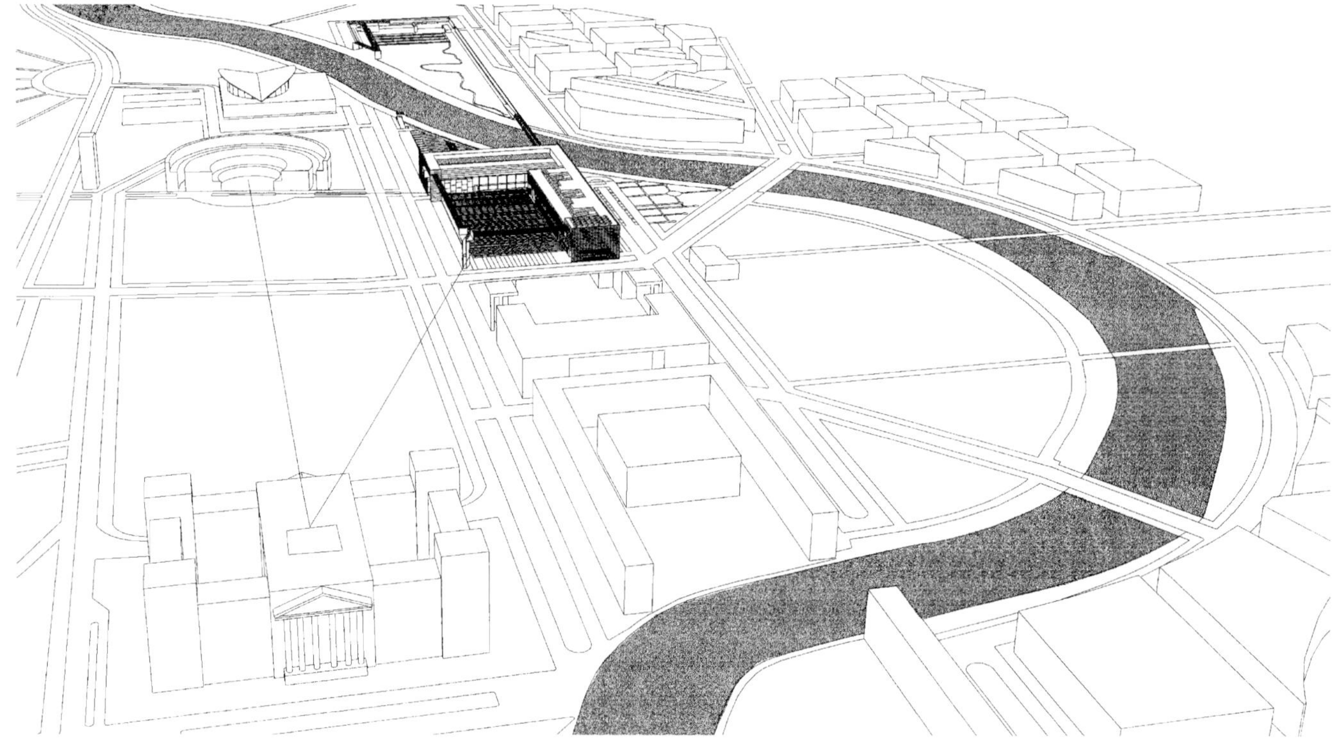

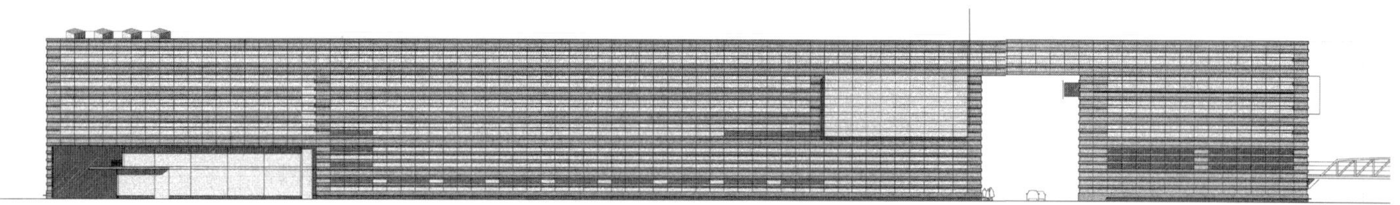

Schnitte und Ansichten / *Sections and elevations*

Modell der Gesamtanlage / *Model of the entire complex*

Lageplan / *Site plan*

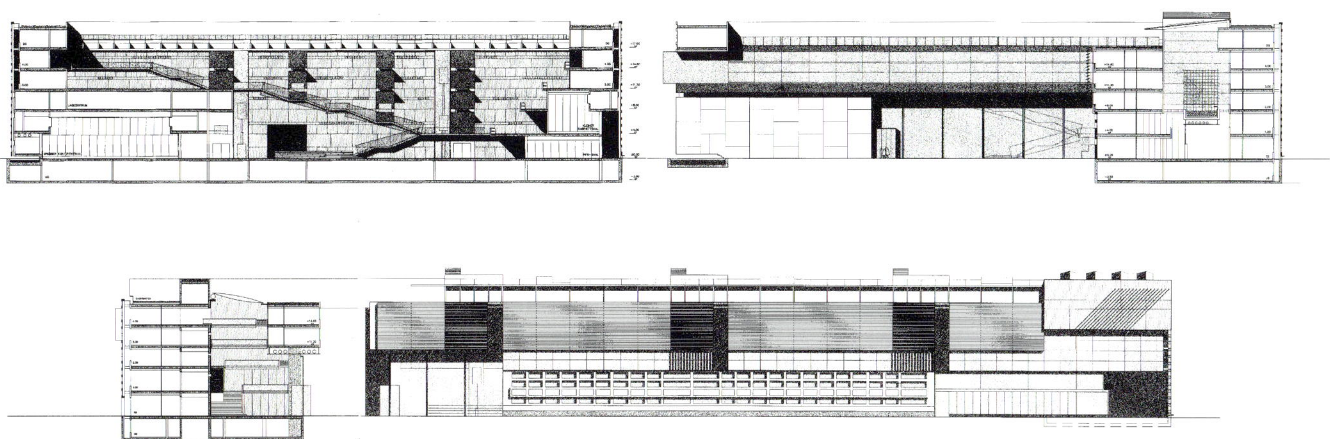

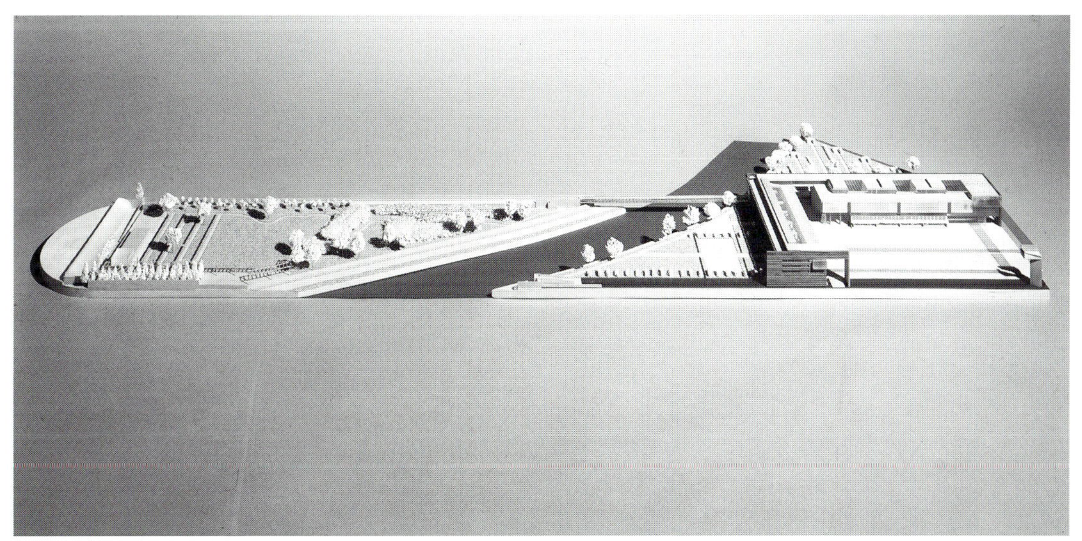

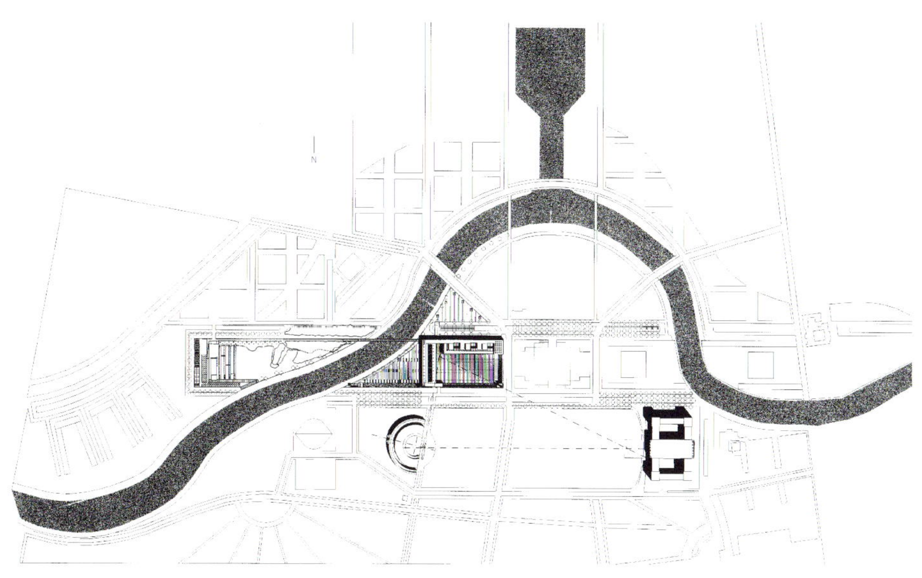

Fontanafredda, Italien / *Italy* 1992

Grundriß / *Plan*

Der flach-zylindrische Zentralbau steht zwischen zwei quergestellten Quadern, so daß sich basilikale Längsordnung und Kreis überlagern. Eine breite offene Halle bildet den Eingangsportikus. Zwei durchbrochene Betonscheiben – im Mittelbereich in Rundstützen aufgelöst – sind durch ein Grabendach verbunden und vermitteln eine gewisse Unbehaustheit. Der nach außen fast schroff wirkende Rundbau, mit seinen schalharten Oberflächen, horizontal gebändert mit bruchrohen Streifen, vertikal unterteilt von schmal-hohen Fenstern, ist im Innern in einfacher Weise verfeinert und veredelt. Nach Durchschreiten der doppelten Säulenharfe im Portikus betritt man den Zentralraum durch eine kleine Pforte. In konzentrischen Kreisen flach gestuft, sinkt der Boden zur Mitte hin ab, die ihrerseits wieder um zwei Stufen erhöht liegt und von einem zentralen Dachreiter Licht erhält. Durch die zwei parallelen Hauptträger des Daches klingt eine achsiale Symmetrie an. Sie wird bestätigt von einer pavillonartigen Kanzel mit flachem Baldachin. Von beiden Seiten führen Treppen hinauf, deren weiße Brüstungsmauern wie empfangende Arme ausschwingen. Oben, unter dem Baldachin ist der Ort der Taufe, unten führen gegenläufig zwei Treppen ins Untergeschoß. Nach hinten schließt der Quader der Werktagskapelle an. Die von außen kastenartigen Fenster erweisen sich von innen als leuchtende Flächen in plastisch rahmenden Wandfeldern. Die entstehenden Lichtreflexe beleben den polierten Fußboden.

The flat cylindrical central building is located in between two transversely placed cuboids creating an overlapping of the basilica's longitudinal order and the circle. A wide, open hall forms the entrance portico. Two concrete slabs with vertical openings, which diffuse into round columns in the center, are connected by an obtuse V-shaped roof and communicate a certain feeling of being vacant. The round building has an almost rugged appearance on the outside, its shell-hard surfaces horizontally stripped with natural-split bands and vertically divided by high, narrow windows. On the inside, however, it is refined and ennobled in a simple way. After passing through the concrete, sieve-like slabs in the portico, one enters the central room through a small portal. The floor steps down towards the center in flat, concentric circles. The center itself is raised by two steps and receives light through a central roof spire. An axial symmetry can be perceived due to the two parallel main supports of the roof. It is strengthened by a pavilion-like pulpit with a flat canopy. It can be accessed from both sides via stairs whose white parapet walls swing to the outside like receiving arms. On the top and below the canopy lies the baptistery; on the bottom, in a counter-movement, two stairs lead to the lower level. Towards the back, the cuboid of the "weekday" chapel adjoins. The windows, which from the outside look like boxes, prove to be shining surfaces from the inside, placed in plastic framed wall fields. The resulting development of light reflections enliven the polished floor.

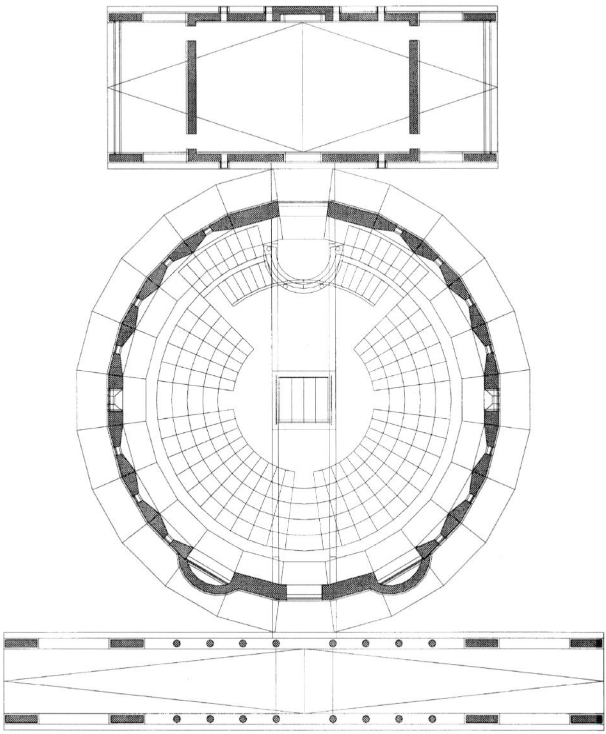

Ansicht / *Elevation*

Portikus, Seitenansicht / *Portico, side view*   Fassadentextur, Detail / *Facade texture, detail*

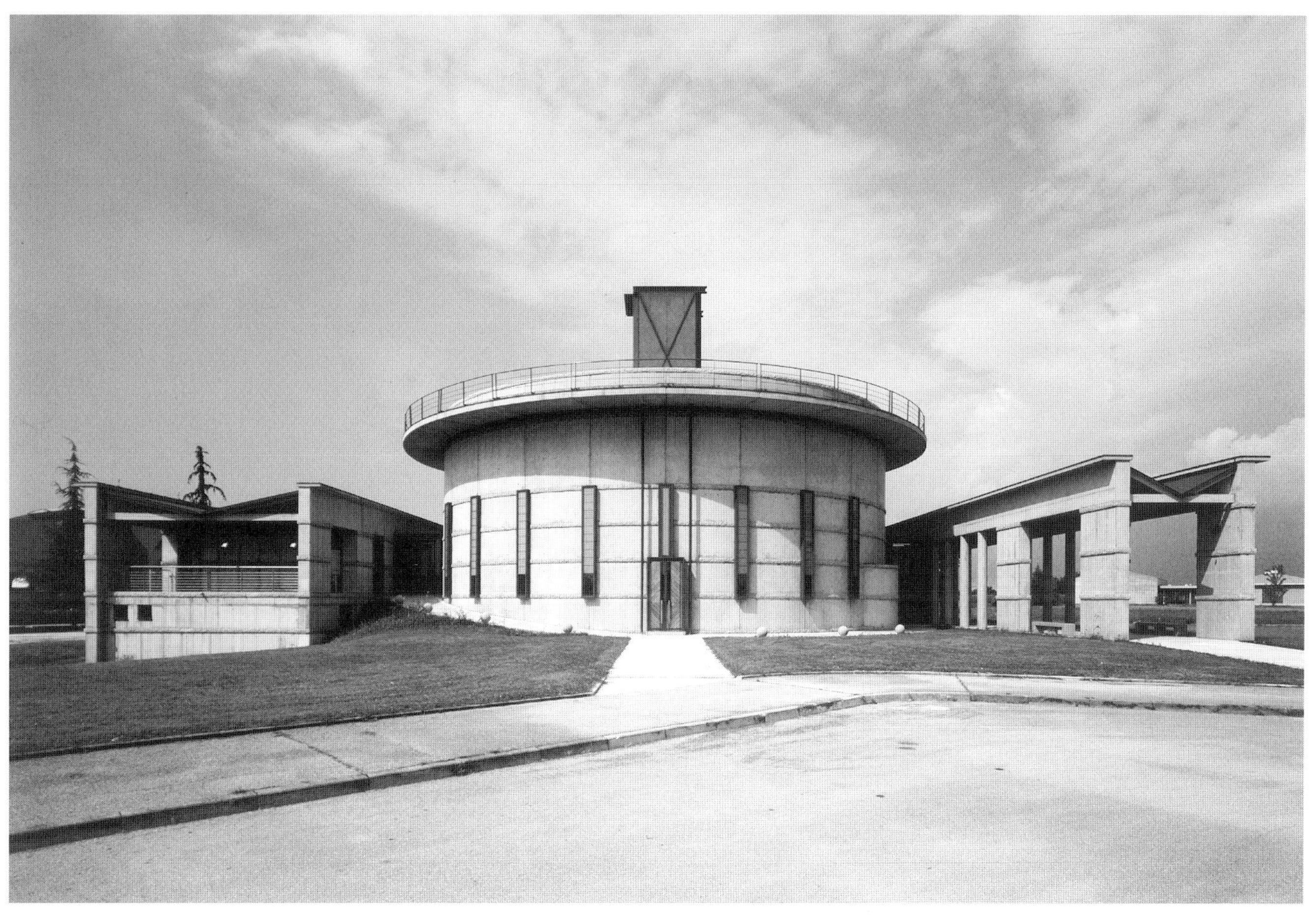

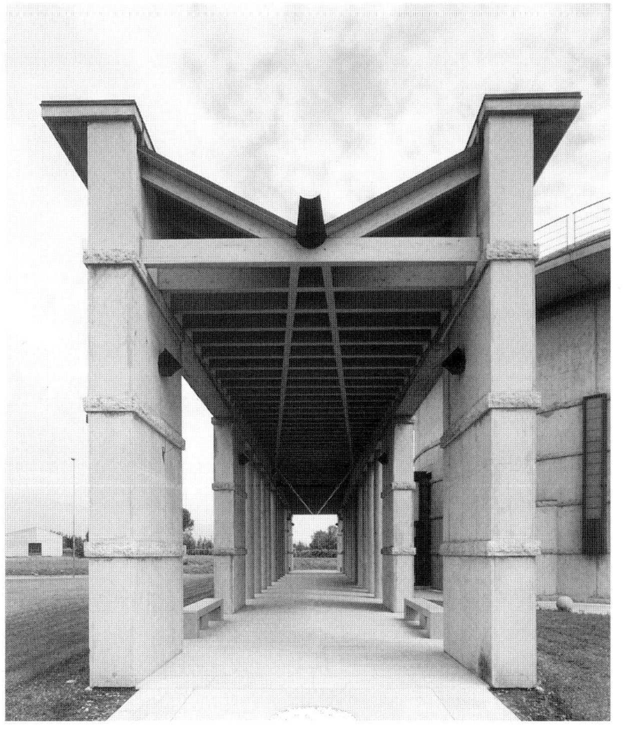

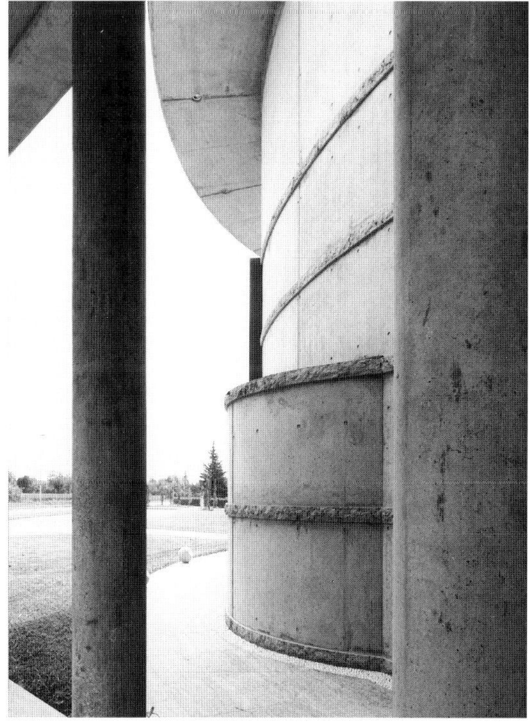

Hauptportal / *Main entrance portal*

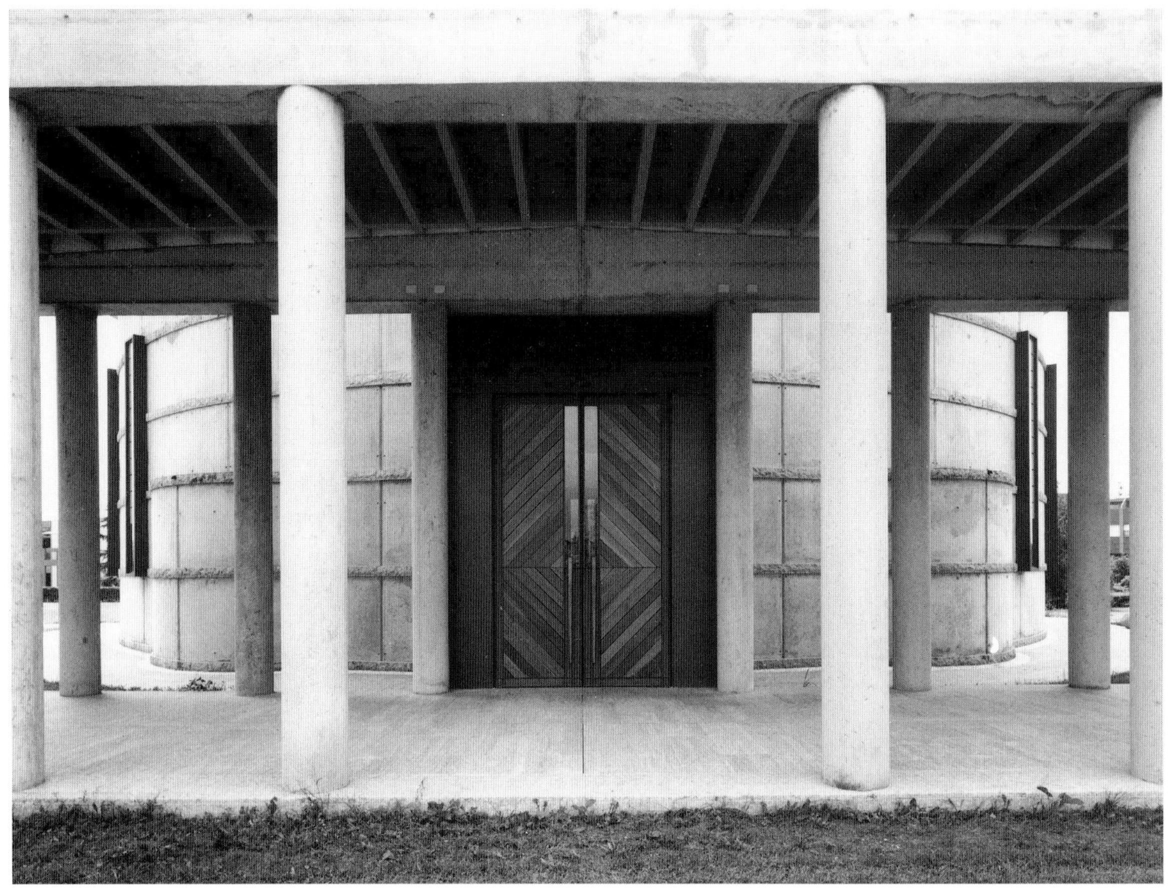

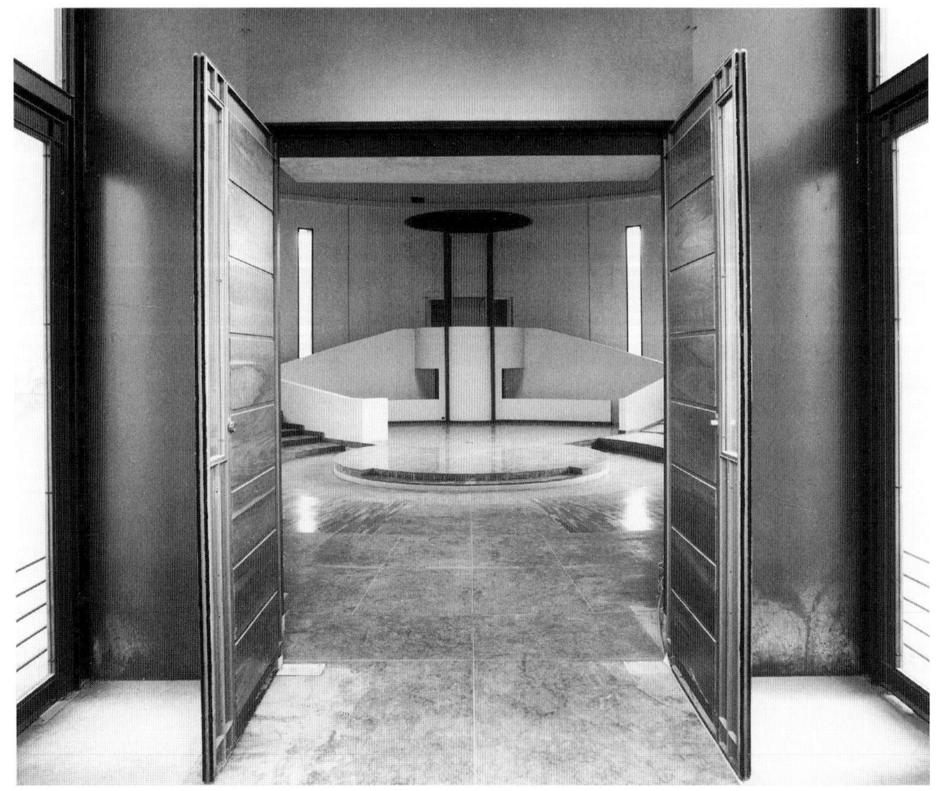

Schnittperspektive Kirchenraum / *Cross sectional perspective of church*

Presbyterium / *Presbytery*

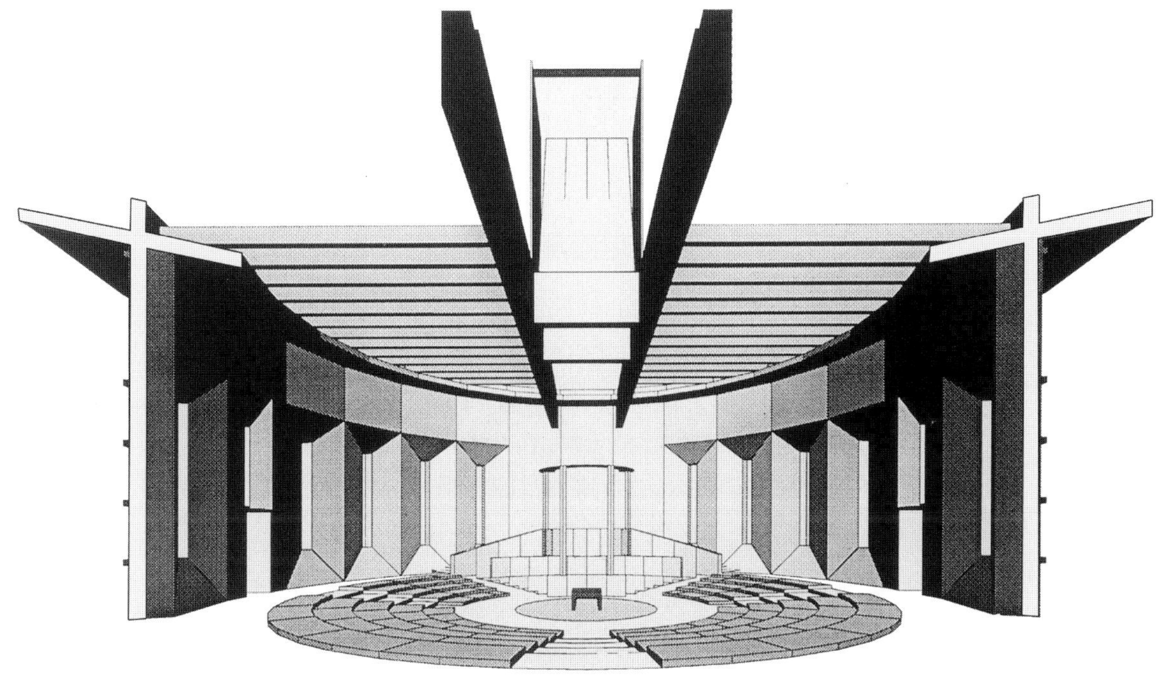

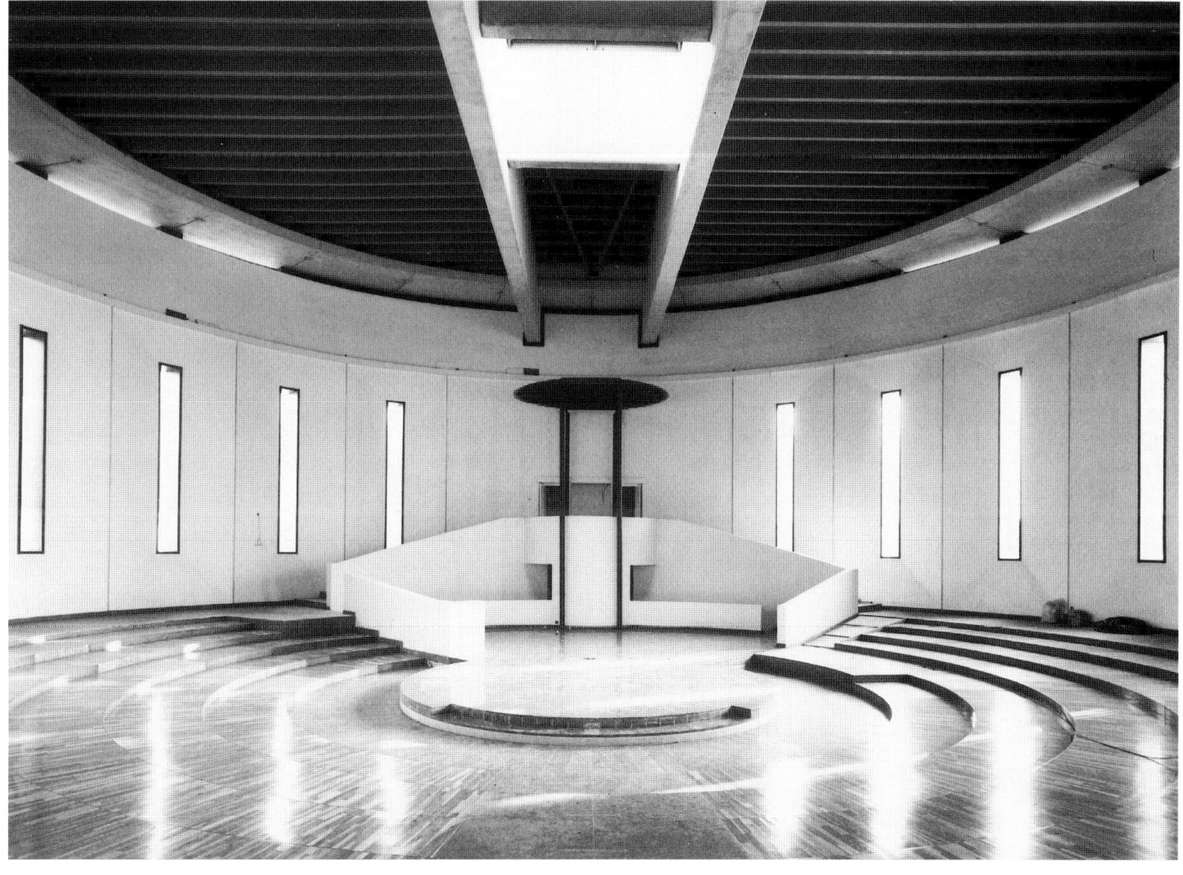

Ljubljana, Wettbewerb / *Ljubljana, Slovenia, competition* 1989

Axonometrie der Hotelprojekte im Stadtzentrum /
Axonometric projection of the hotel projects in the city center

Perspektive, Hotelhalle / *Perspective of hotel hall*

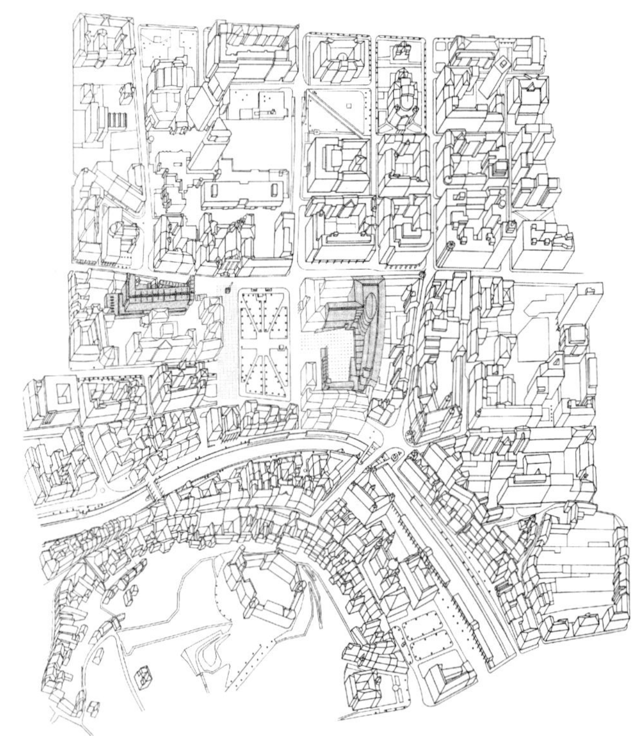

Im historischen Stadtkern, mit Blick auf die über der Stadt thronende Burg, sollte unter Wahrung von Teilen des Bestands ein 300-Betten-First-Class-Hotel in das Geviert zwischen Zvezda-Park und der auf die drei Brücken von Jože Plečnik zielenden Straße geplant werden. Das mit dem 1. Preis ausgezeichnete Projekt sah einen um das Zentrum der elliptischen Hotelhalle sich entwickelnden, dreimal abgewinkelten Baukörper vor, der in gespannter Krümmung nach vorn schnellt, aber dort keinen Kopf ausbildet, sondern die Stirne fast demütig hinter der bestehenden Straßenfront zurückstaffelt. Mächtig dräuend dagegen das Oval eines gläsernen, nur zu einem Viertel sichtbaren Kegelstumpfs. Dennoch dominiert dieser hohe Binnenraum den davor liegenden, hofartigen Platz, der die wichtige städtebauliche Achse der Vegova Ulica über den Park hinweg aufnimmt. Die neuen Wege durch das Geviert sind nicht bloß winkelige Hintergassen, sondern von eigenständiger Kraft. Am stärksten wirkt wohl der unter einer Reihe schlanker Säulen verlaufende Durchgang am Rand des geschwungenen Bettentrakts. So ist der Weg in Querrichtung, vom offenen Platz bei den drei Brücken zum geschlossenen Platz vor dem Hotel, als Folge kleiner Plätze, Gassen und Höfe gestaltet. Der hohe elliptische Binnenraum der Hotelhalle mit nach innen geneigten Säulen und viergeschoßig umlaufenden Galerien ist mit seinen hohen Glaswänden exakt für den Blick auf den über dem Flüßchen Ljubljanica gelegenen Burghügel und die Burg konzipiert.

In the historic city center, with a view of the old castle sitting throne-like above the city, a first class hotel with 300 beds was planned, maintaining parts of the old structure in the quarter between Zvezda-park and the street leading to the three bridges of Jože Plečnik. The project was awarded first prize. It proposed a building volume with three angular masses developing around the center of the elliptic hotel lobby and moving forward in a suspended curve without, however, forming a primary structure. Almost with a humble gesture, the face remained behind the existing street front. Contrary to this, a massive oval of a cylindrical glass base (only a quarter of it visible) was planned. And yet this high interior space dominates the yard-like square in front, which takes up the important urban axis of Vegova Ulica through the park. The new paths through the quarter are not simply angular back alleys, but have their own impact. The passageway beneath a row of slim columns at the perimeter of the curved bedding tract has the strongest effect. Thus, the crossing path leading from the open square at the three bridges to the closed square in front of the hotel is designed as a sequence of small squares, alleys, and yards. The high elliptical interior space of the hotel lobby, with its columns slanted towards the inside and the surrounding galleries on four floors, has been precisely conceived to offer a view of the hill and the castle above the Ljubljanica stream through its high glass walls.

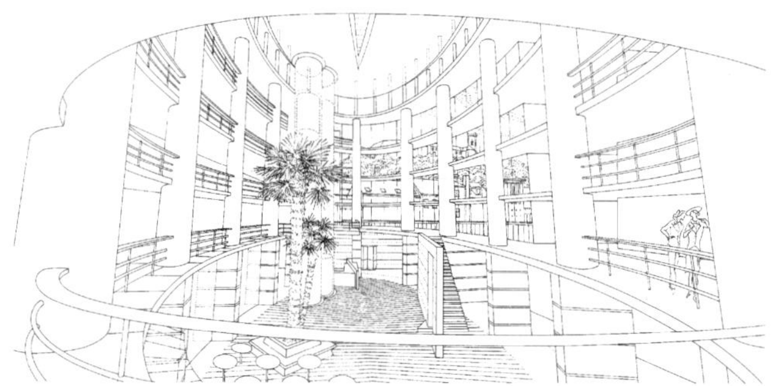

Axonometrie / *Axonometric projection*

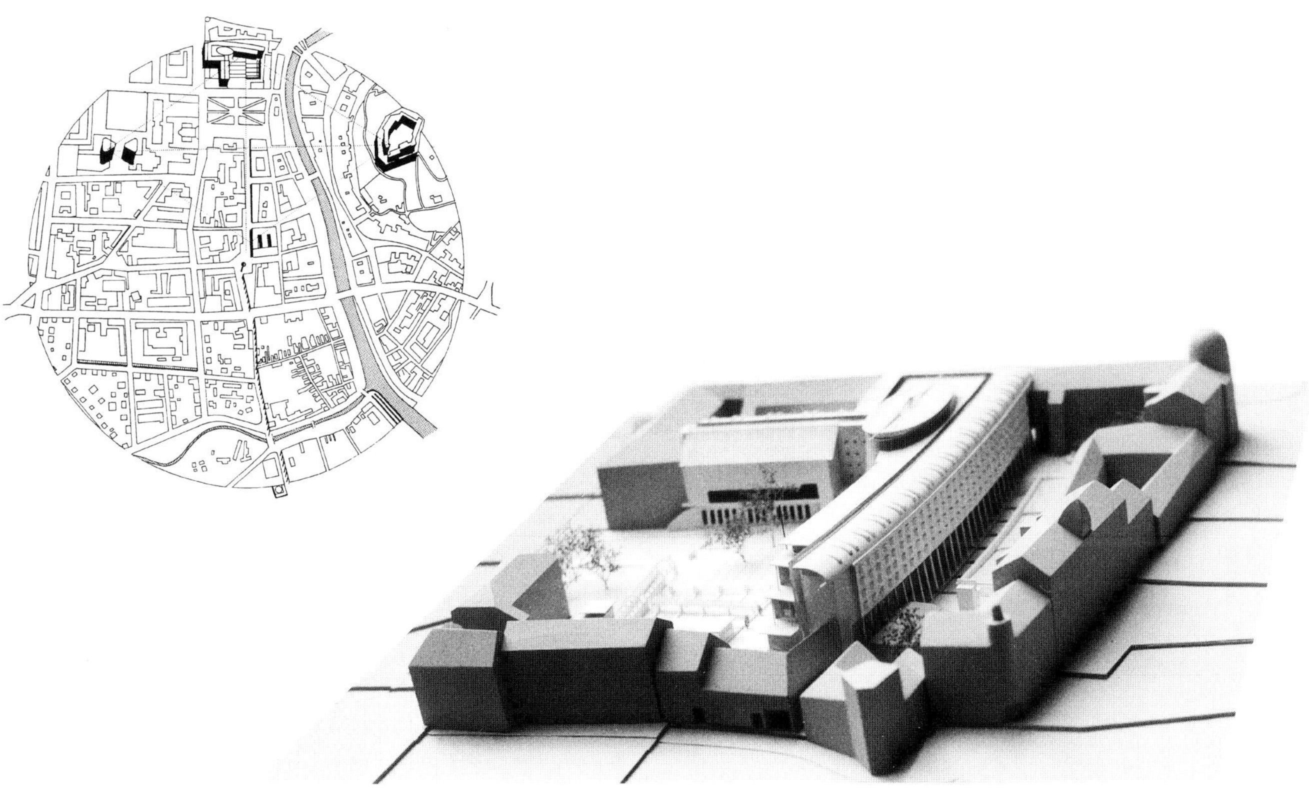

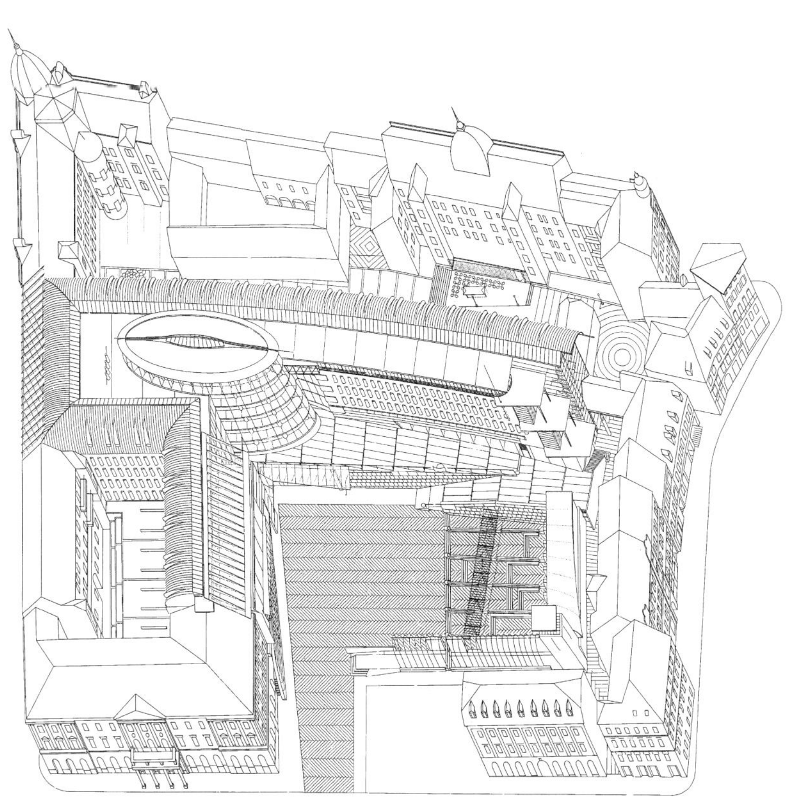

Schnitte und Ansichten / *Sections and elevations*

Grundriß 1. Obergeschoß / *Plan of second floor*

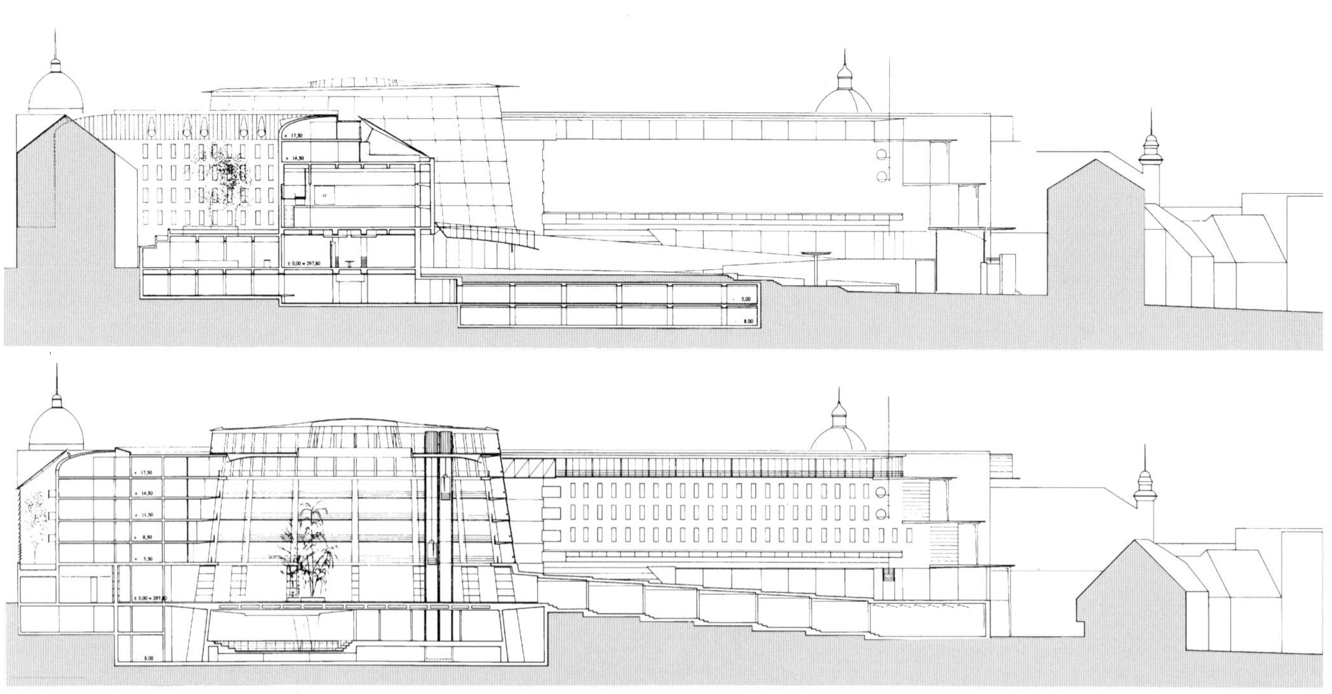

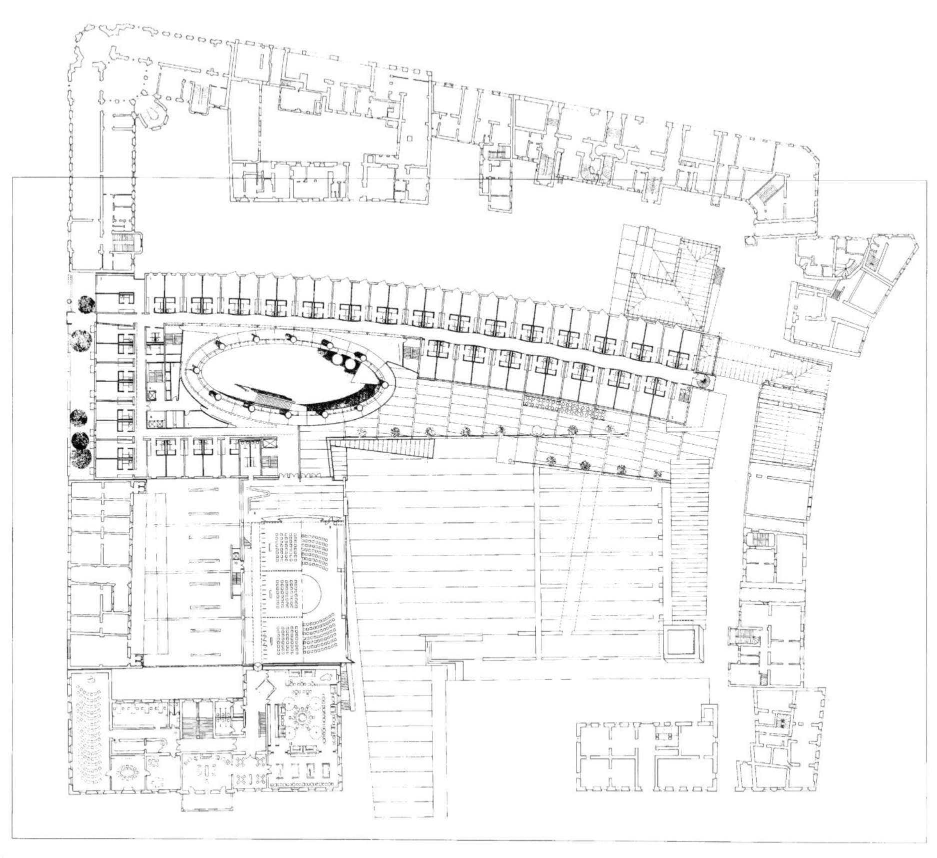

Ljubljana, Projekt / *Lubljana, Slovenia, project* 1992

Modell / *Model*

Baukörperlage im römischen Castrum /
Building volume location in the Roman Castrum

Da sich die Investitionen für das Južni Trg-Hotel verzögerten, wurde ein reduziertes Programm auf einem Grundstück westlich des Kongresni Trg vorgeschlagen. Es liegt innerhalb des ehemaligen römischen Castrum, der gesamte Baugrund ist archäologische Zone. An der Südseite war ein Straßentrakt aus dem 19. Jahrhundert, im Norden die Turnhalle des nahen Gymnasiums einzubeziehen. Zum Kongresni Trg, dem grünen Platz, dessen Ostseite von der Ursulinenkirche und der Universität beherrscht wird, steigt ein Portalbau mit Erschließungen in die Höhe. Eine verglaste Galerie, die im Mezzanin die Straße begleitet, und, zurückversetzt, der Zimmertrakt als Rückgrat der ganzen Anlage, setzen hinter dem Portalbau an. Ein kastenartiges, zwei Stockwerke hohes Volumen bildet die Basis. Ein Geschoß tief in die Erde versenkt, birgt es römische Ausgrabungen. Über diesen schweben lange, durch Treppen und Stege verbundene Plattformen, mit einer Bar und Tischen zum Verweilen. Zwischen diese Decks hindurch fällt der Blick auf die freigelegten römischen Fundamente. Im Mittelteil dient eine große Halle als Foyer für das Hotel, die anschließenden Kongreßsäle, das Restaurant und das in die Turnhalle eingebaute Spielkasino. Mit der Konstruktionsstruktur bezieht sich der gesamte Neubau auf die Lage des römischen Straßenrasters, mit der räumlichen Ordnung jedoch auf die neuere Richtung des Gymnasiums. Daraus ergibt sich bei jedem zweiten Hotelzimmer ein Versatz, der für einen Balkon genützt wird.

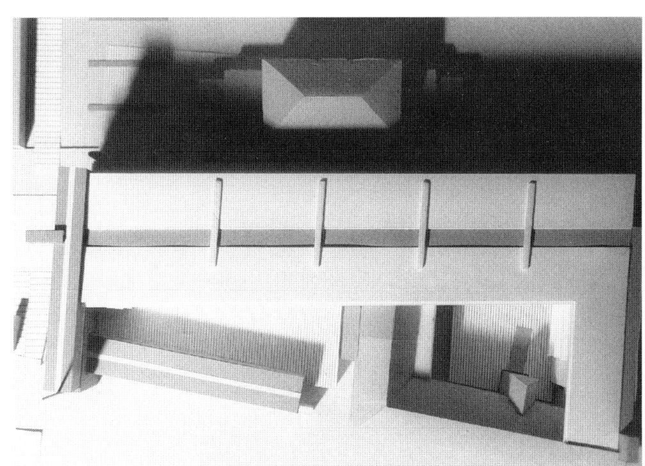

As the investment capital for the Južni Trg-hotel was delayed, a reduced agenda on a property west of the Kongresni Trg was suggested. It is located within the former Roman castrum and the entire building grounds are considered an archeological zone. A section of street on the south side dating from the 19th century and the gymnasium of the nearby high school to the north were to be considered. Towards Kongresni Trg, the green square, dominated on the east side by the Ursulinen church and the university, a portal building rises up into the sky. A portal-like glazed gallery runs along the geometry of the street on the second level, while setback, the hotel rooms provide a spine for the entire complex. A box-shaped, two-story volume forms the basis. Lowered into the ground by one story, it shelters Roman excavations. Above them, long, floating platforms connected by stairs and small bridges, with a bar and a few tables, invite the visitors to stay. Through these decks, one can see the excavated Roman foundations. In the middle section, a great hall serves as a lobby for the hotel, the adjoining convention halls, the restaurant and the gambling casino built into the gymnasium. The entire new building refers to the location of the Roman street grid with its structure of construction. The spatial order, however, refers to the newer design of the schoolbuilding. At each point where the facade shifts foward is a balcony at every other hotel room.

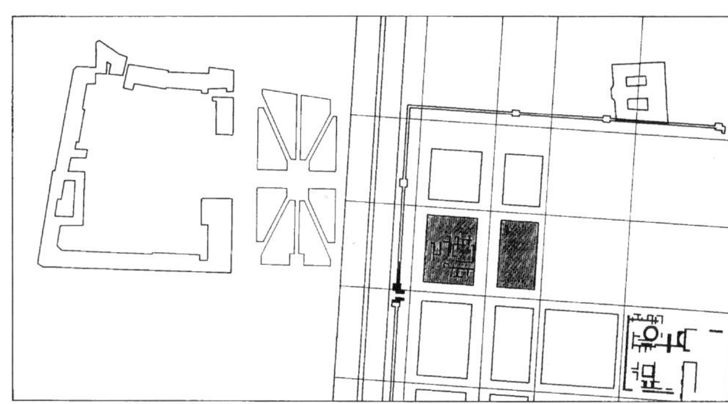

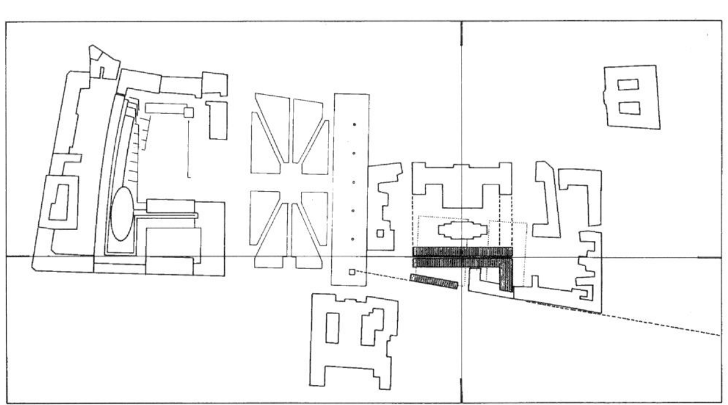

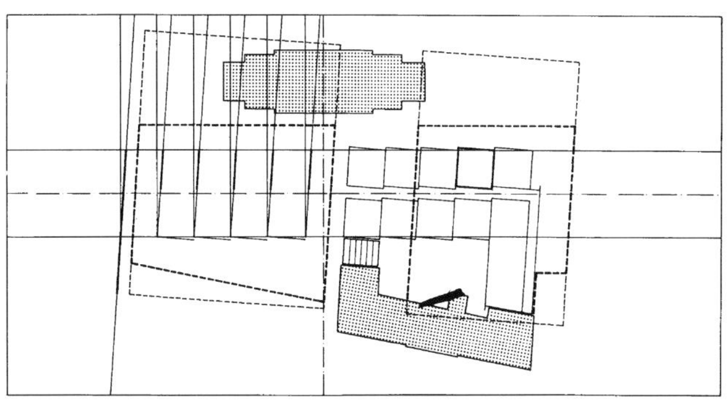

Modell / *Model*

Grundriß Erdgeschoß / *Plan of first floor*

Perspektive mit Blick zur Burg / *Perspective with a view of the castle*

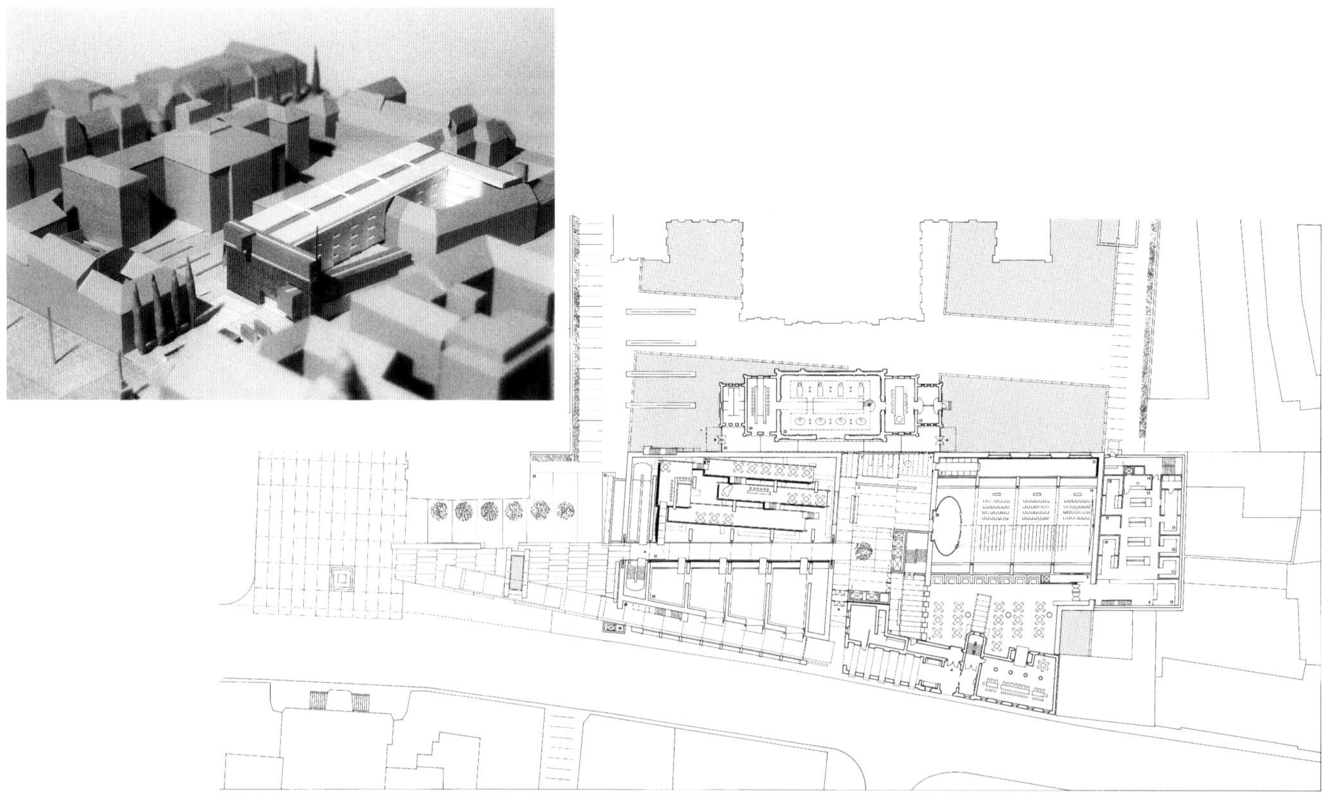

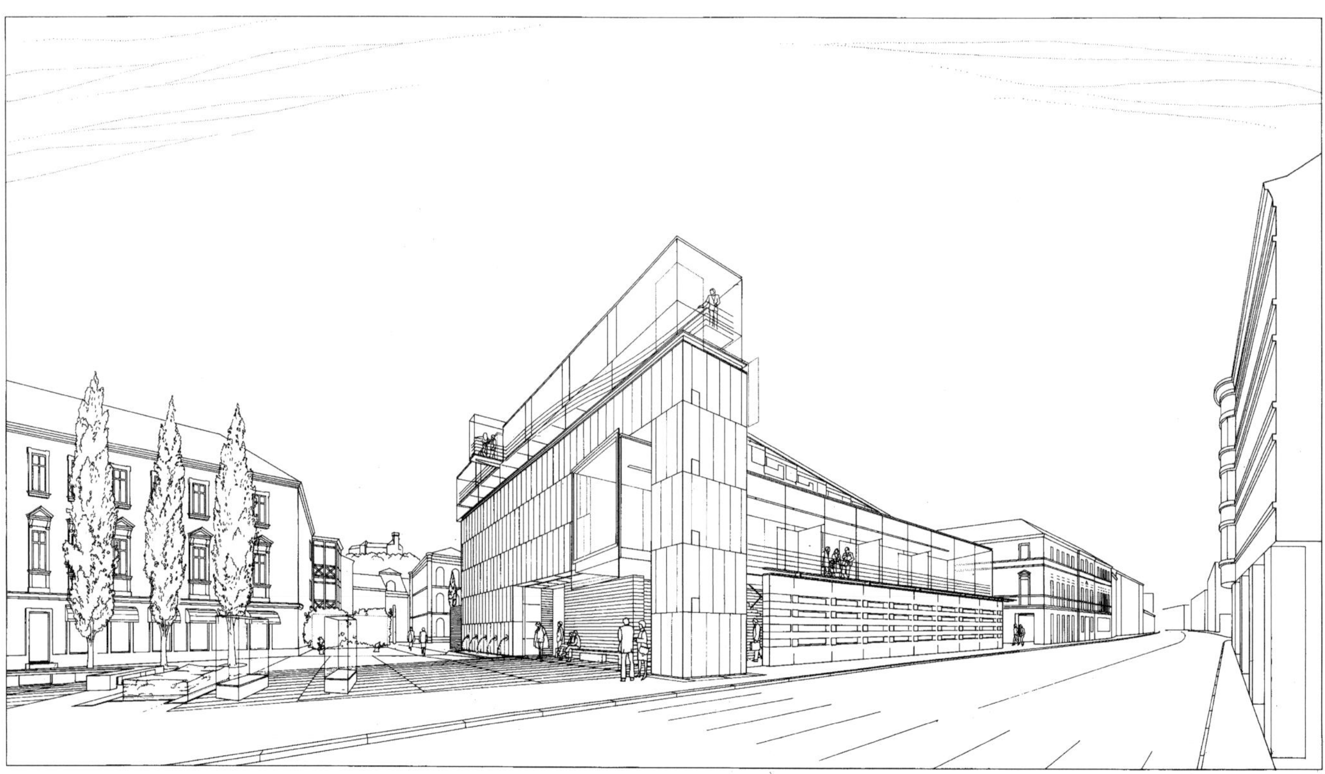

Schnitte und Ansichten / *Sections and elevation*

Modell / *Model*

Perspektive mit Ursulinenkirche / *Perspective with the Ursulinen church*

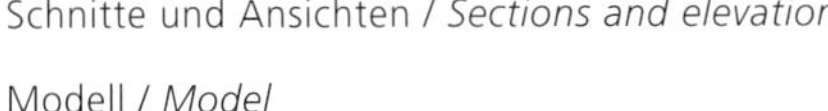

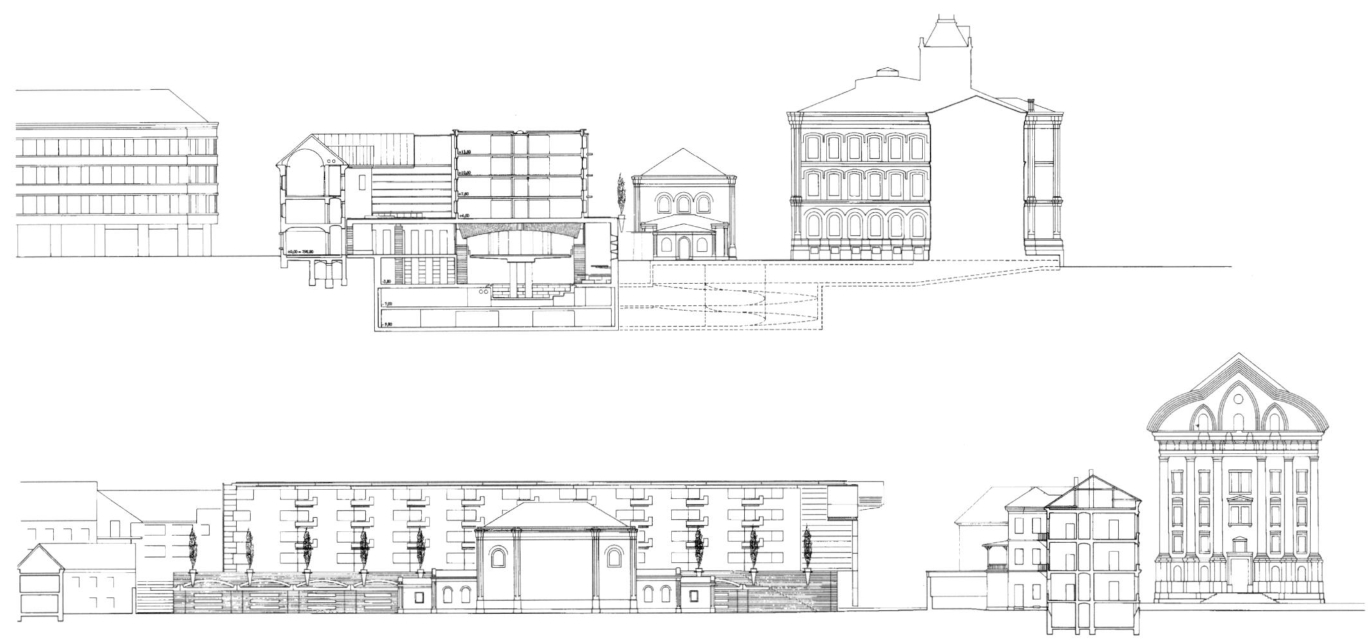

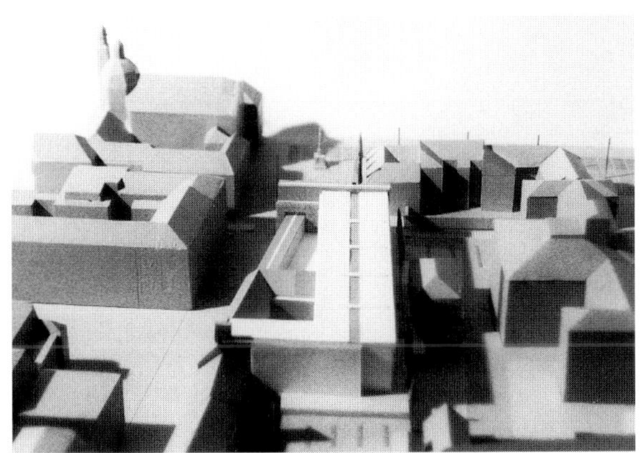

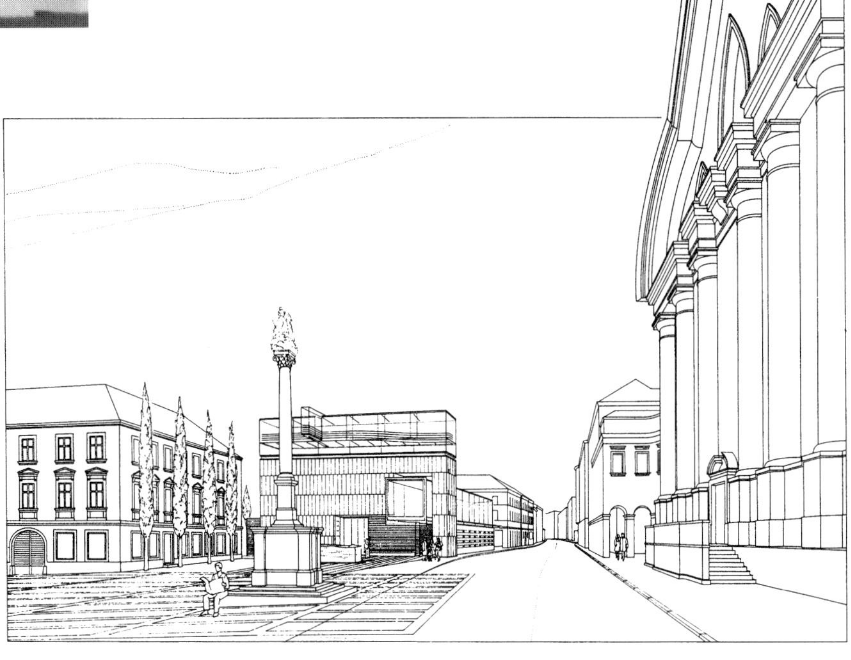

Büro- und Geschäftshaus Arndtstraße, Wien / *Office and commercial building, Arndtstrasse, Vienna*
1994

Wohnbebauung Am Liesingbach,
Wien, Typologien / *Housing development Am Liesingbach, Vienna,
typologies* 1994

Die Spanne zwischen einem kulturvoll gestalteten und eingerichteten Einfamilienhaus und dem sozialen Wohnbau mag auf den ersten Blick sehr weit erscheinen. Hier die sensibel nachempfundene Individualität einer vorhandenen und dem Entwerfer bekannten kleinen Gemeinschaft, dort die unspezifizierte, oft gleichartige Hülle für viele, die in kleinsten und mittelgroßen Familienverbänden in typisierten Wohnungen leben und die individuellen Bedürfnisse in der Regel nur mit der Möblierung differenzieren können. Die Wohnanlage birgt aber auch eine Chance, nämlich die Chance zur Stadt, zu urbaner Identität, was dem Einfamlienhaus wegen seiner geringen stadtbildenden Möglichkeiten abgeht. Natürlich ist ein große Wohnanlage nicht per se urban, und die sozialen Probleme, die auch in bestehenden Stadtquartieren schwer zu bewältigen sind, können mit architektonischen und urbanistischen Maßnahmen nicht auf Vorrat vermieden werden. Deutlich ist jedoch an den Wohnbebauungen Boris Podreccas sein Bekenntnis zur Stadt ablesbar. Beim Projektieren denkt er nicht bloß an optimierte Erschließungswege, dichte Packung der Wohneinheiten, gesicherte Privatheit usw., sondern er sieht die geplanten Gebäude immer auch als Teile der Stadt, wobei er in den oft ungenügend differenzierten Gebieten der Stadtperipherie vorhandene Ansätze zu strukturierenden Elementen aufnimmt und verstärkt und den Wohnbau auf diese Weise in das Gefüge einschreibt und ihm damit zu einer mit dem Vorhandenen vernetzten Identität verhilft.

Mit dem Konzept der Wohnbebauung Kapellenweg in dem urbanistischen Entwicklungsgebiet nördlich der Donau, aber auch bei der Wohnbebauung Am Liesingbach, hat er eine zeitgenössische Form kollektiver Identität gesucht, die von einer weniger streng formierten Gesellschaft ausgeht, als dies in den 20er Jahren bei den Wohnhöfen und Superblocks der Fall gewesen war. Diese Verabschiedung einer Strukturform, für die es keine gesellschaftliche Realität mehr gibt, war die eine Problematik, die es zu lösen galt. Auf der anderen Seite standen die wesentlich gefährlicheren, gesellschafts- und stadtfeindlichen Entwicklungen im Wohnbau, die aus Desinteresse an anderen als ökonomischen Fragen, aus kultureller Unbedarftheit und urbanistischer Ahnungslosigkeit resultierten. Der Wohnbau war in den 70er Jahren zu einer sinnentleerten Reproduktion modernistischer Klischees verkommen, wobei unheilige Allianzen und Begünstigungen die Qualität noch weiter reduzierten. Diesem Zynismus, der Teile des Massenwohnnungsbaus noch heute beherrscht, setzen die identitätsstiftenden und soziokulturell offenen Entwürfe Podreccas eine menschliche, aber nicht unkritische Haltung entgegen.

In kleinerem Maßstab ist auch die Reihenhauszeile Laab im Walde durchaus städtisch, obwohl sie im mehrheitlich ländlich bestimmten Niederösterreich steht. Die dichte Koppelung gleicher Einheiten, die im Inneren nach den Wünschen der Bewohner eingeteilt werden können, ist städtisch. Die Großform

At first glance, the difference between a one-family home designed and furnished with cultural taste, and a social housing project may appear to be very great. On the one hand, a sensible and astute consideration for an individual living in an existing small community who is known to the designer, and on the other hand, the nonspecific and often uniform shell for the multitudes who, living in small and medium-sized communities, reside in stereotyped apartments while differentiating their individual needs and tastes only by means of the interior furnishings. However, the housing development also offers an opportunity towards the city, towards an urban identity, which the one-family home, due to its small possibility for imprinting on the city's urban structure, cannot keep up with. Of course, a large housing development is not urban as such, and the social problems which are difficult to overcome in existing city quarters cannot be prevented beforehand by architectural and urban measures. However, Boris Podrecca's confession towards the city can be easily detected in his housing constructions. When projecting, he does not think only of optimized connections: a dense arrangement of the units, the assurance of privacy, etc. On the contrary, he always considers the planned buildings as integral parts of the city. Doing this, he takes up the disposition for structural elements in the oftentimes insufficiently differentiated areas of the city's periphery, strengthens them, and thus imprints the housing construction into the arrangement thereby helping it towards an identity interwoven with the existing. With the concept for the housing development, Kapellenweg, in the urban development area north of the Danube, and also with the development, Am Liesingbach, he searched for a form of collective identity, assuming a less strictly formed society than was the case with the apartment houses and super-blocks of the '20s. Leaving behind this structural form which no longer functioned for todays society was one problem that needed to be solved. On the other hand, there were the much more dangerous, anti-social and anti-urban developments in the housing construction which were a result of a disinterest in others, economic questions, a lack of

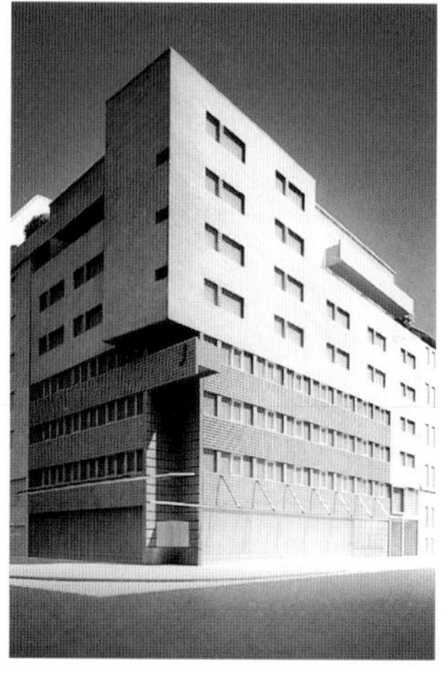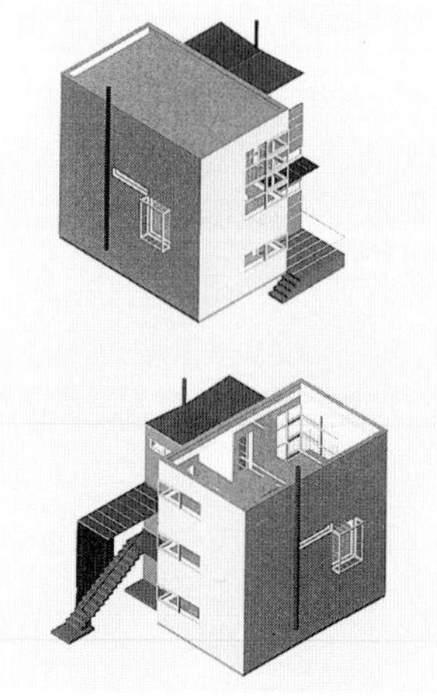

entspricht einem Häuserblock, die Sonderformen an Zeilenkopf und -ende sind typologisch Elemente der Stadt, auch wenn sie dort dichter stehen. Eine Wurzel mag in den Arbeiterwohnhäusern des 19. Jahrhunderts liegen, der größere individuelle Spielraum und die bessere soziale Stellung der Bewohner weist die Häuserzeile aber als Produkt der zweiten Hälfte des 20. Jahrhunderts aus.

Trotz begrenzter Quadratmeterzahlen, wie im sozialen Wohnbau üblich, erreicht Boris Podrecca mit räumlich interessanten Grundrissen, daß die Kultur des Idividuums nicht vernachlässigt wird. Gleichzeitig ist jedoch der Gedanke an die Stadt immer präsent: kollektive Erinnerung und ein dichtes, vielfältig-urbanes Leben. Beim freistehenden Haus sind dagegen Wohnkultur, handwerklich gediegene Herstellung, sinnlich greifbare Präsenz der Materialien, räumliche Spannung, Verwobenheit mit der Kultur- und Architekturgeschichte sowie die speziellen Bedürfnisse der Bewohner individuell konkret umgesetzt. Dennoch wird bei der Villa in Cavtat die übergeordnete Struktur des Territoriums ebenso berücksichtigt: die Küste, der Hügel, der terrassierte Hang.

Die Pole Sozialwohnbau und Villa markieren die große Bandbreite im Schaffen Boris Podreccas, seine Gelände- wie Gesellschaftsfühligkeit, die neben dem Einsatz für den Einzelnen die kulturelle Metaebene nie vergißt.

cultural considerations and urban clues. The housing construction had degraded into a senseless reproduction of modernistic stereotypes in the '70s when unholy alliances and self-gratification reduced the quality even more. This cynicism still dominating parts of the mass housing constructions today was opposed by a humane but critical attitude in Podrecca's designs which are supporting an identity and are socio-culturally open.

On a smaller scale, the linear row house buildings, Laab im Walde, is rather urban in its design although it is located in the mainly agricultural Niederösterreich. The dense coupling of equal units which on the inside can be divided according to the inhabitant's wishes, is an urban concept. The large form corresponds to a housing block; the special forms at the head and end of the linear buildings are typological elements of the city, even though they may be arranged in a denser way there. One root may be the working-class housings of the 19th century. The large room for individual activities and the improved social standing of the inhabitants, however, reveal the line of houses to be a product of the second half of the 20th century. Despite the limited square area, common in the social housing construction, Boris Podrecca assures, through the use of interesting spatial ground plans, that the culture of the individual is not neglected. At the same time, the thought of the city is always present: collective memory and a dense, multifaceted urban life.

In the case of single-family homes, however, the living culture, the genuine manual production, the sensually tangible presence of the materials and the spatial suspense, the interweaving with the cultural and architectural history as well as the special needs of the inhabitants, have all been individually realized. And yet, in the case of the villa, in Cavtat, the superimposed structure of the territory is considered just as much: the coast line, the hill, the terraced slope.

The polarity between social housing construction and villa mark the wide range of Boris Podrecca's creative work. His feeling for the grounds and for society, and his active engagement for the individual, never neglects the thought of the cultural meta-level.

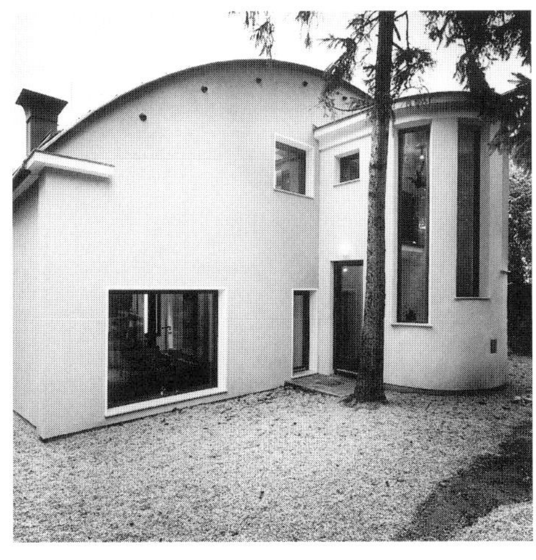

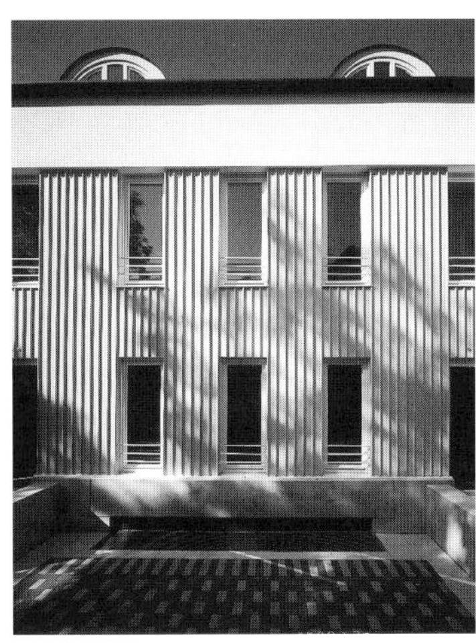

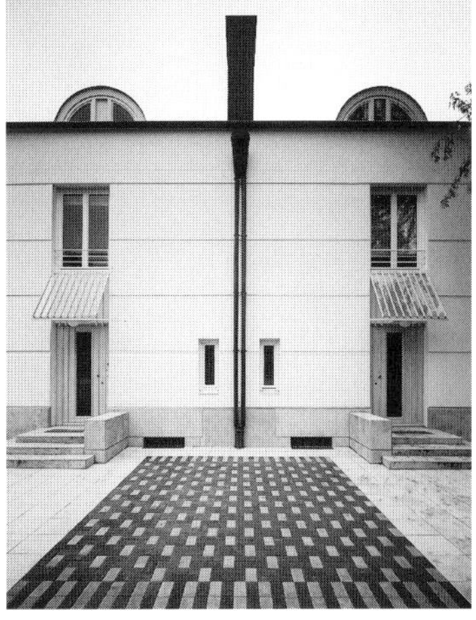

Wien-Donaustadt / *Vienna-Donaustadt* 1993

Perspektivische Skizze des Donauraumes /
Perspective sketch of the Danube area

Lage im Stadtgebiet / *Location in the city*

Als Antwort auf die breiartige Zersiedelung in den Wiener Bezirken nördlich der Donau durch Wohnanlagen grober Körnung, ohne Beachtung stadtmorphologischer Aspekte, wurde eine raumbildende Bebauung vorgeschlagen, die, obwohl auf vorhandene Strukturelemente wie Straßen usw. reagierend, als «Stadtparavent» überörtlich differenzierend wirken sollte. Die 150 bei 300 Meter langen, fünfgeschoßigen Trakte wurden nicht zu Höfen arrangiert, sondern sollten, Grenzen setzend, mit einer Längsfassade zur Stadt, mit der anderen ins Land hinaus blicken. Die kompakte Längsform der rückgratartigen Kernschicht wird relativiert von seitlich angelagerten Wohnungspaketen, so daß ein dreischichtiges Volumen entsteht. Auf unterer Maßstabsebene sind es Vordächer, Loggien und Terrassen, die den kompakten Charakter auflockern. Für die Gebäudeköpfe und anstelle der Wohnungen beim torartigen Durchbruch waren soziale und dienende Nutzungen vorgesehen, die aber nur zum Teil realisiert wurden. Nutzungsmäßige Durchmischung und Vielfalt im Großen sind so wichtig wie die räumliche Qualität der Wohnungen mit ihrer vertikalen Entwicklung. Die größeren Wohnungen sind als «Triplette» organisiert. Sie beginnen im Erdgeschoß mit Gartenanschluß und reichen über ein galerieartiges Zwischengeschoß bis ins dritte Stockwerk. Darüber ist eine Zeile Maisonetten angeordnet, wobei neben mittleren auch kleine Einheiten eingefügt wurden, die für selbständig werdende Kinder oder später als Auszugswohnung für die Eltern gedacht sind.

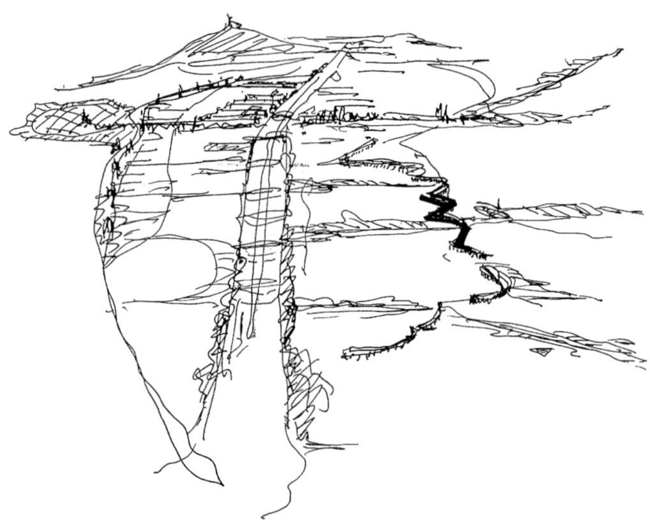

In answer to the amorphous sprawl of rough grained housing developments without consideration of the urban morphological aspects in Vienna's districts north of the Danube, a panorama creating development was suggested. Although reacting to existing structural elements such as streets, etc., it should have a differentiating effect reaching beyond the location, similar to a "city partitioning screen". The 150 by 300 meter long five-story block structures were not arranged into courtyards. Instead, they face the city with one longitudinal facade and face the country with the other, thus setting boundaries. The compact longitudinal shape of the spine-like core layer is made relative by laterally adjoining apartment parcels, creating a three-layered volume. On a smaller scale, there are canopies, loggias, and terraces which loosen up the compact character. Social and service utilities had been planned for the two building heads and gate element. However, they were only partially realized. A use-oriented mixture and variety on a large scale is as important as the spatial quality of the apartments with their vertical connections. The larger apartments begin on the ground floor, have a garden-access and, with a gallery level in between, reach up to the fourth floor. Above them a row of smaller maisonettes is arranged, with alternating mid-sized to smaller units which were designed for older children on their way to living independently, or for the parents to move into later on.

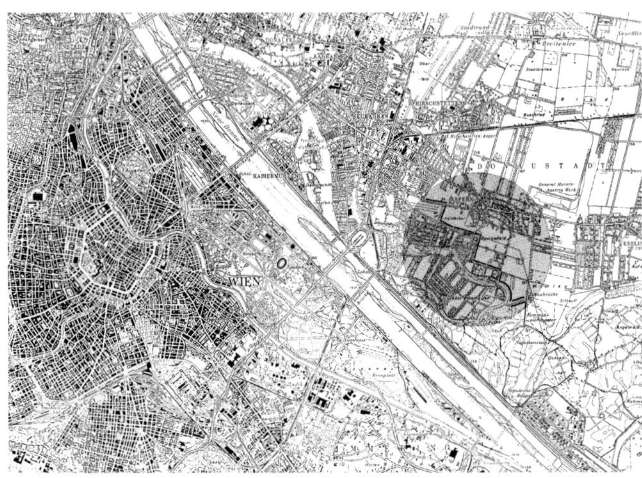

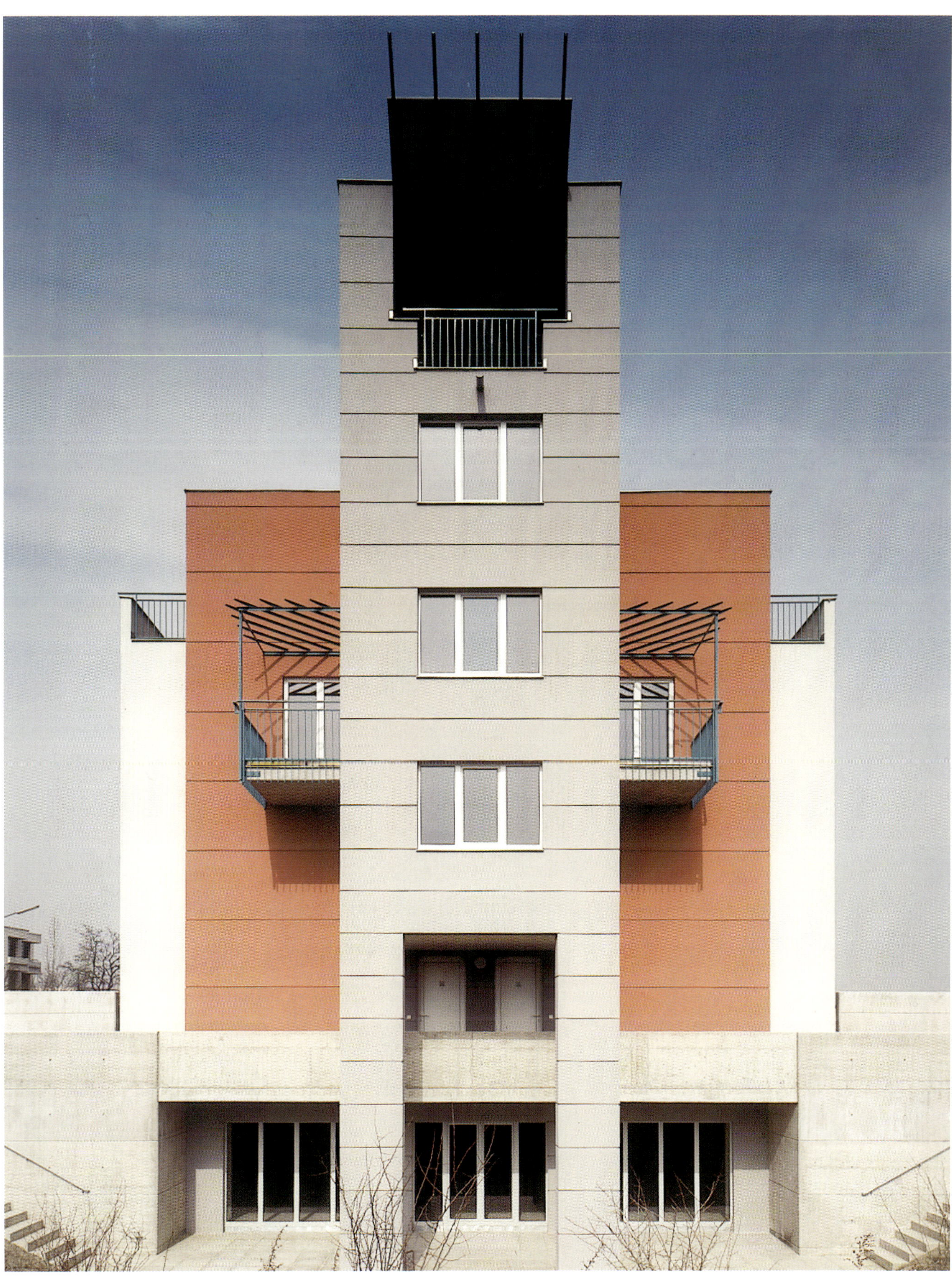

Ansichten und Schnitte / *Elevations and sections*

Ansicht von Osten / *View from the east*

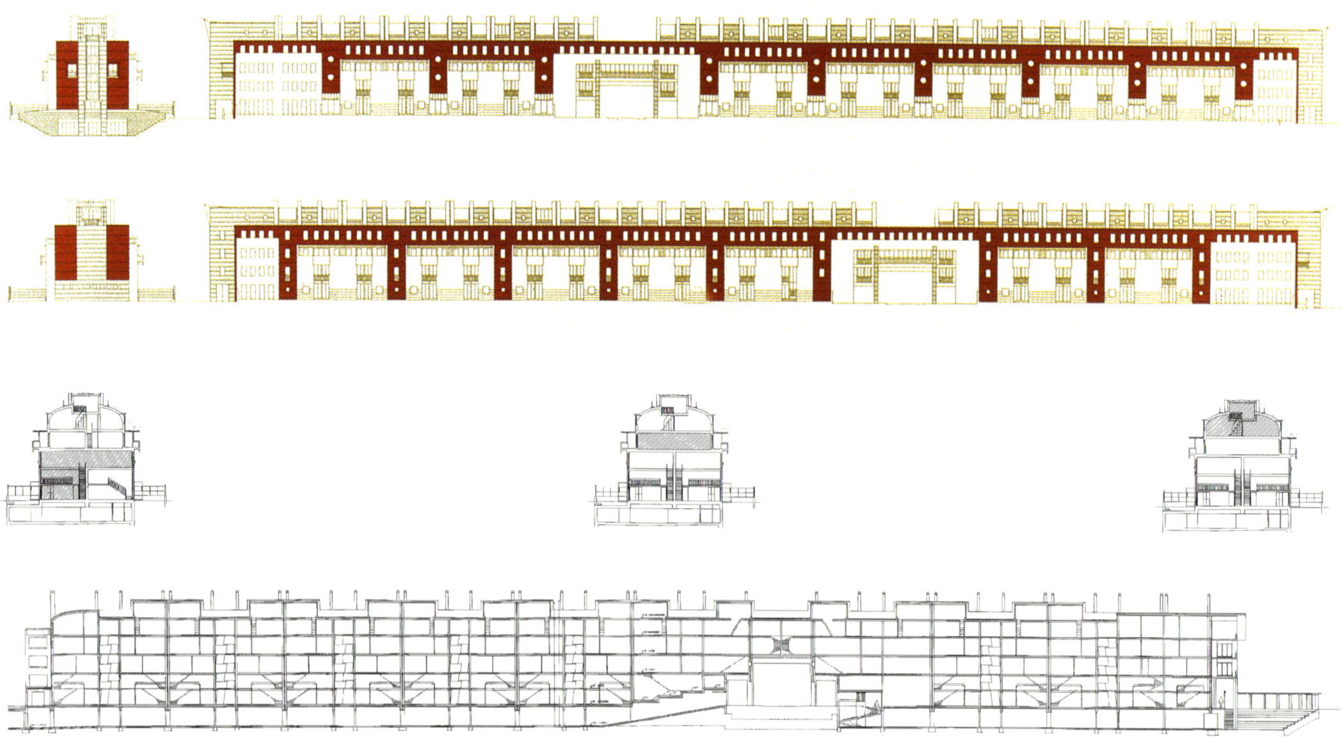

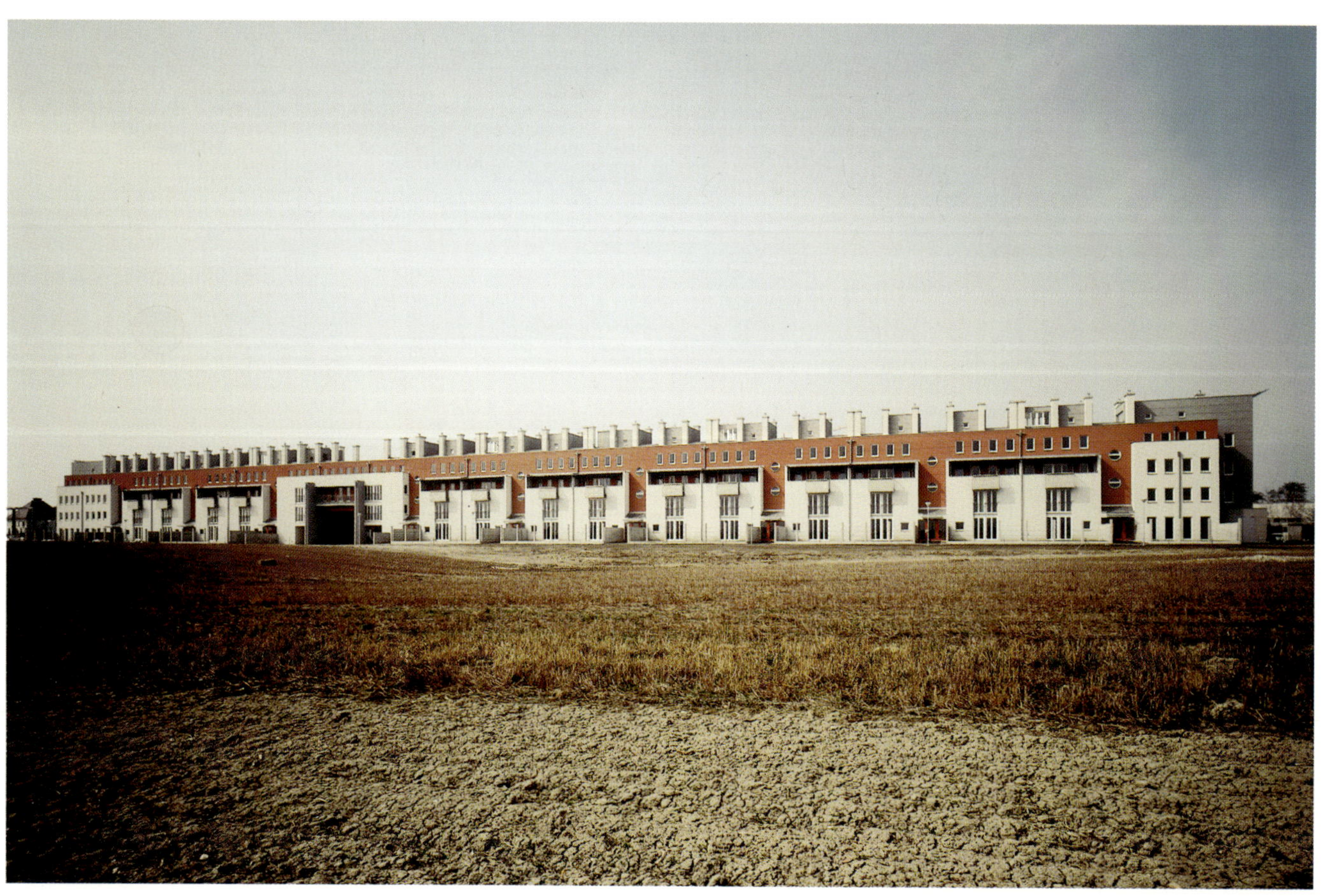

Dreischichtige Randbebauung / *Three-layered perimeter building*

Axonometrien der Prototypen / *Axonometric projections of the prototypes*

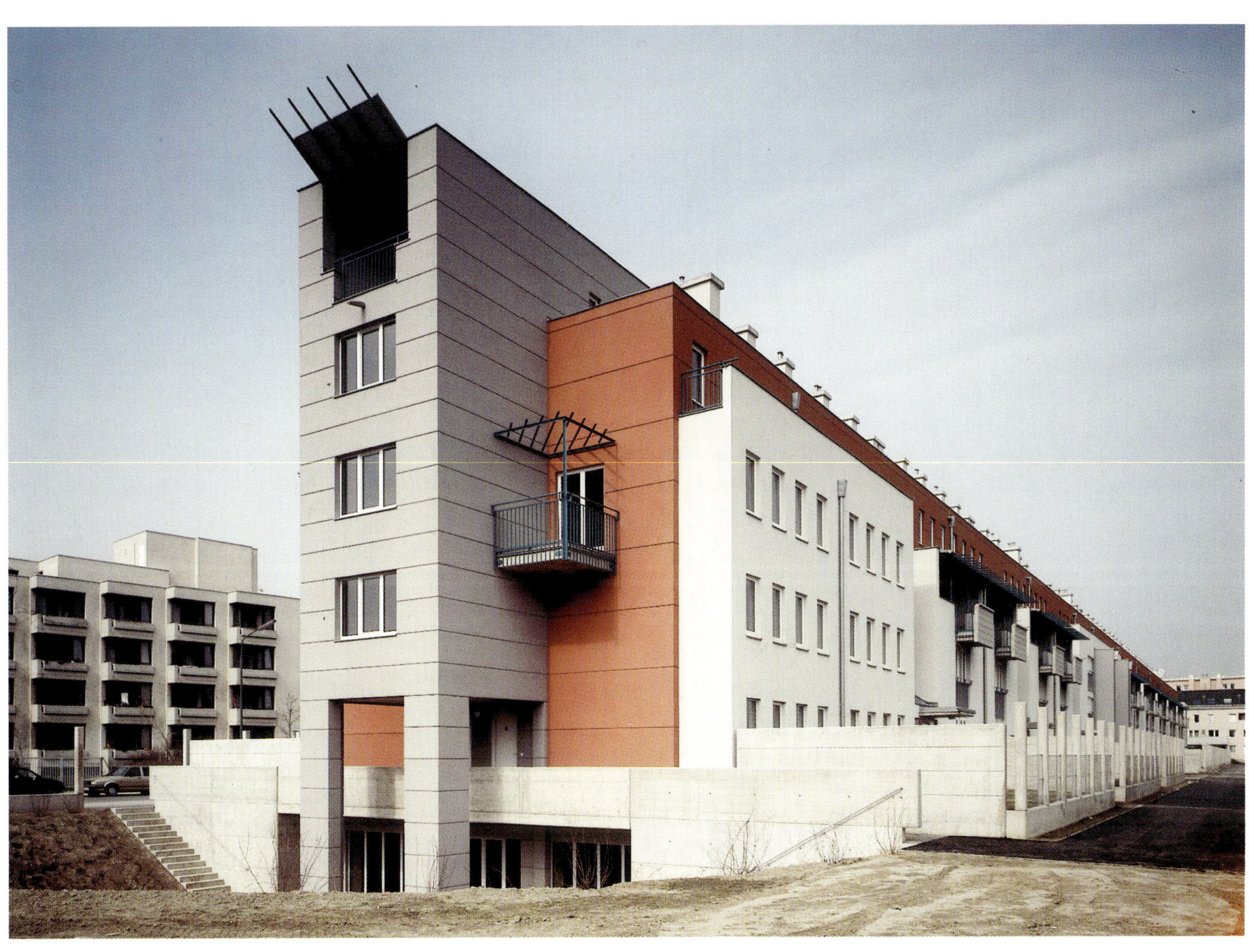

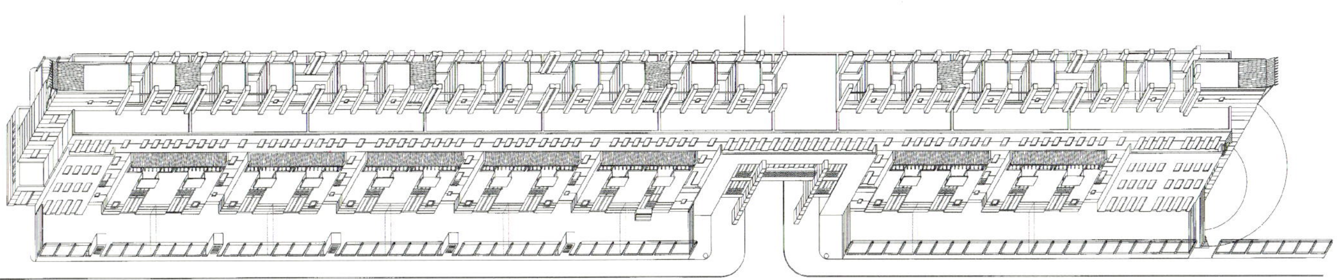

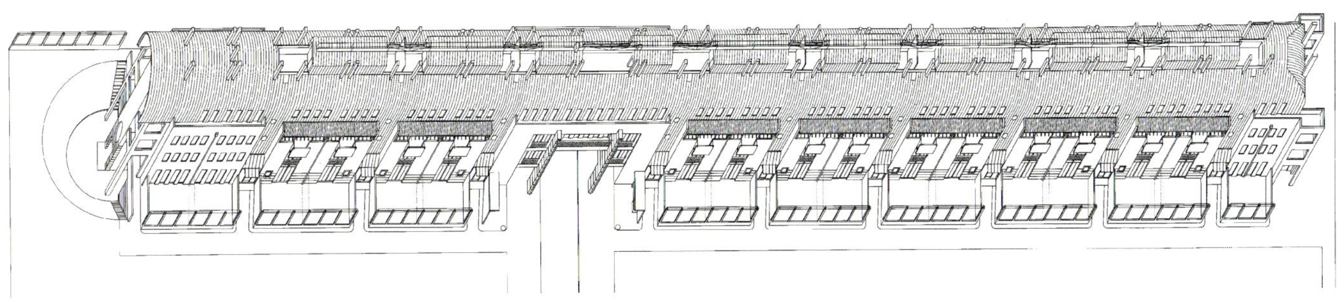

Laab im Walde, *Austria* 1994

Reihenhäuser, Gartenseite / *Rowhouses, garden view*

Ein Dutzend Reihenhäuser unter einzeln-giebelständigen Satteldächern fügen sich zu einer langen Zeile. Die kompakte Reihung wird relativiert durch eine geringfügige Schrägstellung, aus der zwischen den Häusern jeweils ein kleiner Versatz resultiert, sowie durch ein individuell ausgebildetes Element am Südkopf. Damit gerinnt die Zeile zur Figur, sie hat nun einen Körper, und wir reden von «Kopf», auch wenn die einzelnen Einheiten deutlich erkennbar bleiben. Entgegen der ursprünglichen Intention wurden einige weitere Häuser ebenfalls äußerlich individuell abgeändert und teils größer, teils kleiner ausgeführt. Sie besetzen das Ende der Zeile. Im Innern werden zahlreiche unterschiedliche Grundrißvariationen angeboten, die zusammen mit den späteren Besitzern entwickelt wurden. Dabei sind normale, exquisite, aber auch eigenartige Interpretationen des vorgegebenen Volumens entstanden. Während in vielen Fällen die Möglichkeiten des Vorbaus auf der Eingangs- oder des Wintergartens auf der hinteren Seite geschickt genutzt werden – womit beiläufig die Polyvalenz einer gegebenen Hülle demonstriert wird –, gibt es das Beispiel fast tragischen Ankämpfens gegen die Hülle, des krampfhaft Anders-Sein-Wollens, mit architektonisch wenig befriedigendem Resultat. Dennoch haben alle diese Sonderformen im Rahmen der Gesamtfigur platz, da der Anteil des «Körpers», das heißt an weniger differenziertem Gleichmaß ausreichend ist.

A dozen row houses beneath single-gable supported saddle roofs gather in a long line. The compact row is made relative by a slight angular positioning, resulting in a small off-set between the houses as well as by a independently elaborated element on the southern head. Thus the line reduces into a figure – it now has a body and we are speaking of the "head", although the separate units remain clearly recognizable. Contrary to the original intention, several more houses were also changed individually on the exterior and realized in either larger or smaller configurations. They occupy the end of the line. For the interiors, numerous different ground plan variations are offered which were developed in cooperation with the future owners. In this way, normal, exquisite, and also rather unique interpretations of the given volume came into being. While in many cases the possibilities of the fore-building on the side of the entrance or the winter garden to the rear are skillfully used – by the way demonstrating the manifold possibilities of a given shell – there is also the example of the almost tragic fight against the shell, the compulsive desire to be different, with an architecturally, ambiguous result. However, all these special forms fit into the context of the whole figure as shares of the "body", which means that a less differentiated equal measure suffices.

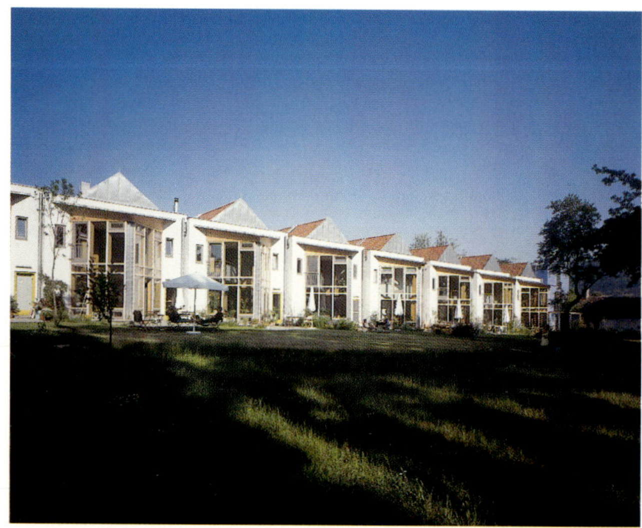

Axonometrie südseitig / *Axonometric projection on south side*

Nachtansicht, Gartenseite / *Night view, garden side*

Gartenansicht / *View of the garden*

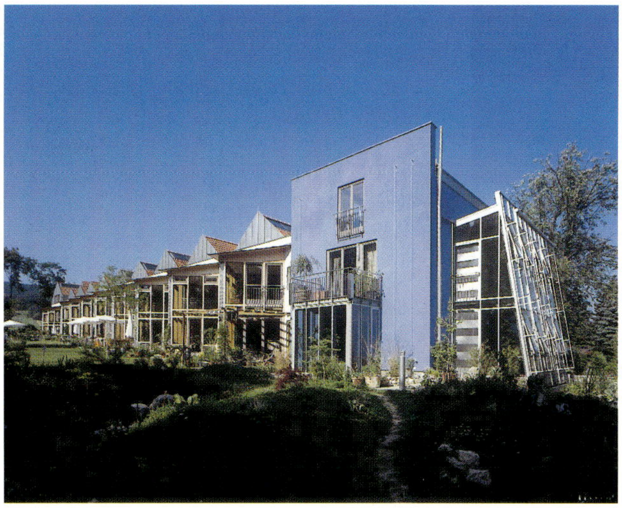

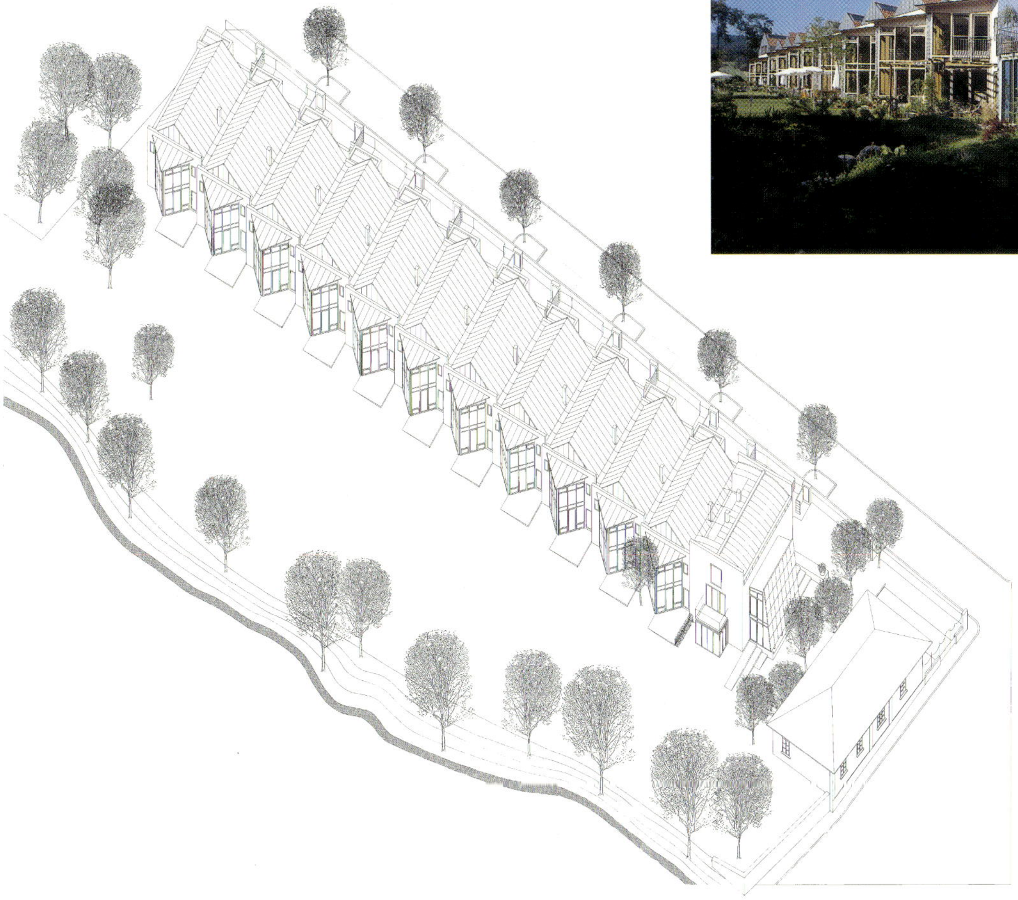

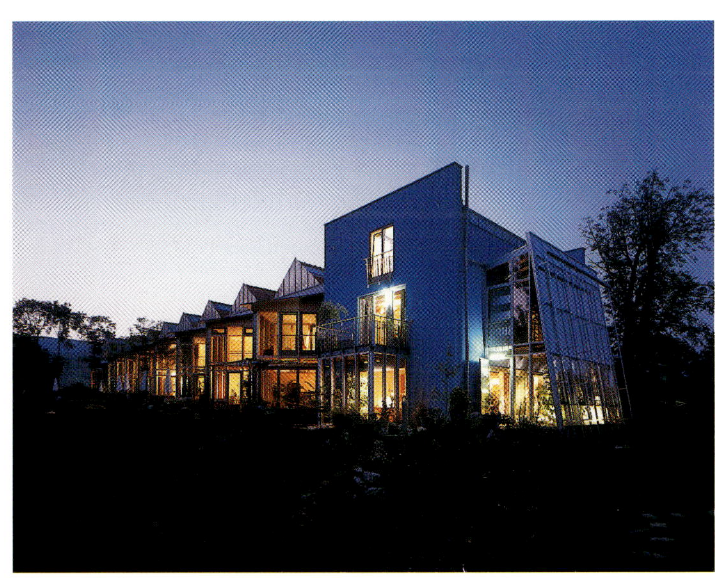

Blauer Kopfbau / *Blue head building*

Nachtansicht, Gartenseite / *Night view, garden side*

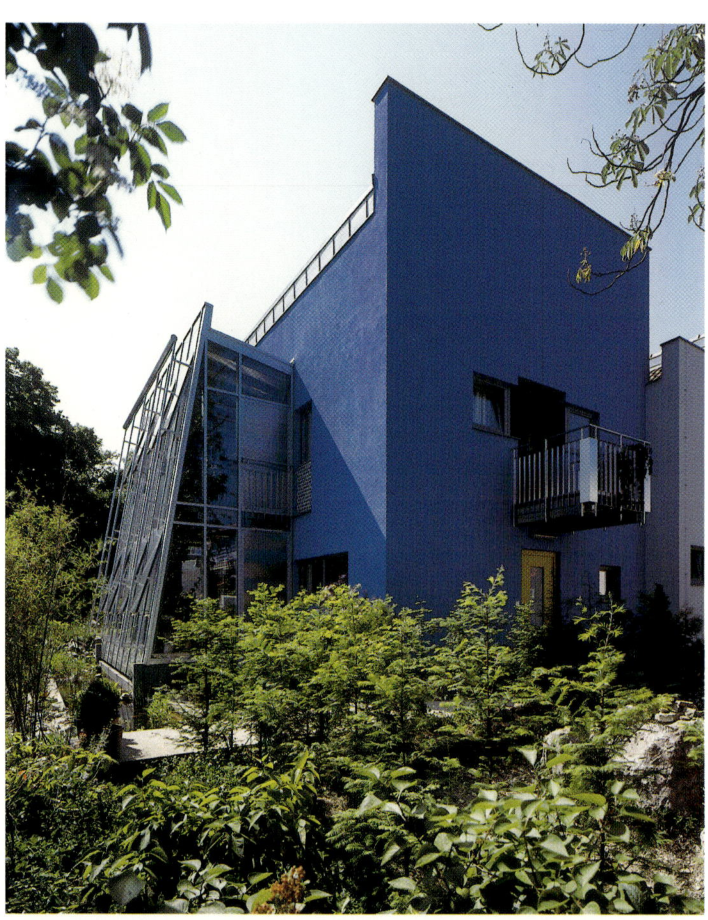

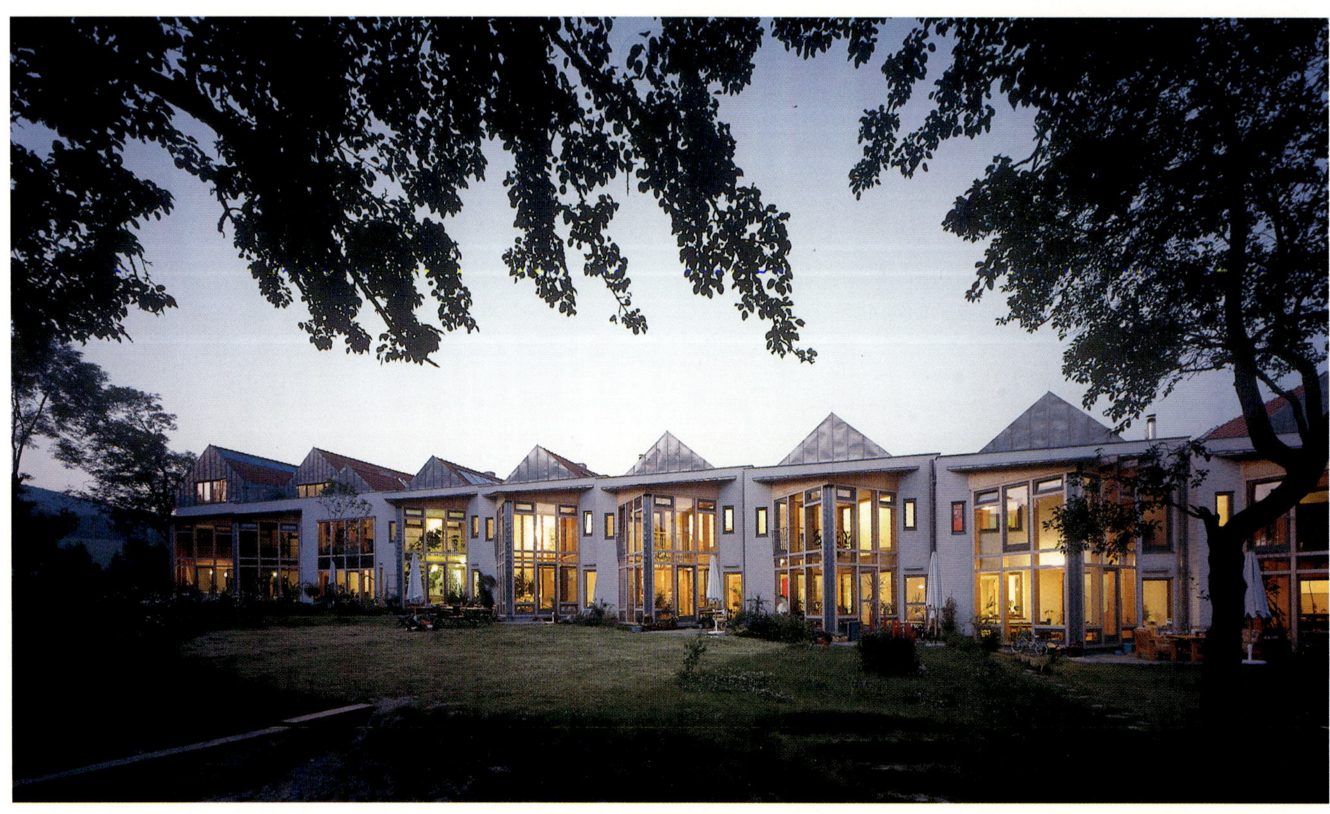

Kopfbau mit Glashaus / *Head building with glass house*

Eingangsvorbauten / *Entrance porch*   Glashaus, Ausschnitt / *Glass house, detail*

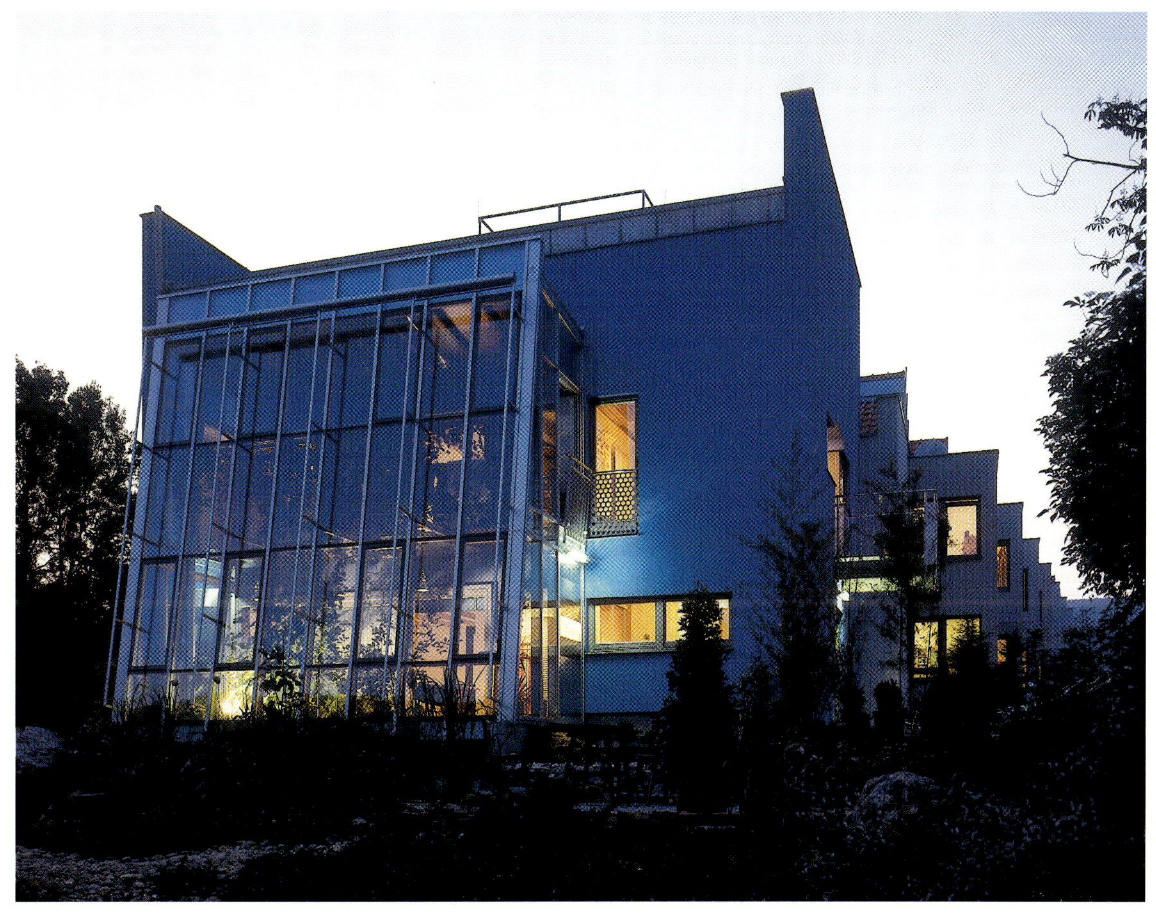

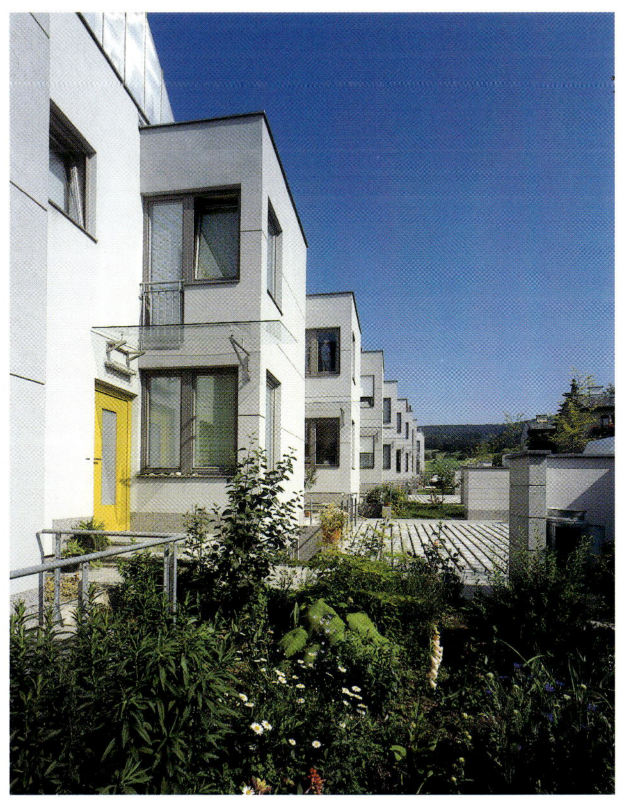

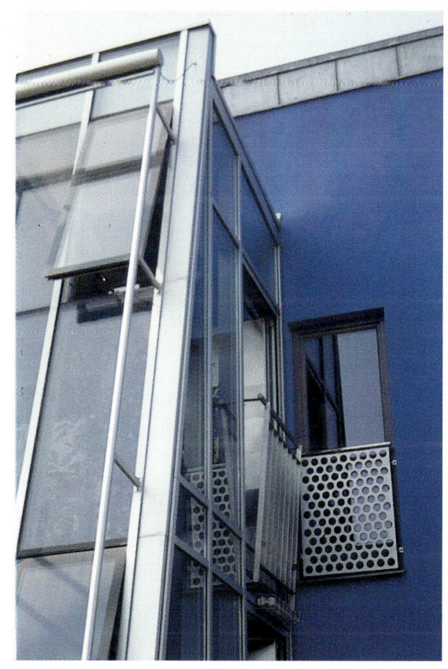

Innenraumtypologie / *Interior typology*

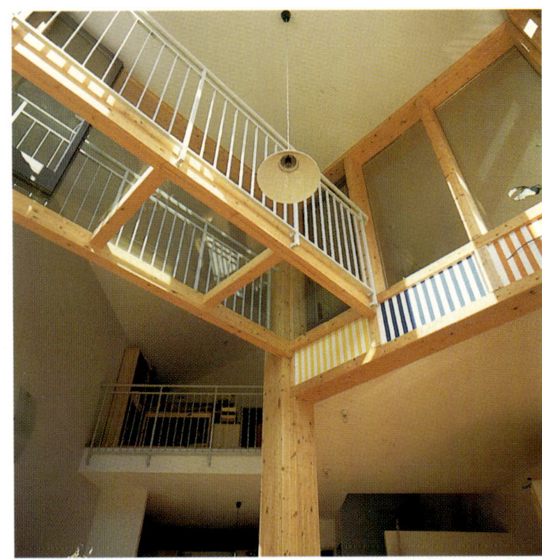

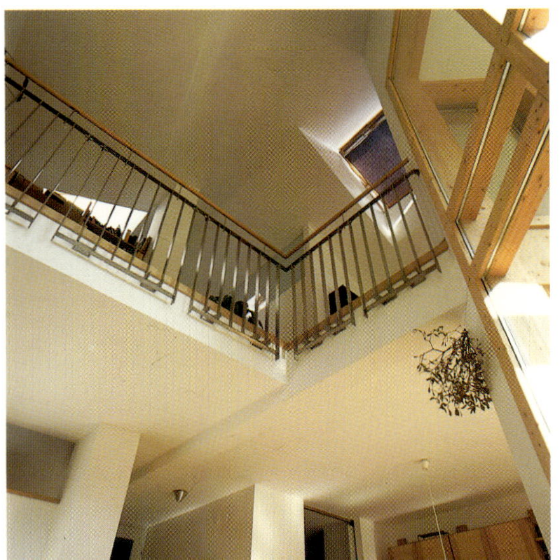

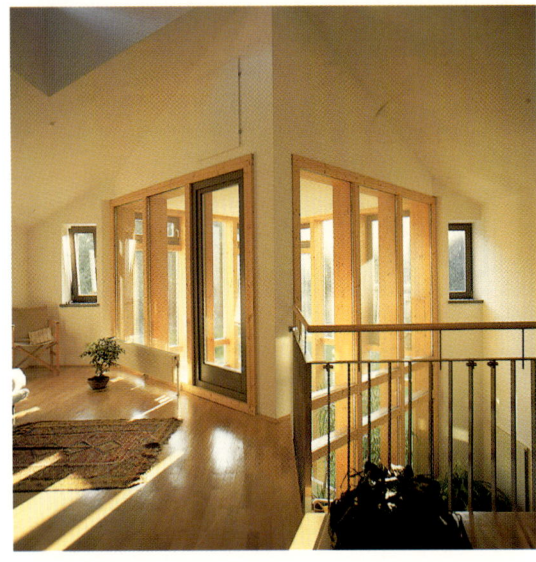

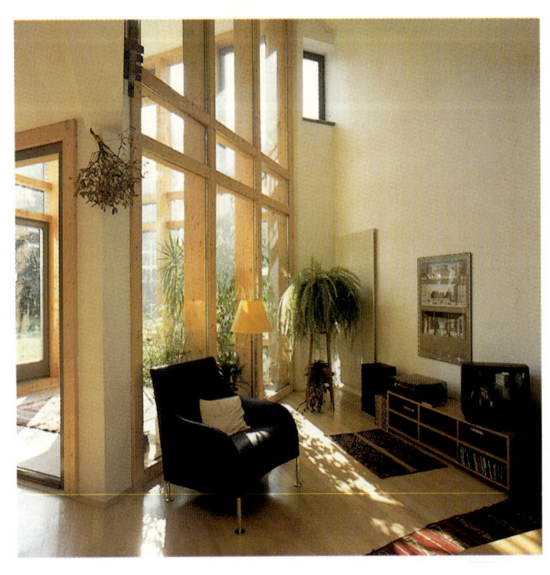

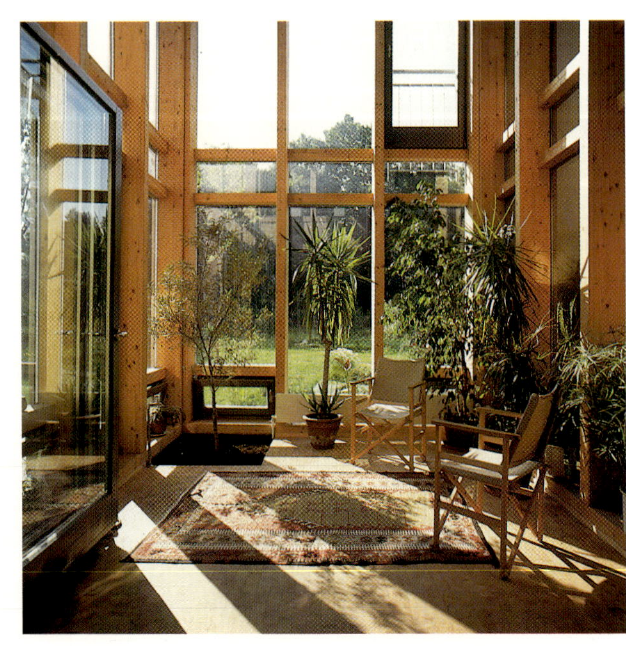

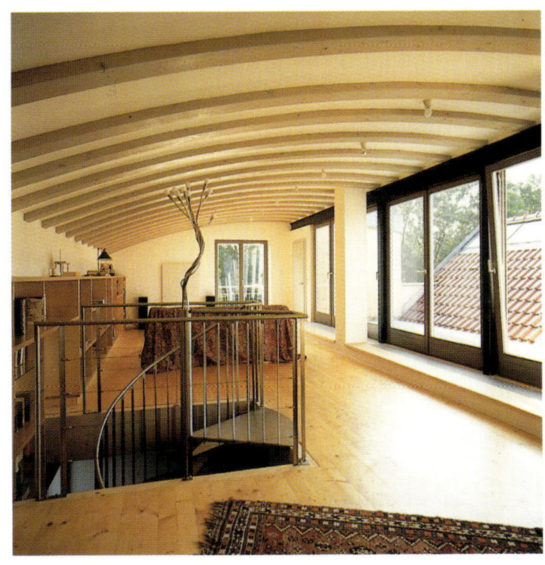

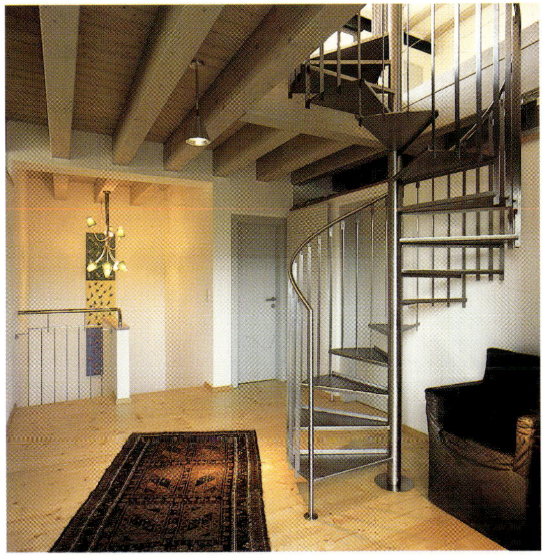

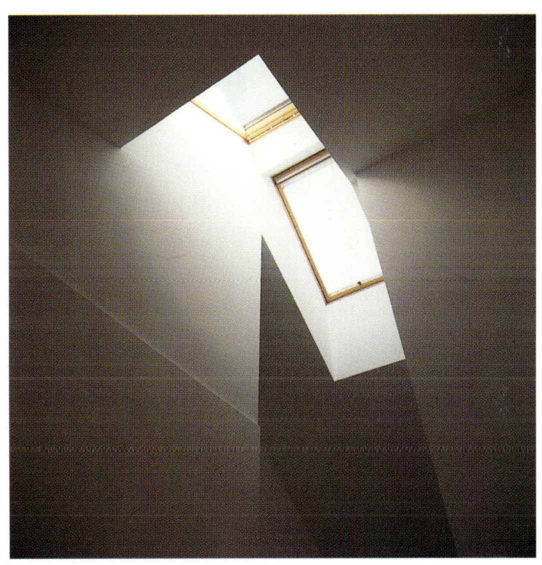

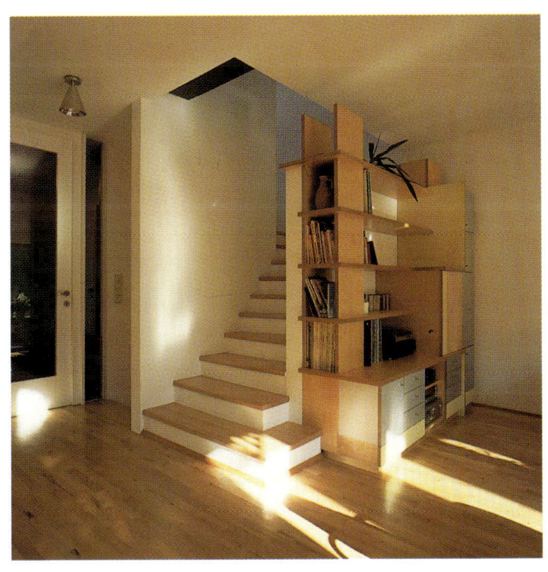

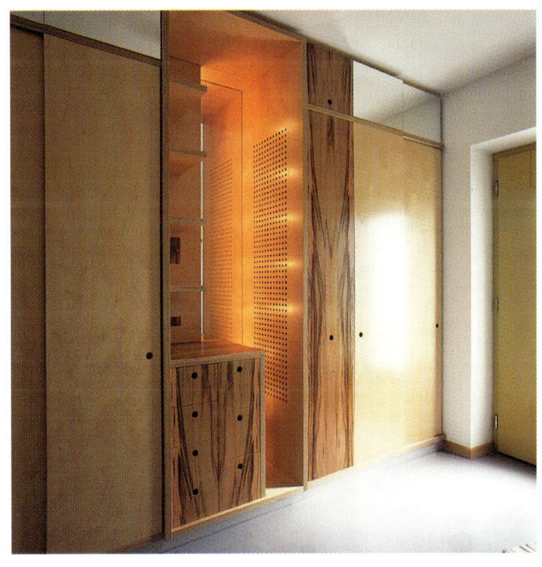

Wien-Liesing / *Vienna-Liesing* 1995

Straßenansicht / *Street view*

Grundriß 1. Obergeschoß / *Plan of second floor*

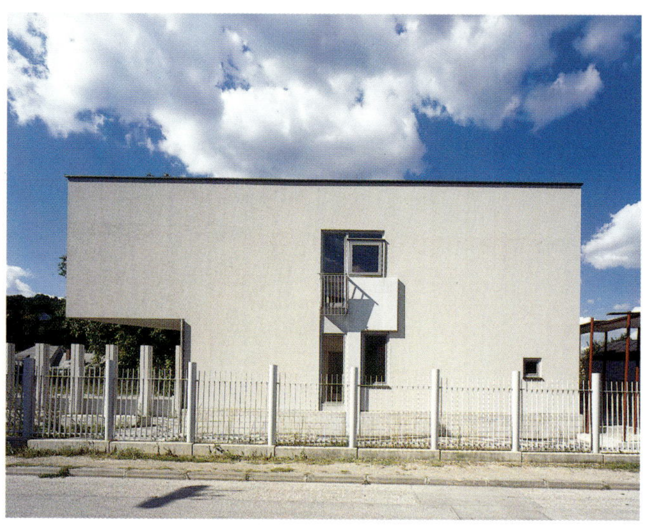

Zwei Normalparzellen eines Einfamilienhausquartiers schließen rückseitig an eine große Wiese, die den Blick auf einen Ausläufer des Wienerwalds freigibt. Das Wohnhaus ist parallel zur Straße in drei Teile gegliedert: Die Rückseite übernimmt ein länglicher, hochgestellter Quader, der in der Negativform des Schwimmbeckens eine Entsprechung findet. Zur Straße schirmt ein Mauerwinkel die übrigen Räume ab, im Obergeschoß verjüngt sich eine gerundete Innenseite zur Spitze, dazwischen dehnen sich Treppen und Gänge. Eine rote Mauerscheibe bildet hier eine vertikale Klammer. Vom seitlichen Zugang her geht der Blick durch den Eingangsbereich, die Kaskaden der Erschließung und den Wohnraum. Dann schweift der Blick hinaus in den Garten, wo die Sicht von einer langen Pergola gebremst wird. Jede Fassade ist entsprechend ihrer Ausrichtung zu einem Bild komponiert: eher geschlossen, aber nicht abweisend die Vorderseite; etwas offener und doch nüchtern die Rückseite; zum Garten sich öffnend und den Außenraum einsaugend die Westfassade mit einem «Bild im Bild», erzeugt von den Steintafeln vor dem gedeckten Sitzplatz. Im Innern entwickelt sich eine Wohnlandschaft über mehrere Ebenen. Sie führt vom halb versenkten Kaminraum über Wohn- und Tagesarbeitsräume hinauf durch die Treppenschlucht bis zur Terrasse auf dem rückseitigen Baukörper und verfügt über zahlreiche Nebenbeziehungen und Ausblickmöglichkeiten.

Two normal parcels in a community of single-family homes adjoin at the rear to a large lawn, opening the view to the Vienna forest. The house is arranged parallel to the street in three parts: the back side is taken up by a long vertically erected block-form which finds a correlation in the swimming pool's negative shape. Towards the street, an angular masonry form shields the other rooms. On the upper floor, a rounded inside tapers to a point; staircases and hallways stretch out in between. A red masonry structural wall forms a vertical link. From the side entrance, the view goes through the entrance lobby, past the cascading stairway, flaring out as it descends, and through the living space. Then the eyes are guided out into the garden where the view is halted by a long pergola. Each facade is a composed picture according to its orientation: the front side is rather closed but not repelling; the back side is more exposed and yet matter-of-fact; the west facade opens towards the garden and sucks in the outer space with a "picture within a picture" created by the stone plates in front of the covered sitting area. On the inside, the living space develops on several levels. It leads from the sunken fireplace room, through the living and working quarters up through the cascading stairway, and then to the terrace on the backside of the volume, thus offering numerous side-relations and possibilities for looking out.

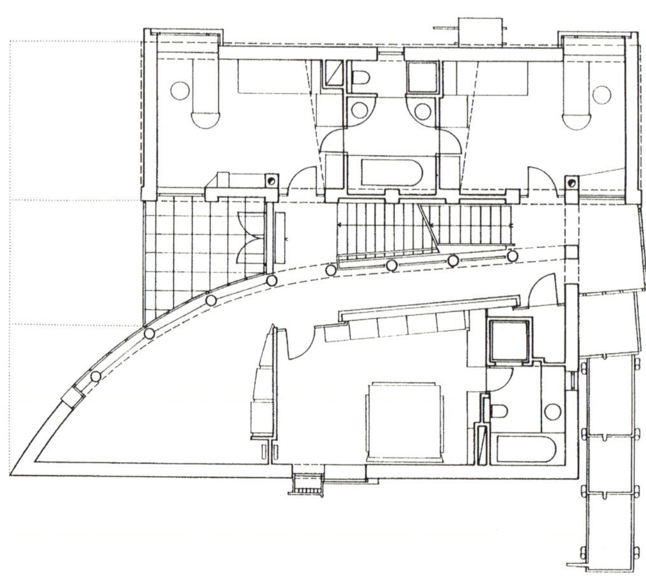

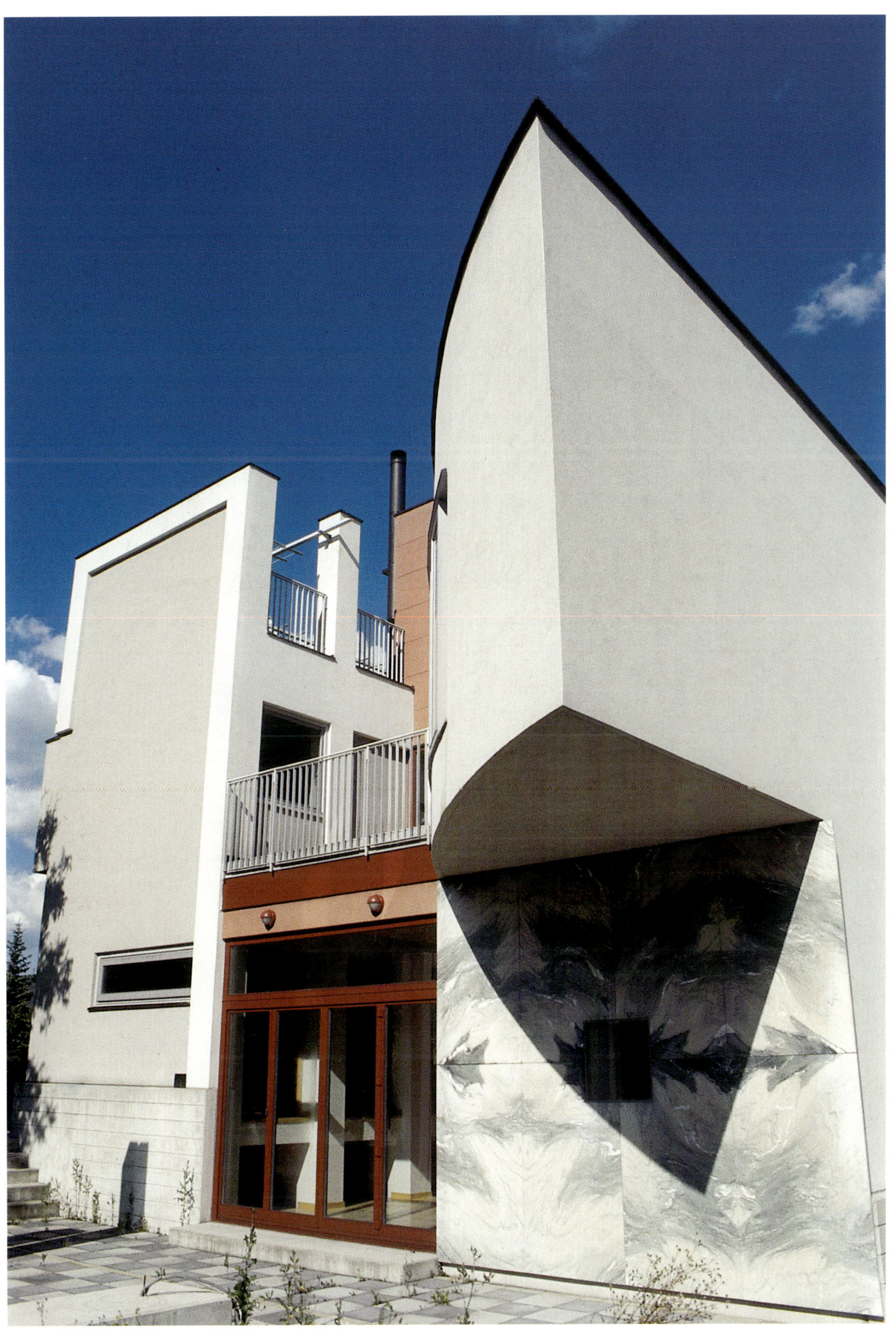

Eingangsbereich / *Entrance area*

Rückseite Garagen / *Rear garages*

Nordostansicht / *Northeast view*

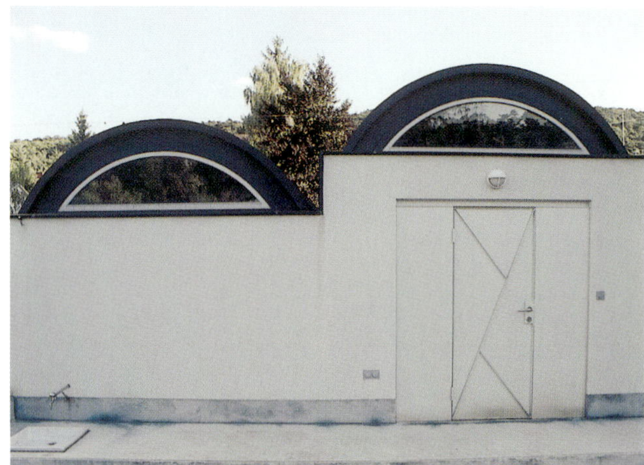

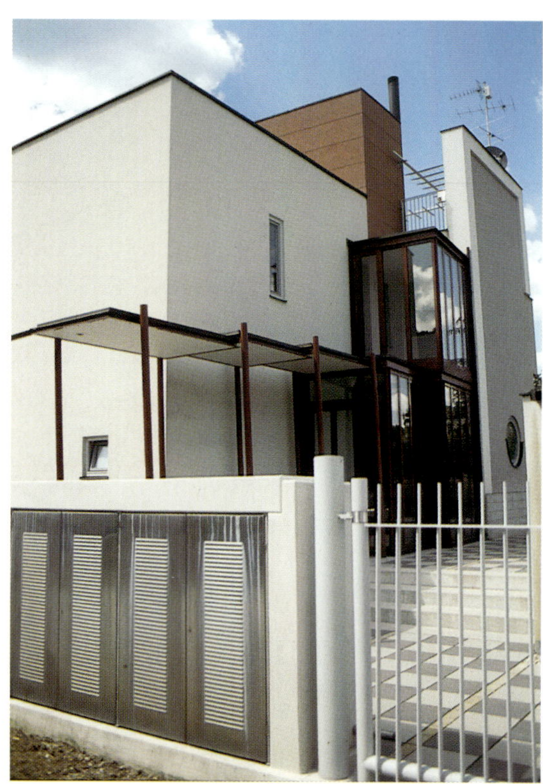

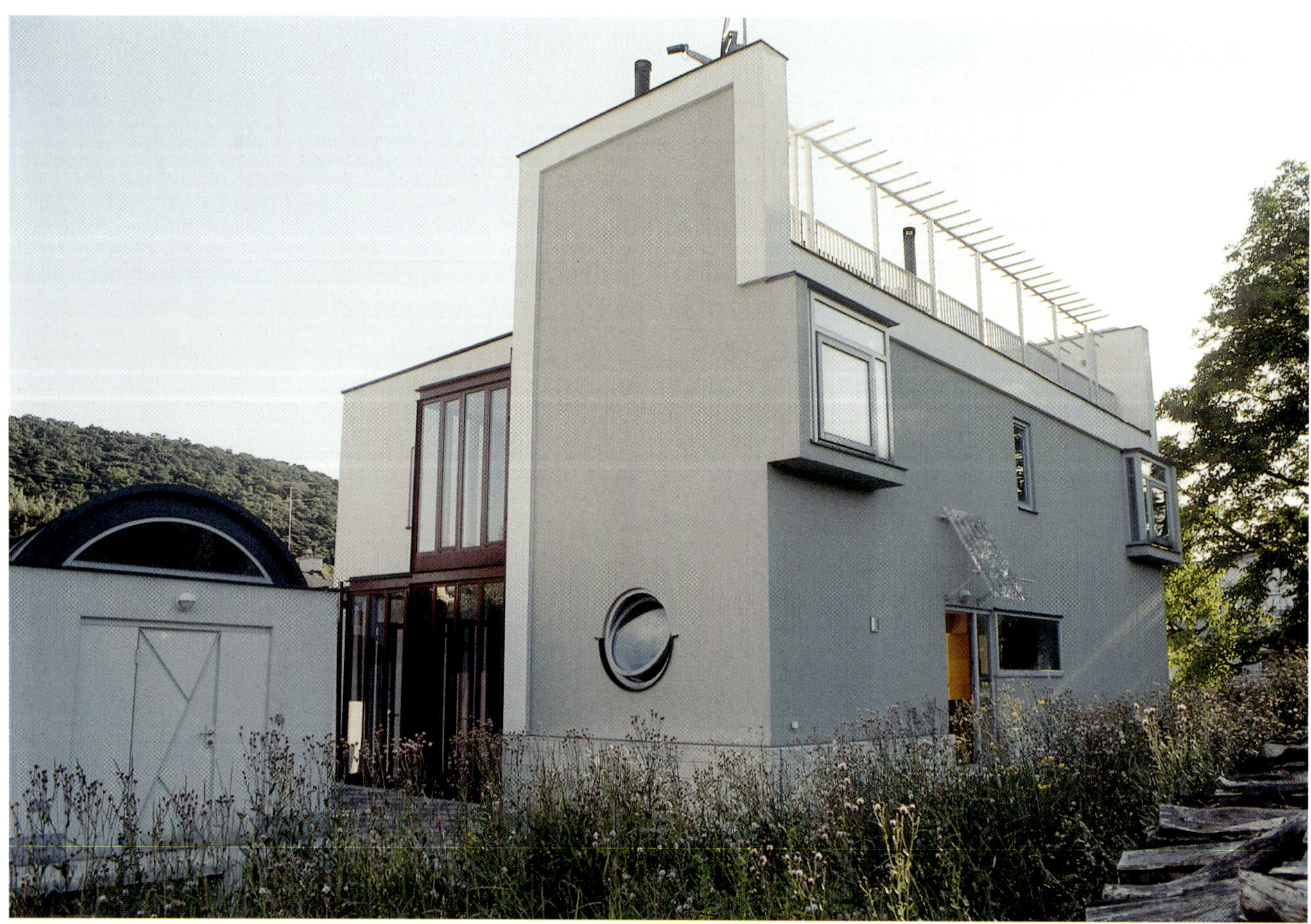

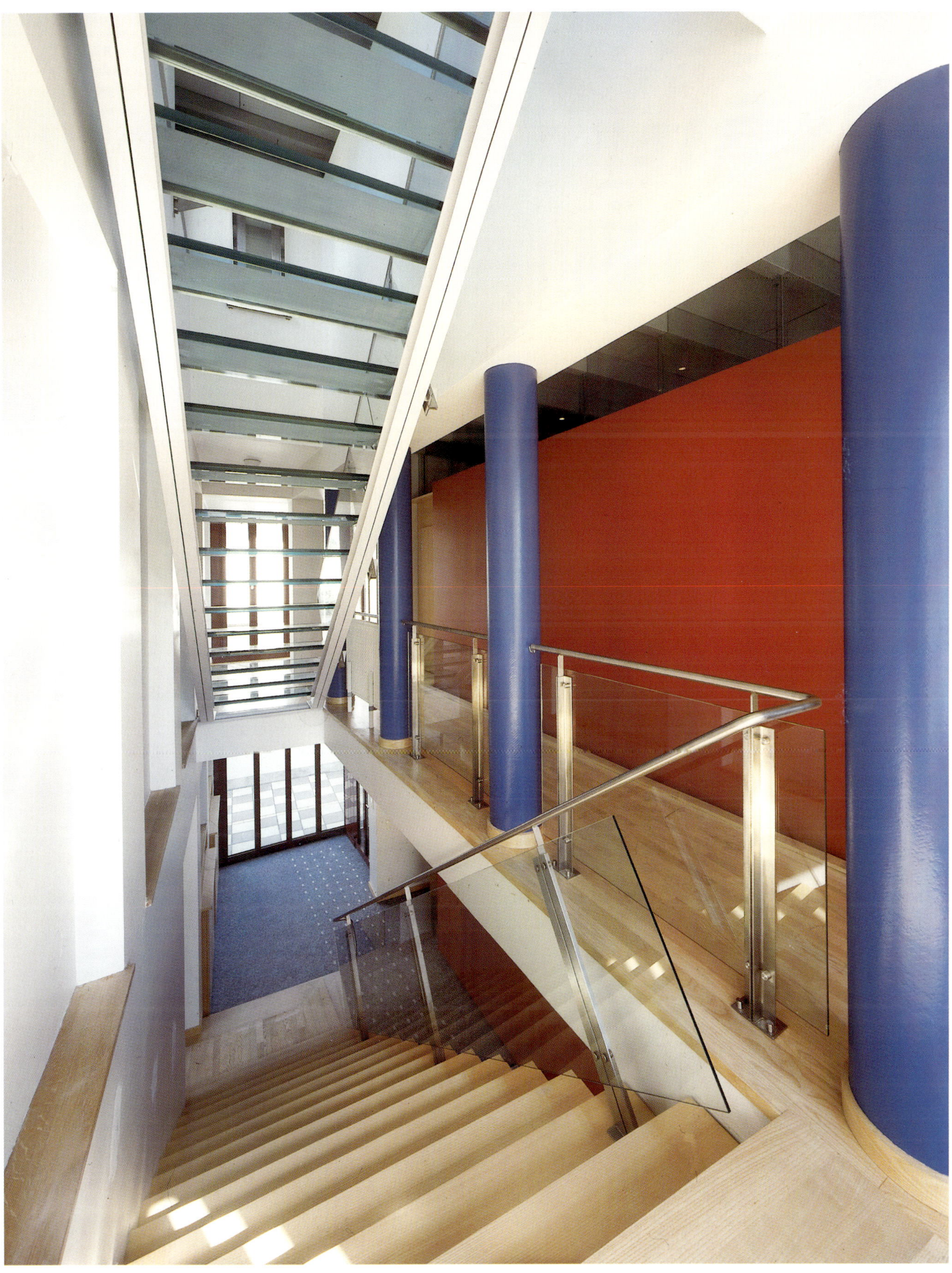

Wartungssteg / *Maintenance bridge*

Aufgang Dachterrasse / *Stairway, roof terrace*

Stiegenhaus, Ausschnitt / *Staircase, detail*

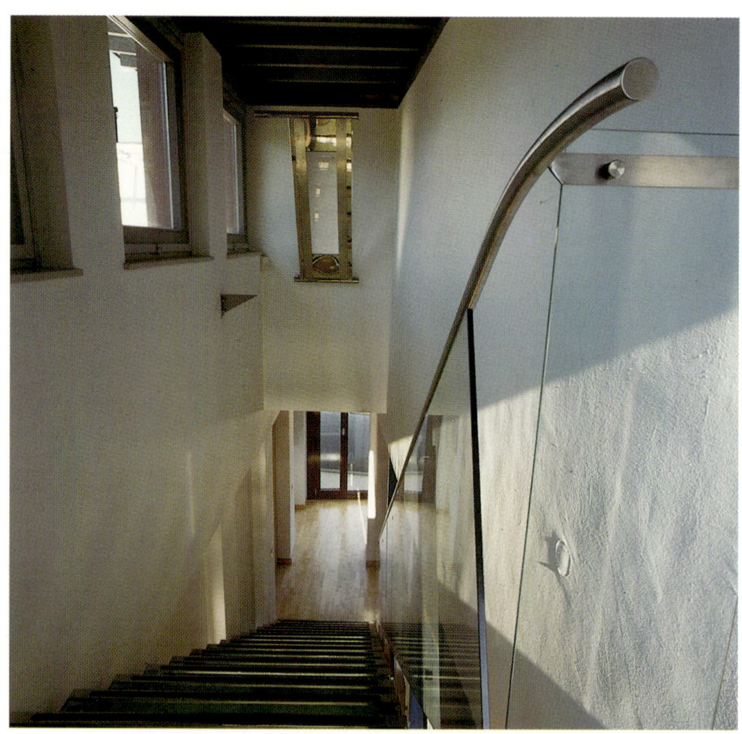

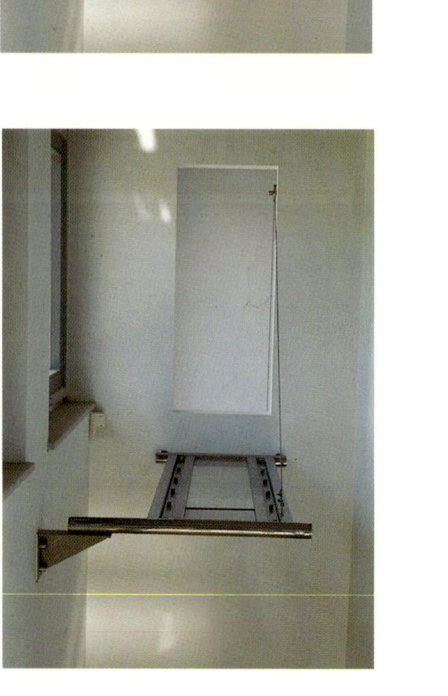

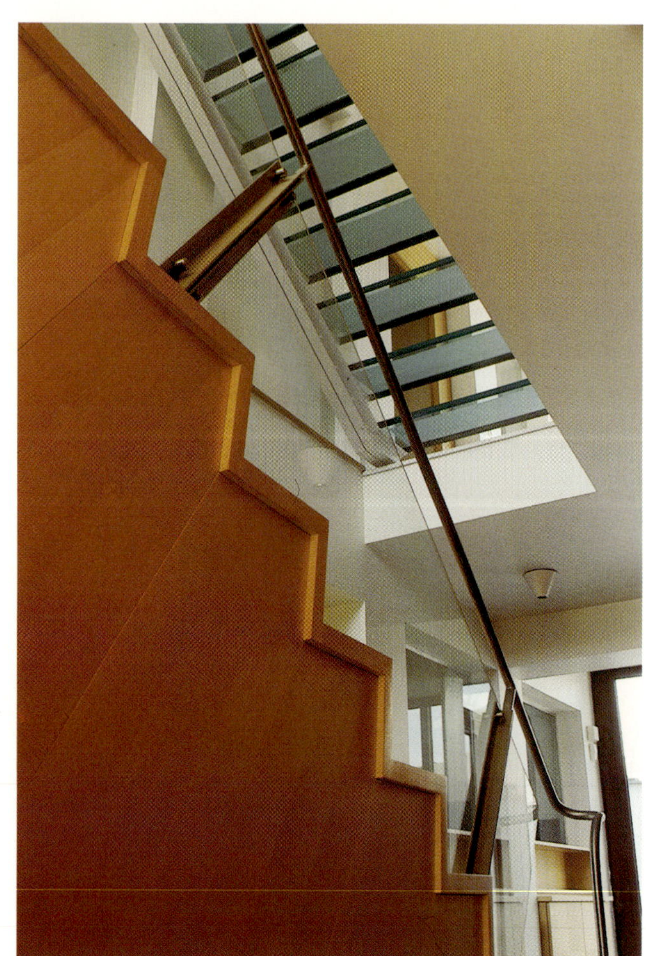

Speisezimmer / *Dining room*
Stiegenhandlauf, Detail / *Staircase railing, detail*

Bibliothek / *Library*
Zugang Wohnraum / *Entrance to living room*
Musikzimmer / *Music room*

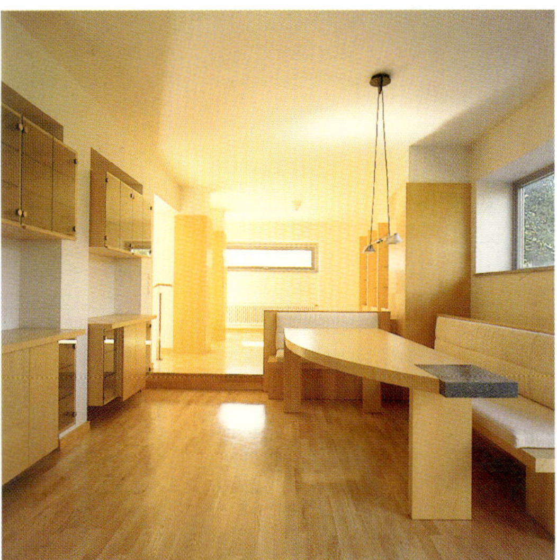

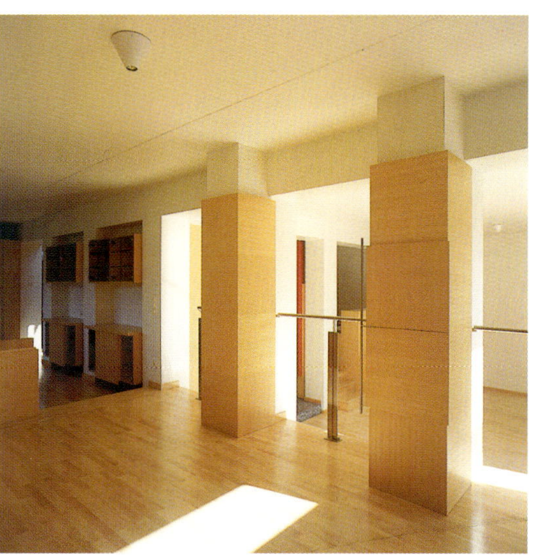

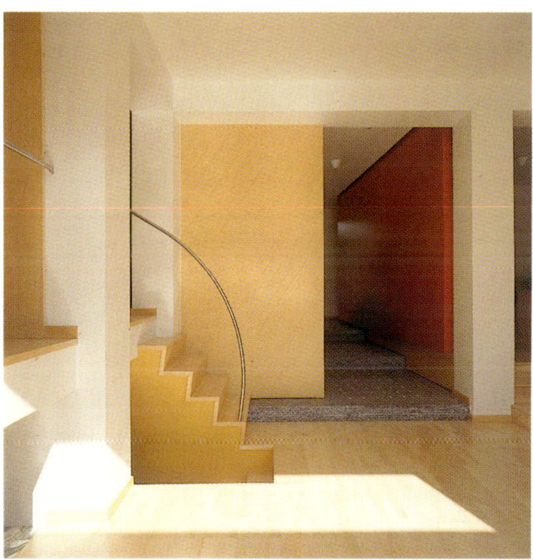

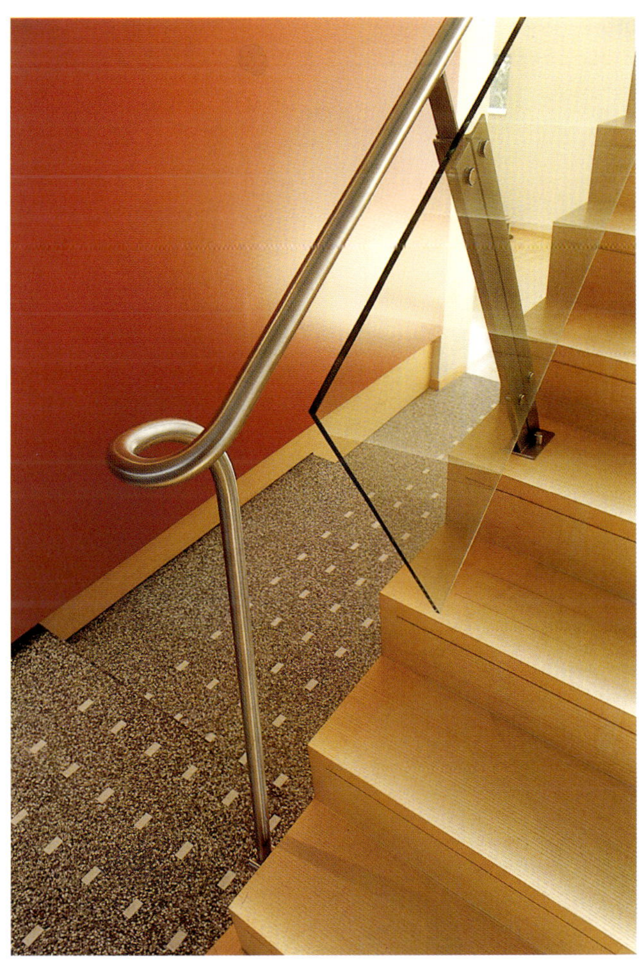

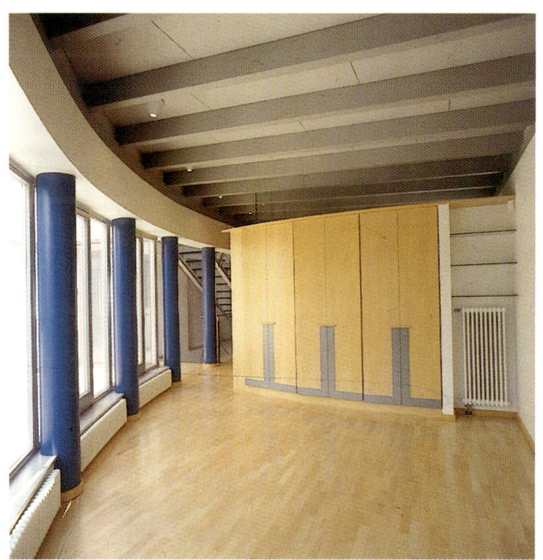

Wien-Döbling / *Vienna-Döbling* 1993

Querschnitt / *Cross section*

Grundriß Erdgeschoß / *Plan of first floor*

Auf relativ kleinem Grundstück mit schräg laufenden seitlichen Grenzlinien steht das 8-Zimmer-Wohnhaus traufseitig parallel zur Straße. Ein hohes Tonnendach überwölbt und schirmt den niedrigen Baukörper. Zur Gartenseite ist er zweigeschossig. Das Dach endet mit klarem Gesims über einem die gesamte Breite einnehmenden Bandfenster. Die Stirnseiten sind unterschiedlich gestaltet: die Nordwand wird nur von kleinen Fenstern und einer Schar Gucklöcher perforiert, während die Südwand mehrere große Fenstertüren aufweist. Die Andeutung einer Vertikallinie in beiden Stirnfassaden verweist auf das Innere, wo eine dicht stehende Pfeilerreihe ähnlich einer Mittelmauer den Grundriß auf beiden Hauptgeschoßen strukturiert. Da die Garagenabfahrt der Grundstücksgrenze folgt, ist auch die anschließende, nördliche Stirnseite schräg geschnitten. In demselben Winkel trifft der Zugang auf das Haus. Die Richtung wird von der Trennwand zur Küche aufgenommen und setzt sich bis ins Wohnzimmer fort, wo sie in einem Sitzmöbel ausschwingt. Ein weiteres Mal erscheint diese Schräge an der Südfassade in einem großen Erkerfenster, das in Leichtbauweise die Mauerschale durchstößt. Auf der anderen Seite der Mittelachse antwortet darauf ein kleiner Balkon. Die interne Treppe steigt aus der Eingangshalle empor ins Obergeschoß, wo das Tonnendach in Bodenhöhe ansetzt. Eine zartgliedrige Stiege führt von hier zur großflächigen Diele unter der Dachwölbung.

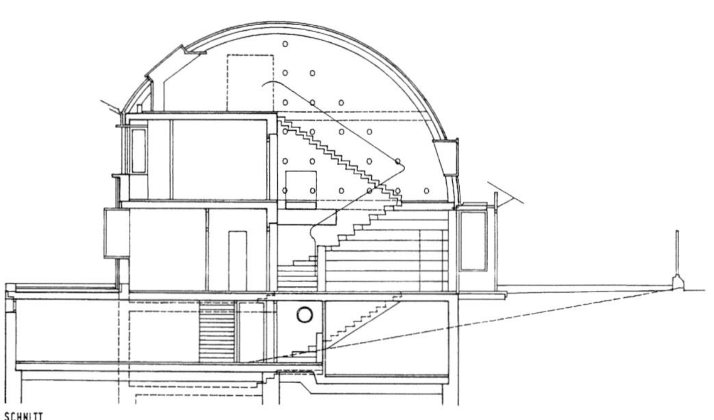

Situated on a relatively small property with angular side border lines, the 8-room-house is positioned parallel to the street on the side of the eaves. A high barrel roof vault and shields the low volume. Towards the garden, it has two floors. The roof ends with a clear cornice above a strip window taking up the entire width. The two facades are decorated differently: the northern wall is pierced only by small windows and a bevy of peep holes, while the southern wall has several large glass doors. The hint of a vertical line in both primary facades points to the interior where a row of tightly placed columns, structuring the ground plan on both main levels, functions in a way similar to a middle wall. As the garage descent follows the property border, the adjoining northern front side is also cut at an angle. The access way meets the house at the same angle. The direction is taken up by the dividing wall towards the kitchen and is continued to the living room, where it swings out into a sitting area. This angle appears again on the south facade in a large lightly constructed oriel piercing through the masonry layer. On the opposite side of the middle axis, a small balcony replies to it. The inside staircase ascends from the entrance lobby to the upper floor where the barrel roof starts at the floor level. A filigree stairway leads from there to the large lobby beneath the roof vault.

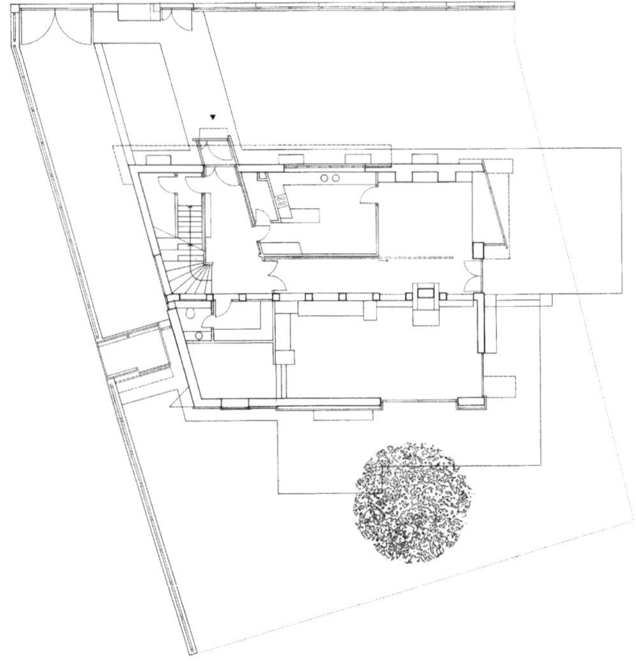

Ansicht Gartenseite / *View of garden side*

Eingangsfront / *Entrance front*

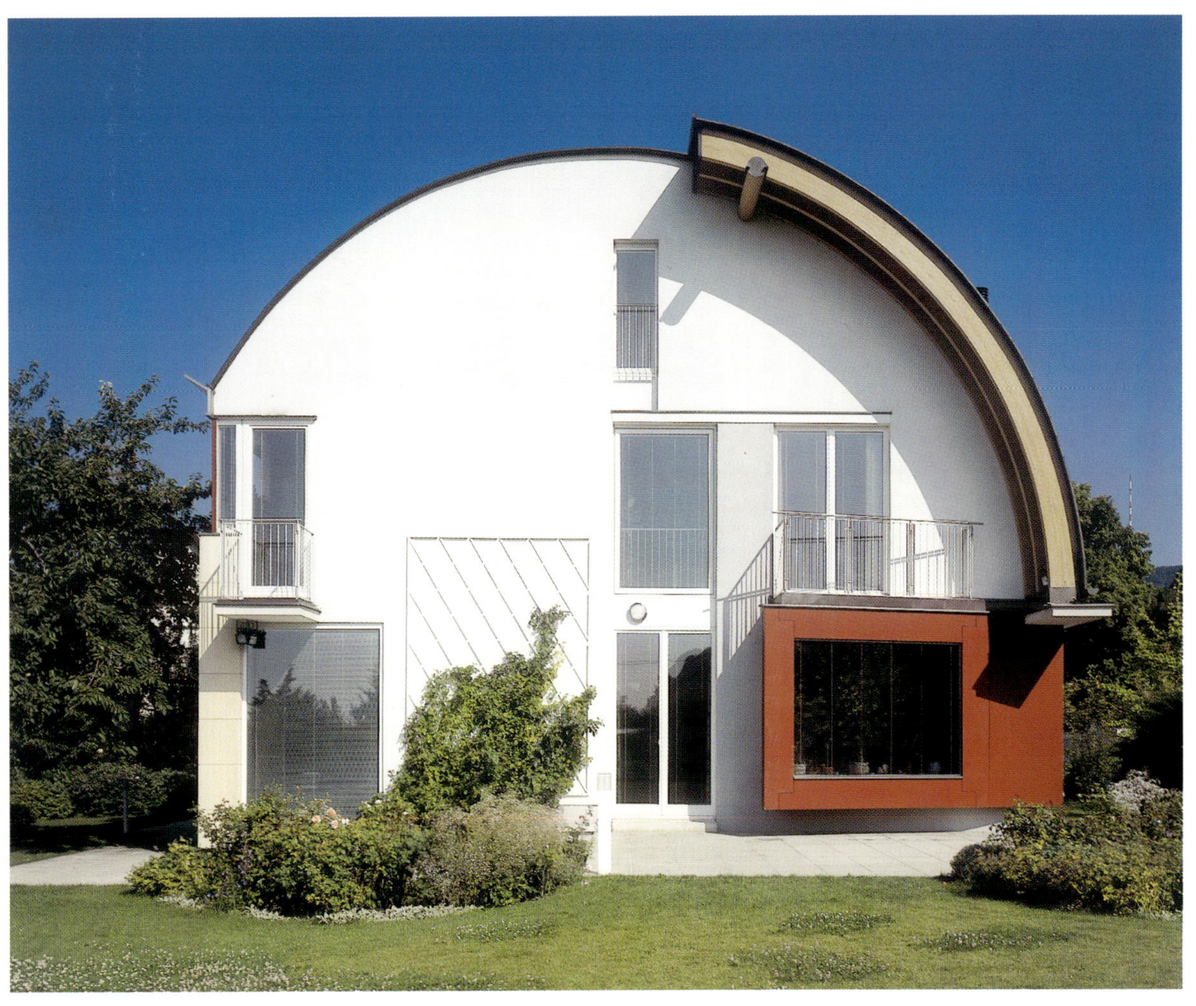

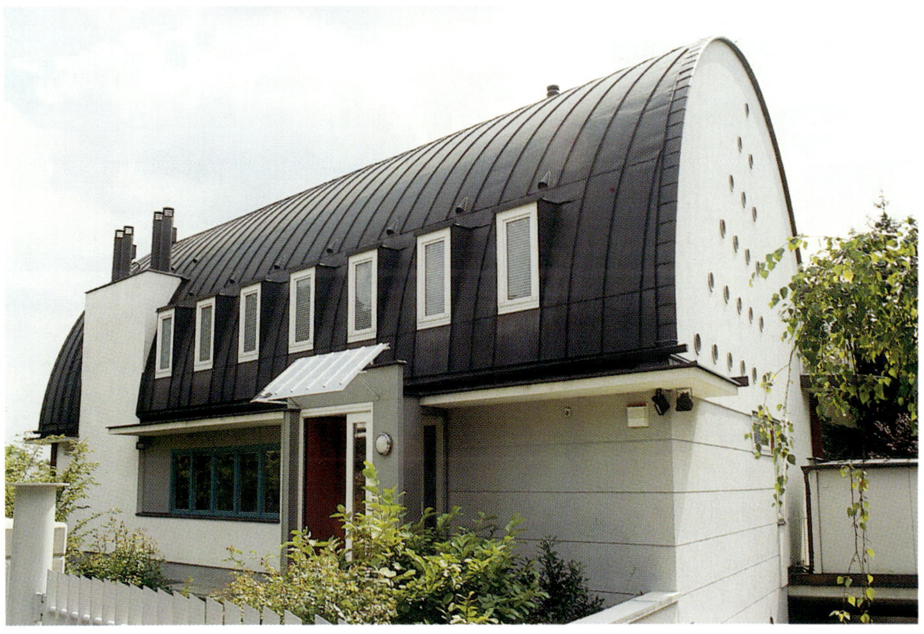

Eckdetail im Obergeschoß / *Corner detail on upper floor*

Holz-Steinfassade / *Wood-stone facade*

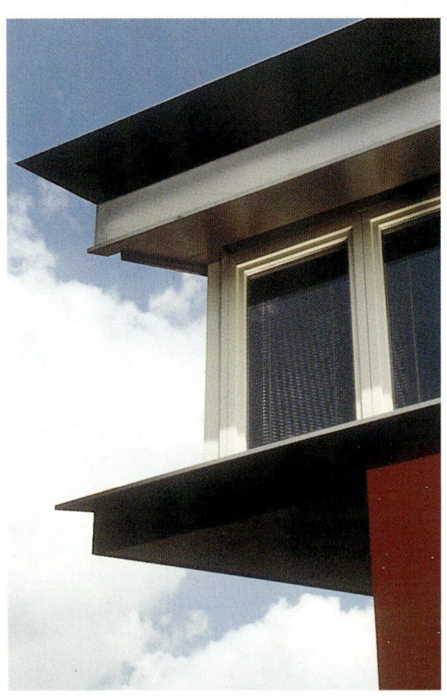

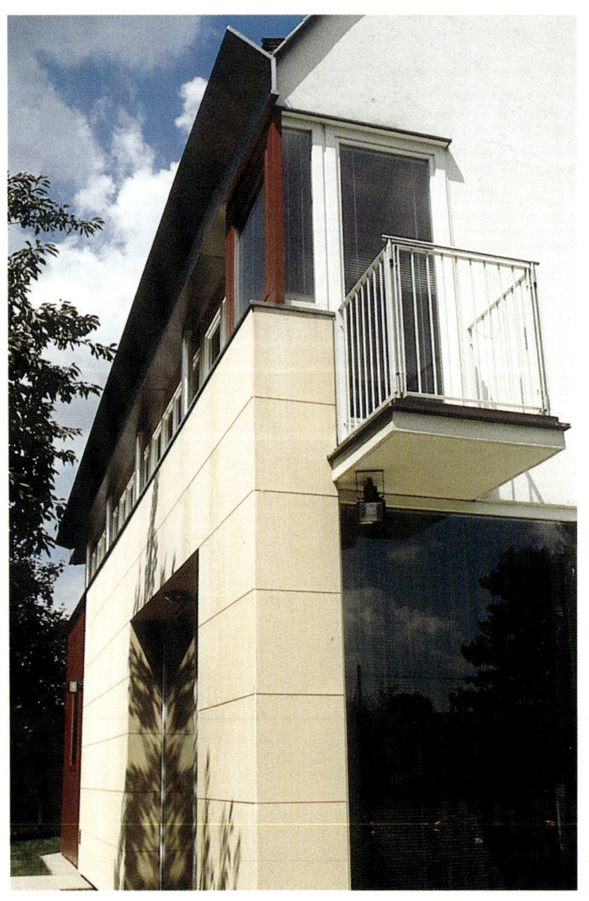

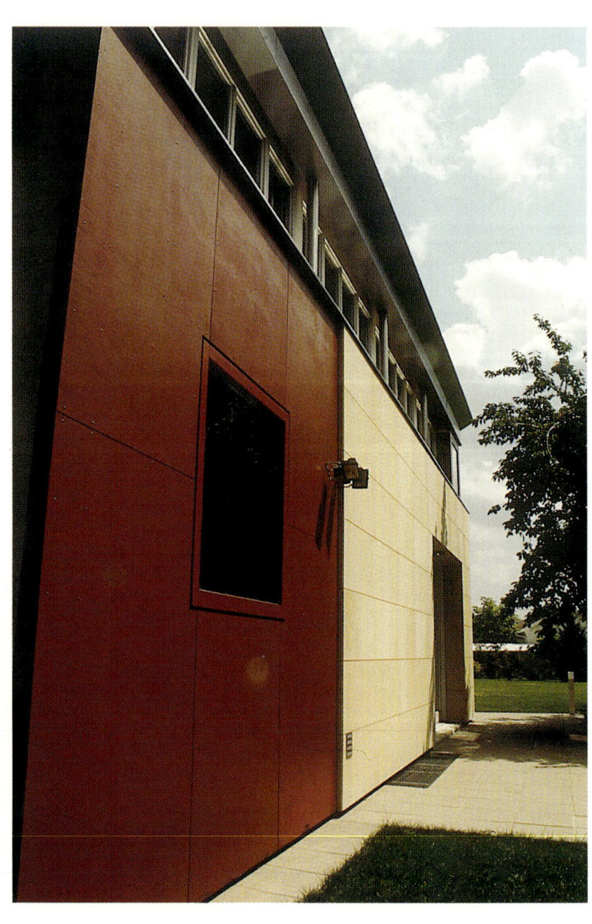

Erkerfenster im Speisezimmer / *Oriel in dining room*

Wohnraum / *Living room*

Wohnraum und Speisezimmer / *Living and dining rooms*

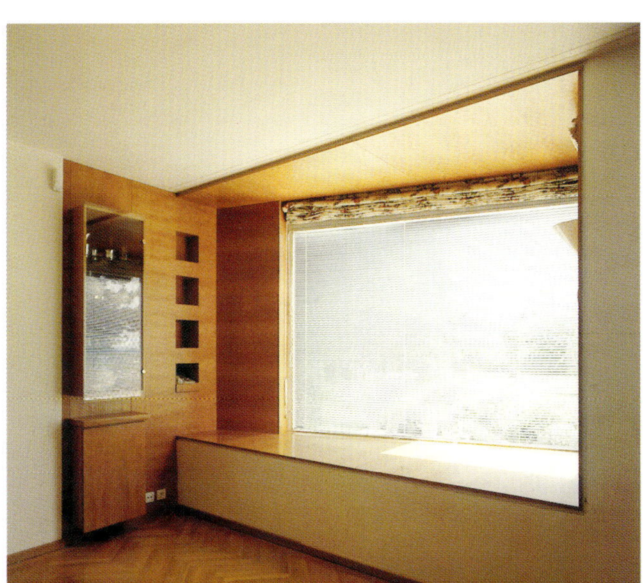

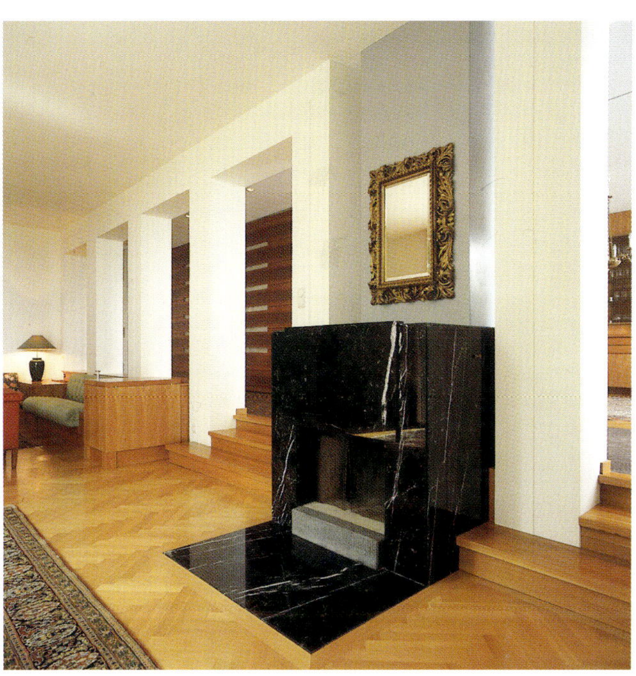

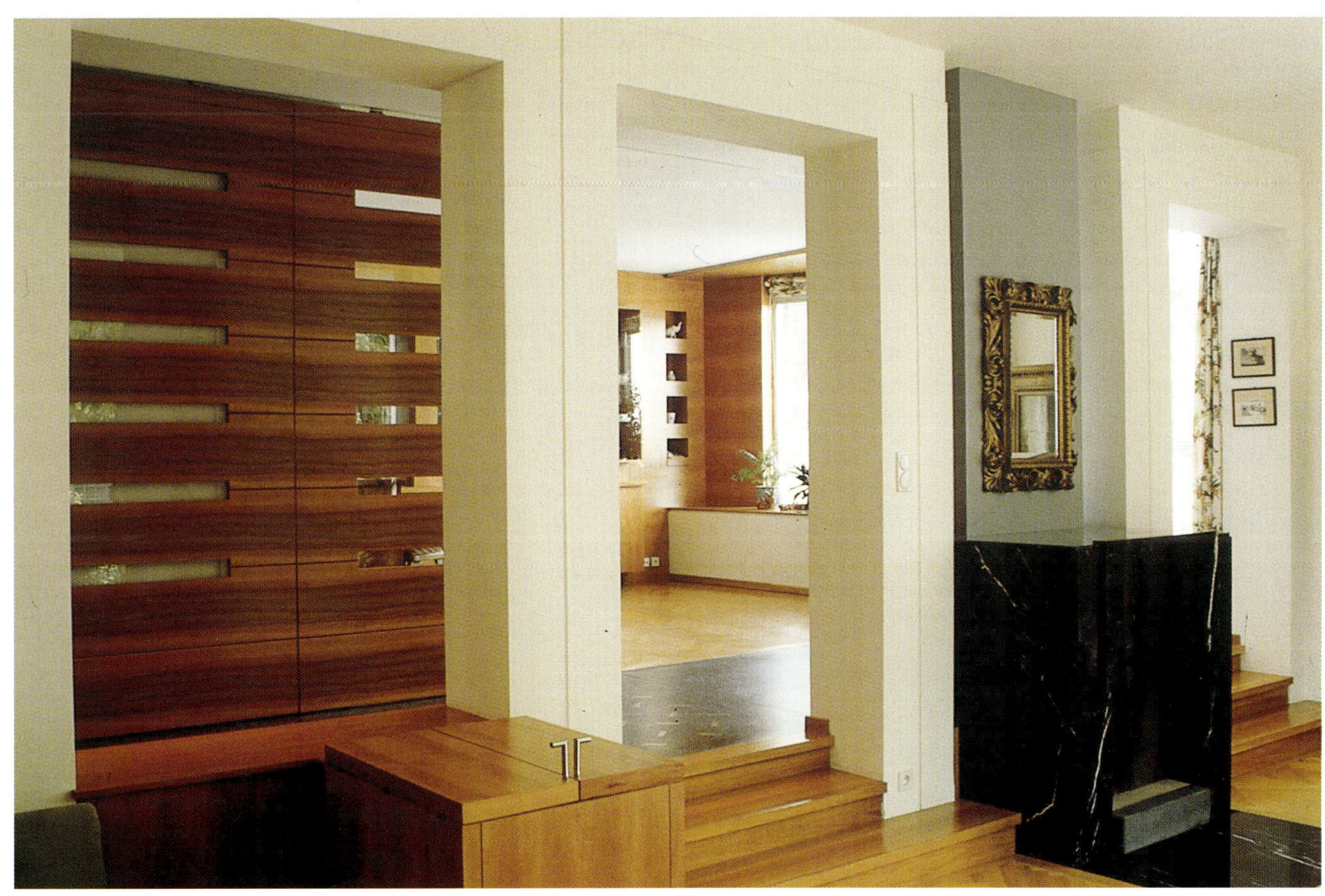

Stiegenaufgang über drei Geschoße /
Stairway ascending through three floors

Geländer, Detail / *Railing, detail*

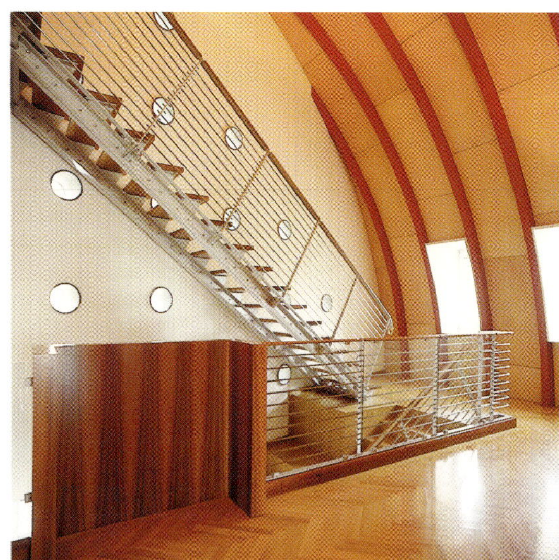

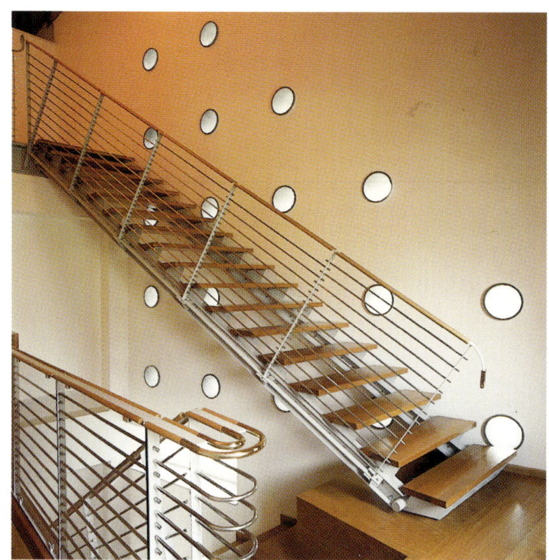

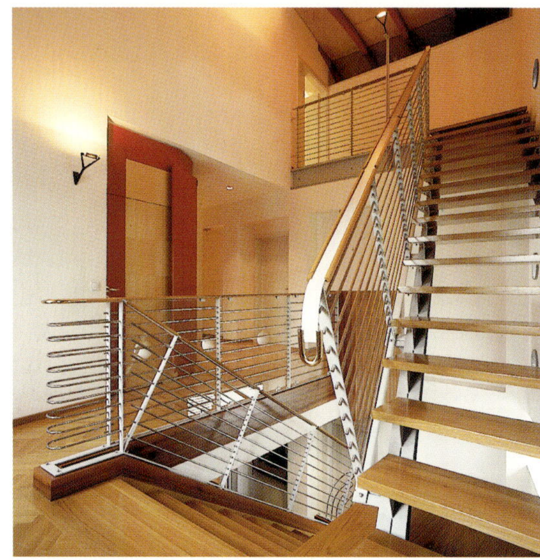

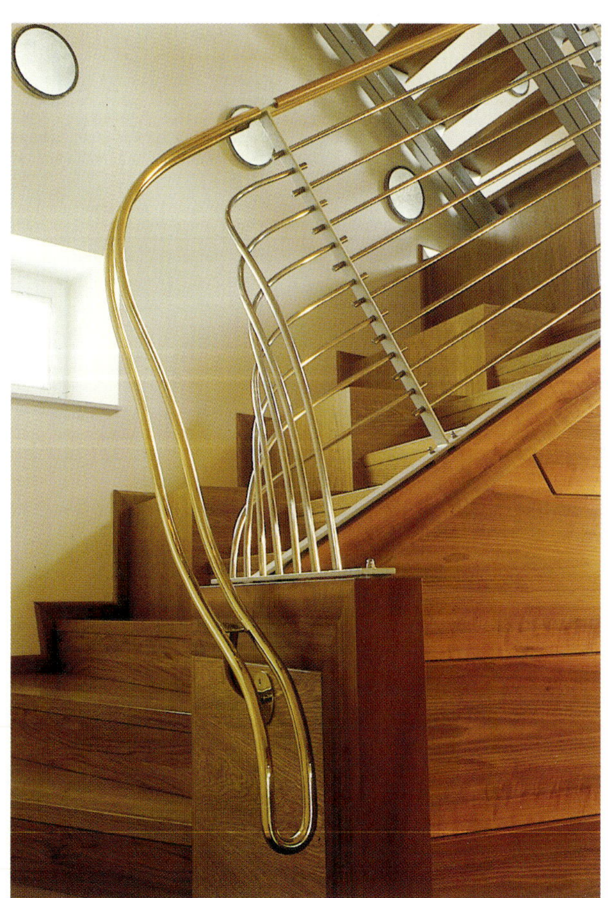

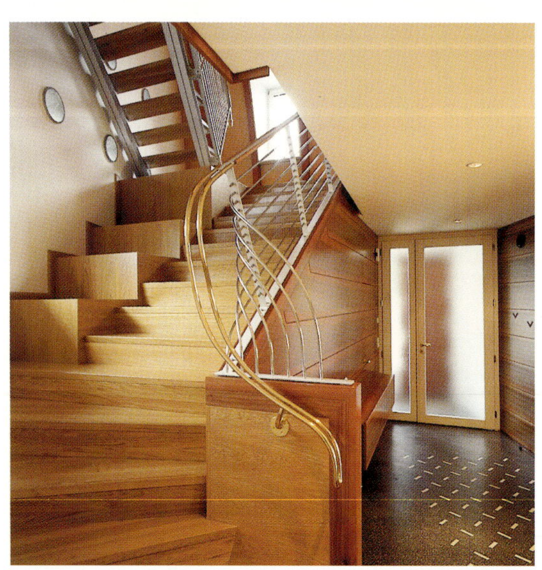

Eingangshalle, Details / *Entrance hall, details*

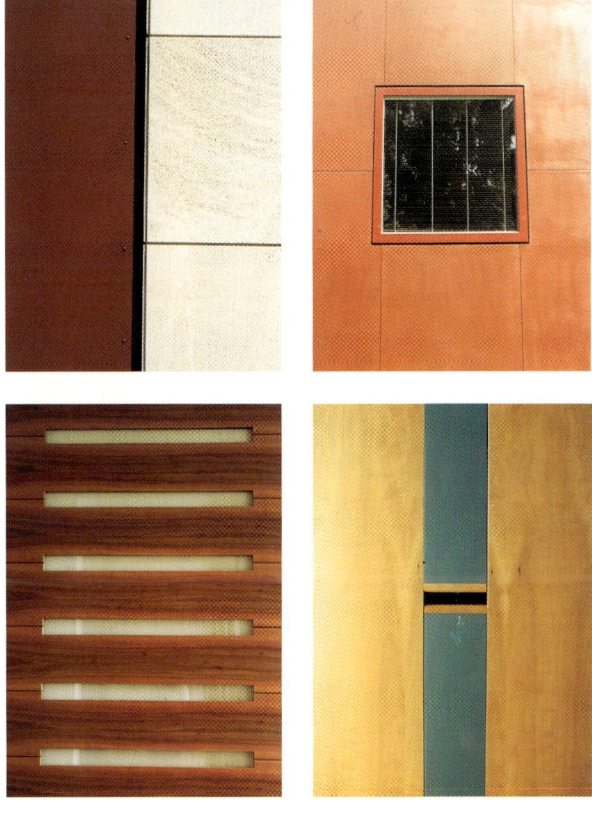

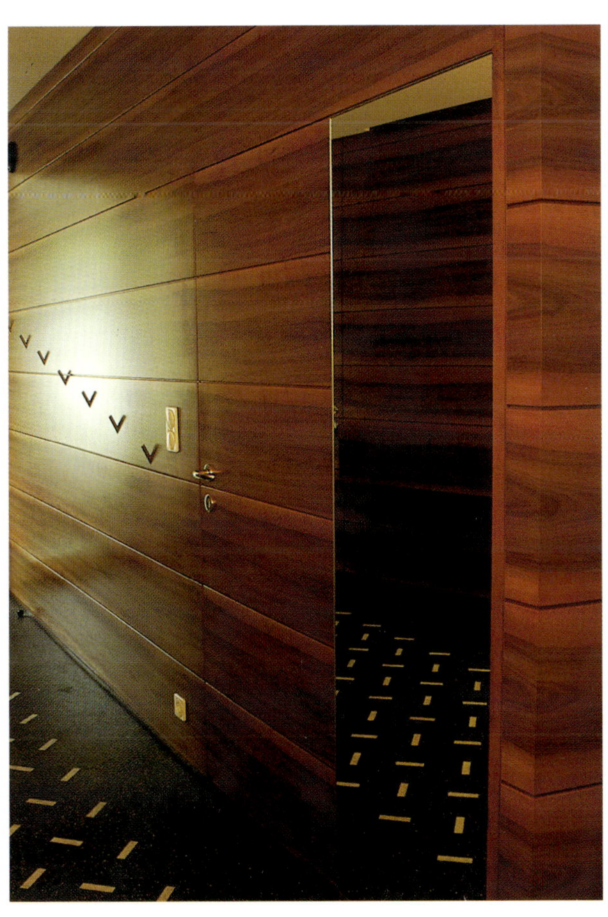

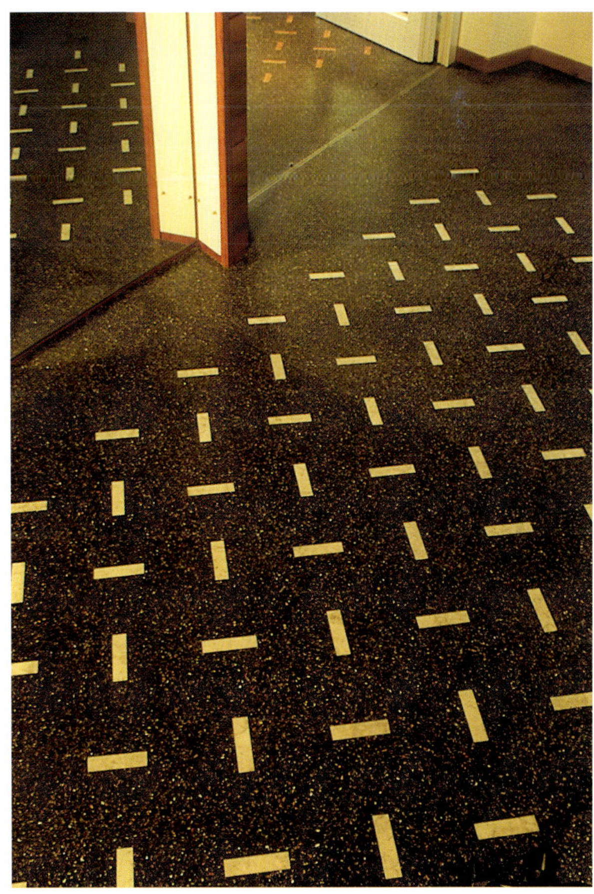

Cavtat bei Dubrovnik / *Cavtat near Dubrovnik, Croatia* 1989

Skizze des Weges: Mausoleum, Villa, Meeresbucht /
Sketch of the pathway: mausoleum, villa, ocean bay

Restaurierte Hauptfront / *Restored main facade*

An einer traumhaft schönen Bucht der dalmatinischen Adria-
küste, etwas außerhalb der 3000 jährigen, verwinkelten Stadt
Cavtat, am Fuß eines grünen Hügels, erbaute sich 1898 eine
Reederfamilie ihr Sommerhaus im Stil des Neopalladianismus.
Eine wechselvolle Geschichte hatte von dem Haus kaum mehr
als eine Ruine übriggelassen, als ein im Ausland tätiger Ge-
schäftsmann darauf aufmerksam wurde. Über die revitalisierte
Villa Vojcsik stieß er auf Boris Podrecca, der den Ort bereits
kannte. Beim Umbau blieben die drei denkmalgeschützten
Ansichtsseiten stehen, der Eingang wurde von der Seite in die
Achse verlegt. Die Rückwand erhielt eine differenzierte Bekleidung aus Stein. Vom Meer her führt ein Weg durchs Haus, von
dem der in Terrassen gestufte Hang von jedem Geschoß her
zugänglich ist. Hinter dem Haus wird eine Erschließungslücke
zur Terrasse durch einen aufgehängten, in einzelne Platten aufgelösten Steg geschlossen. Das Innere des Hauses folgt den von der
Fassade vorgegebenen Grundrißmustern: Gangachsen münden
auf Fenster und manche Zimmer sind symmetrisch organisiert.
Die Fenster wurden zu Fenstertüren vergrößert und die Räume
teilweise vereinigt. Steinböden und glatte Wände erzeugen mediterranen Hall, gemildert durch zahlreiche prächtige Kelims. Die
schnörkellosen Einbaumöbel orientieren sich an der undogmati-
schen Moderne, verkörpert durch Josef Frank, an den gerahmte
Ausschnitte seiner Stoffe erinnern.

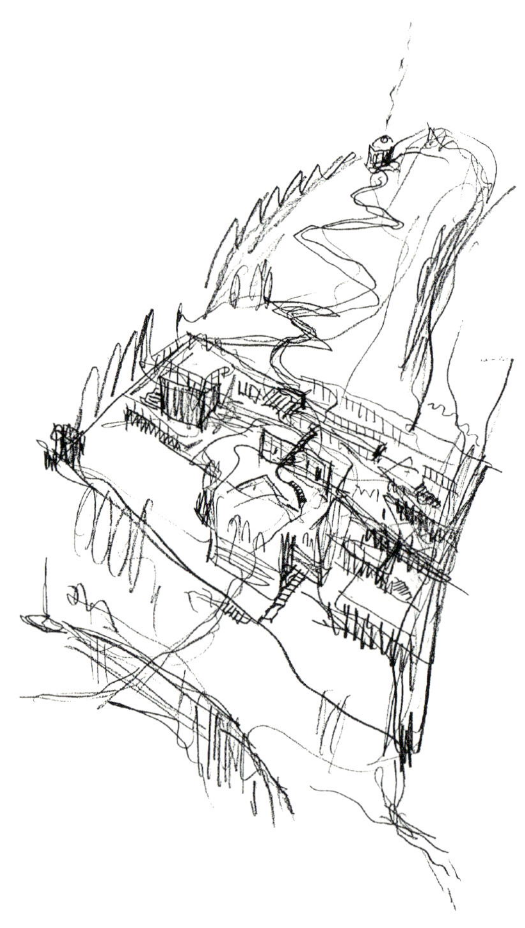

*At an incredibly beautiful bay on the Dalmatian Adriatic coast,
a little bit outside of the 3000 year old intricately structured City
of Cavtat, at the foot of a hill, a ship owner's family had a summer
house built in 1898 in the neo-Palladian style. A long history had
left little more than a ruin of the house, when it caught the
attention of an international businessman. He met Boris Podrecca,
who was already familiar with the location, via the revitalization
project at Villa Vojcsik. During the conversion, the three historically
listed elevations were maintained and the entrance was moved
from the side onto the axis. The back wall received a refined stone
covering. From the ocean, a path leads through the house, from
where the terraced hill is accessible on all floors. Behind the house,
a gap towards the terrace is closed by a small suspended bridge,
divided into separate plates. The interior of the house follows the
ground plan patterns dictated by the facade: walkway axes lead to
windows and some rooms are organized symmetrically. The
windows were enlarged into glass doors and some of the rooms
were joined together. Stone floors and smooth walls create a
Mediterranean echo, softened by numerous stately Kelim rugs. The
simple built-in furniture is oriented towards the undogmatic
modernity, represented by Josef Frank who is commemorated by
framed pieces of his fabrics.*

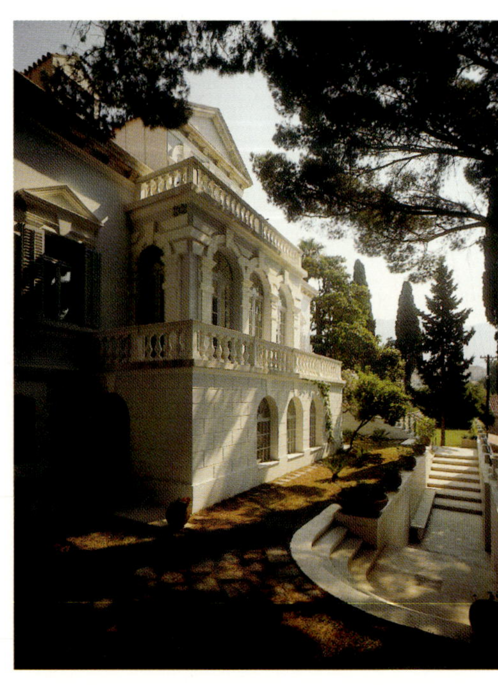

Schnittaxonometrie, Villa und sieben Terrassen /
Sectional axonometric projection, villa and seven terraces

Terrassen / *Terraces*

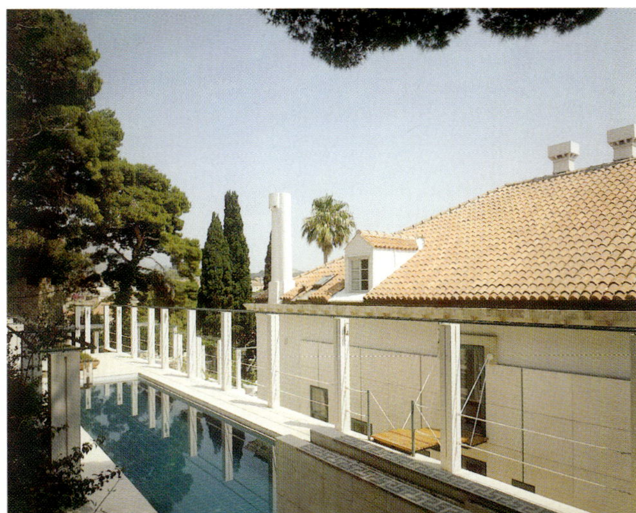

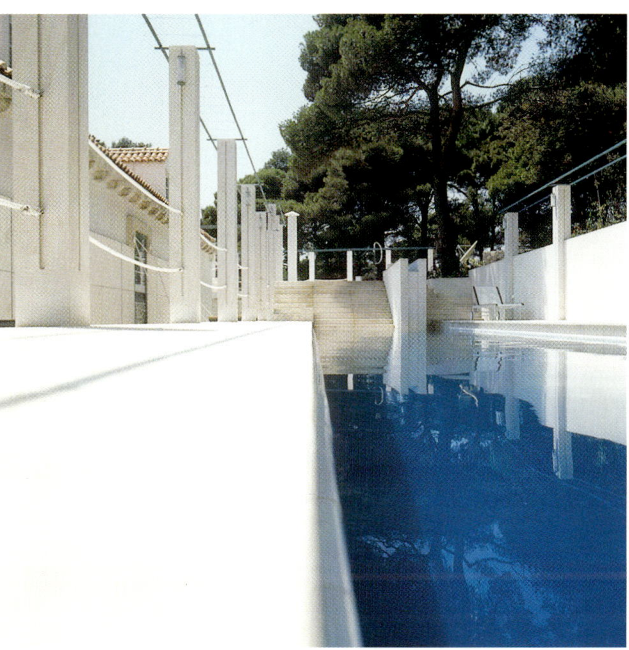

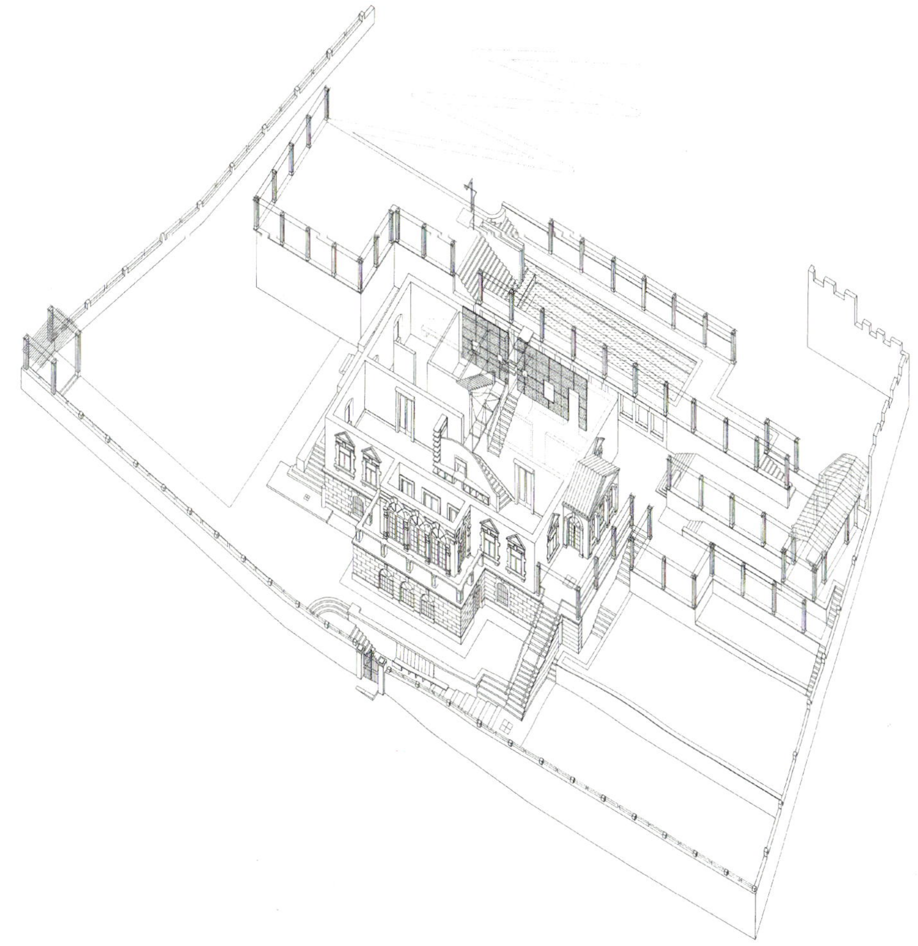

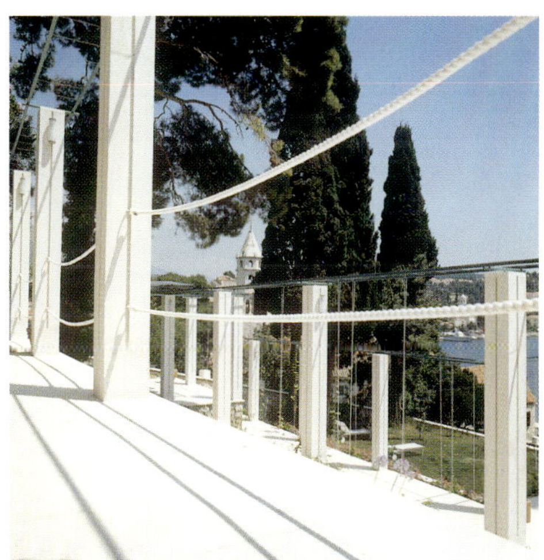

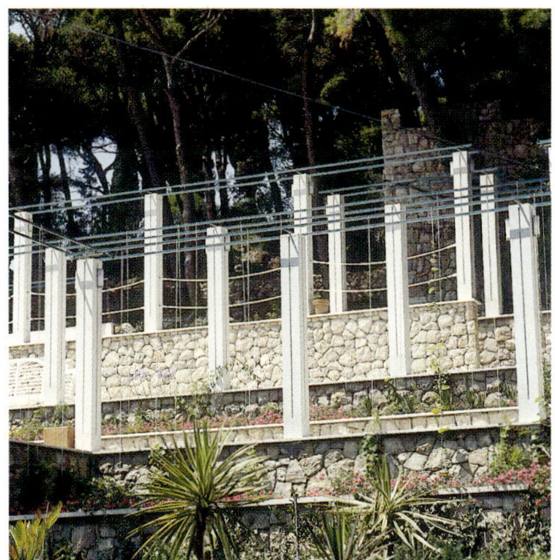

Wandverkleidung mit Steg / *Wall covering with overpass*

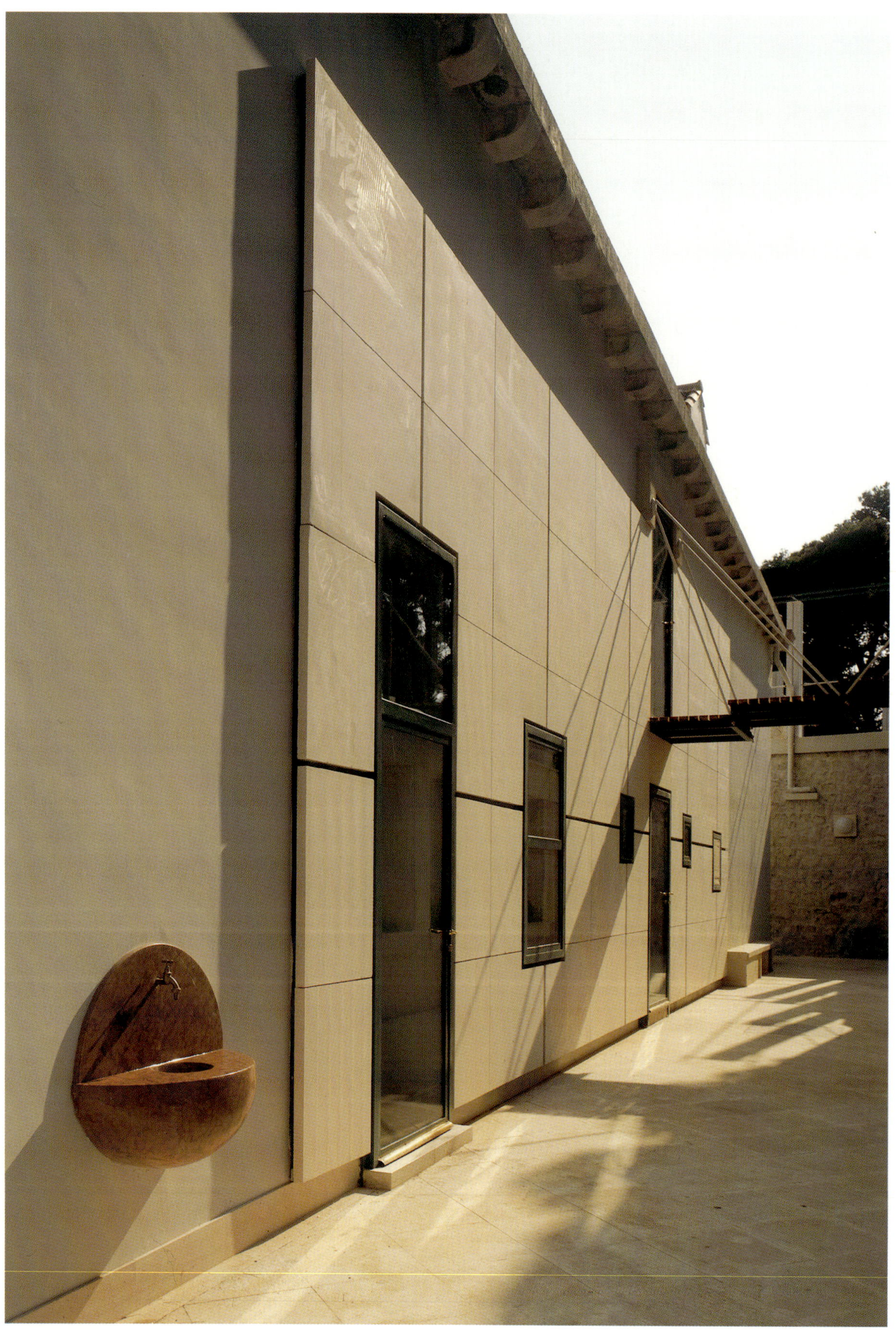

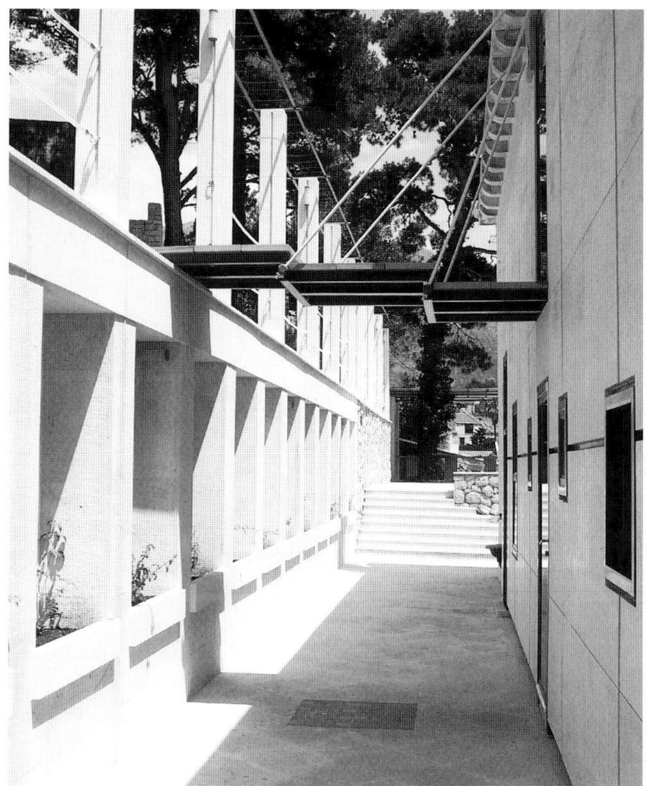

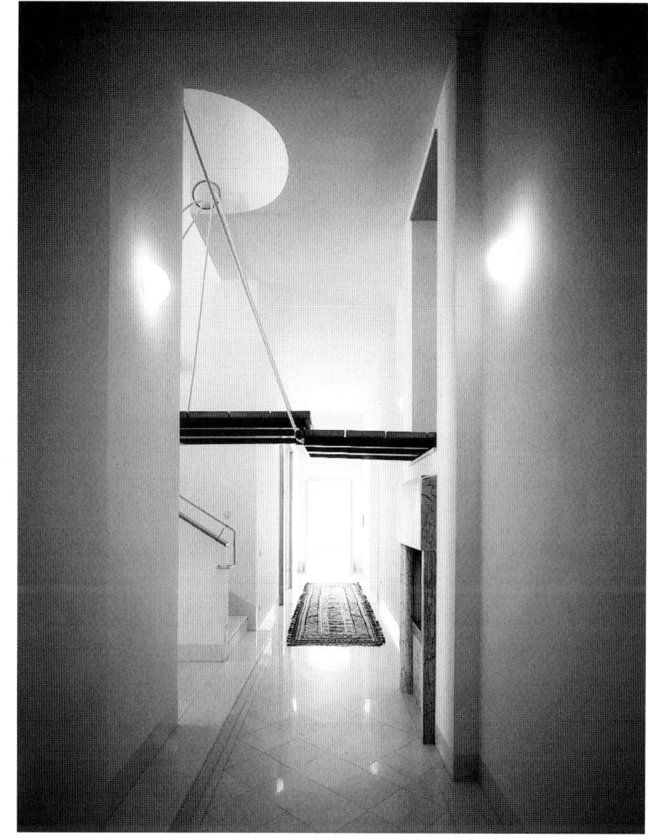

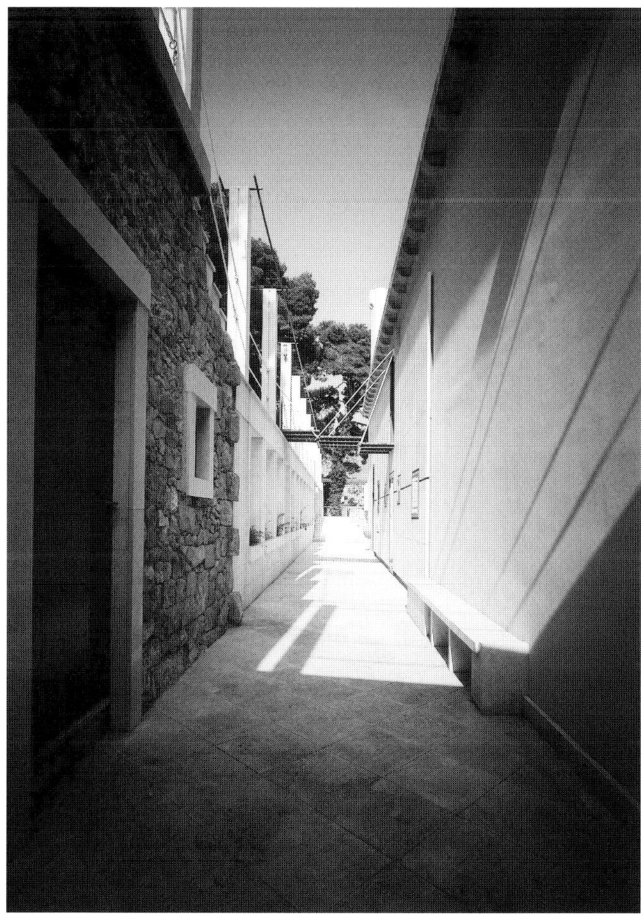

Horizontale und vertikale Erschließung / *Horizontal and vertical connections*

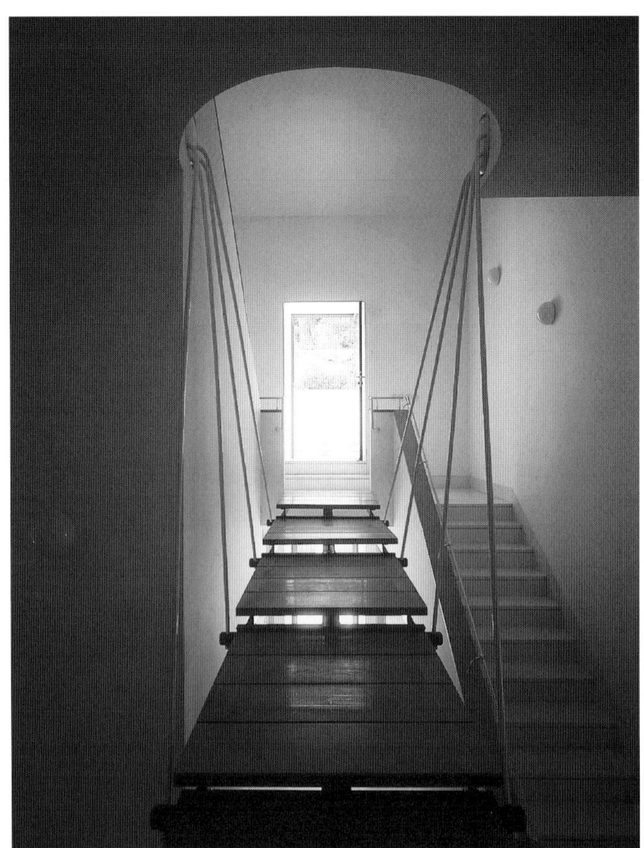

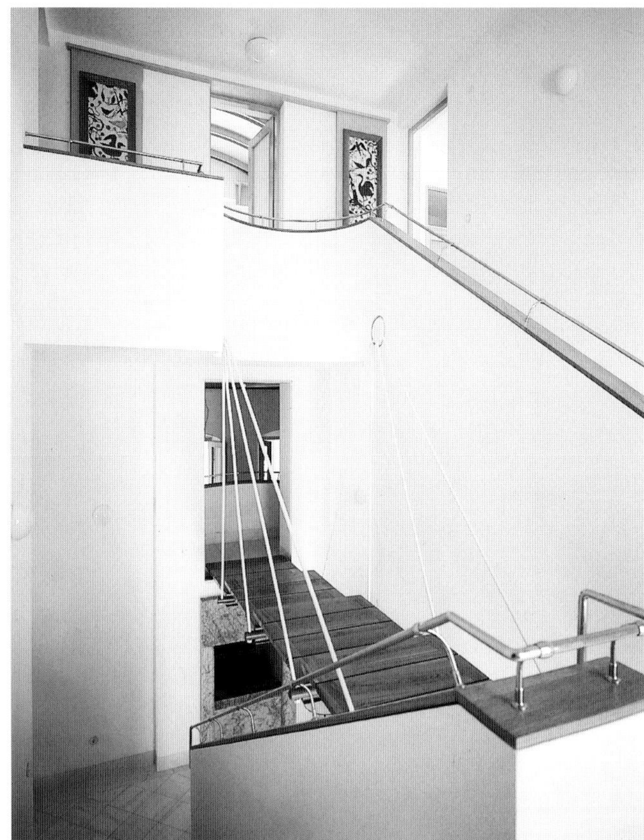

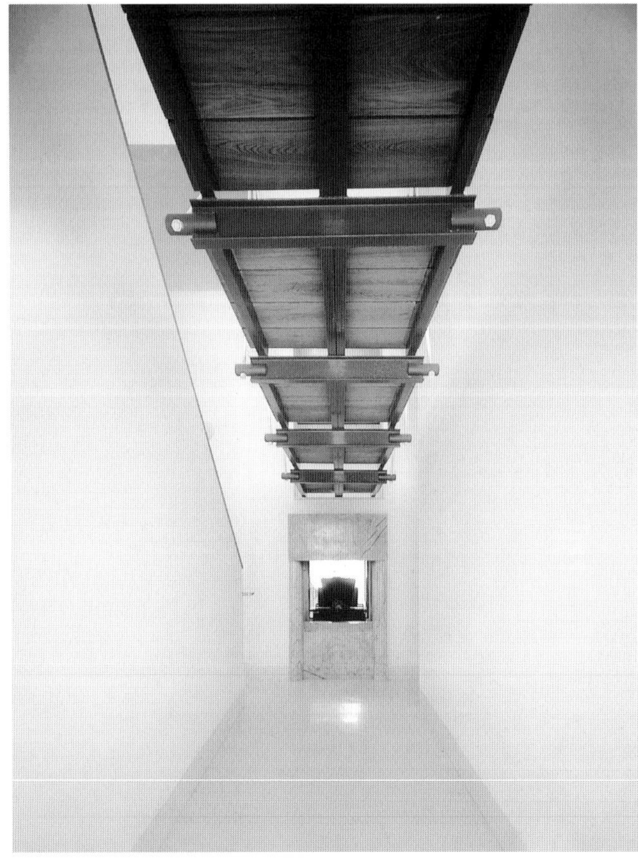

Wohnraum / *Living room*

Bad / *Bathroom*

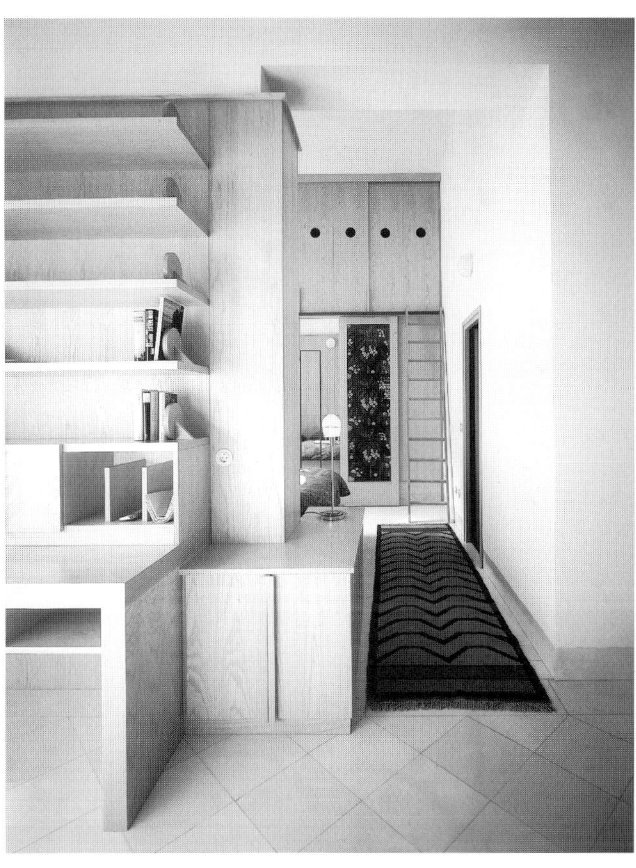

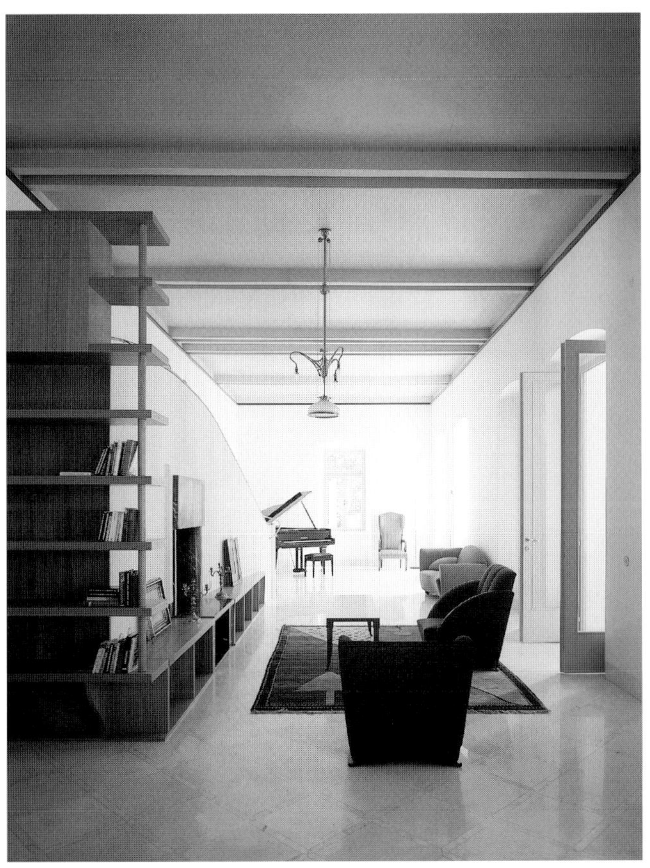

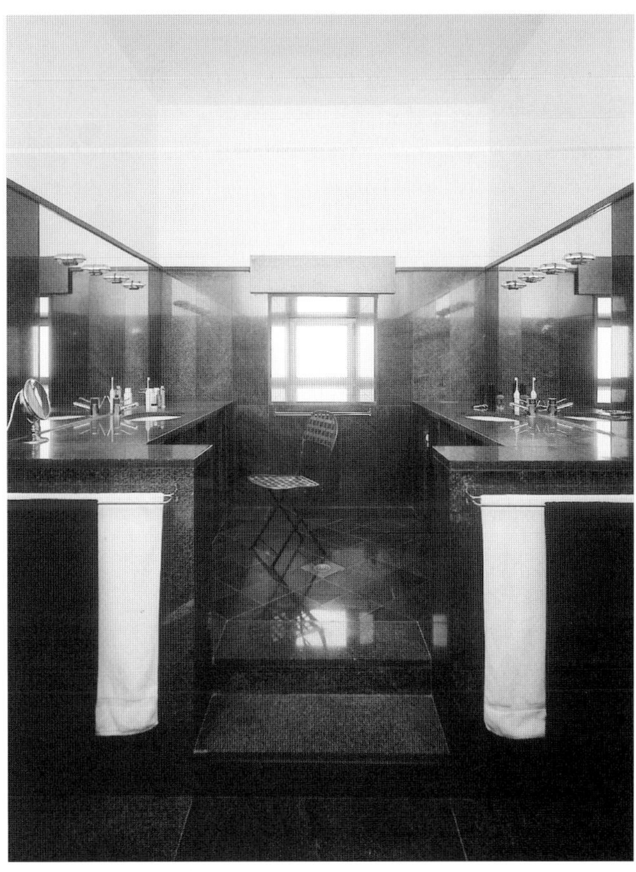

Leipziger Platz, Wien, Oberflächengestaltung und Brunnen /
Leipziger Platz, Vienna, surface design and fountain 1994

Der öffentliche Raum verdient seinen Namen nur dann, wenn er allgemein zugänglich ist. Die Monofunktionalisierung von Flächen durch Fahrbahnen und Autoabstellplätze, aber auch das Zupflanzen mit Bodenbedeckern, hat die als Räume erlebbaren Plätze in den historischen Zentren in ihrer Wirkung stark reduziert. Boris Podreccas Programm für den gestalterischen Umgang mit historischen Platzräumen ist denn auch in einem hintergründigen Sinn didaktisch auf eine posititive Entwicklung des öffentlichen Raumes hin orientiert. Er zeigt, wie ein Platz wahrgenommen und in der Folge interpretiert werden könnte. Da oft mehrere Lesarten des Raumes denkbar sind, bietet er zuweilen auch verschieden sich überlagernde Ansätze an, aus deren Spannungsverhältnis eine weitere Qualitätskomponente entsteht.

Platzräume weisen in der Regel nach oben keine festen Raumbegrenzungen auf. Entsprechend wächst die raumdefinierende Rolle der Platzwände. Die meisten Fassaden sind jedoch jahrzehntealter, oft jahrhundertealter Bestand. Nur selten wird eine davon in zeitgenössischer Gestalt neu errichtet. Bei einer Neubestimmung kommt daher der Aufteilung und Differenzierung der Platzoberfläche sehr viel Gewicht zu. In die Gestaltung dieser Fläche arbeitet Boris Podrecca daher nicht bloß die Lektüre des Bestands mit ein, sondern macht mit seiner durch die Flächenaufteilung räumlich wirkenden Interpretation zugleich den spezifischen Charakter des Platzes deutlich.

In Cormons und in Salzburg bilden die wichtigsten Bauwerke am Platz die Basis. Podrecca läßt sie weitgehend ungebremst auf den Platzraum wirken, indem die Gestaltung des Belags darauf bezogen ist. Dabei scheut er sich nicht, eine räumliche Reparatur anzubieten, und sei es nur mit einer Pergola, die beide Sachverhalte, vor und nach dem Eingriff, verständlich macht. Andererseits weiß Podrecca auch die Rolle der normalen Bürgerhäuser zu würdigen, die Abweichungen oder Unregelmäßigkeiten im Verlauf ihrer Fassadenfolgen ernst zu nehmen und sich mit feinen Korrekturen im Muster der Platzfläche darauf zu beziehen.

Historische Rudimente in den Schichten unter der Platzfläche sind für ihn kein ausreichendes Argument, um etwa die Gestaltung davon abzuleiten; als auf den ersten Blick irrationale Störungen im klaren Muster der bedeutungsmäßigen Hierarchien sind sie ihm aber willkommen. Sie bilden jenen Haken, an dem sich der Betrachter fängt und der ihn provoziert, tiefer in den Wahrnehmungsprozeß einzudringen. Eine ähnliche Rolle spielen jene vertikalen Elemente, die aus einer zweiten Staffel auf den Platz hineinwirken, ebenso die läuferartig aus Durchgängen und aus Portalen wichtiger Gebäude in die Platzfläche vorstoßenden, anders texturierten Flächen, die auf öffentliche Zugänglichkeit verweisen.

Beim Rathausplatz St. Pölten, der eine stark längsrechteckige Konfiguration aufweist, dessen nicht übermäßig hohen Platzwände aber bei der großen Fläche eine reduzierte räumliche Wirkung haben, wird mit einer Art großem Teppich vom Rathaus her,

A public space deserves its name only if it is generally accessible. The mono-functional quality of surfaces created by roads and parking spaces and also the treatment of areas with ground-covering plants has strongly reduced the effect of squares, able to be experienced as spaces, in historic town centers. Boris Podrecca's program for the creative treatment of historic squares is therefore concentrated didactically towards a positive development of the public space. He shows how a square could be perceived and, as a consequence, interpreted. As oftentimes several interpretations of the space are conceivable, he sometimes offers different overlapping approaches and, out of the tension of their relationship, another component of quality arises.

Squares usually do not have any upper spatial limitations. Accordingly, the space-defining role of the squares' walls increases. Most facades, however, are decade-old, often century-old substance. Only rarely is one of them re-erected and redefined in a contemporary form. Therefore, when dealing with a redesignation, the division and differentiation of a square's surface is of great importance. Boris Podrecca does not only work the discourse of the substance into the design of this surface but also with his interpretation which, due to the division of the surface, has a spatial effect while at the same time enhancing the specific character of the square.

In Cormons and in Salzburg, the most important buildings around the square form the basis. Podrecca allows them for the most part to freely have their effect on the space of the square by relating the form of the surface to them. He does not shy away from offering a spatial repair, be it only with a pergola which clarifies both situations before and after the operation. On the other hand, Podrecca knows how to appreciate the role of the typical town houses, how to take the variations or irregularities in their facades seriously, and how to relate to them with subtle corrections in the pattern of the square's surface.

Historic elements in the layers beneath the square's surface are not enough of a reason for him to derive from them the design; however, as irrational disturbances in the clear pattern of the implicit

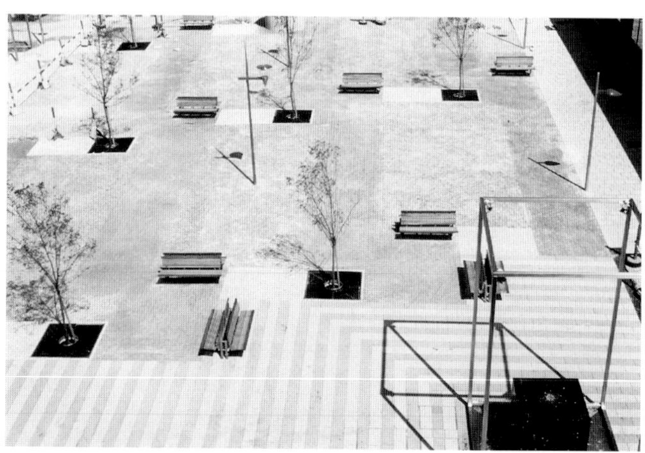

das an der südlichen Schmalseite steht, ein eindeutiges Feld definiert. Zwar verlaufen an den Längsrändern jeweils Fahrspuren, sie bleiben aber gegenüber der Platzfläche untergeordnet. Ein zweites Texturierungsprinzip geht von der anderen Schmalseite aus, die von der Hauptfassade der Franziskanerkirche ausgezeichnet wird. Der lange Platz wird aufgeteilt, die Dreifaltigkeitssäule gewinnt, ohne versetzt worden zu sein, eine spannungsreichere Position, und beim Zusammentreffen der beiden Plattenmuster macht Podrecca eine historische Grenze durch «Vernähen» sichtbar.

In Leoben, wo die beiden Hälften des langgezogenen Platzes durch die Kärntner Straße getrennt waren, verschränkt das Projekt zwei teppichartige Flächen, um den Zusammenschluß auszudrücken. Die außermittige Plazierung der Lichtmasten verbindet die beiden mit Brunnen bezeichneten äußeren Pole, während die Pestsäule wegen ihrer autonomen Position in der Fläche an Kraft dazugewinnt; ihre Aufladung ist aufgrund der zentralen Stellung im Platzraum bereits recht groß. Die doppelte Beziehung zu Fläche und Raum verweist überdies auf die Wirkung beider Systeme. Die in Fußgängerzonen meist üppig verteilten Elemente der Infrastruktur, wie Rigole, Hydranten, Papierkörbe, Pflanzkübel und Telephonkabinen, die zuweilen verschämt irgendwo angelehnt oder in eine Ecke deponiert werden, vereinigt Podrecca bei seinen jüngsten Projekten (St. Pölten, Leoben und Maribor) zusammen mit der unumgänglichen Möblierung in einer Art Leiste oder Infrastrukturschiene, die er der Platzgestalt unterordnet, um die Fläche möglichst integral zur Wirkung kommen zu lassen. Indem er immer den Platzraum als Ganzes betrachtet, dem die einzelnen Maßnahmen nachgeordnet sind, gelingt es ihm, die öffentlichen Räume entscheidend aufzuwerten und den Platz als zentralen Ort für die urbane Kultur zurückzugewinnen.

hierarchies, at a first glance, he welcomes them. They represent the eye-catcher for the observer and provoke him in order to get deeper into the process of recognition. The vertical elements influencing the square from a second rank play a similar role, as do the differently textured surfaces pointing to a public accessibility, pushing like runners from the passageways and portals of important buildings into the square's surface.

In the case of St. Pölten's town hall square, with a strong longitudinal rectangular configuration, a distinct field is created with a carpet texture starting at the town hall. Although there are roadways along the longitudinal borders of the square, they remain subordinate to the surface of the square. Another principle of texture starts at the second narrow side where the church of St. Francis is located. The long square is divided and the Trinity pillar gains a more exciting position. Where the two tile patterns meet, Podrecca makes a historic borderline visible by "stitching".

In Leoben, where the two halves of the long stretched square were separated by the Kärntner Strasse, the project overlaps two rug-like surfaces in order to express their articulation. The off-center placement of the light poles connects the two outer poles marked by fountains, while the plague-pillar gains expressive power due to its autonomous position on the surface. Its tension was already rather great due to its central position in the square. Moreover, the dual relationship with surface and space points to the effect of the two systems.

The widely spread infrastructure elements in the pedestrian zones, such as rocks, hydrants, trash receptacles, potted plants and phone booths, which at times lean against something or are often shamfully distributed in some corner are, instead united by Podrecca in his latest projects (St. Pölten, Leoben und Maribor) together with the unavoidable furnishings into a kind of molding or infrastructure shim. He subordinates it to the design of the square in order to let the space have a high integral effect. By always looking at the space of the square as a whole to which the separate measures are subordinate, he succeeds in decisively opening up the public spaces and regaining the square as a central location for the urban culture.

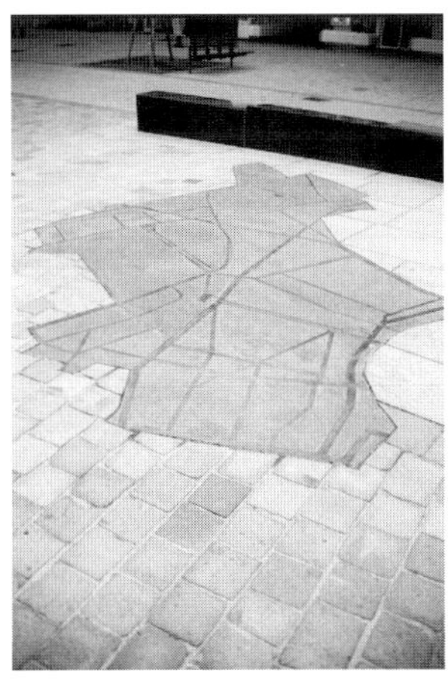
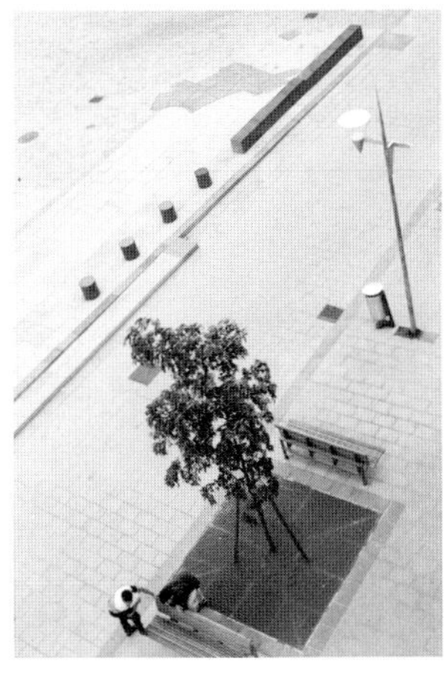
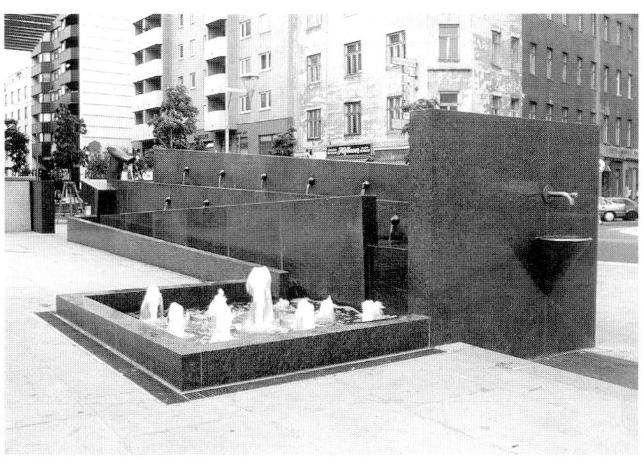

Salzburg 1989

Dreiklangbrunnen / *Three tone fountain*
Grundriß Brunnen, Sonnenuhr / *Plan of fountain, sundial*
Sonnenuhrmeridiane / *Sundial meridian*

Der Straßen- und Platzraum vor der Universität weitet sich an der Stelle, wo die Kollegienkirche von J. B. Fischer v. Erlach die Ecke besetzt hält. Gegenüber dem Universitätsgebäude, einem geraden Straßentrakt mit flachem Mittelrisalit, steht eine unregelmäßige Zeile von Bürgerhäusern auf schmalen gotischen Handtuchparzellen, die gegen die Kirche hin zurückweichen, so daß ein Platzraum entsteht. Zahlreiche Durchgänge machen die Häuserzeile zum angrenzenden Quartier durchlässig. Eine etwas größere Durchfahrt liegt an der Stirnseite des Platzraumes: der Ritzerbogen. Von hier aus zieht sich ein Mittelrigol über den Platz und in den sich verengenden Straßenraum hinein. Quer dazu verläuft das Muster des Platzbelags in Kleinsteinpflästerung, das vor der Kirchenfront radial aufgefächert wird. Ein breiter Saumstreifen bildet und interpretiert den Übergang von den Fassaden zur Platzfläche. In einer der beiden Platzecken liegt ein Gastgarten, in der anderen eine Brunnenanlage mit Beziehung zu dem unter dem Platz verlaufenden, ein paar Meter geöffneten Almkanal, der mittelalterlichen Frischwasserversorgung. Wo die Durchgänge in den Platzraum münden, reagiert das Muster des Bodenbelags jeweils mit einem Sonderelement. Die Randbereiche des Platzes werden von den leichten Ständen des Wochentagmarkts belegt. Am Samstag sind es mehr, aber an Sonntagen ist der Platz frei, und die Front der Kirche, die als einziges Gebäude direkt an das Belagsmuster stößt, regiert ungestört den knappen Platzraum.

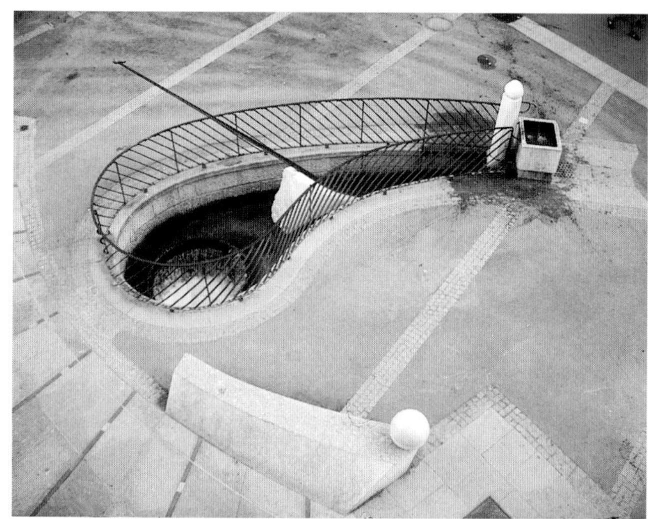

The square in front of the university expands at the point where the collegiate church by J. B. Fischer von Erlach occupies the corner. Across from the university building – a straight block with a shallow, central projection – lies an irregular row of town houses each built on narrow gothic building lots, which, as they approach the church, actually recede, thus creating a square. Numerous passageways make the row of houses permeable towards the adjoining quarter. A larger passageway is located at the front side of the square: the Ritzer arch. From here, a drainage gulley stretches across the middle of the square and into the street. Transversely to it runs the pattern of the square's small cobble stone surface which, in front of the church, fans out. A wide seam forms the transition from the facades to the surface of the square. A garden is situated in one corner, in the other there is a system of fountains entering into a relationship with the Alm canal flowing underneath the square. It opens up for a couple of meters and becomes visible. In medieval times it served as the fresh water supply. The edges of the square are seamed by the light-weight streetstands used on weekdays by the open market vendors. There are more booths on Saturdays; however, on Sundays the square is relieved of these structures and the front of the church – which is the only building directly connected to the pattern of the square surface – can rule undisturbed over the scarce space of the square.

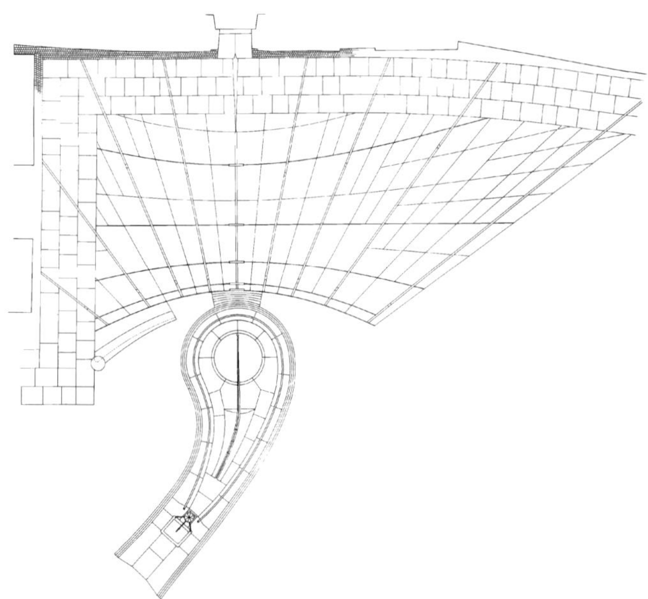

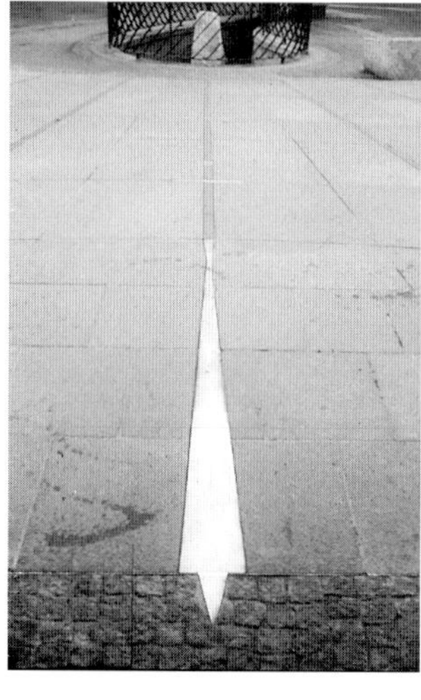

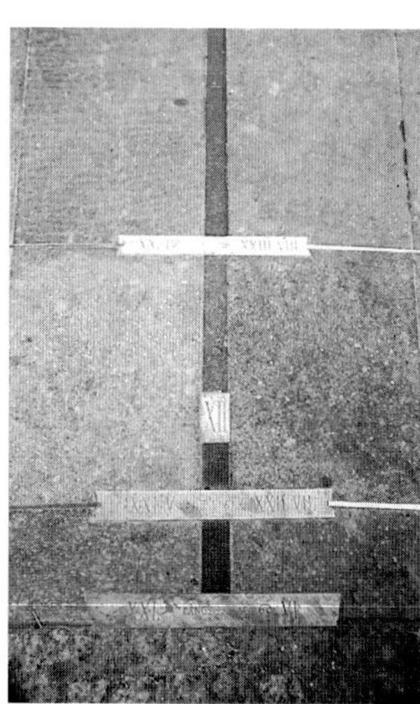

Brunnen, Details / *Fountain, details*

Lageplan / *Site plan*

Brunnen, Details / *Fountain, details*

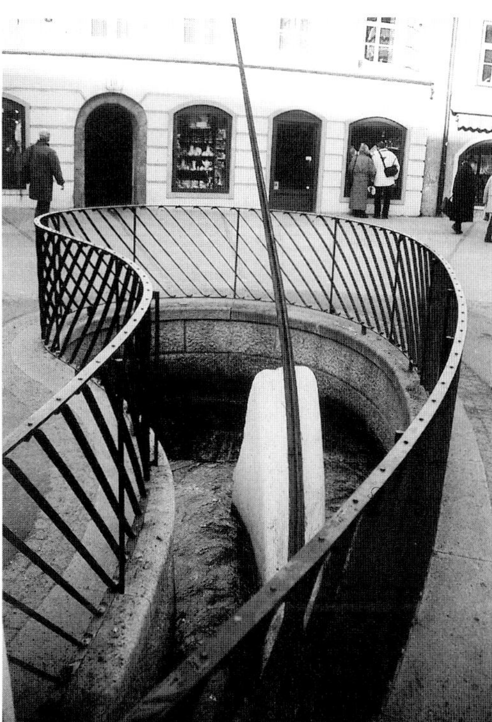

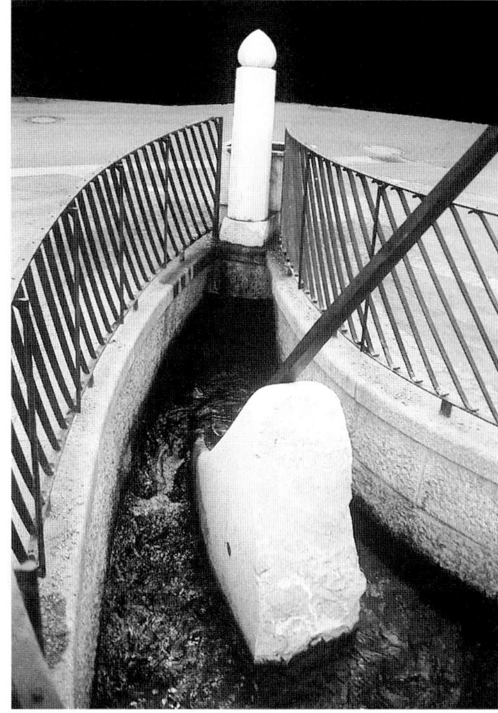

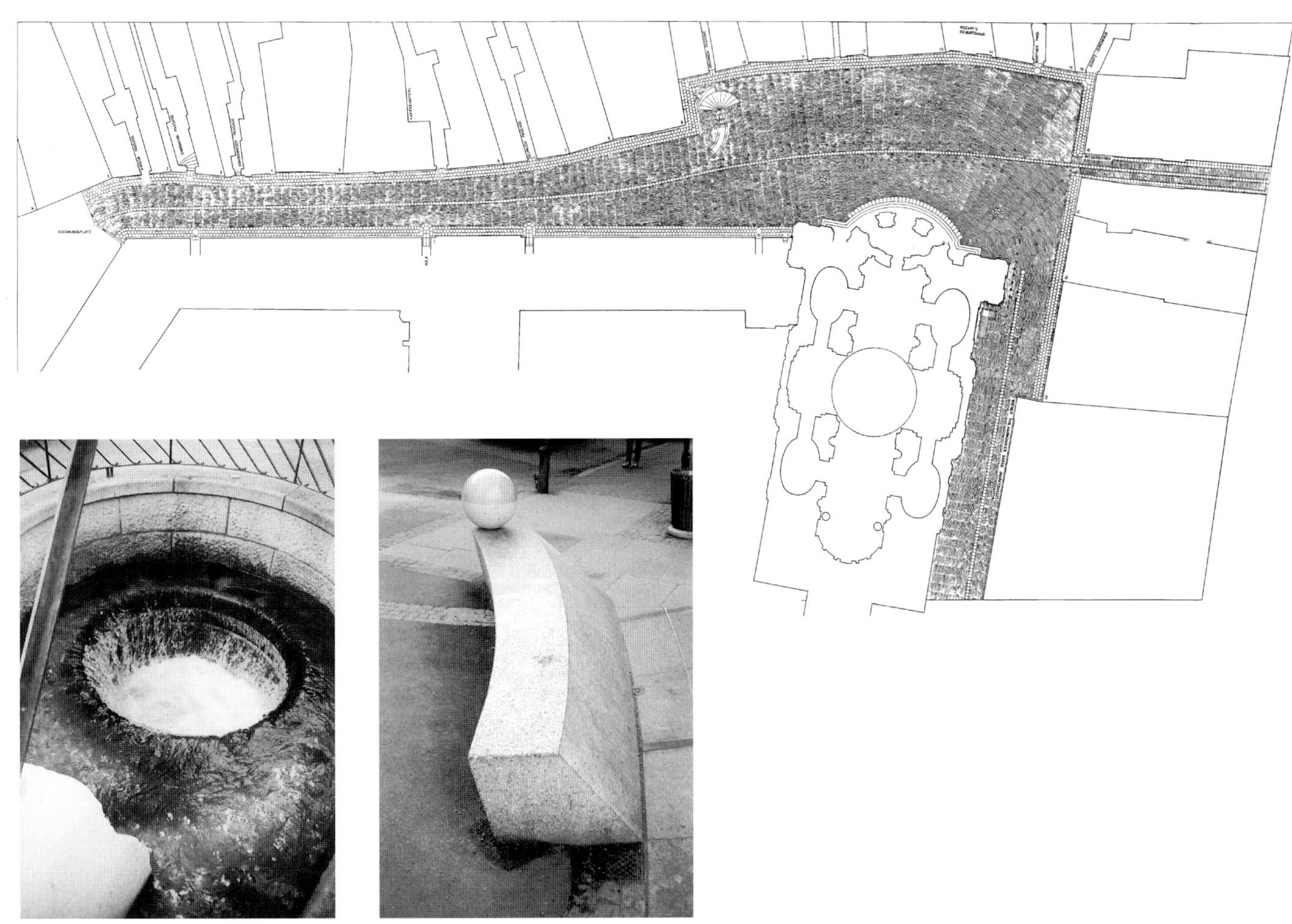

Cormons, Italien / *Italy* 1990

Axonometrie / *Axonometric projection*

Der längliche Platzraum wird an drei Seiten von Fahrbahnen gefaßt. Die vierte Seite bildet das Vorfeld der wichtigsten angrenzenden Bauten, des Palazzo Locatelli und der etwas niedrigeren Enoteca. Die gegenüberliegende Häuserzeile schwingt leicht konkav aus, als würde sie auf die Frontalwirkung des Palazzo sanft reagieren. In Wahrheit ist die weiche Linie wohl älter als die ausgerichtete Platzfront. Eine Reihe von Beleuchtungsmasten zieht eine Gerade über die Platzfläche und trennt die Fahrbahn vom ruhigen Fußgängerbereich. Mit der Zäsur eines Brunnens, flankiert von drei Stufen und einer Steinbank, wird ein oberer Platzteil abgetrennt, so daß vor dem Palazzo eine im Steinplattenbelag speziell texturierte und auf diese Weise ausgezeichnete Fläche entsteht. Die untere Schmalseite des Platzes war eher heterogen. Eine Pergola auf massiven Pfeilern schließt daher die schwach definierte Ecke im Erdgeschoßbereich. Die freistehende, schmalbrüstige Stirnseite der zurückgesetzten Trattoria wird in der zweiten Häuserstaffel überragt von dem hohen Campanile, der den Platz in Längsrichtung dominiert. Sein virtueller Schattenwurf auf den Platz (der Turm steht im Norden) ist lapidar in den Belag eingeschnitten. Darin leuchten einige scheinbar frei eingesetzte Glasflächen heraus. Sie verweisen auf Funde aus römischer Zeit. In einer weiteren Etappe zieht sich die Außenraumgestaltung durch die schmalen Gassen und kulminiert in der breiten Treppenanlage vor der barocken Kirchenfront.

The longitudinal square is framed on three sides by roadways. The fourth side is formed by the area in front of the most important adjoining buildings of the Palazzo Locatelli and the slightly lower Enoteca. The opposing building row swings out slightly concave as though it would react subtly to the frontal effect of the Palazzo. In reality, the soft line is older than the aligned square front. A row of light poles forms a straight line across the square and separates the roadway from the more quiet pedestrian area. An upper section of the square is separated by the caesura of a fountain surrounded by three steps and a stone bench. Thus, in front of the Palazzo, a surface especially textured in stone tile covering and distinguished in this way, comes into being. The lower end of the square used to be rather heterogeneous. A pergola resting on massive columns therefore closes the weakly defined corner on the ground floor level. The free-standing, narrow front of the set-back cafeteria is surmounted by the second row of houses, with the high Campanile dominating the longitudinal direction of the square. Its virtual "shadow" (the tower is situated in the North) is casually imprinted onto the plaza. Apparently freely placed glass panels set in the ground lay within this ensemble. They refer to artifacts from a prehistoric time. In another phase, the outer space design continues in the narrow alleys and culminates in the wide stairway system in front of the baroque church facade.

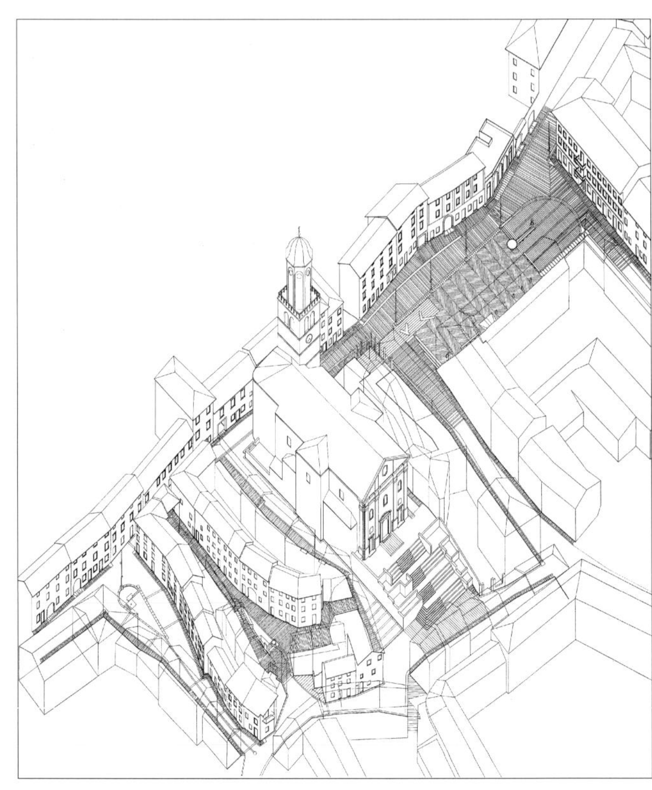

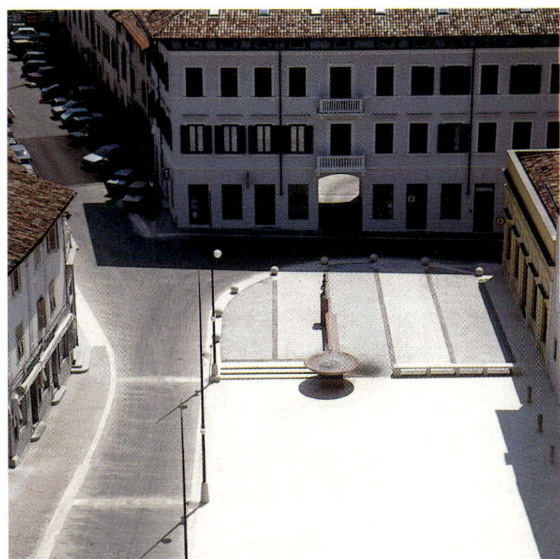

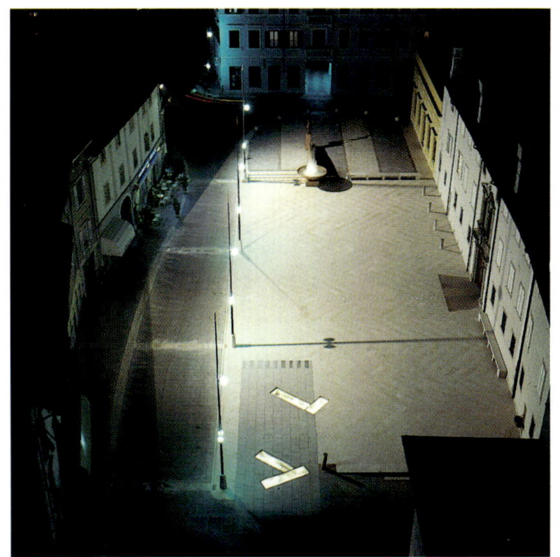

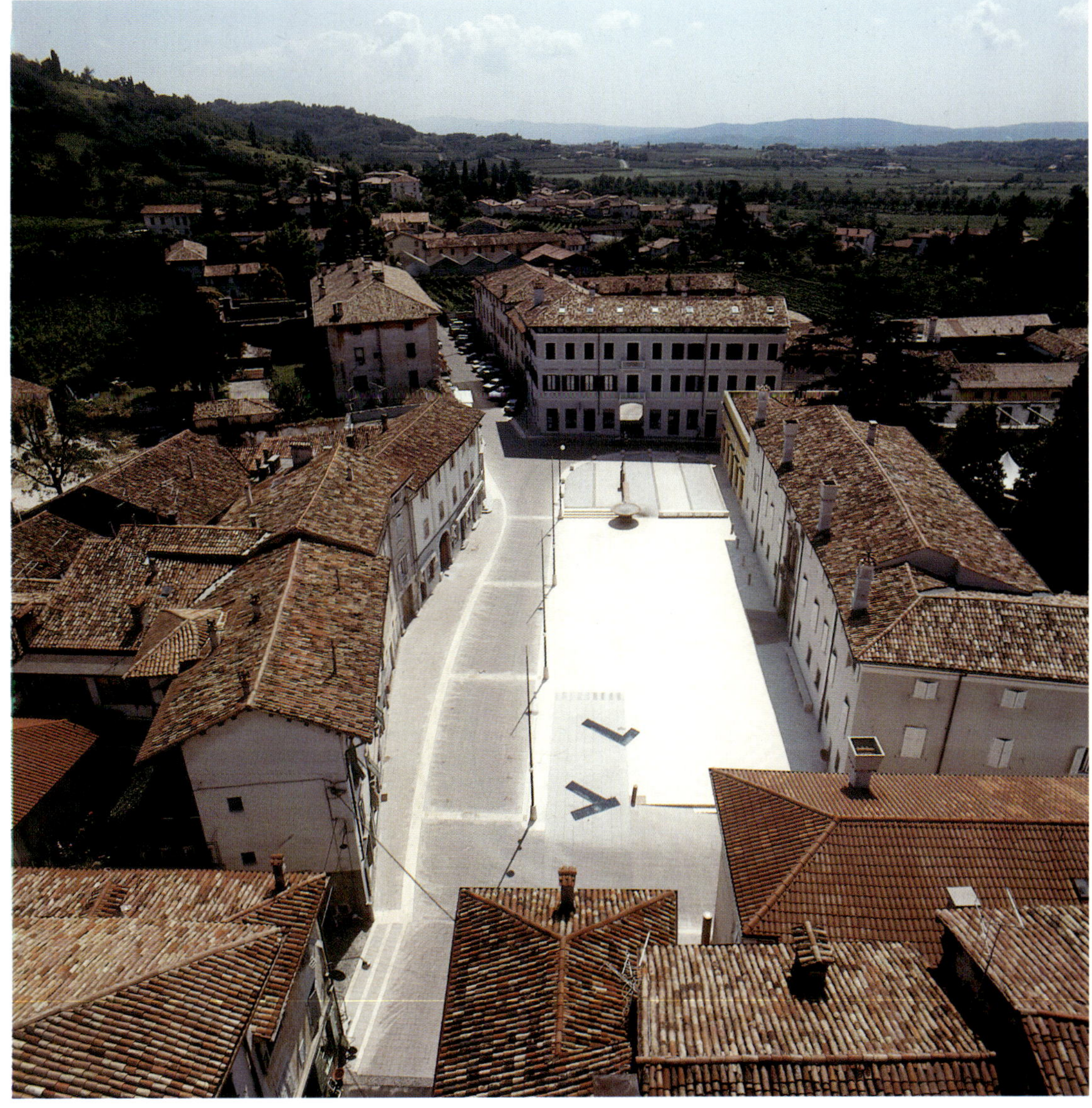

Monolithen der Loggia / *Monoliths of the loggia*

Blick zum Campanile, Brunnen. Plastik: A. Canciani, 1894 /
View of the Campanile, Fountain. Sculpture: A. Canciani, 1894

Römische Mauerreste unter Glas, Rathaus /
Roman wall ruins under glass, town hall

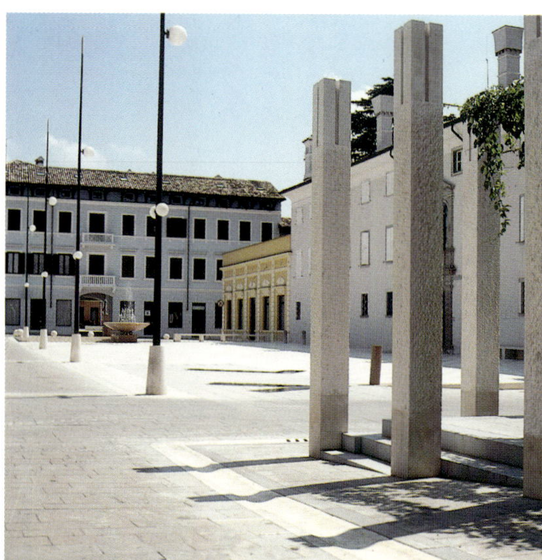

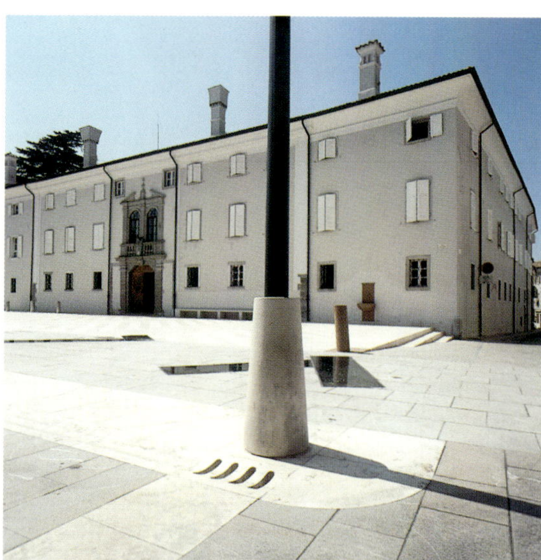

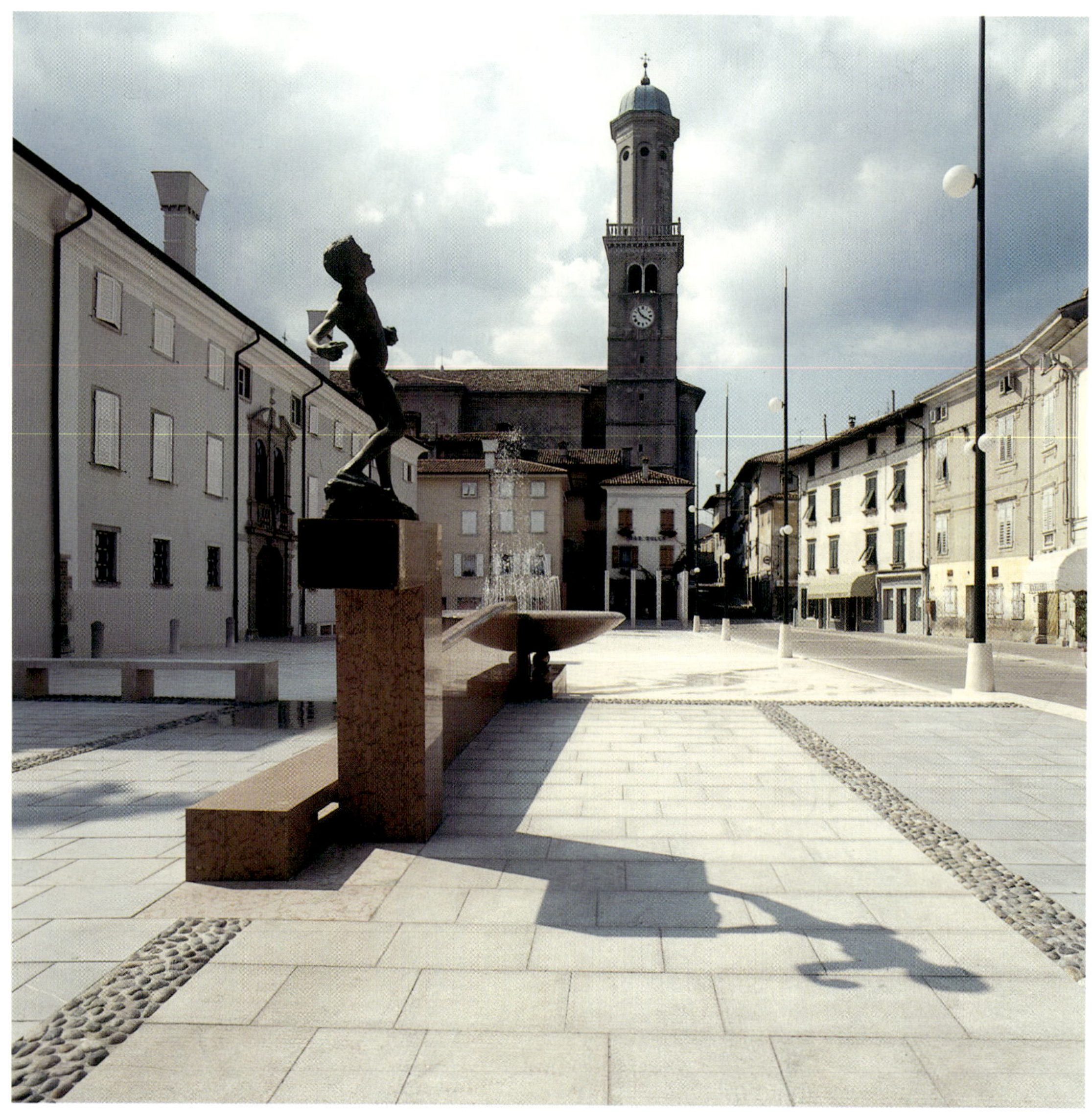

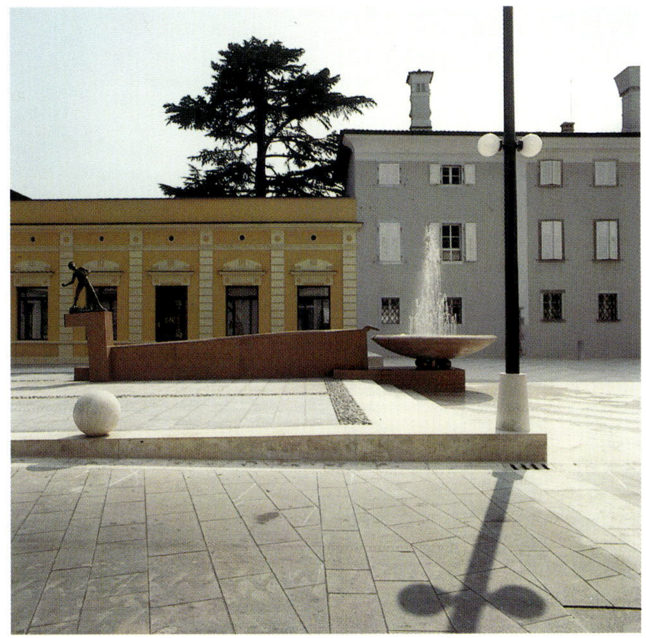 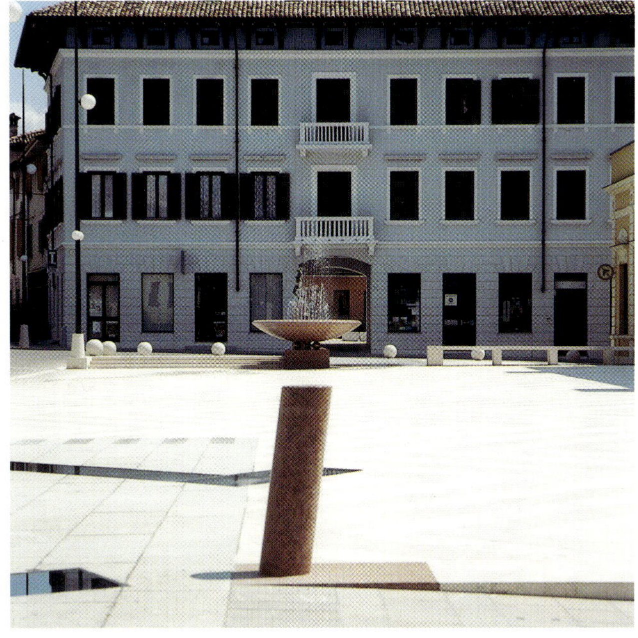

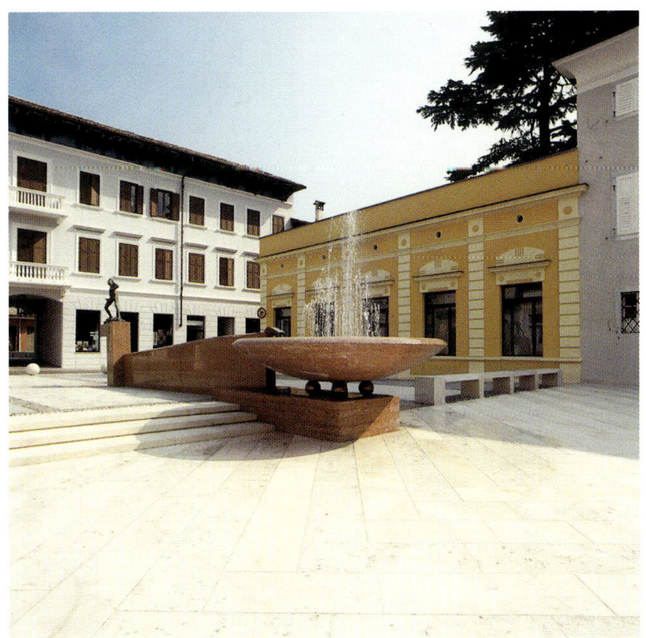 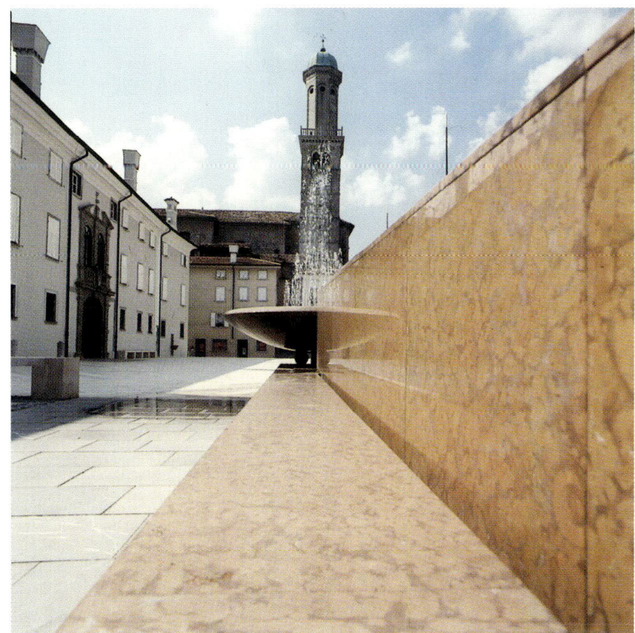

Piran, Slowenien / *Slovenia* 1989

Flugbild von Piran / *Aerial view of Piran*

Axonometrie / *Axonometric projection*

Eine ins Meer hinausführende mächtige Felsrippe und die dahinter entstandene Sandbank bildeten den Baugrund der uralten Handels- und Fischerstadt Piran im venezianischen Herrschaftsbereich. Das winzige alte Hafenbecken steckt tief im Stadtkörper. Längst ist es aufgefüllt und durch einen gößeren Hafen im Bereich der gewachsenen Sandbank ersetzt. Relativ ungeordnet säumen kleine und größere Gebäude den Platz und definieren mit ihren Schaufassaden den Raum. Mit einer elliptischen, leicht bombierten Fläche, die dem unregelmäßig-polygonalen Verlauf des alten Hafenbeckens eingeschrieben ist, gibt Podrecca dem Platz eine dominierende Mitte. Die starke autonome Form wird zum zentralen öffentlichen Raum der Altstadt. Einen Brennpunkt der Ellipse besetzte er mit dem historischen Tartini-Denkmal. Den Mittelpunkt sollte das Bronzerelief einer Windrose fixieren. Steinerne Bänke und Beleuchtungskörper tragende Säulen säumen die Fläche des Platzspiegels, deren harmonisches Verhältnis zum rahmenden Umfeld den angrenzenden Häusern und Palazzi ein breites Vorfeld läßt, das ursprünglich den Reparaturarbeiten der Fischer und dem Markt diente, heute aber von parkenden Autos angefüllt ist. Die über ein mechanisches Erinnern an den ursprünglichen Zuschnitt weit hinausführende Konzentration auf eine Idealform verleiht diesem öffentlichen Raum unnachahmlich-identitätsstiftende Verdichtung.

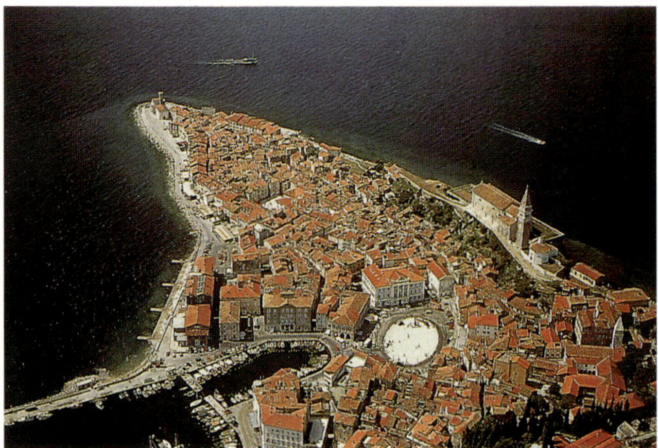

A massive rib of rocks growing out of the sea and the sand bank beyond formed the building base for the ancient trade and fishing town of Piran within the Venetian territorial zone. The tiny old harbor basin is deeply emerged in the town's corporeal substance. It had long ago been filled and had been replaced by a larger harbor in the area of the sand bar. Small and larger buildings surround the square in a rather unorganized fashion and, with their main facades, define the space. Podrecca gives the square a dominating center with an elliptic surface slightly curved in two planes, which is inscribed in the irregular polygonal run of the old harbor basin. The strong autonomous shape becomes a central public space in the old town center. He placed the historic Tartini monument into a focal point of the ellipse. The central point was to be marked by the bronze relief of a compass dial. Stone benches and columns carrying the lighting fixtures surround the surface of the square, whose harmonic relationship with the framing environment leaves a wide zone in front of the adjoining houses and palazzi. This was a place originally reserved for the market and for the repair shops of the fishermen. Today, it is a parking lot. The focus of attention on an ideal form, reaching far beyond a mechanical memory of the original appearance, provides this public space with an unmatchable condensation of elements creating a unique identity.

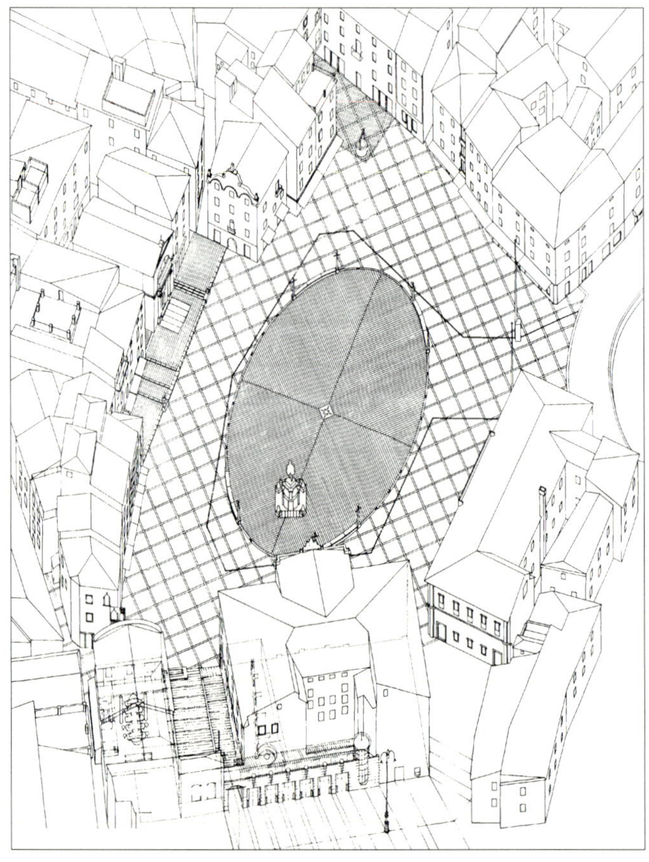

Gesamtansicht des Platzes / *Overall view of the square*

Steinbänke und -kandelaber / *Stone benches and candelabras*

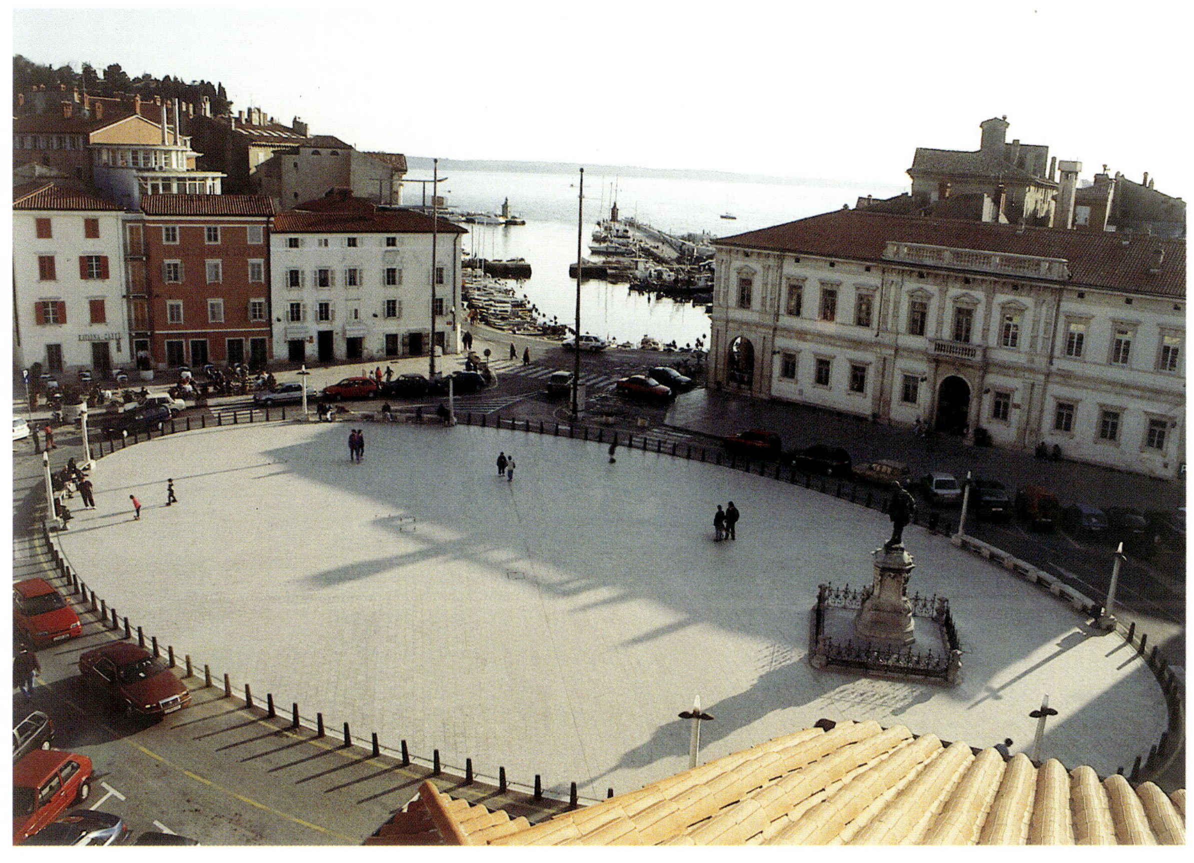

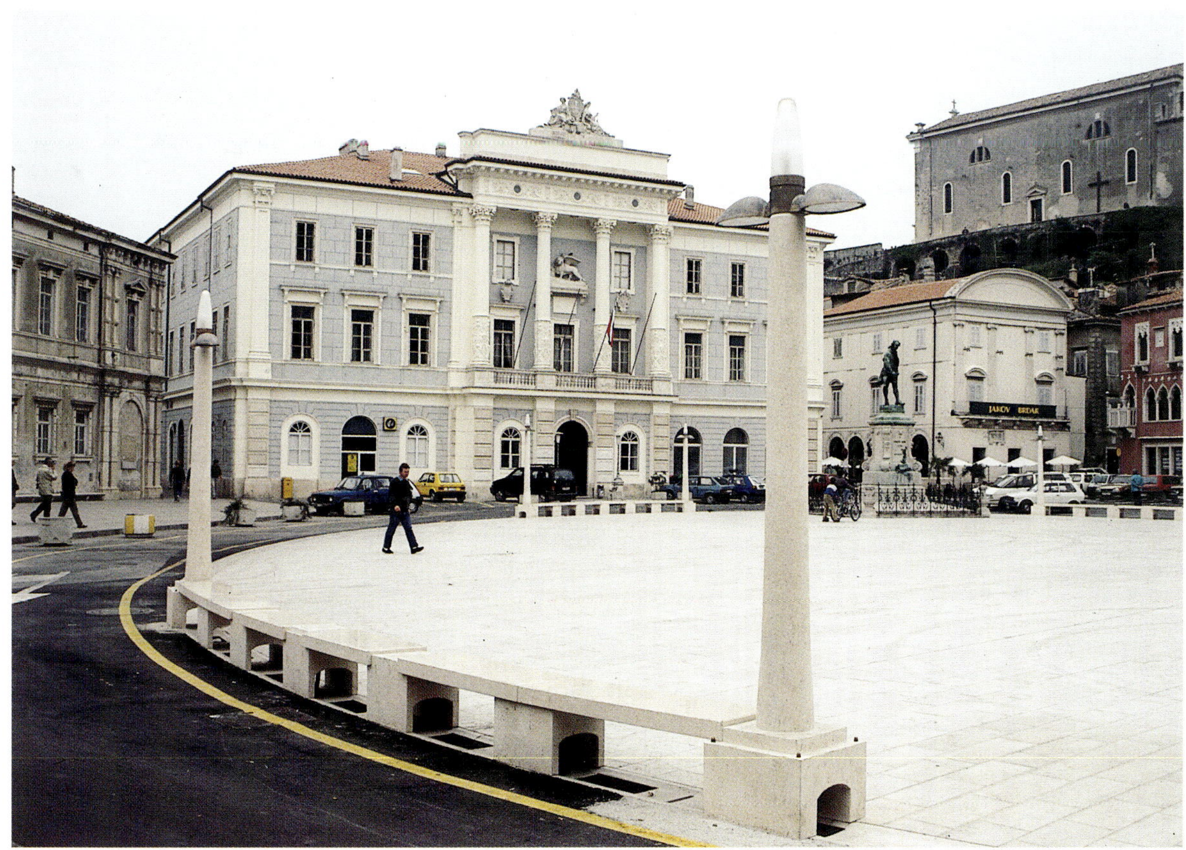

Brunnen / *Fountain*

Ausschnitte und Details der neuen Estrade / *Details of the new Estrade*

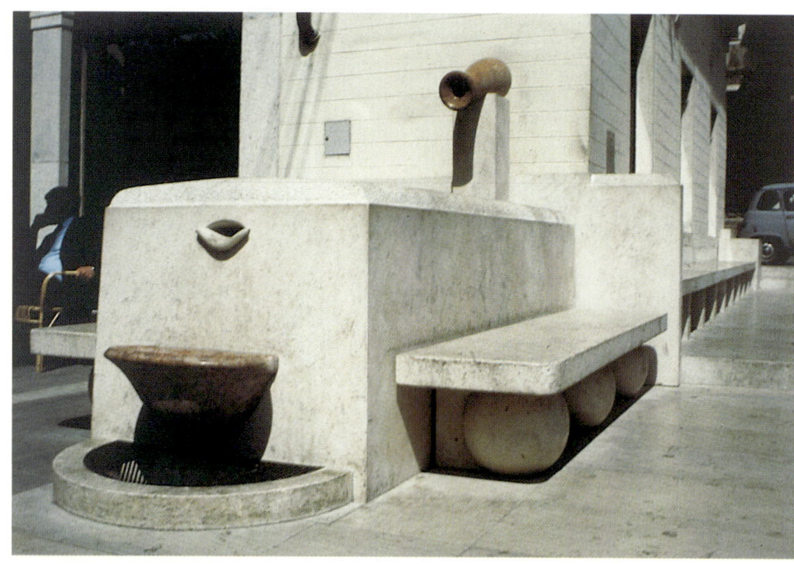

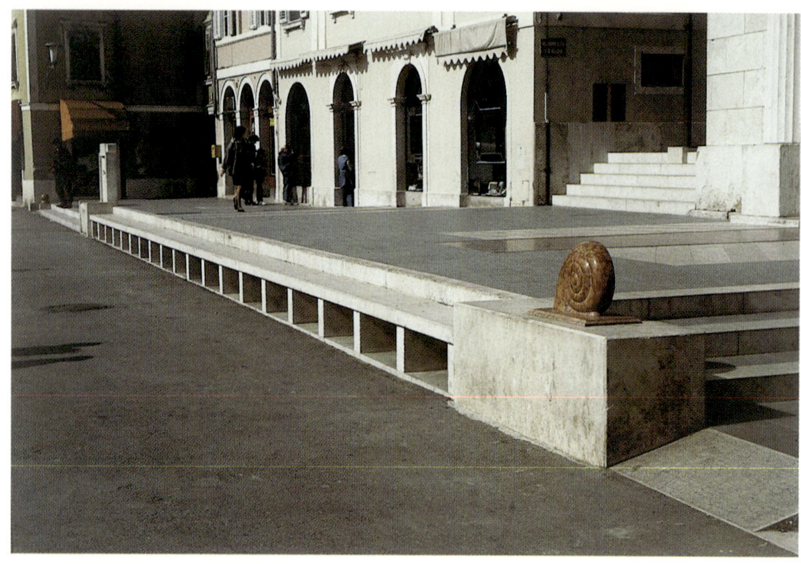

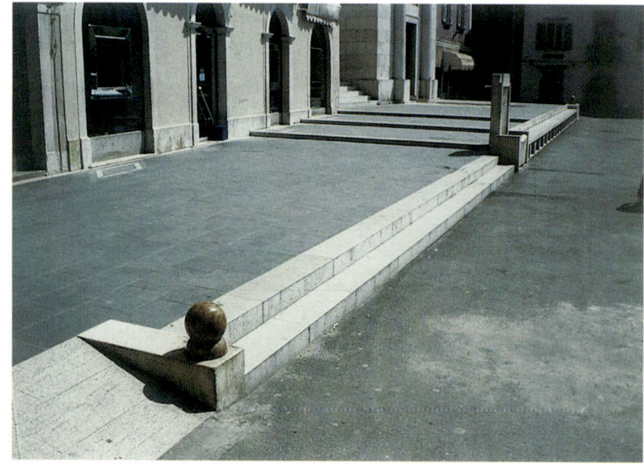

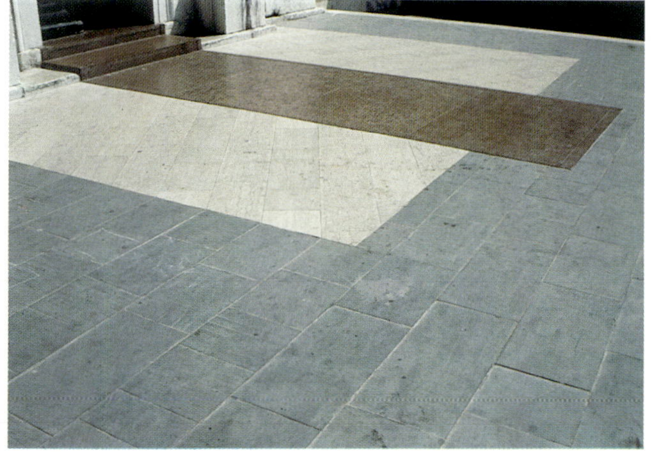

Piran, Slowenien / *Slovenia* 1990

Fassadenrudimente / *Image of the old facade*

Entwurfskizzen / *Design sketches*

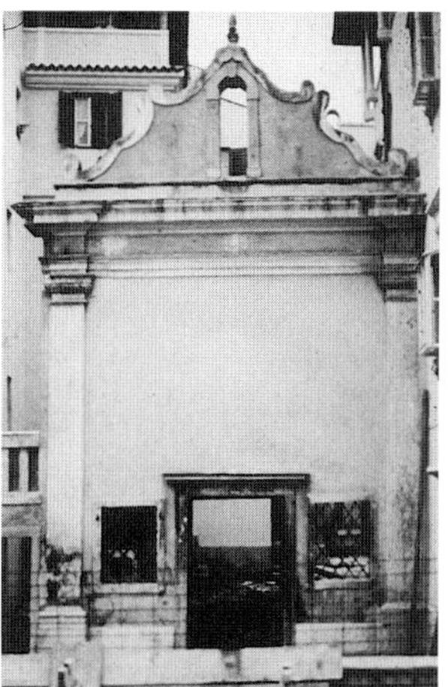

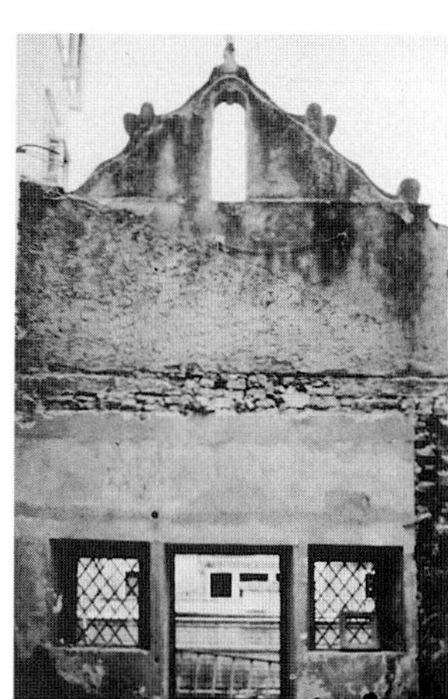

Die bereits im Mittelalter verbürgte Kapelle St. Donat liegt an der Piazza Vecchia, dem Piraner Hauptplatz, wo auch das Rathaus steht. Zwar konnte der schmucke spätbarocke Giebel nicht verhindern, daß das Gebäude Anfang dieses Jahrhunderts als Transformatorenstation dienen mußte. Aber das in den 80er Jahren gewachsene slowenische Selbstbewußtsein verhalf der Ruine zu neuem Leben. Das fehlende Dach wurde mit einem Tragwerk aus gebogenen Rippen und einem doppelten «Kiel» geschlossen, das den Fischerbooten nachempfunden ist, mit dem gerundeten hinteren Abschluß aber auch an eine Apsis erinnert. Die scheinbare Profanierung zur Kunstgalerie wird mit dem sakral wirkenden Element eines Präsentationstisches relativiert, der in der Verdoppelung, als Bodenplattform für das frei im Raum stehende Obergeschoß an Bedeutung gewinnt. Die metaphorischen Anklänge an archetypische Elemente des Sakralbaus – das Untergeschoß wirkt als Krypta – erzeugen eine weihevolle Atmosphäre, die von den edlen Materialien und der sorgfältigen Verarbeitung noch verstärkt wird. Für das schmale Rundbogenfenster im Frontgiebel hat Podrecca aber bewußt einen weißen Alabaster aus Volterra gewählt, mit dem er der Sakralisierung gegensteuert, so daß eine ambivalente Raumstimmung aufkommt, die für den Kauf von Kunstwerken adäquat ist. Interessant ist, daß die axiale Organisation des Raumes durch die an der Seite gerade hochführende Treppe nicht gestört wird. Sie ist Teil des tischartigen Einbaus, der den hohen Raum ausmißt.

The chapel of St. Donat had already been consecrated in the Middle Ages and is located at the Piazza Vecchia, the main square of Piran, where the town hall is also situated. The beauty of the ornate late-baroque gable could not save the building from being turned into a transformer station at the beginning of the century. However, the Slovenian self-consciousness, which grew during the '80s, helped to bring new life and vitality to the ruin. The missing roof was closed by a supporting structure of curved ribs and a doubled "keel" which was designed in response to the ever present fishing boats, but is also reminiscent of an apse with its rounded back end. The seemingly profane transformation into an art gallery is made relative by the ecclesiastic effect of a presentation table which, having a double effect in form of a floor platform, gains importance for the upper floor which is a free-standing platform. The metaphoric hints of archetypal elements of religious buildings – the lower level has the effect of a crypt – create a consecrated atmosphere which is emphasized by the precious materials and the careful fashioning. However, Podrecca consciously chose white alabaster from Volterra for the narrow roundarched window in the front gable, which he works against the ecclesiastic effect, thus creating an ambivalent spatial atmosphere appropriate for the purchasing of works of art. It is interesting that the axial organization of the space is not disturbed by the straight ascending staircase on the side. It is part of the table-like installation which measures out the space.

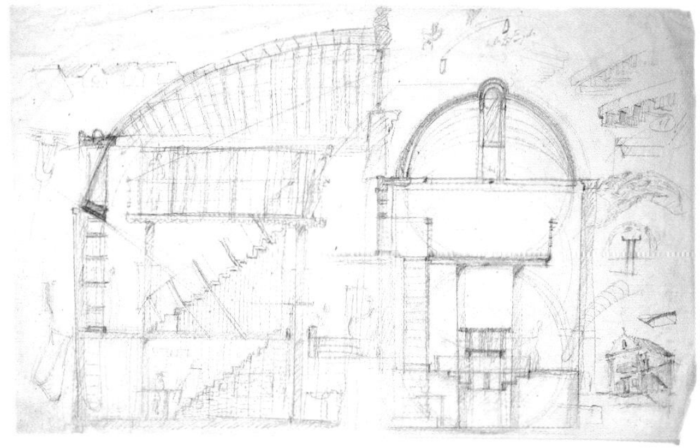

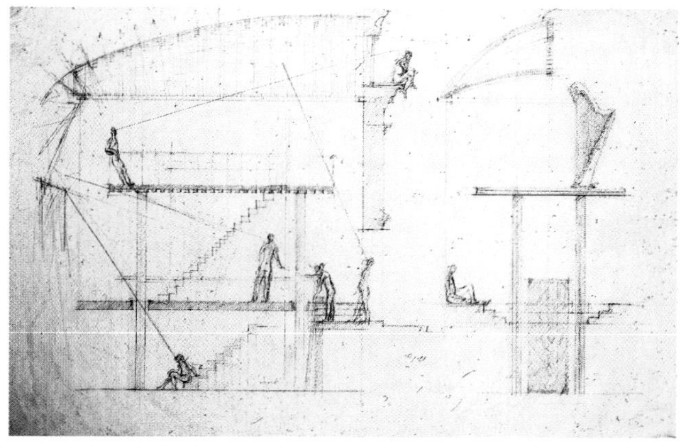

Blick von der Zisterne / *View from the cistern*

Tonnengewölbe, Details / *Barrel vault, details*

Rückfassade / *Rear facade*

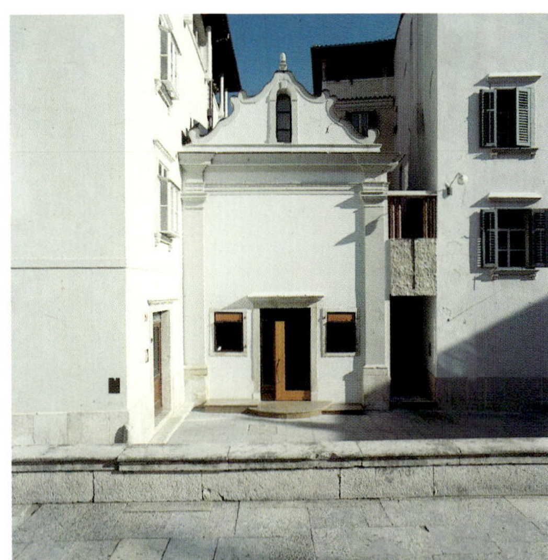

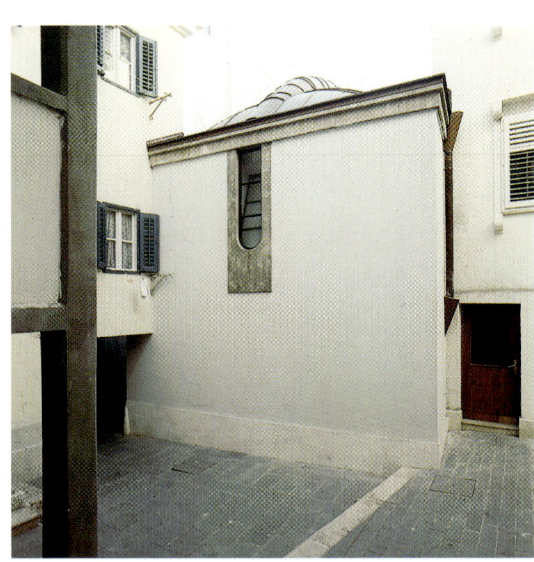

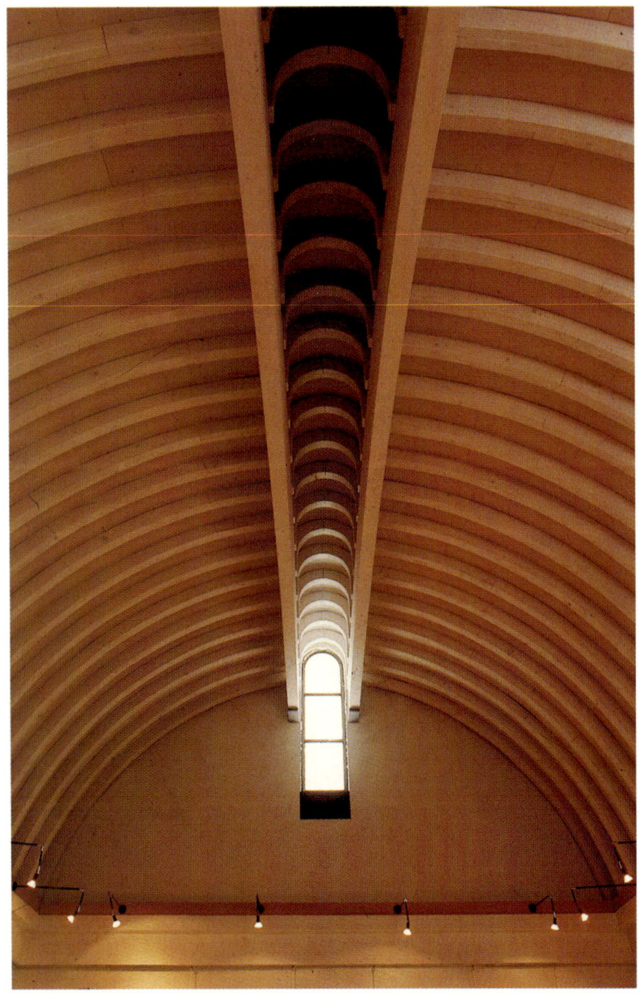

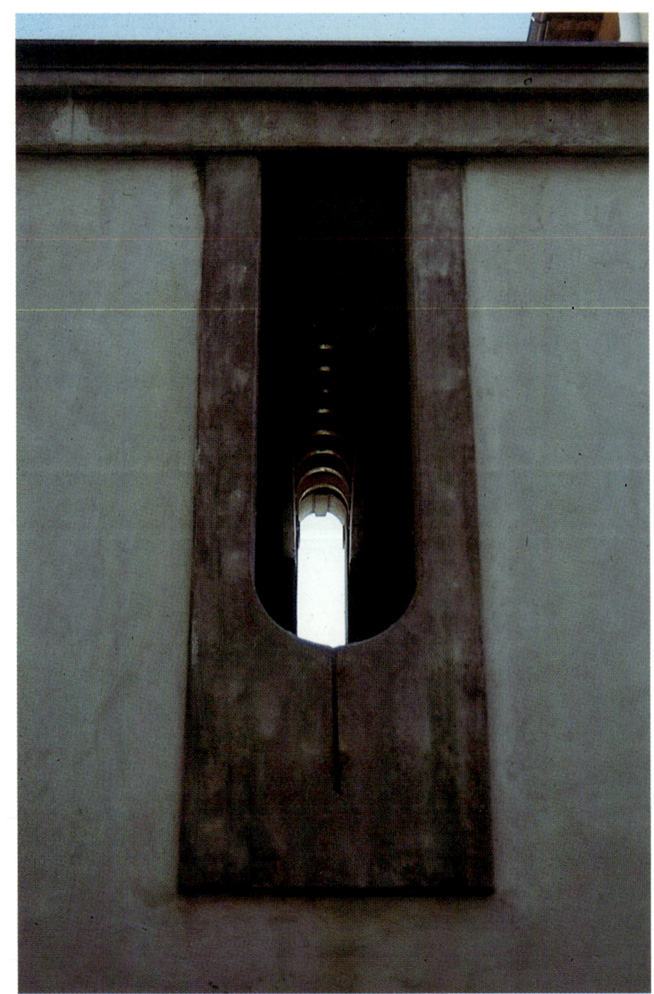

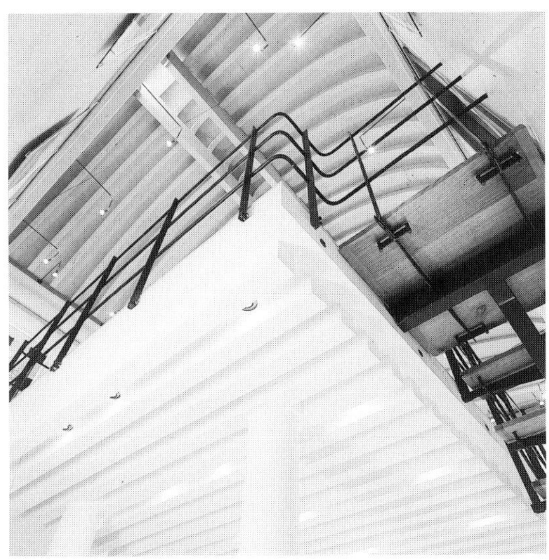

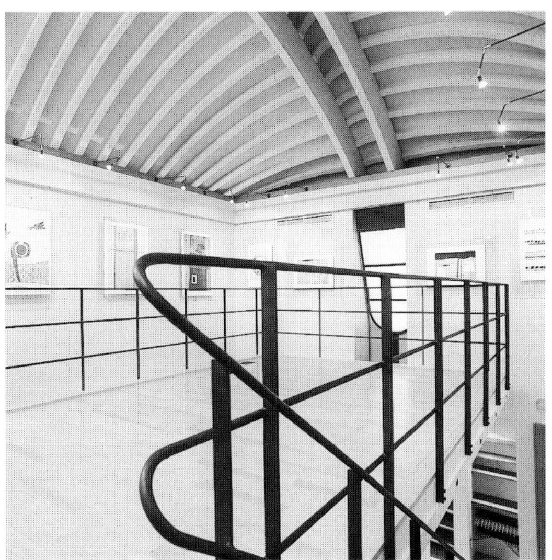

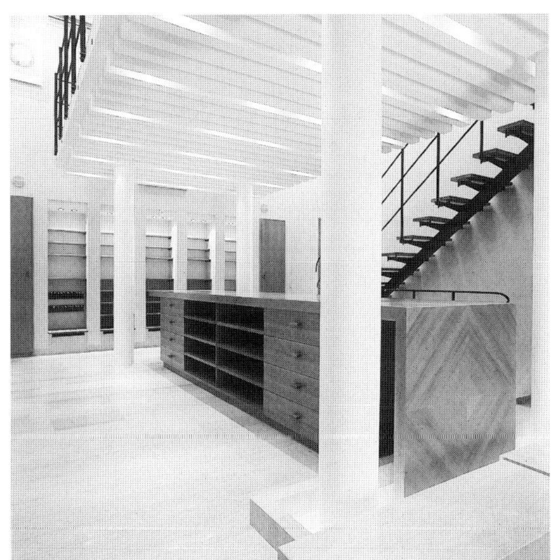

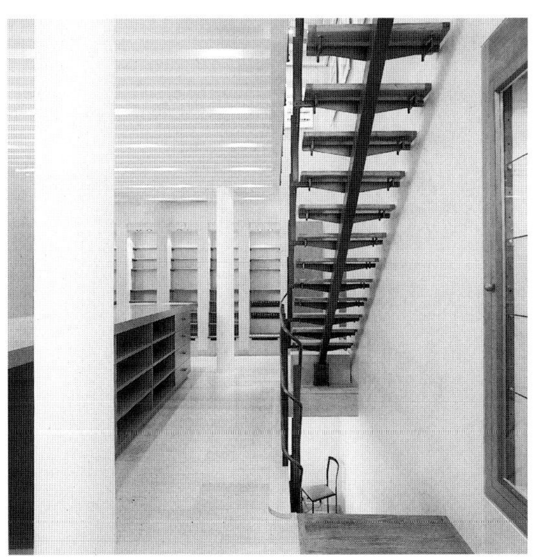

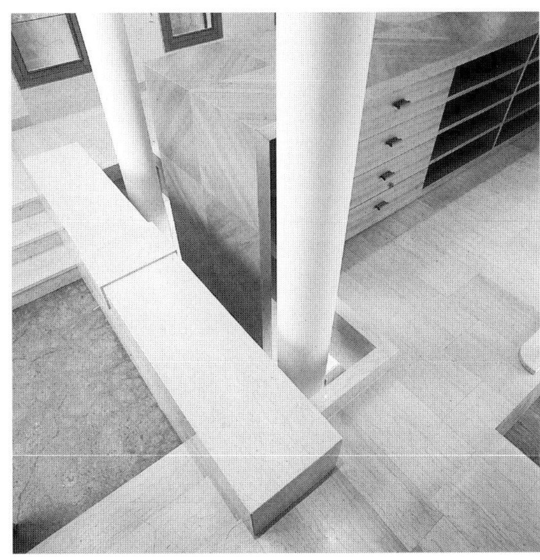

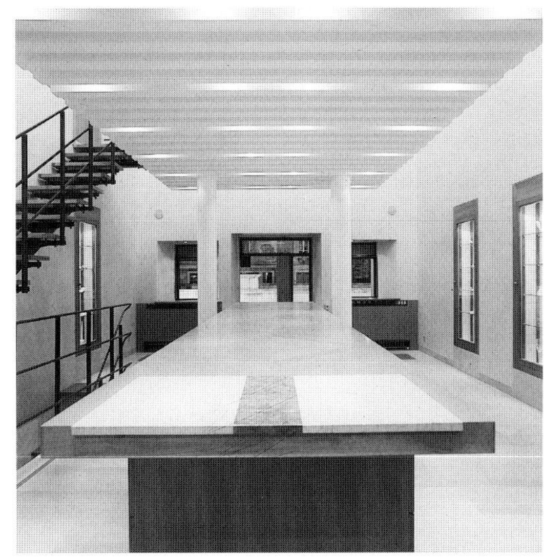

Das temporäre Wesen einer Ausstellung bewirkt, daß sie, generiert aus dem Spannungsverhältnis der Exponate und deren Präsentation, nach dem Abbau auf der Basis von Fotografien und dem Katalog nie mehr dieselbe Lebendigkeit in der Vorstellung hervorrufen kann, wie sie sie während der Laufzeit durch ihre Unmittelbarkeit zu erzeugen vermag. Boris Podreccas jüngste Ausstellungsgestaltung, seine letzte, wie er betont, profitiert von den Erfahrungen zahlreicher monographischer und historischer Präsentationen, und soll als Fallbeispiel dienen. Das Thema lautet: «Die Donau. 1000 Jahre Österreich. Eine Reise.»; Ort: die Gewölbe unter dem Wiener Schottenstift; Zeit: Sommer 1996. Obwohl wieder eine historische Thematik zu bearbeiten war, wurde diese überlagert von der Lebenskraft des Donauraumes, dem die Ausstellung vor allem gewidmet ist. Der Fluß als Metapher des Lebens und des Zeitenlaufs erlaubt im Gegensatz zu diesen, ihn sowohl von der Quelle, als auch von der Mündung her zu betrachten und abzuschreiten, dasselbe gilt für die Ausstellung.
Die Donau verbindet unterschiedlichere Kulturkreise als etwa der Rhein. Die Aufgabe daher ist für Boris Podrecca geschaffen, wie kaum eine andere für einen Wiener Architekten. Seine Liebe zu diesem Fluß und vor allem zum Leben an den Ufern dieses Flusses bewogen ihn, trotz des Zeitdrucks und der begrenzten Mittel die Verantwortung für den sinnlichen Gesamteindruck der Ausstellung zu übernehmen. Im Überblick wird ersichtlich, daß sie eine Quintessenz seiner bisherigen Ausstellungsgestaltungen darstellt.Ort der Ausstellung sind Kellergewölbe, mehrere Geschoße tief unter dem Schottenstift in der Wiener Innenstadt. Die aus Ziegeln gemauerten Wände, Pfeiler und Deckengewölbe bilden das Kontinuum, vor dem sich das Ausstellungsgut entfaltet. Von der Freyung, mehr Straßenausweitung denn Platz, erfolgt der Zugang. Als äußeres Signal hat Podrecca einen Stahlmast vor die Hofeinfahrt gelehnt, mit großen, leuchtenden Tafeln, die den Verlauf der Donau als blaue Neonschlange vor einer Montage grobgerasterter Satellitenbilder zeigen. Die Republik Österreich ist mit dem Logo ihres Kartenbildes hervorgehoben. Wenige Schritte daneben bohrt sich ein umgedrehtes Periskop in die Erde, wo der suchende Blick im Doppelspiegel die Skulptur des «Donauweibchens» erfassen kann. Im Schottenhof, der auch ein beliebtes Gartencafé enthält, folgt vor dem Abstieg eine erste künstlerische Auseinandersetzung mit dem Element Wasser. Aus einem Trog mit mechanisch bewegten Ledermänteln spritzt das Naß vor die Füße der Passanten und gebietet ein erstes Innehalten. Damit schafft Podrecca jenes geheimnisvoll Anziehende, das die Menschen bewegt, hinunterzusteigen und den Eintritt in die Wiener Katakomben zu wagen.
Zur Einstimmung stößt man auf Schwarzweißbilder von vier Fotografen, die sich mit dem Thema des Uferstreifens, des Übergangs vom Wasser zum Land befaßten. Einige ausdruckstarke zeitgenössische Kunstwerke, die ebenfalls mit dem Element Wasser arbeiten, bilden dann den Auftakt. Die zugänglichere Fotografie

The temporary existence of an exhibition – created by the eventual removal of the shown objects and the interruption of their presentation – has the effect that, after being taken down, never again can the same lively imaginations be created through photographs and catalogues. Boris Podrecca's most recent design of an exhibition (and his last one, as he has avowed) profits from the experiences of a long series of monographic and historic presentations. We will look into this as an example. The theme is: "The Danube. 1000 years of Austria. A voyage." The location: Schottenstift, Vienna, The time: summer 1996. Although a historic theme was again posed, it was superimposed by the vitality of the Danube river to which the exhibition was mainly dedicated. The river can be a metaphor for life and the passing of time. However, the river itself as a physical thing offers the possibility for one to walk along it from its source as well as from its estuary, both forward and back.
The Danube, which connects many more cultures than other rivers, is a theme custom-made for Boris Podrecca. It must have been his love for the river and for life along its banks which caused him to take on the responsibility for the sensual impression of the show. Taking an overall view, it becomes clear that this exhibition can be seen as the quintessential of all his exhibition designs.
The show was located in basement vaults, a couple of floors beneath the Schottenstift in Vienna's center. These brick masonry walls, columns, and vaults form a basic continuum in front of which the shown objects can develop. The access to the show goes across the Freyung which is more of a street expansion than a square. Podrecca leaned a steel mast in front of the yard entrance as an outer signal with large lit boards showing the Danube as a blue neon snake on a collage of satellite images. Only the Republic of Austria is distinguished by its map out-line logo. A few steps to the side a periscope is drilled into the ground where a curious look can detect the sculpture of the "Little Danube woman". In the Schottenhof, with its garden café, a first artistic encounter with the water element occurs at the threshold to the descent. From a trough with mechanically moved leather coats, the wet element sprays in front of the pedestrians' feet and requests an initial stop, thus creating an attraction, a mysterious magnetism, stimulating people to descend the stairs and dare to enter into Vienna's catacombs.
As a first impression, black-and-white photographs by four photographers deal with the theme of the river bank. Some works of art follow, which also play with the watery element. The more easily accessible photography and the more challenging works of conceptual art, minimal art and arte povera touch visitors from all cultural levels and make them cognizant for what is to come. Such bi-polarities create a suspension adequate for receptivity while walking through the show. On the lower level, the historic part highlighting politics, technology, culture, natural science and art begins. It is possible to walk through in both directions – forward and backwards. In the basement labyrinth, the collection of 264 reproduced pages of the "Views of the Danube following its course

und die anspruchsvolleren Arbeiten der Konzeptkunst, der Minimal art und der Arte povera berühren Besucher aus allen kulturellen Schichten und sensibilisieren sie für das Kommende. Derartige Bipolaritäten schaffen eine der Aufnahmefähigkeit beim Schreiten adäquate Spannung.

Ein Geschoß tiefer beginnt der historische Teil, der Politik, Technik, Kultur, Naturwissenschaft und Kunst schlaglichtartig berührt. Der Durchgang in beiden Richtungen ermöglicht auch das vor und zurück. Als Ariadnefaden im Kellerlabyrinth dienen die 264 Blätter der «Donau-Ansichten nach dem Laufe des Donaustromes von seinem Ursprunge bis zu seinem Ausflusse in das schwarze Meer.» (1826) von Jakob Alt, Ludwig Erminy, Alois von Saar, Franz Wolf. Auf zwei parallele Kupferleitungsröhren montiert, betonen sie das kontinuierliche Fließen.

Die Präsentationstafeln, bestehend aus dunkelgrauem Eisenblech, heben sich von den in Rottönen changierenden Ziegelwänden ab. Oft sind sie gelocht, das Licht fällt durch und wahrt die Integrität der Gewölberäume. Die Tafeln stehen lose auf dem Boden, kaum daß die Mauer berührt wird oder gar verletzt. Ehrfurcht vor dem Bestand, gerade weil er so profan ist wie die alte Ziegelmauer, bestimmt die gestalterische Haltung.

Die Vitrinen sind in die Metalltafeln eingelassen, ein davor montiertes Glas dient dem Schutz. Oft fällt oder steigt der einfache Betonboden leicht ab oder an, variable Fußelemente gleichen dies aus, so daß die Tafeln horizontal bleiben.

Zwei hohe Gewölbesäle enthalten thematische Schwerpunkte. Sie werden auf deckartigen Plattformen betreten, die einen Raum im Raum andeuten. Wichtige Exponate sind durch ausreichend Umraum hervorgehoben; drohen die Inhalte akademisch trocken zu versanden, werden sie mit sinnlich wirkenden Stücken konfrontiert, in denen menschliche Arbeit inkarniert ist, wie etwa der «erste» Eisenpflug, an dem man die lange Dienstzeit, die Reparaturen und die Schwere der bäuerlichen Arbeit gleichsam körperlich spürt.

Licht scheint mit dem Tropfenzähler verteilt, so daß im Dämmer der Katakomben erwartungsvolle Entdeckerstimmung aufkommt. Oft scheinen die Objekte erst beim Nähertreten geheimnisvoll aufzuglühen, während die Lichtquellen kaum sichtbar sind.

Aus der Gestaltung spricht nicht nur die Liebe zur Donau und zu den von ihr bespülten Kulturräumen, sondern auch zu den einzelnen Exponaten. Durchblicke auf wichtige Stücke werden genützt zur raumzeitlichen Verknüpfung. Hier schaut aus dem Hintergrund nachdenklich der Kopf Arnold Schönbergs aus dem Ölbild von Richard Gerstl durch die Pferdebeine eines türkischen Panzerreiters, dort schimmert Klimts Portrait der Emilie Flöge wie Achat aus einem Quergang heraus. Nicht um zu belehren hat Podrecca seine Gestaltung inszeniert, sondern um die Freude am Schauen und Entdecken zu fördern und zu lohnen.

from its source to the estuary into the Black Sea" (1826), by Jakob Alt, Ludwig Erminy, Alois von Saar, and Franz Wolf represents the Ariadne-thread. Mounted onto two parallel copper pipes, they enhance the continuity of the flow.

The presentation panels generally consist of dark-gray iron metal sheets distinguishing themselves from the changing red shades of the brick walls. Often, they have holes and the light falls through. These boards are placed casually onto the floor; the wall is not touched or interrupted. The designer's attitude is determined by a respect for the existing, especially something as profound as the brick wall.

Show-cases are cut into the metal boards and glass mounted to their front serves as protection. Often the simple concrete floor rises or descends a bit. This unevenness is balanced by floor elements, thus maintaining the horizontal continuity of the boards.

Two high, vaulted halls contain thematic focal points. One enters them on cover-like and slightly raised platforms, thus hinting at a space inside the space. Adequate surrounding space allows important works to stand out; if the contents threaten to become too academic and dry, they are confronted with strongly sensual pieces in which human labor is incarnated, e.g., the "first" iron plow which makes you physically feel the long time of service, the innumerable repairs, and the strain of farm work.

The lighting seems to have been distributed with a drop-counter, which creates an expectant mood of discovery in the dim catacombs. Often, the objects seem to mysteriously glow only when approached and the light sources are hardly visible.

The entire design not only speaks about the love for the Danube and the cultural areas that it flows through. It also tells about the love for each shown piece. Lookouts on important pieces are used for the connection with time and space. From the background, the thoughtful head of Arnold Schönberg in the oil painting by Richard Gerstl is looking through a Turkish armored rider's horses legs in one place. In another, Klimt's portrait of Emilie Flöge shimmers out of a side hallway like agate. Podrecca has not staged his design in order to teach us something, but rather to foster and reward the joy of looking and discovering.

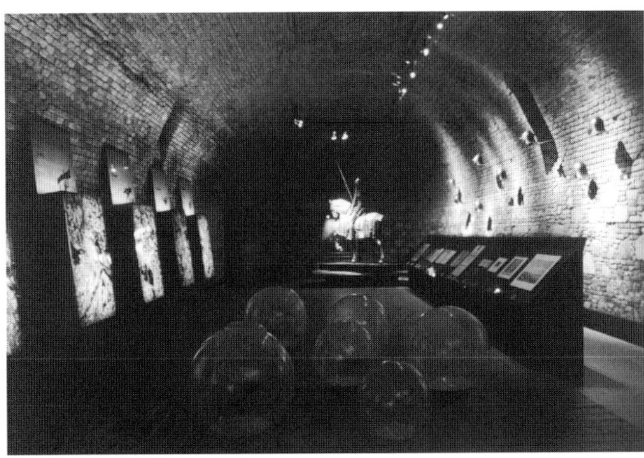

Chiesa della Carità, Gallerie dell' Accademia, Venedig /
Venice 1984

Perspektivische Skizze der Abhängung /
Perspective sketch of suspension system

Pavillon der Glasobjekte / *Pavilion of glass objects*

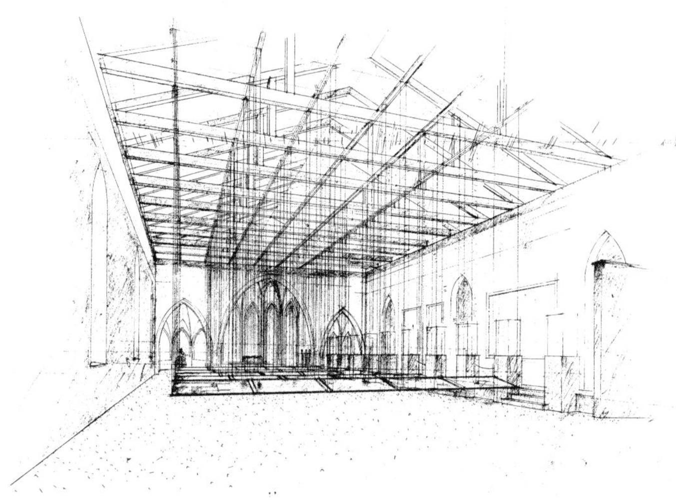

Das Werk des Architekten Carlo Scarpa wurde sechs Jahre nach
seinem Unfalltod erstmals als breit angelegte Ausstellung in seiner Heimatstadt Venedig gezeigt. Der Ort, die durch eine Anfang
19. Jahrhundert eingezogene Zwischendecke stark veränderte
gotische Chiesa della Carità, bot architektonisch interessante
Ansätze für die Ausstellungsgestaltung. Das Konzept rückte vor
allem Scarpas Zeichnungen in den Vordergrund; speziell angefer-
tigte Architekturmodelle und zwölf der schönsten von Scarpa
entworfenen Gläser bildeten weitere Schwerpunkte. Zwischen
gewölbten, in Metallrahmen gespannten Plexiglasplatten wurden
die Zeichnungen geschützt und blendfrei präsentiert. An feinen
Drähten vom alten Dachgebälk herabhängend, erzeugten die
schwebenden Rahmen mit ihren transparenten Füllungen eine
ansteigende Wellenbewegung, die zum Chor hin im Thema des
Brion-Friedhofs kulminierte. Die konsequente Scheu, den die
Kirche profanierenden Boden zu berühren und die doppelte
Lichtführung – als stetiges Himmelslicht und lebendig gespiegelt
von den Wellen des Canale Grande – verdichteten sich zu einer
weihevollen Raumstimmung. Die sichtbare Reflexion an den
Hängedrähten füllte den gesamten Raum. Einem Tempietto
gleich vereinigten sich die zwölf Vitrinen mit den Gläsern zu
einem autonomen Vertikalelement, das zur horizontalen Präsenta-
tionsstruktur der Zeichnungen den Kontrapunkt setzte. Im anschließenden Raum faßte ein kleiner Glasrahmen Scarpas das
Tor der Markuskirche auf dem dahinterliegenden Gemälde und
setzte den Abschlußpunkt.

*Six years after his accidental death the work of the architect Carlo
Scarpa was first shown in a large exhibition in his hometown of
Venice. The location was the gothic Chiesa della Carità, drasti-
cally changed by the installation of a false ceiling in the beginning of the 19th century, which offered interesting approaches for
the design of the show. The concept placed Scarpa's drawings into
the foreground. Custom-made architectural models and twelve of
the most beautiful glasses designed by Scarpa were further focal
points. The drawings were protected and presented in concave,
glare-free plexiglass plates stretched in metal frames. Hanging
from fine wires from the old roof beams, the floating frames with
their transparent fillings created a rising wave-like movement cul-
minating towards the choir in the theme of the Brion-cemetery.
The consequent reluctance to touch the floor and the two light
sources – the constant "heavenly" light and the light lively reflec-
ted by the waves of the Canale Grande – condensed into an ecclesiastic mood in the space. The visible reflection on the hanging
wires filled the entire space. Similar to a tempietto, the twelve
show-cases united with the glass into an autonomous vertical element, creating a counter-point to the horizontal structure of the
presentation of the drawings. In the adjoining room, a small glass
frame by Scarpa surrounded the gate of the church of St. Mark on
the painting behind it and thus formed the finishing point.*

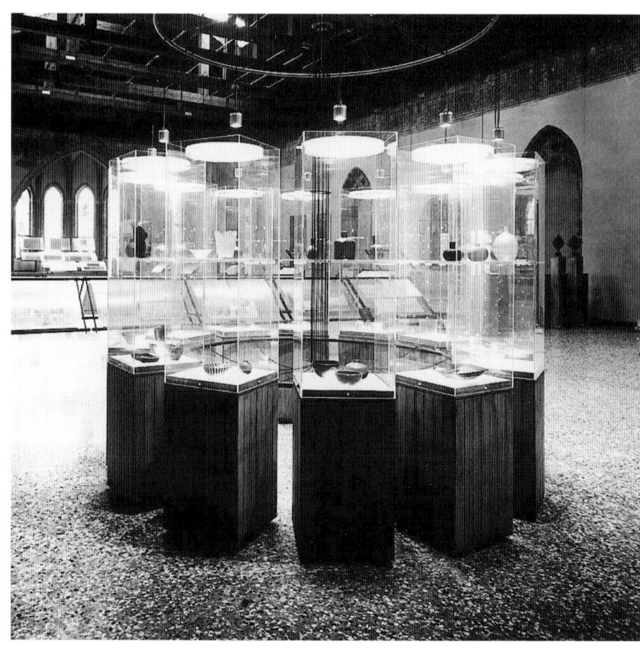

Gesamtansicht / *Overall view*

Rahmenabhängung, Detail /
Frame suspension system, detail

Blick in die Längsachse / *View of the longitudinal axis*

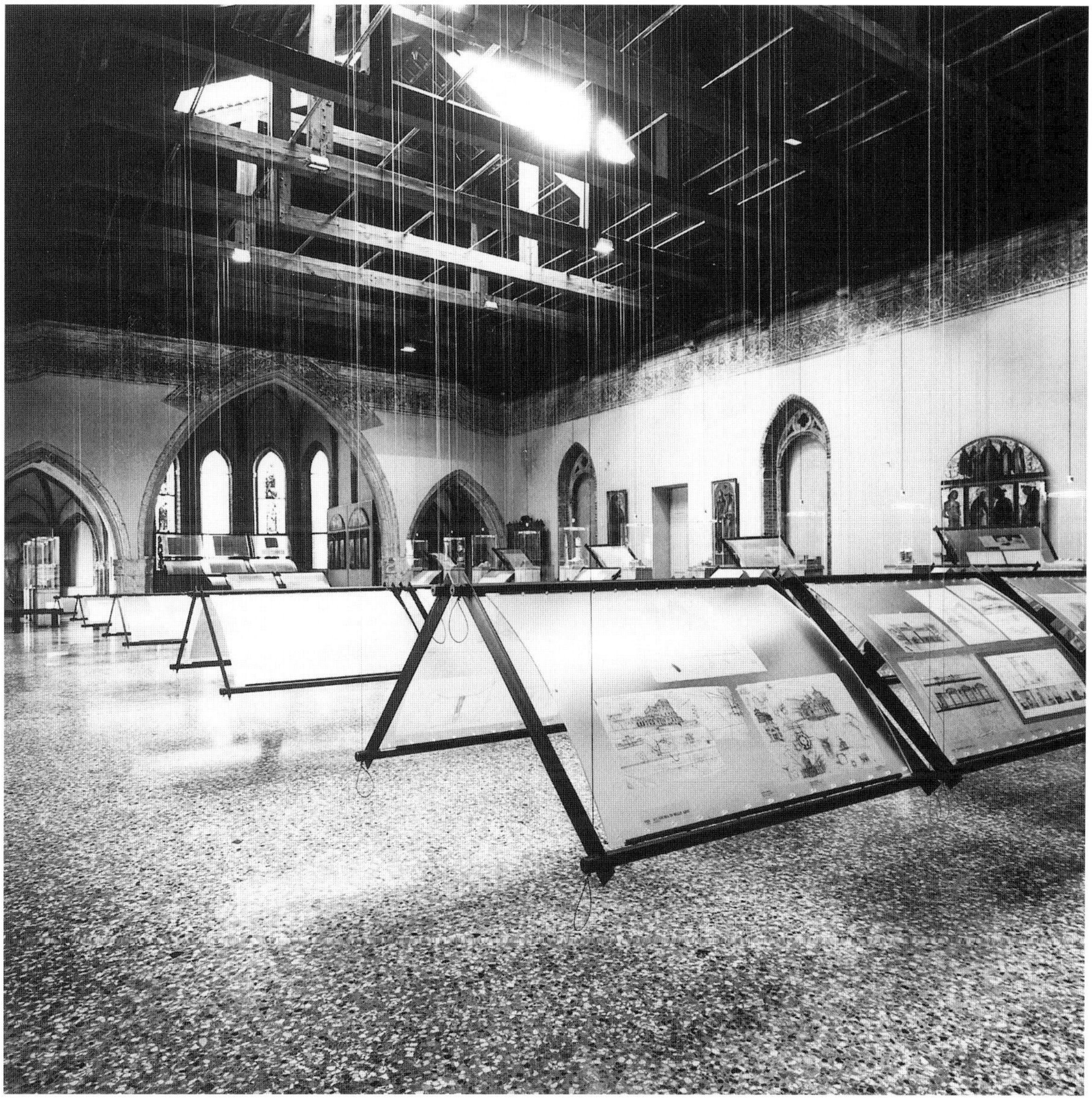

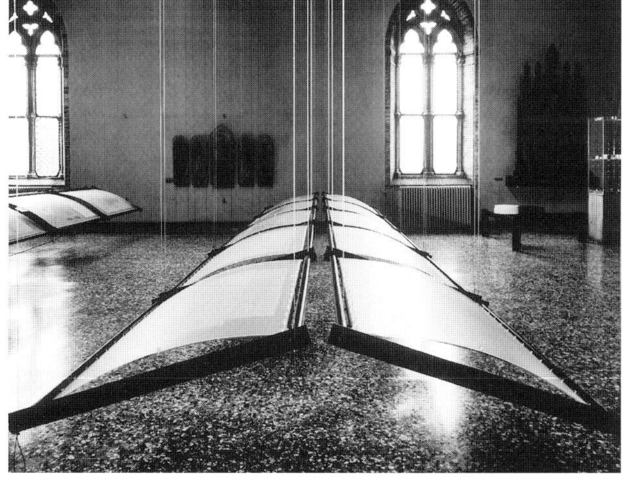

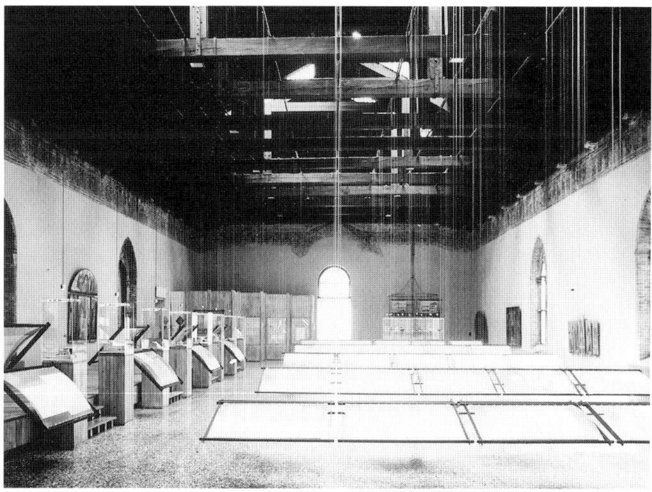

Triennale di Milano 1988

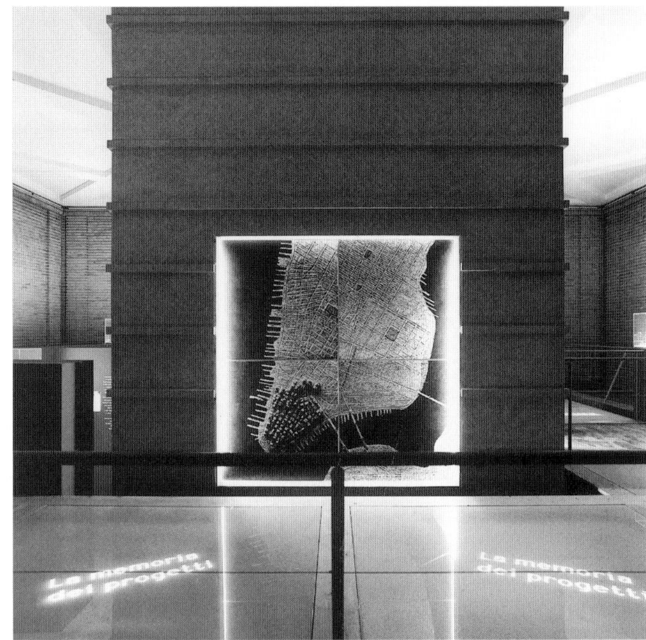

Blick in den Tageslichtturm / *View of the skylight tower*

Schnitte und Ansichten / *Sections and elevations*

Historische Karten, Stadtgrundrisse und alte Vermessungsinstrumente bildeten die Exponate dieses Ausstellungsteils im Palazzo d'Arte im Mailänder Parco Sempione. Während die Objekte auf einer raumfüllenden, vom Boden abgehobenen Plattform im milden Kunstlicht gezeigt wurden, enthielt ein turmartiger Raum in der Mitte kontrolliertes Tageslicht durch eine zenitale Glaspyramide. Hier waren die wichtigsten alten Pläne und Karten zu sehen. Durch eine Öffnung im Boden fiel der Blick auf ein Beispiel des meist unsichtbaren Untergrundes der Städte, der nur durch archäologische Grabungen erschlossen werden kann, dessen Struktur sich aber dem, der ihn lesen kann im Stadtgrundriß erschließt.

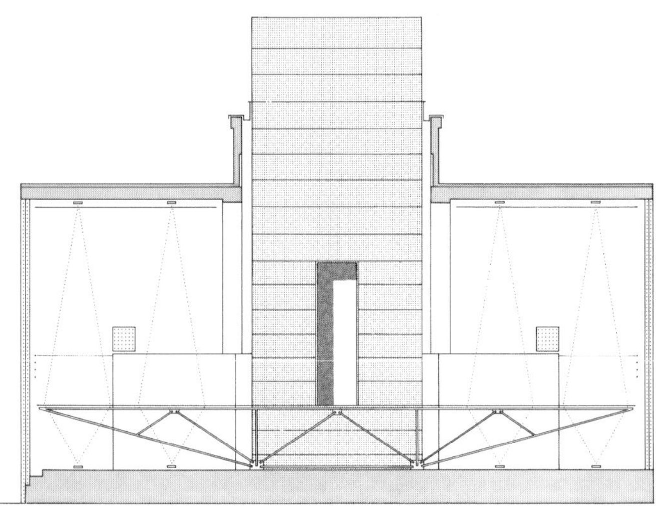

Historic maps, city ground plans, and the old measuring instruments were the objects of this part of the exhibition in the Palazzo d'Arte in Milano's Parco Sempione. While the objects were shown on a space-filling platform raised above the floor and in mild artificial light, a tower-like room was lit in its middle by controlled daylight falling in through a central glass pyramid. The most important old plans and maps could be seen here. Through an opening in the ground, the view was guided to one example of the mostly invisible sub-level of the city which can be revealed only by archeological excavations. However, its structure is disclosed to those who can read it in the city's ground plan.

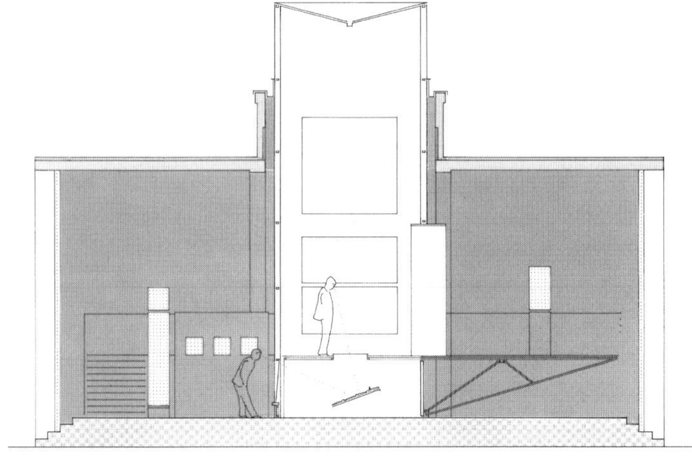

Virtuelle Plattform / *Virtual platform*

Grundriß / *Plan*

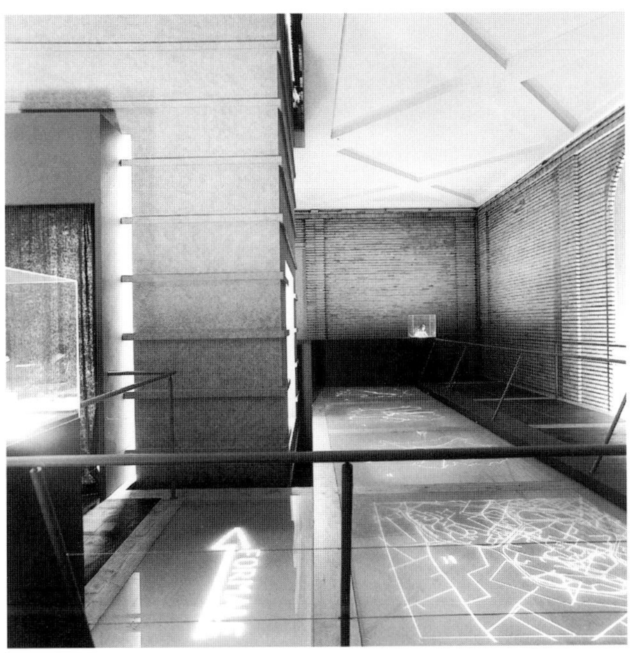

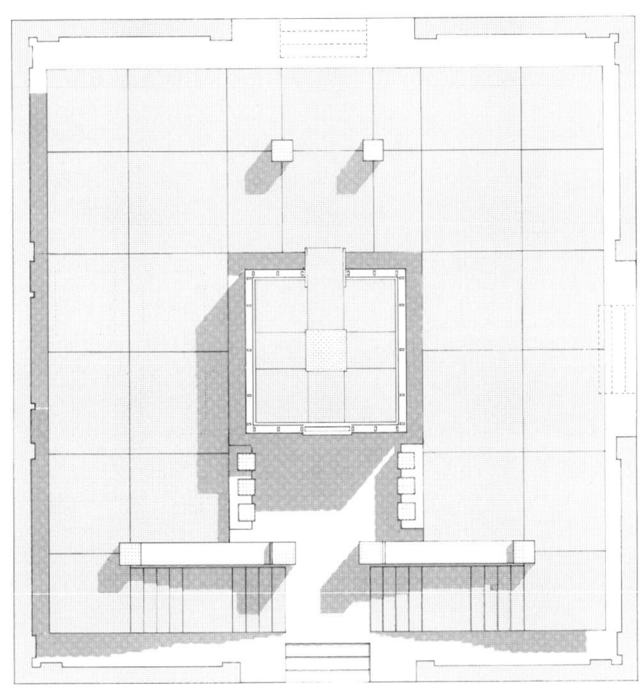

Tageslichtturm / *Skylight tower*

Ausschnitte / *Partial views*

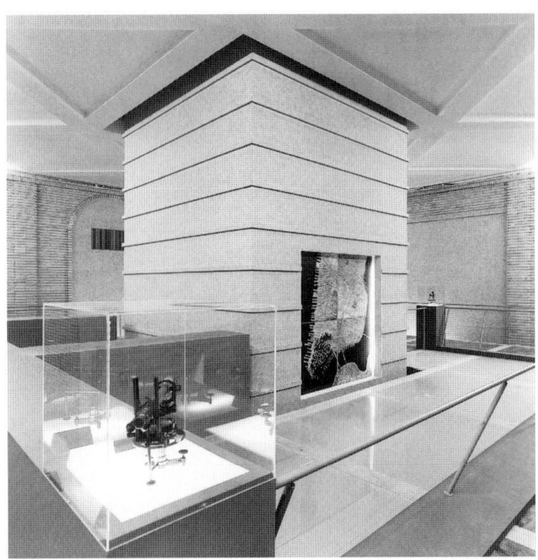

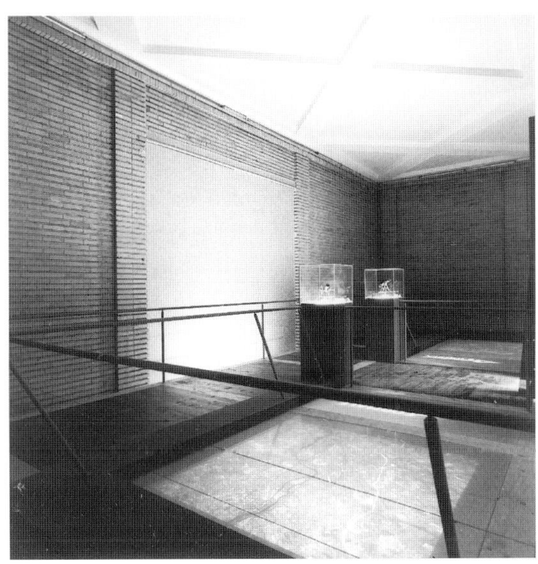

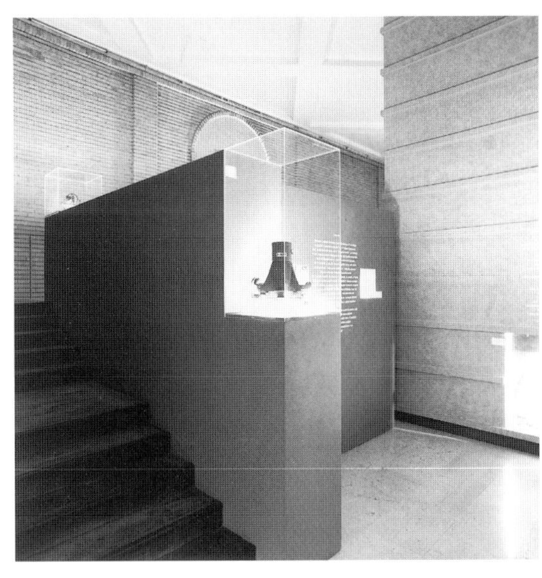

Halles des Beaux-Arts, Paris 1985

Lageplan: Beaux-Arts, Seine und Louvre / *Site plan: Beaux-Arts, Seine and Louvre*
Aufgang zur Aussichtspasserelle / *Stairway to the exhibition passerelle*

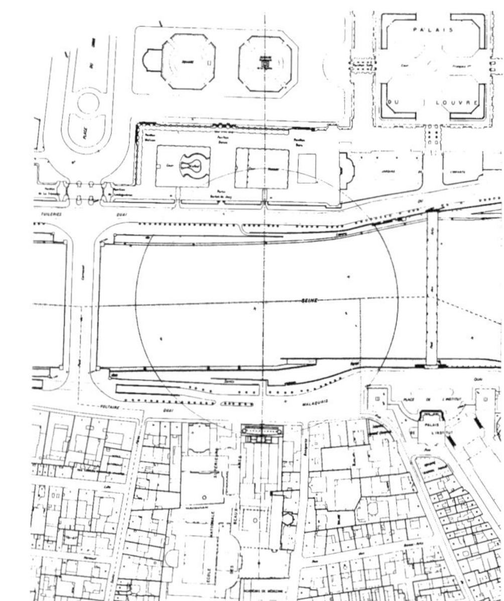

Gegenstand der Ausstellung waren Architektur und Urbanismus der französischen Bäderstädte, die ihre Existenz mineralhaltigen, oft warmen Quellen verdanken und meist auf eine lange Geschichte zurückblicken können, so daß umfangreiches historisches Material vorlag. In den polychromen, tonnenüberwölbten Saal des Palais des Beaux-Arts stellte Podrecca eine reinweiße Struktur, die mit kreissegmentförmigen Flügeln den durch die hohen Fenster eindringenden Außenraum der Stadt über die Seine hinweg und bis zum Louvre hinüber einfing. Wie eine in den Bogen eingehängte Sehne spannte sich ein Steg über die Ausstellungskojen mit den Bild- und Plandarstellungen hinweg. Von hier aus konnte der neue, üblicherweise nicht faßbare Raumeindruck aufgenommen werden. Mit dieser temporären, den Raum in ungewohnter, aber sinnfälliger Weise interpretierenden Intervention erreichte Podrecca einen unverwechselbaren Ausdruck der Ausstellung, die in ihren Exponaten sehr viel Bild- und Planmaterial und eher wenig Objekte enthielt. Die sanfte Verfremdung und der Einbezug des in Augenhöhe des Besuchers bestenfalls latent vorhandenen Stadtraumes schuf eine Möglichkeit der Distanznahme, zum Schweifenlassen der Blicke. Eine neuartige Lesart des Innen- wie des Außenraumes reizt die Sinne und macht die Besucher neugierig, schafft mithin jenes Klima, in dem sich die Betrachter tiefer auf die Ausstellungsinhalte einzulassen bereit sind.

The subject of this exhibition was the architecture and urbanism of the French bath cities which owe their existence to mineral springs and which can look back at a long history. This provided the show with extensive historic material. Into the polychrome vaulted hall of the Palais des Beaux-Arts, Podrecca placed a white structure which, with its circular, segmented wings seized the outside space of the city entering through the high windows from across the Seine up to the Louvre. A small bridge was stretched, like a string on a bow, across the exhibition cabins with the pictures and plans. From this vantage point, the new and usually ungraspable room impression could be absorbed. With this temporary intervention interpreting the space in an unusual but impressive way, Podrecca achieved an unmistakable expression of the exhibition which contained a lot of pictures and plans but rather few objects. The soft estrangement and inclusion at eye level of the latently existing city space created a possibility of distance, of letting the glance wander. A new way of reading the inside and outside space stimulates the senses, making the visitors curious and creating a climate in which the observers are more willing to allow themselves to enter into the contents of the exhibition.

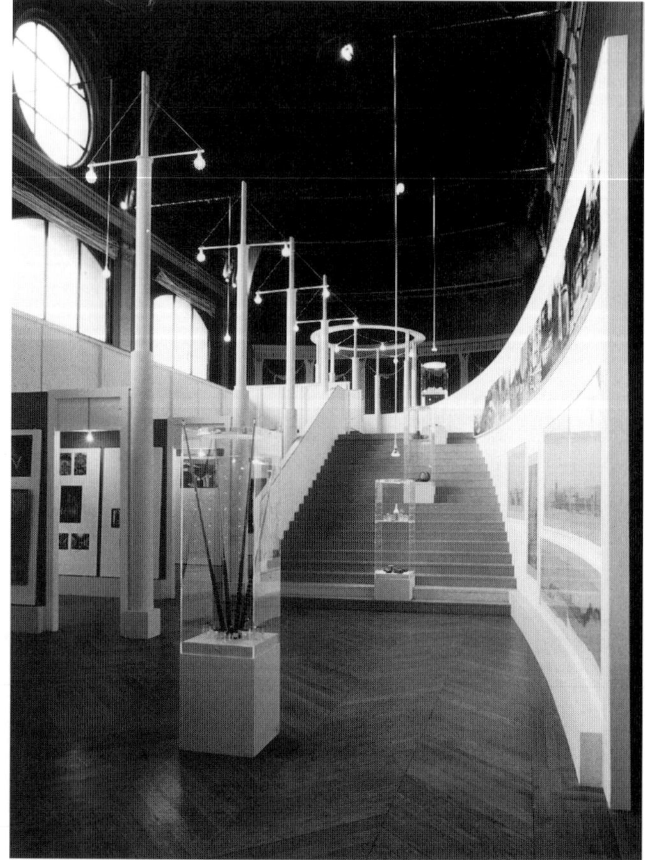

Axonometrie der Einbauten / *Axonometric projection of installations*

Gesamtansicht der Salle Foche / *Overall view of Salle Foche*

Passerelle mit Ausblick zur Seine /
Passerelle with view of the Seine

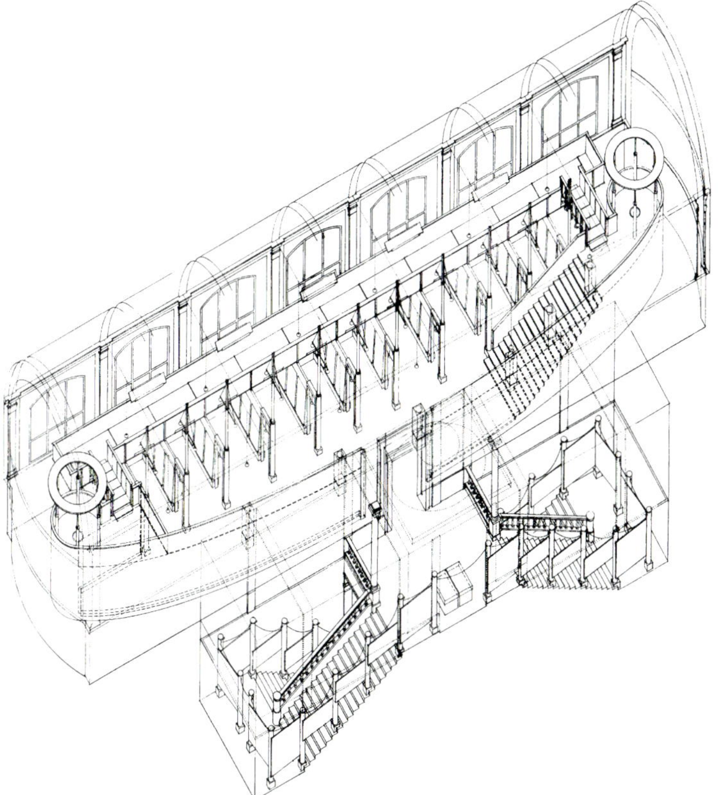

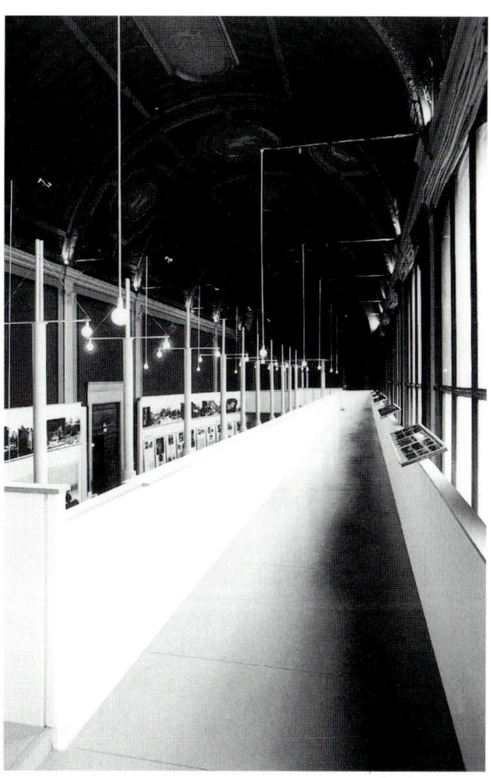

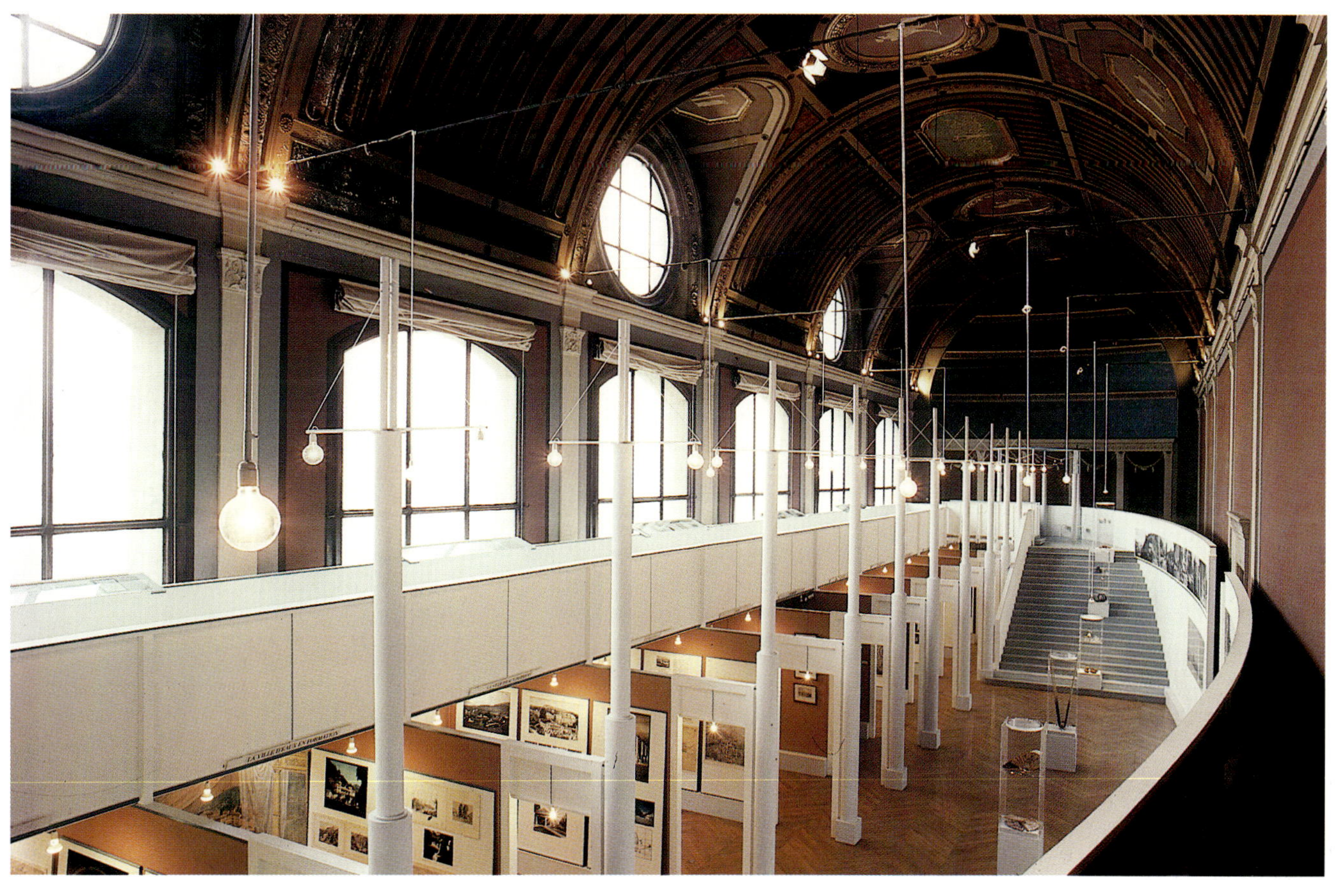

Künstlerhaus, Wien / *Vienna* 1987

Axonometrie Erdgeschoß / *Axonometric projection of ground floor*

Axonometrie Obergeschoß / *Axonometric projection of upper floor*

Sowohl vom Inhalt, der sich in 19 thematische Abschnitte gliederte, als auch von den Exponaten her, die sehr zahlreich und oft sehr klein waren, aber auch wegen der breitgelagerten Grundrißkonfiguration des Künstlerhauses verbot sich der Einsatz einer alles umfassenden klar hervortretenden Großform. Und der Bezug zur schwach strukturierten Weite des Karlsplatzes drängte sich nicht auf. Das gestalterische Konzept sah daher eine große Zahl pavillonartiger Einbauten vor, die, wie Marktstände in einer Halle, den Rahmen für die historischen Themen bildeten. Mit diesen Architekturen versuchte Podrecca jedoch nicht etwa bühnenbildartig das Thema zu interpretieren, sondern bezog sich spielerisch auf das Lebensgefühl der Zeit und lotete beiläufig die Variationsbreite der Pavillonthematik aus. Das zeitlich begrenzte Wesen der Ausstellung erlaubte, «Überzeichnungen, Obsessionen der Gestalt, Mimik usw.» zum Prinzip zu erheben. Ihn faszinierte das Visionäre der Zeit, die technischen Erfindungen, die Freude sich zu zeigen, die im reichen Schmuck gipfelte, aber auch die Bewegungslust, die in Tanz und Gymnastik ihren Ausdruck fand – als Blickfang vor der Eingangsfassade diente als Symbol die Spirale –, sowie die große Farbigkeit, die das Aussehen der Innenräume und der kunstgewerblichen Gegenstände bestimmte. In der Ausstellung kontrastierten die Farben mit den Materialfarben der Exponate: etwa pistaziengrüne Podeste mit dem Nuß- oder Kirschholz der Möbel.

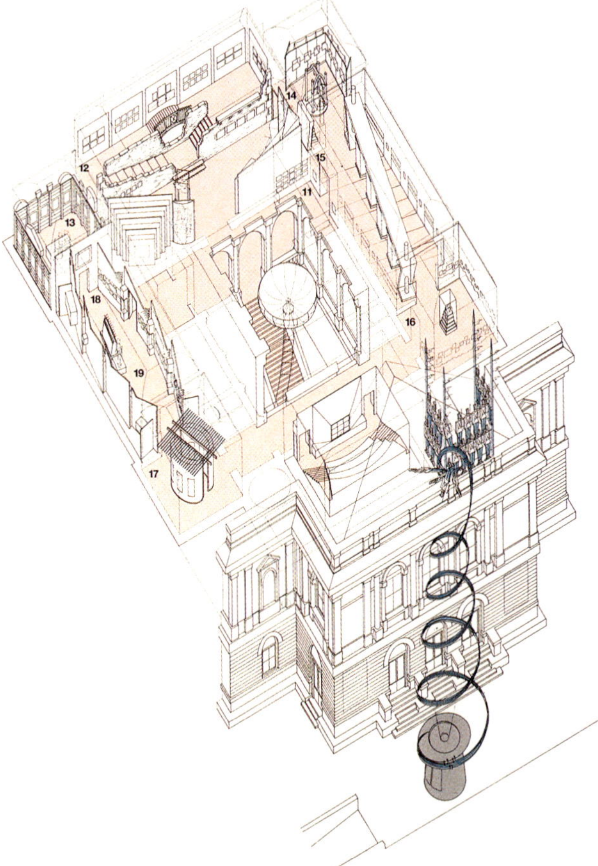

The content of the exhibition – structured into 19 thematic sections as well as the numerous and often very small displayed objects – and the wide ground plan configuration of the Künstlerhaus (house of artists) all together disallowed the use of an all-embracing and clearly prominent large form. And a reference to the weak structure of the Karlsplatz did not impose itself. The design concept therefore included a large number of pavilion-like installations which, like market booths in a hall, set the framework for the historic themes. Podrecca, however, did not try to interpret the theme with this architecture like scenery on a stage. Instead, he referred in a playful way to the feeling of life of the time and just casually echoed the variations in the width of the pavilion. The timely yet limited existence of the exhibition allowed "exaggerations, obsessions with the form, mimicry, etc.," to be elevated as a principle. He was fascinated with the visionary aspect of time: the technological inventions; the joy of showing off which reached its peak in the rich jewelry; the lust of movement which found its expression in dances and gymnastics; the spiral as a symbol which was an eye-catcher in front of the entrance facade; the richness in color which determined the look of the interior and the objects of the arts and crafts. In the show, the colors stood in contrast to the material colors of the displayed objects, e. g., pistachio green platforms with the cherry or nut wood of the furniture.

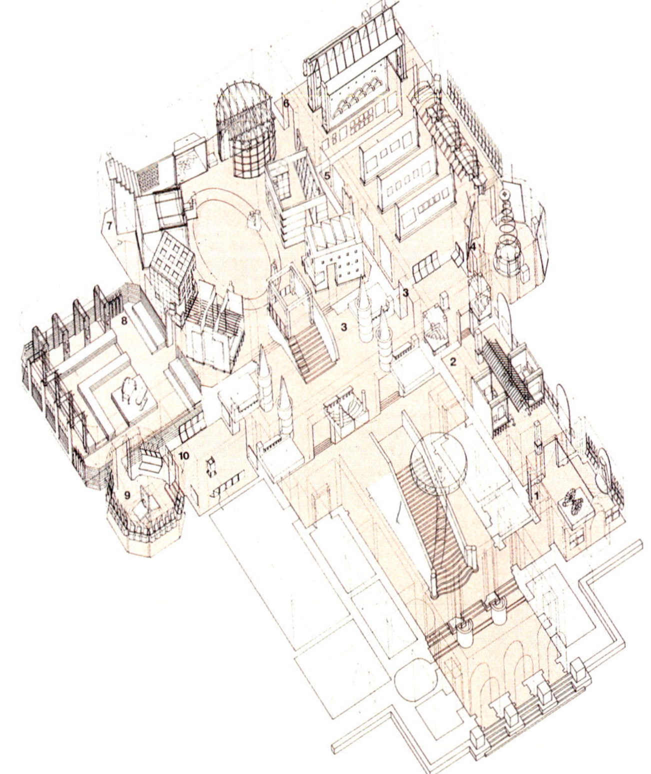

Installation im Außenbereich / *Installation on the outside*

Piazzetta / *Plaza*

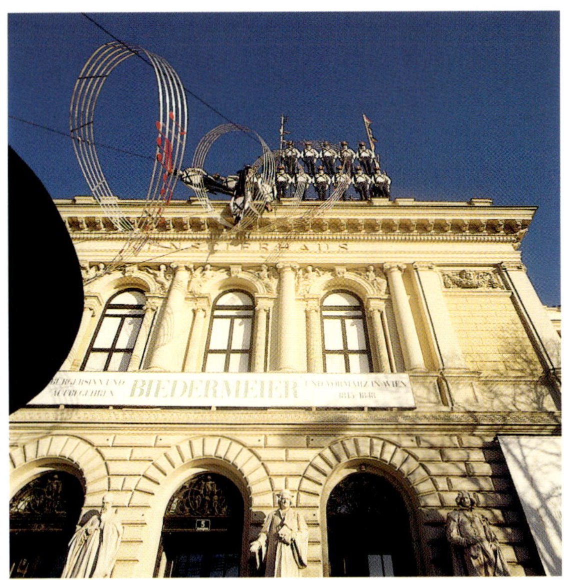

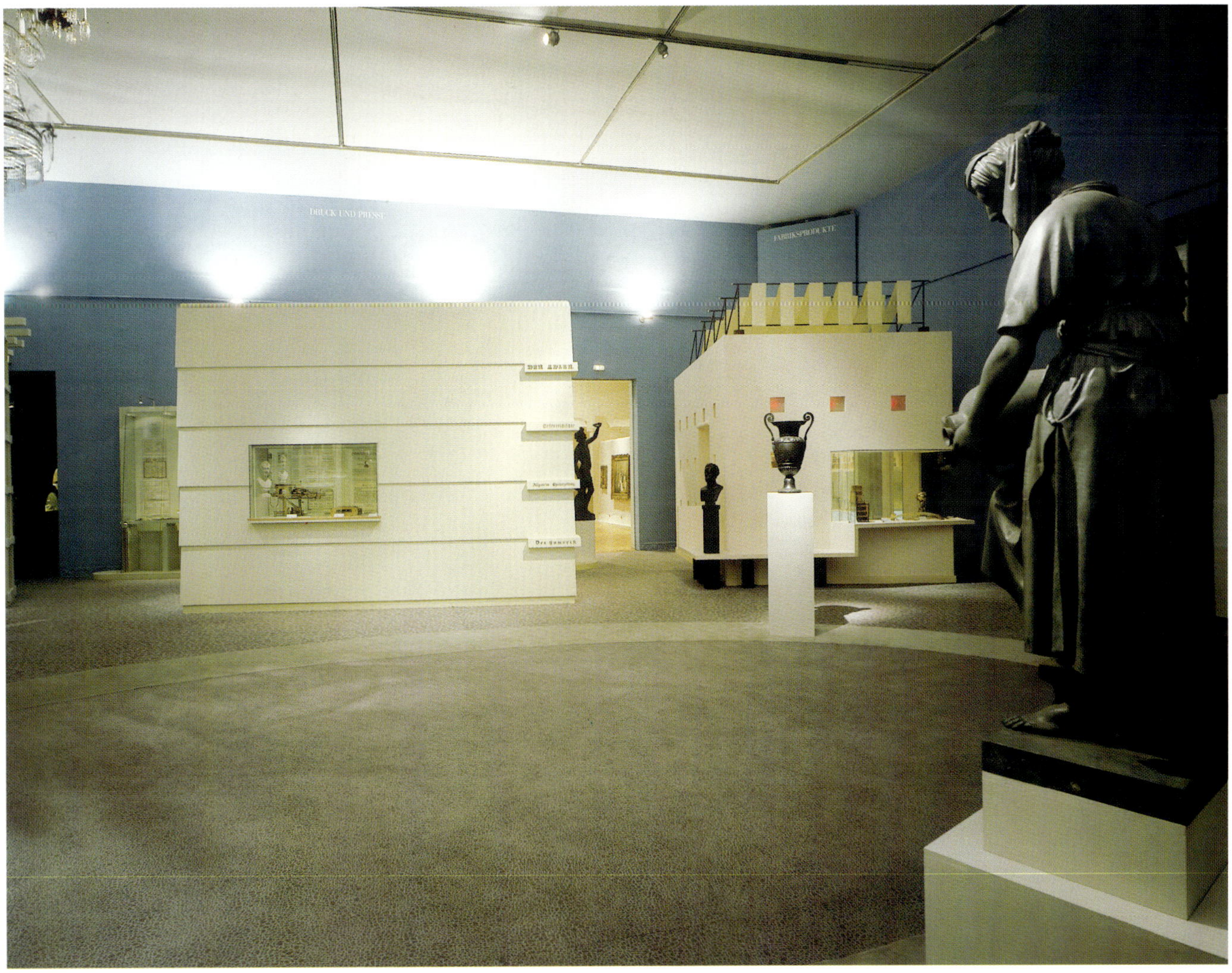

Der Alltag / *Every-day life*

Die Fortbewegung / *The progression*

Industrielle Produkte / *Industrial products*

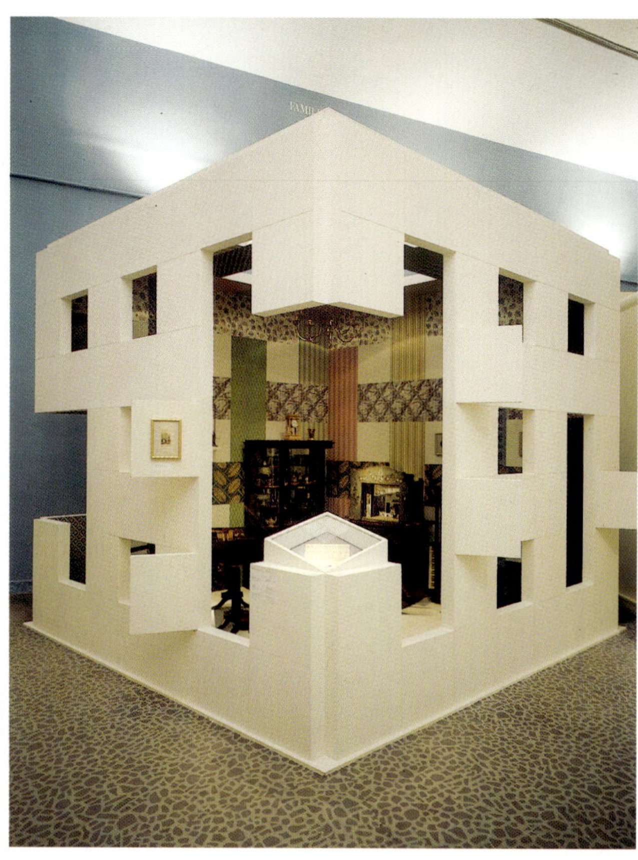

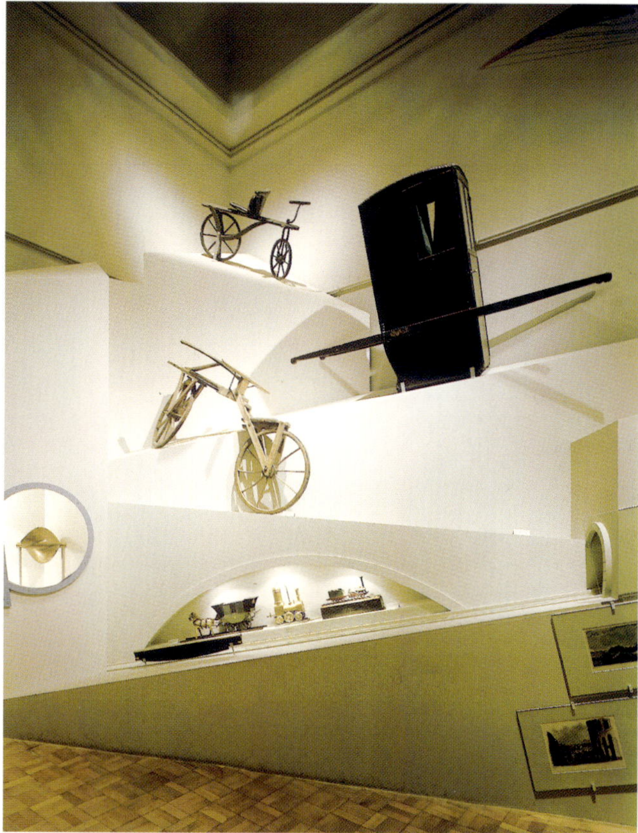

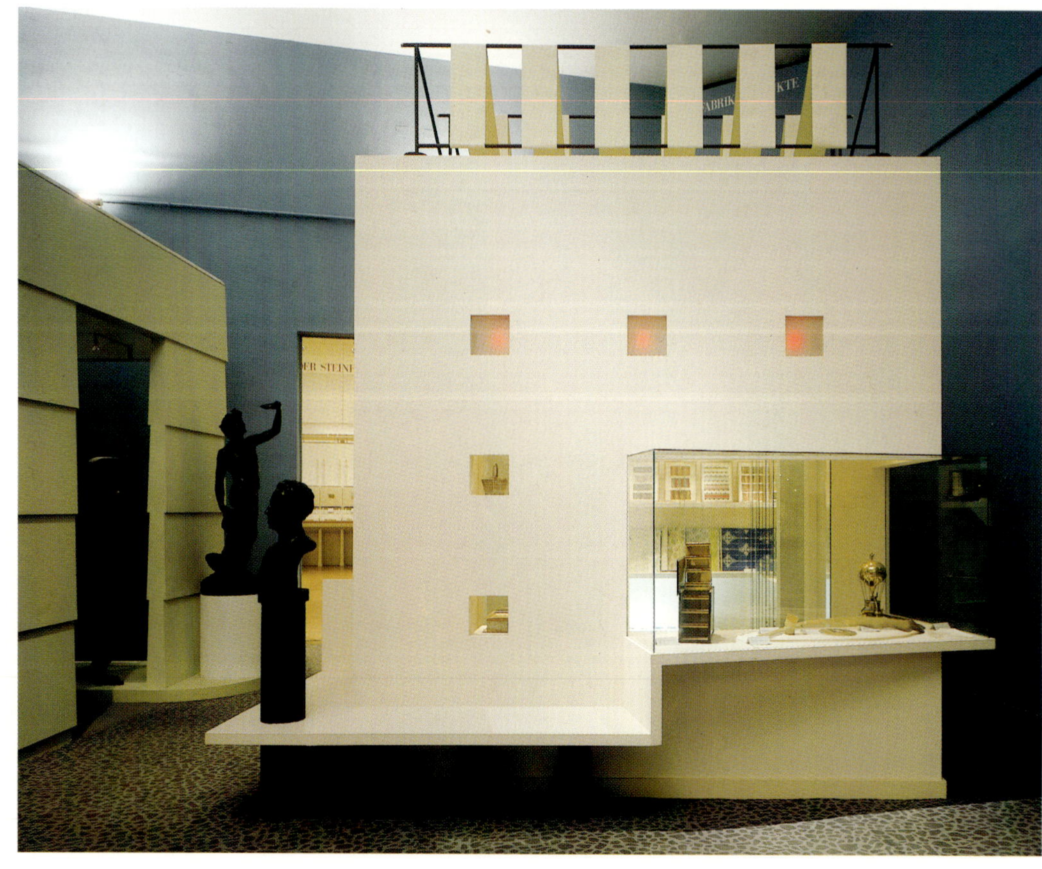

Musikraum / *Music room*

Musikraum, Detail / *Music room, detail*　　　　　　　　Erotikpavillon, Detail / *Erotic theme pavilion, detail*

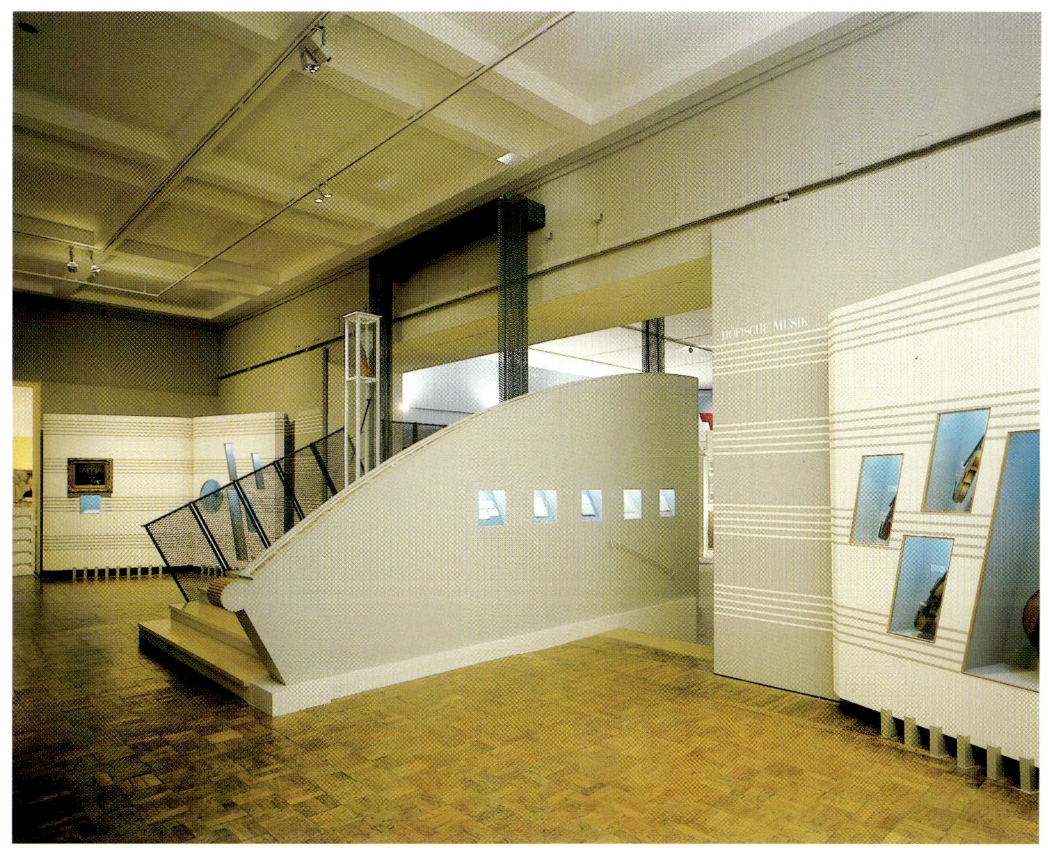

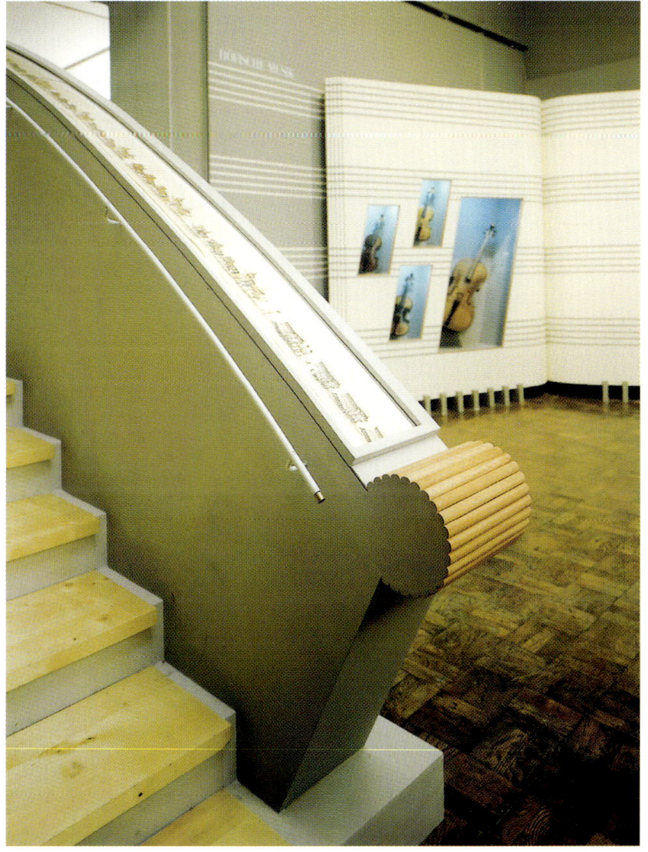

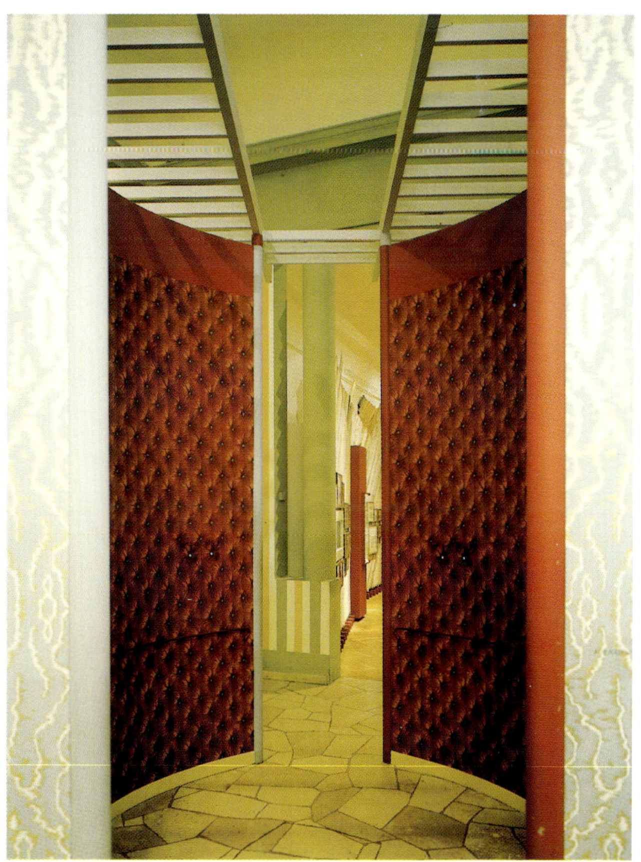

Erfindungen / *Inventions*
Theater und Literatur / *Theater and literature*
Vorführungsraum / *Show room*

Der Walzer / *The Waltz*

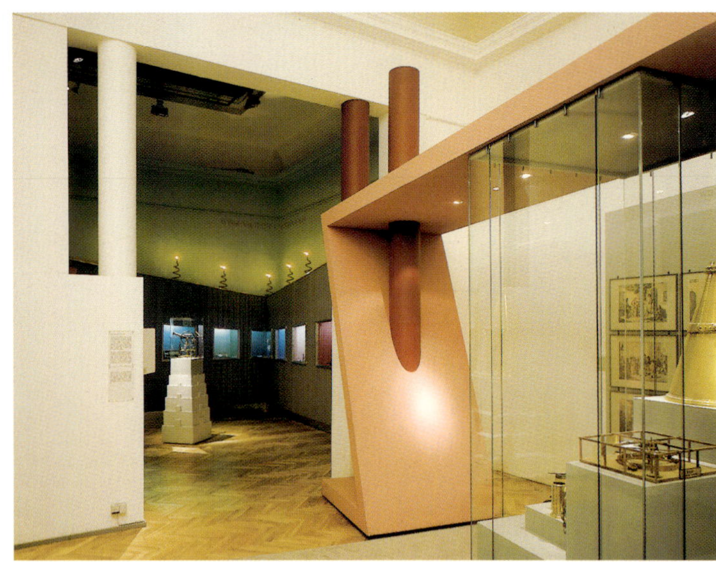

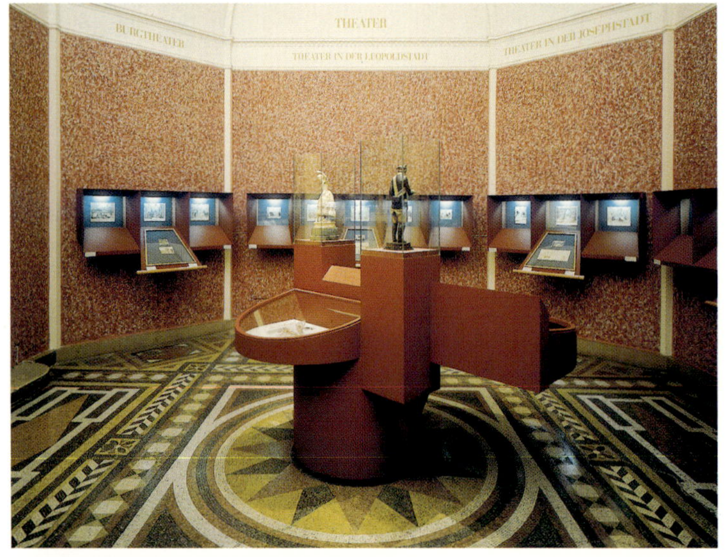

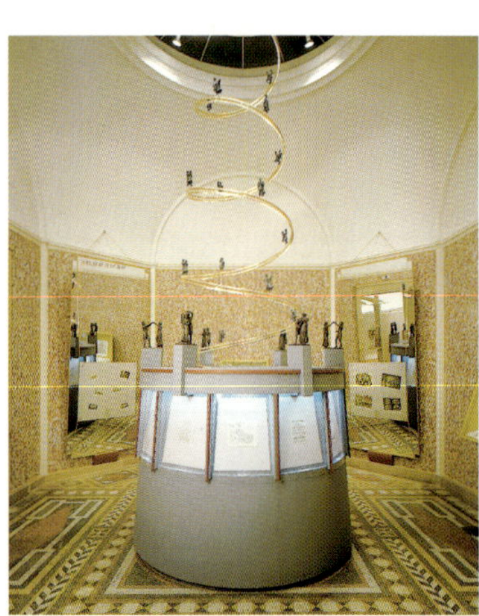

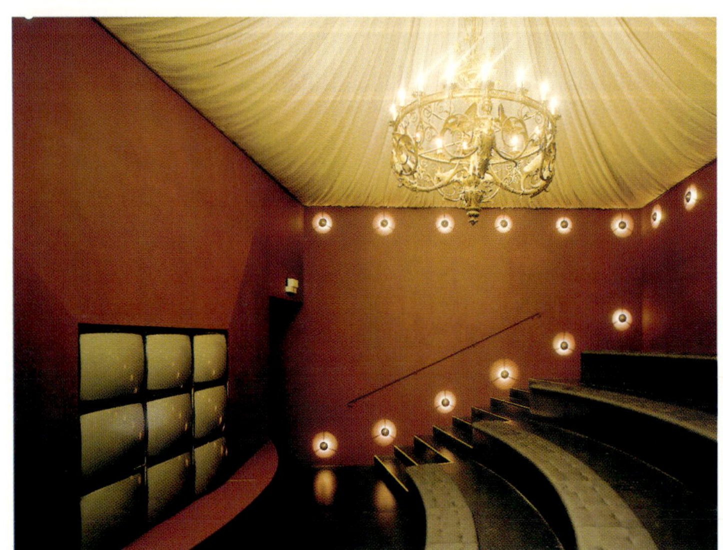

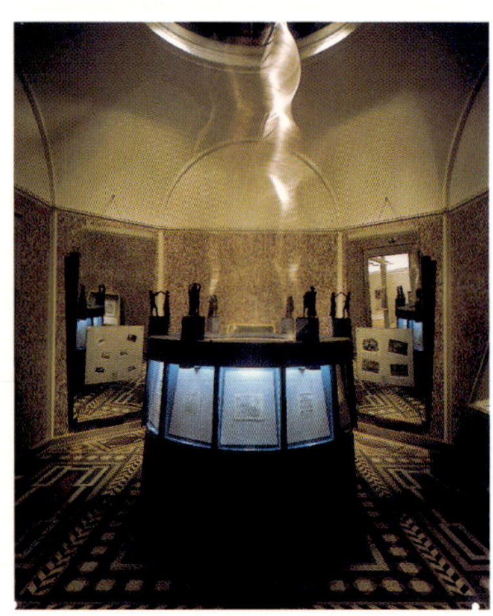

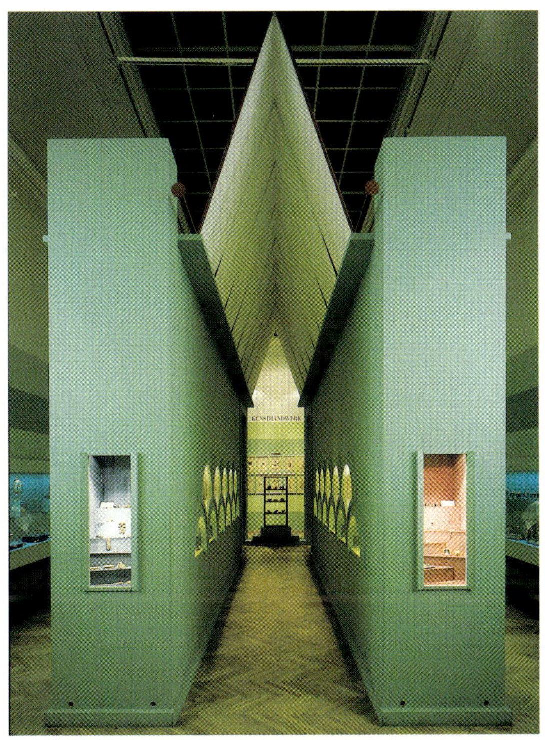

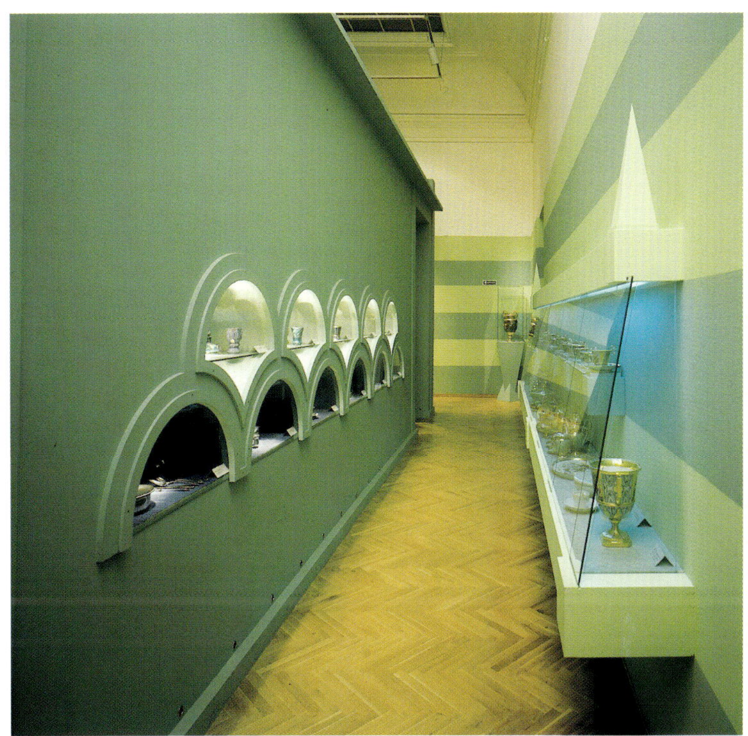

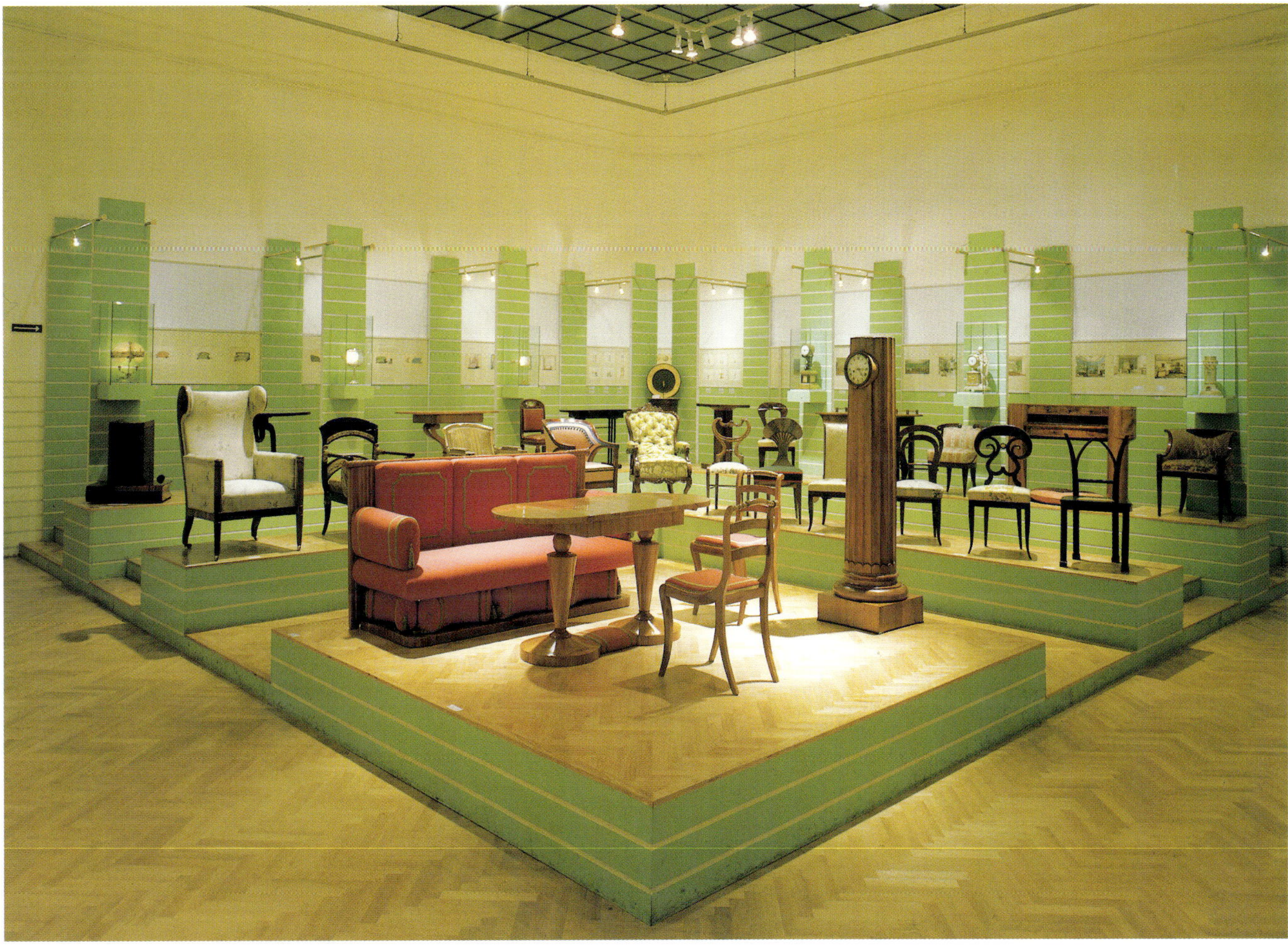

Temporäre Ausstellungshalle, Technisches Museum, Wien /
Temporary exhibition hall, *Vienna* 1989

Schnittperspektive / *Sectional perspective*

Modell / *Model*

Für die Sonderausstellung «Phantasie und Industrie» sollte mit extrem begrenztem finanziellem Aufwand eine provisorische Halle errichtet werden. Das tonnenförmige Dach ruht an der einen Traufseite auf einer Ständerwand, in der Mitte auf schräg gestellten Pendelstützen aus massivem Rundholz und reicht auf der anderen Seite direkt auf den Erdboden. Damit wird die seitliche Aussteifung bereits in unkomplizierter Weise erreicht. Das Dach selbst wird von zwei Reihen identischer Nagelbinder getragen, darüber spannt sich die Dachhaut aus Trapezblech. Über einen geschlossenen Steg ist der große Einraum an den Altbau angedockt. Man betritt die Halle in der Höhe des ersten Obergeschosses wie über eine Empore, so daß sich den Eingetretenen ein Überblick auf die Ausstellung bietet. Nach dem Heruntersteigen gelangt man auf einen Bretterweg, der sich wie ein Landungssteg eine Stufe über dem bekiesten Erdboden hinzieht. Obwohl als kurzzeitiges Provisorium gedacht, ist die Halle weiterhin, leider entstellt, als Teil eines Imax-Kinos, in Betrieb.

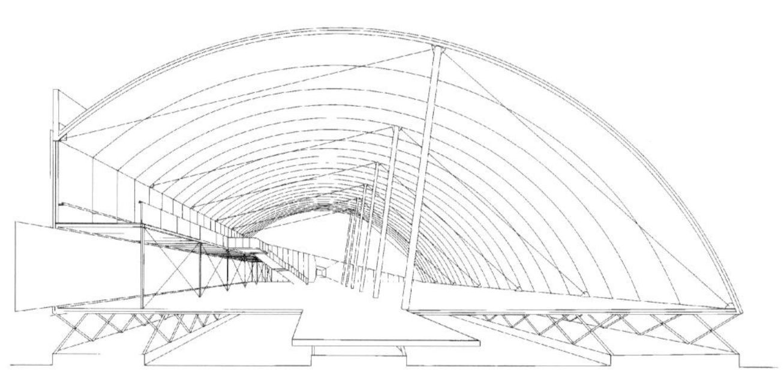

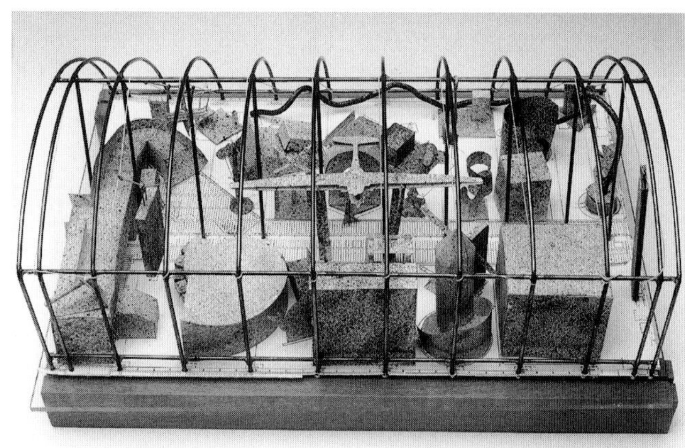

For the special exhibition, "Fantasy and Industry", a temporary hall was to be erected with extremely limited financial means. The vault roof rests on a post and beam wall on one eaves side, its center is supported on inclined pendulum supports made of massive timber wood, and on the other side it reaches directly to the ground. The lateral reinforcing is thus achieved in an uncomplicated manner. The roof itself is supported by two rows of identical nailed wood framing. Above stretches the roof shell made of trapezoidal metal sheets. The large one-room structure is docked to the old building by a closed footbridge. One enters into the hall at the level of the second floor like across a choir loft, thus being offered an overview of the exhibition. After the descent, one enters a wooden boardwalk stretching one step above the graveled ground like a landing pier. Although it was intended as a temporary construction, the hall (unfortunately in a rather distorted manner) continues to be used as a part of an Imax-movie theater.

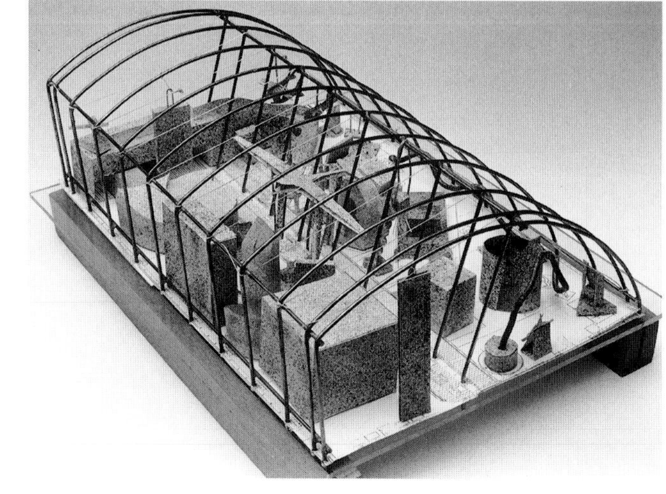

Westansicht und Verbindungsbau / *West facade and connecting building*

Ostansicht / *East view*

Hauptansichten / *Main views*

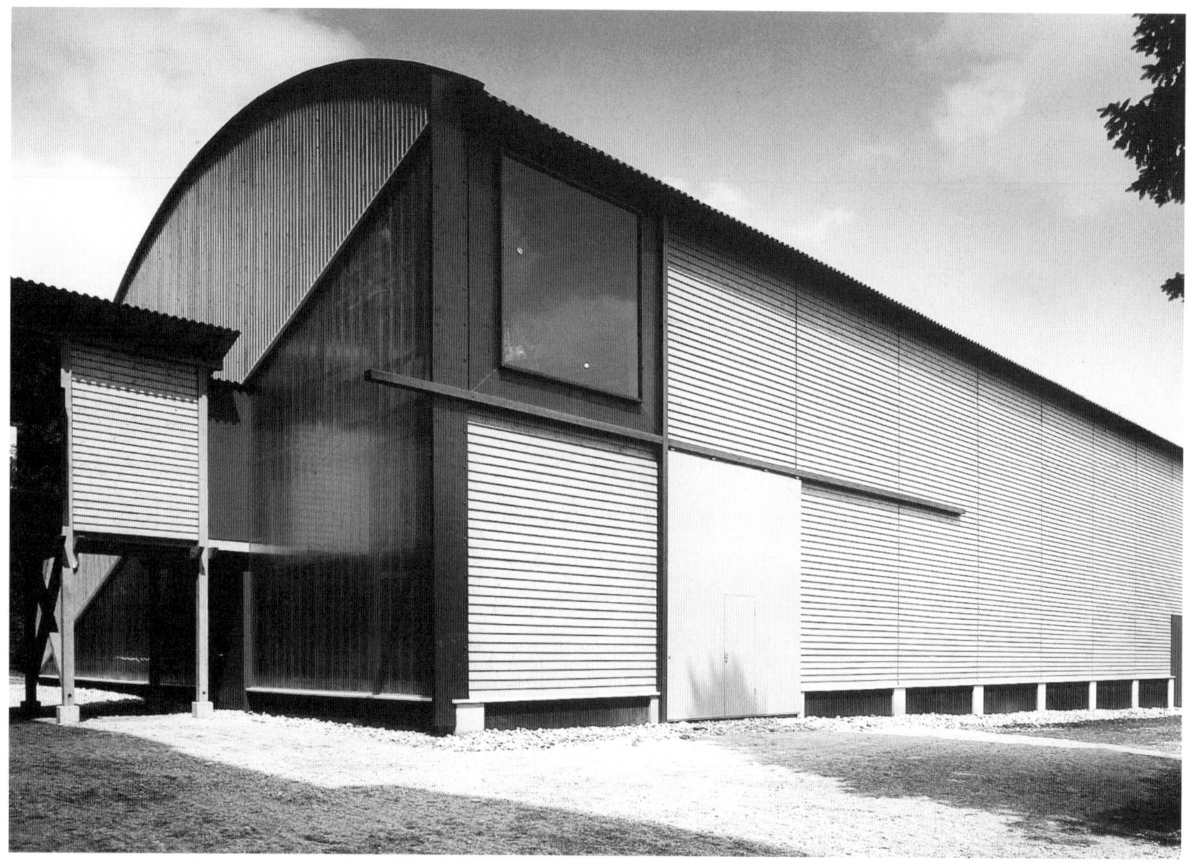

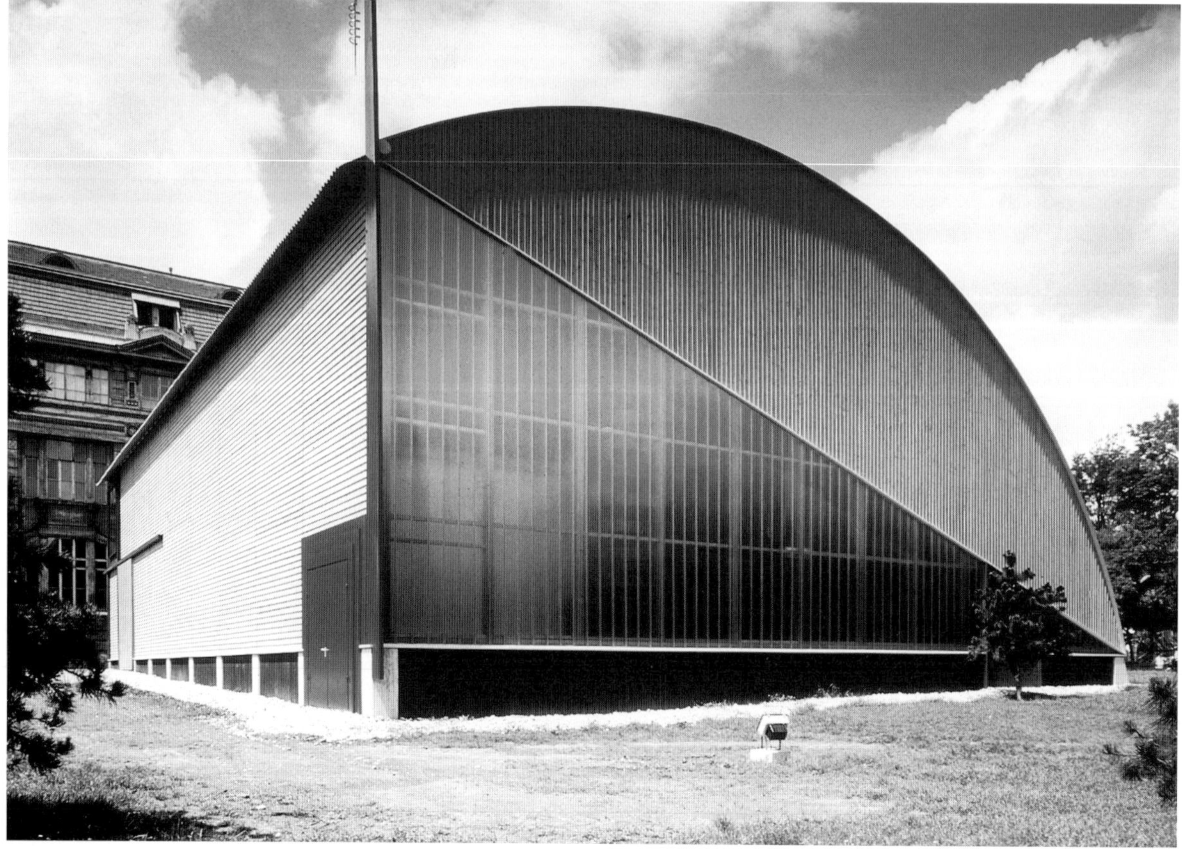

Grundriß / *Plan*

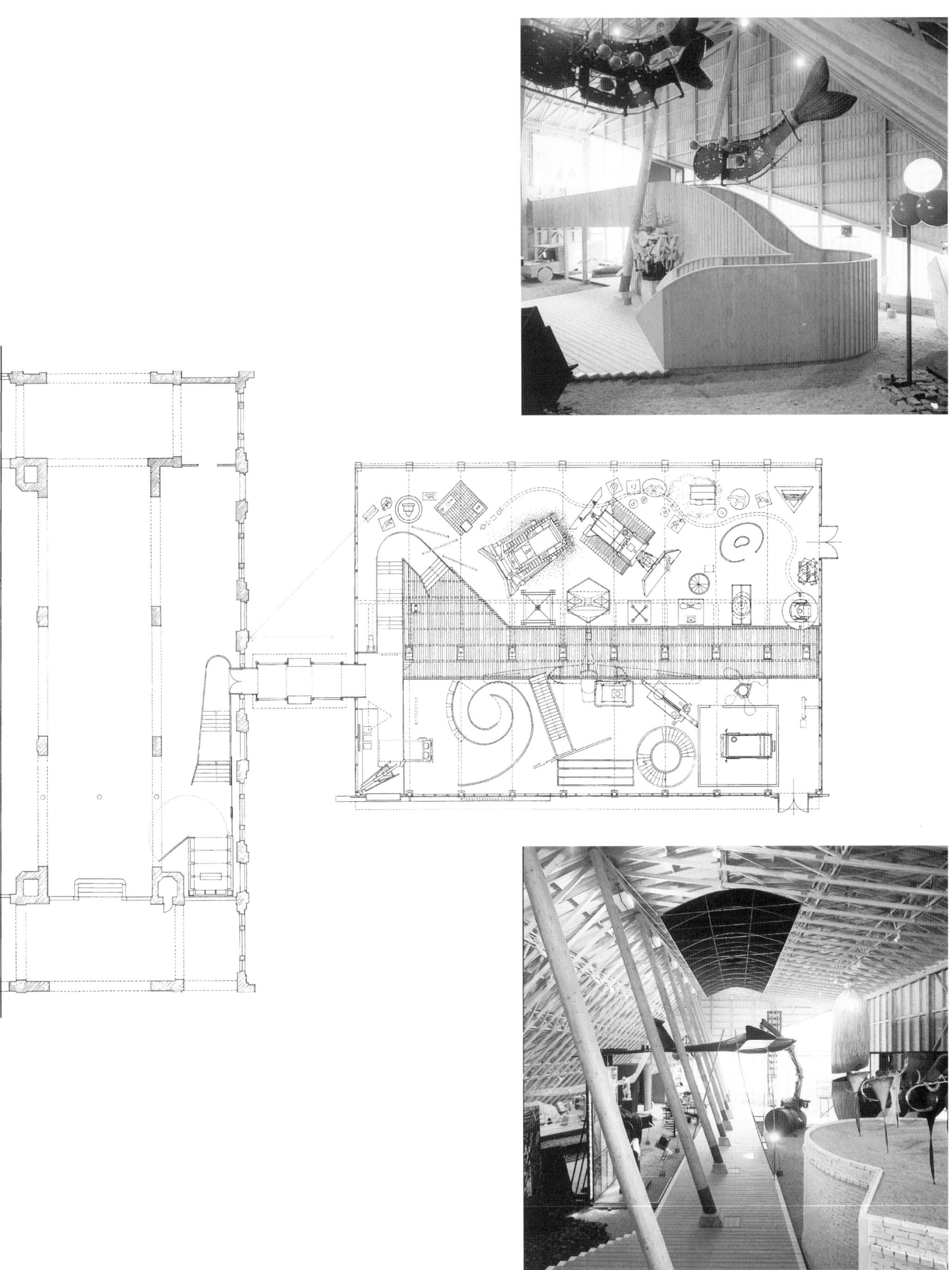

Martin-Gropius-Bau, Berlin / *Martin-Gropius-Building, Berlin* 1990

Elementierung und Disposition /
Fundamental elements and arrangement

Modell, Arkadenhof / *Model, arcaded courtyard*

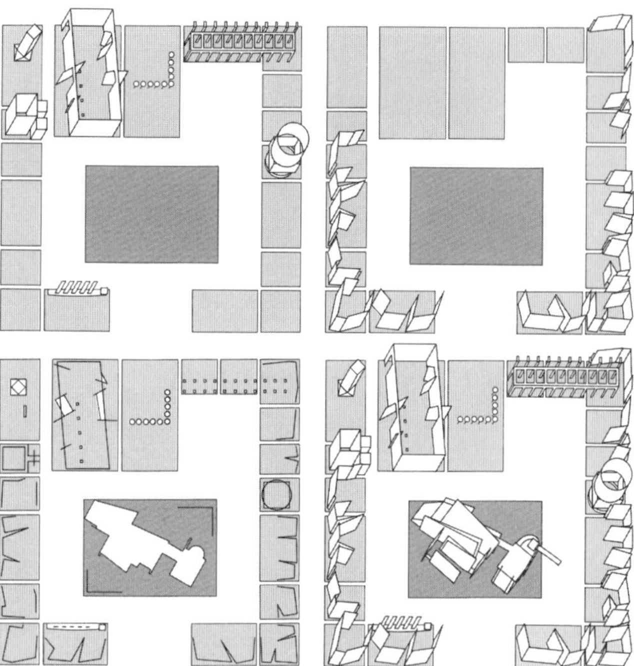

Der historische, polychrome Martin-Gropius-Bau und die große Materialfülle stellten der Ausstellungsgestaltung nicht geringe Probleme. Und die Vielzahl von Exponaten unterschiedlichster Größe zwang bei dieser historischen Ausstellung zu ordnenden Elementen und zugleich zu einer Erweiterung der Hängefläche. Mit dem Prinzip des Paravents als Hintergrundfläche, der mit einer oder zwei Farben einen Themenbereich vom anderen abgrenzte, konnte beiden Bedürfnissen entsprochen werden. Vor und zwischen dieser heterogenen Abwicklung setzte Podrecca einige in sich geschlossene Elemente: Pilasterreihe, Raumkubus, Monolith, Rahmen, Freiraum, Säulenhalle, Tambour. Schon die Bezeichnungen verweisen auf Signifikanz, sei dies als ordnende Maßnahme oder um Inhalte durch eine spezifische Figur zu verdeutlichen. Den Lichthof beherrschte eine Rampenanlage, deren Stahltafeln in dynamischer Komposition den industriellen wie den sozialen Aufbruch symbolisierten, aber auch den unsicheren Ausgang von Kriegshandlungen und den Boom der Waffenproduktion. Sie gipfelt in einer fragilen Konstruktion, an der sich eine Treppe hochwindet – der schwierige Weg in die Moderne – überragt von einer unter vielen Bismarckbüsten und -statuen. Die Vielzahl der Standbilder relativierte die Person des zum «eisernen Kanzler» hochstilisierten Politikers in historisch kritischer Absicht. Gezielte Blicke durch Vitrinen und Wandöffnungen auf Bilder oder Objekte anderen Inhalts zeugen von Podreccas Freude an spontaner Vernetzung.

The historic polychromatic Martin Gropius building and the richness of materials posed some rather large problems to the design of the exhibition. The multitude of displayed objects of a wide variety of sizes enforced the need for ordering elements and at the same time an extension of the hanging surface into this historic exhibition. By using the principle of the paravent as a background surface, setting borders between thematic sections with one or two colors, both needs could be met. In front and in between this heterogeneous sequence, Podrecca placed a few elements closed within themselves: a row of pilasters, a space cube, a monolith, frames, free space, column hall, tambour. These terms already indicate their significance, whether as an ordering measure or as a clarification of contents by a specific figure. The light courtyard was dominated by a ramp system whose steel plates symbolized the industrial and social departure in a dynamic composition and also the invisible result of war activities and the boom of the weapons industry. It culminates in a fragile construction along which a staircase winds up – the difficult path into modernism – surmounted by one of the many Bismarck busts and statues. The multitude of sculptures with a historically critical intention made the stylized persona of the "iron chancellor" relative. Purposeful views into show-cases and through wall openings onto pictures or objects with a different content witness Podrecca's joy of spontaneous networking.

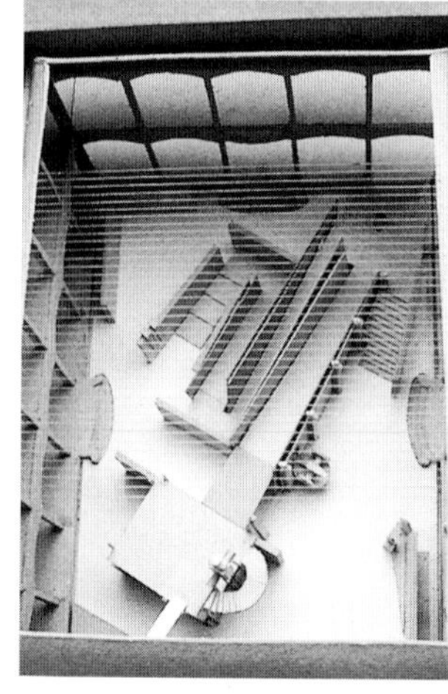 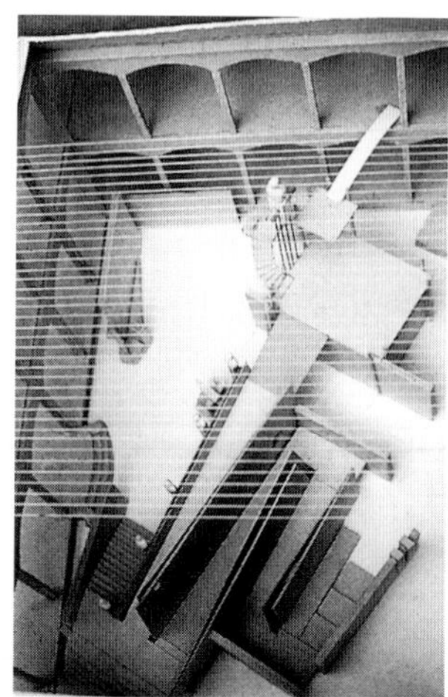

Installation, Gelenke / *Installation, joints* Eingangsinstallation / *Entrance installation*

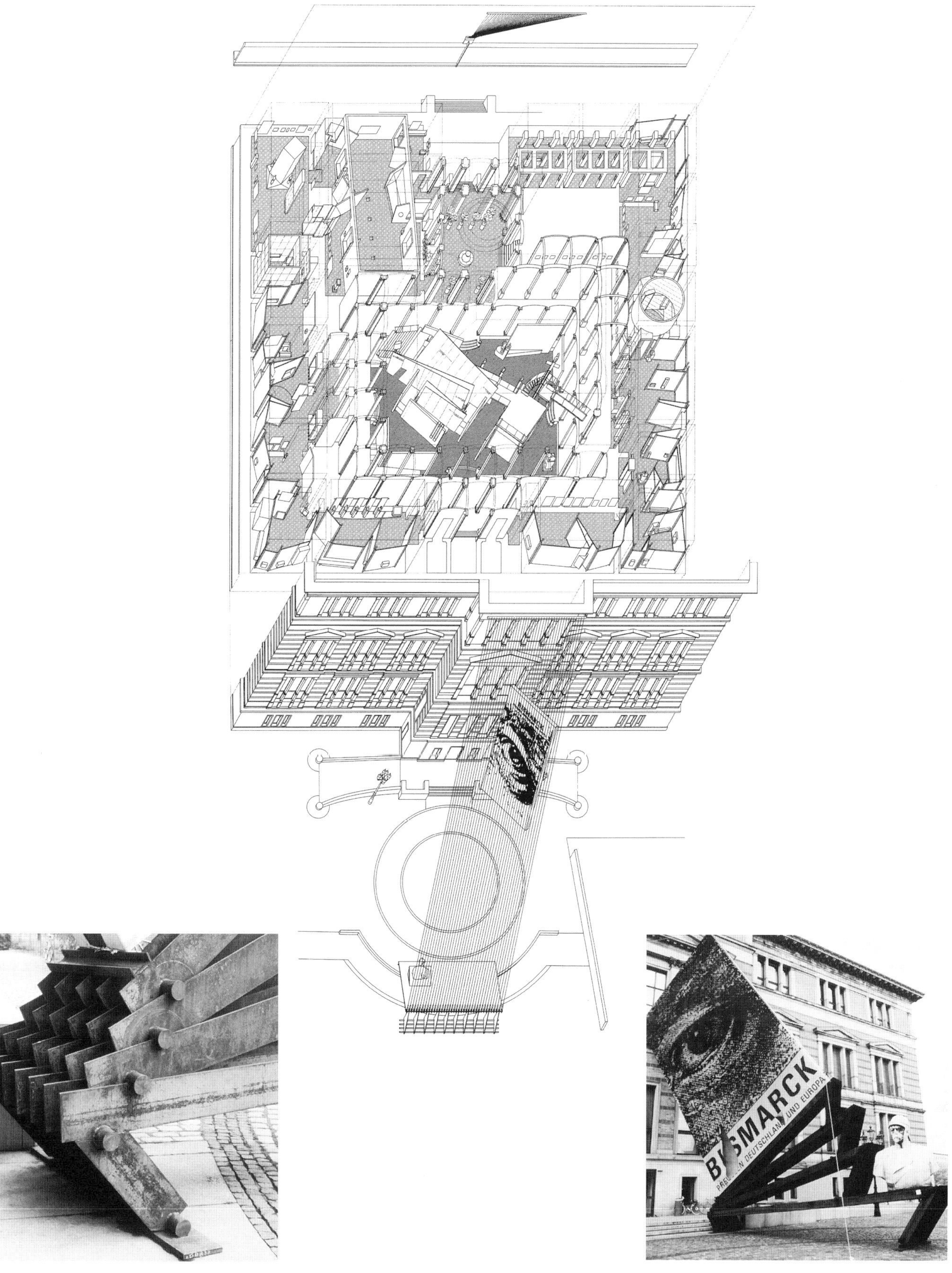

Arkadenhof, Ausschnitte / *Arcaded courtyard, partial views*

Rampeninstallation Arkadenhof /
Ramp installation, arcaded courtyard

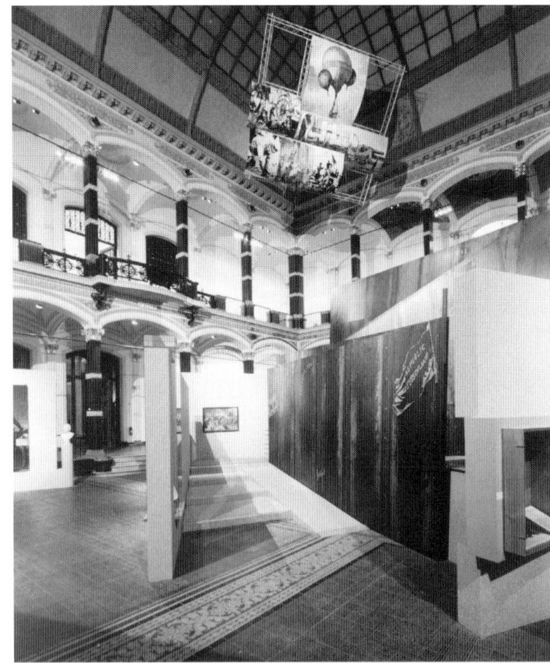

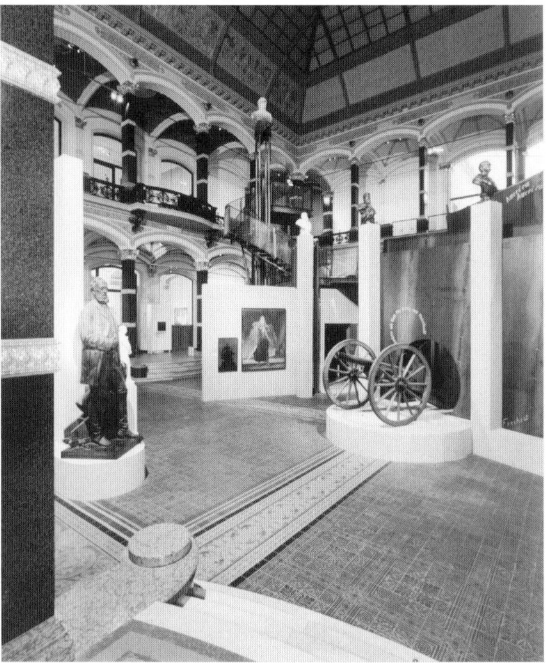

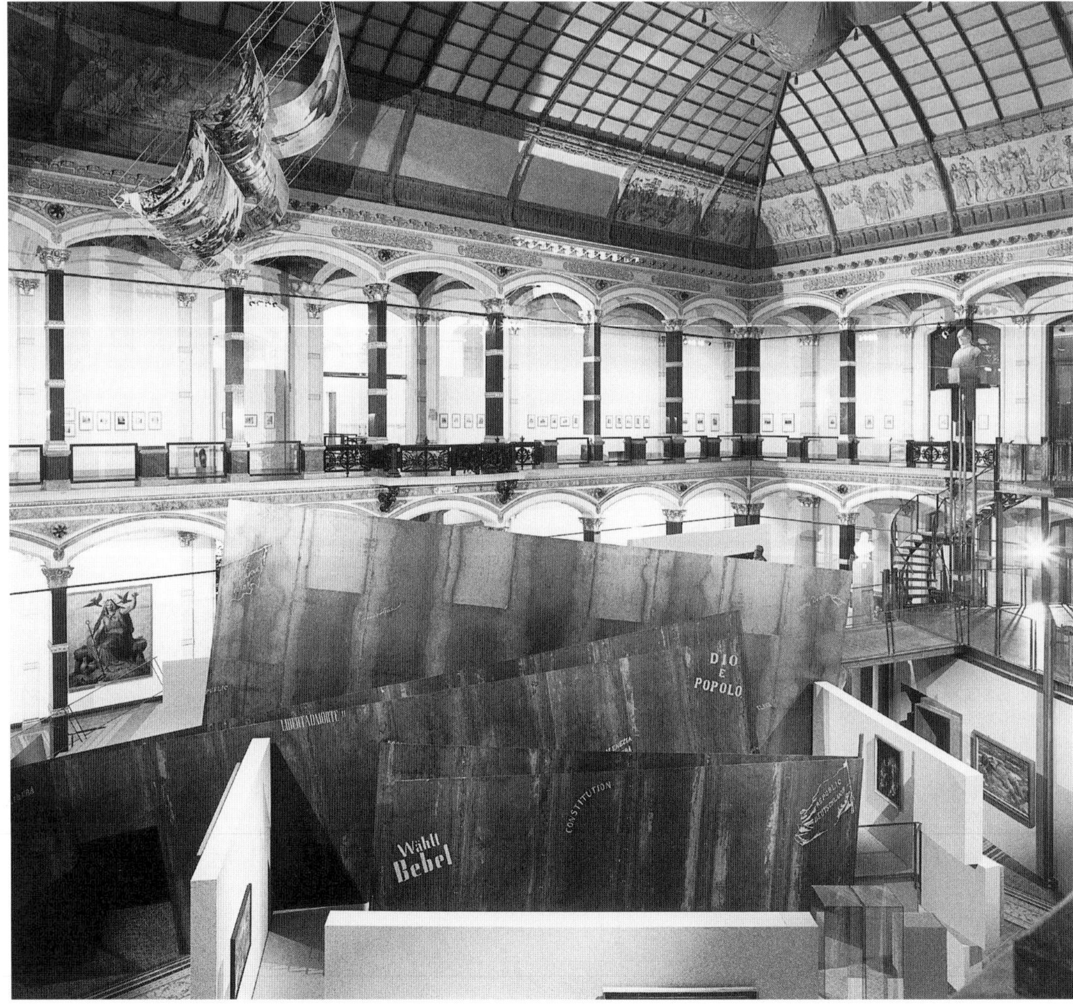

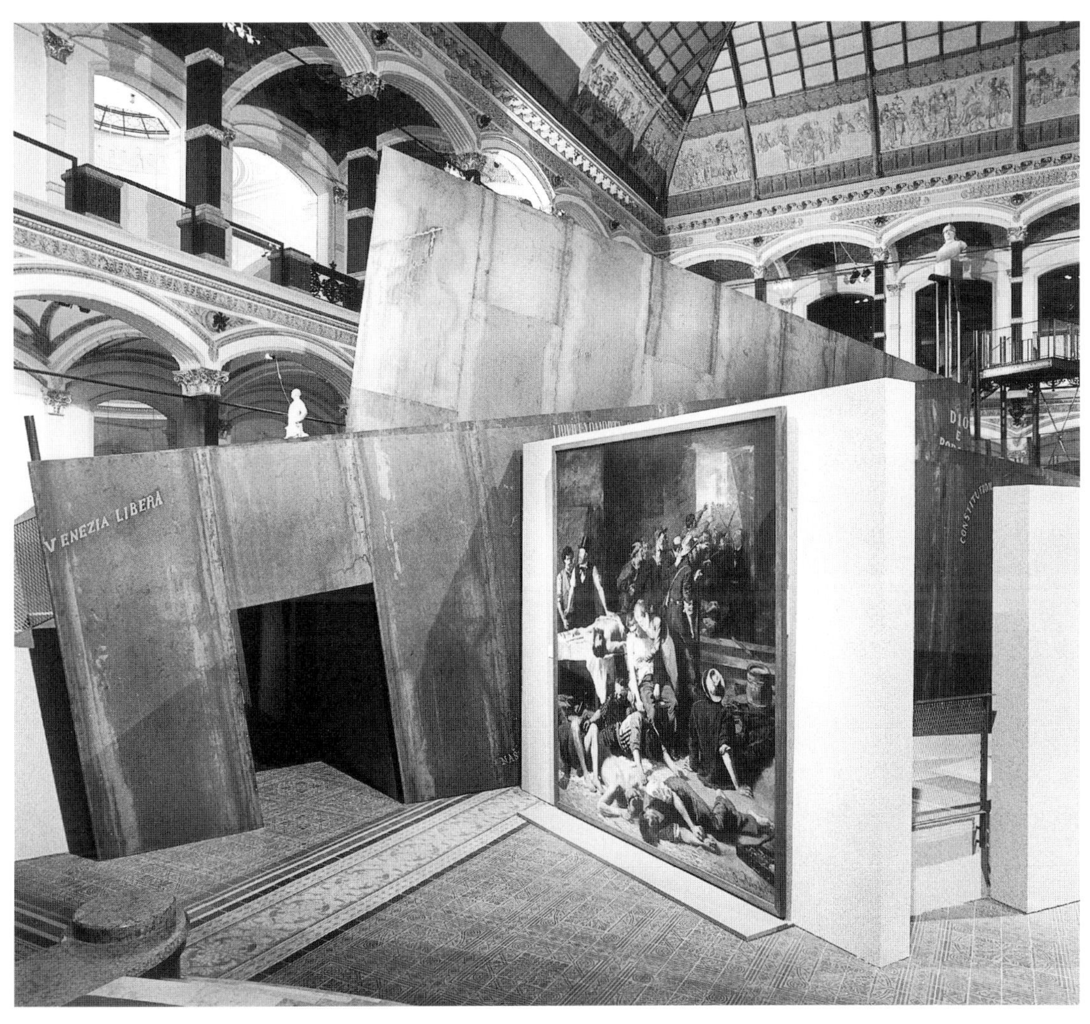
VENEZIA LIBERA

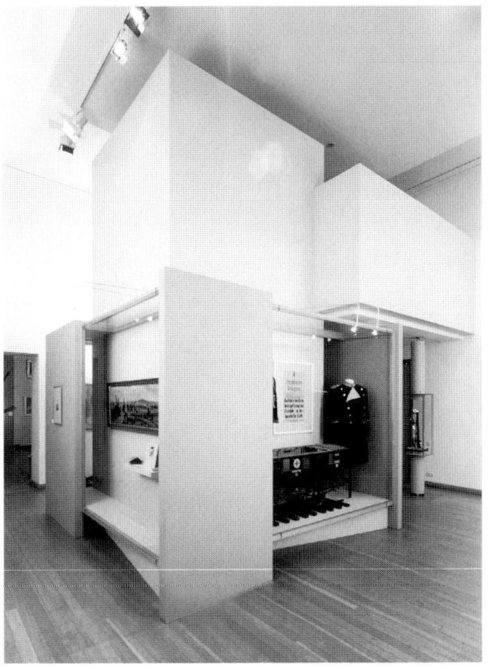

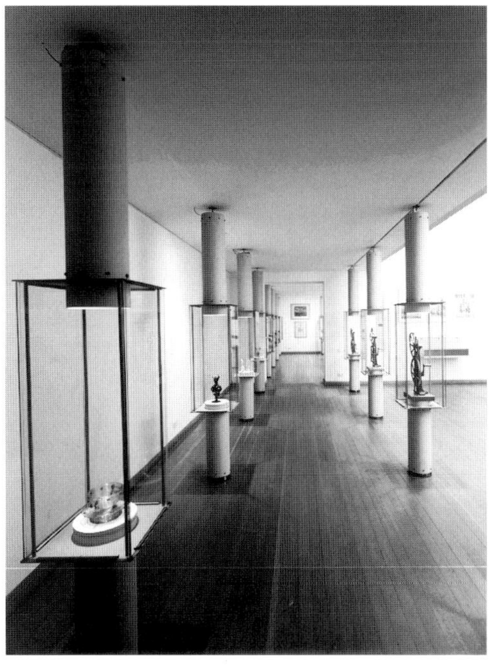

Schloß Karlsruhe / *Karlsruhe castle* 1989

Axonometrie Erdgeschoß / *Axonometric projection, ground floor*

Mit dieser Ausstellung konnte Podrecca ein ihm näher stehendes Thema, sozusagen ein Segment des Städtebaus im Hinblick auf eine breitere Vermittlung gestaltend bearbeiten. Bereits durch die Wahl des Ortes, das Karlsruher Schloß, Zentrum der strahlenförmig sich öffnenden Stadtanlage, ergab sich der von Podrecca bei den meisten seiner Ausstellungen angestrebte städtebauliche Bezug. Dabei war es vor allem die Faszination der sternförmigen Grundrisse militärischer Befestigungsanlagen – denen sich die bewohnten Stadtteile meist unterordneten – die im Vordergrund der optischen Wirkung stand. Ein maßstäblicher Vergleich von einigen dieser Festungsstädte rückte die Proportionen zurecht. Naturgemäß erhielt die Darstellung der Planung von Karlsruhe viel Raum. Aber auch andere Musterbeispiele wurden vorgestellt. Beispielsweise das Fragment gebliebene Zentrum der Salinenstadt Chaux, gegen Ende des absolutistischen Zeitalters von C. N. Ledoux geplant, die alsbald vom offenen Schachbrettmuster der – unbefestigten – amerikanischen Städte abgelöst wurde. An riesigen Strukturmodellen von Washington, Kalmar, Turin, Nancy und St. Petersburg machte Podrecca den Unterschied zwischen grafischer Wirkung des Plans und stadträumlicher Realität deutlich. Damit gelang es, das vornehmlich aus Plandarstellungen in Grundriß und Ansicht bestehende Ausstellungsgut dreidimensional aufzulockern.

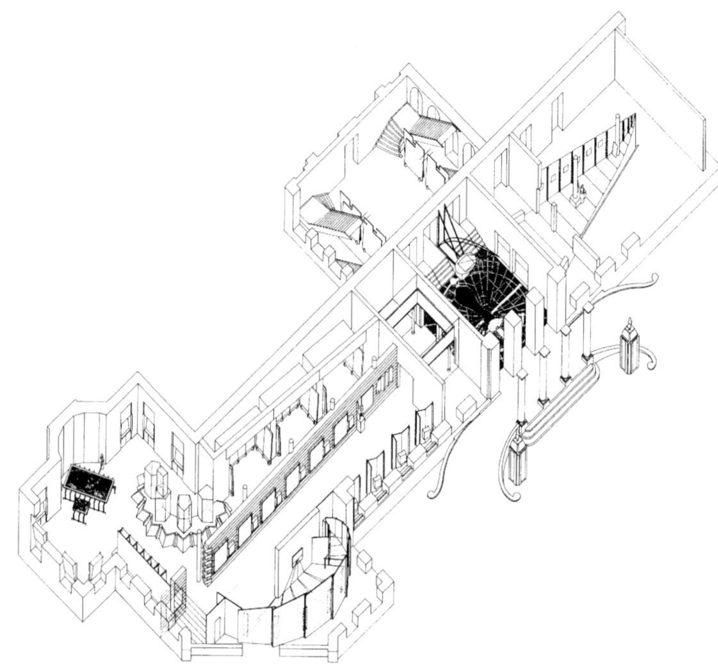

With this exhibition, Podrecca could work on the design of a theme close to himself so to speak; a segment of urban construction with a view towards a wider mediation. The choice of the location, Karlsruhe castle – the center of the city opening up in concentric rays, already provided the urban reference that Podrecca had been striving for in most of his exhibitions. Above all, the fascination of the star-shaped ground plan of military entrenchments to which the lived-in city districts are usually subordinate stood in the foreground of the visual effect. A comparison according to the scale of some of these fortified cities put the proportions into the correct relationship. Naturally, the demonstration of the planning of Karlsruhe was given a lot of space. But other examples were introduced, as well. The center of the saltworks city of Chaux, which has remained a fragment and was planned at the end of the Absolutist Age by C. N. Ledoux, was one such example and was soon to be substituted by the chess-board pattern of the "unfortified" American cities. Huge structural models of Washington, Kalmar, Torino, Nancy and St. Petersburg were used by Podrecca to clarify the difference between the graphic effect of the plan and the urban spatial reality. He thus succeeded in three-dimensionally loosening up the displayed material consisting mainly of ground-plans and views.

Ansicht der Stadt Karlsruhe von Christian Thran /
View of the city of Karlsruhe by Christian Thran 1739

Axonometrie Obergeschoß /
Axonometric projection, upper floor

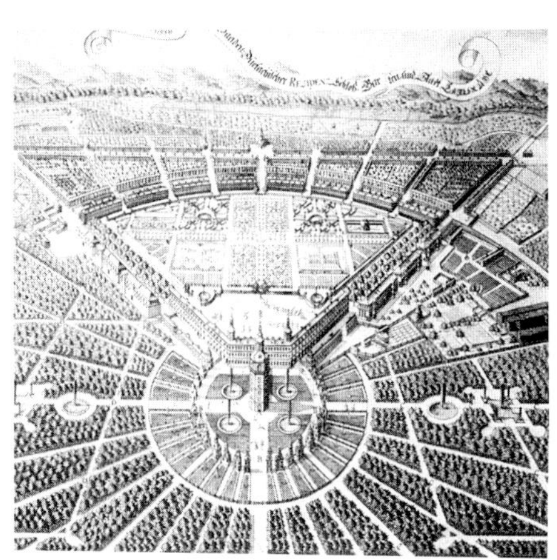

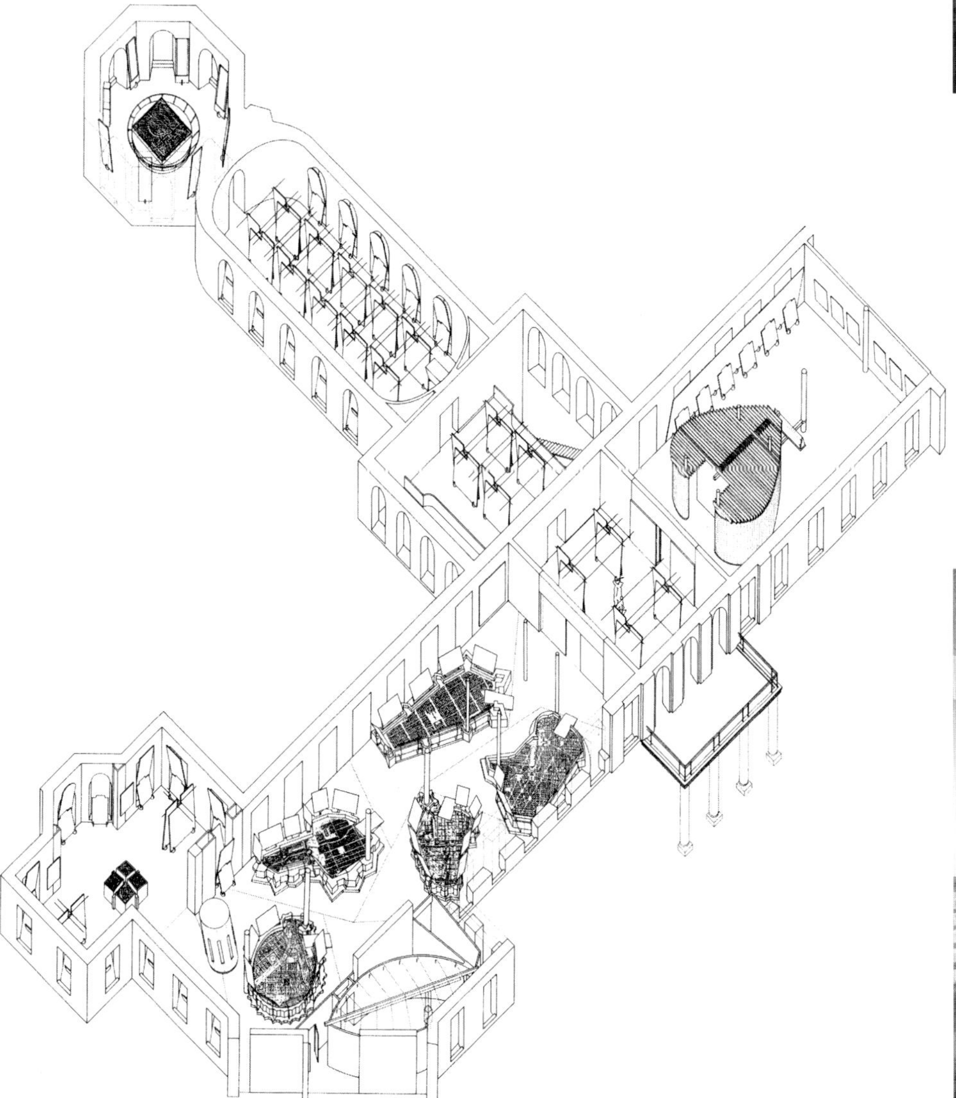

Architekturvisionen / *Architectural visions*,
Piranesi

Projektion Entwicklungsgeschichte /
Projection historical development, Karlsruhe

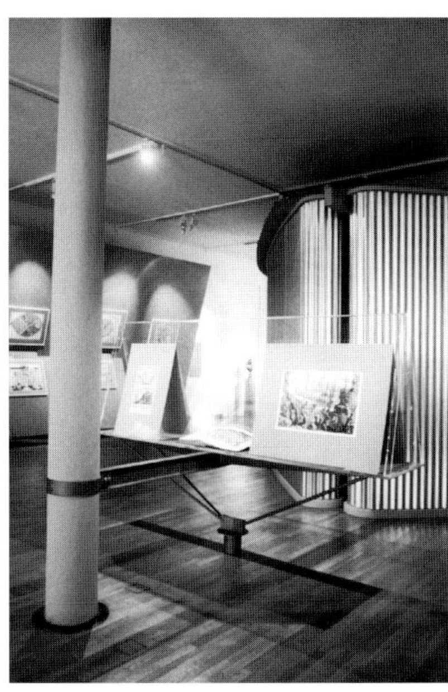

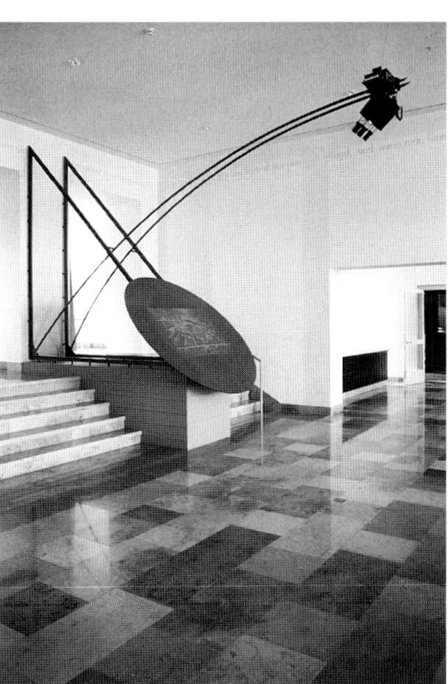

Sokrates und Plato / *Socrates and Plato*

Die Perspektive / *The Perspective*

Die Traktatistik / *The Tractatistics*

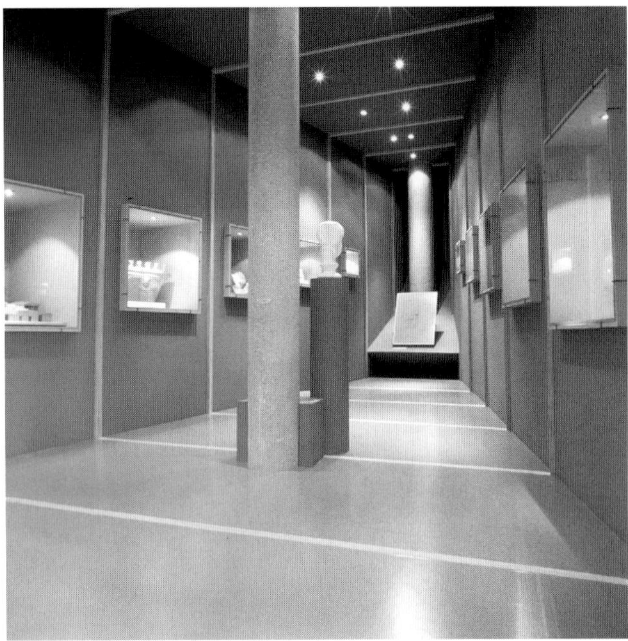

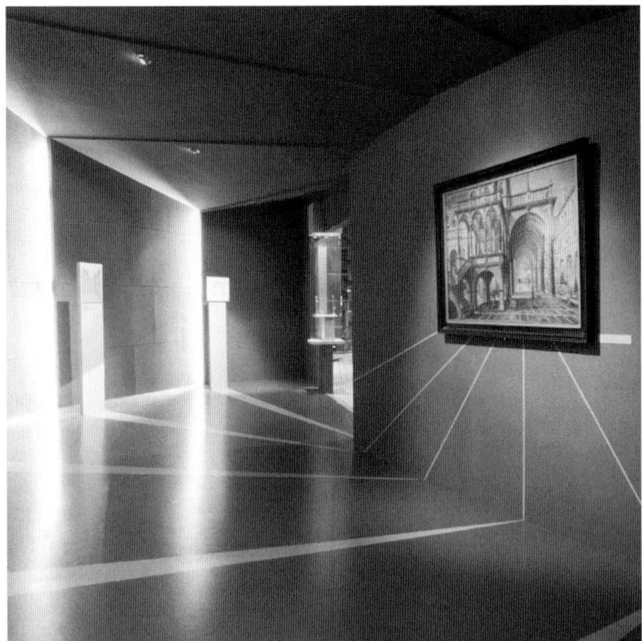

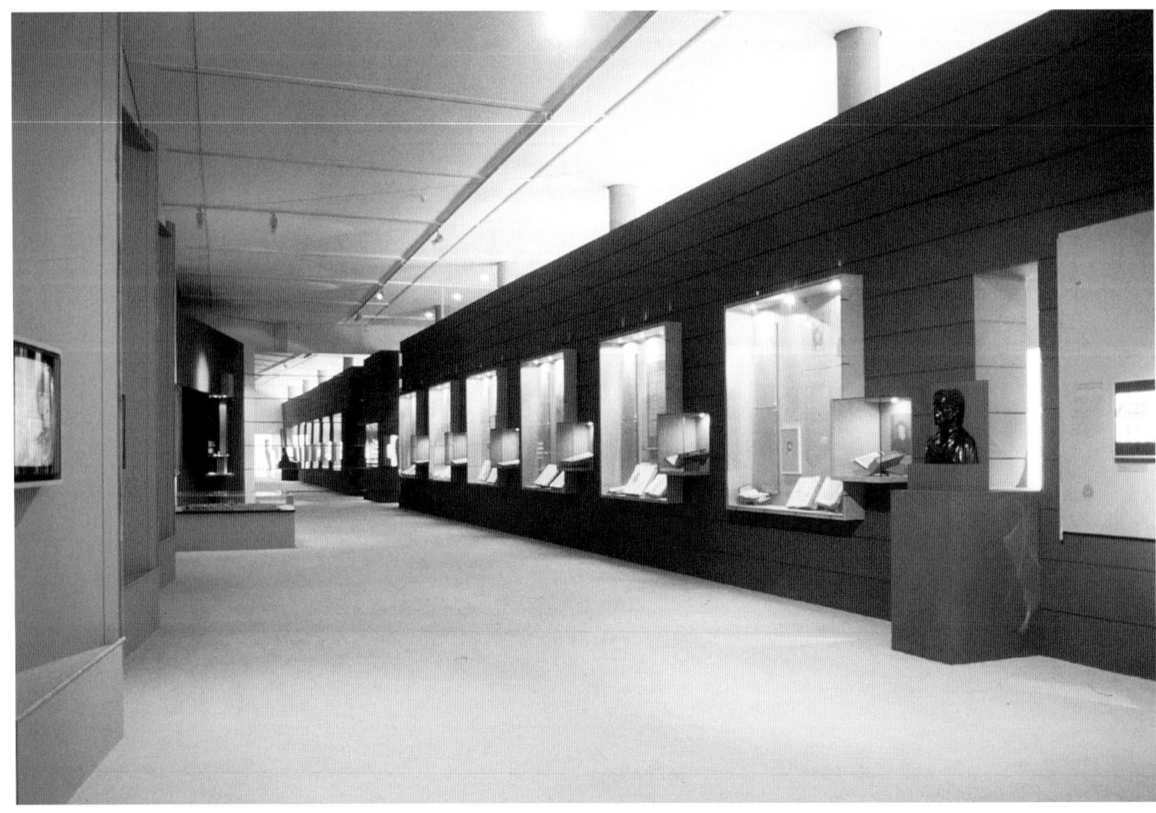

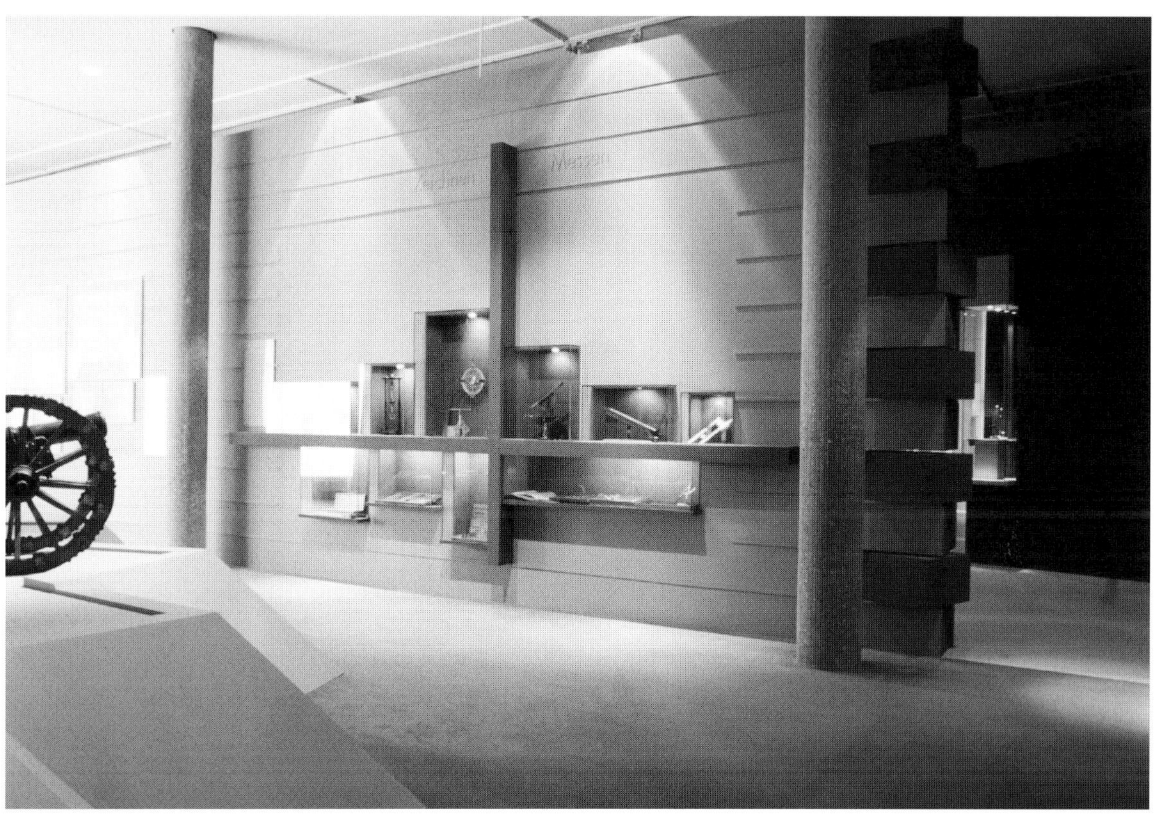

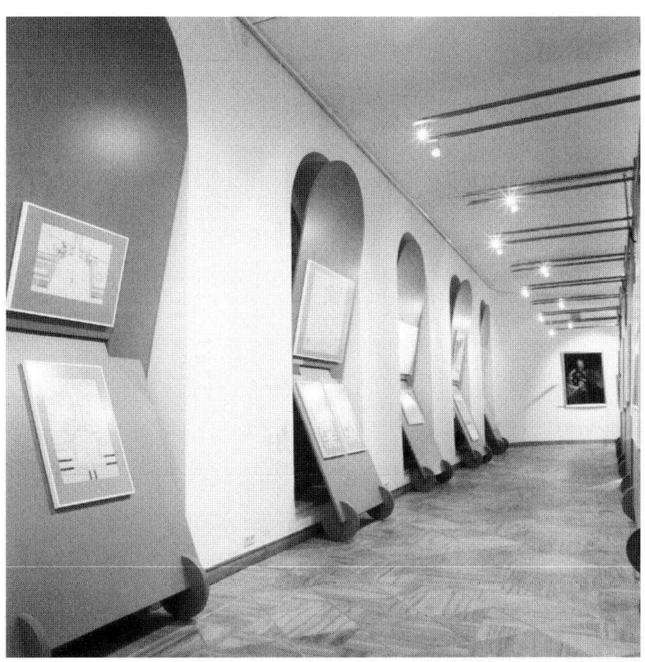

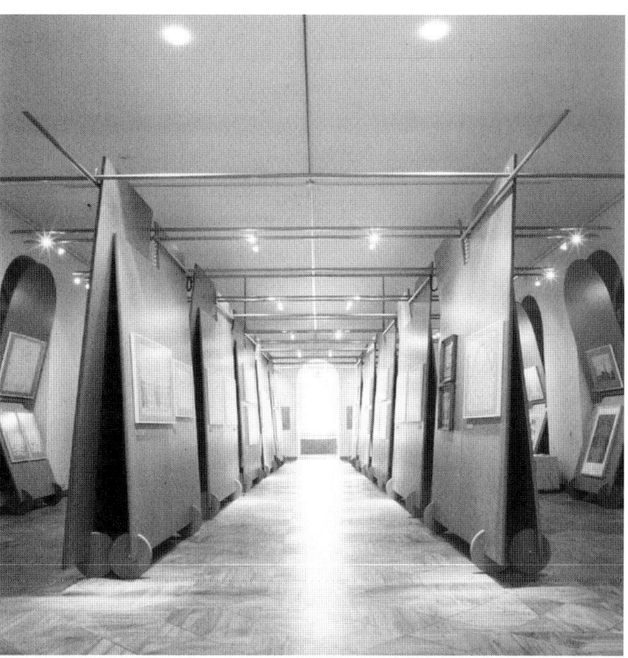

Planstädte / *Planned cities*

Einzelstädte / *Single cities*

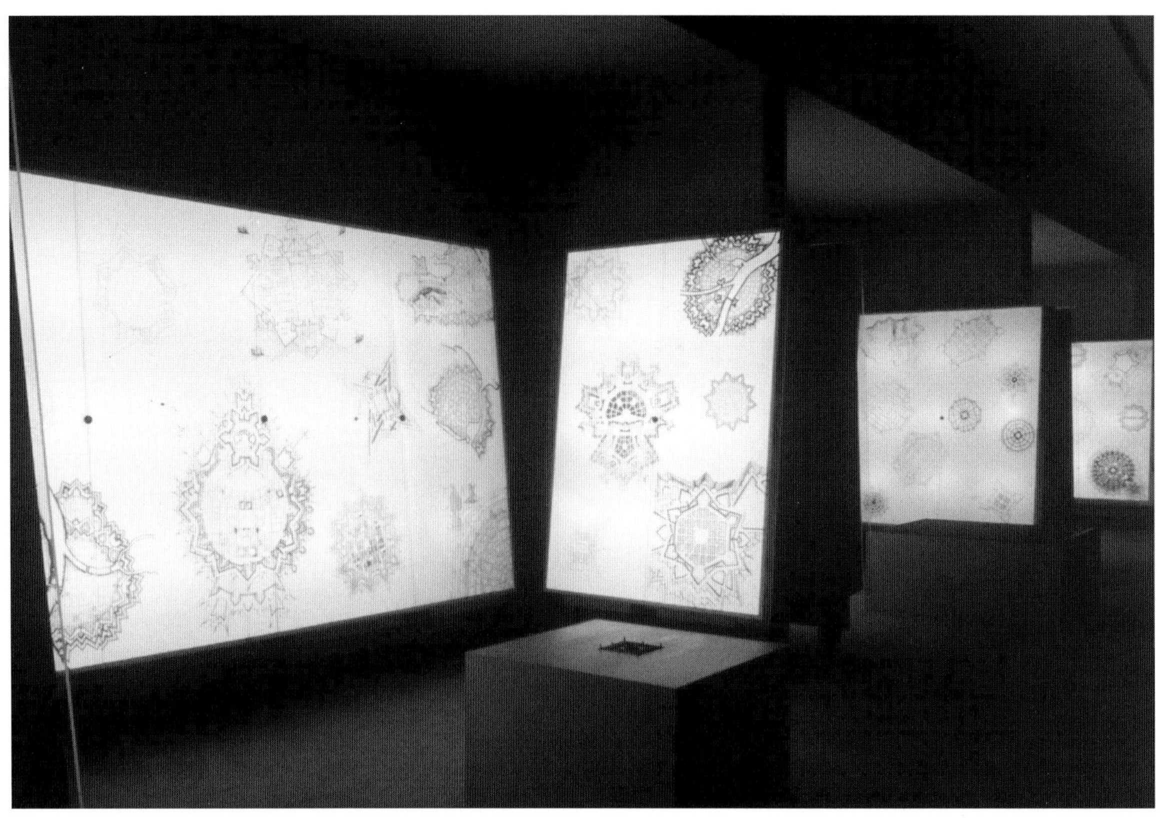

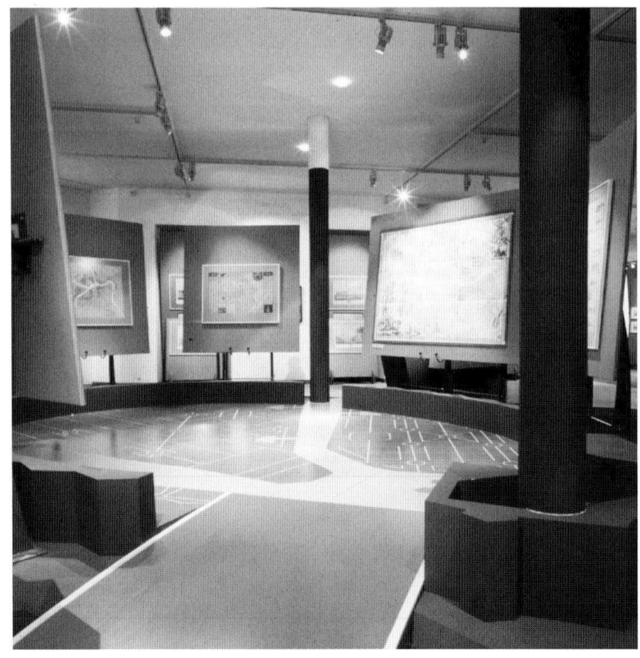

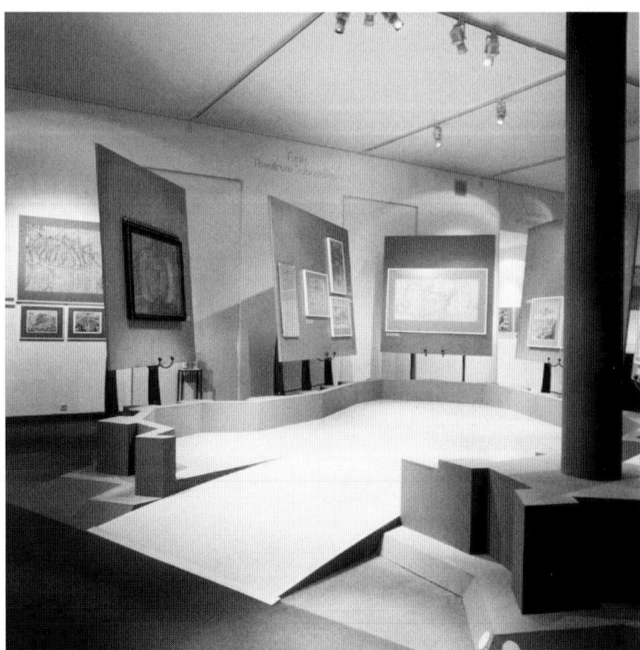

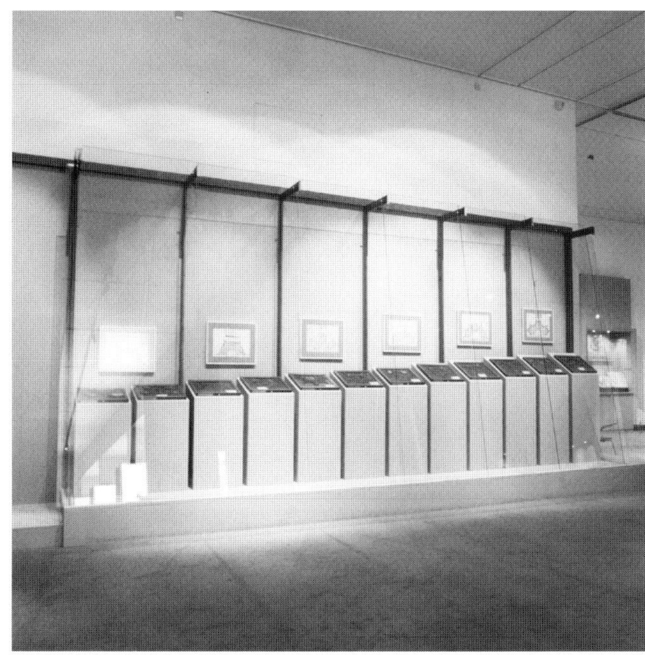

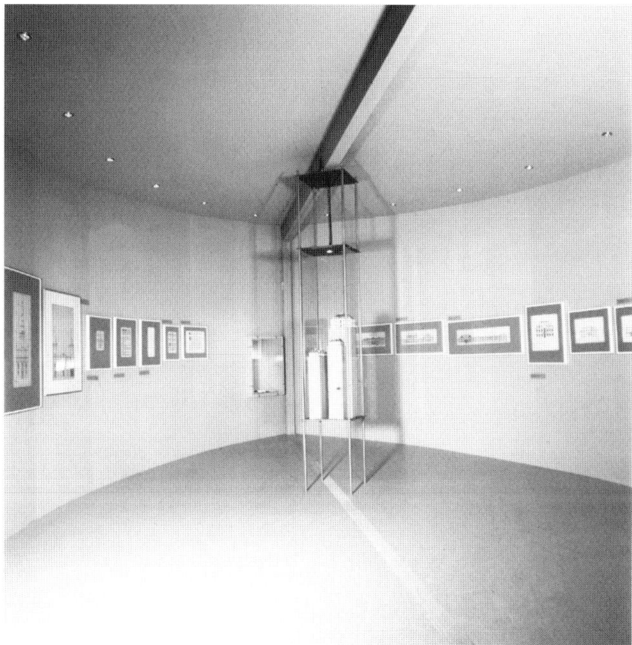

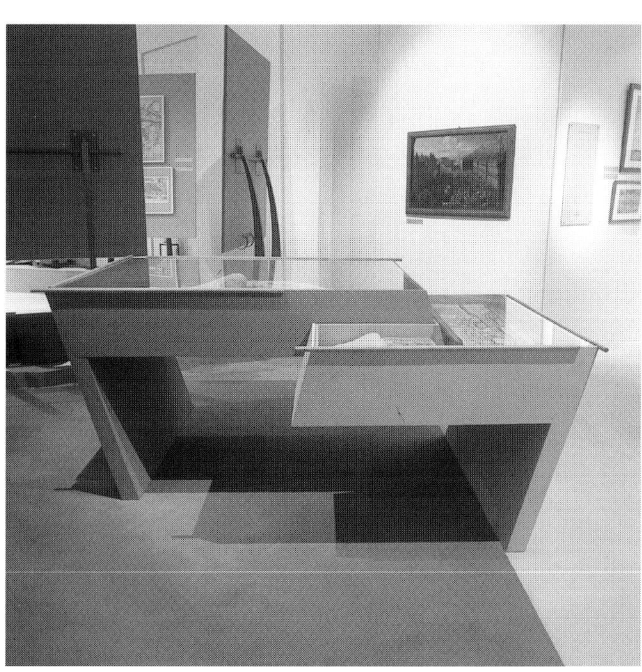

Entwurfskizzen / *Design sketches*

Leuchtmast und Kandelaber / *Lightmast and candelabra*

Aufgrund seiner Beschäftigung mit öffentlichen Räumen hat sich Podrecca immer auch mit der Frage der Beleuchtung und mit festinstallierten Serviceelementen befaßt. Der Leuchtmast mit Strahlern in halber Höhe und vier Reflektorfeldern unter der Spitze wird zum einen von seiner technischen Leistung bestimmt, zum anderen rufen die Reflektorflächen schmetterlingshafte Leichtigkeit hervor.

Der etwas kleinere Kandelaber ist dagegen eine zutiefst poetische Umsetzung des Leuchtens im nächtlichen Stadtraum. Die spitze Nadel des Stehers ist zuerst einmal selbständiges vertikales Element, an dem der Waagbalken mit dem einseitig angebrachten, auf der Spitze stehenden Leuchtkörperkegel wie provisorisch montiert erscheint. Kegel und Nadel sind die Hauptbestandteile, das andere ist Hilfskonstruktion. Im Nahbereich des Kandelabers entsteht nun durch die Reflektorfläche im Deckel ein leuchtender Bereich auf dem Pflaster, ein «Raum bei der Laterne», deren Licht von der Kegelspitze zu tropfen scheint.

Because of his occupation with public spaces, Boris Podrecca has always dealt with the question of lighting and fixed service elements. The light mast with spotlights at medium height and four reflectors below the top is determined for one by its technical performance and also by the aesthetics of the reflector surfaces creating a butterfly lightness.

The somewhat smaller candelabra, on the contrary, is a deeply poetic realization of the lighting in the nocturnal city space. The pointed tip of the stand is an independent vertical element at which the horizontal crossbar with its spotlight cone, standing on its tip and mounted on one side, appears to be temporarily installed. The cone and pin are the main components, the rest is an auxiliary construction. In the close vicinity of the candelabra, a shiny area on the pavement is created by the reflector surface in the cover, a "space at the lantern", whose light seems to drop from the tip of the cone.

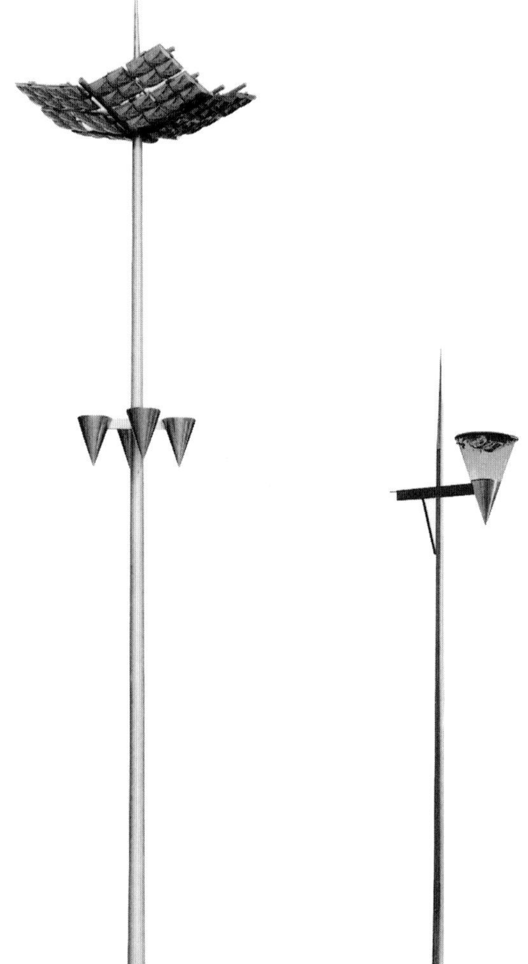

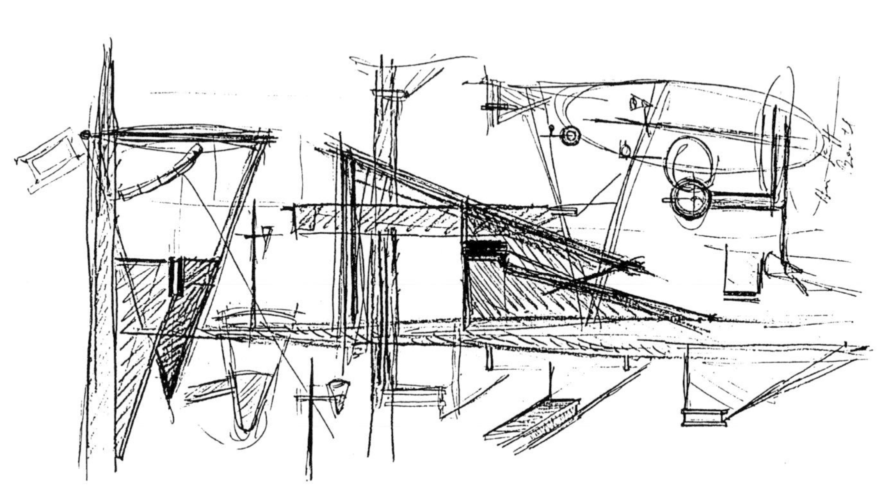

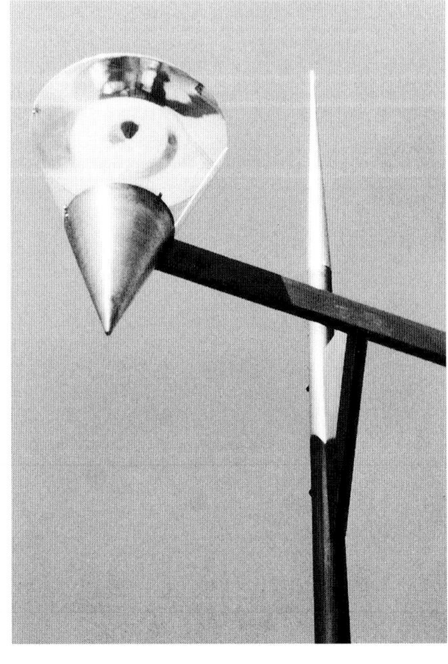

Papierkorb / *Paper basket*

Papierkorb, Doppelsitzbank und Blumenschale sind teils durch die gewellte Blechversteifung formal verwandt. Einen weiteren gemeinsamen Wesenszug bildet der zivile, freundlich verbindliche Charakter. Podrecca vermeidet mit Eleganz und Leichtigkeit eine demonstrative Vandalensicherheit, die den gestalterischen Ausdruck unangenehm dominieren würde. Der Papierkorb neigt sich beispielsweise der entsorgenden Hand freundlich zu, das Design der Bank sieht nicht das erste Ziel darin, zu verhindern, daß sich wer drauflegt – warum denn auch nicht. Es spricht ein positives menschliches Kulturverhalten aus dieser Gestaltung, der seelenlose Obrigkeitsstaat wird damit durch entwaffnende Freundlichkeit relativiert.

Paper basket, double sitting bench, and planter all are used partly in a formal way due to the wavy metal stiffness. Another common characteristic is given by the civil, friendly and obliging character. Podrecca avoids a blatant protection against vandalism which would uncomfortably dominate the design's expression of elegance and lightness. The paper basket, for example, obligingly tilts towards the hand and the design of the bench does not see its first goal as keeping someone from lying on it – and it shouldn't. A positive human cultural behavior speaks to us through these designs. The soul-less, authoritative state is thus made relative by a disarming friendliness.

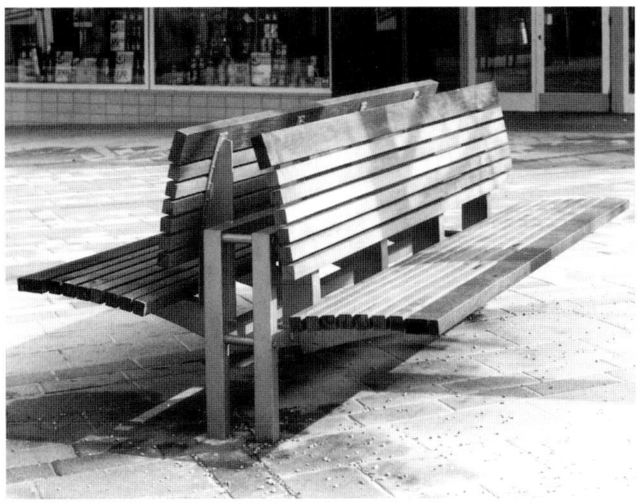

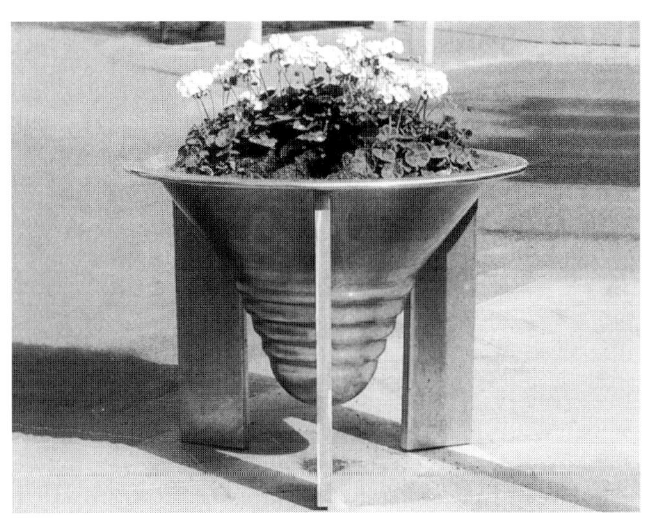

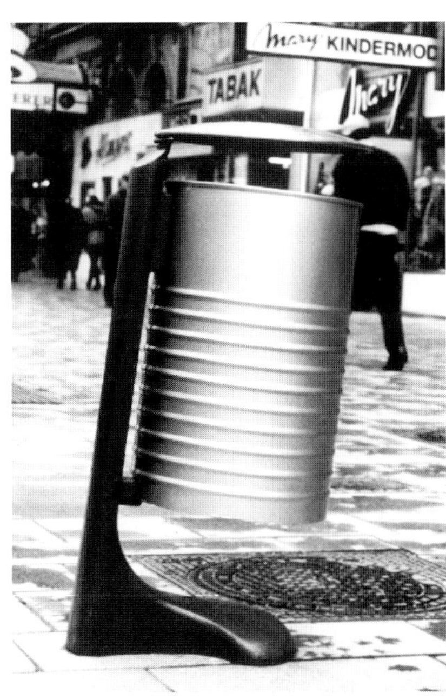

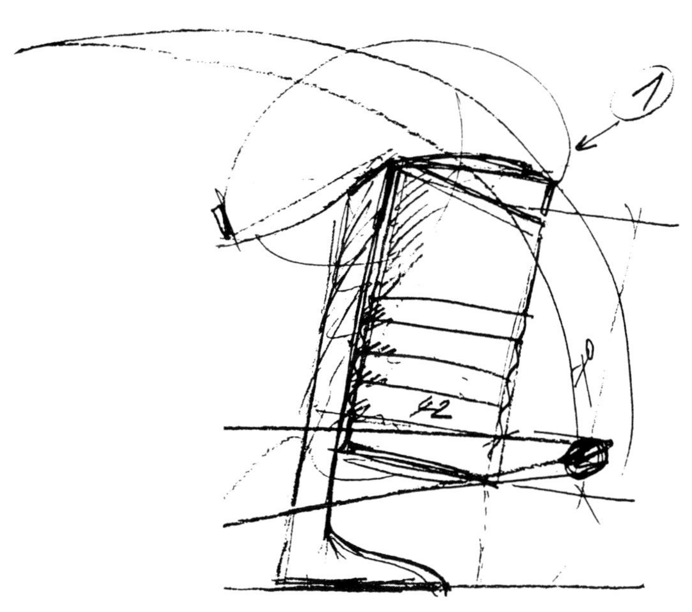

Sitzmöbel Serie Atlantis / *Furniture series Atlantis* (Wittmann)

Sessel Platana / *Chair Platana*

Die Möbel, etwa jene gepolsterten, entworfen für die Firma Wittmann, verfügen über eine knackige Gespanntheit, die sowohl zeitspezifische Jugendlichkeit, aber auch eine nicht bildhafte Erotik vermittelt. Dagegen erhält der Sessel «Platana» durch die frappierende Entwurfsidee, zwei gebogene Sperrholzflächen gleichsam an den Zipfeln zusammenzuknöpfen, so daß sie eine Sitzschale bilden, den zeitlosen Charakter einer genialen Bastelei. Das metallene Untergestell mit sehr präzis geformten und differenzierten Beinen und für verschiedene Bodenbeläge auswechselbaren Fußteilen, rückt die Flapsigkeit der Sitzschale wieder ins Lot. Es hat einen zoomorphen Anflug, etwa den eines Käfers. Die kurze Lehne mit Griffloch macht den Sessel handlich für ein kurzes Dazusetzen zum Kaffeehausgespräch. Praktikabilität und gestalterische Identität kommen damit zur Deckung.

The furniture, like the upholstered piece designed for the Wittmann company, not only has a crisp tautness radiating a contemporary youthfulness, but also a non-pictorial eroticism. Contrary to this, the "Platana" chair has the timeless character of an ingenious handyman's construction with the striking design concept being to button up two curved plywood surfaces at the tips thus creating a sitting shell. The metal substructure, with precisely formed differentiated legs and changeable foot parts for different floor coverings, puts the boorish character of the sitting shell back into balance. It has a suggestion of zoomorphical morphology, slightly that of a beetle. The short back with a grip hole makes the chair handy for quickly joining in a coffee house discussion. Practical use and the identity of the design are both covered in this way.

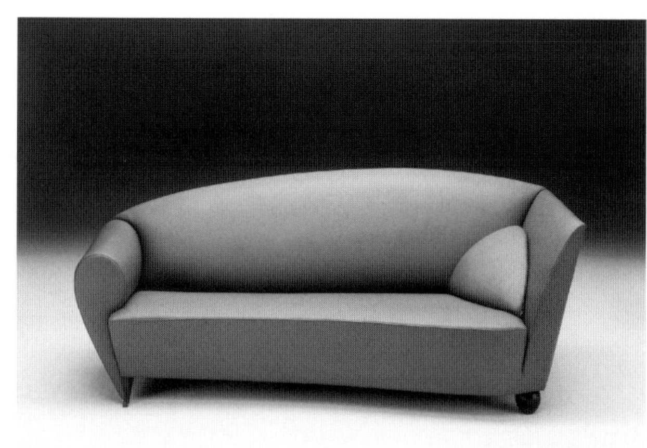

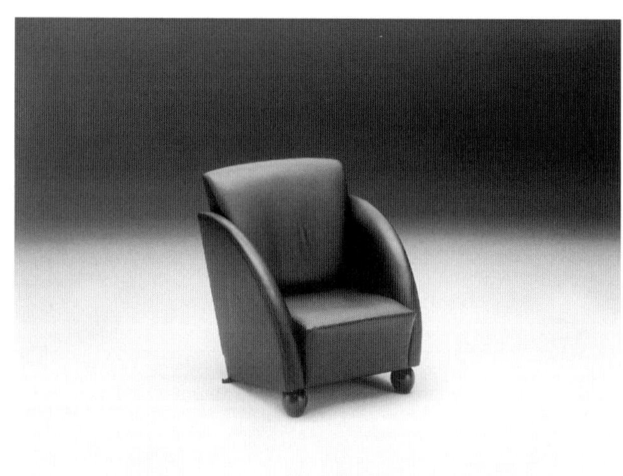

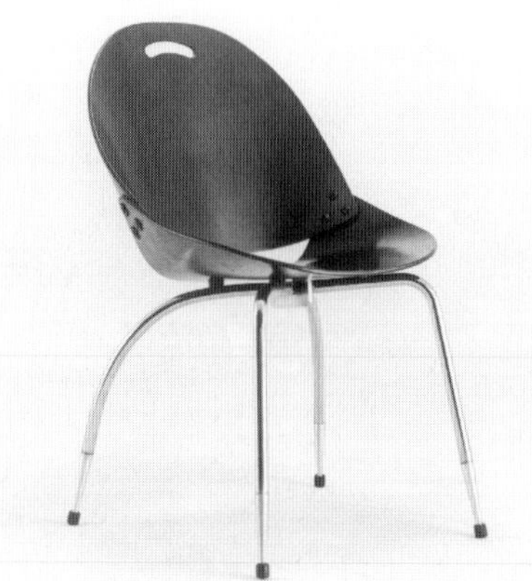
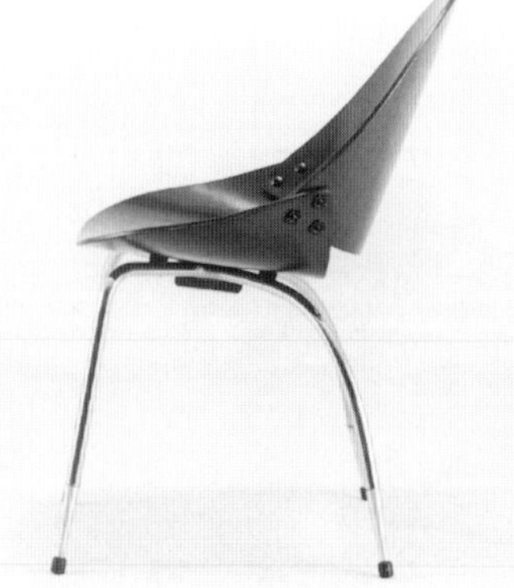
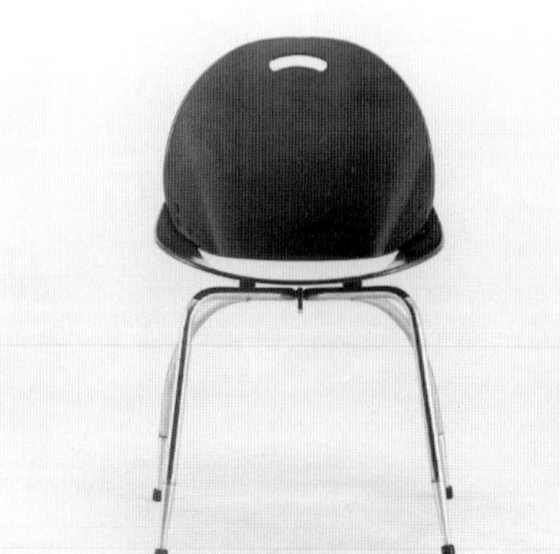

Bett Saba / *Bed Saba* (Wittmann)

Bett Carriola / *Bed Carriola*
(Teatro delle Muse)

Sessel Korotan / *Chair Korotan*

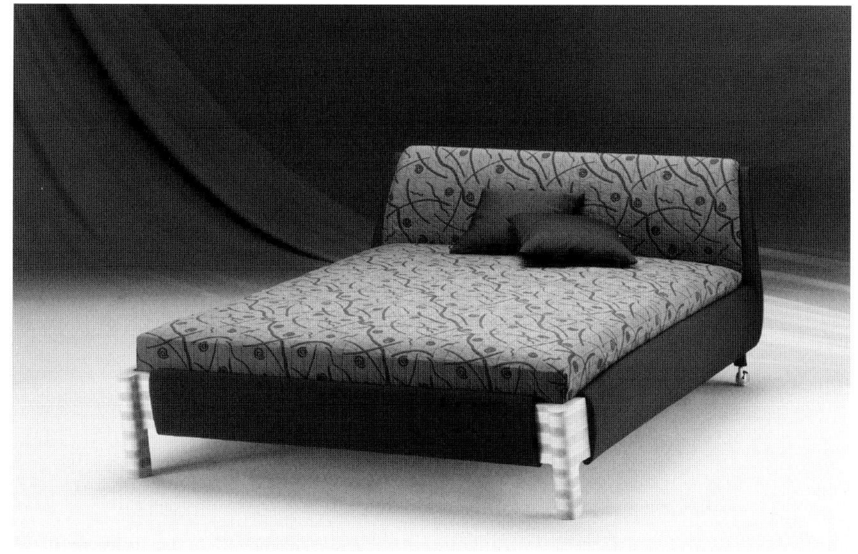

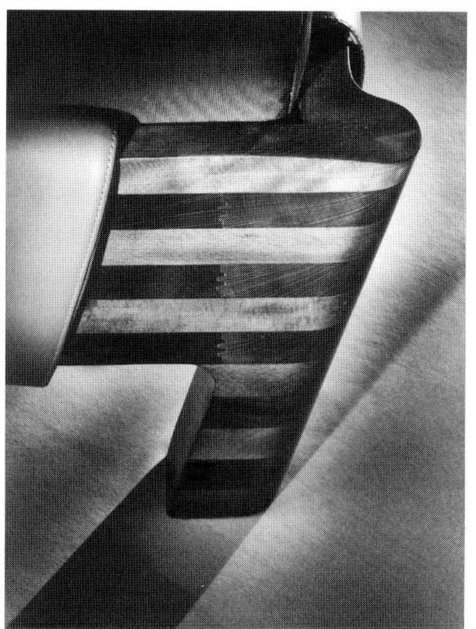

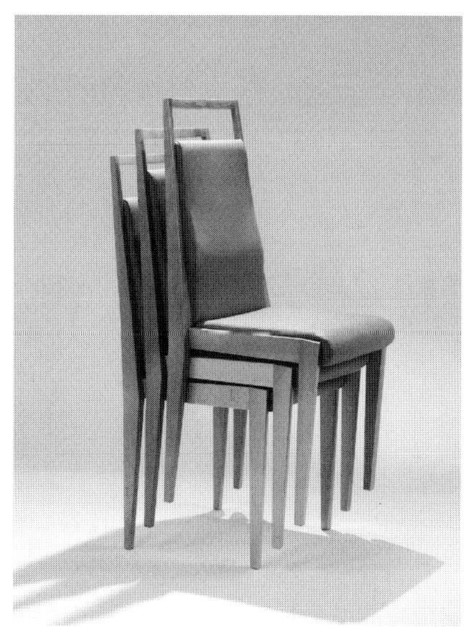

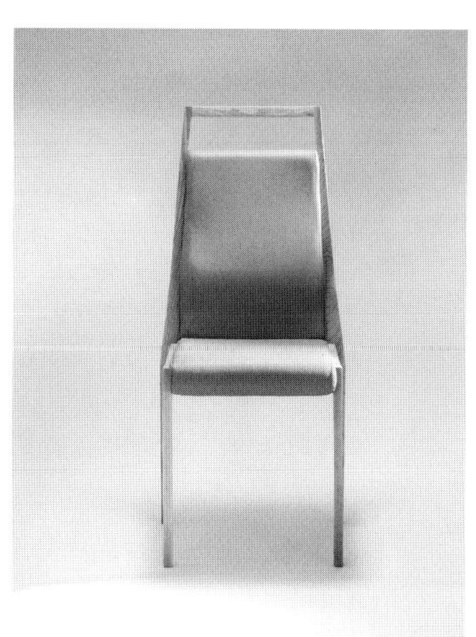

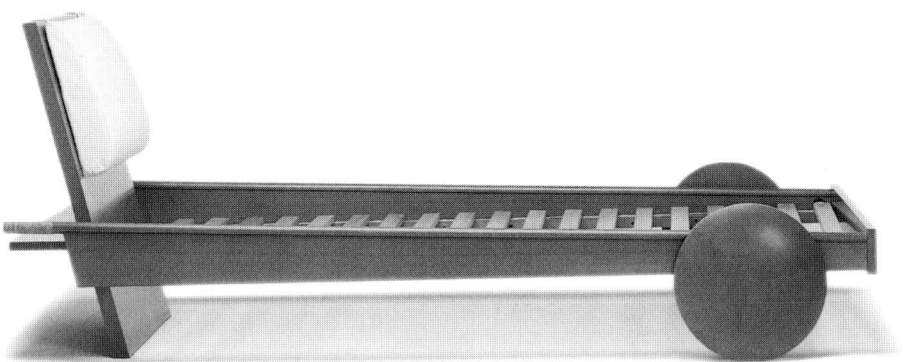

Fußdetail für den Steintisch Ädipus / *Leg detail for stone table Ädipus* (Bigelli)

Tisch Poppea / *Table Poppea* (Bigelli)

Entwurfszeichnung / *Design sketch*

Marmorschüssel Cocca / *Marble bowl Cocca* (Bigelli)

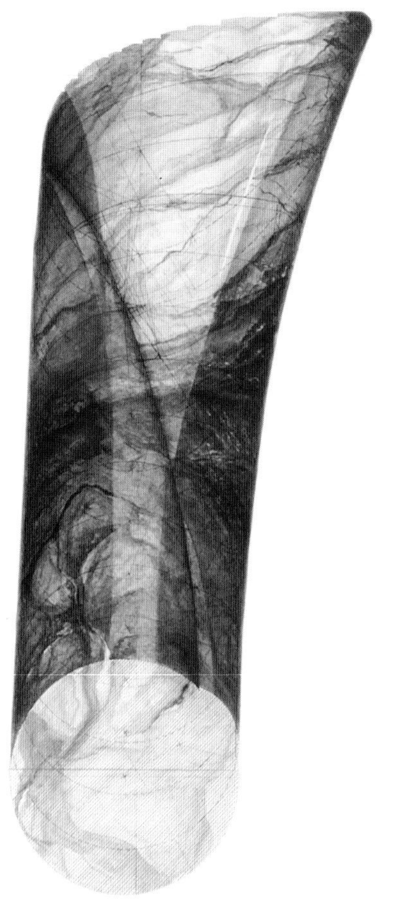

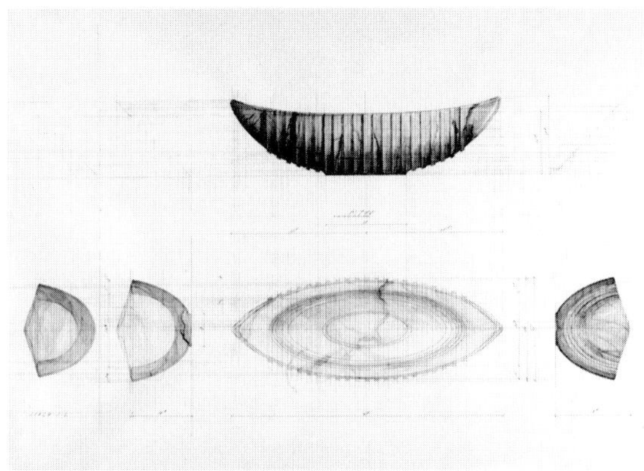

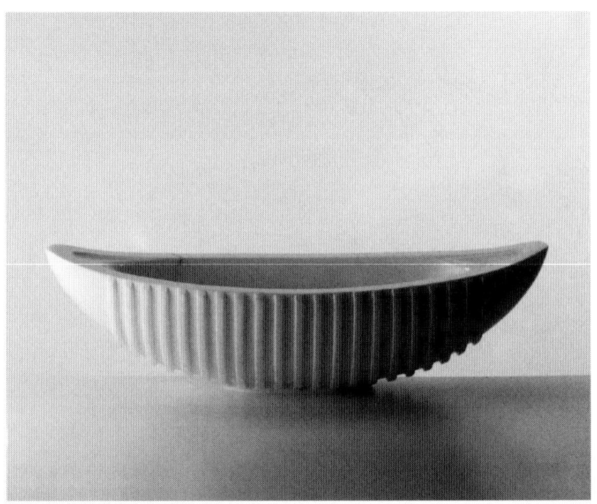

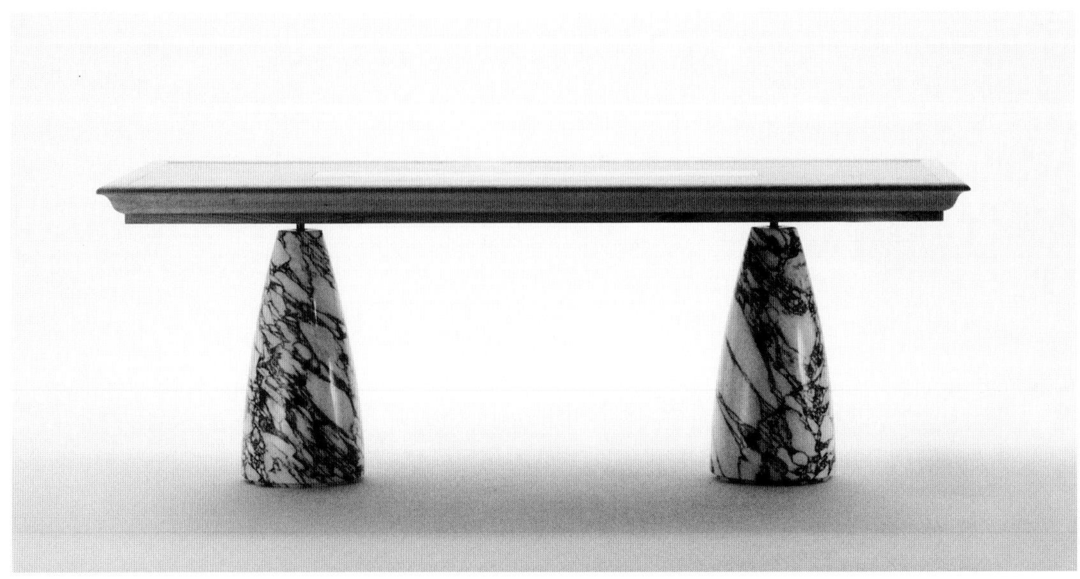

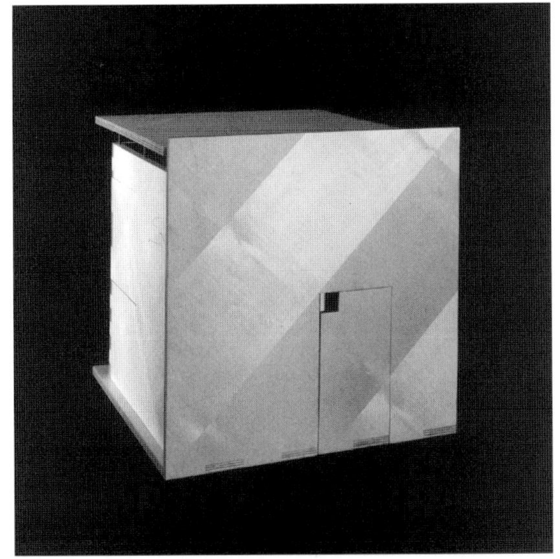

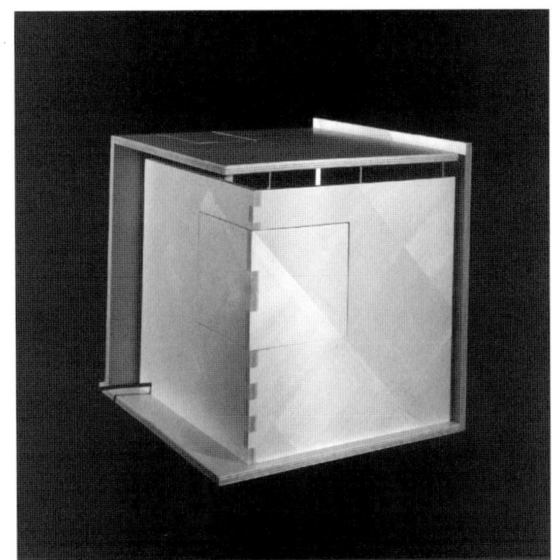

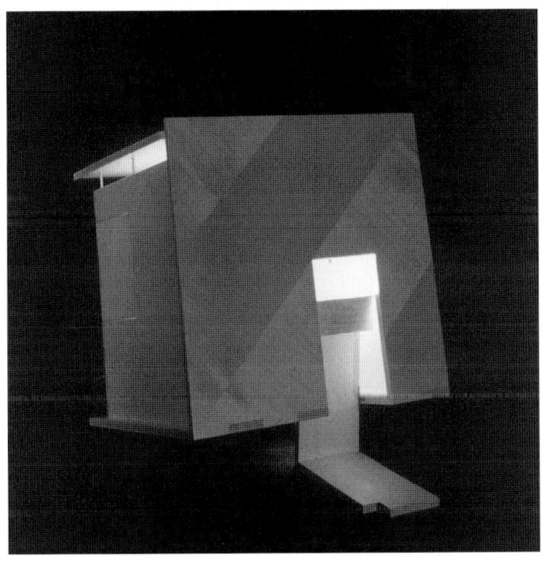

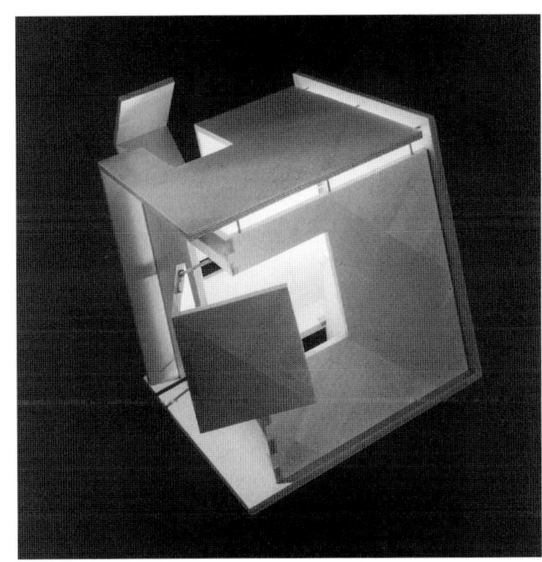

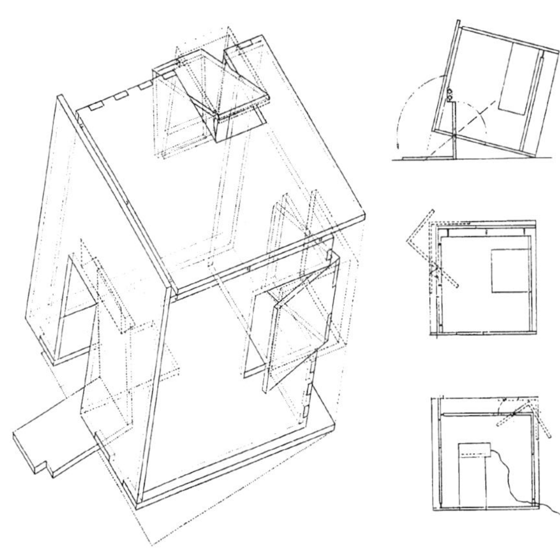

1965 Projekt Gestaltung des Mirabellplatzes, Salzburg	*1965 Project, design of Mirabell square, Salzburg*
1967 Wettbewerb Stadtzentrum und Wohnbebauung Varna, Bulgarien	*1967 Competition for city center and housing construction Varna, Bulgaria*
Diplomarbeit Jugendzentrum, Ljubljana, Slowenien Meisterklasse Roland Rainer	*Degree work, youth center, Ljubljana, Slovenia, Master class of Roland Rainer*
Gestaltung der Ausstellung Jože Plečnik. Wien–Triest–Prag, Österreichische Gesellschaft für Architektur, Wien, Krypta der Heilig-Geist-Kirche, Wien	*1967 Design of the exhibition, Jože Plečnik. Vienna – Triest – Prague, Austrian society for architecture, Vienna, Crypt of the Holy-Spirit-church, Vienna*
1968 Wettbewerb Kolonialstädte in Südamerika, Merida, Mexiko, 1. Preis	*1968 Competition for colonial cities in South America Merida, Mexico, 1st prize*
1969 Wettbewerb Ortszentrum in Hohenems, Österreich, 3. Preis, (mit G. Eiböck)	*1969 Competition for town center in Hohenems, Austria, 3rd prize (with G. Eiböck)*
1972–74 Entwicklungsplan Athen 2001, Athen, (mit G. Eiböck)	*1972–74 Development plan, Athens 2001, Athens, (with G. Eiböck)*
1972 Projekt Einfamilienhaus Vremec, Triest, Italien	*1972 Project for single-family-home, Vremec, Triest, Italy*
1975 Fassadenrenovierung und Einrichtung eines Besprechungs- raumes für die Werbeagentur GGK in der Villa Vojcsik von Otto Schönthal, Wien	*1975 Facade renovation and furnishing of a conference room for GGK advertising agency in villa Vojcsik by Otto Schönthal, Vienna*
1976/77 Einrichtung Werbeagentur Plus, Wien	*1976/77 Furnishing, Plus advertising agency, Vienna*
1978/79 Einrichtung Zahnärztliches Institut Dr. Klaus, München	*1978/79 Furnishing, Dental medical Institute, Dr. Klaus, Munich*
Projekt Vier-Familien-Haus Acropoli, Kalabrien, Italien	*Project, four-family-home, Acropoli, Calabria, Italy*
1979 Einrichtung Institut für Markt- u. Meinungsforschung Dr. Braunegger, Wien	*1979 Furnishing, Institute for market and opinion research, Dr. Braunegger, Vienna*
1979/80 Einrichtung Studioräume L'Oréal, Wien	*1979/80 Furnishing, studio space, L'Oréal, Vienna*
1979–81 Lichtkörper und Glasfenster, Heilig-Geist-Kirche von Jože Plečnik, Wien	*1979–81 Light installations and glass windows, Holy-Spirit-church by Jože Plečnik, Vienna*
1979 Projekt Siedlung Kiefersfelden, Deutschland	*1979 Project for housing community, Kiefersfelden, Germany*
1979–82 Einrichtung Neurophysisches Institut im Palais Starhemberg von Matthias Steinl, Wien	*1979–82 Interior design, Institute for Neurophysiology in the Palais Starhemberg by Matthias Steinl, Vienna*
1980 Wettbewerb Gedenkstätte in Bazovica, Triest, Italien	*1980 Competition, Bazovica memorial, Triest, Italy*
Umbau Werbeagentur GGK in der Villa Vojcsik von Otto Schönthal, Wien	*Conversion, Advertising Agency GGK in the villa Vojcsik by Otto Schönthal, Vienna*
1980/81 Ausstellungspavillon für Metallwarenfabrik Neher, Mailand	*1980/81 Exhibition pavilion for the metal goods factory Neher, Milano*
1980–82 Einfamilienhaus Daneu, Hinterbrühl bei Wien	*1980–82 Single-family-home, Daneu, Hinterbrühl/Vienna*
Einfamilienhaus Braunegger, Hinterbrühl bei Wien	*Single-family-home, Braunegger, Hinterbrühl/Vienna*
1981/82 Einrichtung Ausstellungs- und Sitzungsräume Palmers, Wien	*1981/82 Interior design, exhibition and conference rooms Palmers, Vienna*
Einrichtung Empfangs- und Ausstellungsbereich L'Oréal, Wien	*Interior design, reception and exhibition lobby, L'Oréal, Vienna*
1982 Projekt Einfamilienhaus Nardin, Triest, Italien	*1982 Project, single-family-home Nardin, Triest, Italy*
Gestaltung der Ausstellung Max Fabiani 1865–1962 und Umbauten der Ausstellungsräume Palmers, Wien	*Design of the exhibition, Max Fabiani 1865–1962, and conver- sion of the exhibition rooms, Palmers, Vienna*
Ausbau Untergeschoß für die Werbeagentur GGK in der Villa Vojcsik von Otto Schönthal, Wien	*Expansion, basement level for the Advertising Agency GGK in villa Vojcsik by Otto Schönthal, Vienna*
1982/83 Einrichtung Galerie bei der Albertina, Wien	*1982/83 Interior design of the Albertina-gallery, Vienna*
1983 Einrichtung Ausstellungs- und Simulationsraum für Möbel und Einrichtung–Wohnbühne Fehlinger, Wien	*1983 Interior design, exhibition and simulation room for furniture and interior design – Wohnbühne Fehlinger, Vienna*
Wettbewerb Opéra de la Bastille, Paris	*Competition, Opéra de la Bastille, Paris*
Einrichtung Wohnung Winkler, Wien	*Interior design, Winkler apartment, Vienna*
Einrichtung Redaktionsräume der Zeitschrift Wiener, Wien (zerstört)	*Interior design of the editor's offices, Wiener magazine, Vienna (destroyed)*

1983	Einrichtung Möbelgeschäft Susanne Wirth, Wien	*1983*	*Interior design store, Susanne Wirth, Vienna*
	Umbau Foyerräume Sofiensäle, Wien (zerstört)	*1983*	*Conversion of the lobby rooms, Sofiensäle, Vienna (destroyed)*
1983/84	Projekt Einfamilienhaus Zembaty, Wien	*1983/84*	*Project, single-family-home, Zembaty, Vienna*
	Einrichtung Pausenraum L'Oréal, Wien		*Interior design, break-room, L'Oréal, Vienna*
1984	Projekt Fassadengestaltung Einrichtungshaus Leiner, Wien	*1984*	*Project, facade design, Leiner interior design store, Vienna*
	Gestaltung der Ausstellung Carlo Scarpa, Chiesa della Carità, Gallerie dell'Accademia, Querini Stampaglia, Venedig (mit M. Botta)		*Design of the exhibition, Carlo Scarpa, Chiesa della Carità, Galerie dell'Accademia, Querini Stampaglia, Venice (with M. Botta)*
	Zubau Einrichtungshaus Kika, Wiener Neustadt, Österreich		*Addition, Kika interior design store, Wiener Neustadt, Austria*
	Einrichtung Boutique Lilli Pilli, Wien (zerstört)		*Interior design, Lilli Pilli boutique, Vienna (destroyed)*
1984/85	Geschäftspassage Humanic Casapiccola, Wien	*1984/85*	*Business mall, Humanic Casapiccola, Vienna*
	Projekt Banca Popolare, Sacile, Italien		*Project, Banca Popolare, Sacile, Italy*
	Gestaltung der Ausstellung Villes d'Eaux en France, Ecole Nationale Supérieure des Beaux-Arts, Paris		*Design of the exhibition, Villes d'Eaux en France, Ecole National Supérieure des Beaux-Arts, Paris*
1984–86	Stadtgestaltung Sacile, Italien	*1984–86*	*City design, Sacile, Italy*
	Zweifamilienhaus Schlamminger, München		*Two-family-home, Schlamminger, Munich*
	Erweiterungsbürobau Werbeagentur GGK, Wien		*Extension, office building for advertising agency GGK, Vienna*
1985	Internationaler Wettbewerb Campo di Marte, sozialer Wohnbau, Giudecca, Venedig	*1985*	*International competition, Campo di Marte, social housing, Giudecca, Venice*
	Projekt Sitz der Landesregierung und Industriellenvereinigung, Pordenone, Italien		*Project, main offices of the countygovernment and industrialist association, Pordenone, Italy*
	Einrichtung Ausstellungs- und Simulationsraum für Möbel und Einrichtung – Wohnbühne Fehlinger, Linz, Österreich		*Interior design, exhibition and simulation room for furniture and interior design – Wohnbühne Fehlinger, Linz, Austria*
	Naßeinheit Wohnung Prohaska, Wien		*Wet room unit, Prohaska apartment, Vienna*
	Bühnengestaltung am Rathausplatz und Errichtung von 8 Stadtpavillons für die Wiener Festwochen, Wien		*Stage design at the town hall square and erection of 8 city pavilions for the Vienna Festival weeks, Vienna*
1985/86	Einrichtung Bekleidungsgeschäft 1789, Wien (zerstört)	*1985/86*	*Interior design, clothing store 1789, Vienna (destroyed)*
	Gestaltung der Ausstellung Jože Plečnik. Architecte 1872-1957, CCI Centre de Création Industrielle, Centre Georges Pompidou, Paris, Ljubljana, Wien, Mailand, Venedig, New York		*Design of the Jože Plečnik exhibition. Architecte 1872–1957, CCI Centre de Création Industrielle, Centre Georges Pompidou, Paris, Ljubljana, Vienna, Milano, Venice, New York*
1986	Projekt Einrichtungshaus Kika, Vösendorf bei Wien	*1986*	*Project, Kika interior design store, Vösendorf/Vienna*
	Gestaltung der Ausstellung Jean Dubuffet, Ecole Nationale Supérieure des Beaux-Arts, Paris		*Design of the Jean Dubuffet exhibition, Ecole Nationale Supérieure des Beaux-Arts, Paris*
	Gutachten Staatsbrücke–Radwegunterführung, Salzburg		*Consultant, Staatsbrücke-bicycle underpass, Salzburg*
1986–92	Neugestaltung des Universitätsplatzes, Salzburg	*1986–92*	*New design of University Place, Salzburg*
1986	Einrichtung ÖCAD, EDV Schulungs- und Serviceräume, Wien	*1986*	*Interior design, ÖCAD, PC schooling and service rooms, Vienna*
	Gutachten Studioräume L'Oréal–Paris, Wien		*Consultant, studio space, L'Oréal-Paris, Vienna*
	Projekt Arsenale in Venedig für die Triennale di Architettura, Mailand		*Project, Arsenale in Venice for the Triennale di Architettura, Milano*
1986/87	Wettbewerb und Realisierung Freiaufgang zur Landesausstellung Wolf Dietrich von Raitenau, Residenzplatz, Salzburg, 1.Preis	*1986/87*	*Competition and realization, outside access to the country exhibition, Wolf Dietrich von Raitenau, Residenzplatz, Salzburg, 1st prize*
1986–89	Gestaltung des Tartini Platzes, Piran, Slowenien	*1986–89*	*Design of Tartini square, Piran, Slovenia*
	Villa Moralić, Cavtat bei Dubrovnik, Kroatien		*Villa Moralić, Cavtat/Dubrovnik, Croatia*
	Einrichtungshaus Kika, Linz, Österreich		*Kika interior design store, Linz, Austria*
	Einrichtungshaus Leiner, Salzburg		*Leiner interior design store, Salzburg*

1986–93 Wohnbebauung Kapellenweg, Wien	*1986–93 Housing development, Kapellenweg, Vienna*
1987 Projekt Eingangshalle Veitscher Magnesitwerke, Wien	*1987 Project, entrance hall, Veitscher Magnesitwerke, Vienna*
Wettbewerb Holzfachgeschäft Schömer, Wien und Vomp, Tirol	*Competition, Schömer lumber store, Vienna and Vomp, Tyrol*
Wettbewerb Rathauserweiterung La Roche sur Yon, La Roche sur Yon, Frankreich, 2. Preis	*Competition, town hall extension, La Roche sur Yon, La Roche sur Yon, France, 2nd prize*
Wettbewerb Rathaus Nantes–Reze, Nantes–Reze, Frankreich, 2. Preis	*Competition, town hall Nantes-Reze, Nantes-Reze, France, 2nd prize*
Wettbewerb Revitalisierung Ronacher Theater, Wien	*Competition, restoration of Ronach theater, Vienna*
Gestaltung der Ausstellung Neue Tendenzen in der französischen Malerei, Ecole Nationale Supérieure des Beaux-Arts, Paris	*Design of the exhibition "New tendencies in French painting", Ecole National Supérieure des Beaux Arts, Paris*
Gestaltung der Ausstellung Bürgersinn und Aufbegehren-Biedermeier und Vormärz in Wien, Künstlerhaus, Wien	*Design of the exhibition "Bürgersinn und Aufbegehren - Biedermeier und Vormärz in Wien", Künstlerhaus, Vienna*
1987–92 Kirche SS. Redentore, Fontanafredda, Friaul, Italien (mit A. Santarossa)	*1987–92 SS. Redentore church, Fontanafredda, Friaul, Italy (with T. Santarossa)*
1988 Projekt Einrichtung Bekleidungsgeschäft Palmers, Kärntner Straße, Wien	*1988 Project, interior design, fashion store, Palmers, Kärntner Strasse, Vienna*
Projekt Neubau Hotel Plaza, Salzburg	*Project, new construction, Hotel Plaza, Salzburg*
Wettbewerb Büroneubau L'Oréal, Karlsruhe, Deutschland	*Competition, new office building, L'Oréal, Karlsruhe, Germany*
Wettbewerb Büroneubau Bank für Kärnten und Steiermark, Klagenfurt, Österreich	*Competition, new bank office building for Kärnten and Steiermark, Klagenfurt, Austria*
Wettbewerb Atlanopole, Nantes, Frankreich	*Competition, Atlanopole, Nantes, France*
Wettbewerb Pustijerna, Dubrovnik, Kroatien (mit T. Galijašević und M. Jošić)	*Competition, Pustijerna, Dubrovnic, Croatia (with T. Galijašević and M. Jošić)*
Projekt Staatliche Kunsthalle und Kunstforum Berlin für die Ausstellung Berlin–Kulturstadt Europas 1988/Denkmal oder Denkmodell, Staatliche Kunsthalle, Berlin	*Project, Staatliche Kunsthalle and Kunstforum Berlin for the exhibition Berlin – Kulturstadt Europas 1988/Denkmal oder Denkmodell, Staatliche Kunsthalle, Berlin*
1988–92 Neubau Studentenheim San Massimo, Padua, Italien (in veränderter Ausführung)	*1988–92 New building, student housing at San Massimo, Padua (in a modified realization)*
1988 Projekt Kirche Sv. Janez, Celje, Slowenien	*1988 Project, Sv. Janez church, Celje, Slovenia*
Gestaltung des Themas Cartografia für die XVII. Triennale di Milano 1988, Mailand	*Design of the theme, Cartografia, for the XVII. Triennale di Milano, 1988, Milano*
Gestaltung der Ausstellung Friedrich Kiesler, Museum des 20. Jahrhunderts, Wien	*Design of the exhibition, Friedrich Kiesler, Museum des 20. Jahrhunderts, Vienna*
Möbel Serie Atlantis für Wittmann	*Furniture, Atlantis line for Wittmann*
Messepavillon Funder, Wien	*Fair pavilion, Funder, Vienna*
1988/89 Einrichtungshaus Kika, Klagenfurt, Österreich	*1988/89 Kika furniture house, Klagenfurt, Austria*
Einrichtung Bekleidungsgeschäft Palmers, Alser Straße, Wien	*Interior design for Palmers fashion store, Alser Strasse, Vienna*
1988–95 Einfamilienhaus Glaser, Wien	*1988–95 Single-family-home Glaser, Vienna*
1988–92 Sanierung der Personenaufzüge im Rabenhof, Wien	*1988–92 Restoration of the elevators in Rabenhof, Vienna*
1989 Wettbewerb Hotelneubau am Južni Trg, Ljubljana, Slowenien, 1. Preis	*1989 Competition, new hotel building at Južni Trg, Slovenia, 1st prize*
Wettbewerb Gestaltung des Königsplatzes, Kassel, Deutschland	*Competition design of the Königsplatz, Kassel, Germany*
Projekt Kaufhaus Dogro, Klagenfurt, Österreich	*Project, Dogro store, Klagenfurt, Austria*
Projekt Umbau Geschäftshaus Priesterhausgasse, Klagenfurt, Österreich	*Project, conversion of Priesterhausgasse office building, Klagenfurt, Austria*
Möbelentwürfe in Marmor Serie Roveresca für Bigelli Marmi	*Furniture designs in marble, Roveresca line, for Bigelli Marmi*
Betten Saba für Wittmann	*Saba beds for Wittmann*

1989	Ausstellungshalle Technisches Museum Wien (zerstört) und Gestaltung der Ausstellung Phantasie und Industrie, Technisches Museum, Wien	1989	*Exhibition hall, Technical Museum of Vienna (destroyed) and design of the exhibition – Fantasy and Industry, Technical Museum, Vienna*
	Gestaltung der Ausstellung Veneto e Austria 1841–1866, Palazzo della Gran Guardia, Verona, Italien		*Design of the exhibition, Veneto e Austria 1841–1866, Palazzo della Gran Guardia, Verona*
	Einrichtung Architektenverein und Galerie Dessa, Ljubljana, Slowenien		*Interior design architectural association and Dessa gallery, Ljubljana, Slovenia*
	Umbau Bar und Bistro Platana, Ljubljana, Slowenien		*Conversion, Platana Bar and Bistro, Ljubljana, Slovenia*
1989/90	Gestaltung der Ausstellung Bismarck–Preußen, Deutschland und Europa, Martin Gropius Bau, Berlin	1989/90	*Design of the exhibition Bismarck-Prussia, Germany and Europe, Martin Gropius Building, Berlin*
	Gestaltung der Ausstellung Klar und lichtvoll wie eine Regel-Planstädte der Neuzeit, Schloß Karlsruhe, Deutschland		*Design of exhibition, Klar und lichtvoll wie eine Regel - Planned cities of modern times, Karlsruhe castle, Germany*
	Platzgestaltung Piazza XXIV Maggio, Cormons, Italien		*Square design, Piazza XXIV Maggio, Cormons, Italy*
	Zubau Einfamilienhaus Spazier, Kufstein, Österreich		*Addition to single-family-home, Spazier, Kufstein, Austria*
1989	Projekt Kirche Sv. Janez Bosko, Maribor, Slowenien	1989	*Project, Sv. Janez Bosko church, Maribor, Slovenia*
1989–94	Meidlinger Hauptstraße, Meidlinger Platzl–Neue Fußgängerbereiche, Wien	1989/94	*Meidlinger Hauptstrasse, Meidlinger Platzl, new pedestrian zones, Vienna*
	Wohnhausanlage Laab im Walde, Österreich		*Housing complex, Laab im Walde, Austria*
1990	Wettbewerb Bürogebäude am Mittelweg, Hamburg	1990	*Competition, office building at Mittelweg, Hamburg*
	Wettbewerb Erweiterung Technisches Museum, Wien, 3. Preis		*Competition, extension of Technical Museum, Vienna, 3rd prize*
	Einrichtung Technisches Museum, Bauabteilung, Wien		*Interior design, Technical Museum, building department, Vienna*
	Lampenentwurf Kubus–Cuboluce		*Light design, Kubus-Cuboluce*
	Umbau Galerie Sv. Donat, Piran, Slowenien		*Conversion, Sv. Donat gallery, Piran, Slovenia*
	Gutachterverfahren Graben West, Wien		*Consultant, Graben West, Vienna*
1990/91	Einrichtung Büro Cargonaut im Empire State Building, New York	1990/91	*Interior design, office Cargonaut, Empire State Building, New York*
1990–94	Umbau Hotel Laurin, Bozen, Italien (mit A. Mascotti)	1990–94	*Conversion, Hotel Laurin, Bozen, Italy (with A. Mascotti)*
1990–92	Marktstände Philharmonikergasse, Salzburg	1990–92	*Market booths, Philharmonikergasse, Salzburg*
1990	Umbau Museum Moderner Kunst Ca'Pesaro, Venedig (in Realisierung)	1990	*Conversion, Museum of Modern Art Ca'Pesaro, Venice (in realization)*
1990–93	Autohaus Mazda-Lietz, Waidhofen/Ybbs, Österreich	1990–93	*Car shop, Mazda-Lietz, Waidhofen/Ybbs, Austria*
	Bürozentrum Basler Versicherung, Wien (mit Suter + Suter)		*Office center, Basel Insurance Company, Vienna (with Suter + Suter)*
1990	Gutachten Donaukanal-Innere Stadt, Wien	1990	*Consultant, Danube canal - inner city, Vienna*
1990–93	Einfamilienhaus Reich-Rohrwig, Wien	1990–93	*Single-family-home, Reich-Rohrwig, Vienna*
1990–96	Slowenische Bank TKBCT, Triest, Italien (in veränderter Ausführung)	1990–96	*Slovenian Bank TKBCT, Trieste, Italy (in a modified realization)*
1990–94	Wohnhausanlage Case di Barcola, Triest, Italien	1990–94	*Housing complex, Case di Barcola, Trieste, Italy*
1990	Projekt Platzgestaltung und Stadtmöblierung, Via dell'Indipendenza, Bologna, Italien (mit M. Drabeni)	1990	*Project, square design and city furnishing, Via dell'Indipendenza, Bologna, Italy (with M. Drabeni)*
1991	Gutachten Umbau Kirche in Kirchham, Österreich	1991	*Consultant, conversion of Kirchham church, Austria*
	Gutachten Ideenfindung Schönbrunn, Wien		*Consultant, think-tank Schönbrunn, Vienna*
	Pavillons und Szenographie für das Theaterfestival «Mittelfest», Cividale, Italien		*Pavilions and scenography for the theater festival, "Mittelfest", Cividale, Italy*
1991–94	Ganztagshauptschule Dirmhirngasse, Wien	1991–94	*School Dirmhirngasse, Vienna*
1991	Projekt Bürohaus Universale, Wien		*Project, office building, Universale, Vienna*
	Projekt Kaufhaus Dogro, Klagenfurt, Österreich		*Project, Dogro store, Klagenfurt, Austria*
	Projekt Dachaufbau Hotel Imperial, Wien		*Project, roof addition, Hotel Imperial, Vienna*

1991–93 Umbau Bankfiliale Erste Österreichische Spar-Casse, Wien-Josefstadt

1991–94 Oberflächengestaltung U-Bahn 6, Leipziger Platz, Wien

1991 Projekt Bürohaus und Hotel Parkshop U4, Wien

1991/92 Umbau Galerie A + A, Madrid

1991 Projekt Sportbad Cavtat, Cavtat bei Dubrovnik, Kroatien

Projekt Einfamilienhaus Rinecker, München

1991–94 Umbau Hotel und Studentenwohnheim Korotan, Wien

1991/92 Wettbewerb Nordbahnhofgelände–Die neue Stadt, Wien, 1. Preis

1992 Wettbewerb Kunst.Halle.Krems, Österreich, 2. Preis

Entwicklungsstudie Nordbahnhofgelände–Areal B, Wien (mit H. Tesar)

Wettbewerb Hofbauergründe, Wien, 1. Preis (im Bau)

1992–95 Umbau Stadtbücherei Biberach, Deutschland

1992 Projekt Hotel Lux-Šumi, Ljubljana, Slowenien

Projekt Bürogebäude Mestre, Italien

1992–94 Stadtmöblierung für die Fußgängerzone Meidlinger Hauptstraße, Wien

1992 Bettenentwurf Carriola e Francescano für Teatro delle Muse

Projekt Büroturm für EKZ-Südpark, Klagenfurt, Österreich

Projekt Tankstelle Aral, Klagenfurt, Österreich

Wettbewerb Österreichisches Kulturinstitut, New York

Wettbewerb Gesundheitszentrum Schloß Wolfsberg, Krems, Österreich, 1. Preis

1993 Um- und Zubau Wohn- und Bürohaus Palais Erzherzog Karl, Wien

Realisierungswettbewerb Hauptverwaltung der Berliner Wasser-Betriebe, Berlin, 1. Preis

Veranstaltungsetage Ringturm, Dachebene, Wiener Städtische Versicherung, Wien (mit G. Podreka)

Neugestaltung der Hauptstraße in Fürstenfeld, Österreich

Wettbewerb Bürohaus «Tor zur Landeshauptstadt» im Regierungsviertel St. Pölten, Österreich, 1. Preis, (in Realisierung)

Wettbewerb Wohnbebauung Am Liesingbach, Wien-Oberlaa, 1. Preis (in Realisierung)

Expertenverfahren Wohnbebauung Grundäcker, Wien

Realisierungswettbewerb Breite Straße, Berlin-Mitte, Berlin

1994 Wettbewerb Kraftwerk Nußdorf, Wien, 1. Preis

Realisierungswettbewerb Bundeskanzleramt, Berlin

Wettbewerb Neugestaltung Rathausplatz St. Pölten, Österreich, 1. Preis (im Bau)

Einkaufszentrum und Hotel Greif-Areal, Bozen, Italien, (in Realisierung)

Büro- und Geschäftshaus Arndtstraße, Wien (in Realisierung)

1991–93 Conversion, bank branch Erste Österreichische Spar-Casse, Vienna-Josefstadt

1991–94 Surface design, subway 6, Leipziger Platz, Vienna

1991 Project, office building and hotel Parkshop U4, Vienna

1991/92 Conversion, A + A gallery, Madrid

1991 Project, sports bath Cavtat, Cavtat/Dubrovnik, Croatia

Project, single-family-home Rinecker, Munich

1991–94 Conversion, hotel and student housing, Korotan, Vienna

1991/92 Competition, North station grounds – The new city, Vienna, 1st prize

1992 Competition, Kunst.Halle.Krems, Austria, 2nd prize

Development study, North station grounds – Area B, Vienna, (with H. Tesar)

Competition, Hofbauergründe, Vienna, 1st prize (under construction)

1992–95 Conversion, Biberach municipal library, Germany

1992 Project, Hotel Lux-Šumi, Ljubljana, Slovenia

1992 Project, office building, Mestre, Italy

1992–94 City furnishings for the pedestrian zone, Meidlinger main street, Vienna

1992 Bed design, Carriola e Francescano for Teatro delle Muse

Project, office tower for Südpark shopping center, Klagenfurt, Austria

Project, gas station Aral, Klagenfurt, Austria

Competition, Austrian Cultural Institute, New York

Competition, Health center, Wolfsberg castle, Krems, Austria, 1st prize

1993 Conversion and addition, housing and office building, Palais Erzherzog Karl, Vienna

Realization competition, main administration building of the Berlin Water Works, Berlin, 1st prize

Company events facility, Ringturm, top floor, Vienna Municipal Insurance, Vienna (with G. Podreka)

New design of the Fürstenfeld main street, Austria

Competition, office building "Tor zur Landeshauptstadt" in the government district of St. Pölten, Austria, 1st prize (in realization)

Competition, housing development Am Liesingbach, Vienna – Oberlaa, 1st prize (in realization)

Procedural expert housing development, Grundäcker, Vienna

Realization competition, Breite Strasse, Berlin-Center, Berlin

1994 Competition, power plant, Nussdorf, Vienna, 1st prize

Realization competition, Bundeskanzleramt, Berlin

Competition, new design for Rathausplatz St. Pölten, 1st prize (under construction)

Shopping center and hotel, Greif-Areal, Bozen, Italy (in realization)

Office and commercial building, Arndtstrasse, Vienna (in realization)

1994	Masterplan Areal–Zanussi, Conegliano, Italien
	Inneneinrichtung Klinik Buchinger am Bodensee, Überlingen, Deutschland
	Projekt Bauvorhaben Breitenfurter-/Altmannsdorfer-Hetzendorferstraße, Wien
	Um- und Neubau Universität Maribor, Slowenien (in Realisierung)
	Wettbewerb Keramikmuseum Schloß Ludwigsburg, Ludwigsburg, Deutschland, 1. Preis
	Projekt Kiosk Rathausplatz Wien, Wien
	Büroetage im Ringturm Wiener Städtische Versicherung, Wien
1995	Realisierungswettbewerb Dresdner Bank, Pariser Platz, Berlin
	Wohnbebauung Remise–Nordbahnhofgelände, Wien (in Realisierung)
	Um- und Zubau Schloß Moralić, Bozjakovina, Kroatien (im Bau)
	Geschäfts- und Wohnhausanlage mit Bürohochhaus, Zentrum Handelskai, Wien (mit G. Peichl und R. Weber)
	Umbau des Österreichischen Kulturinstituts, Prag (im Bau)
	Wettbewerb Hauptplatzgestaltung und Fußgängerzone, Leoben, Österreich, 1. Preis (im Bau)
	Realisierungswettbewerb Krankenhaus Kaulsdorf, Berlin
	Gestaltung Via Mazzini–Verbindungsachse Piazza Bra (Arena) und Piazza dell'Erbe, Verona, Österreich (in Realisierung)
	Bürohaus Electrolux–Zanussi, Conegliano, Italien (im Bau)
	Wohnhausanlage in Conegliano, Italien (in Realisierung)
	Wettbewerb Wohnhausanlage Area Ex Junghans Giudecca, Venedig, 2. Preis (in Realisierung)
	Schmuckdesign für Juweliere Köchert, Wien
1995/96	Millenniumsausstellung «Die Donau–1000 Jahre Österreich», Historisches Museum der Stadt Wien im Schottenstift, Wien
1995	Wettbewerb Neugestaltung Slomškov Trg, Maribor, Slowenien, 1. Preis
1996	Brunnen Slomškov Trg, Maribor, Slowenien
	Gestaltung Bahnhofplatz Krems, Österreich (in Realisierung)
	Eingangshalle und Ausstellungssaal der Wiener Städtischen Versicherung, Ringturm, Wien
	Umbau des Donau Versicherungsgebäudes an der Ringstraße, Wien (im Bau)
	Parkstadt Unterliederbach für Hoechst, Frankfurt a. M. (in Realisierung)

1994	Master plan, Areal-Zanussi, Conegliano, Italy
	Interior design, Buchinger clinic, Lake Constance, Überlingen, Germany
	Project, construction, Breitenfurter-/Altmannsdorfer-Hetzendorferstrasse, Vienna
	Conversion and new building, Maribor university, Slovenia (in realization)
	Competition, ceramics museum in Ludwigsburg castle, Ludwigsburg, Germany, 1st prize
	Project, kiosk at Rathausplatz Vienna, Vienna
	Office floor in Ringturm, Vienna Municipal Insurance company, Vienna
1995	Realization competition, Dresdner Bank, Pariser Platz, Berlin
	Housing development, Remise-North station grounds, Vienna (in realization)
	Conversion and addition, Moralić castle, Bozjakovina, Croatia (under construction)
	Store and housing complex with high rise office building, Handelskai center, Vienna (with G. Peichl and R. Weber)
	Conversion of the Austrian Cultural Institute, Prague (under construction)
	Competition, Main Square design and pedestrian zone, Leoben, Austria, 1st prize (under construction)
	Realization competition, Kaulsdorf hospital, Berlin
	Design, Via Mazzini-connecting axis Piazza Bra (arena) and Piazza dell'Erbe, Verona (in realization)
	Office building, Electrolux-Zanussi, Conegliano, Italy (under construction)
	Housing complex in Conegliano, Italy (in realization)
	Competition, housing complex Area Ex Junghans-Giudecca, Venice, 2nd prize (in realization)
	Jewelry design for Köchert jewellers, Vienna
1995/96	Millennium exhibition "The Danube – 1000 years of Austria", Museum for History Vienna, in the Schottenstift, Vienna
1995	Competition, new design, Slomškov Trg, Maribor, Slovenia, 1st prize
1996	Fountain, Slomškov Trg, Maribor, Slovenia
	Design, Bahnhofsplatz Krems, Austria (in realization)
	Entrance lobby and exhibition hall of the Vienna Municipal Insurance company, Ringturm, Vienna
	Conversion of the Danube Insurance company building at Ringstrasse, Vienna (under construction)
	Park city, Unterliederbach for Hoechst, Frankfurt a.M. (in realization)

1980   *La presenza del passato.* Biennale di Venezia, Venezia (I)

1981   *Après le modernisme.* Festival d'Automne, Paris (F)

1982   *Après le modernisme.* San Francisco, Denver (USA)

        Aus der Wiener Architekturszene. Wiener Festwochen, Wien (A)

1982–84 *Versuche zur Baukunst.* Wien, Linz, Innsbruck, Klagenfurt, Salzburg (A), Bologna (I), Budapest (H)

1984   *Boris Podrecca–Der Dialog mit der Stadt.* Museum für Moderne Kunst, Beograd (YU), Zagreb (CRO), Ljubljana (SLO), Budapest (H), Trieste, Roma (I)

        Oeuvres sur papier. Architekturzeichnungen, Galerie Beaufreton, Nantes (F)

1986   *Transgression and Identity.* Galerie 9H, London (GB)

        3 Arbeiten in Wien. Obalne galerije in Piran (SLO) und 12. Salon arhitekture in Beograd (YU)

        Créer dans le Créé. Centre Georges Pompidou, Paris (F)

        Architekturzeichnungen. Galerie Interart, Wien (A)

1987   *Le città immaginate. Nove progetti per nove città. Il progetto nell'Arsenale Venezia.* XVII. Triennale di Milano, Palazzo dell'Arte, Milano (I)

        The Work of Boris Podrecca. Gund Hall, Harvard University GSD Graduate School of Design, Cambridge, Massachusetts (USA)

        Boris Podrecca. Pinacoteca Nazionale, Palazzo Pepoli, Bologna (I)

1987/88 *3 Städte–3 Plätze–ein Architekt, Universitätsplatz, Teil einer Gestaltungstrilogie.* St. Blasius Kirche, Salzburg (A), Sacile (I), Piran (I)

1987   *Zeichnungen österreichischer Architekten.* Architekten- und Ingenieurkammer Schleswig-Holstein, Kiel (D)

        L'Arsenale Riordinato. Nuovi progetti per Venezia. Triennale di Milano, Piazza San Marco, Venezia (I)

1988   *Boris Podrecca. Il progetto di architettura versus l'architettura del progetto.* Comune di Padova (I), Associazione cultura Italia–Austria, Consolate Generale d'Austria, Ferrara (I)

1989   *Roveresca. Arbeiten in Marmor.* Ausstellung der Firma Bigelli Marmi, Senigallia (I)

        Wien 1960–1990. Museum für Moderne Kunst in Bolzano, Beitrag: Textile Metaphern, Milano, Valsugana, Roma (I)

        Wien Möbel. Wiener Secession, Wien (A), Paris (F), Helsinki (S)

1990   *SABA–Neue Betten.* Möbelhaus Henn, Wien (A)

        L'Arte della Tavola. Abitare il Tempo 1990, Verona (I)

1991   *Boris Podrecca. Beitrag zur Architektur–Biennale.* Galleria di Architettura Fondazione Masieri, Dorsoduro, Venezia (I)

1992   *Wien, Architektur–Der Stand der Dinge.* Planungswerkstatt, Wien (A)

        ZwischenStromLand. Wien im Aufbruch. 1. u. 2. Wiener Architektur Seminar, StadtRaumRemise, Wien (A)

1992   *LeMarcheEuropee.* Abitare Il Tempo 1992, Fiera di Verona, Padiglione Progetti e Territori, Verona (I)

1992/93 *Architettura e Spazio Sacro nella Modernità.* Biennale di Venezia, Antichi Granai della Giudecca, Venezia (I)

        Neue Ritualbauten für die drei monotheistischen Weltreligionen. Galerie an der Finkenstraße, München (D)

        Sacred Space in the Modern Age. Accademia Italiana, London (GB)

        Neue Sakralbauten–Synagogen, Moscheen, Kirchen. Orangerie im Neuen Garten, Potsdam (D)

        Greek Association of Architects, Athen (GR)

1992   *Boris Podrecca–Arquitectura.* Galerie de Arte A+A, Madrid (E)

1993   *Auf dem Weg ins 21. Jahrhundert–Stadtentwicklungsplan für Wien.* Rathaus und Planungswerkstatt Wien (A)

        Die Ökologische Stadt. Arkadenhof, Rathaus, Wien (A)

1994   *Neuer Wohnbau in Wien–Vienna Housing: Trends and Prototypes.* Wiener Planungswerkstatt, Wien (A), UCLA Los Angeles, UC Berkeley, Arizona State University (USA)

        Stadteinfälle. 14 internationale Projekte für Wien. Architektur Zentrum Wien (A)

1994/95 *Boris Podrecca, Wien: Basler Bürozentrum–Diener & Diener, Basel: Bürohaus Basler Versicherungen.* Architekturforum Maculan–Aedes, Wien (A), Galerie und Architekturforum Aedes, Berlin (D)

1995   *Dizajnerski Crtež–Designer's Drawings.* 13th International Biennal of Drawings, Moderna Galerija Rijeka, Rijeka (CRO)

        Wiener Stadtmöbel–Der Stand der Dinge. Wiener Planungswerkstatt, Wien (A)

        Wien, Architektur–Der Stand der Dinge. Wiener Planungswerkstatt, Wien (A), Los Angeles, New York (USA), Madrid, Sevilla (E), Roma, Napoli, Firenze (I), Berlin (D)

        Österreich–Architektur im 20. Jahrhundert. Deutsches Architektur Museum, Frankfurt (D)

        Exhibition on Viennese Architecture. Kyushu University, Fukuoka, Japan

1995/96 *Österreichiches Kulturinstitut New York. Ein baukünstlerischer Wettbewerb.* Wien (A), New York, Washington (USA), Stuttgart, Bonn, Berlin (D), Zagreb (CRO), Krakau (PL)

1996   *Sarajevo. Neuresničeni projekti za razdejano mesto/Projets non réalisés pour une ville détruite/Unbuilt Projects for a Destroyed City.* Moderna Galerija Ljubljana, Ljubljana (SLO), Sarajevo, Bosnien

La Presenza del Passato. La Biennale di Venezia. Venezia 1980, p. 262–263.

La présence de l'histoire. L'après modernisme. Ausstellungskatalog. Festival d'automne à Paris. Paris 1981, p. 234–235.

La modernité ou l'esprit du temps. Biennale de Paris. Paris 1982, p. 84–87.

Glancey, Jonathan, *Three Viennese interiors*, in: The Architectural Review, No. 1023. London 1982, p. 58–65.

Fillion, Odile, *Les atmosphères de Podrecca*, in: créé architecture intérieure, No. 188. Paris 1982, p. 102–109.

Dialoghi viennesi, in: Casabella, No. 483. Milano 1982, p. 30–31.

Boris Podrecca, in: Versuche zur Baukunst, Ausstellungskatalog. Wien 1982, p. 129–152.

Boris Podrecca, in: Versuche zur Baukunst, Ausstellungskatalog. Wien 1983, p. 157–184.

Haus Daneu, Villa Vojcsik, in: Toshi-Jutaku–urban housing, (Ed.) Kajima Institute, No. 186. Tokyo 1983, p. 52–57.

Hrausky, Andrej, *Predavnje. Boris Podrecca v Ljubljani*, in: ab architektov bilten, No. 64/65. Ljubljana 1983, p. 21–22.

Maggiori, Bepi, *A Vienna. Casa come città*, in: Casa Vogue, No. 155. Milano 1984, p. 290–297.

Savi, Vittorio, *Carlo Scarpa da svelare*, in: Casa Vogue, No. 157. Milano 1984, p. 186–188.

Dal Co, Francesco, *Dopo la festa*, in: Casa Vogue, No. 157. Milano 1984, p. 189–191.

Lucan, Jacques, *Travaux viennois. Boris Podrecca*, in: AMC, No. 4. Paris 1984, p. 24–37.

Lucan, Jacques, *Carlo Scarpa 1906–1978. Une exposition à Venise*, in: AMC, No. 5. Paris 1984, p. 72–75.

Doubilet, Susan, *Vienna: Sons and fathers, Magnificent obsession*, in: Progressive Architecture, No. 3. Cleveland 1984, p. 57–63.

Gavrić, Zoran, *Boris Podrecca. Arhitektura u rasponu tradiranog*. Katalog. (Ed.) Muzej savremene umetnosti Beograd. Beograd 1984.

Intérieur/Extérieur, in: Biennale de Paris. Architecture 1985. Katalog. Paris 1985, p. 36–41.

Masopust, Dietrich, *Perspektiven für Salzburg. Boris Podrecca. Zur Gestaltung des Salzburger Universitätsplatzes*, in: Salzburger Bildhauer-symposion 1985.

Lootsma, Bart, *Boris Podrecca en de Weense traditie/Boris Podrecca and the Viennese tradition. Vier projecten van deze Weense architect en een interview met hem door Pieter Jan Gijsberts/Four projects by this Viennese architect and an interview by Pieter Jan Gijsberts*, in: Forum, No. 303. Amsterdam 1985, p. 122–129.

Müller, Dorothee, *Tradition trägt. Boris Podrecca*, in: Gala, No. 6. München 1985, p. 30–34.

Grimmer, Vera, *Prigradnja ulazne lode trgovine pokućstvom Kika u Wiener Neustadtu*, in: čovjek i prostor, No. 1. Zagreb 1985, p. 30–31.

Steiner, Dietmar, *Always on the move*, in: Transgression and Identity. Ausstellungskatalog. 9H Gallery. London 1986, p. 1–3.

Steiner, Dietmar, *"Viennese Architect" Boris Podrecca*, in: a+u Architecture and Urbanism, No.190. Monographische Ausgabe. Tokyo 1986, p. 81–130.

Wang, Wilfried, *Cultural Evolution*, in: AJ The Architects' Journal, No. 3. London 1986, p. 20–23.

Romanelli, Marco, *Boris Podrecca. "Humanic"–Casa Piccola, Vienna*, in: domus, No. 670. Milano 1986, p. 56–60.

Merkac, Janko, *Ustvarjati v ze ustvarjenem*, in: Celovski Zvon, No. IV/11. Klagenfurt 1986, p. 63–76.

Grimmer, Vera, *U dijalogu s Plečnikom*, in: čovjek i prostor, No. 4. Zagreb 1986, p. 22–23.

Caldenby, Claes, *Wien genom tre*, in: arkitektur, No. 3. Stockholm 1986, p. 3–9.

Wenz-Gahler, Ingrid, *Licht- und Farbklänge für Haarkunst*, in: Gestaltete Läden. Leinfelden-Echterdingen 1986, p. 77–79.

Boris Podrecca, in: Le città immaginate. Un Viaggo in Italia. Nove Progetti per nove città. Katalog. XVII. Triennale di Milano 1987, p. 137–139.

Moneo, José Rafael/Wang, Wilfried, *Boris Podrecca*. Ausstellungskatalog. (Ed.) Harvard University Graduate School of Design. New York 1987.

Bürgersinn und Aufbegehren. Biedermeier und Vormärz in Wien 1815–1848. Ausstellungskatalog. Historisches Museum der Stadt Wien, Wien 1987.

Boris Podrecca. Il progetto di architettura versus l'architettura del progetto, in: Parametro, No. 153. Monographische Ausgabe. Faenza 1987.

Boris Podrecca. Architektur, in: bauforum, No. 121. Monographische Ausgabe. Wien 1987, p. 13–44.

Bru, Eduard/Mateo, Josep Lluis, *Zapateria „HUMANIC–Casa Piccola", Viena (Austria)*, in: Arquitectura europea contemporànea. Barcelona 1987, p. 50–51.

Gijsberts, Pieter Jan, *Boris Podrecca. Intervju z arhitektom/An Interview with the architect*, in: sinteza, No. 75–78. Ljubljana 1987, p. 57–73.

Hoddé, Rainier, *L'Ombre des lieux, la peau des choses. Entretien avec Boris Podrecca*, in: Cahiers du CCI. Monuments éphémères: BD, mode, théâtre, lumières… et architecture, No. 3. Paris 1987, p. 61–64.

Steiner, Dietmar, *Boris Podrecca. Mit Wiener Gespür*, in: architektur & wohnen, Heft 5. Hamburg 1988, p. 118–123.

Cappellato, Gabriele, *Un bilancio del Biedermeier*, in: domus, No. 693. Milano 1988, p. 7–9.

Savi, Vittorio, *A Vienna. Il Biedermeier di Podrecca,* in: Casa Vogue, No. 195. Milano 1988, p. 254–261.

Cherubini, Roberto, *Alpe Adria. Un colloquio con Boris Podrecca*, in: Arredo Urbano, No. 25, Roma 1988, p. 52, 54–55.

Bugatti, Angelo, *Segno e disegno. Uno spazio commerciale*, in: Costruire, No. 64. Milano 1988, p. 116–119.

Oltre la città, la metropoli. Cartografia: Il significato dei sistemi imformali e invisibili. in: Le città del mondo e il futuro delle metropoli. Milano 1988, p. 92–95.

Boris Podrecca. Architecture and exhibit design, in: Via. Re-Presentation. Journal of the Graduate School of Fine Arts. University of Pennsylvania, No. 9. New York 1988, p. 129–138.

Tabor, Jan, *Baukunst für Belesene*, in: Rendezvous Wien, Heft 1. Wien 1988, p. 16–18.

Contemporary Interiors in Vienna. Boris Podrecca, in: SD Space Design, No. 290. Tokyo 1988, p. 37–44.

Kunsthalle Berlin/Kunsthalle de Berlin, in: Berlin–Denkmal oder Denkmo-dell?/Berlin–Monument ou modèle de pensée?. Berlin 1988, p. 218–221.

Kapfinger, Otto/Kneissl, Franz E., *Dichte Packung. Architektur aus Wien.* Salzburg/Wien 1989.

Tabor, Jan, *Anmerkungen zum Werk Boris Podreccas. Das Wiener Dilemma eines begabten Architekten. Boris Podrecca. 3 x Laibach*, in: Möbel Raum Design, No. 2. Wien 1989, p. 19–32.

Über Kaufhäuser in Klagenfurt, Linz und Salzburg, in: wettbewerbe, No. 86/87. Wien 1989, p. 60–71.

Boris Podrecca, in: Roveresca. Opere in pietra e marmo. Katalog. Senigallia 1989.

Robert, Jean-Paul, *La grammaire et le style, Boris Podrecca. Dans cet entretien, Podrecca illustre ses rapports avec la culture viennoise*, in: L'Architecture d'Aujourd'hui, No. 264. Paris 1989, p. 123–128.

Il Veneto e l'Austria. Vita e cultura artistica nelle città venete 1814–1866. Ausstellungskatalog. Palazzo della Gran Guardia, Verona. Milano 1989.

Phantasie und Industrie. Ausstellungskatalog. Technisches Museum Wien. Wien 1989.

Klar und lichtvoll wie eine Regel. Planstädte der Neuzeit. Ausstellungskatalog. Badisches Landesmuseum Karlsruhe. Karlsruhe 1990.

Bismarck–Preußen, Deutschland und Europa. Katalog. Deutsches Historisches Museum Berlin. Berlin 1990.

Bismarck–Preußen, Deutschland und Europa. Ausstellungsdokumentation. Deutsches Historisches Museum Berlin. Berlin 1990.

Achleitner, Friedrich, *Österreichische Architektur im 20. Jahrhundert. Ein Führer in vier Bänden. 1.–12. Bezirk.* Band III/1. Salzburg/Wien 1990.

Gijsberts, Peter Jan, *Metaforen en metamorfosen in het werk van Boris Podrecca*, in: de Architect, No. 9. Den Haag 1990, p. 69–81.

Grimmer, Vera, *Kretanje prema jugu Borisa Podrecce*, in: covjek i prostor, No 1. Zagreb 1990, p. 18–19.

Arlotti, Maria Laura/Angelini, Maria, *Boris Podrecca. La storia ininterrotta*, in: Incontri internazionali di architettura. Pescara 1990, p.11–24.

Mikeln, Tone/Prelovšek, Damjan, *Boris Podrecca. Galerija Sv. Donat. Galleria San Donato. Gallerie St. Donat.* Piran 1990.

Chramosta, Walter M., *Neue nautische Notationen oder das Wasser, die Stadt und eine Versicherung*, in: Perspektiven, Heft 4. Wien 1991, p. 6–7.

– Eine profane Dreifaltigkeit des Geldes, in: Basler Bürozentrum. (Ed.) Basler Versicherungs-AG für Österreich. Wien 1991.

– Una trilogia profana del denaro, in: phalaris, No. 14. Venezia 1991, p.14–19.

– Delikates Dreigestirn im kakanischen Kosmos. Drei rezente Projekte von Boris Podrecca in drei benachbarten Ländern, in: Architektur & Bauforum, No. 145. Wien 1991, p. 17–29.

Tabor, Jan/Haslinger, Regina, *Möbelhaus Kika Klagenfurt*, in: Architektur und Industrie, Wien 1991, p. 92–93.

Tolmein, Gabriele, *Frischer Wind weht durch altes Gemäuer*, in: Häuser, No.1. Hamburg 1991, p. 12–21.

Mulazzani, Marco, *Boris Podrecca. Galleria San Donato, Pirano*, in: domus, No. 728. Milano 1991, p. 52–57.

Galerie Saint Donat à Piran, in: L'Architecture d'Aujourd'hui, No. 275. Paris 1991, p. 78–79.

Radović, Darja, Boris Podrecca–Protiv „esperanto grimasa" u arhitekturi, in: život umjetnosti, No. 50. Zagreb 1991, p. 80–83.

Commercial Spaces. Kika, in: European Masters/3. (Ed.) Francisco Asensio Cerver. Barcelona 1991, p. 206–215.

Frediani, Gianluca, *Complesso residenziale a Vienna*, in: La sfida architettonica. Il progetto di Architettura tra ideazione e conoscenza. La formazione dell'architetto nella prospettiva europea. Roma 1991, p. 254–255.

Cividale si trasforma in città-teatro, in: Mittelfest. Cividale 1991, p.12–13.

Petrovic Casanova, Beatrice, *Archicultura e città. Progetto e contesto nel lavoro di Boris Podrecca*, in: AD/Vienna. Milano 1992, p. 87.

Architettura e spazio sacro nella modernità. Quadrilatero cerchio ellisse, in: Biennale di Venezia. (Ed.) Renato Minetto. Venezia 1992, p. 299–300.

Vatter, Klaus, *Der Stadtteil der Zukunft: Stadtentwicklungszone Nordbahnhof*, in: Perspektiven, Heft 2. Wien 1992, p. 52–53.

– Beispiele zur inneren Stadtentwicklung, in: Perspektiven, Heft 10. Wien 1992, p. 51–54.

Steiner, Dietmar/Chramosta, Walter M., *Auto und Architektur, Wallfahrtsort der Voralpenbeschleuniger*, in: Architektur & Bauforum, No.152. Wien 1992, p. 69–79.

Steiner, Dietmar, *Auto, Architektur und Niemandsland/Car, Architecture and No-One's Land*, in: Piranesi, No. 1/I. Ljubljana 1992, p. 48–57.

Angelillo, Antonio, *Progetti per spazi pubblici di Boris Podrecca*, in: Casabella, No. 590. Milano 1992, p. 52–59, 69–70.

Pirhofer, Gottfried, *Vienna: il futuro verso il Danubio*, in: Casabella, No. 594. Milano 1992, p. 34–47.

Boris Podrecca, Pustijerna, Dubrovnik, in: Tefchos, No. 9. Athen 1992, p. 108–111.

Cappellato, Gabriele, *Incontri: Boris Podrecca. L'allestimento come dialogo*, in: Progex, No. 8. Milano 1992, p. 12–25.

Moneo, Jose Rafael/Chramosta, Walter M./Rozanc, Marjan/Kozelj, Janez/Vodopivec, Ales, *Boris Podrecca. Architecture.* Katalog anläßlich der Ausstellung in Madrid 1992. (Ed.) Obalne Galerije, Piran 1992.

Sarnitz, August, *Museums–Positionen in Österreich*, in: Museums–Positionen. Bauten und Projekte in Österreich. Salzburg 1992, p. 55–56, 71.

Angelillo, Antonio, *Boris Podrecca: la forma dello spazio eloquente*, in: Interni, No. 420. Milano 1992, p. 132–139.

Zacek, Patricia, *Der Denkansatz entspringt dem Rucksack des Unbewußten, Gedanken zum Möbeldesign Boris Podreccas*, in: Möbel Raum Design, No. 4. Wien 1992, p. 61, 74–81.

Huidobro, Enrique, *Galeria A + A. Refinamiento constructivo en el mínimo espacio*, in: Diseño Interior, No. 24. Madrid 1993, p. 66–73.

Purtscher, Vera, *Mein Triangel. Im Gespräch mit Boris Podrecca*, in: Architektur der Gegenwart. Konzepte, Projekte, Bauten. Stuttgart 1993, p.160.

Chramosta, Walter M., *Podrecca*, in: Österreichisches Kulturinstitut New York. Ein baukünstlerischer Entwurf/Austrian Cultural Institute New York. An Architectural Competition. Innsbruck 1993, p.100–101.

Pirhofer, Gottfried, *Stadtentwicklungsbereiche*, in: Wien wächst–Wohnen und Arbeiten, No. 2. Wien 1993, p. 21–27.

Zacek, Patricia, *Ein Augenaufschlag in die Umgebung–Neue Elemente für städtische Muster*, in: Architektur & Bauforum, No. 158. Wien 1993, p. 115–122.

Salisburgo la verde, in: Lotus Quaderni, No. 19. Milano 1993, p. 66, 68–69, 80–82.

Richards, Ivor, *Developing typologies of sacred space and form*, in: Architettura e spazio sacro nella modernità. Katalog. München 1993, p. 50.

Vitas, Elena, *Boris Podrecca: realtà e sogni transdanubiani appoggiati su di una sedia di Adolf Loos*, in: Vienna. I misteri di Vindobona. Neapel 1993, p. 117–129.

Sparsam. Umbau einer Bankfiliale in Wien, in: AIT Architektur Innenarchitektur Technischer Ausbau. Banken Versicherungen Behörden, No. 12. Leinfelden-Echterdingen 1994, p. 62–67.

Grimmer, Vera, *Skriveni život kuča*, in: čovjek i prostor, No. 5/6. Zagreb 1994, p. 26–27.

Wirkungsvoll. Die Kunstgalerie A+A in Madrid, in: AIT Architektur Innenarchitektur Technischer Ausbau, No. 9 Spezial. Leinfelden-Echterdingen 1994, p. 50–53.

Zschokke, Walter, *Ein Bauwerk bildet Stadt/A Building Creates Urbanity*, in: Boris Podrecca. Basler Bürozentrum Wien. Katalog. (Ed.) Aedes-Galerie und Architekturforum. Berlin 1994.

– Ein Bauwerk bildet Stadt, in: Architektur & Bauforum, No. 165. Wien 1994, p. 73–81.

– Signifikant–Zwei Verwaltungsgebäude der Basler Versicherungsgruppe in Wien und in Basel, in: AIT Architektur Innenarchitektur Technischer Ausbau, No. 12. Leinfelden-Echterdingen 1994, p. 68–73.

– Urbanes Signal im Stadtgrau/An Urbane Signal in Vienna's Tenement District, in: Piranesi, No. 4/III. Ljubljana 1994, p. 50–61.

Masiero, Roberto, *Uffici della Basler Versicherung a Vienna*, in: Casabella, No. 618. Milano 1994, p. 62–66, 71.

Lootsma, Bart, *Housing in Vienna. Urban Development in the Socialdemocratic Tradition*, in: de Architect, Special issue 56. 's-Gravenhage 1994, p. 44–51.

Thurn und Taxis, Lilli, *Wohnzeile in Wien–Donaustadt. Dichter Wohnen*, in: Baumeister, No. 12. München 1994, p. 40–44.

Tillner, Silja, *Vienna Housing: Trends and Prototypes*. Ausstellungskatalog. Los Angeles 1994, p. 8–9.

Purtscher, Vera, *Lebenszyklen einer Villa – und ihre wundersame Errettung*, in: Möbel Raum Design, No. 2. Wien 1994, p. 102–108.

Boris Podrecca. Riqualificazioni ambientali a Salisburgo, Pirano, Cormons e Bologna, in: paesaggio urbano, No.3/4. Bologna 1994, p. 74–81.

Dvorak, Wolfgang, *Wien ins 21. Jahrhundert. Stadtplanung für eine ökologische und soziale Gründerzeit*. (Ed.) Magistrat der Stadt Wien–Stadtplanung Wien. Wien 1994.

Ašič, Ana, *Intervju: Boris Podrecca. Delo prihaja pome*, in: jana ambient, No. 3. Ljubljana 1994, p. 38–49.

Purtscher, Vera, *Filiale di banca a Vienna/Bank branch in Vienna*, in: domus, No. 769. Milano 1995, p. 40–45.

Brate, Tomaž, *Slovenija na Dunaju/Slovenia in Vienna*, in: Piranesi, No. 5, 6/IV. Ljubljana 1995, p. 52–60.

Segantini, Maria Alessandra, *Complesso commerciale e per uffici Basler Versicherung*, in: Habitat Ufficio, No. 72. Milano 1995, p. 38–47.

Achleitner, Friedrich, *Österreichische Architektur im 20. Jahrhundert. Ein Führer in vier Bänden. 13.–18. Bezirk*. Band III/ 2. Salzburg/Wien 1995.

Harather, Karin, *Haus-Kleider–Zum Phänomen der Bekleidung in der Architektur. Das kleidsame Tuch*. Wien/Köln/Weimar 1995. p. 117–120.

Waechter-Böhm, Liesbeth, *Architektur des Milieus*, in: Architektur Aktuell, No. 177. Wien 1995, p. 36–49.

Hellmayr, Nikolaus, *Bildungsbauten Schule in Wien. Eine Schule der Neugierde*, in: Leonardo, No. 5. Augsburg 1995, p. 22–26.

Favole, Paolo, *Boris Podrecca – Drei städtische Projekte*, in: Plätze der Gegenwart. Frankfurt/New York 1995, p. 82, 86–91.

Sarnitz, August/Kapfinger, Otto/Chramosta, Walter M.,*Wien, Architektur. Der Stand der Dinge/Vienna, Architecture. The State of the Art*. Wien 1995, p. 10, 19–21, 54–56.

Österreich. Architektur im 20. Jahrhundert. Deutsches Architektur-Museum Frankfurt am Main. Architektur Zentrum Wien. (Ed.) Annette Becker/Dietmar Steiner/Wilfried Wang. München/New York 1995, p. 112–113, 300–301, 341.

Zugmann, Gerald, *architecture in the box. architectural photography 1980–1995*. Wien/New York 1995, p. 31–38.

Bigatton, Walter/Bordugo, Maurizio/Lutman, Guido/Moranduzzo, Sara, *Fontanafredda. Chiesa Parrocchiale del SS. Redentore*, in: 1945–1995. Architettura nel Friuli Occidentale. Pordenone 1995, p. 113–117.

Casciani, Stefano/Ducoté, Barbara/Irace, Fulvio/Zunino, Maria Giulia, *Arredo Urbano? Dizionario di Luoghi e Cose*, in: Abitare, No. 340. Milano 1995, p. 53, 164–166.

Orben, Claudia, *Die Ethik in der Architektur. Österreichische Professoren im Ausland*, in: Architektur & Bauforum, No. 173. Wien 1995, p. 32–37.

Bucher, Viktor, *10 Fragen an 10 Architekten*, in: Architektur & Bauforum, No. 174. Wien 1995, p. 72–85.

Behal, Vera, *Podrecca o Plečnikovi*, in: Architekt, No. 14/15, 16/17. Praha 1995, p.1, 8–9 / p.1, 10.

Dimster, Frank, *Boris Podrecca. Kaufhaus Kika Klagenfurt. Autohaus Mazda Lietz. Bürohaus Basler Versicherung*, in: Die neue österreichische Architektur. Stuttgart 1995, p. 176–197.

Wien, Stadtmöbel–Der Stand der Dinge/Vienna, Urban Furniture. The State of the Art. (Ed.) Stadtentwicklung und Stadtplanung Wien. Wien 1995. p. 13–15, 26–27, 32–37.

Klopf, Peter/Pirhofer, Gottfried/Schenekl, Manfred, *Stadtachsen–Die U-Bahn*, in: StadtBauwelt, No. 126. Berlin 1995, p. 1380–1383.

Bernik, Stane, in: Dizajnerski crtež/Designer's Drawings.13. Medunarodni Biennale Crteža/13th International Biennal of Drawings. Rijeka 1995, p. 81–82, 126.

Boris Podrecca, in: 581 Architects in the World. (Ed.) Atsushi Sato. Tokyo 1995. p. 147.

Chramosta, Walter M., *Ganztagshauptschule Dirmhirngasse Wien 23*. Projekte und Konzepte, Heft 5. (Ed.) Stadtplanung Wien. Wien 1995.

Waechter-Böhm, Liesbeth, *Boris Podrecca. Stadtgespräch. Umbau eines slowenischen Studentenwohnheims und einer Bankfiliale in Wien Josefstadt*, in: Architektur Aktuell, No. 187/188. Wien 1996, p. 27, 84–95.

– Boris Podrecca. Erster Preis in Maribor, in: Architektur Aktuell, No. 189. Wien 1996, p. 6.

Rožanc, Marjan, *Una migrazione*, in: Piano Progetto Città, No. 15. Pescara 1996, p. 62.

Dimitrijević, Braco/Chaslin, François, *Sarajevo. Unbuilt Projects for a Destroyed City*. Ljubljana 1996, p. 76.

Faiferri, Massimo, *Opere recenti di Boris Podrecca*, in: L'Industria delle Costruzioni, No. 292. Roma 1996, p. 4–32.

M 1 : 333–Innovative Austrian Architecture. (Ed.) Ramesh Kumar Biswas. Wien 1996, p. 37, 41, 71, 94, 172–173, 212, 214.

Dešman, Miha, *Wien bleibt Wien. Intervju z Borisom Podrecco*, in: ab arhitektov bilten, No. 131/132. Ljubljana 1996, p. 10–17.

Grimmer, Vera, *Nakit je radost življenja*, in: čovjek i prostor, No.1/2. Zagreb 1996, p. 34–35.

Tilman, Harm, *Bevroren stedebouw. Boris Podrecca, Hauptschule Dirmhirngasse Wien–Liesing / Weense ontwikkeling stagneert. Experimentele ontwerpen stilgelegd*, in: de Architect, No. 62. 's-Gravenhage 1996, p. 26–29, 38–49.

Die Donau. 1000 Jahre Österreich. Eine Reise. Ausstellungskatalog. Historisches Museum der Stadt Wien. Wien 1996.

Modern–Post-Modern–Prä-Antik. Über die erste Architektur-Biennale 1980 in Venedig. "Die Präsenz der Vergangenheit", in: bauforum, No. 81. Wien 1980, p. 19–25.

Max Fabiani. Die Wiener Jahre, in: Max Fabiani 1865–1962. Bauten und Projekte. Ausstellungskatalog. Wien 1982.

Jože Plečnik, in: Casabella, No. 476/477. Milano 1982, p. 96–103.

Plašč Zaprtega, in: ab arhitektov bilten, No. 62/63. Ljubljana 1982.

La presunta particolarità, in: Carlo Scarpa. Opera completa. (Ed.) Francesco Dal Co/Giuseppe Mazzariol. Milano 1984, p. 241–245.

Wien – Venedig am Beispiel Carlo Scarpas, in: Reflexionen und Aphorismen zur österreichischen Architektur. Wien 1984, p. 428–431.

La disponibilità del fatto oggettivo riflessioni su Adolf Loos, la sua missione e la sua scuola, in: Parametro, No. 126. Faenza 1984, p. 10–15.

"Le savoir est pouvoir". Les maisons du peuple à Vienne, in: Maisons du peuple. Architecture pour le peuple. Bruxelles 1984, p. 125–139.

O spletu odnosov nastajanja arhitekture, in: ab arhitektov bilten, No. 72. Ljubljana 1984, p. 28–33.

Aufsätze über Bauen in Wien. Gottfried Semper, Jože Plečnik, Adolf Loos und seine Schule, Carlo Scarpa, in: Boris Podrecca. Arhitektura u rasponu tradiranog. (Ed.) Muzej savremene umetnosti Beograd. Beograd 1984.

Vienne–Paris, une question de température, in: La recherche en architecture. Un bilan international. Marseille 1986, p. 113–115.

Adolf Loos. Villa Müller, in: AMC, No. 3. Paris 1984, p. 51–57.

L'elemento colettivo di una continuità, in: Casabella, No.512. Milano 1985, p. 14–17.

In anteprima su una mostra/Jože Plečnik, architetto sloveno. Riflessioni sull'opera, in: Casa Vogue, No. 170. Milano 1986, p. 65.

Vernunft der Intuition. Carlo Scarpa und das Bauen in Venezien, in: Alte Bauten–Neue Kunst. Denkmalpflege und zeitgenössisches Kunstgeschehen. Wien 1986, p. 63–74.

Transgression and identity. Boris Podrecca. Ausstellungskatalog. (Ed.) 9H Gallery. London 1986.

Temporality and the Proximity of Things, in: Boris Podrecca. Ausstellungskatalog. (Ed.) Harvard University Graduate School of Design. New York 1987, p. 10–11.

L'Arsenale riordinato. Nuovi progetti per Venezia. XVII. Triennale di Milano, Venezia 1987, p. 66–69.

Falsa memoria e vera architettura/False memory and true architecture, in: Architettura Monumento Memoria. Venezia 1987, p. 119–124.

L'architettura di tre piazze. Salisburgo, Piran, Sacile, in: Arredo Urbano, No. 25. Roma 1988, p. 56–59.

Zu Hause und anderswo. Bundesallee und Etliches, in: Großstadtarchitektur. Sommerakademie für Architektur. Berlin 1989, p. 99–105.

Podrecca, Boris/Cappellato, Gabriele/Macchietto, Marisa, *Ipotesi di intervento sull'immagine urbana della città*, in: Manifesto dell'Arredo Urbano. Quaderni die AU Rivista Arredo Urbano. Roma 1989. p. 36–45.

Vienna: il senso del limite, in: phalaris, No.12. Venezia 1991, p. 44–46.

Podrecca, Boris/Drabeni, Mirna, *Via dell'indipendenza a Bologna. Studio per la sistemazione e la riqualificazione degli spazi pubblici*, in: Bologna. Immagine Urbana e Flussi della città. Roma 1992, p. 82–89.

Boris Podrecca. Institut für Innenraumgestaltung und Entwerfen, in: Stuttgarter Architekturschule. Stuttgart 1992, p. 82–85.

Topos und Typus, in: Zukunft der Gegenwart–Über neues Bauen in historischem Kontext. (Ed.) Egon Schirmbeck, Stuttgart 1994, p. 169–180.

Nymphen, Styx und Tröpferlbad. Architektenbäder, in: Bad exclusiv, Architektur & Bauforum, No. 167. Wien 1994.

Qualità urbana... innanzitutto!, in: Città di confine. Conversazioni sul futuro di Gorizia e Nova Gorica. (Ed.) Alfonso Angelillo/Antonio Angelillo/Chiara Menato. Portogruaro 1994, p. 175–192.

Alpe Adria. Architekturparallelen, in: Alpe Adria, Ausstellungskatalog. Klagenfurt/Udine/Ljubljana 1995.

DAS ATELIER / *THE STUDIO* 1980–95

Gotthard Eiböck, Mitautor bei vielen Arbeiten und Projekten. / ***Gotthard Eiböck**, Co-author of many works and projects.*

Volker Auch-Schwelk / Marc Berutto / Ramesh Kumar Biswas / Matthias Bjørnsen / Leonardo Blasetti / Miloš Bobić / Ursina Brunner / Gabriele Cappellato / Elena Carlini / Zette Cazalas / Federica Cerami / Marjeta Černe / Walter M. Chramosta / Beatrice Ciruzzi / Mirna Drabeni / Anela Dukan / Marko Dumpelnik / Miloš Dunaj / Herman Duquesnoy / Thomas Exner / Elise Feiersinger / Peter Fleiß / Irmgard Frank / Ivo Frei / Guido Galet / Teufik Galijašević / Remo Gavaz / Jochen Goede / Georg Görny / Mie Goto / Winfried Gruber / Gerhard Hagelkrüys / Ullrich Hanselmann / Neil Harkess / Bard Helland / Gabriele Hochholdinger / Sepp Horn / Radan Hubička / Josef Hyks / Susan H. Jones / Mladen Jošić / Nataša Jovanović / Branka Kaminski / Anne Kaun / Franz Knauer / Dieter Koll / Robert Kraus / Janez Kusar / Ralf Kürbitz / Domenico La Marca / Marko Lavrenčič / Franz Loranzi / Gerhard Luckner / David Lukas / Evita Lukež / Marisa Macchietto / Xavier Menard / Alejandro Monteagudo / Markus Myndl / Werner Neiger / Manfred Novak / Aledsander Ostan / Alfred Oszwald / Hans Oszwald / Max Pauly / Luis Pereira / Mihailo Perović / Rosanna Pettirosso / Gregor Pintar / Gisela Podreka / Jean-Claude Pondevie / Nikola Popović / Marko Prestor / Christian Radics / Claus Radler / Tomas Ramljak / Magdi Rashied / Tilmann Rohnke / Gerhard Schaller / Heike Schlauch / Friedrich Schmidmair / Christoph Schmidt-Ginzkey / Ingrid Schmutzer / Michael Schreger / Nevil Selimić / Michael Shamieyh / Ján Šoltés / Ferdinand Stabauer / Andreas Stöcklin / Christian Tengelmann / Norbert Thaler / Tamara Tišina / Alain Tisserand / Milena Todorić-Toplišek / Saša Uran / Piero Valle / Dimitri de Vecchi / Stefano de Vecchi / Pietro L. Vitali / Matej Vozlič / Vesna Vozlič / Virginia Vrecl / Zsolt Wanger / Felix Wettstein / Erich Wiedeschitz / Lisette Wong / Hannes Ziesel / Marco Zordan

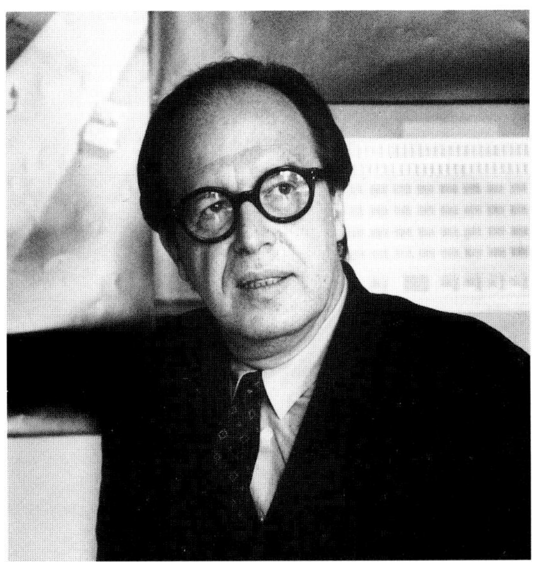

BORIS PODRECCA

1940	geboren in Belgrad
1946–58	Volksschule und Gymnasium in Triest und Wien (Abitur)
1960–67	Architekturstudium an der Technischen Universität Wien und an der Akademie der bildenden Künste, Wien
1968	Diplom der Meisterklasse Prof. Roland Rainer
1979–81	Assistent an der Technischen Universität München und an der Technischen Universität Wien
seit 1982	Gastprofessuren in Lausanne, Paris, Venedig, Philadelphia, London, Wien, Harvard-Cambridge (Boston)
seit 1988	ordentlicher Professor an der Technischen Universität Stuttgart, Direktor des Institutes für Innenraumgestaltung und Entwerfen
1990–95	Leiter des internationalen Wiener Architekturseminars

PREISE UND EHRUNGEN

1964	Preis der Architektur, Sommerakademie, Salzburg
1982, 1992	Plečnik–Preis, Ljubljana
1986	Preis des 12. Architektursalons, Belgrad
	Chevalier des Arts et des Lettres, Paris
1990	Kulturpreis der Stadt Wien für Architektur
1991, 1995	Pilgrampreis, Wien
1996	Ernennung zum Ehrenmitglied des Bundes Deutscher Architekten

BORIS PODRECCA

1940	*born in Belgrade*
1946–1958	*Elementary and High School in Trieste and Vienna*
1960–67	*Study of architecture at the Technical University, Vienna, and the Academy for Fine Arts, Vienna*
1968	*Masters Degree under Prof. Roland Rainer*
1979–81	*Assistant at the Technical University, Munich and the Technical University, Vienna*
since 1982	*Guest professorship in Lausanne, Paris, Venice, Philadelphia, London, Vienna, Harvard-Cambridge (Boston)*
since 1988	*Professor at the Technical University Stuttgart, Director of the Institute for Interior Design and Planning*
1990–95	*Chairman of the international Vienna Seminar for Architecture*

AWARDS AND HONORS

1964	*Architecture Award, Summer Academy, Salzburg*
1982, 1992	*Plečnik-Award, Ljubljana*
1986	*Award of the 12th Salon for Architecture, Belgrade*
1986	*Chevalier des Arts et des Lettres, Paris*
1990	*Cultural Award of the City of Vienna for Architecture*
1991, 1995	*Pilgram Award, Vienna*
1996	*Nomination as an honorable member of the Federation of German Architects*

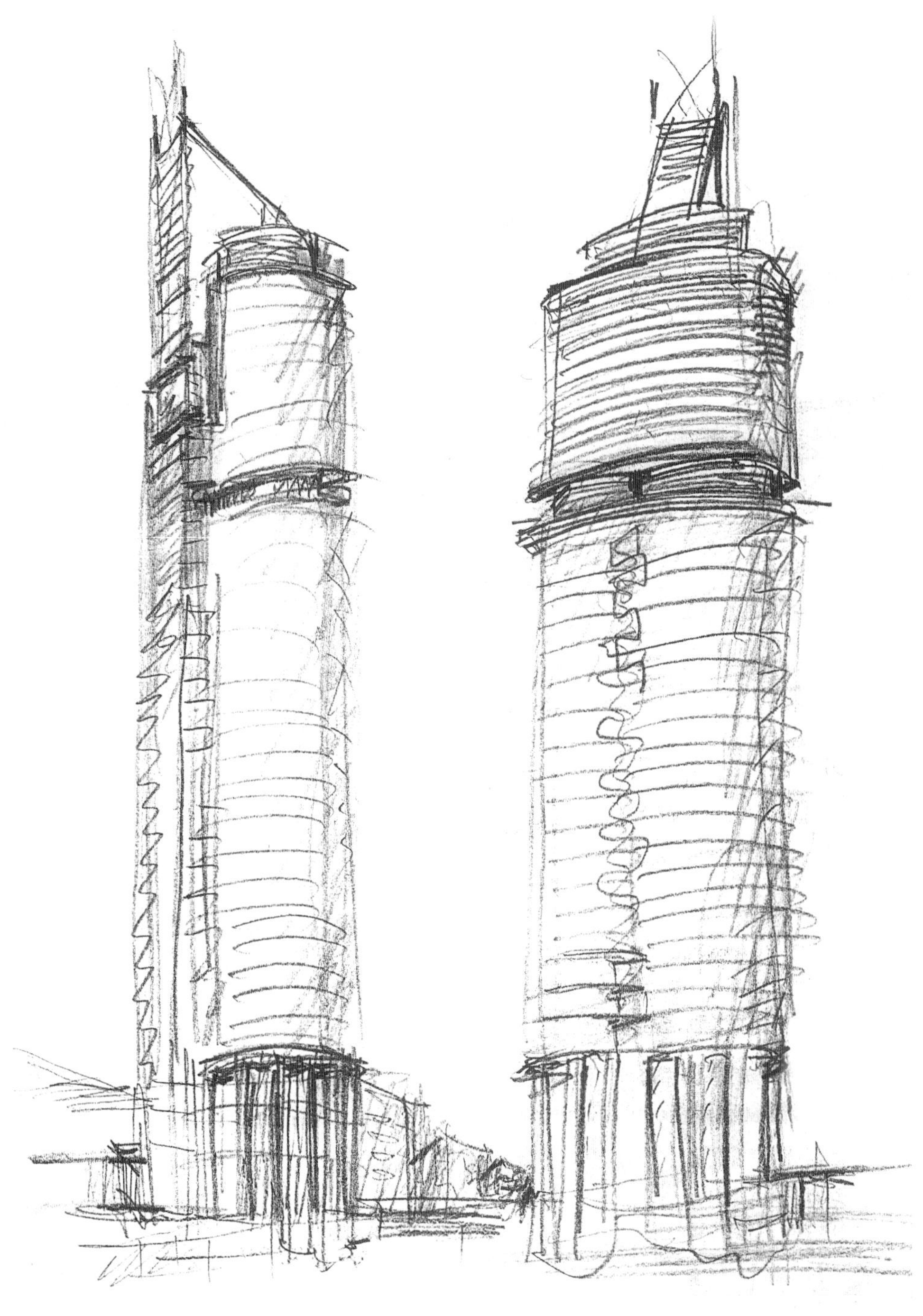